The Dirty War

COVERT STRATEGIES AND TACTICS USED IN POLITICAL CONFLICTS

MARTIN DILLON

Routledge
New York

Published in the United States of America in 1999 by
Routledge
29 West 35th Street
New York, NY 10001

First hardcover edition published in Great Britain by Hutchinson 1990.
First paperback edition published by Arrow Books Limited 1991.

Printed in the United States of America on acid-free paper.
Text Design by Tara Klurman

10 9 8 7 6 5 4 3 2 1

Library of Congress Cataloging-in-Publication Data

Dillon, Martin, 1949—
   The dirty war / Martin Dillon.
       p.   cm.
   Includes index.
   ISBN 0-415-92281-X (alk. paper)
   1. Northern Ireland—History—Military.   2. Military intelligence—Northern
Ireland—History—20th century.   3. Political violence—Northern Ireland—
History—20th century.   4. Terrorism—Northern Ireland—History—20th cen-
tury.   I. Title.
DA990.U46D53 1999
941.70824—dc21   98-49268
                                                                CIP

The Dirty War

*I dedicate this book to my parents, Maureen and Gerard,
for their constant love and support while I write about
difficult times in a difficult society*

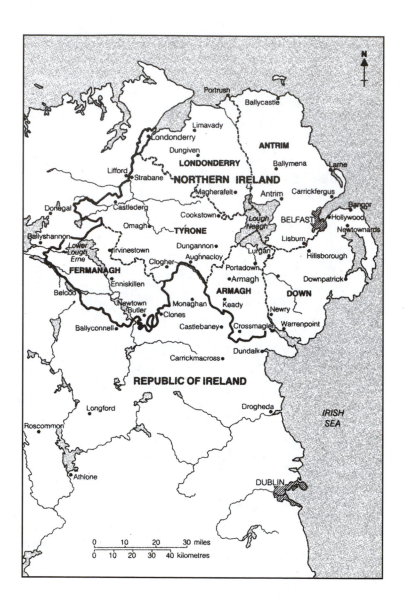

Contents

Acknowledgements

It is not possible to name everyone who assisted me. Many work within the security forces and to name them would place their lives in jeopardy or compromise them professionally. The majority of them spoke to me out of a genuine interest in what I was writing and to clarify previous reports of episodes in which they or their colleagues were involved. In all instances I sought them out for interview and established my own terms of reference for our conversations. Politicians on both sides of the political divide in Northern Ireland provided me with off-the-record briefings and I respect their wish to remain anonymous.

I thank David Ross of the BBC in Northern Ireland for assisting me in researching the material for this work, providing creative journalistic perspectives and spending many hours making sense of legal reports of terrorist trials. Linden Stafford was invaluable as an adviser and editor on this book. She possessed a genuine interest in the work and constantly encouraged me to broaden the material to explain a wider conflict which is the backdrop to the dirty war. She deserves special praise for her unceasing effort and her consummate professionalism. The writer, Frank Delaney, provided the impetus which set me on the road to write a trilogy of books on Ireland and Richard Cohen, my editor at Hutchinson, and Anthony Cheetham believed in the project and gave this book their full support. I am indebted to my wife, Kath, and our children, Crawford and Nadia, for living with the pressures created by writing this trilogy in a violent society, and to Kathy in particular for her imaginative appraisal of the work in its many and varied stages. In the world of print journalism and broadcasting I was given assistance by many people. Foremost among them was Chris Moore, a television reporter with the BBC in Northern Ireland. As a fellow writer and journalist with a genuine affection for Northern Ireland and a deep knowledge of the conflict he supplied me with interesting angles on several stories and some exciting documentation in relation to very sensitive matters. Others who deserve special mention are Martin O'Hagan, a reporter with the *Sunday World* newspaper, who provided me with some research material and was abducted and interrogated by the IRA while this book was in progress. The northern editor of *Sunday World*, Jim Campbell, made it possible for me to reach an acute understanding of several complex issues. Others who were willing to discuss matters with me included David McKittrick of the *Independent,* John Ware of the BBC Panorama' programme and Chris Ryder of the *Daily Telegraph.* Duncan Campbell was kind enough to provide me with copies of material which he published and Pacemaker Press in Belfast proved once again that they have one of the best photographic library services in these islands. The typing of this manuscript and the tasks associated with having much of this material in advance of publication rested with a trusted friend, Jean Jordan, now retired from the BBC Newsroom in Belfast but a true professional who helped with a difficult task. Adele Gilding in the BBC Library was kind in finding a range of reference books and ensuring that I kept possession for long periods. Finally, in writing the first two books in this trilogy there are those who by their very proximity to my life and their views on all matters connected with Northern Ireland are, were and remain an invaluable source of creative thought. They include Gerard and Maureen Dillon, Brian and Kate Garrett, Dr Conor Cruise O'Brien, Ian and Cecilia Kennedy, Professor Paul Bew, Brian and Anne Turley, Dr Tony Stewart whose book, *The Narrow Ground,* should be a classic addition to the personal library of any student of Irish history, Colin Lewis, John Bach, Stephen Dillon, Moore Sinnerton, Don Anderson, Brian and Ursula McLoughlin, Susan Delaney Collier, David Malone, the writer Gordon Thomas and Jennifer Brown.

I owe heartfelt thanks to Crispin Avon for ensuring that parts of the manuscript found their way to my publisher and to David Sykes for listening to and contributing to lengthy conversations between Linden and myself. Finally, I am grateful for the advice and assistance of the former politician and writer Paddy Devlin who proved to be an excellent commentator on matters political, and to Lord Fitt who has supported all my creative projects from the moment I moved from scribbling to journalism and writing political and historical works.

Foreword
Conor Cruise O'Brien

As a writer, Martin Dillon possesses a quality which was commended by Albert Camus: 'the reserve that befits a good witness'. He has no axe to grind; he follows the evidence as far as it takes him and he acknowledges that, in a number of cases, the evidence does not permit of more than an open verdict. In his conclusion, he writes: 'My role, I felt, was to prise open some of the issues, to unravel some of the stories which have become distorted by the propaganda of either side and to tease out the complexity of the backdrop to the war.... Finally, in reiterating that the dirty war often generates more questions than it answers, I hope the reader will understand that in some instances where no answer was available I included the question in the belief that the question of itself was important and that perhaps its existence may encourage someone, somewhere to provide an answer.'

Those who know Martin Dillon—including those wary denizens of Northern Ireland who are the subjects of his enquiries—know well that he will never distort what anyone says to him in order to build up some kind of case to support a theory or assumption. This well-established reputation has greatly assisted him in the pursuit of his enquiries. Most of his subjects, 'the dirty warriors', are not in the least trustworthy themselves. They are either terrorists—whether of the Catholic or Protestant variety—or they are policemen or soldiers, who have either broken the law themselves—usually by murdering suspects or releasing information likely to get them murdered—or, more usually, have connived at such activities, or condoned them. These are by no means people who cannot tell a lie; they lie habitually, as part of the conditions of their survival within the struggle of terrorist and counter-terrorist. Yet I have the impression that, in recalling past events, a number of them have told Martin Dillon much more of the truth than they are normally in the habit of telling. It is clear that he won the confidence of several of his subjects, by getting them to realise that he was not out to get *them* personally, only to get at the truth.

The Dirty War is the most thorough enquiry yet made into the armed struggle in and over Northern Ireland, during the past twenty years. Future historians will draw on it—especially on the 'confessional' statements by protagonists on the various sides—as rare and indispensable source material. But it is not only historians who will draw on it; so will writers of spy stories. Here is a real-life underground world of double and treble agents, and many of them are singing. For the general reader, too, *The Dirty War* has much of the attraction of a good spy story. If you can think of it as fiction, it makes most entertaining reading. It is only when you keep in mind that this is not an invention of Graham Greene or John le Carré, but the cold and sober truth about something that is still going on, that you begin to get the horrors.

I shall not, in this Foreword, attempt to pursue the various absorbing and horrifying episodes which make up *The Dirty War.* These are complex stories and any attempt at summary would be bound to spoil them, through the distortion of compression. Instead, I should like to consider the general theme which pervades the story of the dirty war. The theme is complicity.

Respectable people in Ireland—politicians, clergy, businessmen—condemn, for example, as regularly as clockwork, the latest atrocity of the Provisional IRA. Yet Irish politicians helped to start the Provisional IRA with the help of some Catholic priests. As for the businessmen in both communities of Northern Ireland, their readiness to co-operate financially helps to keep both the Provisionals and Loyalist paramilitaries in, well, business. All that is told in this book.

As a citizen of the Republic, and a former member of its parliament and government, I am particularly concerned with the far-reaching complicities of the politicians in the Republic and shall concentrate on that aspect in the remainder of this Foreword.

In his Preface, Martin Dillon says: 'For example, in 1969–70, while television screens were depicting the conflict as a series of street battles between rioters in both communities and the British Army, the Irish government was consorting with gunrunners and members of the IRA, and British intelligence was operating a policy of spying which was amateurish, outlandish and downright dangerous.'

Martin Dillon's strictures on many of the activities of British intelligence, both in 1969–70 and in some later periods, are well merited and amply demonstrated in his narrative. It is also true that senior British politicians often condoned, or turned a blind eye to, breaches of the law on the part of the security forces, and then either lied about them, or repeated lies reaching them from the security forces.

Yet the often shabby role played at various times by certain British politicians should not be allowed to distract attention from the fact that the primary responsibility for the foundation and arming of the Provisional IRA rests squarely on the shoulders of a particular group of Irish politicians, members of Jack Lynch's government in 1969–70, aided by some of the Catholic clergy. That story is told in Chapter One of *The Dirty War*. Again, there is no need for me to summarise that, but I shall quote certain passages, and comment on their general implications.

Martin Dillon quotes Paddy Devlin, who at the time looked for guns to be used in the defence of Catholic homes, but then realised that the guns—and the money to buy them—that were coming in were being steered towards people who would use them, not defensively, but in a 'war' to be waged against the British and the Protestant population. Devlin told Dillon: '"Initially it was easy for the IRA to take over the defence committees because they had the men with experience of conflict. Slowly they took over all the areas, but it was the type of leadership that worried me. They were the men of the right who would become the Provisionals. They tended to remain in the background using the barricades as cover for reorganising and for planning the reshaping of the IRA. I believe the church knew who it was getting into bed with. However, I don't believe the vast majority of people realised what was going on." In the course of seeking assistance for his organisation Paddy Devlin met the Dublin government's Minister for Finance, Charles J. Haughey, at the latter's home. He says that Haughey promised financial assistance for the relief of distressed families, but that guns were not discussed.' (p.10)

Devlin added: 'I eventually resigned my post but remained in the organisation in name only. I was appalled on one occasion when I arrived at a meeting to see that some of those leaving the house with members of the clergy were men I knew were about to return the IRA to an offensive role.' (p. 11) The clergy believed that the good Catholic nationalists who became Provisionals would be less dangerous than the Marxists. In this, the clergy were wildly mistaken.

Martin Dillon's considered judgement as regards responsibility for the establishment of the Provisional IRA is as follows: 'On 29 December 1969 the name Provisional Army Council hit the headlines after a meeting of the full IRA Army Council. The dissidents issued a statement to the newspapers declaring their position. Several weeks later, at a full convention of IRA Sinn Fein, the break was finally made when the dissidents walked out. The Provisional IRA was born. In relation to violence, weaponry, contacts with the Irish government and support from the Catholic population, it appeared to hold all the ace cards.

'During its infancy it was nurtured by an Irish government which behaved as though it had unfinished national business to resolve. That suited the Provisionals. They watched and felt morally secure in the knowledge that a sovereign state was trying to acquire arms for them. Some might argue that Fianna Fail was merely engaged in supplying arms to protect Catholics, but the facts are that they knew with whom they were dealing and they had in their mind's eye a "doomsday" situation on which those weapons would be used not only against Ulstermen but also against British troops.' (pp. 14–15)

And also against the Protestants of Northern Ireland, perceived to be tools of the British.

The former leadership of the IRA—before the Provisional breakaway—had been Marxist-orientated and had aimed, in theory, at class war and revolution in the whole island of Ireland, overthrowing the bourgeois government in Dublin and creating a socialist United Ireland. As there was never the slightest likelihood of any of that happening, the Marxist-inclined IRA—later the Official IRA—was much less dangerous than its successor, which drew its strength from the gut nationalism and sectarian animosities of a large element in the Catholic population of Northern Ireland (and some in the Republic also).

The deal that launched the Provos was essentially this: certain members of the Lynch government approached those leading members of the IRA who were known to be disgusted with the Marxist leadership, on both nationalist and Catholic grounds, and also on operational grounds. These leaders—who were to become the leaders of the Provisional IRA—were offered money, arms and general support if they would abjure operations against the Republic, and concentrate on operations inside Northern Ireland. The Provisional leaders-to-be agreed. The new policy, in exchange for which the emerging Provos received support from the then Dublin government, is enshrined in the IRA's General Order No. 8, which is still in force and is set out in the IRA's *Green Book*, published for the first time in the Appendix to *The Dirty War*. General Order No. 8 runs as follows:

1 Volunteers are strictly forbidden to take any military action against 26 County forces under any circumstances whatsoever. The importance of this order in present circumstances especially in the border areas cannot be over-emphasised.
2 Minimum arms shall be used in training in the 26 County area. In the event of a raid, every effort shall be made to get the arms away safely. If this fails, the arms shall be rendered useless and abandoned.
3 Maximum security precautions must be taken when training. Scouts must always be posted to warn of emergency. Volunteers arrested during the train-

ing or in possession of arms will point out that the arms were for use against the British forces of occupation only. This statement should be repeated at all subsequent Court proceedings.

4 At all times Volunteers must make it clear that the policy of the Army is to drive the British forces of occupation out of Ireland.

Thus the Provos were born, and the dirty war began.

That deal was a radical, indeed a revolutionary, departure from the policy of previous Fianna Fail governments. Eamon de Valera, after he became head (in 1932) of a democratically elected government in the Irish Free State (now the Republic), laid down the principle that an armed minority would not be allowed to usurp a power—that of waging war—which belonged to the State alone. He assured the British government, on the outbreak of the Second World War, that he would not allow the territory of the Irish State to be used for attacks on Britain (meaning, in practice, the United Kingdom of Great Britain and Northern Ireland). De Valera was as good as his word: he interned all known IRA people, allowed hunger-strikers to die, and death sentences handed down by courts to be carried out. In peacetime, de Valera's successor, Sean Lemass, held to the same basic policy. In 1957–60, he introduced internment, successfully, to quell a campaign which the IRA had begun against Northern Ireland. He treated as irrelevant the fact that the IRA of that period was not attacking targets in the Republic. He would not let them attack Northern Ireland, either. That was the policy that was jettisoned in 1969–70.

The covert accord between the Dublin government and the emerging Provisional IRA was of brief duration. When it ended it was replaced by a tacit understanding, the consequences of which are still felt, and do much to sustain the dirty war. That war began in earnest in 1971, when the Provinsionals' offensive led to the deaths of 174 people. Under the principle laid down by de Valera and followed by Lemass, this attempt to usurp the power of the Irish state, by waging war (in part, from the Republic's territory) should have been met as in the past by internment. This did not happen. The Stormont authorities, with the approval of the British government, introduced internment in Northern Ireland in August 1971. This was clumsily done, on the basis of old lists, and was represented by Catholic leaders in Northern Ireland as a witchhunt against Catholics. All parties in the Republic—not just Fianna Fail this time—joined in the outcry against the use of internment in Northern Ireland. Partly as a result of that agitation, and partly for other reasons, internment itself soon became a dirty word. A consensus that internment is abominable in Northern

Ireland, and unthinkable in the Republic, speedily became established, and still exists. This consensus is extremely advantageous to the IRA in its prosecution of the dirty war.

In the Republic, the anti-internment case is presented as a courageous adherence to liberal principles. It is part of a general 'liberal' stance pervading the Irish media which provides copious coverage and commentary on the *British* side of the dirty war (Stalker, Wallace, Guildford Four, Birmingham Six; see *The Dirty War, passim*). The media pundits of the Republic dilate on such impeccable themes as that the security forces must never 'descend to the level of the terrorists': a theme which, as well as being impeccable, is very helpful to the terrorists.

There is little if any *conscious* hypocrisy in this 'liberalism' of the Irish media, but there is a great deal of the unconscious kind. For those concerned know very well that if the IRA were to drop General Order No. 8 and start an offensive *down here*, in the Republic, internment would be introduced, before the death-toll reached fifty. Public opinion would approve the most ruthless measures against any of the IRA who might remain at large. The beating of suspects and a 'shoot to kill policy' would be routine, and public opinion in the Republic would have no fault to find with it, provided it worked, and the IRA was stopped from shooting and bombing people in the Republic. Few of the media voices which have been so vocal about the Stalker Report etc., would be heard from about excesses of repression against the IRA if the IRA campaign, and its consequent repression, were going on down here. This type of liberalism is for export only.

There is another side to the medal of internment. Internment would be introduced in the Republic if General Order No. 8 were dropped. But conversely, as long as General Order No. 8 is observed internment will not be introduced in the Republic. People know that if it were introduced, a number of the IRA would escape the net and would start killing people 'down here'. So the tacit assurance conveyed to the IRA is: 'We won't intern you as long as you are killing people up there, and only up there. But if you start killing people down here, woe betide you....' The IRA gets the message, and General Order No. 8 stands.

This tacit understanding between the IRA and the authorities in the Republic is a great part of the foundations and of the durability of the dirty war. The IRA cannot be beaten without the firm application of internment on *both sides* of the border. If internment is ruled out in the Republic, then it cannot be made effective in Northern Ireland either. As long as the security forces have to fight the IRA without the aid of internment, they are going to bend the law. There is no such thing as a dirty war on one side only.

But the dirtiest secret of the whole dirty war is the tacit understanding which has grown up since 1970 that the IRA shall be safe
from internment in the Republic, as long as the people they murder are
all outside the Republic's jurisdiction.

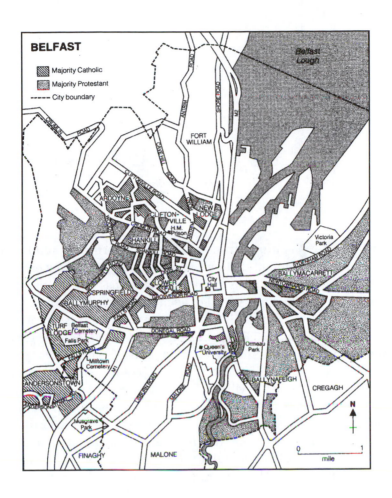

Author's Preface

When I began planning a trilogy of books on terrorism and the Irish conflict I was determined that one of the works would concentrate on the war which is fought away from the headlines. It is the war which takes place in the shadowy world of agents, double agents and informers; the world in which intelligence agencies and terrorists seek to outwit and kill each other. From the outset of what people term the 'Troubles' in Ireland, beginning in 1969, part of the terrorist war has been fought at a pace and ferocity not always represented in the media. For example, in 1969–70, while television screens were depicting the conflict as a series of street battles between rioters in both communities and the British Army, the Irish government was consorting with gunrunners and members of the IRA, and British intelligence was operating a policy of spying which was amateurish, outlandish and downright dangerous. Those were times of major conspiracies which provided the basis for the 'dirty war' and created a need for deniability on the part of both governments which would recur each time there was a crisis. Ultimately, it was to be the British government and not the Irish government of those early years which, whether under Labour or Tory leadership, was to be drawn inexorably into a dirty war in which the rules of engagement were not those of a conventional conflict. Some have rightly referred to this part of the war against the terrorists as the undercover war because it is fought by men from secret agencies of government and the military. The fact that this war is not always apparent and is not contested openly on the streets determines that different rules can be applied, and often are, without the consent or approval of government. In the late 1960s and early 1970s, while the conventional forces of government were openly combating terrorism in Ireland, other agencies within the intelligence community in the United Kingdom believed that unorthodox methods and techniques were required in the war. The intervention of these groupings, which included Special Branch, military intelligence, MI5 and MI6, was uncoordinated. Much has been written about that period, some of it honest journalism but most of it propaganda inspired by the terrorists and their supporters. I persuaded the IRA and former members of the organisation to talk for the first time in detail about that period, and what I discovered was startling. The evidence pointed clearly to the involvement of the British military in amateurish counter-terrorist methods which cost lives on both sides of the conflict and left a legacy which seriously damaged the role of the British Army in Northern Ireland. I also uncovered evidence that the IRA secretly executed and buried those of its members who became involved in working at that time for military intelligence. The IRA also revealed for the first time the details of how it smashed a major spy network and how the IRA itself was almost destroyed by what it still regards as a brilliant British intelligence operation or 'sting'.

One area of the dirty war which I was obliged to confront was the use of black propaganda by the terrorists as well as the intelligence agencies and how propaganda led to the deliberate or accidental creation of conspiracy theories. Much of the evidence in print or by word of mouth pointed to the involvement of British intelligence groupings in political murder and the manipulation of Loyalist paramilitaries for counter-terror. My conclusions may not please people in both communities or some of the left in Britain, but I believe it has to be said that the vast majority of the conspiracy theories in this regard are inaccurate and in some instances are a deliberate creation of black propaganda for the purpose of discrediting the security forces. In a few instances I uncovered evidence which pointed to the involvement of members of the security forces in terrorism but the overwhelming evidence indicated that such involvement was personal and not part of a stated policy.

One aspect of the conflict which fascinated and puzzled me was the extent to which the terrorists on both sides were engaged in criminal pursuits and the degree to which mutual profit created unholy alliances and collusion in murder spanning the political and religious divide. I found evidence to show that such alliances exist between sworn enemies and that deals were made as a result of criminal collusion which guaranteed the safety of terrorist leaders on both sides and sometimes led to joint terrorist operations. This avenue of research also led me to an analysis of the way in which terrorism is funded and how the IRA has made use of international terror contacts to purchase arms.

By far the most controversial aspect of the dirty war is the use of agents, double agents and informers. My investigation provided me with insights and information which shocked and dismayed me. I uncovered a world in which a dangerous 'game' is played out every day which costs as well as saves many lives. It is a game in which things are not always as they appear or are represented: a world of mirrors and of clever and dangerous men. In this world the innocent and the guilty can be compromised and sacrificed for very high stakes. In the last ten years it is this part of the dirty war which has formed the most critical area of the conflict not only in Ireland but on the international stage when terrorism is confronted. It is a 'game' of high-tech surveillance equipment, of tiny bugs and tracing devices which can be placed in terrorist weapons or explosives so that elite counter-terrorist teams from groups such as the SAS can trace and eliminate IRA active service units. One of the stories in this book illustrates the danger of such techniques: the IRA almost wiped out an SAS unit by discovering the existence of a bugging device in a weapon. In this part of the war the intelligence agencies employ not only their own staff but also informers to enable them to learn about terrorist operations, weapons supplies and the constant threat of political assassination following the bombing of the Royal Hotel at Brighton during the Tory Party Conference, a terrorist act which almost claimed the lives of the cabinet and might, if it had succeeded, have changed the course of British history for the remainder of this century. It is essentially because the stakes are so high that the dirty war is the critical arena where the war against terrorism can be won or lost. Consequently, in the gathering of intelligence about terrorists it is the agent, double agent or informer who is the vital tool or pawn. In this dimension of the dirty war the rule-book of orthodox military procedure is not applied even by those agencies which are ultimately responsible to government.

In this book I have tried to represent every aspect of the dirty war including the IRA's use of the honeytrap to lure soldiers to their deaths. In so doing I hope I have presented a readable book with chapters devoted to stories which illustrate varying aspects of the war. No grouping emerges from the book unscathed and that includes those organisations which exist to defeat terrorism. However, I hope that by attempting to present an honest analysis of the undercover or dirty war I will have dispelled many of the myths and conspiracy theories which distort the history of the period.

In order to assist readers who may not be aware of all of the major events which characterise the conflict since the emergence of the civil rights protests of 1968 I am including a chronology of milestones in the

'Troubles'. Overall I have dealt with events which I believe broadly to represent the progress of the dirty war from the outset of the violence, although, in some cases, I have been obliged to deal with events which are not clearly defined in a chronological representation of the conflict.

Martin Dillon
Belfast
January 1990

Chronology of Major Events in Northern Ireland
1969–1989

1969 Deaths 13   As the civil rights campaign brought worldwide media attention, it was a year of mounting tension, with violence at marches and Loyalist bomb attacks on a reservoir and power stations. In August three days of rioting in Derry's Bogside led to the deployment of the first British soldiers (members of the Prince of Wales' Own Regiment of Yorkshire). Violence then switched to Belfast—leading to further troop deployments there. During the honeymoon period that followed, the IRA split and the Provisionals were formed out of Catholic vigilante groups which had been partly funded by the Irish government. The first shots fired by the Army were in October and were directed at Protestant gunmen on the Shankill Road who had claimed the first RUC victim of the Troubles, Constable Victor Arbuckle, during disturbances over the disbanding of the B Specials.

1970 Deaths 25   A 34-hour curfew and search operation in the Lower Falls area of Belfast in July is generally regarded as marking the end of the honeymoon period and the end of the Army's initial role as a protector of Catholic areas against Protestant attacks. On 1 April the Ulster Defence Regiment came into service to replace the B Specials, and politically the year saw the formation of the nationalist Social Democratic and Labour Party (SDLP) and the election of a Conservative government in Britain.

1971 Deaths 174   The first soldier to be killed, Gunner Robert Curtis (aged nineteen), was shot dead in Belfast on 5 February. In March three Scottish soldiers were lured away from a city centre bar by young women and shot dead. Northern Ireland's Prime Minister, James Chichester-Clark, resigned because of what he saw as Westminster's lack of understanding of the seriousness of the security situation and he was succeeded by another Unionist, Brian Faulkner. On 9 August Faulkner ordered internment without trial. Three hundred and fifty people were picked up in initial raids but intelligence was poor—many had nothing to do with the IRA and more than a hundred were released within 48 hours. In the climate of resentment which followed there was widespread violence and an increased IRA bombing campaign. In September the Protestant paramilitary Ulster Defence Association (UDA) was born out of an amalgam of vigilante groups and on 4 December fifteen people were killed in a UVF (Ulster Volunteer Force) bomb attack on McGurk's Bar in Belfast.

1972 Deaths 467   The worst year for violence so far. On 30 January thirteen civilians were shot dead by soldiers of the Parachute Regiment in Derry on 'Bloody Sunday'. A fourteenth died later. The Widgery Inquiry said there would have been no deaths if there had not been an illegal march but none of the victims was shown to have been handling a weapon when shot. On 21 July nine people were killed when 22 IRA bombs exploded in Belfast on 'Bloody Friday' and in Dublin two people were killed and eighty injured when two bombs exploded on 1 December while the Irish Parliament (Dail) was debating tighter security measures. No one claimed responsibility. On 24 March direct rule from London was established after the Unionist government at Stormont resigned over the transfer of security powers to Westminster. In June the Provisional IRA called a truce and on 7 July the Northern Ireland Secretary, William Whitelaw, held a secret meeting in London with six of its leaders, including Gerry Adams. The truce collapsed two days later and at the end of the month the Army launched 'Operation Motorman' to occupy 'no-go areas' in Belfast and Derry.

1973 Deaths 250 In March a British government White Paper proposed a new 78-seat Assembly elected by proportional representation and without security powers. Elections were held in June and by November a majority had agreed on the creation of a new power-sharing executive. This was ratified by a four-day conference at Sunningdale in Berkshire attended by the power-sharing parties and the British and Irish governments. In March the Irish authorities seized five tons of arms for the IRA on board the *Claudia* off the coast of Waterford.

1974 Deaths 216 The new Northern Ireland executive took office in January with Brian Faulkner as Chief Executive. The following month the anti-power-sharing Unionist parties united in the UUUC (United Ulster Unionist Council) to take eleven out of twelve Northern Ireland seats in the Westminster election. On 14 May the Executive voted 44 to 28 in favour of the Sunningdale Agreement, which included a Council of Ireland, and this was followed by the Ulster Workers' Council strike. The strikers used a combination of industrial action (particularly in the power stations) and open paramilitary intimidation to bring the province to a virtual standstill until 29 May when Unionist members of the executive resigned and the executive collapsed. The previous week 22 people had been killed in Dublin and another five in Monaghan when bombs exploded without warning in cars which had been hijacked in Loyalist areas of Belfast. Later in the year, on 5 October, five people were killed and 54 injured when bombs exploded without warning in Guildford, Surrey, and on 21 November another 19 people were killed and 182 injured in explosions at two Birmingham pubs. In December the Provisional IRA announced a Christmas ceasefire after six IRA leaders had met a group of Protestant Churchmen for talks at Feakle in Co. Clare.

1975 Deaths 247   The year began with the IRA's Christmas truce being extended from 2 January to 10 February. It was then extended indefinitely with 'incident centres' set up by Sinn Fein and with links to an operations room in Stormont Castle, to monitor breaches of the cease-fire. With a steadily growing number of 'incidents' during the year the centres were closed in November and the ceasefire was officially ended on 23 January 1976 with a raid by the Army on the Sinn Fein offices in Belfast's Falls Road. Among the notable acts of violence during the year was the murder of three members of the Miami Showband near Banbridge in July by the UVF. Two of the killers also blew themselves up with their own bomb. In September five Protestants were murdered at Tullyvallen Orange Hall in South Armagh. This was claimed by a group calling itself the South Armagh Republican Action Force, which was widely thought to be a cover for the South Armagh IRA who had abandoned the ceasefire at an early stage. Politically the year saw the calling of a constitutional convention in May. It was intended to encourage local politicians to write their own constitution for Northern Ireland's future and although it was recalled again in February 1976 it could reach no real agreement and was finally dissolved in March 1976 after a majority report which rejected power-sharing and called for the restoration of the old Stormont system.

1976 Deaths 297   In a bloody opening to the year five Catholics were shot dead near Whitecross in South Armagh on 4 January and the following day ten Protestant workmen were taken off a bus at Kingsmills nearby and also murdered. In response the government drafted a unit of the SAS into South Armagh on 7 January. In March the Secretary of State, Merlyn Rees, announced the ending of special-category status for all prisoners convicted of offences after that date and by the end of the year protests had begun in the Maze, with Republican inmates refusing to work or to wear prison clothes. In August the deaths of three children in Andersonstown (they were crushed by a car whose driver had been shot dead by the Army) led to the formation of the

Peace People and the staging of a number of highly publicised peace marches and rallies. In September Roy Mason took over from Merlyn Rees at Stormont Castle and in October Mrs Maire Drumm, the vice-president of Provisional Sinn Fein, was shot dead in the Mater Hospital in Belfast where she was a patient.

1977 Deaths 112   This is the year in which the policy of 'Ulsterisation' was begun, with the day-to-day direction of security policy being put in the hands of a coordinating committee chaired by the Chief Constable. April saw the formation of the UUAC (United Unionist Action Council, made up of the DUP, sections of the Vanguard Party, the Ulster Workers' Council, and the UDA), who announced another Loyalist strike in support of their demands for the implementation of the convention report and the introduction of tougher security measures. The strike was launched on 3 May but collapsed within ten days owing to much more vigorous government response than in 1974 and because of divisions among the Unionists themselves and their failure to close the power stations. Later in May, Mason began a new round of talks with the political parties and he announced increases in the strength of both the RUC and UDR and the increased use of undercover soldiers.

1978 Deaths 81   On 18 January the European Court of Human Rights in Strasbourg ruled that interrogation techniques used on internees in 1971 had been 'inhuman and degrading', though the court said they did not amount to torture. In February twelve people were killed in an IRA incendiary attack on the La Mon Hotel just outside Belfast. March saw the stepping up of the prison campaign for the restoration of special-category status, with Republicans starting their 'dirty protest'. In November the deputy governor of Belfast Prison, Albert Miles, was shot dead by the IRA.

1979 Deaths 113   This was a year of spectacular successes for the Republican paramilitaries. On 30 March the INLA came to prominence when they killed the Conservative Party spokesman on Northern Ireland, Airey Neave, with a bomb which exploded under his car as he was driving out of the House of Commons car park. Humphrey Atkins became Northern Ireland Secretary when the Conservatives took office in May. On 27 August the IRA killed eighteen soldiers in a double bomb attack in Warrenpoint, Co. Down (the biggest death toll in any single incident in Northern Ireland), and on the same day they also murdered Lord Mountbatten of Burma when they blew up his boat off Mullaghmore, Co. Sligo. His fourteen-year-old grandson Nicholas and another fourteen-year-old, Paul Maxwell, were also killed and the Dowager Lady Brabourne died later from her injuries. Mrs Thatcher came to Northern Ireland on 29 August to see how security could be improved and in October she appointed former head of the Secret Intelligence Service, Sir Maurice Oldfield, as 'security coordinator'.

1980 Deaths 76   The year opened with another constitutional confer-ence at Stormont. It ran between 7 January and 24 March. It was boycotted by the Official Unionist Party but attended by the DUP, the SDLP and Alliance, who could not reach agreement. However, the year was really dominated by prison issues. On 26 March the government abolished all special-category status. In May the European Commission on Human Rights rejected an application by four of the Republican pris-oners on 'dirty protest'. The Commission said they were not entitled to political status but it also criti-cised the British government for having an 'inflexible approach'. On 27 October seven H-Block prisoners began a hunger strike which was only called off in December after 53 days, following apparent conces-sions including an agreement that 'civilian-type' cloth-ing could be worn. When prisoners realised this would be issued by the authorities they felt duped and this helped lay the foundations for a second hunger strike. Earlier in the year, in June, a prominent Republican campaigner on the prisons issue, Dr Miriam Daly, was shot dead at her home by gunmen who were never apprehended.

1981 Deaths 101   On 16 January another prominent prisons campaigner, former MP Bernadette McAliskey, and her husband, were shot and seriously wounded by Loyalist gunmen at their home near Coalisland in Co. Tyrone. The second hunger strike began on 1 March when the Provisional IRA commander within the prison, Bobby Sands, began refusing food. He and the others that followed were making five demands—the right to wear their own clothes; to refrain from prison work; to associate freely; to have one letter, visit and parcel a week; and to have lost remission time fully restored. Four days later the Independent Republican MP for Fermanagh/South Tyrone, Frank McManus, died and Sands won the seat in a by-election on 9 April in a straight fight with the former Unionist leader, Harry West. On 5 May Sands died on the 66th day of his fast and this led to widespread disorder in Catholic areas—a pattern which continued as nine more prisoners died on hunger strike between May and August. In August Sinn Fein's Owen Carron won Sands's Fermanagh seat with an increased majority. The following month Jim Prior took over from Atkins as Northern Ireland Secretary and on 3 October, after intervention by churchmen and families, the hunger strike was called off. On 6 October Prior announced that prisoners could wear their own clothes and, if they abided by prison rules, could retain 50 per cent remission. On 14 November it was the Unionist community's turn to be outraged, when the MP for South Belfast, the Rev. Robert Bradford, was shot dead by the IRA. This was followed two days later by the appearance of the DUP's 'Third Force' in Enniskillen and on 23 November there was a 'Loyalist Day of Action' in protest at security policy. Rallies were held at Belfast City Hall and other venues and in Newtownards 5000 men marched in a military-style parade in front of Ian Paisley.

1982 Deaths 97   Politically the year was marked by the emergence of Sinn Fein as an electoral force. In April Jim Prior issued a White Paper setting out his plans for implementing a policy of 'rolling devolution' through the creation of a 78-member Assembly which he hoped would reach agreement on how powers could gradually be devolved to it. In elections to the Assembly in October, Sinn Fein captured 10.1 per cent of the vote compared to 18.8 per cent for the SDLP (both parties boycotted the actual Assembly). In July eight soldiers were killed and 51 people injured by two IRA bombs in London—one at Regent's Park bandstand and the other near the Household Cavalry barracks at Knightsbridge. On 6 December seventeen people including eleven off-duty soldiers died when the INLA bombed a disco at the Droppin Well Inn at Ballykelly, Co. Derry. Also towards the end of the year six people died in shootings by the RUC which gave rise to allegations that a 'shoot-to-kill' policy had been put into effect and which led to the later Stalker investigation. The first shooting was near Lurgan on 11 November when three unarmed IRA members were killed. It was alleged they had driven through a roadblock. In December two associates of INLA leader Dominic McGlinchey were shot in similar circumstances in Armagh, and also in December a seventeen-year-old, Michael Tighe, was shot by police at a hayshed near Lurgan.

1983 Deaths 77

In March the Republic's government announced it was setting up an all-Ireland Forum along the lines proposed by the SDLP after their Assembly boycott. It was to allow all parties on the island to redefine Irish nationalism and it held its initial meeting on 30 May. April saw the conclusion of Northern Ireland's first 'supergrass' trial with the conviction of fourteen UVF men on the evidence of Joseph Bennett, who had been given immunity from prosecution. (The convictions were later quashed in December.) In August 34 people were convicted on the word of IRA supergrass Christopher Black—at 128 days it had been the longest and most expensive trial in British legal history. In June Sinn Fein's Gerry Adams won one of what was now seventeen Northern Ireland seats at Westminster, taking 13.4 per cent of the poll. The SDLP leader John Hume also took a seat, while the other fifteen went to Unionists. On 25 September thirty-eight IRA prisoners escaped from the Maze in the biggest escape in British prison history. One prison officer was stabbed and died during the breakout and nineteen of the prisoners were recaptured within days. In November three elders were shot dead during a church service in a Pentecostal hall at Darkley in South Armagh—an attack claimed by the Catholic Reaction Force. On 7 December the rising Unionist politician Edgar Graham was shot dead at Queen's University and on 17 December five people were killed and 80 injured by an IRA bomb outside Harrods in London.

1984 Deaths 64   On 14 March the Sinn Fein President Gerry Adams was shot and wounded by the UFF while being driven through the centre of Belfast. On 29 March an RUC man, Constable John Robinson, went to trial for the murder of INLA man Seamus Grew in Armagh in December 1982. Robinson, who was acquitted, claimed senior officers had ordered him to lie about events to protect Special Branch officers and an RUC informer in the Republic. A few days later the British government apologised to Dublin for RUC undercover action in the Republic at the time. The shoot-to-kill controversy was raised again in August, when the Armagh coroner Gerry Curran resigned after finding 'grave irregularities' in the RUC file relating to the two shootings in Armagh. In May the New Ireland Forum issued its report—re-expressing the desire for Irish unity by agreement as the favoured option but also including the possible variants of confederation or joint British-Irish authority over the North. On 29 September the Irish authorities seized seven tons of arms on the trawler *Marita Ann* off the Kerry coast. On 12 October the entire British cabinet narrowly escaped death when an IRA bomb exploded at the Grand Hotel in Brighton during Conservative Party conference week. Four people were killed and 34 injured. Among the dead were Sir Anthony Berry MP and Mrs Robert Wakeham, wife of the government Chief Whip, Robert Wakeham. In Belfast on 14 December Private

Ian Thain became the first soldier to be convicted of murdering a civilian while on duty. (In 1989 it was revealed he was released after serving just 26 months of a life sentence and he is still serving with the Army.)

1985 Deaths 54   On 28 February nine RUC officers were killed when the IRA used mortars to attack Newry police station. On 12 and 13 July there was sporadic rioting in Portadown after police prevented Orange and Black parades through the mainly Catholic 'Tunnel' area. The big political development of the year was the signing of the Anglo-Irish Agreement at Hillsborough Castle on 15 November, under which the Irish government was given a consultative role in Northern Ireland policy through an inter-governmental conference and permanent secretariat. The House of Commons ratified the agreement by an overwhelming majority (473 to 47) and it was widely welcomed abroad, but Unionists were outraged and have been protesting about it ever since. In the immediate aftermath they organised a massive rally in the centre of Belfast on 23 November attended by between 50,000 and 100,000 people.

1986 Deaths 61   In January Unionist MPs resigned their seats in protest at the Anglo-Irish Agreement. In the resulting by-elections they lost one of those fifteen seats, with Newry/Armagh going to SDLP deputy leader Seamus Mallon. On 25 February Unionist leaders Ian Paisley and James Molyneaux met Mrs Thatcher, but after at first appearing optimistic of some sort of agreement they returned to Belfast and announced that they would not continue talks and would withdraw all consent from the government. A 'Day of Action' on 3 March disrupted industry and transport and was marked by violence and the appearance of paramilitaries and barricades. At the end of that month there were serious clashes between Loyalists and the RUC in Portadown over an Apprentice Boys parade and twenty-year-old Keith White became the first Protestant to die after being hit by a plastic bullet. (Up to then fifteen Catholics had been killed by such weapons.) During the next month 50 RUC families and 79 Catholic households were petrol-bombed by Loyalists. On 29 May the Secretary of State, Tom King, announced that he had decided to dissolve the Northern Ireland Assembly, which had increasingly been used by Unionists as a vehicle for their anti-Agreement protest. The SDLP had never taken part and by now the Alliance Party had also withdrawn. The Assembly was finally closed on 23 June with some of the protesting Unionists being carried out of the Stormont building by police. As protests over the Agreement continued, there was more violence in Portadown over the re-routeing of Twelfth of July marches and in November a new paramilitary-style grouping, Ulster Resistance, was formed at a rally in the Ulster Hall in Belfast attended by leading members of the DUP including Ian Paisley.

1987 Deaths 93   At the beginning of the year twelve people were killed in a feud between factions of the INLA. The feud ran from January until March. In the Republic Fianna Fail won 81 seats in the election of 19 February and although they were still three short of an overall majority Charles Haughey was able to form a government on the casting vote of the Speaker. In May eight members of the Provisional IRA were shot dead by SAS who were waiting in ambush when they tried to blow up the local police station. 12 June saw another election—this time for Westminster, when the SDLP won a third seat through Eddie McGrady's defeat of Enoch Powell in South Down. On 1 November French customs and police officers intercepted 150 tons of arms and ammunition bound for the IRA on board a coaster, the *Eksund*. It was later revealed the guns had come from Libya and that probably three previous shipments had got through. In the Republic police and soldiers organised a massive search of houses and outbuildings along the border counties. On 8 November 11 people were killed and 63 injured by an IRA bomb which exploded without warning at the Remembrance Day ceremony in Enniskillen, Co. Fermanagh. Mrs Thatcher attended the rearranged church service on 22 November. On 19 November Loyalist politician George Seawright was shot dead by the IPLO, an offshoot of the INLA, and on 22 December a leading UDA figure, John McMichael, was killed by an IRA bomb which had been left under his car.

1988 Deaths 93   The largest seizure of Loyalist weapons was made on 8 January when police found 100 guns in the boots of a number of cars near Portadown. Later in the month the Irish government expressed 'deep dismay' at a decision by the Attorney-General Sir Patrick Mayhew not to prosecute eleven RUC officers investigated by the Stalker inquiry for 'reasons of national security'. On 6 March three members of the IRA, Mairead Farrell, Sean Savage and Daniel McCann, were shot dead by the SAS in Gibraltar. The government at first said the three had left a bomb on the Rock but it later transpired that there were no explosives in the car they had just left. On 16 March Loyalist Michael Stone attacked mourners at the funeral of the three at Milltown in Belfast. Using a handgun and grenades, he killed another three people before being arrested. (He was gaoled for life in March 1989.) Three days later, at the funeral of one of Stone's victims, two Army corporals were attacked and beaten and then shot dead, when they blundered into the cortege in their car. The summer saw a series of IRA attacks on military personnel. On 1 May two RAF men were killed in Holland and West Germany. On 15 June six soldiers were killed when a bomb exploded under their minibus at a charity fun-run in Lisburn, Co. Antrim. On 1 August the first IRA bomb in Great Britain since 1984 killed a soldier at Inglis Barracks in North London. On 20 August eight soldiers were killed when a landmine was detonated under their bus at Ballygawley, Co. Tyrone. This was followed in October by a government ban on direct statements in support of violence being heard on television or radio—effectively banning Sinn Fein from the airwaves—and by changes in a suspect's right to silence.

1989 Deaths 62   On 2 February the BBC disclosed that representatives of the four main constitutional parties had met for secret talks at Duisburg in West Germany, but claims of 'a historic breakthrough' were dismissed by party leaders. On 12 February Belfast solicitor Pat Finucane was shot dead by the UFF at his home in North Belfast. Many politicians later criticised earlier remarks by junior Home Office Minister Douglas Hogg, who said that some solicitors were 'unduly sympathetic' to terrorists. On 20 March two senior RUC officers were shot dead by the IRA as they were crossing the border in South Armagh after meeting Gardai colleagues in Dundalk. In April three members of Ulster Resistance, including a Territorial Army instructor, were arrested in Paris allegedly trying to trade missile parts for weapons. The DUP said they had severed their links with Ulster Resistance soon after it was set up. The RUC Chief Constable, Sir John Hermon, retired at the end of May, to be succeeded by Hugh Annesley of the Metropolitan Police. In July Secretary of State Tom King was replaced by Peter Brooke in the cabinet reshuffle. At the end of August a new row began over links between members of the security forces (particularly the UDR) and Loyalist paramilitaries after the murder of a Catholic, Loughlin McGinn, at his home in Rathfrailand, Co. Down. A few weeks after this a BBC reporter was shown a security forces document by Loyalists. In the document Mr McGinn was listed as an IRA suspect. A number of people including two UDR men have since been charged in connection with his murder and the Stevens inquiry has been set up to investigate collusion with Loyalist paramilitaries. On 22 September ten Royal Marine bandsmen were killed by an IRA bomb at their headquarters at Deal in Kent. In October the Court of Appeal quashed the convictions against four Irish people who had served fifteen years in prison for the 1974 Guildford pub bombings.

1990 Deaths 16
(to end of January)

On 13 January three members of a criminal gang were shot dead by undercover agents outside a betting shop in West Belfast. The circumstances surrounding the shooting revived allegations

of a shoot-to-kill policy by the security forces.
Two of the robbers were carrying imitation guns and
two of those shot dead were said to be unarmed.

**Overall death
total 2781**

Prologue

Northern Ireland began the 1960s much like any other decade this century with a Protestant Unionist Party in power and a Roman Catholic minority which did not consider itself to belong to the state and appeared to owe allegiance to the other part of the divided island, known as the Irish Republic. Catholics regarded themselves as an oppressed people, discriminated against in housing, employment, education and the public services. Protestants considered Catholics subservient and subversive and resented the fact that they showed no willingness to be a part of a state which came into being in 1920. The events of the early years of the Northern Ireland state formed the basis on which both communities perceived and judged each other. In the period 1920–3 the IRA opposed the Northern Ireland government with a campaign of violence which brought the six counties of Northern Ireland to near-anarchy. The violence was not confined to the IRA but became a tribal conflict, with both communities as warring factions. Hundreds of people, most of them innocents, lost their lives. The majority of the dead were Catholics, but the numbers killed on both sides testified to an equally prejudiced position adopted by both communities. To assist the police, the Royal Ulster Constabulary, a Protestant Special Constabulary was created. This constabulary was to be subsequently known as the B Specials and until its disbandment in 1970 was rightly regarded by nationalists as a Protestant paramilitary force. The violence of the 1920s also led to the enactment of a Special Powers Act which permitted internment without trial; Catholics, with justification, viewed this piece of legislation as directed entirely at them. The political climate of the 1920s reinforced sectarianism and a society which developed on conflicting lines. Protestants ran the country, perceived the state as their own and regarded nationalists as second-class citizens. The Unionist Party as a corollary to Protestant attitudes devised structures of government which allowed little scope for Catholics to benefit from the state. Electoral boundaries were interfered with to ensure that nationalists were never in a position to elect the number of public representatives that would reflect the size of the Catholic population. This device became known as gerrymandering.

Catholics made no effort to seek accommodation with the newly formed state or with Unionism and resented Northern Ireland as a political entity, regarding the partition of Ireland as a political wrong directed at them. By the beginning of the 1960s Catholic grievances were obvious and justified. By that time the one-party Unionist government had spent fifty years shaping a state with a single religious ethos, and discrimination against Catholics was rife in housing, education and other areas of life. The situation was a recipe for disaster, but not all the ingredients were in place for the conflagration which would engulf Northern Ireland by the end of that decade. First, the IRA, which was considered the major threat to stability, was in a period of decline. It had staged an abortive campaign during the 1950s which found little support within the nationalist community. The campaign resulted in the deaths of IRA men and the internment of many of its members. The internees were released at the beginning of the 1960s into a world which was changing rapidly. However, the IRA leadership who languished in gaol after the 1950s failure re-entered society with a new set of values. They decided that the gun was a failure in Irish politics and a new strategy of social action was required to win the hearts and minds of people in Ireland and to improve the tarnished image of Republicanism. They saw Catholic grievances in Northern Ireland as an ideal catalyst for developing a philosophy and strategy of social action. Under the leadership of Cathal Goulding they devised a Marxist approach to politics in both parts of the island which divided the IRA along left and right lines and eventually led to the creation of two IRA groupings: the Official IRA with Goulding as its leader; and the Provisional IRA, who adopted the mantle of traditional right-wing Republican ideology, which in effect made them the inheritors of the blood-sacrifice tradition of the men who led the 1916 Rising in Dublin.

However, while the IRA were developing a new approach to Irish politics, there were others in the Catholic community in Northern Ireland who were equally concerned about the plight of nationalists and decided that change was needed. They were men such as Austin Currie, who had benefited from the 1948 Education Act which made it possible for Catholics to be educated to university level. Another element in this melting-pot towards the latter part of the decade was the influence of students at Queen's University in Belfast who sought to mimic the stance being adopted by students elsewhere in the world who were campaigning for change and civil rights. Prominent among the students were people such as Bernadette Devlin and Eamonn McCann, who demanded a more radical change in the structure of Northern Ireland. They believed that Stormont was a failed British experiment at self-government and should be abolished. McCann and Devlin were in the students' People's Democracy movement which was formed in 1968. It argued for the repeal of the Special Powers Act, the disbanding of the B Specials, the right of Catholics to one man one vote, the redrawing of electoral boundaries to rid Northern Ireland of gerrymandering, and the outlawing of discrimination in jobs and housing. The most popular and prominent body to reflect the need for change was the Northern Ireland Civil Rights Association, established in January 1967. It was similar in character to the London-based Council for Civil Liberties, with an almost identical constitution. Its demands were for changes to take account of what Catholics saw as basic human rights such as one man one vote in council elections, and fair treatment in the allocation of jobs, houses, and so on. A small number of Protestants were involved in the leadership of NICRA, and several of the Catholics who were engaged in shaping the organisation later formed the Social Democratic and Labour Party (SDLP) in 1970.

However, with the Civil Rights Association in place in 1967, Republicans and particularly members of the IRA saw an opportunity to influence the organisation. Initially they joined NICRA, and in 1967–8 they assisted in the stewarding of civil rights marches. They were people with political experience and long-term aims. They moved quietly into NICRA and were prepared to bide their time before attempting to control it.

The Protestant community viewed the sixties with a degree of trepidation. Some of their leaders warned of trouble from the IRA on the basis that 1966 would represent the fiftieth anniversary of the 1916 Rising in Dublin and the IRA would conspire to overthrow the Northern Ireland state. Some students of Northern Ireland history would argue that successive Unionist leaders used the threat of the IRA as a means of ensuring Protestant solidarity and a hardline attitude towards Catholics to ensure there was no room for change. Undoubtedly there was a rise in anti-Catholic militancy in response to nationalist demands for change, but there was another factor which is rarely mentioned and is conveniently forgotten by Unionists who were prominent in politics at that time. Within Unionism itself there was a moderating influence led by Captain Terence O'Neill, the Northern

Ireland Prime Minister, who was regarded by many people on both sides as a liberal. O'Neill was prepared to give ground slowly to the clamour for change, but he did not take account of the fact that there were those within the Unionist establishment who were prepared to plot against him and overthrow him if he was seen to be capitulating to nationalists. There were plots and counter-plots to oust him, but they failed and he lasted in office until April 1969, when calls for his resignation from both communities encouraged him to step down. During his period of office he witnessed the coming together of the dangerous elements which would set the society alight. What he did not know was that three prominent Unionists who reckoned that he was not hard enough on the issues re-formed the Ulster Volunteer Force, a paramilitary organisation which was involved in the killing of Catholics in the 1920 Troubles. Those three men, who for legal reasons cannot be named here, introduced the one ingredient which the IRA was not prepared to provide in the mid-sixties: violence. The UVF was no sooner re-formed than it began killing Catholics in West Belfast. The year was 1966. The terrorist group also planted explosives at reservoirs outside Belfast, but this was decreed to be the work of the IRA by a Unionist government which did not believe that the UVF was in place or that Protestants would seek to destroy their own reservoirs. Although the killings soon became known as the work of the UVF, belief remained that the IRA was active in planting explosives. All this tended to support early warnings that the IRA was planning to overthrow the state. That view served the purpose of hardening attitudes towards nationalist demands for change and replaced them with a clamour from within the Protestant community for stricter security measures to deal with the IRA.

An interesting footnote to the explosives saga is that two of the leading Unionists who were involved in re-forming the UVF in 1965 were also party to the acquisition of the explosives planted at the reservoirs. Both men were in a car which was stopped by police and found to contain gelignite. A file was sent to the authorities but no action was taken. It may be that the two prominent gentlemen were acting on behalf of others of equal importance within Unionism. The fact that they were allowed to go free bears testimony to their importance or to the fact that they were acting in consort with others who wielded considerable power. I am reliably informed that a file on this matter still exists within the Director of Public Prosecution's archives.

The most potent symbol of Protestant fear and hatred of everything Catholic and nationalist was the fiery orator, Ian Kyle Paisley, who preached that the Vatican and the Dublin government were co-conspirators in a plot to overthrow the Northern Ireland state. Outrageous as this may now seem, many people believed Paisley. The majority of political pundits of the period would agree that Paisley was an important figure in raising the political temperature of the period, and his obvious bigotry found fertile ground at a time when Northern Ireland was riddled with fear, uncertainty and a growing clamour for a change in the status quo. The moment that most observers agree was the one which pushed events towards the edge was the civil rights march in Duke Street in Derry on 5 October 1968. John Hume, leader of the SDLP, says it was the spark which lit the bonfire. The RUC reacted to the march by batoning peaceful protesters. From that moment nothing would be the same. More violence followed and in January 1969 a march by the People's Democracy through a Loyalist area attracted the violence some say it was designed to provoke. This event turned the situation into a sectarian conflict. It was soon apparent that the violence against the students of the People's Democracy was led and organised by members of the B Specials. The violence occurred at Burntollet Bridge outside Derry and the scene was bloody; it also evidenced the sectarian nature of the intention both of the marchers and of those who used brutality to halt it. One other aspect of the People's Democracy march to Burntollet attracted attention. Armed IRA men guarded the marchers while they stopped overnight at Magherafelt en route to Burntollet. That proved that the IRA was an integral part of the civil rights struggle. In April O'Neill resigned but tension continued to rise. In August a Protestant march led to confrontation and violence. Catholics in the Bogside area of Derry erected makeshift barricades and for days fought pitched battles with the RUC, who attempted to remove the barricades and enter the area but found itself unable to cope with what is now known as the Battle of the Bogside, in which the rioters used stones and petrol bombs. The government ordered the mobilisation of 8500 B Specials just as rioting began in Belfast.

The violence in Belfast was organised by the IRA to draw police away from Derry to relieve pressure on the Bogsiders. However, the situation in Belfast, a city where the two communities live within shouting range of each other, erupted into a more brutal conflict. Protestant mobs invaded Catholic neighbourhoods in West Belfast, assisted by the B Specials, with the RUC standing idly by. Hundreds of homes belonging to Catholics were set alight and within days Belfast witnessed the largest population displacement since the Second World War. The RUC used armoured cars in the Lower Falls area and fired heavy-calibre Browning machine-guns in a densely populated area. The IRA found itself unprepared and incapable of defending its own areas. It possessed few weapons, because it had sold most of its guns to Welsh nationalists several years earlier in the belief that the gun would no longer be required in Irish politics. However, several weapons were removed from old dumps, oiled and used in the Lower Falls area. A shotgun and .22 rifle were made available to IRA men for use against Loyalist gunmen who gave cover to a mob which burned out every house in Bombay Street in the Clonard area of the city. Nationalist politicians called for the introduction of British troops to maintain order on the basis that the RUC and B Specials were prejudiced in favour of their own community. The IRA, which had found itself wanting when it came to the need for reciprocal violence, was discredited. Slogans appeared on walls in Catholic housing estates parodying the letters IRA as 'I Ran Away'. British soldiers were on the streets of Belfast and Derry within days of the serious rioting in Derry and Belfast. Their arrival was welcomed by Catholics and they were treated much like the soldiers who liberated Paris. However, their role was simply defined as peacekeeping, which necessitated their being a buffer between the two tribal factions.

While the Army settled into this role, both communities made their own preparations to ensure that individual areas were safe from attack. Barricades were erected in both Catholic and Protestant neighbourhoods. The barricades created defined areas which were run by those who controlled them. In the Catholic areas that role was first undertaken by vigilante groups who were established in response to an awareness that the IRA was not capable of delivering the required protection. These groups became known as defence committees and were responsible to an umbrella organisation called the Central Citizens Defence Committee. Initially it comprised members of many organisations including the IRA but was eventually taken over by Republicans who were disillusioned with the leftward trend of the IRA and its failure to develop a strong military strategy. These men used the defence committee structure as the basis for forming the Provisional IRA in January 1970 and continued to control it after that date. It was the CCDC which sought weapons for the defence of the barricades in Catholic areas and had the initial dealings with the Dublin government. In Protestant areas the barricades also provided cover for vigilante groups, and these eventually became the largest Loyalist paramilitary group, the Ulster Defence Association.

The presence and maintenance of barricades in Catholic and Protestant areas is one of the most critical elements in the development of the war. They created areas of virtual self-government where the paramilitary organisations could act freely. The Provisionals used the cover of the barricades to shape a highly professional terrorist organisation and the UDA and UVF did likewise. These areas of confinement enabled criminal enterprises to be devised, and the only law and order was that decreed or delivered by the paramilitaries. The British Army chose not to interfere because of the politically sensitive nature of the society and the fact that its role was simply to keep the two warring communities apart.

The Hidden Agenda
Civil Rights, the Dublin Government and the IRA

The year 1968 has been described as 'The Year of Dreams' because the youthful involvement in protest movements throughout the world evidenced vitality, optimism and great expectations. In the United States civil righters fashioned a style of protest which was mimicked throughout Europe. The song 'We Shall Overcome' epitomised the idealistic quality of a new age and a new generation who saw protest as a means of correcting injustice and who were enraptured by their dreams and convictions.

Unnoticed by many observers on both sides of the Atlantic was the protest movement which was gaining momentum in Northern Ireland. There was little reason for astute observers to pay attention to this small and almost forgotten part of the United Kingdom. It rarely featured in the news in those days and, as Tariq Ali admitted to me in 1988, he knew nothing of what was happening in Ireland and was not particularly well informed of the prevailing political climate in Northern Ireland in 1968. The fact was, however, that young Catholic intellectuals such as John Hume and Austin Currie were agitating for social reform of what was in essence a one-party state in which Catholics believed themselves to be second-class citizens. Hume, who later became the leading social democrat in Northern Ireland, was watching the progress of civil rights protests elsewhere in the world and recognised that the time was ripe for similar types of demonstrations in Northern Ireland. However, the young

educated Catholics were not alone in believing that change could be
effected by protest, neither were they all social democrats. On the fringe
of the civil rights movement were university students and graduates who
believed that protest required something much more radical than peaceful shows of commitment to fine ideals. Men such as Eamonn McCann
and Michael Farrell, who espoused a Trotskyist ethos, believed the state
could not be changed by gradualist politics but confrontation would bring
about the collapse of the Unionist domination of Northern Ireland.

Another ingredient in the civil rights framework was a coterie, small
in number, of young Protestant liberals who believed earnestly in the
need for democratisation of the state and were convinced that peaceful
agitation was preferable to confrontational politics which would only
lead inevitably to tribal warfare through the heightening of fear and the
arousal of the spectre of sectarianism.

The one dimension to the civil rights struggle which many involved in
it in 1968 failed to perceive with clarity was the presence of the IRA, an
organisation with a history of protest and long-term objectives. Since
1968 there has been much debate about the degree to which the IRA
influenced the civil rights campaign, the extent to which they penetrated
it and whether a war was fought at a subliminal level before it began in
earnest in August 1969. The young Protestant liberals who marched in
1968 now believe that they were duped and that they failed to detect the
hidden agenda of the IRA and its involvement in civil rights. Within
nationalism, there has developed a self-conscious revisionism which
articulates the view that the IRA played little if no part in the civil rights
movement but was merely there as an observer. This view emanates from
a conviction that an admission of IRA involvement would devalue, if not
debase, the part played by those who genuinely believed in what they were
doing at that time and identify them as part of a Republican conspiracy.

In fact, not only did the IRA become a part of what John Hume
describes as 'the spark that lit the bonfire' but so did members of the ruling party in the Republic, Fianna Fail.

Only one month after the fateful 5 October march in Derry's Duke
Street, when civil righters were batoned and television pictures of the
event informed the world about the nature of life in Northern Ireland,
Neil Blaney, the Minister for Agriculture in the Dublin government,
entered the fray.

Blaney, who was, and is, unashamedly a supporter of the IRA, saw the
civil rights movement as taking a political path which veered away from
Irish nationalism. In a speech aimed at people in both parts of Ireland he
pointed out that the Northern Ireland Civil Rights Association did not
include the unity of Ireland in its list of objectives. He went on to attack

meetings between the Northern Ireland Prime Minister, Captain Terence O'Neill, and leading politicians in Dublin. Blaney asserted that such meetings were futile and the Republic's claim of sovereignty over Northern Ireland should be on the political agenda in the twenty-six counties of Ireland. Blaney's statements were evocative of a realisation that events in Northern Ireland could easily spill over the border and it was time for his party, Fianna Fail, to recognise this and be prepared to play the Republican Card when the time was right. This was to be the beginning of a strategy which one year later would lead to formal discussions with the IRA and the emerging Provisionals and create a relationship between members of the Fianna Fail government and terrorism which Dr Conor Cruise O'Brien would describe as being 'highly dangerous for a democracy'.

During the 1960s the IRA from its Dublin leadership base was revising its political strategy. Its leaders in Dublin such as Cathal Goulding and Tomas MacGiolla were considering taking the gun out of politics, ending their policy of political abstentionism and adopting a Marxist analysis of Ireland later translated as the 'Stages Theory'. The first stage of the 'Stages Theory' was to be the breaking down of sectarian barriers in Northern Ireland followed by agitation in the Republic to move workers away from the innate conservatism of Catholic Ireland, thus enabling a realignment of working-class attitudes in Ireland and a transformation of communal class interests. A further development or stage in the process was a detachment from Catholicism and a coming together of workers throughout Ireland. The 'Stages Theory', naïve though it was, evolved in discussions between members of the IRA, the Communist Party of Ireland and left-wing political theorists such as Roy Johnston, who sought to apply Marxist principles to Irish politics with particular emphasis on the ideas of James Connolly, a renowned socialist who was executed as one of the leaders of the 1916 Rising in Dublin. This drift away from traditional Republican thinking and romantic nationalism worried the Fianna Fail Party and particularly men such as Charles Haughey and Neil Blaney, who perceived this change in philosophy as the beginning of a drift towards communism which could eventually pose a threat to the Republic. Within the ranks of the IRA in Northern Ireland were dedicated Republicans who shared the Haughey/Blaney analysis and felt that Goulding and his partners who discussed many of their new-found theories in Dublin pubs were out of touch with the developing political realities in the North.

Not withstanding the differences of opinion about the IRA's new policies, IRA members joined the civil rights movement in the belief that it would ultimately provide a vehicle for new politics of the kind envisaged by the Dublin leadership. However, those in the IRA who adhered to the politics of the smoking gun did not have to wait long for a situation which demanded that the IRA play a role for which it was formed, namely the defence of the Catholic population and the armed struggle. In January 1969 the situation in Northern Ireland was transformed utterly by one event which not only evidenced the presence of the gun in civil rights politics but provided the real spark for a conflagration which would engulf the society for the foreseeable future. That spark was the student-led People's Democracy march from Belfast to Derry on New Year's Day 1969. Among the organisers, who included people such as Eamonn McCann, Bernadette Devlin and Michael Farrell, were young men from the ranks of the Republican movement. The organisers sought confrontation through their intention to parade through staunchly Loyalist areas. In Dublin, Goulding and others within the IRA leadership saw the New Year's Day march as jeopardising the newly created policies of the IRA. Predictably the marchers were attacked by Paisleyites and members of the Ulster Special Constabulary (the B Specials), a part-time paramilitary force which was anti-Catholic and anti-Republican in character. When the march stopped for one night at Magherafelt, the guns came out. IRA men paraded armed in the vicinity of a camp set up by the marchers. Those IRA men evidenced not only the developing split within the organisation, which would later lead to the formation of the Provisionals, but also the IRA presence within the civil rights campaign. The march organisers achieved their goal of confrontation and determined the way in which politics developed. It became known as the Burntollet March, named after the bridge on the outskirts of Derry where the marchers were ambushed by Loyalists.

Dr Conor Cruise O'Brien says that the events at Burntollet pushed things 'over the edge' and convinced him of the presence of the IRA and the developing 'hidden agenda' which would later include the Dublin government. The 'dirty war' was in progress and would be masterminded away from prying eyes and the glare of the media, who simply perceived two communities in conflict.

In the spring of 1969, while Captain Terence O'Neill was attempting to woo middle-class Catholic voters to accept his 'new-look' Unionist Party, Neil Blaney denounced O'Neill and expressed the view that he should not receive Catholic support. Blaney was again playing the Green Card for his own party and articulating a view shared by the anti-Goulding faction within the IRA. Charles Haughey, then Finance Minister, Neil Blaney and Kevin Boland, a fellow cabinet minister, privately discussed how they could influence developments in Northern Ireland, and whether they should attempt to establish an offshoot of the Fianna Fail Party there. They knew that if the Dublin based leadership of the IRA shaped events in Northern Ireland and considerably affected views in the Republic there was a danger that Fianna Fail would not be in a position to capitalise on any political overspill, since the IRA's Marxist policy in the Republic was opposed in every way to the ruling Fianna Fail administration. As each demonstration for civil rights led to violence, so talk of guns for defence permeated many conversations in Catholic neighbourhoods in Belfast and Derry. In South Derry a businessman approached the IRA officer commanding that area and asked for a meeting to discuss the availability of weapons. When the meeting was held, the businessman intimated that, if the IRA in that area required guns, a source in the Republic would provide them. The IRA commander did not respond to the offer and was not told the nature or name of the source who would provide weaponry. He contacted Goulding, who was not prepared to negotiate with an unidentifiable source and was not in favour of reintroducing guns into the political process. However, Goulding instructed the South Derry OC to continue his dialogue with the businessman with the purpose of exposing the source of the weapons. Though no transfer of weapons came from this dialogue, a private IRA communication defined the source. An anonymous document later circulated in Northern Ireland claimed that the South Derry OC and Neil Blaney met in the spring of 1969, but this was simply not true. In fact it was not until after the dreadful violence on the streets in August 1969 that contact was renewed with the businessman and subsequently Blaney.

Even before the dramatic events of August the civil rights movement had changed beyond recognition. There were prominent Republicans within the civil rights struggle such as Liam McMillen, an IRA commander from the Lower Falls area of Belfast, and Jim Sullivan, an active Republican campaigner from the same neighbourhood. Their presence did not go unnoticed by those few Protestants who remained within the Northern Ireland Civil Rights Association in spite of Unionist claims that NICRA was merely a front for the IRA. One of those Protestant members of NICRA, who to this day is frightened to be identified, told me: 'I knew that between April and August 1969 the IRA was beginning to exert influence within NICRA. I am not even prepared to tell you the whole story for fear I could be identified but I can tell you that money was being siphoned off to provide the IRA with funds to purchase weapons. I was powerless to do anything about it, even though I knew that this money was being made available to the IRA by, among others, a prominent member of NICRA such as Frank Gogarty.' This assertion was made to me by a respected professional, and the person he was referring to was a prominent Catholic who ran a dental practice in North Belfast. Frank Gogarty was of sufficient interest to the security authorities that his phone was being tapped in 1970–1 while the Provisional IRA was being formed. I sought evidence to authenticate the claim of my unnamed source and discovered that Gogarty did provide NICRA funds for the Republican movement just prior to August 1969 in the belief that guns might be needed to protect Catholic areas, and it must be said that he was later involved with the defence organisations which also sought guns from the Dublin government.

IRA activity throughout Ireland in the months before August 1969 did not fully equate with the Goulding ethos. Bank robberies were carried out in the Republic under the guise of a defunct organisation, Saor Eire, foreign-owned farms were burned, and post offices were petrol-bombed in Belfast. (Saor Eire, first known in 1931 as a small left-wing Republican grouping, was declared illegal by the government of the Irish Republic. The use of the name emerged again in the 1960s, by which time it was believed to be a label of convenience—a cover name for the IRA when it wished to engage in criminal activity within the Republic.) All these activities, particularly those in the Irish Republic, frightened the Fianna Fail administration and forced them to consider the use of internment without trial. Meanwhile requests for weapons from IRA units in Belfast and Derry were ignored by the Goulding leadership. Journalists in Dublin were told by the Irish Premier, Jack Lynch, at a private gathering, to ignore and refuse to print IRA statements about events in the Republic, but events were running away from the control of politicians north and south of the Irish border. Street fighting in Derry on 12/13 August between young men and the police produced a massive reaction of sympathy in the Republic and resurrected the spectre of volatile national solidarity. The Irish cabinet met and considered the prospect of invading Northern Ireland but were informed that the Irish Army was unprepared for such a course of action. Blaney, Boland and Haughey argued that events were slowly heading for all-out civil war, with the Catholic population in the North being left at the mercy of Loyalist mobs, the RUC and the B Specials. Blaney contended that at the very least the Irish Army should take Derry and force a situation where there would be United Nations mediation leading to the direct involvement of UN and not British troops. Haughey and Boland were in favour of this course of action. The alternative was to make a direct approach to the British government and seek their approval for sections of the Irish Army to enter Northern Ireland at two points—one giving it access and eventual control of Derry in the north-west; the other, through Dundalk, to Newry. It was accepted that Catholics in Belfast would have to wait until Newry and Derry were secured. The plan was irresponsible and did not take account of Protestant resistance or the Catholic death toll in other areas which would ensue from such drastic action.

Blaney, to this day, claims that the British government waited for forty-eight hours before sending troops to Northern Ireland to allow the Irish government time to make the proposed incursions. He also claims that a decision was taken to proceed with this military strategy and Irish troops were sent to the border. In the event, Jack Lynch did send troops but claimed they were field hospital units for Catholic casualties fleeing Belfast and Derry. Blaney says Lynch had 'cold feet' when the time came to take Derry and Newry. Until cabinet documents from that period are made public we shall not know the truth, but subsequent events and actions by Blaney and Haughey suggest that they felt betrayed by Lynch's refusal to take more direct action. Lynch's failure to apply strong states-manship to events on 13 August 1969 unleashed other problems of a more serious nature. An article in *Hibernia* assessed his role thus:

August 13 provided the kind of opportunity which rarely occurs even in the careers of successful politicians: the golden moment to cross the gulf between politics and statesmanship; the moment for which great men are afterwards remembered in his-tory. The really important issue was not the political one. It was that Irishmen were fighting Irishmen; Irish blood was being spilled on Irish soil; Irish lives were being threatened by their own kith and kin. The right thing for Jack Lynch to do in those cat-aclysmic circumstances was to rise above petty political considerations. He should have spoken for All Ireland, North and South, Protestant and Catholic, living and dead. And for once the right thing would have been the most effective, politically. That he failed to do so is hardly any surprise. But that he missed a unique opportunity is as much a personal tragedy for himself as for the nation as a whole.

What Lynch also failed to do was to recognise that Blaney's chauvin-istic proposal for direct action to end partition would have a logical con-sequence of inciting support if not actively providing the means for sub-version in Northern Ireland, and those who adhered to such a policy were to be found in the ranks of the IRA. The split in the IRA during the civil rights campaign from October 1968 to August 1969 now led to a sit-uation where the real subversives were identifiable and, unlike the Marxist-led Goulding faction, were the type of people with whom the Dublin government could do business.

The attacks by Loyalist mobs, aided by B Specials and police, on Catholic areas of Belfast exposed the inability of the IRA to defend Catholic areas. Across the city from north to west the IRA was able to muster only a small supply of weapons—an old Thompson sub-machine-gun, a few revolvers and .22 sporting rifles and shotguns. Goulding discovered that the arms available to the IRA in the Republic were only sufficient to equip four active service units which were sent immediately to the bor-der and not to Belfast or Derry. Goulding's strategy, which never materi-alised, was to attack military targets across the border in Northern Ireland and draw RUC and B Special units from the troubled cities of Belfast and

Derry. The 'border' plan, which was to be masterminded by Sean MacStiofan (later Chief of Staff of the Provisionals), was called off after violence subsided in Belfast. Goulding reckoned that to proceed with military action would only serve to exacerbate the situation. His judgement was not appreciated by those IRA men in Belfast who were now determined to lay their hands on as many guns as they could find. Goulding's leadership and the IRA were at a crossroads. In Northern Ireland the Catholic population rejected them for failing to protect Catholic districts in which almost 1600 Catholic families were forced to flee their homes. (315 Protestant families also fled because of burnings, damage, intimidation and looting.) The Fianna Fail government upstaged the IRA by placing the Irish Army on the border and calling up the Reserve.

Goulding tried to salvage IRA fortunes by issuing a statement on 19 August claiming that 'IRA units are active all over the North'. The statement added that the IRA was ready to defend Catholic districts and to defend the 'liberation of the North'. Dr Conor Cruise O'Brien publicly dismissed Goulding's claim as outrageous, and so did Catholics in the beleaguered areas of Northern Ireland. The result was the setting up of defence committees and the erection of barricades in many areas.

An example of how Goulding's statement and his decision to abort the border campaign were received within IRA ranks can best be illustrated by an episode which occurred at that time. Goulding decided that he would personally explain to the active service units his reasons for aborting their border mission. He travelled to Louth and headed for a farmhouse close to the Louth-Armagh border. His arrival was detected by one of the active service volunteers positioned in a field near the farmhouse. He radioed his commanding officer with the news that the Chief of Staff was in the vicinity, to which the OC replied: 'Shoot the fucker.' The comment, which was not interpreted as an order, was indicative of the mood within the rank and file of the organisation. In Belfast and Derry, particularly, there was talk of setting up a new organisation or ridding the IRA of the Goulding faction. Ironically, Goulding's authority is best illustrated by the fact that, while he was explaining his reasons for aborting the border mission, one of the active service units undertook an unsuccessful bid to blow up Crossmaglen police station.

There was little left to Goulding and those men loyal to him in Northern Ireland but to resurrect the IRA's fortunes; and that could be achieved only by acquiring arms for the units in Northern Ireland and for the defence committees which were blossoming and appeared to be controlling events.

Goulding was contacted by an Irish priest in London who informed him that he had a source willing to supply an unlimited sum of money for arms, provided they were for use not in the Republic but in Northern

Ireland. The implication, Goulding believed, was that the source was likely to be someone connected with Fianna Fail who did not wish the 'Marxist' IRA to have the weapons in the Republic and preferred that the conflict be confined to Northern Ireland. Goulding was introduced to the source of the money. The contact (who for legal reasons cannot be named) turned out to be a man who, because of family ties to someone high in Irish government circles, could only, Goulding deduced, have been acting on behalf of the Fianna Fail administration. Goulding told him that a sum in the region of £50,000 was required to buy the right kind of weaponry. His contact handed him £1500, and promised a further sum within days and the whole amount within a relatively short period.

Other people of prominence in the Republic contacted the Goulding leadership to discuss the prospect of providing money for weapons, but always with the stipulation that any weapons acquired would be solely for use in the North. Addressing a rally in O'Connell Street in Dublin city centre, Paddy Devlin, then Northern Ireland Labour MP for Falls, took the unprecedented step of calling for money for guns. The result was his eventual departure from the Northern Ireland Labour Party, who were dismayed at his behaviour. Devlin, who had been in the IRA from boyhood until the end of the fifties campaign, says he felt justified in seeking money for guns because there was no one prepared to defend the Catholic population. He argues that he took such a step before the British Army arrived on 19 August.

Devlin became the secretary of the Central Citizens Defence Committee in Belfast. The chairman was the leading Republican Jim Sullivan. It was in Belfast that events under the surface began to transform everything including the IRA. Devlin says the barricades and the emergence of the defence committees pushed the IRA into the background, despite attempts by McMillen and Sullivan to give support to the committees. However, there were others joining the defence committees with the objective of taking them over. Some were members of McMillen's battalion staff who were opposed to the Goulding philosophy—men from West Belfast such as Leo Martin, Joe Cahill, Billy McKee, Seamus Twoomey and the young Gerry Adams. There were also men in other areas of the city and in Derry who were of like mind and prepared to adopt similar tactics. The Catholic Church too, always eager not to lose control of its flock, placed representatives on the co-ordinating body of the Central Citizens Defence Committee. The church, with its propensity for orthodox guidance and leadership quickly confirmed that it was determined that the Marxist element within the IRA would not assume control of the situation. As a result a gradual division appeared which was recognised only by a few within the defence structures. Two leaderships emerged: that of Devlin, Sullivan and others with a gradualist if not left-of-centre ethos; and that of the Catholic Church and those within the IRA and the business community who were more attached to an inherited sense of romantic nationalism.

Paddy Devlin puts it this way: 'Initially it was easy for the IRA to take over the defence committees because they had the men with experience of conflict. Slowly they took over all the areas, but it was the type of leadership that worried me. They were the men of the right who would become the Provisionals. They tended to remain in the background using the barricades as cover for reorganising and for planning the reshaping of the IRA. I believe the church knew who it was getting into bed with. However, I don't believe the vast majority of people realised what was going on.' In the course of seeking assistance for his organisation Paddy Devlin met the Dublin government's Minister for Finance, Charles J. Haughey, at the latter's home. He says that Haughey promised financial assistance for the relief of distressed families, but guns were not discussed.

The Dublin government's desire to do something about events north of the border initially centred on the setting up of a Cabinet Sub-Committee to deal with Northern Ireland. Two of the leading members of that Sub-Committee were Charles J. Haughey and Neil Blaney. Aside from giving aid to Northern Ireland to relieve distress, the Irish government was also interested in knowing precisely what was happening across the border. One man who became central to Irish government contacts in areas such as Belfast was an Irish Army intelligence officer, Captain James Kelly. His introduction to people in Belfast was made easy by his brother, who was a priest in St Malachy's College, a leading grammar school for boys in Belfast. In this way he was introduced to Paddy Kennedy, the Catholic MP representing the Central constituency, and to members of a staunchly Republican family in North Belfast, the Kellys, and in particular John Kelly, who later became Adjutant-General of the Provisionals. Paddy Devlin claims that in 1969–70 John Kelly was the liaison man between political figures in Fianna Fail and the emerging group who announced the formation of the Provisional Army Council in January 1970.

In Belfast in September and October 1969 events moved rapidly. Primarily the leadership of the Central Citizens Defence Committee began to change. The Catholic Church organised a *putsch* against the Sullivan leadership and, despite pleas from Devlin, ousted him in favour of a Catholic businessman, Tom Conaty. Sullivan had presented a moderate leadership of the organisation and had orchestrated the removal of the barricades. That did not suit the traditionalists within the IRA who were an integral part of what Devlin calls 'the other leadership'. Devlin observes: 'The departure of Sullivan was not merely another blow to the

IRA in terms of McMillen and the Goulding faction; it also left the organisation at the mercy of the traditionalists. I eventually resigned my post
but remained in the organisation in name only. I was appalled on one
occasion when I arrived at a meeting to see that some of those leaving the
house with members of the clergy were men I knew were about to return
the IRA to an offensive role.'

Devlin's fears were formed not merely by askance observation but by
events which personally affected him. On 24 August 1969 the dissidents
within the Belfast IRA command had held a secret meeting in a social
club in Casement Park in the Andersonstown area of the city. They discussed their control of the CCDC and their disillusionment with the IRA
leadership in Dublin and those loyal to it in Belfast such as McMillen and
Sullivan. The meeting was held secretly because each man present was
liable to be court-martialled for failing to inform the IRA leadership and
for contemplating its overthrow. Those present included Daithi
O'Connell, later to become a Provisional IRA Chief of Staff, Seamus
Twoomey, Joe Cahill, Jimmy Steele, Gerry Adams, John Kelly, Jimmy
Drumm and Billy McKee. They considered how to replace the IRA leadership throughout Ireland. This, however, was ruled to be unnecessary and
a decision was taken to tell McMillen to step down. On 22 September the
plotters took advantage of a meeting being held in a room in Cyprus Street.
Paddy Devlin was present with McMillen and members of the CCDC.

Twenty-one armed men representing every Catholic area in Belfast arrived in the
room. They burst open the door and faced us. They addressed their comments to
Liam McMillen in a threatening fashion. The leader of the group was Billy McKee. He
told McMillen to resign his role as IRA commander. He also said McMillen and his
people started the conflict but couldn't handle it. McKee added that it was the role
of the IRA to defend Catholic areas, and in that regard they had failed. 'You are a
Dublin communist and we are voting you out. You are no longer our leader.' When
McMillen heard this he shrewdly played for time, agreed to their demands but asked
for one week to put his house in order and comply with their wishes.

McKee agreed to McMillen's request, but McMillen spent the following week organising those units loyal to him—which transpired to be
only two out of twenty-one units in Belfast. Goulding attempted to defuse
the situation by sending his Director of Intelligence, Sean MacStiofan, to
Belfast. MacStiofan arrived with the proposal that there would soon be
an Army Council meeting where all matters divisive to volunteers would
be on the agenda. MacStiofan phoned Goulding twenty-four hours after
arriving in Belfast to inform him that there had been a coup and the
majority of Belfast units would no longer take orders from Dublin headquarters staff. However, violence between the various factions was avert-

ed once again with a meeting in Dundalk, where dissidents from Belfast agreed to participate in pooling resources with General HQ for a major arms deal and accepted a proposal to send representatives to an Army Council meeting in Dublin on 4 October.

After the Dundalk dialogue Goulding travelled to Monaghan to a gathering which was intended to endorse the setting up of a body to co-ordinate all activities of defence committees and thus bring them under the control of the Dublin IRA leadership. On arriving in Monaghan, Goulding learned that he had been out-manoeuvred by the dissidents, who had set up a similar organisation in Lurgan the same day.

In the midst of the IRA crisis in the weeks following the August violence, the Irish Army supplied weapons training at Fort Dunree in Donegal at the express wish of the Irish government. That ended when a newspaper enquired from Irish Army headquarters whether the training was officially sanctioned and if it included the provision of weapons.

There was also growing concern in the Defence Ministry in Dublin, where the minister in charge, Jim Gibbons, was in receipt of disturbing reports from Captain James Kelly which were being channelled through the Army's Director of Intelligence, Colonel Michael Heffernan. Gibbons and Heffernan were both worried about how arms supplied from the Republic would be used in the North, and by whom. From all accounts, Captain Kelly acted as a professional soldier in pursuit of Irish government policy and his frequent visits to Belfast did not go unnoticed by British military intelligence and operatives of MI5 and MI6.

Kelly held a meeting of representatives of the defence committees in October 1969 and among those present were prominent members of the IRA. Kelly deduced that all they wanted from the Irish government were guns for defence, and he relayed his belief to the Dublin government. There is little doubt that the behaviour of the Irish government was to say the least confused, if not downright irresponsible and dangerous. Despite the presence of the British Army there was a willingness to supply money without knowing exactly how it would be spent, and some were ready to supply weapons, knowing that the only people capable of using them were the IRA. In this context many people felt it reasonable to deduce that the Irish government through some of its representatives was intent on ensuring that its eventual dealings would be with those members of the IRA, the dissidents, who would guarantee that the conflict would be confined to Northern Ireland and whose traditionalist thinking determined that their allegiance would be to Fianna Fail in the event of a 'doomsday situation'. It is known that plans for an invasion of Northern Ireland by the Irish Army were envisaged until January 1970, when they were finally shelved. In the intervening period the excursions of Captain

Kelly into Northern Ireland and the contacts between Irish government figures and the IRA provided the opportunity for Fianna Fail leaders to determine who its friends would be in the event of a major conflagration encompassing both parts of the island.

One example of an attempt to define the relations of the IRA *vis-à-vis* Fianna Fail occurred towards the end of September 1969 when a Fianna Fail grouping led by Captain Kelly visited the home of the South Derry OC of the IRA. Kelly examined the feasibility of establishing a separate Northern Command of the IRA with a view to detaching it from the Goulding leadership. It was implied that if this happened money and guns would be readily available.

In October a consignment of arms arrived at Dublin airport and was handed over to the IRA. Evidence that this actually took place remains hidden in Special Branch files in Dublin. Who supplied these weapons and paid for them has never been made known.

Meanwhile a £100,000 fund for distress in Northern Ireland was available to the Dublin government Sub-Committee for social action in the North. At least £24,000 was given to Cardinal Conway in Northern Ireland to be used as he saw fit. At a subsequent Dail inquiry into the use of the £100,000, the sum to the Catholic hierarchy was not investigated because of the highly embarrassing quasi-political role of the church in the defence organisations. Charles Haughey, as Minister for Finance, decided that the fund would be administered by a committee of reputable people inside Northern Ireland, though his own government's Information Bureau announced on 21 August 1969 that it would be handled by the Irish Red Cross. Ironically, the government pledge of money, which first amounted to £89,000 and then supplemented with public donations reached £100,000, was transferred by the Red Cross into accounts in the Munster & Leinster banks in Baggot Street, Dublin, and Clones. This resulted in the fund's not being under the control of the Red Cross. The Northern defence committees also had accounts, three in all, in the Baggot Street branch of the Munster & Leinster and shifted sums between the three accounts. The defence committees spent much of their money on relief work, but since they also sought guns it was inevitable that the Irish government contribution which was handed over to the defence committees would be used in part for buying weapons.

The Clones account contained a sum of £5000, and the authorised account holders were, according to the Irish Red Cross documents, Paddy Devlin, a politician and a Belfast solicitor. The first withdrawal from the account was made by the politician and the second by Devlin, but then an alternative withdrawal system was established. Neither the politician nor solicitor acted improperly and in the case of the solicitor there is no evidence that he made a withdrawal from the account. Devlin states:

I accept that the money was to be used for relief work, though I also admit that at that time I was also asking for guns. I only asked for guns because I believed that the police failed to protect the Catholic population in Belfast on 13/14 August and even when the British Army arrived I was still asking for guns because there was no guarantee that they would act as protectors if violence flared again. After the second withdrawal of monies I was approached by people within the defence committees and it was suggested that the signatories to the Clones account should not be actual names but pseudonyms. I now know that this was a ruse to remove me from the scene and obscure the passage of monies from the account. It was agreed that the three pseudonyms should be John White, John Loughran and Roger White. This ensured that other people could withdraw cash from the account. It is my belief that people connected with the Haughey faction through Captain Kelly did not see me as being ultimately dependable. After all, I was a Republican in earlier years but in 1969 I was a member of the Labour Party and did not espouse nationalism. I think they, whoever they were, preferred that I was disentangled from the financial dealings. I don't know what happened to the account after my departure because I never had any other dealings with it.

When in 1971 a Dail inquiry asked Devlin to give evidence about this account he declined to do so. He argues that his decision was based not on the possibility that he would be compromised but on other considerations. His primary reason, he says, for refusing to discuss his role in the Clones affair was because at the time when the Dail Committee of Inquiry was sitting, in 1971, Devlin was raising funds for the families of men who were interned. He claims that to have raised the spectre that the Clones account was used for anything other than relief purposes could have halted the flow of funds to support internees' families. He says that the public in 1971 would have panicked or suspicion might have discouraged them from contributing to a fund aimed again at relief in Northern Ireland. Several people who were members of the Goulding faction in 1969 maintain that the Clones bank account was originally intended to provide support for the defence committees.

Representations were made by the Goulding-led IRA commanders to Captain James Kelly, but, though they say he behaved impeccably towards them, he was unable to stem the growing support for the dissidents who appeared to represent nationalist opinion in Northern Ireland through the defence committees. Those months between August and September were littered with intrigue. Both IRA factions watched each other closely, but throughout the period the dissidents appeared to hold the upper hand, using the defence committees to obscure their real intentions and to convince the Dublin government that they were part of a populist movement with traditional views. They thus established significant contacts with the Lynch/Haughey government.

On 29 December 1969 the name Provisional Army Council hit the headlines after a meeting of the full IRA Army Council. The dissidents issued a statement to the newspapers declaring their position. Several weeks later, at a full convention of IRA Sinn Fein, the break was finally made when the dissidents walked out. The Provisional IRA was born. In relation to violence, weaponry, contacts with the Irish government and support from the Catholic population, it appeared to hold all the ace cards.

During its infancy it was nurtured by an Irish government which behaved as though it had unfinished national business to resolve. That suited the Provisionals. They watched and felt morally secure in the knowledge that a sovereign state was trying to acquire arms for them. Some might argue that Fianna Fail was merely engaged in supplying arms to protect Catholics, but the facts are that they knew with whom they were dealing and they had in their mind's eye a 'doomsday' situation in which those weapons would be used not only against Ulstermen but also against British troops.

The Irish government's intention to provide arms to the IRA began on 14 November 1969 when Captain James Kelly withdrew money from two of the accounts in the Munster & Leinster bank in Baggot Street, Dublin. The accounts were in the names of George Dixon and Anne O'Brien, names which were merely pseudonyms. He made contact with an arms dealer in the United States and another in Hamburg. Kelly and his superiors decided it would be easier and more discreet to ship weapons from continental Europe. Blaney was convinced that Europe was a better shopping ground and insisted that Kelly make use of Albert Luykx, an acquaintance of the Blaney family. Luykx knew a Baron William Regniorers, who in turn knew a Hamburg arms dealer. Kelly travelled to Hamburg, where he met a Herr Schleuter and made a down-payment of £3000 to secure a deal for a large consignment of guns. Schleuter said time and caution would be needed for assembling the weapons and insisted they meet again on 19 February 1970 in Dortmund, where Captain Kelly would be required to produce £10,000 in English notes which he would lodge in a bank in Schleuter's name. On 19 February Kelly did as requested and several days later met the arms dealer at a pre-arranged venue in Dortmund to finalise arrangements for the transfer of weapons to Dublin. Kelly was aware that official sanction had been granted for the consignment to be cleared by Dublin customs, and he suggested that the weapons be crated with a manifest describing the contents as 'Mild Steel Plates'. The crates would leave Antwerp by boat and arrive in Dublin docks on 19 March.

Captain Kelly returned to Dublin unaware that his trips were being monitored by MI6, who were passing the information to their mole within the Gardai, the Irish police. The arms did not arrive in Dublin on the promised date, but instead a quantity of bullet-proof vests. Kelly contacted Schleuter and was told that the shipping company had refused to transport the weapons because the correct end-users' certificate had not been provided. Unknown to Kelly and Schleuter, British intelligence had obstructed Kelly's initial gun-running plan by enticing one of Schleuter's employees to ensure that the shipping documents for the Antwerp transportation did not meet official requirements. However, MI6 were as much interested in the people financing the weapons' consignment as the threat the guns would pose to British troops on the streets of Belfast. They were faced with a choice of acting to halt Kelly's arms negotiations or—as a journalist would define it—'running with the story'. They were sure that Kelly was not simply acting for the IRA defence committees but for people in senior positions in the Irish government. Their objective was to identify the real source and exploit the information politically. To this end they observed Captain Kelly and Herr Schleuter and tapped their phones. They learned that Kelly had received a communication from Schleuter that the arms were being moved to Trieste. Kelly asked for the cargo to be halted at Vienna and said he would arrange for it to be flown to Dublin.

In the first two weeks of April, Kelly connived at encouraging the Department of Transport and Power to support his venture and make it possible for a private plane to land unhindered at Dublin airport with the weaponry. Kelly adopted this course of action after an unsuccessful attempt to persuade Aer Lingus to be the carrier. Albert Luykx made the necessary importation arrangement after meeting a government figure who would later become prominent in successive Haughey administrations, and he also hired a private plane. Both he and Kelly met Schleuter in Vienna in mid-April to finalise their deal and the trafficking of the weapons. Kelly did not realise while he sat with Schleuter in Vienna that his well-laid plans were known not only to British intelligence, but also to Chief Superintendent John Flemming, head of the Irish Special Branch. He, in turn, was keeping the Gardai (the Irish police) informed about the whereabouts of Kelly and the weapons.

Another dimension to life within the Irish Republic which was not to Kelly's advantage was the fact that the Gardai were disillusioned with the inaction of the government in respect of increased IRA activity in the Republic. The Gardai regarded all Republican groups as subversives, but in April 1970 the force felt bitter about the loss of one of its members, Garda Richard Fallon, who was shot during a robbery in central Dublin. The group known as Saor Eire was identified as responsible for the robbery and shooting and was adjudged to be guilty of a series of robberies at that time. Those in higher ranks within the Gardai and Special Branch who observed the killing of Fallon as well as increasing lawlessness were concerned that senior figures in the Irish government were conspiring to supply arms to organisations they regarded as subversive. It was in this context that British intelligence kept both the Gardai and Special Branch informed of the activities of Captain James Kelly and his cargo of guns.

In this atmosphere of intrigue, conspiracy and suspicion, enquiries were made from official channels, mostly Gardai and Special Branch, about the role of Dublin airport in allowing the guns to be flown into airport property. In turn, the airport authorities enquired about a document supplied by Captain Kelly from Haughey's Ministry of Finance which requested that the cargo would be permitted to leave Dublin airport without a customs check. With most bureaucracies, one enquiry or memorandum tends to generate a hundred others in reaction. Thus one enquiry led to many until the Department of Justice was being asked for a directive from the Gardai regarding the weapons due to arrive in Dublin. The Gardai, while awaiting a directive from the Justice Minister, Michael O'Morain, placed a cordon round Dublin airport on the evening of 18 April. Word quickly reached the Provisionals that the arms would be seized, and their leader John Kelly, who was in Dublin, flew to Vienna to meet Captain James Kelly and cancel all arrangements for transporting weapons. One must ask who was responsible for the tip-off to John Kelly about the trap laid at Dublin airport and on whose behalf he flew to Vienna to talk to Captain Kelly. One can only assume that someone in the Irish government, perhaps in the cabinet, needed the arms shipment stopped to avert a major political crisis. It was later reported that the Gardai chief, Peter Berry, announced to the Justice Minister that he had placed a ring of steel round Dublin airport, and O'Morain responded: 'You'd think we were in fucking Casablanca or somewhere.'

John Kelly conveyed the seriousness of the situation to Captain Kelly and they returned to Dublin several days later without the guns. For the Irish government, matters did not end there. Almost at the same time as the two Kellys returned from Vienna, the opposition leader, Liam Cosgrave of Fine Gael, received anonymous information about the arms plot. Sources within the Irish Special Branch claim that British intelligence sent Cosgrave a letter which appeared to come from the Gardai. He made enquiries through his contacts in both Special Branch and the Gardai and soon discovered that the anonymous source was accurate. Cosgrave, a man of considerable integrity, recognised that he was in possession of information which was not just damaging to Fianna Fail as a political party but, if made public, would bring down the Irish government. His information implicated important men and included references to cabinet figures such as Blaney and Haughey. Cosgrave, who would have benefited his party politically by making public his information, chose instead to present it to the Taoiseach, Jack Lynch. In the days that followed there were bitter scenes in the Irish Parliament, Dail Eireann. The Minister for Justice, Michael O'Morain, was encouraged to resign for health reasons. Blaney and Haughey were dismissed from the cabinet, Boland resigned in protest, and Captain James Kelly was arrested. Cosgrave, when explaining his actions to Dail Eireann, said: 'I considered it my duty in the national interest to inform the Taoiseach of information I had received and which indicates a situation of such gravity for the nation that it is without parallel in this country since the foundation of the State.'

As the story unfolded, so did criminal proceedings, which resulted in Captain Kelly, John Kelly and Charles Haughey appearing together in the same dock, charged with importing arms. John Kelly and Charles Haughey were acquitted.

The 'Arms Trial', as it became known, did, however, produce other information on the nature of the conspiracy and the hidden agenda which existed even into 1970, when British troops were facing serious civil unrest and their first major confrontations with rioters in Catholic areas of Belfast. During the Dail Committee of Inquiry into the £100,000 fund, which was held after the Arms Trial, reference was made to a directive of 6 February 1970 from the Defence Ministry to the Irish Army command.

When the Committee of Inquiry sought to question the Army Chief of Staff, General Sean McKeown, about the February 1970 directive, he pleaded privilege. In making his claim, General McKeown said that none of the matters covered by the directive was in any way related to the expenditure of funds being examined by the Committee. General McKeown was correct in that the directive was not connected with government funds and the Committee's brief was to examine the £100,000 of government money channelled towards the defence committees and, by implication, the IRA in 1969–70. He was advised to seek privilege by the Defence Minister, who at the time of the inquiry in 1971 was Mr Cronin. However, General McKeown was also aware of references made to the directive at the Arms Trial. During that trial, Colonel Heffernan, who was Director of Army Intelligence in 1969–70, gave evidence which supported an assertion made by one of the accused, Captain James Kelly, that the directive had a vital bearing on the question of official and alleged unofficial importation of arms to Northern Ireland and had a considerable bearing upon his actions. Although General McKeown was reacting strictly to the Committee of Inquiry's brief regarding the £100,000 fund, he must also have known that the Committee had been given a much wider brief. The advice to him to claim privilege must be considered in relation to the nature of the directive and its implications for the Irish Army both in 1970 and for the future.

The famous directive was not committed to paper but was a spoken order which was delivered to the Chief of Staff in the presence of the Director of Intelligence, Colonel Heffernan. From all accounts there was no verbatim record of the order, though the Arms Trial was told that an 'appreciation' of it had been returned to the Ministry for clarification and ratification. The Arms Trial was informed that a search had been made and no such document had been uncovered.

How does that equate with the fact that Colonel Heffernan told the Arms Trial on 29 September 1970 that shortly before the trial he contacted the Chief of Staff's branch requesting an opportunity to view the directive to check his recollection of it? Heffernan added that he was not afforded an opportunity to view it but was told the terms of it, and it was his considered opinion that the original directive committed to writing still existed in the Chief of Staff's section, in the Plans and Operation Branch. So what was Colonel Heffernan's understanding of this secret directive, how did it fit into the overall conspiracy, and why should the Chief of Staff seek to protect himself and the Army from it?

The general terms of the directive were that surplus arms and ammunition should be put aside and made readily available for certain contingencies. The directive stipulated that the Irish Army should prepare for incursions into Northern Ireland and that the surplus arms and ammunition and a supply of gas masks should be provided for these incursions.

The directive will never be seen, but there are sufficient grounds for believing that it was primarily concerned with the arming of a section of the Catholic population. If it was merely concerned with the procurement of weapons that would have been a relatively straightforward matter which would not have required the presence of the Director of Intelligence at the meeting during which the directive was issued. The Quartermaster-General, who is responsible for arms supplied, was not present at the meeting. However, if the intention was to supply weapons clandestinely, then there was every reason to have Colonel Heffernan present to offer advice.

During the Arms Trial, when one of the witnesses was repeatedly cross-examined about the directive, he categorically refused to confirm or deny that it allowed for the possibility of Irish Army incursions into Northern Ireland or the distributing of arms to the Catholic population. When asked directly if the Army was requested to acquire arms which the government could decide to distribute in Northern Ireland, the witness replied: 'I don't think that could have happened. These arms would not have been used for any purpose at all without the full agreement of the Irish Government. I think Counsel is trying to put words in my mouth.'

There is every reason to believe that the directive was essentially an apparatus to realise the purpose of those members of the government and the armed forces who were preparing for a 'doomsday' situation in Northern Ireland.

An example of how the directive was almost put into effect occurred on 1 April 1970. When serious rioting erupted in the highly populated Catholic enclave of Ballymurphy in West Belfast, 500 .303 rifles and ammunition were moved to the town of Dundalk close to the border with Northern Ireland. Gibbons did not order the Army to send 500 soldiers to use the rifles—which suggests that the weapons were intended for use by others. The Defence Minister sent the rifles in the knowledge that the Irish Army was equipped with 7.62 mm rifles and not Second World War .303 Lee Enfields.

Aside from the directive, the Arms Trial and the Committee of Inquiry left much unsaid and a feeling that the full facts would never emerge. People remember the great feeling of expectation when the head of the Special Branch, Chief Superintendent John Fleming, appeared before the Committee of Inquiry. Like all men involved in a dirty war, an undercover war, he prefaced his testimony with stern warnings that he was obliged to protect his sources, that his information came from confidential sources, and that anyway he was not at liberty to disclose his sources or divulge the nature of their work. Everything he alleged was based on hearsay. As one journalist said at that time: 'After a long investigation it appeared that there was a great deal more that the head of Special Branch didn't know compared to what he did know.'

And what of Herr Schleuter and the guns? Arms dealing, as this book will later explain, is a risky venture. Before the story was exposed in Dublin, the machine-guns, sub-machine-guns and automatic rifles were removed from the crates bound for Dublin. When members of the Irish Special Branch flew to Vienna, where the crates were impounded at the request of the Irish government, they only found crates containing 500 pistols with a supply of ammunition. Gone were the heavy weapons and several hundred thousand rounds of ammunition of high-velocity calibre. Therefore the Arms Trial centred only on the importation of pistols. Nothing more was heard of the weapons or the money paid by Captain Kelly. The Provisionals refuse to confirm or deny whether they retrieved the money or the weapons, but privately they accept that British intelligence thwarted the operation.

There were many forces at work to create a conspiracy. Who were Saor Eire? That question is never likely to be answered. It is known they existed as a small breakaway group, but their emergence and subsequent disappearance raised questions about the convenience of the Republican label. The significance of Saor Eire in the eventual uncovering of the government's dealings can only be looked at briefly in respect of certain factors. Although it was never proved, it was Saor Eire who were believed by the Gardai to be responsible for numerous bank robberies and, especially, the murder of Garda Richard Fallon. When Captain James Kelly was first interrogated by the head of Special Branch, he was asked what he knew about Garda Fallon's murder. Kelly knew nothing, but he wondered why this should have been relevant to the importation of arms.

The only thing that one can say for certain is that there was a hidden agenda, a conspiracy of a kind which was dangerous for the Irish state, and it provided an indication of just how dirty the war would become on both sides of the Irish border. One can only speculate on what might have occurred had the consignment of 'Mild Steel Plates' been available on 1 April 1970. As we know it was in Vienna; and the .303 rifles were recalled from Dundalk because it was believed that they could be traceable to the Irish Army—so says the official version. We may never know the true version, if such a concept as truth exists in the labyrinthine levels of a dirty war.

What Haughey, Blaney and Captain Kelly did not know in 1970 was that the Provisionals had plans for the continental arms shipment. On the occasion when it was expected from Antwerp, the Provos had an armed unit on the dockside and a lorry to convey the guns to the border. There is little doubt that they would have endured no interference on the part of Captain Kelly, who intended moving the guns to a monastery in Cavan until a decision could be taken about their distribution. John Kelly and his brother Billy, the OC of the Provos' 3rd Battalion, who were on the dockside, had already arranged for a convent on the outskirts of Dublin to store the cargo until Provo units were allocated a percentage of the cargo.

Likewise, at Dublin airport in April, the Provos were again prepared to seize the weapons and move them northwards without delay. The Provos were not simply preparing for defence. Like Fianna Fail, they believed they had some unfinished national business to conclude.

2

Gangs, Counter-Gangs and Secret Burials

The formation of the Provisional IRA in 1970 signalled a significant change in the situation in Ireland. It reintroduced romantic nationalism and placed it firmly on the stage of political conflict. By 1971 the Provisionals were illustrating that they viewed the British Army as a force of occupation rather than a peacekeeping force. As violence increased, the Northern Ireland Prime Minister introduced internment without trial. Predictably it was directed at Republicans, but ironically many of those interned were neither Republicans nor members of either the Provisional or Official IRA. Four months later fifteen innocent Catholics were killed when a bomb exploded at McGurk's Bar in Belfast. The explosion was the work of the Ulster Volunteer Force, but the authorities tried to suggest that it was an 'own goal', a bomb which the IRA had placed in the bar to be collected by one of its units. By January 1972 the situation was further exacerbated when paratroopers shot dead thirteen unarmed civilians in Derry in what became known as 'Bloody Sunday'. In retaliation the Official IRA took the war to England and placed a bomb in Aldershot military barracks which claimed the lives of seven people. In March 1972 the British government finally ended one-party government in Northern Ireland by imposing direct rule from Westminster and abolishing the Unionist administration at Stormont. The reaction of the Loyalist population was fear and a feeling that the British had finally succumbed to terrorist pressure. Loyalist reaction was violent: killer gangs took to the streets claiming the lives of hundreds of innocent civilians, mostly Catholics, particularly in the summer months of 1972. Murder squads were stalking the streets, the war had spread to mainland Britain, and at the end of 1972 bombs exploded in central Dublin while the Dail was discussing the implementation of tougher anti-terrorist laws. The bombs killed two people and injured eighty, and the anti-terrorist legislation was passed in a Dail shocked by news of the carnage. At first the explosions were believed to be the work of the Provisionals, who were said to be angry that the Dublin government was seeking to impose curbs on IRA activities. The IRA denied planting the bombs and accused British intelligence of responsibility on the grounds that the bombs were intended to force the Dublin government to pass the stricter anti-terrorist legislation. Within a short time senior political figures also sought to blame the British once it was realised that British agents were operating what was viewed as a dirty tricks campaign in the Irish Republic.

The situation in Ireland had come a long way since 1969. British security chiefs who had watched the Army being sent to Northern Ireland in a peacekeeping role quickly realised that it was unprepared for what had developed into an urban guerrilla war. When the British Army arrived on the streets of Northern Ireland in 1969 in response to pleas from Catholic politicians, in traditionally Republican areas soldiers were welcomed much like the troops who arrived to liberate Paris in 1944. The scenes of jubilation witnessed on film and captured by newspaper cameramen, in trouble spots such as West Belfast, were soon replaced by a belligerent nationalist population who saw the Army as the old enemy. By the middle of 1970 Catholic youths were frequently in serious confrontation with soldiers. The Army was not equipped for dealing with civil disturbances within the United Kingdom, much less the threat of terrorism which began with the emergence of the Provisional IRA. The Provos, as they soon became known, simply assumed that they were the rightful inheritors of the 1916 Republican tradition and that war with the British in Ireland was still in progress. However, in 1970 the IRA waged a war on the sidelines because they were unsure of their support in their own community for a military campaign and they were too busy acquiring the weaponry to form themselves into a guerrilla army. They preferred to condition attitudes towards the British troops by advising people not to 'fraternise' with soldiers. Such a word as 'fraternise' carried a historical message, if only subliminally, that associating with British soldiers was a crime which throughout IRA history carried the penalty of tarring and feathering or something more sinister.

Inside the Catholic ghettos, the role of vigilantes within the defence committees was reduced by the Provisionals to a minor element in the power structure and, ironically, these same Provisionals were representing the Catholic community, in the guise of community leaders, at meetings with the British Army and the RUC. The Army also assisted a gradual erosion of confidence in itself by being seen to behave with ill-discipline and over-zealousness in dealing with riots. Perhaps most significantly, the Army was seen to concentrate its policing role mainly in Catholic areas. By the end of 1970 British troops were engaged in searching nationalist areas for guns while Protestant paramilitaries operated freely and often manned road blocks with the express permission of the Army. There was no one in authority, political or military, who was capable of examining the situation, unravelling its complexities and providing equitable solutions. Matters too often gravitated towards a breakdown because of historical prejudices, historical ignorance, or a lack of political clarity at a level where it should have existed. Within Army HQ at Lisburn, some fifteen miles from Belfast, there was a growing concern that irrespective of street rioting the Army would suddenly find itself in a historical struggle from which it might not easily be extricated. After all, by September 1970 the Army Command was aware of the attempts by the Dublin government to import arms, and it was assumed that it was only a matter of time before both wings of the IRA would be fully equipped to sustain a campaign of terror. In 1970 the Goulding faction, now the Official IRA, were concerned about improving their image within the nationalist community and were as equally anti-British as their counterparts, the Provos.

In April 1970 a soldier who had the credentials for dealing with difficult situations arrived in Belfast. He was Brigadier Frank Kitson, and he took command of 39 Infantry Brigade, which gave him effective control of the city of Belfast. His arrival went virtually unnoticed, and few people in journalistic circles judged his presence to be of news value. Fewer within paramilitary circles recognised the name Kitson—which now seems absurd, when one considers the significance the terrorists and propagandists have since attached to his tour of duty in Northern Ireland. Before being posted to Ulster he had spent a year at Oxford and finished a book entitled *Low-Intensity Operations.* In 1960 he had published what became a counter-insurgency manual, *Gangs and Counter-Gangs,* about his experiences of fighting the Mau Mau in Kenya. In that conflict Frank Kitson at twenty-seven years old was a district intelligence officer who devised techniques for terrorising the terrorists. These involved using 'counter-gangs' which could be attributed to the enemy, namely the Mau Mau, in order to discredit them. After Kenya he fought in Malaya and was given command of a battalion in Cyprus between 1962 and 1964. His tour of duty in Northern Ireland turned out to be brief—which was unusual for a man with so much military experience. However, during his short stay he devised a system of intelligence gathering, of penetrating the IRA and of exploiting propaganda that was in some respects extremely successful. His critics have attributed him with the role of devising every conceivable dirty trick ever used in Northern Ireland. Indeed, sections of the Provisional IRA became paranoid about Kitson. They saw events as though in double vision, and happenings which seemed inexplicable at any point in time were deemed to be part of a Kitsonesque experiment. The IRA incorrectly credited Kitson with the introduction of internment in August 1971; in fact he was opposed to the policy because, as he told his military superiors, it would prove counter-productive. That is not to suggest that he was not central to the idea of using the interrogation techniques which were applied to twelve of the first batch of men arrested on the day internment without trial was implemented.

However, it is in the areas of intelligence gathering and propaganda that Kitson was a supreme strategist. His stay in Northern Ireland ended in April 1972. There were those within the Army and within political circles who felt that this quiet but self-assured soldier was a liability. The IRA were using the publication of *Low-Intensity Operations* and *Gangs and Counter-Gangs* to support claims that Kitson was responsible for illegal in-depth interrogation techniques, killings and counter-gangs. Fanciful stories emerged, and Kitson's actions in Kenya were seen as being applied to Northern Ireland. Senior nationalist politicians fed the mythology which began to surround him, and his published work provided a framework which the Provisionals duly exploited and exported to the international press. Even twenty years later Kitson is defined by some writers as the man responsible for devising counter-insurgency techniques involving the use of the SAS in covert actions. This chapter is an attempt to explore a period which the Provisionals, in respect of this book, have agreed to talk about for the first time, since they too believe it is crucial to an understanding of the 'dirty war'. Leading Provisionals provided me with information on the subject, and the Army's views on the events which are unfolded in this chapter are drawn from press coverage and off-the-record briefings.

So where does the influence of Frank Kitson become apparent in relation to undercover activities, considering that he was the expert in this field? Kitson had left Ireland by the time the incidents dealt with in this chapter took place in Belfast, but most of the episodes I am about to describe have their origins in structures and events which began while Frank Kitson was in command of 39 Infantry Brigade.

At 11.20 am on Monday, 2 October 1972, West Belfast was quiet. In the Twinbrook estate on the edge of the Andersonstown area many housewives were arranging dirty clothing and placing it in bags to be collected by the firm of Four-Square Laundry. It was an efficient service and cheaper than others that operated in the neighbourhood. A van called twice a week to collect and return the laundry. The van was always driven by a pleasant young man who remained at the wheel while his companion, a pretty, slimly built young girl, went to houses and collected the clothing. Customers believed they were brother and sister because they looked so alike. The Four-Square Laundry's Bedford van was distinctive: it had a symbol of the company, four squares overlapping each other, cut into the metal above the windscreen. Most housewives did not have time to talk to the female employee of the laundry company, but those who did found her chatty and pleasant. Those who were wary of strangers were relieved to discover that both the van driver, Ted, and his colleague, Sarah, had Belfast accents. They appeared to be a quiet, hard-working young couple.

On that morning, 2 October, Ted drove the van into Juniper Park in the Twinbrook estate. Everything seemed normal, and once he had completed the Twinbrook run he would travel to nearby estates in Finaghy and Lambeg before completing his day's work. He would return with the laundered clothes to the three estates on Thursday. As he drove slowly into Juniper Park, Sarah directed him towards no. 8, where there was always a large supply of dirty clothing to be collected. When the van came to a halt, Sarah made her way towards the front door of no. 8. The occupant, a mother of two children, opened the door and exchanged pleasantries with Sarah. Ted remained in the van and watched Sarah produce the relevant forms to record the items of clothing.

Sarah was busy checking the laundry items when she heard the sound of gunshots and what sounded like machine-guns. For a split second her mind flashed back to the moment when Ted was driving into Juniper Park. A blue car driven by a man with a beard had passed the Four-Square van and the driver of the car peered at her and at Ted. But this recollection was suddenly shattered by the reality of what was now happening fifteen yards away. Two men, their backs to her, were facing into the driver's side of the van. They were crouched in a firing position and there was a lot of smoke surrounding them. As she stood, motionless, the gunmen fired at least twenty shots. Then one of the gunmen appeared to swivel his body in her direction. Sarah reacted quickly and dived into the doorway of no. 8, dragging the occupant and the children with her. She waited there for a few minutes and then made her way out of the rear of the house, explaining that it was probably a Loyalist hit-squad that had carried out the attack. Before she left no. 8, she looked into the street to see the van being driven away.

The van was being driven by a local man, Frank Finlay, who with a friend had arrived on the scene to find the laundry van riddled with bullets and the driver slumped over the wheel. Finlay, his friend and a local priest decided that there was no time to waste if they were to save the life of the laundry van driver, who appeared to be alive. They drove towards Lisburn and were fortunate to meet an ambulance en route. They transferred the injured man to the ambulance and drove the van to Lisburn police station in the knowledge that it represented crucial evidence of the terrorist attack. There were fourteen bullet holes in the driver's side of the vehicle and a further two bullet strike marks. Before the van reached the station, the young man who had been its driver was found to be dead on arrival at the hospital.

On 2 October it was also a quiet morning on Belfast's Antrim Road in the north of the city. At approximately 11.30 am a car containing four men drew to a halt outside no. 397. Three of the occupants of the car alighted from the vehicle and walked quickly to the entrance. A casual observer would not have noticed that the three men each carried something concealed inside their heavy overcoats.

The ground floor of the premises at no. 397 was used as a massage parlour which offered a range of services including sex. The floor above was used as an office and was staffed by a young girl and a middle-aged man. The massage parlour often advertised that it had attractive masseuses. That was more than simply an exaggeration: there was just one masseuse providing services with the consent of her husband who owned the business. On the morning of 2 October business was not brisk and the only customer was a middle-aged man sitting in the shabby waiting-room. He did not notice as three strangers entered 397, passed the waiting-room and made their way to a staircase leading to offices on the floor above. Then one of the men removed a Thompson sub-machine-gun from the folds of his coat and his companions produced a short American M1 carbine and a .45 semi-automatic pistol. As they slowly climbed the staircase, the gunman carrying the Thompson was so busy gripping the weapon in front of him with two hands that he slipped on a loose stairboard. He failed to control his weapon and his finger accidentally squeezed the trigger. The gun was not switched to automatic fire, otherwise the three gunmen would have been killed. Three bullets were loosed off, one of them penetrating the staircase and striking the customer in the waiting-room of the massage parlour. The gunmen panicked as the gun discharged, hurried from the building and made good their escape in the car which had driven them there. The injured man was rushed to hospital but was not seriously injured.

As the shooting was taking place on the Antrim Road, another group of gunmen fired wildly into office premises in College Square East, close to Belfast city centre. The offices were not occupied at the time and no one was hurt.

Within forty-eight hours of these incidents the Provisional IRA claimed that they had killed 'five British spies' in the three shootings. The British Army replied to this claim: 'The IRA says it executed five spies but as everyone knows we always disclose any deaths and on Monday there was one.' The Army was admitting that Ted—or, as the kids in Twinbrook called him, Teddy—was a spy.

The Provisionals, however, were more explicit than journalists expected: 'The Republican movement has been aware for a number of months of a Special British Army Intelligence Unit, code-named MRF. This Unit, comprising picked men, has been operating under the guise of civilians. The Unit was run by a Captain McGregor who used flats and offices in Belfast and ran a laundry service.'

Were the Provos correct in claiming that a secret unit existed, and what was the purpose of the laundry service and the other premises attacked on 2 October? Yes, the MRF or, to give it its correct designation, the Military Reconnaissance Force, did exist. It was attached to 39 Infantry Brigade and was formed in 1971. The Four-Square Laundry was just one of many MRF operations. It was a simple but clever way of conducting surveillance in difficult areas. Laundry was collected, and the clothing items of people known to be connected with the IRA were forensically tested. The laundering of the clothing was then contracted out as part of a job lot to a large laundry firm in Belfast which was unaware that there was a military connection. The Four-Square Laundry offered competitive prices which made them more attractive than their rivals. The operation had been in progress three months when the Provos uncovered it. The laundry van driver was twenty-one-year-old Sapper Ted Stuart, a native of Northern Ireland. His companion was Lance-Corporal Sarah Jane Warke, W/439979, Provost Company, Royal Military Police.

The attack on 397 Antrim Road was intended to wipe out another MRF operation which was run from the rooms above the massage parlour, but what the IRA did not know was that the massage parlour itself was also part of the intelligence operation. The attack on the offices in College Square East was also aimed at an MRF operation, but the operatives had moved from the premises several days before the attack.

In the days following the three incidents, *The Times* and other national papers carried a claim from the Provisionals that they had executed 'two high-ranking British agents' in the Antrim Road premises and two other operatives who were hiding in the van in which Sapper Stuart was killed. Until recently the Provos insisted that they killed five people on 2 October 1972, and several books have unquestioningly accepted their assertion. However, they now admit that only one agent was shot and that IRA units bungled the other operations on the Antrim Road and in College Square East.

The real story, which until now has not been revealed, is the degree to which the Provos were penetrated by the MRF operations and the extent to which they were eventually damaged by them.

In 1972, following the ravages of internment without trial, the IRA leadership was changing rapidly. Internment in August 1971 failed in that it led to the arrests of innocent men, of people who had left the IRA after the 1950s campaign, and civil rights activists who were classified as subversives on RUC Special Branch files. Internment failed because the Army relied heavily on outdated intelligence files in the hands of the RUC. By 1972 the Army, which was facing an urban guerrilla force, required precise intelligence identifying people at various levels of leadership within the Provisional IRA. The Provos knew that the favourite method of screening the population of areas such as the Lower Falls was the constant stopping and searching of pedestrians, the frequent checking of vehicles, house searches, temporary arrests and interrogations, or the placing of soldiers or small units in derelict buildings. A soldier or unit would be supplied with food and told to establish a temporary observation post for several days. Such posts were set up in shops damaged in rioting or houses which were bricked up after being vacated by families who had fled from an area because of intimidation. A unit would move into a building under cover of darkness and set up listening devices which would be angled towards the street; a brick would be carefully removed from an outside wall to provide a view of a street; a slate or part of a slate would be removed from a roof so that a soldier could perch in the rafters of a building and be afforded a panoramic view of a neighbourhood.

The IRA knew from years of experience that the most successful form of surveillance took place when someone within its own organisation was informing to the security forces. That was difficult to detect and isolate and when it happened the damage was often irreparable.

In the Lower Falls, British Army intelligence was particularly interested in penetrating 'D' Company of the 2nd Battalion of the Provisionals because much of the violence in that part of the city appeared to emanate from within the confines of the area which the Army knew contained that company.

In the summer of 1972 the intelligence officer of 'D' Company reported to his OC that one of their volunteers was frequently absent and had lately been arrested. The OC suggested that a casual watch be kept on this volunteer, a married man in his early twenties called Seamus Wright. He lived in Leeson Street and was regarded as a quiet but dedicated Republican. When volunteers were arrested by the Army they were interned or released if little was known about them. When they returned to their areas they were not debriefed in the style which now exists and which proves as gruelling for the IRA men as when they face police or British Army interrogators.

However, 'D' Company was an exception to the rule in 1972, and when it was suggested that a 'casual' watch be maintained on Seamus Wright the intelligence officer did the opposite. When Wright was released from Army custody he returned to his wife and reported briefly to his unit in 'D' Company. He explained in a plausible manner that he was questioned about guns and explosives and asked to name the leading IRA men in his area. Shortly after this episode, Wright again disappeared from home. The inquisitive IO of 'D' Company enquired from Mrs Wright if she knew of her husband's whereabouts. She replied that he had gone to England to seek work and produced a letter from her husband with an English postmark. The IO allowed the matter to rest for several weeks and then again approached Mrs Wright, who said that her husband was trying to get a job so that he could arrange for her to join him. Some weeks later the IO learned from a neighbour that Mrs Wright had gone on a trip. After a few days she returned and told neighbours and acquaintances that she had visited her husband in London but did not wish to live in England. She hinted that her husband would soon be returning home.

Seamus Wright surfaced in his old haunts in the Lower Falls several weeks later, but this time there were prying eyes watching his every move, and every question he asked was analysed. The intelligence officer was a naturally suspicious man and he knew that 'D' Company had been suffering setbacks; people who had recently joined the IRA in the area were being pulled in for questioning and the Army seemed to know exactly where to look for weapons. The IO's analysis was that of everyone he could identify in the company, the one person whose habits were erratic was Seamus Wright. He conveyed his suspicions to the OC of 'D' Company, who suggested that Wright should be questioned.

When Wright was hauled before several officers from 'D' Company in a shabby room in a house off Leeson Street, he panicked. He believed he was about to be executed. The irony was that Wright, when suddenly faced, as he believed, with death, realised that he had a value. As one IRA man put it later: 'When we catch a guy who has been turned by the Brits, we know that he knows he has a value to us. He has learned that by the fact that the Brits have also convinced him of his value. In essence, when you look at the two poles of that argument, he is expendable as far as both sides are concerned. When it comes to the sting, winning matters, not the survival of the double agent.'

Wright's interrogation lasted forty-eight hours, during which he unfolded a fascinating story for his captors. He told them that early in 1972 he was arrested while walking along Leeson Street. He was taken to Castlereagh interrogation centre where he was told that there was evidence to connect him with a murder in 'D' Company area. Wright was

connected with an explosion which had killed a member of the security
forces, and the fact that his interrogators knew of his involvement suggested that someone had 'grassed' on him. His interrogators offered him
a deal whereby no charge would be preferred against him if he co-operated and named everyone in 'D' Company. He admitted to the IRA that he
did in fact name everyone he knew to be in 'D' Company. Wright's reaction
to events in Castlereagh was from the outset that of a naïve young man who
firmly believed that the authorities were in a position to charge him simply on the assertions being made by the security forces' interrogators.

The IRA found Wright's story much more fascinating when he began
to reveal how he co-operated with Special Branch and military intelligence and how he became part of an intriguing operation. Wright said
that on his release from Castlereagh he was taken to Palace Barracks at
Holywood on the outskirts of Belfast and placed in a heavily guarded
compound with other men. He was treated well and informed that he was
to be part of a special team to assist in the defeat of all violence. Wright
did not personally meet the other men in the compound, but within
twenty-four hours he was flown to England, where he was given training
in basic man-to-man surveillance techniques. After several days he was
flown back to Belfast with instructions to be seen around his neighbourhood. He would then disappear on the pretext of going to England to find
work. Wright travelled initially to Palace Barracks. According to the IRA,
he admitted that when he returned to Palace Barracks his training continued. He was asked to write letters to his wife which he was told would
be posted from an address in England. As a result of this correspondence,
he received replies from his wife, who insisted that she would visit him
at his English address. His Army contacts suggested that to avoid his
cover being blown they would arrange for his wife to travel to London to
the accommodation address which appeared on his letters to her. He was
flown to London and from there he wrote to his wife and arranged for her
to meet him. Although he tried to encourage her to remain in England,
she refused to do so. His Army handlers would have preferred that she
left Belfast so that Seamus Wright did not have the added complication
of constantly worrying about his wife or the danger of her finding out
about his double life. She represented a particular danger to the Army's
operations because she, unlike Wright, was from a prominent Republican
family and there was always the risk that someone from her family might
ask awkward questions about her husband. Wright was told that if he could
persuade his wife to live in England he could operate more freely and
return to Belfast as often as he liked without having to answer to her for his
movements.

The revelation which most fascinated Wright's IRA interrogators was his reference to a compound within Palace Barracks housing informers. The IRA knew informers existed within its ranks, but the concept of a compound where they were temporarily housed and trained appeared much more intricate and serious than typical Special Branch ploys which the IRA constantly experienced. Wright told them that the group with whom he worked was known within the Army as the Military Reconnaissance Force. He was allowed free access to Palace Barracks and to the compound, which was segregated from other military buildings within the camp. He was constantly questioned about his childhood, his family, schoolfriends and everyone he knew in his neighbourhood. He was shown photographs of IRA suspects and asked to identify them or shown photos or newsreel of funerals and parades in order to discover if he knew any of the faces. Occasionally he was driven into the Falls area in armoured personnel carriers and asked to scrutinise pedestrians or people standing on street corners to determine whether they were members of either wing of the IRA. Wright soon had his Provo interrogators acutely interested in him, especially when he pointed out that there was a great deal more he needed to learn about the MRF. Wright was trying to buy himself time, to buy his life. Equally the IRA was faced with a dilemma. On the basis of his confession, they were obliged by their rules to shoot him; yet, as he was pointing out, there was much to be gained. The IRA were also beginning to realise that they were dealing with someone who was extremely capable and who was offering himself as a double agent while expressing, in the face of danger, a feeling of invincibility; after all he had survived Special Branch's threats at Castlereagh and was now about to repeat the performance by making himself useful to the Provos. However, his captors in Castlereagh did not tell him that they could kill him if they so desired whereas the Provos made that clear to him. The OC of 'D' Company decided to run the operation without reference upwards to battalion level in the belief that this was such a sensitive matter that it had to be handled secretly and with only the knowledge of those present at Wright's interrogation.

In late August and early September 1972 Wright made frequent trips to the MRF compound at Holywood Palace Barracks and passed on low-level information which the IRA deliberately provided for him. On several occasions ammunition was conveniently planted in derelict buildings by the IRA and, on Wright's information, the Army picked it up. This maintained the double agent's credibility with his handlers at Holywood. Each time he reported back to the IRA he provided them with information which enabled them to construct a dossier on the Army's secret unit. The IRA learned that the MRF operation was under the auspices of 39 Infantry Brigade and had been devised by Frank Kitson, who had left the province in April after having shaped the structure of the new force. The MRF was composed of several elements. The first was a group of regular soldiers who were divided into four-man units comprising a junior officer, a sergeant and two privates. They operated in plain clothes and drove civilian cars. The section to which Wright was attached was known as the 'Freds' and was composed of members of Republican and Loyalist paramilitary organisations who had been 'turned' by Special Branch and Army intelligence. Wright told the IRA that the complete MRF operation and its members were billeted in an area close to the entrance to Palace Barracks and that this area was out of bounds to other members of the military within the camp. The 'Freds' did not associate freely but tended to avoid each other. Each 'Fred' had separate accommodation and his duties included travelling inside armoured personnel carriers with an Army intelligence officer. They would travel through Republican and Loyalist areas and observe pedestrians or men gathered at street corners. From gun-slits in the sides of the carriers a person could easily view the outside world. If a 'Fred' pointed out someone of importance, a photographer in the vehicle quickly snapped that individual. At the end of each day the trip was analysed and the 'Fred' was shown photographs of people whom he identified. A dossier was painstakingly assembled from all the knowledge the 'Fred' had of the 'target'.

The OC and IO of 'D' Company constantly warned Wright to be careful about what he divulged to the Army, and only when there was little choice was he willingly to identify an important member of the Provisional IRA. They encouraged him that when he was faced with a difficult situation he should identify a Provisional as a member of the Official IRA. This could later prove valuable in confusing Army intelligence about the allegiance of certain individuals.

Within two weeks of working as a double agent Wright asked for a meeting with his IRA handlers on the grounds that he had something important to convey to them. While 'D' Company's OC and IO listened intently, Wright claimed that there was a special operation in progress to which the specialist military teams within the MRF constantly referred in code, but in a fashion which suggested that it was extremely successful. The IRA men listened to this and then put it to Wright that this was of little value to them unless he could reveal something meaningful about the operation. Wright said: 'There is a guy I have seen in there and he is one of us. He comes and goes freely and even wears a shoulder holster.' Before the IRA men could ask who this man was, Wright blurted out his name, Kevin McKee. The shock on the faces of the OC and IO confirmed what Wright knew: McKee was important, not simply because he was working for the Army but because he came from a well-known

Republican family. Both IRA officers were visibly embarrassed by the revelation and even more embarrassed as Wright began to recount how McKee was allowed freedom of movement within the compound, was permitted to carry a pistol in a holster and did this while he was in the company of Republicans and members of the IRA. Wright provided a description which implied that McKee enjoyed his work and that the military units within the MRF enjoyed his companionship and admired his bravado.

The OC of 'D' Company was faced with a dilemma as to whether he should relay this information to the others within his area and in particular to the OC and IO of the 2nd Battalion to which he was responsible. The IO of 'D' Company expressed the view that there was a risk in 'spreading the net' and thus compromising an operation which had begun with 'D' Company. He also added that until the scope of MRF penetration of the IRA was fully established the matter should be confined to as few people as necessary. The OC agreed, but insisted that McKee should be pulled in for questioning about the 'special MRF operation' which Wright said was in progress. If McKee maintained constant contact with the MRF military units, then there was a possibility that someone had divulged information to him which might, when assembled, lead to the uncovering of the MRF's real intentions towards the IRA.

Within days, Wright and McKee were both in IRA custody. From the outset the interrogation of McKee began in earnest. Initially the interrogators did not reveal the source of their information because they were intent on discovering not simply whether Wright was a genuine double agent but the personality and underlying motivations of McKee. When he was seized by the IRA McKee was wearing his shoulder holster and pistol which he claimed he had bought from an IRA man who was killed in a gun battle several months after the transaction. The interrogators were more concerned about the detailed allegations regarding the MRF. McKee spent two days under interrogation before he broke, and that happened after he was confronted with the presence of Seamus Wright. Within twenty-four hours the IRA extracted from McKee a fascinating portrait of an MRF operation which concerned a laundry service. McKee said that in his conversations over drinks with the military members of the MRF details emerged of how this cleaning service, the Four-Square, actually worked. It was not simply a means of forensically testing laundry but the van was especially equipped for surveillance. The Four-Square symbol above the windscreen offered a view of the street to two operatives who lay face down in a specially constructed compartment built into the roof of the vehicle. These observers were equipped with miniaturised photographic equipment and also a two-way radio which linked them with the MRF base. McKee told his interrogators that the laundry van covered

estates in West Belfast. He also said he had overheard that two other operations were linked to the Four-Square missions, and these comprised
offices above a massage parlour on Belfast's Antrim Road and offices in
College Square East. McKee also confirmed Wright's assessment of the
role of the 'Freds' in the MRF, identifying known IRA, UDA or UVF operatives. However, the IRA was puzzled when McKee also admitted to having been trained in the use of a range of weapons.

'D' Company was now presented with a major problem in the form of
two volunteers who were working with the MRF, information which
required detailed assessment, and the probability that if they executed
Wright and McKee the Army would know that MRF operations were
blown, provided of course that such operations existed and that Wright
and McKee were not working on an elaborate plan to entrap the
Provisionals in a more devastating fashion.

The OC of 'D' Company decided it was time to refer matters to the
command of the 2nd Battalion. His primary reason was that most of the
alleged MRF operations occurred outside his battalion's area: although
College Square was in the 2nd Battalion's area, Antrim Road was in the
3rd Battalion's and the major housing estates in West Belfast were the
responsibility of the 1st Battalion. The IRA rules dictated that the operatives of a battalion area were permitted to operate outside their defined
zone only with the permission of the Belfast Brigade staff. Secondly, if
Wright and McKee were correct then the matter was too intricate to be
handled simply by 'D' Company. Within twenty-four hours, while Wright
and McKee were still being held in IRA custody, the Belfast Brigade staff
met with representatives from the three battalion areas of the city. The
OC of 'D' Company outlined the nature of the information gleaned from
the questioning of Wright and McKee. It was agreed that one member of
the Belfast Brigade staff would immediately assume responsibility for
assessing the evidence and acting on it quickly. Wright and McKee had
now been held captive for four days. The brigade officer suggested that
they should be held for a further twenty-four hours to establish whether
there was any truth in the claims about a Four-Square Laundry and
offices in two areas of the city. If there was no corroborating evidence,
both men should be court-martialled and executed without delay. If they
were telling the truth, a 'temporary' arrangement could be made.

The IRA man who was now in charge told the intelligence officers representing the three areas of the city to move cautiously. On the one hand
it could be a trap, but if the operations were genuine then they should not
risk 'blowing their cover' and jeopardising what could transpire to be a
crushing blow against military intelligence.

With five days having passed since the arrest of Wright and McKee, the brigade staff officer learned that there was a Four-Square Laundry vehicle which toured Twinbrook as well as estates bordering on Finaghy and Lambeg. No one knew from whence it came or how it laundered clothes. The intelligence officer of the 3rd Battalion confirmed that offices existed above a massage parlour at 397 Antrim Road and, according to local people, only two persons used the offices, a middle-aged man and a young girl. The intelligence officer from the 2nd Battalion said there were offices in College Square East which were not listed to a company, but a laundry van bearing the Four-Square symbol was frequently seen outside the premises. The brigade officer ordered that Wright and McKee be released with suitable warnings, but watched. It should be pointed out to them that it was fully understood that they could at any time be required to report to Holywood, and they should do so with the utmost caution. When I asked the IRA why they took the risk of releasing Wright and McKee they replied that they had no choice. It was a calculated risk taken in the knowledge that if, as it seemed, Wright and McKee were telling the truth both men had compromised their Army handlers and their only salvation was with the IRA. Both were assured that they would be protected and moved from Belfast if their position with the MRF was to be jeopardised. I also put it to the IRA that the Army would surely have been suspicious if two agents disappeared for five days. The IRA spokesman whom I talked to replied: 'You have to understand the period we are talking about. There was a lack of communication with all groupings involved in the war because there were so many things happening. In the case of these two men, their role was to infiltrate and inform on the IRA. It was easy for them to make excuses for delaying meetings with their handlers. We also checked their homes during the five-day interrogation to ensure that nothing untoward happened which would have implied that the MRF was checking on their movements. Once we released them we knew we had to act quickly.'

As the end of September approached, senior officers within the Provos' three battalions were nervous that the longer IRA intelligence officers surveyed the Four-Square Laundry operations, and the offices, the greater the risk of indicating IRA interest. By the last day in September the brigade officer-in-charge reckoned that enough was known about Four-Square and what he believed were its offshoot workings to move against it.

The commanding officers of the three battalions were assembled with their attendant intelligence officers. From the discussion which ensued a decision was taken to hit the MRF operation on 2 October and to co-ordinate attacks against the three targets so that they coincided at the same time of day. The intelligence officer of the 1st Battalion said Twinbrook was the best for an assault on the laundry van and, since customers claimed it arrived punctually, the assessment, based on a week's observation, was that it would arrive on the estate between 11.15 and 11.30, and would complete its tour of the neighbourhood by midday. He reckoned that if the van was attacked in Twinbrook an IRA unit could make an escape with ease and be in the safety of the Andersonstown district within a matter of five to ten minutes. There was, he pointed out, a dilemma in the form of a girl who went from door to door to collect the laundry.

The brigade reacted by telling the 1st Battalion OC that the girl, the driver of the van and whoever was in it were to be 'wiped out'. He stressed that his information (he did not mention his source) was that two soldiers were lying face down in a special compartment in the roof. The 'hit' was to be executed with speed, but the volunteers had to ensure that they riddled the roof of the van. If possible, said the brigade officer, the attack on the van should take place at approximately 11.30 so that the other attacks could coincide. If the van was moving and had to be stopped, the assault would require two cars. Otherwise the car containing the active service volunteers should complete the job while laundry was being collected from door to door, in which case the driver and the persons in the roof would be shot first; it would be easy to deal with the girl afterwards because she would be on foot. The important thing, stressed the brigade officer, was to act swiftly and decisively. No one was to be left alive, however the attack was made.

The representative of the 3rd Battalion reckoned that one squad comprising a driver and three volunteers could 'neutralise' the man and girl who occupied the offices above the massage parlour in the Antrim Road. A similar grouping was chosen from the 2nd Battalion to make an assault on the premises at College Square East. The brigade officer insisted that twenty-four hours before the operation Wright and McKee should both be arrested and held in secure custody.

On the afternoon of 2 October the three IRA units returned jubilant to their commanders in the respective battalion areas. The squad from the 1st Battalion reported that they had shot the van driver and riddled the roof of the vehicle—which would have ensured the death of the other operatives—but the female agent had escaped by running into a house and claiming that a Loyalist hit-squad was after her. In fact, the roof of the van was never riddled and L/C Sarah Jane Warke was never fired on. The evidence available suggests the IRA team loosed off bursts of automatic fire at the van, then panicked and hightailed it out of Twinbrook. Unfortunately L/C Warke did not trust her instincts when she saw what was an IRA vehicle and its driver observing her and Ted Stuart.

The 3rd Battalion unit reported that they had 'shot up' the offices at

397 Antrim Road and must have killed anyone who was there. The 2nd Battalion unit made a similar claim.

Meanwhile the news media were reporting the death of Sapper Ted Stuart and the shooting of a man at premises on the Antrim Road. The Provisional IRA brigade staff were at first content to believe the versions given by their men, though they were willing to discount any killings at College Square. The admission by the authorities of a death at Twinbrook and a shooting at the Antrim Road tended to support the units' claims. The IRA tendency at that time (and after subsequent events) was to suspect that the Army never revealed the numbers of its dead. They believed that the Army was obliged to admit to the death of Stuart and the wounding on the Antrim Road because there were public witnesses to both incidents. However, for reasons of pride and propaganda they would hide the failure to kill the operatives in the roof of the laundry van and the couple above the massage parlour. In the days following the attack on the laundry van, therefore, the IRA issued statements revealing its knowledge of the MRF claiming its units executed 'five British spies'.

Only now is the IRA willing to admit the truth. It says that within a short time the brigade officer conducted a detailed examination of the entire operation of 2 October and was not convinced of the claims made by the three units. It was obvious that, if the unit in Twinbrook had riddled the roof of the van and killed two operatives, the local men and the priest who drove the van from the scene of the shooting would have been aware of blood dripping through the roof or of the sounds of wounded persons. Journalists provided their readers with information that the offices in College Square had been out of operation for some time before the shooting—and that, of course, left the Antrim Road episode to be properly examined.

What the IRA never knew is that the Antrim Road operation was an MRF exercise but was not connected with the Four-Square Laundry. The offices above the massage parlour and the massage parlour itself were both part of one operation which was another form of intelligence gathering. The two MRF operatives in the rooms above the massage parlour were a retired Army major known as Jim or Bossman who had agreed to undertake duties with the MRF. His companion was a serving soldier and the daughter of a British Army brigadier. They installed listening equipment linked to bugging devices in the massage parlour, which was being run by an ex-Republican internee and his wife, who had been recruited by the MRF. This operation took place without the knowledge of local CID officers or members of the Special Branch. The massage parlour offered services including masturbation and full sexual intercourse, and its clients were encouraged to talk generally about the 'Troubles' in

Belfast. Since it was situated close to Catholic areas, people of interest to Army intelligence were expected to frequent it.

One client who came to the attention of the 'watchers' at 397 was a leading political figure in the nationalist community, Paddy Wilson, a Belfast City Councillor. He was in his late thirties, married, and loved to carouse and spent much of his time in McGlade's Bar, off Royal Avenue, the haunt of politicians and journalists. Paddy Wilson's visits to the massage parlour provided hard intelligence about terrorism within the Catholic community. Wilson was close to that community and was frequently in the company of members of the SDLP who knew what was happening on the ground and the prominent people within the IRA. On one of his visits his masseuse asked about his reaction to the brutal slaying of three young Scottish soldiers in March 1971. Wilson felt comfortable with her, and she encouraged him to believe that she was discreet. As a result he revealed the names of the three Provisionals who carried out the killing. The three Scottish soldiers were lured from a busy city centre bar on the promise of being taken to a party where girls would be available. On a lonely road outside Belfast the three young men, all in their late teens, left their car to urinate by the roadside. While they were relieving themselves, beer glasses in their hands, they were individually shot through the back of the head. Two of them were brothers.

Paddy Wilson was accurate in naming the guilty men, one of whom, Paddy McAdorey, was later shot by the Army during a gun battle in August 1971. The other two are still alive and one of them is living in the Irish Republic. What is particularly fascinating about this story is that Paddy Wilson divulged this information in 1971 before McAdorey was killed. This places the MRF operation firmly within this period. Paddy Wilson was brutally slain by a Loyalist murder squad operating from within the UDA on the night of 26 June 1973. He left McGlade's Bar with twenty-nine-year-old Irene Andrews, whom he frequently dated, and they drove to a lonely road outside Belfast. Their bodies were found, his with over thirty stab wounds lying twenty yards from her car, and hers with twenty stab wounds to the head and chest beside the car. It later transpired that he was held on the ground face upwards while he was stabbed to death and she was forced to watch before the assassins used the knife on her.

Another dimension to MRF operations which eluded the gaze and scrutiny of the Provisionals in 1972 was revealed after an incident which occurred in West Belfast on the morning of 22 June 1972. Shots were fired from a civilian car near a bus terminus on the Glen Road. Two men were injured and a stray bullet entered the bedroom of a house and wounded Thomas Gerard Shaw, who was lying in bed. Journalists who covered the story assumed that the attack was either carried out by Loyalists or was part of a feud between the Provos and the Official IRA.

This incident occurred just when the Provos announced they were talking to the British government about a truce—which necessitated the British government flying IRA leaders to London. It was not until twelve months after the failed truce that the Glen Road shooting was fully explained, and even then it only merited coverage on an inside page of Northern Ireland's only evening newspaper, the *Belfast Telegraph*. Ironically, the front page on that day, 26 June, was given over to coverage of the murders of Paddy Wilson and Irene Andrews.

The Glen Road shooting, according to the *Belfast Telegraph* report, was the subject of revelations in the Belfast High Court, where twenty-six-year-old Sergeant Clive Graham Williams was on trial accused of attempting to murder three men on the Glen Road on 22 June 1972. Brian Hutton (now Northern Ireland Lord Chief Justice) opened the case for the Crown by telling the jury that Sergeant Williams was in civilian clothes, travelling in a civilian Ford Cortina car, on the day in question. Three men—Hugh Kenny, Joseph Smith and James Murray—were gathered round a car at the bus terminus on the Glen Road. Sergeant Williams, Mr Hutton alleged, opened automatic fire at them from the rear passenger window of his car, wounding Murray and Smith, and injuring Mr Shaw in the nearby house. Sergeant Williams also faced the charge of maliciously wounding Mr Shaw.

The Crown prosecutor went on to say that Williams subsequently made statements claiming he saw two gunmen at the terminus, one armed with a carbine and the other with a revolver. The sergeant further alleged that six to eight shots were fired by these gunmen at the Cortina, one bullet penetrating the rear window, and that only at this point was fire returned. The Crown, added Mr Hutton, would say that Kenny, Smith and Murray were unarmed and that a forensic examination of Sergeant Williams's vehicle produced no evidence that a bullet had entered the rear windscreen. The Crown would allege that the window was knocked out deliberately. Evidence would be offered to show that none of the men at the terminus could have fired a weapon, and likewise in respect of Mr Shaw. The Crown would also claim that Williams made no attempt to retrieve terrorist weapons from the scene; he drove away after the shooting and did not summon military assistance.

On the second day of the trial Sergeant Clive Graham Williams walked into the witness box and identified himself as the commander of a unit of the Military Reaction Force attached to 39 Infantry Brigade. (Note his use of the word 'Reaction' rather than 'Reconnaissance' as in the official title given to the unit by the media, the Provos, the two double agents and

Army statements released after the Four-Square attacks. Was the designation 'Military Reaction Force' an error on the part of Williams, or was it the Army's term for this elite grouping, or was it a term which defined a role for one of the sections within the Military Reconnaissance Force?)

The judge, the late Ambrose McGonigal, and the jury listened intently as Williams revealed that the Military Reaction Force was set up to carry out surveillance in areas where it was difficult for uniformed troops to travel freely. In June 1972 there were about forty men in the force, and they were supplied with civilian cars to move about areas and had their own armoury. He had fifteen men in his squad and generally two to four men travelled in a vehicle. He told the court that in June 1972 his squad was inoperative because an IRA truce was in prospect. At that time there was a fresh intake of NCOs into the unit. On the morning of 22 June he gave the new recruits a briefing and then took them to Kinnegar firing range near Palace Barracks at Holywood. His intention was to familiarise them with general weapons and those used by terrorist organisations, particularly the Thompson sub-machine-gun. His unit had two Thompsons in its armoury and he demonstrated the use of one of them on the range that morning. Later he travelled to Army HQ at Lisburn to have a radio fixed to his car. He dispatched two squads of men to patrol Belfast city centre and districts in the south of the city. On his return trip from Lisburn to Holywood he was accompanied by two new recruits, and the Thompson sub-machine-gun which he had demonstrated earlier was in a holdall under the seat of his Cortina issue car. He decided en route to introduce his two companions to West Belfast by making two passes through the Andersonstown area. In this way, he believed, they would begin to understand the nature of the work for which they were being trained. At this point, Sergeant Williams assured the court that a Thompson was not normally carried by an MRF squad. The regular-issue weapon was a Sterling sub-machine-gun. When a squad consisted of three persons, one man carried the Sterling while his companions were armed with automatic pistols.

When asked by a lawyer why the Thompson was concealed that morning, Sergeant Williams replied: 'Soldiers were our biggest enemy because if they spotted a gun in our vehicle they would open fire and we would be shot dead.' He claimed that he was fired on by terrorists on several occasions while he was engaged in armed MRF duties.

On 22 June, after making two passes of Andersonstown and Suffolk, he ordered another squad to move down the Glen Road. It was then that he received a communication from that squad that they had sighted a man armed with a revolver at the Bunbeg bus terminus. He asked the squad to make another pass and they confirmed their previous observation.

Sergeant Williams went on to explain how he made for the area and saw two gunmen, who fired on his vehicle, one bullet shattering the rear windscreen: 'As I approached the bus terminus, I saw a man crouching near a car and looking through a pair of binoculars. A man in front of him was carrying a pistol. I just glanced away and as I did there were several single shots from what appeared to be a semi-automatic weapon. I looked round and saw a man looking over the roof of a car and firing what I took to be an M1 Carbine. I fired three bursts of automatic fire, discharging about ten rounds from the Thompson.'

A forensic scientist told the court that no lead residue was found on the hands of Kenny, Murray and Smith. Lead residue was generally an indication of a weapon discharge. Under further questioning, the forensic expert admitted that lead residue could be removed by rubbing or washing.

Before the jury retired to consider the case against Sergeant Williams the judge decided there was insufficient evidence to justify one of the charges against the accused—that of wounding Murray and Smith with intent. The jury retired for two hours and returned with an 11 to 1 majority verdict which found Williams not guilty of the attempted murder of Kenny, Smith and Murray and of maliciously wounding Shaw.

Prior to the trial of Sergeant Williams, arms charges were dropped against a leading member of the MRF, Captain James McGregor, who was a passenger in the Cortina with Williams on 22 June.

In October 1972 the name Captain McGregor had featured prominently during the interrogations of Wright and McKee, who claimed that a Captain McGregor was one of the leading figures in the whole set-up. They were not to know that the same name would surface a year later in connection with the Glen Road shooting. Nor was it the last time that Captain McGregor would feature in the undercover war between the Provos and the Military Reconnaissance (Reaction) Force.

Until now, no one has been certain of what became of Wright and McKee. I can now reveal the fate of both men. During the course of my research, IRA intelligence agreed to talk for the first time about the missing men and what befell them. What I discovered about their activities, their roles within the IRA, the damage they caused to IRA operations and how the IRA handled them is new material which until now has remained locked in IRA files.

The moment the Provos mounted their attacks on the MRF operations, the fate of Wright and McKee was sealed. They had outlived their usefulness, and to imagine that they could continue to operate after the workings of the MRF had been exposed was absurd. Perhaps, more significantly, the IRA realised that the two men were a liability. From the IRA standpoint, they had transgressed and the penalty for their behaviour was execution. They could not be trusted and they were in possession of information about the IRA which could be of value to their handlers. There was no guarantee that they would not be induced or coerced into 'turning' once more. The IRA knew that it would be only a short time before the MRF identified the source of the leak, if they did not already know it, and to release Wright and McKee was too great a risk to take.

McKee was removed from Belfast to a house owned by Republicans in South Armagh. His family were informed by the IRA about the MRF operations and, according to the IRA, accepted that he would be shot. However, it was agreed that it would not be made public, since this would embarrass the family, who were prominent Republicans. McKee spent several weeks with the family in the countryside, constantly under guard. Orders were sent from the Belfast Brigade that he was to be executed in the IRA tradition and given a secret burial. One week later a communication reached the Belfast Brigade that the family in South Armagh had formed a relationship with their young captive and could not undertake his execution. The brigade officer who masterminded the planning of what became known as the 'Four-Square Operation' chose two volunteers from the 1st Battalion area to execute McKee. These men, Jim Bryson and Tommy Toland, travelled to South Armagh and took charge of the prisoner. A priest was summoned to appear at the execution so that McKee could be given the last rites of the Catholic Church and prayers be said at his burial.

Bryson and Toland carried out the killing of McKee after reading out passages from the IRA's Green Book which recorded the IRA rules in relation to court martial and execution. The last rites were given to McKee in a remote field near the house where he had spent his captivity. The priest was witness to the shooting, which was carried out in accordance with the rules of the Green Book: McKee was made to kneel, his hands were tied behind his back, a black-cloth hood was placed on his head, and Bryson and Toland fired two pistol shots simultaneously into the back of his head. McKee's body was buried at that spot.

One of the men who had interrogated McKee later remarked to another leading IRA man that there were aspects of McKee's character he could never fully understand. One was that McKee enjoyed the role he played within the MRF and was thrilled by the fact that he was permitted to carry a pistol and had immunity from prosecution or any form of retribution. Other personality traits that struck this IRA interrogator were McKee's display of bravado even when under pressure and, when he knew his life was about to end, the way in which he accepted his execution without protest: 'He was naïve, he was brash, and you knew that he enjoyed his notoriety, his immunity, but what I will never understand is that he accepted death as if it was a fact of life.' This observation seems to imply a naïvety, an abandon, a carelessness which made McKee more of a potential recruit for the role he undertook than Seamus Wright, the young married man who appears to have been an unwitting victim of circumstance.

The IRA's treatment of McKee in the last months of his life signified, if not identified, aspects of Republicanism which provide an interesting insight into the nature of the IRA. The court-martial procedure, the secret burial on unconsecrated ground, on a plot of land which would never be identified for the dead man's relatives, indicated the seriousness with which the IRA viewed a crime which merited such a penalty, and constituted an added punishment which was made known to McKee before he was shot. The decision not to bury McKee in a cemetery is obviously rooted in Catholic belief that burials must take place in consecrated ground. The presence of the priest to administer the last rites presents a bizarre image. While writing this book I was told by a senior Provisional that, on one occasion, as a result of representations from a Republican family, a body was removed from a secret grave, transported across Ireland and given to a family to inter in a cemetery. The IRA traditionally shoots informers and leaves their bodies in back streets or country roads. This is the first time, to my knowledge, that they have admitted to carrying out secret burials. I was given to understand that the secret execution and burial applied only to informers who were IRA members and who were judged to have seriously damaged the organisation. However, in many instances it was not possible for an informer to be taken into the countryside, and therefore executions took place where it was deemed convenient.

So what became of Seamus Wright? He is the only person referred to in subsequent articles or books as a man 'believed to have been connected with the MRF who disappeared from his home in October 1972'. The IRA have always argued that Wright disappeared from his home, the implication being that the Army spirited him away. It must be remembered that in October 1972 and until now they were unwilling to reveal that they had executed McKee; moreover, they were not obliged to do so by his family, who knew not to question the IRA command, since one of the dead man's relatives was Billy McKee, one of the founders and leaders of the Provisionals. However, Seamus Wright's wife and family were willing to talk to the media about what little they knew of Seamus. The Provos had no control over them, so they preferred to let it be known that it was probably the MRF who spirited him away. In fact, he too was executed and given a secret burial somewhere in the South Armagh countryside three months after the 'Four-Square Operation' happened. He was married into a prominent Republican family and his execution was kept secret to prevent public embarrassment.

I would contend that since 1970 many people have been buried secretly, though it is unlikely that we shall ever know how many people met their deaths in lonely fields or hillsides. This is the first time the Provisionals have admitted to a writer that they secretly buried people, and in particular McKee and Wright.

Until October 1972, when the Provisionals learned about the MRF and made public their knowledge of it, many claims had been made by the SDLP, civil rights leaders, the Association for Legal Justice, the Official IRA and the Provisionals that counter-gangs were operating as part of a counter-insurgency strategy and that these gangs were from the 22nd Special Air Service. What is certain is that Kitson's MRF strategy did not involve the operational use of the SAS on the streets. A small number of SAS personnel were flown into Palace Barracks to train members of the MRF in the use of weapons, surveillance and tactical methods of counter-insurgency - which does not necessarily imply counter-terror.

With what is known about the MRF, it is worth examining unsolved incidents which occurred prior to the Four-Square Laundry episode to discover whether they fit a pattern. Some of them happened around the time in which Sergeant Williams and Captain McGregor were undertaking MRF operations in Belfast.

Between midnight and 1.00 am on 13 May 1972 a group of men, mostly members of the Catholic ex-Servicemen's Association, were on vigilante duty at Riverdale Park in the Andersonstown area of West Belfast. Among the group was Patrick McVeigh, a forty-four-year-old father of six children and a welder by profession. Suddenly a car approached the vigilantes from the direction of the Finaghy Road North junction with the Andersonstown Road. According to later reports a burst of sub-machine-gun fire struck the vigilantes. McVeigh was mortally wounded; his companions suffered gunshot wounds, none of a serious nature. The car from which the sub-machine-gun was fired drove down Riverdale Park, made a three-point turn, drove past the scene of the shooting where McVeigh and his companions lay dead or wounded, and returned to Finaghy Road North. Eyewitnesses saw it approach a military checkpoint where the driver produced identification and was permitted to proceed.

For the next twenty-four hours the Army press desk at HQ in Lisburn continued to tell journalists that gunmen in a passing car had fired indiscriminately at civilians, wounding five, one fatally. It was stressed that it was an 'apparently motiveless crime'. As a journalist at that time, I remember the frequency with which the phrase 'apparently motiveless crime' was used by both the Army and RUC public-relations staff. It was used when the Army did not know who was responsible, or when they did and it was not 'responsible' to tell the public. The phrase contributed to heightened tension because it was open to whatever interpretation bigots wished to place upon it. In this instance the implication was that Loyalists were responsible because the car came from the direction of Finaghy Road North, which was then a predominantly Protestant district. When eyewitness accounts of how the killers went through a checkpoint became common currency, this reinforced the view that the British Army was acting in collusion with Loyalist murder gangs. The *Observer* and journalists such as Frank Doherty, who was then writing for *Hibernia*, began to look much more closely at the McVeigh shooting. Doherty, a streetwise journalist who knew Andersonstown, began to look at the possibility that the Army was involved. However, the *Observer* got to the story first and revealed the Army's role in the shooting. Within a month McVeigh's companions were told officially that they were shot by soldiers 'in plain clothes'. It was expected that the inquest into the death of McVeigh, which was held in December 1972, would reveal all. This is how it was interpreted by Frank Doherty:

> The military officer who was on duty in the area that night admitted under cross-examination by counsel for the next-of-kin that he had regarded the killing as a sectarian assassination until he heard military statements read at the inquest. The statements from the soldiers involved in the killing, who as in all such cases at that time did not appear for cross-examination, claimed that they saw a group of men armed with revolvers and rifles and that one of these men fired at their car. If the soldiers had appeared at the inquest the McVeigh family's barrister would no doubt have asked how they saw such detail from a speeding car in an area which had total blackout. He might have asked them why they did not inform their uniformed colleagues by radio that there were gunmen operating in the area. And he might also have asked them why they had allowed the incident to be recorded in military log-books as a sectarian assassination, and why, if they had come under fire as they claimed, they did not drive to the safety of Casement Park military fort, which was less than one minute ahead of them, but chose to make a cumbersome turning—within range of their alleged attackers' guns—past the point where the initial shooting took place and head into the Protestant district of Finaghy. Forensic evidence given by police experts at the inquest showed that neither the dead man nor his companions had fired weapons. There was no evidence to show that a window in the car had been shattered when the machine-gun had been fired from it, so the conclusion drawn was that it was open at the time of the shooting. If this was the case, it indicated the possibility that the occurrence was anticipated by the occupants of the vehicle before they were in a position to see McVeigh and his companions.

The inquest returned an open verdict and the matter was not proceeded with further. The coroner suggested that two men who were a part of the McVeigh grouping, and who were not before the court, may have been the gunmen. The McVeigh incident only served to complicate an already

complex situation where each day saw shootings, very few were motiveless, but it was difficult to define which paramilitary group was responsible. Several weeks before the McVeigh shooting there was an incident
in Ballymurphy which did not attract as much publicity but was well
documented at the time by the Association for Legal Justice. It served to
prove the presence of MRF-type units.

Gerry and John Conway left their home in the Springhill estate to get
a bus to the Falls Road. As they walked casually, they claimed, past the
gates of St Thomas's School on the Whiterock Road, a car pulled alongside them and three men dressed in pullovers and light trousers leapt
from the vehicle with pistols. The brothers say they ran back towards
their home but were fired at and both wounded.

The incident was witnessed by a Mr Noel O'Reilly and his wife, who
were in an upstairs bedroom of their home. They told investigators that
the man who shot the Conway brothers was dressed in light-grey trousers
and a brown pullover and that he returned to his car after the shooting
and spoke into a handset radio. A short time later, O'Reilly and his wife
saw two armoured personnel carriers arrive on the scene. There was a
conversation between the soldiers in the carriers and the occupants of the
car before the three vehicles left the area. The Conway brothers were
taken to the Royal Victoria Hospital and treated for their wounds. They
made statements recounting their version of the shooting incident. The
press desk at Army HQ in Lisburn responded with a statement to journalists that an Army mobile patrol had encountered two men, one of
them on an Army wanted list, the other a suspect, and that this person
fired on the patrol, which returned fire, wounding the suspect, who
dropped a pistol and escaped. If this was an exact and honest account of
what occurred, one would have expected the terrorist weapon to have
been recovered and fingerprinted and one of the two wounded men in the
Royal Victoria Hospital to have been interviewed and subsequently
charged. The matter ended with the Army statement.

In May 1972 an incident involving an Army patrol in civilian clothes
took place in the Protestant Shankill district. As in the McVeigh and
Conway incidents, events were disputed after an Army mobile patrol
fired shots at four people in a car. The occupants of the car drove to
Tennant Street police station to claim they were victims of a sectarian
assassination attempt. The army version was that a mobile patrol tried to
question the occupants of a car containing four men, two of whom produced guns and fired at the patrol. However, after the shooting, in which
no one was injured, the Army vehicle crashed and the soldiers had to be rescued by uniformed troops. An angry mob believed they were members of an
IRA gang. Inside the vehicle, which was later removed from the scene by

Army breakdown trucks, local people found an Army handset radio, nylon masks and a military identity card.

Another shooting involving an Army plain-clothes patrol occurred on 27 September 1972. After midnight on that day nineteen-year-old Daniel Rooney and a companion, eighteen-year-old Brendan Brennan, were shot from a car which sped past the junction of St James Crescent and St Katherine's Road where the boys were standing. Rooney was killed and Brennan wounded.

An Army statement claimed that five shots were fired by Rooney and Brennan at an Army mobile patrol. Soldiers in plain clothes returned fire, claiming 'two hits'. Lieutenant-Colonel Robin Evelegh, who was commanding the 3rd Battalion of the Royal Green Jackets in the St James district, was asked to comment on the incident. He told journalists that Rooney was a known gunman and Brennan, who was less prominent in the IRA, 'got his just deserts'. He also told a BBC interviewer that plain-clothes patrols operated in his area on reconnaissance missions, and that one of his men had on one occasion seen Brennan with a gun and had heard him boast of how he had shot soldiers. For the television cameras, Evelegh produced a car with bullet holes in it and claimed it was the vehicle that Rooney and Brennan had fired on. As with most incidents of this nature, there were many eyewitness statements contradicting the Army version. One element which continuously surfaced was that the firing from the vehicle took place from the rear and there were four men in the car. These mobile patrols, which were undoubtedly part of the MRF operation, had been frequently observed in the St James district for several weeks prior to the Rooney shooting.

The Roman Catholic churches in the Falls area reacted angrily to the shooting and in a statement read from all pulpits on 1 October 1972, the day before the IRA attack on the Four-Square Laundry van, the church expressed its revulsion and its assertion that Daniel Rooney was an innocent victim.

The one thing which is clear about this period in 1972 is that the MRF was active in Belfast. There will always be arguments about such incidents, though not all of them will reinforce the Provisional IRA belief that the units were employed in a counter-insurgency role to carry out selective assassinations. The IRA argument of the 1970s and even until recently was as follows:

The MRF squads carried out hits for two purposes:

1 To encourage people to the view that there was a sectarian war and not a revolutionary struggle taking place.
2 To force us to engage in a sectarian war with the Loyalists so that this would

divert our energies and be an easier problem to resolve.

3 To prove to ordinary Catholics that our purpose as defenders of the Catholic people was merely a hollow promise. Remember that the Official IRA lost support and fragmented because it failed to protect Catholics in '69 and Kitson knew that. When you can send a squad into a neighbourhood and shoot, in the case of McVeigh, five people, one of them dead, and then kill Rooney and wound Brennan, people begin to lose faith in their protectors.

There are many weaknesses in the IRA case, in that they did not always properly interpret Kitson's strategies as outlined in *Low-Intensity Operations*. Certainly it can be argued that some of his theorising lacked clarity and thus afforded terrorists an opportunity to exploit his work for propaganda purposes. However, one must ask why the British Army chose to admit its involvement in many of the shootings. Is there a case to be argued that what Kitson put into place was a system of elite squads which operated with an uncontrolled independence that resulted in the shootings I have outlined? If one examines these cases one tends to feel that there was an amateurish quality about the MRF. It was, undoubtedly, the type of special force which Kitson in *Low-Intensity Operations* argued was essential to combat insurgency. Kitson was a man who foresaw international terrorism, the types of wars which would not be fought by armies that were traditionally structured and had the same orthodox dynamic. He believed the British Army required a special counter-insurgency force which could eventually be used inside and outside the United Kingdom. The question that inevitably arises is whether he was in effect afforded an opportunity in Northern Ireland to examine how his theories could have a practical application.

What the Provisionals fail to recognise is that the Royal Ulster Constabulary, through its detective work, initiated the procedures for the charges to be preferred against Captain McGregor and Sergeant Williams and provided evidence in respect of the McVeigh shooting. The RUC also commented on some of the other incidents, ensuring that for their part there would be no cover-up.

While writing this book I spoke to several leading and highly respected policemen, one of them from Special Branch, and I raised the issue of the conflicting stories concerning the MRF in the early 1970s. To a man they all replied that the RUC was happy not to be involved. A Special Branch officer told me that their 'fingerprints were not on that period'. They all agreed that the MRF operations were amateurish and not tightly controlled. The tendency to train MRF members in the use of IRA weapons and encourage them to think like the IRA may well, in the view of one expert, have had a detrimental effect. According to several policemen who observed the period, there was an arrogant if not brash attitude among the MRF operatives. They knew they were members of an elite group.

Irrespective of the debate about the mobile surveillance patrols, the MRF had more than one objective and method of gaining intelligence and damaging the IRA—as the Provisionals soon found, at a considerable cost to manpower, morale and the near collapse of the IRA.

3

The Sting
British Intelligence and the IRA

In 1974 two groups were emerging within the IRA with differing views of the future of the armed struggle. There was the old guard led by Seamus Twoomey, Billy McKee and Maire Drumm, who believed that the conflict was falling into a historical pattern in which a good fight had been fought and the time had come for a cessation of hostilities as a prelude to a negotiated political settlement. They did not see the IRA as an organisation capable of winning the war. The other grouping within the IRA was led by young men such as Gerry Adams, who believed the armed struggle must be viewed as a long war in which both the military and the political struggle could be fought side by side, while the attitude to the British should be intractable until they agreed to meet the IRA at a political conference table. As the gulf between these factions widened, so did the struggle for control of the IRA. British intelligence saw the opportunity to influence events and with the help of RUC Special Branch devised a 'sting'. In the words of an IRA leader, the 'sting' was a 'brilliant intelligence operation' which caused the Adams faction, many of whom were in prison, to be discredited within the IRA; as well as weakening the Adams group it almost destroyed the IRA. The immediate result was that the old guard gained the upper hand and negotiated a ceasefire in 1975 which the IRA has since described as 'its darkest hour' because the organisation developed a sectarian strategy and became involved in criminal enterprises. When those who supported Adams's philosophy finally gained control two years later—a control they still maintain to this day—they acted against many young men whom they believed were a part of the 'sting', instigating a series of executions and one secret burial.

In the aftermath of the Four-Square Laundry episode journalists as well as paramilitaries were equally puzzled by the British Army's willingness to reveal many details about the existence of the MRF and plainclothes patrols. The reason may lie in the fact that, though the Provisionals claimed a victory, they and the rest of the population were left in no doubt that a secret war was being waged; that the Four-Square Laundry operated with impunity for several months in the middle of IRA areas, and that British military intelligence could be ingenious when spying within the enemy camp. Colin Wallace, who worked at Lisburn HQ as an Army public relations officer, privately hinted that similar operations were probably being aimed at the Loyalists as well as Republicans. A clear admission that undercover operations were in progress instilled a wariness within the ghettos where the terrorists held sway, and over a period of time it also created paranoia, particularly within the IRA, which was the major target for Army operations.

The panic which set in after the Four-Square Laundry incidents and the shootings involving MRF mobile patrols resulted in a hitherto unexplained killing of a civilian on 22 October 1973. Shortly before midnight on that day, Mrs Jean Smith was the passenger in a car being driven down the Glen Road. A gun was fired from the Andersonstown estate and a bullet passed through the driver's window, striking Mrs Smith on the head and mortally wounding her. The driver's first reaction was to think that his car had had a tyre blowout, so he stopped the vehicle and got out to examine the tyres. When he returned to his seat he found Mrs Smith slumped in the front passenger seat. The dead woman was the mother of a young child and was separated from her husband. On that night she was returning with her young companion from a nearby lounge bar. Twenty-five-year-old Jean Smith had short dark hair, and in an area where there was no street lighting both she and her companion were likely to have been mistaken for soldiers. The car belonged to the driver, who lived in the Finaghy district, and therefore neither he nor his vehicle was familiar to the IRA unit on the Glen Road. The Provisionals never admitted responsibility, though I was told, when making enquiries for this book, that Provisionals were responsible and it was 'an unfortunate hit'.

During this period there were other incidents which no one could explain satisfactorily. Two undercover soldiers in a car were stopped by unarmed vigilantes in the Lower Falls, disarmed—and handed over to the IRA. The Provisionals say that one of the soldiers, a Sergeant Davies, was placed in their custody and put under armed guard in a house in the Leeson Street area. He escaped but was wounded as he fled. Even though his armed captors searched for him relentlessly, he managed to find his way to a nearby Army base. The other soldier was handed over to the Official IRA, who said later that his name was Captain Dent, that they executed him for spying and dumped his body in an alleyway off Leeson Street. They elaborated on the killing by adding that several bullets were fired into the back of his head and the body was later recovered by an armoured personnel carrier. The Army press desk responded by telling journalists that no such incident occurred, but later suggested that the Officials had executed a Provisional on that night and not a soldier.

The incident certainly occurred, and the defence committee for the area admitted that both soldiers were handed over to the IRA. The Provos' story is accurate, so what of Captain Dent, whom the Officials say they executed? The fact is that they released their captive but could not publicly admit it in the highly charged atmosphere of 1972. Although the Army did not wish to fully compromise what was a decent gesture by the Officials, they did, to a degree, exploit the event. In claiming the incident did not occur and in suggesting that the Officials probably executed a Provisional, they were sowing seeds of doubt between the two factions, between whom there was little if any affection.

Similarly, a story which had all the ingredients of the Four-Square Laundry affair, and was linked to it, surfaced in the *Sunday Times* on 13 May 1973 under the heading: 'Why the Provos shot their own Double Agent'. The article was written by Paul Eddy and Chris Ryder, a journalist familiar with Belfast. The first paragraph read: 'The British Army deserter who was left for dead in a Belfast alley two weeks ago was not shot because he spied on the IRA. Although 19-year-old Louis Hammond did pretend to work for Army Intelligence for seven months last year, he was in fact a double agent planted by the IRA.' Ryder and Eddy went on to claim that Hammond was 'beaten for three days and shot' by the Provisionals because he had given the journalists a story about the 'wholesale embezzlement of IRA funds by leading Provisionals'.

Why should a man who according to Ryder was an IRA double agent give damaging information about the Provos to *Sunday Times* journalists? And, if he was a double agent, was he connected with the MRF, as were Wright and McKee?

It is worth examining the manner in which Ryder and Eddy brought Hammond to public attention, how they interpreted his story and how other journalists covered it before I attempt to place it in a historical perspective. A brief biography of Hammond is necessary to understand the origins of these events. Hammond, a Belfast Catholic, was born in 1954 and joined the Royal Irish Rangers in 1970. After initial training he was posted to Watchet in Somerset. In January 1972 he went absent without leave from his unit and was understood to have returned to his home in the Andersonstown area of West Belfast.

Ryder claimed in the article of 13 May 1973 that in April 1973 Hammond 'helped us reveal that at least £150,000 had been stolen from IRA funds, mainly by officers serving in the Provisionals' 1st Battalion'. 'Although he knew he was taking a risk', Ryder and Eddy added, 'Hammond helped us, in his words, because somebody had to speak out about the hard men who are lining their pockets and not fighting for the cause.' According to the *Sunday Times* journalists, Hammond believed that during a brief and bizarre terrorist career he had served the 'cause' well and was in no danger from the Republican movement.

Two weeks ago—a few days before his 19th birthday—he nearly paid the traditional price that the IRA extracts from informers. Four Provisionals, one of them a close friend of Hammond, lured him into a house in Joy Street, Belfast. They beat him for three days and interrogated him about the information he had given to us during the three months we had known him. Finally, on Saturday, April 28, as he lay unconscious from the continued beatings, he was shot three times in the head and once in the stomach. His body was taken to Ormeau Road, half a mile away, and just before midnight he was dumped in the entrance to an alleyway and left for dead. Astonishingly, he survived, although one of the bullets passed through his head, two lodged in his skull and three in his liver. For eight days he lay critically ill in a heavily-guarded ward in the Royal Victoria Hospital, Belfast, but by last Friday he had recovered sufficiently to be able to get out of bed for an hour. Hammond is now partially paralysed, and will almost certainly lose the sight of one eye, but he is well enough to be moved for his own safety, to another better-guarded hospital. It was comparatively easy for the would-be killers to abduct Hammond because he thought he had nothing to fear from the 'dedicated Provisionals' who he believed shared his anger and disillusionment over the embezzlement.

Ryder and Eddy also told *Sunday Times* readers in the same issue that Hammond became an intelligence officer in the Provos' 1st Battalion, 'E' Company, while absent without leave from his regiment in 1972. On 19 May 1972 he was arrested by the Army while he was on vigilante duty. 'The Security Forces soon realised he was a deserter, but Hammond bought himself immunity from prosecution by offering, in his words, to work as "a spy for the Army". This was a pre-arranged Provo plan. The Provos' Belfast Brigade was anxious, at that time, to get information on the British Army's secret and increasingly effective weapon—the plain-clothes surveillance groups, codenamed MRF.'

Their assertion that the Provos knew of the existence of the MRF at this time will be discussed later in this chapter and should be borne in mind as a potentially significant element in assessing the veracity of the story as written and understood by both these journalists. I make this point because the line in the *Sunday Times* article which followed the previous assertion is also important: 'Provisional Volunteers including Hammond and two other men we know about—Seamus Wright and Kevin McKee—had been instructed, if arrested, to offer their services to the MRF and then become double agents.'

Ryder and Eddy were basing these claims either on interviews with Hammond or on Army briefings. Why would Hammond claim that McKee and Wright were double agents? The likely explanation is that Ryder and Eddy saw this story as fitting the scenario they sought to out-line. Nowhere in their article did they confirm that they knew of the fate of McKee and Wright. Surely if Hammond was working with McKee and Wright in the MRF he would have learned something of their whereabouts by the time he met the journalists? Ryder and Eddy add that Hammond 'went to live with nine other informers including Wright and McKee in two secluded houses—9 & 10 Harwell Road—inside Palace Barracks'.

They tell their readers that they were given a frank briefing by a senior officer at Army HQ in Lisburn the week before the 13 May article and were told the following:

The MRF is made up of regular soldiers who volunteer for these dangerous duties. They always wear plain-clothes and patrol Belfast in civilian cars, or, on occasions, bogus commercial vehicles. Their main job is surveillance of suspected terrorists but they are always armed and will certainly fire back when shot at. The Officer told us that the Unit is part of the normal military chain of command but he would like to retain the benefit of some doubt in the matter. When we asked him about the use of civilians, he refused to comment and said we were 'getting into deep matters'.

Ryder and Eddy met Hammond on several occasions between January and 14 April 1973, and they claim he told them that he, along with Wright and McKee, gave the British Army genuine but second-grade information. However, although they were not allowed out of the camps, they managed to pass on to the Provos, in coded letters to relatives and friends, vital information about MRF operations, registration numbers of cars used by the MRF, the addresses of policemen, their car registration numbers and details about informers. According to Ryder and Eddy, Hammond said the three double agents gave the Army these letters and the Army posted them from England. The double agents knew their information had been received when a coded message was painted on walls in West Belfast. In Hammond's case the coded message was 'Che' and was observed by him on occasions when he was taken on surveil-lance duties by his MRF handlers. All of this suggests an extremely elab-

orate plan involving three double agents who each required separate
codes and, one must assume, had undergone intensive training by the
Provos to enable them to undertake such a major role under the noses of
British military intelligence. If, as the article claimed, the double agents
were not allowed out of Palace Barracks, why did Wright and McKee disappear from their homes? The *Sunday Times* article expected a suspension of disbelief, considering that the information required to undertake
the 2 October Provo offensives against the MRF could not have been
assembled in the form of coded letters from McKee, Wright and
Hammond. The three young men were not known for a high degree of
intelligence, and in any case the Provos would have needed a detailed
knowledge of the workings of the MRF for a considerable period of time.
There is no evidence to suggest that such knowledge existed, and the
Provisionals admit that it was only through Wright and McKee that they
learned of it and, as I shall seek to demonstrate, of the presence of
Hammond.

When Hammond talked to Ryder and Eddy he was, according to
them, in hiding in Belfast. He gave them a story about the MRF which
to a degree was true; but I believe it was an MRF intelligence 'sting'
and the truth was therefore laced with half-truths and inventions. His
handlers within the MRF found a use for him in 1973 long after they
had extracted all he knew about the IRA. Let us look at how the
Hammond story was unfolded to Chris Ryder and Paul Eddy, whom I
believe acted as most journalists do when they believe they have an
interesting story to tell.

At the outset Hammond contacted Chris Ryder, who was a prominent
journalist in Northern Ireland and was privately enquiring into the disappearance of Seamus Wright. This is what Chris Ryder had to say in 1973:

We first met Hammond when we were making enquiries about the disappearance of
Seamus Wright. He offered us information about the MRF, and during the next two
months contacted us at least once per week. He identified himself by the codename
'Chris'. The meetings were usually held in either the Unicorn Bar in Castle Street or
Keenan's Bar in King Street, both frequented by Republicans. He never drank more
than one bottle of lager and was constantly afraid that soldiers would raid the bar.
Last March after we had learned of the embezzlement of IRA funds, we asked him to
confirm information we had got from other sources. Hammond was in a unique position to help us because he had been Intelligence Officer of 'E' Company whose members had stolen most of the money. We interviewed him twice in the Europa Hotel,
Belfast on April 3/4. On the second day, with Hammond's permission, we tape-
recorded the interview, having first warned him that anything he said might be printed and might also be given to the Security Forces. When the interview was completed we warned Hammond that he might be in danger from some of the Provisionals,
but he remained convinced that the only real threat was from the Army.

Is it credible that Hammond would have believed that he could divulge details of a £150,000 embezzlement, discredit the Provos and not face retribution? Did Hammond know exactly what would be published, and, as Ryder claimed, was he willing to be tape-recorded and have his statement possibly turned over to the people the journalists say he feared most, the Army?

The story about a major embezzlement which was being prepared for publication was being authenticated, as it were, by the timely presence of Louis Hammond, since it just happened to concern the company in the IRA to which he had been attached. Liz Curtis, in her book, _Ireland: The Propaganda War,_ observes:

One of the Army's most successful leaks surfaced in a story in the _Sunday Times_ in April, '73 under the by-line of reporters, Paul Eddy and Chris Ryder. Their front page article, headed 'IRA Provo Chiefs milk £150,000 from funds', concerned a document that the British Army claimed to have intercepted as it was being smuggled out of Long Kesh on its way to the IRA's Belfast Commander, Seamus Twoomey. Said to have been written by a senior IRA detainee, the document alleged that seven named Provisionals had embezzled funds acquired by the IRA through armed robberies. 'From extensive enquiries we have made in Andersonstown', wrote Eddy and Ryder, 'we are convinced that the document is genuine.' _Guardian_ reporters, Derek Brown and Christopher Sweeney, later suggested that the information given by the Army to the _Sunday Times_ was doctored and described the affair as one of the most serious dirty tricks reported to them.

To substantiate the embezzlement story, Eddy and Ryder identified one of their sources as a former intelligence officer of 'E' Company. Their article of 15 April told readers that they had tape-recorded an interview in which he confirmed their story. From this revelation the IRA would have had little difficulty in identifying Hammond.

In June 1981 a London _Times_ article made this reference to the embezzlement document that Ryder and Eddy had in their possession: 'Whatever the provenance of the document, the Military were delighted with their leak. Counter-insurgency expert Major-General Anthony Deane-Drummone cited the _Sunday Times_ story as an example of how "true stories can be put about on the methods or motives of the terrorists which can help to destroy their morale and lead to disintegration", and claimed that it had directly led to the virtual disbandment of the IRA unit. He believed it was a benign use of the psychological weapon.'

The two _Sunday Times_ stories which were directly connected to Louis Hammond were extremely damaging to the Provisional IRA's 1st Battalion. In essence, the stories were not strictly concerned with the undercover war and the disappearance of Seamus Wright but with allegations that IRA leaders were stealing the organisation's funds and were responsible for the subsequent murder of an IRA double agent for having exposed their racketeering. From the British Army's point of view both stories realised the type of counter-insurgency objectives that a 'psychops' unit in any conflict would have been proud to achieve. The first story was designed to show that IRA leaders were not ideologues but criminals—gangsters who were willing to 'milk £150,000' from IRA funds. It also illustrated what the Army wished people to believe about the Provos: that they were acquiring large sums of money through criminal activities and that, like Mafia chiefs, the IRA leadership was in turn 'milking the IRA'. For the journalists, the story gained credibility when Hammond suddenly became available to authenticate it. Moreover, Hammond gave the journalists enough details about the MRF to keep them interested in what he had to say, as the 15 April article demonstrates:

To disguise the fact that Hammond and his colleague were 'spying' in Belfast, the Army arranged for them to be given false addresses in London and Birmingham. Hammond's address was 71 Fulham Road, London SW6—Wright's address was Ambury Way, Green Lane, Great Barr, Birmingham. In both these cases the Army's plan misfired. Hammond's father travelled to London last September to see his son, only to find that 71 Fulham Road is a record shop which provides an accommodation address for small weekly charges.

The article went on to argue that Wright, fearing he would be arrested by the Army, had fled to Scotland with the assistance of two friends and was living there under an assumed name. The journalists, however, had formed a different perception of the Hammond case: 'Louis Hammond was not so lucky. Like Wright, he was released by the MRF when he had outlived his usefulness as a "spy", taken to Liverpool by Captain Moore and advised to "lie low" in England for a few months. In fact, he immediately returned to Belfast, reported back to 'E' Company and gave the Provisionals the remaining information he had about the MRF activities.'

Now here the journalists were asking their readers to accept elements of the story which appeared to fit perfectly but raised some interesting questions. Why should the Army suggest that Hammond should 'lie low' only for a few months? If we are to accept the *Sunday Times* story, the Army believed Hammond was a genuine agent. As such, he would have been in possession of information which would have necessitated his remaining outside Belfast. If Hammond was a genuine Army agent then he had not outlived his usefulness. Accordingly, when the Provos exposed the Army's Four-Square operations, there was a price to be paid, and one might ask if the embezzlement story was the price the Army exacted in revenge for the murders of Sapper Stuart, McKee and Wright.

If the MRF were preparing in late 1972 to send Hammond back to the IRA he needed a cover story since Wright and McKee would presumably have divulged Hammond's name when they revealed details of the 'Freds' operations.

The letters 'Che' were never painted on the walls of West Belfast by the Provos, according to leading figures in that organisation. However, Hammond could tell Ryder and Eddy that he believed he was working for the Provos and that his information was reaching them because he requested the coded signal 'Che' to be painted in relevant areas. Hammond, if interrogated by the Provos, had a cover story; even though it could not be substantiated, he could at least have appeared to the Provos as someone who had been fooled by Army intelligence.

If we assume there was a sting, it is worth examining the story from the perspective of what the Provos say happened in 1972–3. The Provos claim they knew all about Hammond after prolonged interrogations of Wright and McKee. They never expected Hammond to surface again, since Army intelligence would have known that Wright and McKee had been 'taken out' and that they were likely to have blown the cover of Hammond and other agents. According to the Provos, Hammond was brought out of 'retirement' for a final job for the MRF:

We half hoped that Hammond would be put on the streets, but we knew that once we blew the Four-Square the Army would know that we had exposed two of their agents. In fact we never made it known that we killed Wright and McKee, in the hope that there would be a slight doubt in the minds of the military that the two guys had run for cover. However, that was a slim hope. We knew the MRF leadership would be in no doubt that we had compromised Wright and McKee for us to be in a position to hit the laundry service and the other operations. We half expected that Hammond was operative or was being used as a source once the *Sunday Times* article appeared. It was easy for us to determine that the only former intelligence officer of 'E' Company who was going to be used to discredit us would be Hammond. What we were not sure of was whether Hammond was in actual contact with Ryder or whether that was just the Army playing a game. We decided to investigate. We knew that if he was being allowed the freedom to contact journalists he would at some stage contact his family, namely his father. That's how we got to him. We knew too much about him and about the MRF set-up from our interrogations of Wright and McKee. We also knew the damage that was being done by the embezzlement story. He told us that he was sent to Ryder to feed him details about the MRF and was warned that he would be obliged, after some time, to confirm a story about the IRA's 1st Battalion and the embezzlement of funds. The 'Che' story was one designed to convince the journalists that he was genuine. It was a clever set-up. That sting was prepared well in advance. The journalists were sucked into it. They believed the embezzlement story because Hammond convinced them he was a genuine double agent who worked for us and so he gave them all this bullshit about the coded signals involving the use of 'Che' on the walls. The Army was willing to risk Hammond, if necessary to sacrifice him, to seriously damage the IRA's 1st Battalion and, as a result, the whole organisation. He was like the spy who came in from the cold. There were two things the Army could not control: the way Ryder would write the story, because that warned us that Hammond was possibly back in action, and the fact that Hammond would break his cover by trying to contact his family.

Whatever the truth of the story, there can be little doubt that the Army played a final and devastating card in the war between the MRF and the Provos. Hammond's usefulness would have been limited after Wright and McKee had been taken out of circulation. I believe the intelligence operatives within the MRF planned the use of the trump card, namely Hammond, with precision. They gave him his story about the use of 'Che' and they primed him with sufficient information about the MRF set-up to interest the *Sunday Times* reporters, so that they could make use of his one distinct advantage—his former role as an intelligence officer in the IRA battalion which the Army intended to damage ineradicably. They succeeded in doing that, creating an image of leading Provisionals as gangsters, and began a period of investigation by the media into racketeering. Fortunately Hammond survived, but the issue raised questions about the nature of journalism, how it could so easily be compromised (unknowingly in my view) and how young men could become pawns in a highly dangerous game.

Around the end of 1973 and the beginning of 1974 the Provisionals were forced to rethink their military strategy because of numerous setbacks. First, many leading members of the organisation were either interned or imprisoned as a result of the MRF operations involving agents such as Wright, McKee and Hammond. Secondly, military surveillance techniques were rapidly improving with the use of sophisticated technology, and Republican areas were being constantly saturated with troops, making movement extremely risky for those IRA men and women who were on police and Army wanted lists. Finally, the beginning of 1974 saw a more prominent profile for Loyalist paramilitary organisations and Loyalist politicians who were violently opposed to the newly constituted political administration in Northern Ireland, the power-sharing executive led by Brian Faulkner and his deputy, Gerry Fitt. This executive brought together in government, for the first time, nationalists and Unionists. To Catholics Faulkner was the epitome of Unionism, and to Protestants Gerry Fitt of the SDLP was the epitome of nationalism and Republicanism. The executive was responsible for creating a role for the Dublin government in policy-making which was to be achieved through what was termed the executive's Irish dimension. The concept of Dublin being consulted, much less having a say in the affairs of Northern Ireland, was enough to convince hardline sections of the

Protestant population that a united Ireland was on the political horizon. As a result, groups within the Protestant community began to prepare for the overthrow of the executive and others toyed with the possibility of establishing an independent Northern Ireland through a unilateral declaration of independence.

The prospect of the Loyalists overthrowing the power-sharing executive did not worry the Provisionals unduly but it forced them to consider the prospect of having to defend the Catholic population if such a move led to communal violence. Since the Provisionals knew they were seriously weakened by British Army successes, the IRA leadership in Belfast reached the conclusion that, if the organisation was to prevent further setbacks and prepare for a major confrontation with the Loyalist population, steps had to be taken to enable the IRA to restructure the organisation in Belfast. It was the Belfast Brigade which was under the greatest pressure and it was that brigade which would be at the forefront of defending Catholic neighbourhoods in the event of a 'doomsday' situation. The IRA turned to one man in Belfast to provide a solution: twenty-six-year-old Brendan Hughes, who was regarded within the IRA as a shrewd tactician. His brief was initially to find a means of making it easier for senior IRA figures to travel throughout Belfast and meet together away from the prying eyes of military intelligence and then to devise a contingency plan for the defence of Catholic areas. Hughes quickly decided that, since the IRA operated traditionally within neighbourhoods which were obviously defined as Republican and therefore easy for the security forces to target for maximum surveillance, it was imperative that the Provisionals establish safe-houses and bases in parts of the city which were middle class, predominantly Protestant or simply politically undefined. After being given clearance to set up the bases, he began to establish a new identity for himself.

Brendan Hughes took on the identity of a dead man, Arthur McAllister. He dyed his hair black and grew a moustache. His new persona was that of a toy salesman. With the help of IRA intelligence operatives Hughes studied the role he was about to play. He acquired a large collection of toy samples, order books containing details of shops and prospective buyers, and a diary to show his movements and the shops he intended visiting on a daily basis. He bought a new car and acquired a driving licence in the name of Arthur McAllister. His next purchase was a house in the Knockbreda district of Belfast; until now that aspect of his life has not been known. An IRA woman posed as his wife so that he could be seen to be living like most young men in a developing middle-class area. Then Hughes fully adopted the role of toy salesman. For two months he travelled to shops in Belfast and sometimes further afield, selling toys from Monday to Friday of each week. He established many contacts in the sales business and travelled every day to businesses he had approached the night before. In this way he discovered that he could travel freely and his real identity was never in danger of being exposed. After two months he rented a ground-floor flat in an expensive property in the exclusive Malone Road district of Belfast. His plan was to move important IRA operatives out of Republican neighbourhoods so that like himself they could live in anonymity and plan operations without incurring Army and Special Branch scrutiny. He also rented other accommodation addresses on Belfast's Antrim Road so even more IRA men could be moved to the periphery of troubled areas. It was a clever ploy in that it allowed the IRA to begin to rebuild its tattered leadership and set up operations in districts where the Army did not feel the need to concentrate its surveillance. Hughes, alias McAllister, maintained the Knockbreda property as his home and did not allow it to be used as a base or safe-house: if other accommodation addresses were uncovered, the Knockbreda house would still provide him with a base for his operations. The Malone Road safe-house was in Myrtlefield Park, the most unlikely place for terrorists to be based. It became an emergency dump for weapons and explosives. When an active service unit required guns or bombs and it was too risky to transport them from one troubled area to another, the Myrtlefield Park dump could be used. I was told that the flat once contained an Australian sub-machine-gun which the IRA did not wish to fall into the hands of the security forces because its serial number and other identifying features would have led them to the source of the weapon and halted a planned deal for a further consignment.

There was one other dimension to the IRA strategy at that time which has never been made known until now. After examining Hughes's scheme the IRA proposed what must have appeared then as it does now a bizarre idea: the setting up of a company to manufacture car doors. The IRA was beginning to believe that the best means of disguising its operations was through the creation of respectable businesses.

We were pleased that the creation of bases outside Republican areas was achieving results and we decided the next step was to set up a business through which we could move weapons and explosives. We purchased a factory site on a development at Finaghy. It was a purpose-built site so we sent guys in to design offices and get the place ready for business. We had the whole thing well worked out. While some of our lads were painting and building wooden partitions, others were building an underground bunker. This was to be a sealed dump. In other words it was not to be opened for normal operations and was to be there for a major emergency. The plan was to house only explosives in it and it was about the size of an average living-room.

We intended to ask Brian Faulkner to open the place to reinforce the image of the factory as a normal business venture. We knew that he would have had difficulty in refusing, as this was to all purposes a job-creation scheme in an area of high unemployment. We put the explosives in the bunker, sealed it and continued with the work of making the site look like an interesting business operation.

Meanwhile Hughes and one of his colleagues were busy preparing a 'doomsday' plan for the IRA's defence of nationalist areas, and the Myrtlefield Park flat was used for keeping written notes, maps and drawings relating to this. The flat also contained evidence of another IRA operation—the bugging of telephones at Army HQ in Lisburn. When working on this book I asked the IRA how they managed to place taps on Army lines.

We cannot tell you how we did it because that would only serve to reveal important details about those who work for us. We were able to bug lines leaving Army HQ but our recordings of conversations on those lines were of little value to us without specialised equipment. The Army was using scrambling devices. We got several people into Army HQ and acquired the necessary equipment. We learned that there was a highly placed source in our midst but, by the time we learned that from the bugging, the Army were on to us.

On 10 May 1974 the Army and police swooped on the flat at Myrtlefield Park and discovered two men on the premises. Arthur McAllister, alias Brendan Hughes, and another IRA officer, thirty-four-year-old Denis Loughlin, who described himself as a company director. A search of the flat revealed four rifles, a sub-machine-gun, two pistols, 3600 rounds of assorted ammunition, command wire for bombs and detonators.

Members of Special Branch and military intelligence who searched the premises were much more interested in the IRA documentation they found there. Two maps of Belfast showed areas shaded in green and red with accompanying notes indicating that the shaded areas were those the IRA would 'take and hold'. Notes also stipulated how long certain areas could be held and those areas which would be vacated and firebombed. The documents revealed the IRA's plans for a 'doomsday situation'; the Army learned, for example: 'Key buildings such as factories, mills, business premises, schools, fire-fighting facilities and petrol stations were all to be coded and listed and battalion commanders were to mark such buildings as targets for either offensive or defensive action.'

Among the items in the flat was a draft of a press statement which the IRA intended to circulate in nationalist areas in the event of their 'doomsday' scenario becoming a reality: 'An Emergency has been forced upon us and the IRA has no alternative but to defend its people. It may be necessary to impose harsh measures to ensure that this succeeds militarily'. The press statement indicated that an IRA-established radio station would broadcast information about food supplies, and men who had lost their jobs because of the social unrest were to contact their local IRA commanding officer and place themselves at his disposal for the defence of the area.

Documents relating to overall strategy forecast that the IRA would be required to take over Protestant areas in West Belfast and, presumably, force out the indigenous population, to 'hold such areas as New Barnsley' for the influx of Catholic families which the Provos expected to be forced out of areas such as 'the Short Strand in East Belfast or the Bawnmore Housing Estate on the outskirts of the City'.

The capture of Hughes, Loughlin and the documents was a major intelligence coup for the Army, who used the media to exploit the extreme elements of the Provo 'doomsday documents'. For days after the arrest, many of the national papers carried stories depicting Hughes as a person who drove a Daimler and wore a pinstripe suit. The coverage of the story was elaborate and fanciful, but the element which the Army exploited was damaging to the Provisionals—their plans for Armageddon.

When news of the Myrtlefield Park raid became public, many facts were kept from media scrutiny. The presence of tape recordings of telephone conversations was not revealed until much later. Unfortunately not all tapes in the IRA's possession were in the flat, though the IRA was obliged to abandon the bugging of Army HQ. What has never been made known, much less admitted by the Army, is the presence of a bunker loaded with explosives. The factory site was indeed raided and the explosives removed. I asked the IRA why they did not make the matter public.

No one dared go near the site and there was damage limitation to be considered in respect of other ongoing operations. The Knockbreda safe-house was not discovered nor the bases on the upper Antrim Road. But in this type of war nothing is as it seems. Those of us who knew about the bunker were left to ponder on who was the informer. The Army was clever. They simply maintained the secrecy of the presence of the bunker to confuse, to create paranoia. We had to ask ourselves: 'How much do they know?' You see, there was the possibility that they knew all along and that they were following us. It took time to resolve that one. The real story is that they kept us thinking because, firstly, they had a high-level informer in place. They knew we had bugged their HQ, and they knew we were watching for their agent to surface, to make a mistake. No one at first could check the bunker for fear that they had not discovered it or that they had and were waiting for someone to try to unearth the explosives. It was some time before we discovered that they had lifted the gear in the bunker. By then we had discovered the spy in our midst.

It turned out that he worked in the brigade Quartermaster's department. The bastard was not under suspicion for a long time. By degrees we isolated everyone who could have known about the dump. Just think how clever the Brits can be. They hit the dump because they knew that the Myrtlefield débâcle would create sufficient confusion so that suspicion would not lead to their man within the brigade. When we identified the guy who confirmed our worst suspicions we set an elaborate trap for him. We reckoned that if he was a spy he would react predictably to a given situation of our making. We sent him to meet someone across the border, but we mapped out the route for him. In South Armagh his car was flagged down by what he believed was a British Army patrol. One of the patrol dragged him from the car, told him they knew he was IRA and threatened to shoot him. The others told him they were SAS, that there were no witnesses and advised the guy holding him at gunpoint to 'shoot the bastard'. That did it and he blurted out to the bogus patrol that he was Army, gave them a code and told them to check it. We court-martialled him after he was interrogated. He was married but had no kids. We gave him a secret burial. The Army must have wondered about his disappearance but that's the war. It wasn't until 1976 that we eliminated him and by then he had done us a lot of damage.

You must realise that the British know it's a long war. When they have an agent like that in place, they use him cautiously. They are careful not to expose him. We know that they will not use all his information at once because that would be too expedient. It is a complex and dangerous game all the time. Equally when we identify a spy we are faced with the choice of confronting and liquidating him or her. On the other hand we also have the option of feeding the spy with information which may result in creating a situation to our advantage, watching where the information goes in order to identify the spy's controllers or to discover whether the penetration extends to more than one person. In all these circumstances there are considerable risks and often it is best to minimise them by eliminating the person who is the risk factor. You'll hear talk of double agents but in most instances it is not worth asking an informer to turn again because the person has already proved unreliable.

Another situation which often presents itself is when a person approaches us and admits to having been recruited by Special Branch or military intelligence. The question has to be asked as to whether the person is a plant, someone who has been told to admit to spying so that the IRA will attempt to run him or her as a double agent, thus enabling the spy to assess and identify those people in IRA intelligence who are prominent and responsible for handling informers, spies and double agents. Every case has to be assessed on its merits. We often asked ourselves to what extent we were sucked into MRF plans by almost being offered the obvious opportunity to have an easy success. On the other hand look at the damage inflicted by Wright, McKee and Hammond. We identified Wright, who gave us McKee, who told us about Hammond. You could argue that they gave us a knowledge of the MRF, the Four-Square, and exposed each other. In turn the Army may have extracted from Wright and McKee much more valuable information about their interrogators in the IRA. That is fanciful reasoning but it just goes to show how much you begin to wonder what is going on and where the reality lies. This aspect of the war is like a room of mirrors, not just for us but also for the Army.

As I shall demonstrate later in this book, the Army reveals no details of its undercover operations except when it decides there is propaganda value to be achieved or when it can make the revelation in a newspaper story or in a political leak which is intended to confuse the IRA or obscure public knowledge of an event. Until now the IRA has taken a similar view. Like many writers I approached the writing of this book on the basis that there are always people willing to reveal the truth, whether for the purpose of putting the record straight, for self-aggrandisement or because of disillusionment with an ideology.

An example of the difficulties facing an investigator of the undercover conflict is contained in a series of hitherto unlinked episodes which had their origins in 1974, followed a pattern established in 1971–2 and almost led to the collapse of the Provisionals and serious damage to Loyalist paramilitary organisations. This episode, which the Provisionals now say was a 'brilliant piece of counter-insurgency by the Brits', began after the murder of two policemen. Constables John Malcolm Ross and Edmund Bell were on foot patrol on Finaghy Road near Andersonstown at the beginning of May 1974 when they were shot dead by IRA gunmen. Four young men and a juvenile were charged with a range of offences connected with the killing. Only two of the accused, eighteen-year-old Vincent Heatherington and nineteen-year-old Myles Vincent McGrogan, who lived in the Andersonstown area and knew each other, are relevant to the story which is about to unfold.

As with many accused in Northern Ireland they were initially remanded in custody to Crumlin Road Prison in Belfast. At that time the procedure was for the IRA commander in a prison wing to interview accused men when they first arrived. In 1974 'A' wing of Crumlin Road prison housed Republican remand prisoners and convicted terrorists, while Long Kesh (renamed the Maze prison by the government in 1972, one year after internment) housed Republican and Loyalist internees. Crumlin Road prison also had a wing devoted to men convicted of non-political crimes. The prison authorities interviewed men when they arrived at Crumlin Road and informed them of the structure of the prison, defining the nature of each wing and leaving remand or convicted prisoners in little doubt about the allegiance of the men in particular areas of the prison. This arrangement obviated any necessity to ask a prisoner to admit his political allegiance personally and formally, which could have constituted admission of membership of an illegal organisation. At that time the only two proscribed terrorist organisations were the IRA and UVF, while the largest Loyalist paramilitary grouping, the UDA, was legal, as it is to this day. Once a principal prison officer had established where a prisoner chose to be billeted, the officer sent for the 'terrorist officer' commanding a wing; for Heatherington and McGrogan this was the Provisional IRA commander of 'A' wing. After the prison official took his leave the IRA OC could interview 'prospective candidates' for admission to his wing of the prison.

Heatherington and McGrogan told the IRA commander that they were Provisionals from the 1st Battalion and lived in the Andersonstown area— Heatherington at Navan Green and McGrogan at Coolnasilla Avenue.

They were asked to define the nature of the charges against them but were not questioned about guilt or complicity. Both were accepted to 'A' wing, and this decision was conveyed by the Provo OC to the principal prison officer, who in turn arranged for specified cell accommodation to be provided. The IRA then, as now, was organised on military lines within prison, and care was taken in accepting prisoners into a particular wing in order to try to eliminate the risk of informers being placed in IRA ranks. The UDA and UVF adopted similar tactics and, as with the IRA, the initial interview was simply the beginning of a process designed to determine whether a new prisoner was trustworthy or was a 'plant'. From the moment a prisoner arrived in a wing he was subject to a debriefing to establish whether he was being truthful and if he had compromised others during police or Army interrogations prior to being sent to prison.

Before Heatherington and McGrogan reached their prison cells the IRA OC asked his intelligence officer to check whether any prisoners in 'A' wing blocks had knowledge of the newcomers. Within twenty-four hours it was established that both men had been punished by the IRA in the early 1970s while they were members of the boys' section of the organisation, Fianna Eireann (Youth of Ireland). They had been found guilty of larceny and had been tarred and feathered. (This was a punishment used by the IRA for decades, until the early 1970s when it was replaced by more severe measures such as ' kneecapping', in which bullets were discharged through or behind a person's kneecaps. Tarring and feathering involved a less serious form of injury, and was intended more as a public humiliation. A person was tied to a lamppost or a gatepost, hot tar was poured over the individual's head and body, and bags of feathers, from pillows, were emptied on to the tar. In the case of girls who fraternised with soldiers, their heads were shaven before the tar was applied. When tarring was applied to a member of the IRA the person was also banned from further membership of the organisation.) When the IRA leadership in the prison learned of the past history of Heatherington and McGrogan, they immediately suspected that neither of them could have been involved in the killing of the policemen, since they were no longer members of the IRA. However, to ensure that this was the case, the OC and IO interviewed other remand prisoners and sent secret messages from the prison to try to elicit details about McGrogan and Heatherington, and to find out whether they had played a part in the Finaghy Road murders. No attempt was made at this time to debrief either of the two men because it was believed that a debriefing would prove successful only if information was available from IRA sources outside the prison.

Within several days information was smuggled into the prison inside a tampon worn by the girlfriend of one of the 'A' wing Republicans. The message confirmed that McGrogan and Heatherington were not in the IRA and were not involved in the killing of the policemen. It was relayed from the 1st Battalion which had organised the murder of the policemen and knew the identities of the men who had driven the unit to the scene and of those who had fired the guns. On the basis of this information, the OC approached McGrogan and Heatherington and asked them if they were involved in the killing of the policemen. Both replied that they were not but that they were forced by police to sign statements to the effect that they were guilty of the killings. This allayed IRA fears that McGrogan and Heatherington were 'plants'. They were then asked why they chose to be with the Provisionals in 'A' wing, to which they responded that facing charges of murdering policemen would place them in jeopardy both in Loyalist wings and in the wing which housed ordinary criminals. When asked why they had not chosen the wing containing members of the Official IRA, they replied that their allegiance was to the Provos. They made no mention of earlier membership of Fianna Eireann or the fact that they had been tarred and feathered, but the OC reckoned that the omission was a result of embarrassment.

However, the IRA intelligence officer of 'A' wing was not satisfied and conveyed to the OC his feeling, intuitive though it was, that there was something about the demeanour and personalities of both young men which disturbed him. The OC said the debriefing should proceed normally, adding that there was no reason to suspect that either Heatherington or McGrogan was lying or had anything to gain, since they were being truthful about their non-involvement in the murders of the police constables. The IO chose several experienced interrogators and divided them into two teams to question Heatherington and McGrogan separately about the killings of the policemen, to discover who had interviewed them when they were arrested, the questions they had been asked and whether they had divulged information about people they believed or knew to be in the IRA. Debriefings were conducted not in lengthy sessions but whenever time afforded. The IO decided that he would personally undertake, with assistance, the debriefing of Heatherington. This soon became a hard interrogation, partly because of the IO's inherent suspicions, and partly because the young man became increasingly evasive and vague about the nature of the police questioning he experienced before being remanded to prison. At the end of one week the IO consulted both teams of interrogators. Those handling the McGrogan inquiry reported that he was impassive under difficult questioning, was not uncooperative, but was cool and divulged nothing of significance. By contrast, the other team observed that Heatherington appeared nervous, evasive and at times agitated. The IO consulted the OC of 'A' wing and received permission to continue with the debriefing sessions with the greatest concentration being placed on Heatherington.

After several days, Heatherington was told that his interrogators knew he had a 'criminal' background as far as the IRA was concerned and had been publicly humiliated by tarring and feathering, and he then began to show signs of stress. This means of discrediting him was followed by assertions that if he could hide this fact he could also be hiding other matters. He was asked whether he could be an informer. Persistent periods of questioning in this fashion brought Heatherington almost to the point of mental collapse. Just as the IO was preparing to abandon the interrogations, Heatherington proffered a confession. He said he had been forced at the age of sixteen to work with Special Branch from 1971 onwards. While he was in the Fianna he was caught in possession of an old Lee Enfield .303 rifle and was taken to Springfield Road police and Army base, where he was offered a deal: immunity from prosecution in return for providing information on the IRA. He agreed, but the information he was able to give them was in his opinion low-grade, because the Fianna did not have access to important matters. Moreover, he was forced to leave the Fianna after being caught robbing a local shop.

Heatherington told his interrogators that he accepted the immunity deal only because he was frightened of being sent to prison and of the hurt it would cause his parents, and because the Special Branch investigators warned him that they could brand him an informer by making it known to the IRA that he was giving them information. He said that after he was discarded by the Fianna he kept in touch with his Special Branch contacts but did not have information to offer them. One day he was picked up by two Special Branch officers and taken in a car to Hannahstown on the outskirts of Belfast. They stopped at a point where they could observe a Gaelic game being played in front of a small crowd of onlookers. One of the Special Branch operatives handed him a gun and told him to fire on the crowd. He refused, the gun was snatched from him, one of the Special Branch men fired over the heads of the crowd from the car, and the car then sped away. He was told that the gun contained only his fingerprints, since both Special Branch operatives wore gloves, and that it had just been used in what could be construed as an attempted murder. The gun would be kept in a secure place and used as evidence if Heatherington failed to provide information on the IRA.

To the IRA in Crumlin Road prison, it appeared that Heatherington was co-operating with them and that he was the unfortunate young victim of cleverer and more devious people. As he began to unravel his story, he offered his interrogators names and implicated McGrogan as a fellow agent. Unknown to Heatherington, however, a senior interrogator within the team was listening intently to his revelations in a fashion which was not mirrored by the actions or questions of the others. This man had been the central figure in the interrogation of Wright and McKee. He was to observe, later, that 'alarm bells began to ring in my head' and 'the Four-Square experience loomed large in my thoughts'.

Heatherington was now in full flow, providing a list of names of IRA men, some of whom were in Crumlin Road, others in the Maze and several on the outside, whom he claimed were British agents (informers). He also proffered information about incidents that the IRA believed to have been caused by the Army or Loyalist groups. One such incident was the bombing of a bar in Corporation Street in the Docks area of Belfast on a Halloween night in which two young children died. Heatherington said McGrogan drove the car and the target was a Catholic-owned bar. The intention was to plant a no-warning bomb, which would serve to heighten tension and would lead initially to speculation that it was an IRA 'own-goal' or an attack by Loyalists. According to Heatherington, as the car he was driving approached the bar he observed two children swinging from a lamppost and he told McGrogan that if he threw the bomb at the bar the children would be killed. McGrogan replied, 'Fuck it', and then threw the bomb.

After this revelation, questioning was diverted away from other matters, for a time, to a search for the source of Heatherington's handlers and whether they were merely Special Branch; in other words, as the senior interrogator later remarked, 'to discover if suddenly the MRF, which we thought we smashed, was back in business on a grander scale'. It was vital for the IRA to establish without doubt that Heatherington was telling the truth; if he was, all those he mentioned as agents would have to be dealt with.

In response to questions about the nature of his work, Heatherington claimed that he was taken to England for weapons training and to learn anti-interrogation techniques. An Englishman controlled their group, which included McGrogan, a woman (also English) and a Protestant, Gregory Brown from East Belfast. They often met in a caravan owned by the Englishman and situated near Finaghy Road North, but it was only one of many meeting places. Occasionally they met at a flat near Connolly Station in Dublin. They held parties in the flat and the Englishman gave them money. In Belfast they had their own weapons supply and were permitted to carry out their own robberies so that these would create disruption and confusion and cause the IRA to suspect that some of its own members were lining 'personal pockets'. They also had explosives for carrying out no-warning bomb attacks to discredit the IRA.

All of this was exactly the kind of information the IRA was eager to hear. Heatherington was kept apart from McGrogan as much as possible, and Heatherington's revelations were not used against McGrogan at this stage. McGrogan's interrogators continued to report that he was not proffering information which could incriminate him. As the interrogation of Heatherington continued, the IRA also maintained a watch on his cell and scrutinised his belongings to determine whether he was communicating with McGrogan. One evening the IO of 'A' wing was presented with a note which had been found concealed in Heatherington's bedclothes. It was a message from McGrogan warning his fellow accused that 'if he talked he was a dead man'.

McGrogan was not confronted about the note, but it confirmed the IRA belief that in Heatherington they had the right man and McGrogan was confirming his own guilt.

After receiving reports of Heatherington's revelations, the officer commanding 'A' wing organised a meeting with his intelligence officer and the two teams of interrogators to evaluate the information they were extracting. The OC insisted that the one question needing to be answered was why the Special Branch or military intelligence should have risked sending two operatives into a prison where it was known that the IRA debriefed people. Even if Heatherington and McGrogan were trained in anti-interrogation techniques, why take the risk of exposing them to interrogation? The OC said he would accept that Heatherington had genuinely broken under interrogation if he could be given a reason for the presence of the two in his wing. He added that the matter was 'deadly serious' for many IRA personnel named by Heatherington, if it could be proved beyond reasonable doubt that he was telling the truth. On the other hand, he argued, Heatherington was telling them many things they really wished to hear but which could not easily be substantiated.

The IO returned to his questioning of Heatherington and probed for a reason for his appearance in the prison. Heatherington replied that the charges against him and McGrogan for the murder of the policemen were merely designed to get them into prison and would never be made to stick. They had both been told that after they had been in prison for some time they would be contacted by a member of the prison staff who would supply them with a quantity of poison which they should use to kill three senior Provisionals. Their targets were Brendan Hughes of the Belfast Brigade, Tommy Roberts from Derry, the IRA's prison commander, and Junior Fitzsimmons, a prominent Belfast Provisional who held a high rank in the IRA's prison hierarchy.

Since the poison plot was aimed specifically at the men now responsible for assessing Heatherington's information, their reaction to this motive was predictable. Poison was discovered when details of a poison plot were conveyed to the governor of the prison. Moreover, the Provo leaders were particularly susceptible to believing that their lives were in danger because they knew that a UVF leader, Lenny Murphy (who later became known as the founder of the Shankill Butchers gang), had poisoned an accomplice in Crumlin Road prison.

A Provo leader later commented:

We battened down the hatches in 'A' wing. We suddenly believed Heatherington. The names of all those he mentioned were passed on to relevant people in the IRA in Long Kesh [the Maze] and on the outside. Interrogations began, and in the Maze many men were badly treated by their interrogators. The IRA was carried away in hysteria. Men admitted, under interrogation, crimes they could not have committed. No one was safe from scrutiny. We passed on our information to the Loyalists in respect of Gregory Brown and others named by Heatherington. They reacted as we did but not on the same scale. The result of the maltreatment of some of our own people later led to an internal IRA inquiry. We got nothing from McGrogan except his note, which served to support our suspicion that Heatherington did, indeed, have a lot to tell us. I ordered Heatherington to be pulled in for further interrogation and we really leaned on that guy. What does he do? He tells me it is all a lie and that he was told before being sent into the prison that when interrogated to breaking point he was to divulge all the information which he had given us over a period of weeks. I couldn't believe what I was hearing. I was confused. After all, here was a guy I was beginning to know well. I had made assessments of him to the effect that I felt sorry for him. He admitted personal things to me about how he and McGrogan raped a young girl at the bottom of Kennedy Way. Looking back I don't know what to believe.

While the IRA leadership in Crumlin Road prison were considering Heatherington's latest revelation, an event occurred in 'A' wing which had consequences that placed the matter of Heatherington and McGrogan beyond the control of that wing's leadership. A prison officer named Hanna was attacked and received a throat wound. The man responsible should not have been on 'A' wing at that time, since he was from the Ardoyne area and was not a Republican. He had attacked the prison officer with a tin-foil cover from a packet containing a meat-pie. The result was that everyone was locked into their cells in 'A' wing as a punishment. When the measure was relaxed, the IRA leader discovered that McGrogan and Heatherington had been removed to protective custody.

The 'A' wing leaders, the younger generation of Provos who in the late 1970s would become synonymous with Gerry Adams's leadership, were discredited. It was believed in large sections of the Republican movement that they had created hysteria and paranoia through their interrogations of Heatherington and McGrogan.

On the outside the IRA leadership was changing. The Adams leadership now view the happenings in Crumlin Road in 1974 as part of an important military strategy. One IRA source had this to say:

The damage to the leadership in 1974 took various forms. Military intelligence and Special Branch eventually put the younger leadership away and, as with Heatherington, discredited many of us. We believe now that they were softening us up. The leadership that took over comprised the type of men who stand up with every generation and say that at least they fought but lost and then left it to another generation. The Brits needed that leadership in place to negotiate a ceasefire and they got it in February 1975. The men who negotiated that were physical-force men pure and simple. They believed the Brits were going, the economy was collapsing. They overreacted to sectarianism with the result that the H-Blocks began to fill with kids involved in sectarian warfare. That truce was described at Bodenstown in 1978 as a major mistake. It led to four years of feuds and sectarianism.

In *The Provisional IRA* by Eamonn Mallie and Patrick Bishop, the period that ushered in the ceasefire of 1975 is described as the Provos' 'darkest hour', which brought it close to 'collapse and defeat'.

In March 1975, after one of the longest-running trials, Heatherington, McGrogan and four others were acquitted of all charges in connection with the murders of the two constables at Finaghy Road North in 1974. McGrogan and Heatherington were free men, and to their relief they were not on an IRA hit-list. What they did not know was that the Provos in the prison who were responsible for the interrogations which led to a witch-hunt within the IRA sent messages to the Belfast Brigade asking for both men to be executed. The brigade, which was still under the control of the older leadership, refused the request for two reasons. First they believed the younger men in the prison who had carried out the interrogation were wrong in their assessment of McGrogan and Heatherington and had forced them to make false statements, and that the whole process led to paranoia and the near-collapse of the IRA because of the bitterness and dissension generated by the numerous interrogations of IRA men who had been innocent of the charges of collusion which had been levelled at them. The second reason was that the Belfast Brigade and IRA leadership saw an opportunity to exercise authority over the people in prison who were part of what they saw as the 'Adams-led' faction, which believed the Republican movement should be going in a different direction. However, it was not long before the older leadership was ousted in favour of the Armalite and the ballot box strategy and a more sharply defined approach to the British. By the beginning of 1976 the old guard in the Provisionals was on its way out and the 'Young Turks' who supported Adams were on their way in. Those in the prison who were involved in the interrogations of Heatherington and McGrogan were now in a position to demand that the Heatherington/McGrogan episode be reopened.

In the course of my research I met one of the Provisionals who had
been close to the Heatherington/McGrogan affair, and he made the following observations:

We were had. We knew we had fallen for it. It was very much in the mould of the MRF
operations: clever, well planned and brilliantly executed. The IRA knew and found it
difficult to admit that British military intelligence was brilliant. They almost destroyed
us. They created paranoia in the ranks and left us severely damaged. Retrospectively,
you see how simply it was worked. Heatherington gave us what we wanted only after
pressure was exerted. Now that was clever—McGrogan played a game designed to
make us feel that he was holding back so that we could feel pleased that we were
making progress with one of them. When we began to succeed, as it were, that kept
him protected and he left the note. It reinforced our views. Heatherington gave us all
those names of innocent guys and we believed him because he also supplied us with
information which supported our own theories about various incidents. In effect
Heatherington did not need to be very intelligent. He only needed to be given information and instructed on how to divulge it. The Brits and Special Branch had obviously done their homework on us because we reacted with predictability. For example, Heatherington told us that there were explosives in Dublin and he was informed
that they were required south of the border. That equated with our theory about the
Brits bombing Dublin.

Heatherington also told them that the murder of the UDA leader,
Tommy Herron, was carried out by the 'grouping', which included a
Protestant, Gregory Brown. Herron's murder has always been shrouded
in mystery. It is known that he was lured to a car by a woman and that
a killer was concealed in the boot of the vehicle. The rear seat had been
unscrewed, and when the woman drove Herron into the countryside
outside Belfast for a sexual encounter the killer emerged from the boot
and attacked. That information surfaced before the Heatherington
escapade and it was, one could argue, available to Heatherington and his
handlers. Considering that this was allied to the Dublin bombing theories and the statement that the IRA did not bomb the Catholic bar in
Corporation Street, one could validly suggest that all the stories
Heatherington gave were convenient fabrications. However, because the
stories were fashioned to equate with IRA theories, mythology and prejudice, the Provos were more likely to be susceptible to them. Aside from
McGrogan and himself, two others were implicated by Heatherington:
Gregory Brown and a Catholic, Seamus Brendan O'Brien, from
Andersonstown.

At the beginning of January 1976 Seamus O'Brien, known in his locality of Andersonstown as Shay, was visiting his brother Paddy at a flat in
the area when two armed men burst into the premises and kidnapped
them. Seamus and Paddy were hooded, their hands were tied behind
their backs and they were transported to another house in the

Andersonstown/Glen Road district. They were held in separate rooms and constantly interrogated. Two days later Paddy O'Brien, still hooded, hands tied, was dumped from a stationary car at Kennedy Way in West Belfast during rush-hour. He was told by his captors that he would be shot on sight if he reported to the police or military. When he told his parents about the threat the family waited for a further five days without consulting the security forces. It was exactly one week from the day of his kidnapping that the body of Seamus O'Brien was discovered by a roadside ditch in the Glen Road area. It was a Saturday afternoon, 17 January, a day his mother would never forget:

I knew from the day of Paddy's release that, like him, Seamus had a filthy hood over his head. Paddy said that when he was there the heating in the house was turned up and their mouths became dry. They were refused water and food and Paddy heard Seamus screaming as he was being tortured. If they had beaten or kneecapped Seamus it would not have been so bad. But if they thought he was a British agent why did they not kill him cleanly instead of torturing him. The Provos are hypocrites bringing cases before the European Human Rights Commission, accusing the British Army and RUC of torture, when they are carrying out worse torture. When Paddy was released his hands were swollen like balloons. I dread to think of what Seamus went through. We asked a priest to try to find out what was happening and he brought back word that Seamus was being accused of being a British agent.

For Mrs O'Brien this was the second death she faced in one month. Her daughter had been found gassed in a flat in the Falls Road area on 9 December 1975.

The Provisionals issued a statement claiming that Seamus O'Brien was a British agent who had been caught planting a bomb outside the Martin Forsythe Social Club in the Falls area. It was hardly a credible explanation: if he had been caught, why was he kidnapped at his brother's flat?

To confuse matters, a spokesman for an unknown Loyalist grouping, the Ulster Army Council, phoned journalists to claim that O'Brien had passed information about both wings of the IRA to Loyalist paramilitaries as well as identifying IRA arms dumps. He added that the dead man was a 'true Ulsterman and loyal Catholic who wanted to break the stranglehold of the Republicans over ordinary Catholics'. The Provos, UDA and UVF say they never issued such a statement. So who did? Could it have been military intelligence? Did they perceive an advantage to be gained by suggesting that there were informers in Provo ranks, or did they intend to offset any attempt by the Provos to claim that O'Brien worked for the Army? No one is ever likely to answer these questions.

What is known is that the Provos' detailed statement alleged that O'Brien was apprehended by an IRA intelligence unit while planting a

20lb gelignite bomb and that he was armed with a Japanese pistol. He admitted, they said, that he was involved with the British Army through Loyalist paramilitary organisations. One must ask whether the Provos based their statement about the 20lb bomb on an admission extracted from O'Brien under severe physical and mental torture. If it had been put to O'Brien that a bomb had been planted outside the Social Club, he could surely have been forced to admit that he was the guilty person. The additional detail about the 'Japanese pistol' is puzzling, though it could have been added for effect. It is my contention that the Provos had decided to kill O'Brien, not simply because Heatherington identified him but because his death was to be the precursor of a series of assassinations intended to reinforce the IRA's judgement that Heatherington and McGrogan were British agents. By extracting a confession from O'Brien, the Provisionals who felt duped by Heatherington in the prison interrogation were preparing a case for the execution of several other people. After all, Heatherington and McGrogan had survived without fear of retribution, while the men who suffered and who sought revenge against them had been discredited.

The IRA leadership was beginning to come under the control of the faction that included the Crumlin Road interrogators; and those men were moving stealthily to prepare a case against Heatherington and McGrogan and to reverse the view in the Provisional movement that they had been victims of a paranoid leadership in Crumlin Road prison. The Provos were now engaged in a witch-hunt, but Heatherington and McGrogan appeared oblivious; they showed no sign of panic, and IRA intelligence was unable to detect any indication that they were acting as informers. This is how one Provisional IRA officer saw it: 'They were normal citizens. They were not in the IRA and therefore, aside from gossip and general observation, they would not have possessed sensitive information. We couldn't watch them twenty-four hours a day. Anyway the feeling was that by now they could have learned sophistication.'

Four months after the death of Seamus O'Brien a killing took place in West Belfast which puzzled everyone, including, it seemed, the police. On the afternoon of 5 May 1976, at the junction of Shaw's Road and Glen Road on the periphery of the Andersonstown area, a twenty-two-year-old taxi driver, James Green, who lived in the predominantly Catholic Lower Falls district, was driving his black London-type taxi countrywards when a woman hailed him. As he slowed his vehicle to a standstill, a red Renault car pulled alongside and one of its three occupants emerged with a gun and shot Green at point-blank range. One bullet struck him in the head and three in the chest, killing him instantly. The gunman and the unknown woman rushed to the Renault, which sped off citywards. Journalists speculated that the killing was the work of a Loyalist murder gang, or that the taxi driver had been mistaken for someone else, or that his death was the result of a feud between the Official IRA and the Provisionals. Journalists could not discover a clear motive and no terrorist grouping claimed responsibility. The murder was well organised, and if a Loyalist gang had been intent on killing a Catholic on that day there was no need for them to prepare an elaborate plan. It was mid-afternoon and there were hundreds of potential victims walking the roads of Belfast at that time. On the other hand, a journalist would have quickly dispensed with the feud theory, since both IRA groupings always advertised atrocities committed in feuds. The possibility that the murder was the result of mistaken identity would have held much more weight in respect of the available evidence. However, what journalists did not possess was a fine piece of detail about the career of James Green. Like Louis Hammond, he had spent some time in the Royal Irish Rangers before returning to Belfast to work for the Falls Taxi Association, which the Army believed to be a front and fundraiser for the Provisionals. When the London-type taxis were first used in West Belfast, drivers paid a weekly contribution to IRA funds. In return the Provisionals ensured that the taxis had plenty of business by organising the burning of public transport and the use of council-controlled buses as barricades. Moreover, Green was another man who had been named by Heatherington during the lengthy interrogations in Crumlin Road prison.

The Crumlin Road interrogations had also unleashed a paranoia within Loyalist paramilitary ranks in 1974, but this subsided once the Provisionals in the prison had been discredited. With the killing of O'Brien and Green in 1976, however, the UDA also decided to act on Heatherington's claim, as they began to suspect that maybe the prison interrogators were right after all. Nine days after the killing of James Green, an assassination team from the UDA's Ulster Freedom Fighters Belfast Brigade gunned down twenty-seven-year-old Gregory Brown as he walked with friends along the Cregagh Road in East Belfast. The shooting took place before midnight on 14 May 1976. A silver-coloured Cortina, the favourite vehicle of terrorists in Northern Ireland, drew alongside Brown and his friends. A gunman armed with a revolver emerged from the car and shot Brown from a range of 8 to 10 feet. Gregory Brown died leaving a young wife who was expecting their first baby. The UFF claimed responsibility for the murder and said they shot Brown because he was involved in the murder in 1973 of the East Belfast UDA leader, Tommy Herron.

On 8 July the *Irish Times* carried a headline, 'Murdered Man in Herron Death Cycle'. From a casual glance this headline might have appeared to concern the fate of Gregory Brown, shot two months earlier. However, it related to Vincent Heatherington, whose body had been found at Colin Glen on the outskirts of Belfast two days earlier. Two youths were walking past Colin Glen Bridge when they saw a hooded body lying behind a wire fence. The victim had his hands tied in front of him and the hood, which covered part of his head and face, was a rough piece of cloth. When the police arrived a forensic expert and a pathologist quickly confirmed that the body was warm and had been dumped only shortly before the youths had found it. The police were left in little doubt that the dead person was the victim of a paramilitary execution.

It is extraordinary to think that for this IRA ritual of placing a hood over a victim's head someone had meticulously fashioned and sewn the hood with a needle and thread. Occasionally Loyalists have adopted a similar ritual when killing a Catholic, and this may be a form of mimicry, an indication that the killers believed the victim to be a member of the IRA, or simply a trademark of a particular killing team. Such hoods are used by death squads throughout the world. While working as an investigative journalist I remember constantly depicting such a murder where a victim was hooded as 'macabre'. I now think that the paramilitaries always intended it to be so: terror is understood or illustrated not simply by killing, but by the wicked symbolism that remains fixed in one's thoughts long after the name of the deceased is forgotten.

In this instance the IRA was letting everyone know the penalty for 'treachery'. Unlike the case of Kevin McKee, where a public avowal of his 'crimes' would have caused embarrassment because of his family's prominence within Republicanism, with Vincent Heatherington the IRA harboured no reservations. 'The Belfast Brigade, IRA, accepts responsibility for the execution of Vincent Heatherington. After extensive and exhaustive enquiries, he was found guilty of the highest form of treachery—complicity with British Forces.' This statement reached newspaper news desks within hours of the 'execution' and a British Army spokesman responded to press enquiries by saying that the IRA claim was 'rubbish'.

Several days before his death, Heatherington had been abducted by two armed men from his girlfriend's home in Andersonstown. Police were informed of the kidnapping by the Heatherington family and an exhaustive search was mounted by the security forces. It is a measure of the potential success of such searches that Heatherington's body was eventually found less than one mile from where he was abducted.

The article in the *Irish Times* of 8 July, which asked penetrating questions about the dead man, was written by David McKittrick. He sought to infer a connection between the murder of Gregory Brown and Heatherington: 'The killing has been admitted by the Provisional IRA which claims that Heatherington was shot because of complicity with the security forces, but the story behind his death is much more complicated than that. A strange story lies behind these facts and it looks as though the full details will never be known. It begins with the death of Tommy Herron in 1973 for which no one has been brought to trial.' David McKittrick had every reason to believe that Herron's death was linked to both Brown and Heatherington. Though he did not possess all the facts, what he knew from his contacts about these events was given an added ingredient by the interest shown by RUC Special Branch. After Gregory Brown's death the *Irish Times* carried a claim that Brown, an RUC detective constable, a Catholic and a woman had murdered Herron. Following publication of this, two Special Branch officers questioned the *Irish Times* reporter responsible for the allegation. According to McKittrick, they were 'particularly interested in the alleged involvement of a policeman in Herron's death'.

As David McKittrick wrote on 8 July 1976, the full details of the Heatherington saga may never be known. One such element, which I deliberately refer to almost as a postscript, is that Gregory Brown lived in Andersonstown for a short period in the early 1970s. I was told this by an impeccable source, but I could not find evidence to substantiate the claim—that is, until I conducted a search of newspapers of the period. I uncovered an *Irish Times* report from the summer of 1976 that made a slight reference to Brown to the effect that Provisionals had informed the UDA that Heatherington and two of his co-accused in 1974 had told them they knew Brown because Brown once lived in Andersonstown. Fourteen years on from that report it is not possible, I believe, to ascertain the veracity of the alleged Brown/Andersonstown link. It begs so many questions. If the allegation is true, one could conclude that Heatherington and McGrogan knew Brown because he was a neighbour, but one might then ask why a Protestant was living in a predominantly nationalist area during the height of the Troubles. If it is untrue, why and who was responsible for adding such an ingredient to an already complex and murky story?

One further puzzle concerns the fate of twenty-two-year-old Myles Vincent McGrogan. One would expect that the death of Heatherington would have galvanised him into action and that he would have quickly left not only his home at Coolnasilla Avenue in Andersonstown but the island of Ireland. On the other hand he had said little during the 1974 Crumlin Road prison interrogations and had been left in peace by the IRA. He may well have concluded that Heatherington was vulnerable and that if he, McGrogan, decided to run he would be signposting his guilt.

The Provisionals say they kept 'tabs' on him, if only on an infrequent basis. He would have known that, so one must also wonder if he remained in Andersonstown on the advice of others? His decision to remain in Belfast cost him his life. On 9 April 1977 a motorist travelling countrywards along the Glen Road saw a body at a roadside adjacent to the spot where Heatherington had been found dead. McGrogan had been shot in the head and, according to police evidence, had been killed where he was found.

Thus ended an unusual saga which left many unanswered questions, and which cost the lives of young men who were caught in an undercover war in which nothing was as it appeared. They were, one could argue, in a room full of mirrors, and they were expendable. With so many questions unanswered it is impossible to attribute blame except to recognise that they were all murdered by terrorists. One must, however, consider the fact that their youth made it easy for them to be influenced and manipulated by more experienced people who saw them as pawns in a greater game where, perhaps, the risks were higher than several lives. The Heatherington/McGrogan escapade almost destroyed the Provisionals, and that did not occur by chance; it was cleverly designed—but at what cost to life? Many people may argue that there are a limited number of options when dealing with terrorism and that, of necessity, one must recognise that the stakes are higher. One only has to remember the sixteen people who died in McGurk's Bar or the Enniskillen tragedy. In such a war, one might argue that there must be an acceptable level of violence and damage in terms of human life and, in particular, counter-terrorist operatives.

The British Army, Special Branch and other agencies will never answer questions about matters as secret as those I have outlined. Their reasoning is that the war goes on and many events of the last twenty years remain unsolved and unresolved; in addition, many of the IRA intelligence operatives of 1974–7 remain active, and discussion of secret activities could reveal patterns of thinking or behaviour which could prove relevant, because some operations never end.

In that context I would appreciate (though it is not possible) an answer to the following question. Assuming that the Heatherington saga was a fictional IRA story, or 'rubbish' as described by an Army spokesman, why was McGrogan not warned of the danger to his life after Heatherington's murder?

The reason why such a question is relevant is that in July 1976, after Heatherington's death, newspaper reports were indirectly hinting that McGrogan had worked for the Army and had pointed the accusing finger at Gregory Brown. Surely McGrogan would have known his days were numbered unless he was motivated by other factors or advised by others.

Was McGrogan advised that there was a possibility he might escape a death sentence? Did the IRA wait for nine months after Heatherington's execution to see if McGrogan would run for cover and expose other people? The answers, I believe, may lie with the dead.

4

Playing It Dirty
British Agents in Ireland

When the violence began in Ireland in 1969, knowledge of the precise nature of the conflict and the organisations central to it was not an intelligence priority. The use of internment without trial in 1971 showed a distinct lack of hard intelligence for the Northern Ireland Special Branch and the British Army because the majority of those arrested in the first swoops were neither IRA personnel nor Republicans but innocent nationalists, some of whom were subjected to inhuman and degrading treatment during interrogation which led to the British government facing the Court of Human Rights in Strasbourg. Even at the outset of the violence, Special Branch files on the IRA were outdated because they related to the 1950s and many of the IRA men of that period were no longer active. In the minds of security chiefs in Britain and particularly within MI6, which considered Ireland as part of its remit, the IRA was the one organisation which represented terror and threatened stability in Northern Ireland from the safe haven of bases in the Republic and a headquarters in Dublin.

In order to acquire intelligence on the threat posed to the British Army and British interests in Northern Ireland, MI6 placed the IRA in the Republic under close scrutiny, and MI6 contacts within Irish intelligence and the Irish police force, the Gardai, were asked to provide whatever up-to-date information was available on the IRA. Initially the mistake made by British intelligence was the targeting solely of what was the Marxist-led Official IRA and not the element which was to emerge as the Provisional IRA. In the course of this primary offensive, British intelligence permitted the use of criminals as agents in an effort to penetrate the Official IRA under Goulding's leadership. Since the Official IRA at that time harboured a number of criminal elements, the British agents and those members of the IRA whom they sought out recognised each other as fellow travellers or likely bedfellows. This was a period of dangerous and amateurish spying exploits by British agents; and it happened at a time when bombs were exploding in Dublin while the Dail was discussing anti-terrorist legislation, and when the Official IRA were planning a political assassination campaign which almost claimed the life of John Taylor, Minister for Home Affairs in the Northern Ireland government. It was also a period when Dublin was a hotbed of activity with the planning of arms shipments and the development of terrorist contacts outside Ireland. Some would say it was a dangerous time for criminals to be operating as British spies. London-Dublin relations were at their worst ever. The Dublin government was constantly in receipt of complaints from Catholic leaders and politicians that British soldiers were harassing the Catholic population. For their part the British were unhappy about the government of Jack Lynch and its association with the IRA and those who were in the process of shaping the Provisionals. Within this framework of political uncertainty there were rumours of a British dirty tricks campaign. Yet agents were placed in Ireland with disastrous consequences for British-Irish relations.

Most people are familiar with the James Bond image of the undercover agent, but Ian Fleming's character, attractive as he may be, bears little or no resemblance to the real life 'Joes'—MI6 parlance for intelligence operatives. The men and women who are recruited by the security services are not necessarily persons of good character or without criminal blemish. Agents are often chosen for their skills and abilities to mix in a grubby, immoral and amoral level of society far removed from the quick-shooting celluloid arena where the fast cars, expensive suits and Dom Perignon come straight off the pages of a thriller and not from a financial retainer. Sometimes there are exceptions to the rule; for example, a fast car and a champagne lifestyle may be exactly what is required for an agent to fit perfectly into a particular part of society. To many people, however, the prospect of persons with criminal backgrounds working for the security services will be anathema, but in the murky world of espionage and counter-terrorism the edges of public morality become frayed and blurred. At least that is how it appeared when the first major case of British espionage surfaced in Ireland at the beginning of the present conflict. The episode illustrated the amateurishness of MI6 policy in Ireland and the risks involved in using 'Joes' with criminal backgrounds. This story concerns two brothers, Kenneth and Keith Littlejohn, who became entangled in a web of intrigue which severely damaged British-Irish relations and forced the head of MI6, Sir Maurice Oldfield, to reassure his staff in 1973 that 'no violence is involved now in the operations conducted by the SAS'. The spy-watcher extraordinary, Chapman Pincher, commented on the perception of the Littlejohn saga in MI6 HQ: 'There was concern among staff. Some of the women and junior staff did not relish working for an organisation involving violence and assassination.'

The exact function of the Littlejohn brothers may never be known except to those in MI6 who 'handled' them and the keepers of the files at Century House in London where MI6 has its headquarters. Equally, there is a danger in relying too much on what the Littlejohns have said about their role as agents. However, if one examines their words in combination with interviews with people who knew them, members of the IRA who worked alongside them and Irish police sources, an interesting story emerges which could have come directly from the pen of a Le Carré or Frederick Forsythe.

The story begins in 1968 when twenty-seven-year-old Kenneth Littlejohn was released from prison after serving three years for robbery. He immediately decided to improve his life and that of his wife Christina and their two children, and began dealing in cars, but business was not very brisk, and disillusionment set in. On 28 August 1970 a robbery took place at the Midland Motor Cylinder Company in Smethwick, near Birmingham, and a substantial sum of money—£30,000 to £40,000—was stolen. Littlejohn's brother-in-law, Brian Anthony Perks, was found bound and gagged at the scene of the crime and was arrested; he was convicted of complicity but was discharged on appeal. Immediately after the robbery West Midlands police issued a warrant for the arrest of Kenneth Littlejohn for questioning in relation to the crime. On 11 September the *West Midland Police Gazette* named Kenneth Littlejohn as wanted and referred to aliases he used: Kenneth Austen and Charles Durverne.

Police raided twenty to thirty homes in Birmingham, London and Torquay in the search for Littlejohn. He says he stayed with friends in London who introduced him to a policeman, who in turn showed him the contents of the West Midlands arrest warrant. Littlejohn claims he paid this police officer money and was advised by him to travel to Dublin. He further alleges that the officer used contacts in Birmingham to arrange introductions for him in Dublin.

Whether one believes this sequence of events relating to the police officer, the fact is that Kenneth Littlejohn arrived in Dublin purporting to represent a clothing firm. In December 1970 Whizz Kids (Ireland) Ltd was established. The directors of the London parent company were Kenneth Austen (alias Littlejohn) and Robert Stockman. (Stockman was later acquitted of charges of robbery in Ireland and claimed never to have visited the country except in custody when charges were preferred against him and Littlejohn.)

In Dublin, Littlejohn announced that he was setting up a factory in County Kerry on the west coast of Ireland, an area of great natural beauty but high unemployment. When Kenneth Littlejohn arrived in Kerry he was received with warmth and friendliness. Although he said he had worked in the textile business all his life, Whizz Kids company records described him as a property consultant and property investor. He encouraged Kerry locals to believe that he was a big spender and told the Cahirciveen Development Association he intended to build a factory to manufacture hot-pants. Cahirciveen is a village which sees many tourists but is not known for opulence or fast-living. Kenneth Littlejohn exploited this by impressing the locals with his expensive clothes, red MGB sports car and his tendency to dispense largesse in local bars: 'all the lads got a drink from Kenneth when he arrived in a pub'. He was perceived as a dashing young man who was about to bring prosperity to Cahirciveen. When people waited for the foundations of the proposed factory to be laid Littlejohn stayed in smart Killarney hotels, took flying lessons at Farranfore airport and spent much of his time in an attractive hideaway at Killorglin, the property of the owner of a major salmon factory. The residents of Cahirciveen soon became disillusioned with him when the factory did not become a reality. Littlejohn turned down four possible sites and left Kerry as quickly as he had arrived, leaving a string of debts and a few items of 'ladies' clothing' in the office leased to him by Farranfore airport.

Littlejohn claims that while he was in Kerry something happened which made him put aside his business interests. He says he was visiting a possible factory site in Galway when he was shown an AK 47 or AK 49 (Kalashnikov) assault rifle which he was told had been landed from a Russian submarine. At this point, Littlejohn, a former paratrooper who had been dishonourably discharged from the Paratroop Regiment, decided to return to England. It is worth noting that during this time there was considerable disquiet in Britain about the Lynch/Haughey administration's perceptions of the problems in Ireland, and newspapers carried stories about arms being bought abroad and smuggled into Ireland. Littlejohn, an astute man always with an eye to 'advancement', would have been aware of the political situation. His stay in Kerry, a staunchly Republican county, would have acquainted him with the fervour, complexities and developing violence in Ireland. If his claim about the assault rifle were true, it would perhaps have offered him an advantage, if not impetus, for the career on which he was about to embark. However, I doubt his claim on the basis that there is no evidence that guns were ever landed from a Russian submarine. AK 47 assault rifles were introduced to Ireland in small numbers at that time, but the source was Europe and the Middle East. Is it likely that someone is going to show a veritable newcomer, a flashy Englishman, an assault rifle and tell him how it came to be in Ireland? Whatever the truth of this matter, Kenneth Littlejohn abandoned his business plans and returned to London, where he was joined by his younger brother, Keith. One must wonder why he risked going back to London knowing an arrest warrant was still on police files. Was he considering the prospect of exploiting his knowledge of Ireland in the certainty that his proposed business ventures had folded and he was facing arrest, if not the prospect of criminal charges?

His brother Keith had a similar attitude to life but had made social contacts which would prove valuable in his future career. Keith Littlejohn at twenty-six years of age was going through his own personal crisis. His life from the age of fourteen was littered with problems which led him into borstal training for larceny, being considered beyond parental control, and committing robbery. By 1969 he was reviewing his life, had served a period in Brixton Prison and was studying for A levels at Bromley Technical College. His attempt to reconstruct his life ended when his girlfriend left him. He was emotionally devastated and left Bromley for London, where he lived rough until he was assisted by a voluntary organisation, Teamwork Associates, whose aim was to rehabilitate ex-borstal boys.

It was through this organisation that he met Lady Pamela Onslow, who was well known for her great interest in youth. She was an official at the Ministry of Defence, a personal friend of the Defence Minister, Lord Carrington, and the wife of William Arthur Bamhyde, 6th Earl of Onslow and former assistant chief whip to the Tory Party in the Lords. Kenneth Littlejohn says that when he arrived in London and told his brother about the rifle Keith arranged for him to meet Pamela Onslow because of her friendship with Lord Carrington. According to Kenneth Littlejohn, he told Lady Onslow about the rifle, his knowledge of Ireland and the contacts he had established, and convinced her of his value to British security interests because she spoke to Carrington and arranged a meeting in her home which was attended by one of the Defence Minister's staff, the junior minister, Geoffrey Johnson-Smith (whom Littlejohn says he believed was the Secretary of State for War). This meeting lasted three hours and its duration, as well as the presence of a junior minister, was indicative of the seriousness being attached to Kenneth Littlejohn's story of his experiences in Ireland. So impressed was Johnson-Smith that he relayed his conversation with Littlejohn to Century House, headquarters of MI6. One man who insiders believe knew about the Littlejohn episode from an early stage was Christopher Ewart-Biggs, who later became British ambassador to Ireland and was murdered by the IRA.

Subsequent meetings between the Littlejohn brothers and Lady Onslow resulted in the junior minister asking Kenneth Littlejohn if he would be prepared to operate in Ireland on behalf of Special Branch. Littlejohn claims he stated that he 'wanted nothing to do' with the police, to which Johnson-Smith replied that he could arrange instead for him to meet people from the Ministry of Defence. Such an appointment was made, and Kenneth Littlejohn met for the first time an employee of MI6 named Douglas Smythe. According to Littlejohn, Smythe wanted to know if he was willing to return to Ireland to work as an agent for MI6. Littlejohn says that Smythe talked of conditions in Northern Ireland and political assassinations there, and was anxious to know if Littlejohn knew about the communist-made weapons in the hands of the IRA.

An important issue relating to the initial dealings between Smythe and Littlejohn is whether Smythe knew he was dealing with a person with a criminal background. One would expect that MI6 would have checked out their prospective agent and discovered that not only was he a professional criminal but that one of his crimes was characterised by a military efficiency which shocked a court. This was a wages snatch in 1965 from the firm of Fisher & Ludlow Ltd in Edrington, Birmingham. When Kenneth Littlejohn was being sentenced for his part in organising the crime the presiding judge, Mr Justice Ashworth, said the raid had required skill, determination and luck. 'It is not to be compared to the Great Train Robbery in amount, but it can be compared in execution'. Littlejohn maintains that Smythe was fully aware of his criminal past and his recent predicament, namely the outstanding arrest warrant. He says Smythe gave him a telephone number which he could use to make contact with Detective Inspector Sinclair of Special Branch if police in England arrested him, and that Smythe assured him that Sinclair would negotiate a speedy release in the event of such a happening. What Littlejohn did not know was that Smythe was not simply a Special Branch bureaucrat but a fully fledged operative who worked in Ireland, especially Northern Ireland, and handled several agents.

Littlejohn claims he met Smythe in Belfast, Dublin and other places early in 1972, and that on each occasion they discussed the prevailing political situation. Both Smythe and Johnson-Smith, he says, were particularly interested in the Official IRA, because it was felt that the Provos were a temporary phenomenon, whereas the Officials had communist affiliations and would pose the greater threat in the longer term to British interests in Ireland. This would accord with the political climate of the time and, as I explained in chapter 1, was partly the reason why members of Fianna Fail encouraged the growth of the Provisionals.

Whatever Smythe may have wished, he was not fully in control of Kenneth Littlejohn, who was joined in Dublin in early 1972 by his brother Keith. They received a substantial retainer from Smythe which enabled them initially to lead an active social life for a short time in Dublin and establish contacts with people who were mostly on the fringes of the Official IRA. However, whether on Smythe's instructions or their own ingenuity, they moved in the spring of 1972 to Clogherhead in County Louth, close to the border with Northern Ireland, where they rented Smuggler's Cottage, a pleasant residence, and according to the Gardai 'led a fairly high life and associated with a good class of society'. Kenneth Littlejohn persuaded his wife Christine to stay there, so they could present to the local community an air of being a normal family. They were generous in pubs and made it known that they were in favour of Republican ideals. Their acceptance into the world of the terrorists and criminals was also made easier by the fact that police in England contacted the Gardai to warn them about the Littlejohns' criminal background. This ensured that any enquiries from the IRA or affiliated groups were met with the kind of biographical details which would not have encouraged anyone to believe that the Littlejohns were British agents. In that respect one has to accept that the choice of the Littlejohns as agents was ideal, since they exhibited attributes which made it seem they were merely 'wide boys', one of whom was on a wanted list in Britain, and they spoke a language which was common to criminals everywhere. In positioning themselves at Clogherhead they were also paving the way for association with the IRA. At the time many IRA men who had fled Northern Ireland to escape internment or to 'rest' from terrorist action were living around Dundalk and Clogherhead, some of them billeted in caravans.

There was a caravan site at Clogherhead which was the staging point for men on the run and from there they would operate from the South into the North. I was told to get involved with these people but I said I didn't fancy getting into the lines there unless I had a bloody gun. I asked for a 9mm model Browning but Smythe said he fancied a heavier weapon for stopping power. He was telling me that he had put about nine 9mm bullets into some man's head and he carried on moving. He preferred a .45 but to carry a .45 when you are constantly subjected to body searches would have been not only impossible but also uncomfortable. It was decided that I should carry a .22 which, although it hasn't got any stopping power, in an emergency would give me some measure of protection. Every time I asked him for this gun, he would still make excuses. Eventually, he asked me if I would pick it up in Dublin and I went to a solicitor's office in Dublin and the man just opened a drawer and gave me a .22 Berretta with 100 rounds of ammunition.

There are several features of this account by Kenneth Littlejohn of his alleged dealings with Smythe which show the absurd nature of how the self-confessed spy perceived his role, and, if it is true, the bravado of his spymaster. Littlejohn appears as the romancer who needs a gun. He could have bought one from his IRA contacts, but if it was given to him by Smythe it would be a symbol of his job as an official agent. It was as though Littlejohn needed an officially sanctioned weapon before he could believe in his role. If he accurately quoted Smythe, then the spymaster would have had a similar obsession with bravado, notably his preference for a .45 pistol because of its stopping power, and his nonsensical claim that nine 9mm bullets in a man's head failed to stop him 'moving'. Littlejohn's account depicts two men who are busily obsessed with role-playing in a contextual mode which is almost celluloid in character. Moreover, these alleged meetings between Smythe and Kenneth Littlejohn were always reserved to the two, as though the older Littlejohn was ensuring that his younger brother was cushioned from the dangerous world of spying.

Kenneth Littlejohn says that his 'handler' was interested in who was on the terrorists' hit-list: 'I was told to stick with the Officials and to get close to Seamus Costello [later a founder of the INLA who was shot dead in a feud] and Sean Patrick Garland. I was told by Smythe that there was going to be a policy of political assassination and that I was to offer myself as someone available for this.' Littlejohn's claim about a political assassination policy would fit the historical context. In early 1972 the Official IRA shot and wounded John Taylor, the Unionist Minister for Home Affairs. At the time there was no reason to believe that Joe McCann of the Official IRA, who masterminded the assassination attempt on Taylor, was about to embark on a campaign of political killings. McCann was shot dead by a British soldier in the Markets area of Belfast before he had time to put his plan into operation.

Whatever the Littlejohns' boasts, however, in fact they were associating with members of the Official IRA who were not frontline operatives and who, like the Littlejohns, were interested in ordinary criminal activity. The main IRA contact for the brothers was Brian Mathers, from Newry, who had fled across the border when internment was introduced in 1971. Mathers was surrounded by several IRA men who had been expelled from the organisation for carrying out 'unofficial' bank raids. It was a motley crew but it provided the Littlejohns with the right kind of cover and detailed information about IRA figures and organisational matters. Kenneth Littlejohn says that he was involved in transferring

weapons and men across the Irish border, and IRA sources have supported his claim. He argues that his Army training enabled him to assist
in such exercises:

Most of them were getting disillusioned with the command structure in Dublin. They
felt that the command people were getting fat and lazy and living off what everyone
else was earning and they weren't really in touch with the situation on the border.
They were getting pretty disillusioned. I talked to Smythe about this and we thought
we might set up another IRA splinter group, somehow keep it within the movement
but give it some sort of independence and operate it more or less like an SAS unit.

This statement by Littlejohn is indicative of the way in which he not
only perceived his role as an agent but imagined himself running an SAS-
type unit which would ultimately be self-sufficient and rob banks to
finance its existence. From enquiries I have made, Littlejohn undoubtedly harboured this concept and, though it was later adjudged to be part of
a British counter-insurgency policy, it was in reality only an idea which
Littlejohn conveyed to Mathers and it did not derive from briefings by
Smythe. Littlejohn also claims that Smythe suggested that he plan the
assassinations of Sean MacStiofan, Chief of Staff of the Provisionals, and
Seamus Costello and Sean Garland of the Official IRA. It is interesting to
note the flattering if inaccurate fashion in which Kenneth Littlejohn
describes the lifestyle of the IRA leaders, attributing to them training in
Havana and Moscow. This is how he recounts the plan to kill MacStiofan:

I was told to assassinate him in the summer of 1972 and I waited in a car outside
his house which is at 32 Blackcastle, Navan, County Westmeath, but we never saw
him. The instructions we were given was that MacStiofan's body was to be blown up
so that it was completely unrecognisable. We should also take his car to Dublin airport and thereafter money would be sent from Canada to his family so that it would
appear that he had absconded with IRA funds. They would also spread rumours to
this effect which they had previously tried to do.

These claims are not simply outrageous but signify, I believe, his tendency subsequently to exaggerate his role in Ireland. When one considers the
type of people with whom he was operating, he was only in a position to
deal in low-grade intelligence, valuable as it may have been, but he needed to accord himself greater importance. The charge that he was being
asked to assassinate three well-known Republicans does not merit analysis other than a recognition that much of what Littlejohn eventually said
demands close scrutiny. What is significant and cannot be called into
question is that he was, with official sanction, associating with terrorists
and, as impeccable sources have confirmed, undertaking basic terrorist
roles in the border areas of Newry and Dundalk.

The Littlejohns' stay in County Louth was becoming increasingly fraught with danger by the summer of 1972, partly because the Provisional and Official IRA leaderships were suspicious of their presence in Ireland, and partly as a result of one tragic incident. A car which Kenneth Littlejohn admits was in his possession was somehow removed from Clogherhead and left across the border in Northern Ireland at an area known as Hillside. Littlejohn, using the imperial 'we' but not defining whom that related to, says 'we sent three men to pick it up'. The three men who went to retrieve the car were Edmund Woolsley, a married man with six children who owned the Ulster Bar at Warrenpoint, and two of his customers who were simply obliging Woolsley by accompanying him. They contacted the British Army to ensure that the abandoned vehicle had been checked for explosives—a normal procedure in Northern Ireland, where cars were often stolen and booby-trapped. The Army and the police confirmed that the vehicle was in a safe condition. However, when the three went to the vehicle, the two customers adopted a cautious approach which saved their lives. Woolsley was blown to pieces when he tried to open the driver's door.

The Official IRA leadership suspected that Littlejohn was involved, and he admits that he became aware that the accusing finger was pointing towards him. He says he never executed anyone and named another party as responsible for the killing of Woolsley. This is merely a suspicion for which Kenneth Littlejohn has never provided evidence. One would conclude that if he had informed Smythe about the car or been in direct contact with him at this time he would have said so in order to harden his accusation that this was the work of British intelligence. On the other hand there is no proof that it was not, though one is obliged to ask whether there were people within either wing of the IRA who had reason to kill Littlejohn and who believed that he would personally retrieve his car from Newry. There is a valid reason for arguing that there were people within the Official IRA leadership who wanted him dead. It is known that Costello and others were aware of Littlejohn's associations with 'criminal elements' within the organisation and of his grandiose plans for creating an independent unit. The Provisionals distrusted the Littlejohns when they first came to their attention in the border areas and, I am told, only desisted from executing them because of their association with members of the Official IRA. Would it therefore have been easier to booby-trap a car? I can only leave it to the reader to assess which of three groupings, Official IRA, Provisional IRA or MI6, would have had sufficient reason to engineer such a crime.

It was at this time that Douglas Smythe handed over control of the Littlejohns to a man whom they came to know as Oliver. According to Kenneth Littlejohn, the transfer took place after he had warned Smythe that a man answering to his description was known to visit Belfast pubs and was about to be executed by the IRA. Littlejohn may well have delivered such a warning, but the real reason for the 'transfer' was that Smythe was, unknown to the Littlejohns, in a spot of bother. In Dublin, a John Wyman and a Detective Sergeant Patrick Crinion of Irish Special Branch were under scrutiny. Irish Special Branch operatives had been aware for some time that one of their colleagues was passing classified documents to a member of the British Secret Intelligence Services who operated under the alias of John Wyman. What they also knew, but have never admitted, was that John Wyman had another alias—Douglas Smythe— and that his activities included the running of other agents in Ireland, including the Littlejohn brothers. While Kenneth Littlejohn was attempting to establish a rapport with his new handler, Douglas Smythe, alias John Wyman, was arrested in the act of receiving Irish Special Branch documents on the IRA from Detective Sergeant Patrick Crinion.

Wyman gave his address as Swan Walk in Chelsea, which the Littlejohns would have recognised as the address of Douglas Smythe. However, the Littlejohns never knew that Smythe and Wyman were the same person: no photograph of Wyman was issued even after he and Crinion were charged in respect of the classified documents, nor at a later stage because of other events which transpired to obscure the identity of Smythe/Wyman.

Kenneth Littlejohn's relationship with his new spymaster was beset with difficulty, and, according to Littlejohn this derived from their differences of opinion about what Littlejohn should be doing for MI6:

I rowed with Oliver every time I met him. We just didn't get on. His ideas and my ideas were not the same. He wanted the results that would come from illegal acts. I just hadn't the patience to deal with him. He was an ordinary lad, probably a very nice fellow, but I wasn't in it for friendship. It didn't bother me whether he liked or disliked me. All I wanted was someone I knew so that I could pick up the telephone and he would get on with the business. If I was in the stook he would immediately put his mind to try to help me and wouldn't be continually thinking I was trying to con him.

The final sentence of that statement is vital in assessing Littlejohn's mentality and the dilemma that faced him. It implies that he was being run by a no-nonsense spymaster who demanded results and that Littlejohn was not providing anything of significance; he was feeling under pressure and, perhaps more importantly, he needed to deliver something significant or else find a way out of the spying profession. He admits in his statement that he is tired and disillusioned. I detect in this that Littlejohn had been allowed considerable freedom by Smythe but 'Oliver' was more demanding and was tightening the reins of control.

My thesis about Littlejohn's state of mind by October 1972 is based on the event which brought him and his brother to prominence and which occurred during his period of disillusionment. On 12 October 1972 three armed men kidnapped the wife, sister-in-law and the two children of a Dublin bank manager, Noel Curran, at his home on the outskirts of the city. They tied up their hostages and forced Mr Curran to help them rob his bank. In all, six robbers were involved in the enterprise.

On the morning of the robbery Noel Curran was forced to admit members of his staff to the Allied Irish Bank in Grafton Street in Dublin city centre. Clerks were locked in a strongroom while the three robbers filled bags and trunks with notes. The heating in the bank had not been switched on, and female members of staff complained that it was bitterly cold, so the manager suggested that cups of tea would relieve the problem. The raiders responded by providing the women with ledgers on which they could sit and ordering a porter to make tea. It was obvious to the bank staff that the three robbers had not taken a great deal of trouble to disguise themselves. During the two hours they spent removing bank notes from the vault, the men referred to each other by the military titles of major, corporal and sergeant. Such was the relaxed atmosphere that the robbers discussed with bank staff a boxing match which had been televised the previous night and included the British fighter, Joe Bugner. They also talked about the failure of the Republic to improve its antiquated telephone system.

The robbery netted £67,000 and the Dublin newspapers that evening revealed that a military-style raid on a city bank had led to the biggest bank robbery in Irish history. Five days after the robbery—during which time British and Irish newspapers speculated about it, most of them reaching the conclusion that the Provisional IRA were responsible—Kenneth Littlejohn, his wife Christine and his brother Keith were in London. On 18 October Kenneth Littlejohn met his SIS spymaster 'Oliver'. The meeting took place under Nelson's Column in Trafalgar Square and lasted three hours. It was not a pleasant affair and their conversation centred on the Dublin bank robbery. Littlejohn says that 'Oliver' told him he was unhappy about the brothers' involvement in the robbery, though Littlejohn's account of the verbal exchange implies something sinister.

There was a complete change of attitude from the start. Originally, Oliver had said, 'Goody, goody. Can you get away with it?' Now, after it has happened, he is taking a holier-than-thou attitude as if he hadn't known or that he hadn't want to be involved. I told him it was too late and that he should have said so from the beginning, and I would have dropped it and gone back to normal living. He said there was nothing they could do and I said it was a bit late him telling me that I was about to be extradited. We argued and he said he would go back and see what he could do and I would see him the next day. In the meantime I should keep my head down.

This account is perfectly shaped to fit Littlejohn's claim that the Dublin bank robbery, which he personally masterminded with the direct assistance of Keith, Brian Mathers and three others, was part of an SIS plot. It was, however, a piece of retrospective analysis which he forged to discredit British intelligence and to defend his own actions. At the 18 October meeting he undoubtedly learned that there was a warrant issued for the arrest of himself, Christine, Keith and Robert Stockman. A Gardai officer had already arrived in London with extradition warrants and relevant addresses. On 19 October, Kenneth Littlejohn's thirty-first birthday, officers from the Flying Squad arrested him and took him to Edgware police station. When he arrived at the station he met Inspector Parker and gave him the telephone number of Inspector Sinclair, the contact provided by Douglas Smythe. The number, Littlejohn was told, was inoperative.

Meanwhile, in Dublin, Wyman and Crinion were in custody serving a six-month sentence imposed by the Special Criminal Court.

What both governments have never admitted is that, with Kenneth and Keith Littlejohn in custody and Wyman and Crinion behind bars, a deal was struck to the effect that if the Littlejohns were returned to Ireland to face charges in connection with the robbery Crinion and Wyman would be sent to Britain. The government with most to risk from the prospect of the Littlejohns being tried in Ireland and possibly revealing their involvement with British intelligence was the British government. Even greater risks would be incurred if the identity of Wyman could be proved to include the Douglas Smythe alias. On the other hand the Irish government was determined to prove how it was handling the IRA and other criminals and wanted a show trial with the Littlejohns in the dock. What the Irish government was not being told by Irish Special Branch was that Wyman had also handled the Littlejohns, because such an admission would have discredited Irish Special Branch and created the impression that matters of espionage in Ireland were out of control. The result was that the British government struck the better deal: it would extradite the Littlejohns on condition that they were charged only with robbery and provided that Wyman and Crinion were flown to Britain.

The qualification that the Littlejohns should be charged only with robbery was extremely significant. Before the inter-governmental deal was completed, the British government intimated through its ambassador in Dublin that the Littlejohns were connected with British intelligence but not in a way that should concern the Irish. What the British really required was the release of Wyman/Smythe, the spymaster. If it became apparent that he was a spymaster and not merely a courier receiving documents, other operatives in Ireland would be placed at risk. The British government also knew that once its Irish counterpart made a deal there was no going back. Wyman was important. If the Irish had refused to agree to what were essentially British proposals, the likelihood is that the British government would have found a means of charging Kenneth Littlejohn with the Birmingham robbery, convicting him if necessary, and making it impossible for him to be extradited to Ireland. The British government played it cleverly. They were in a position where they could be compromised and were obliged to choose which course of action would be preferable in respect of damage limitation. The fact that they chose to get Wyman extradited reinforces the view that he was much more important than the Littlejohns—that he was the 'big fish'.

There is, of course, another view—that the inter-governmental deal which returned the Littlejohns to Ireland and Wyman and Crinion to England was contrived by both sides so that each could be seen to be walking away from the mess without further damage being caused to Anglo-Irish relations and without a serious diplomatic row which might lead to the unveiling of all aspects of British operations in Ireland. This theory is enticing and assumes that both governments were aware of the role played by the four operatives, or at least the generality of their intentions in Ireland. According to the theory, the Irish were content to agree to the deal but required a show trial to convince people in Ireland that they were not prepared to allow the British to do as they wished in the Republic of Ireland. By bargaining for the extradition of the Littlejohns the Irish government appeared as though it was after the 'bigger fish' and was willing to release two other known spies to get them. The British played their part in the charade but privately stipulated that the Irish could have only a limited show trial, with the Littlejohns subjected only to charges connected with the Dublin robbery. Some would say this was a winning hand for the British. They were given Wyman and his Gardai operative; they also managed to limit the Irish to dealing with the Littlejohns as criminals and not spies—which eventually made it easier to discredit the Littlejohns' stories of spying. Most people were not prepared to believe two bank robbers who claimed to be spies. If one is to believe the theory, one must also accept one of its most important ingredients: the reason why the Irish agreed to an intergovernmental deal which offered them little. The theorists would say that the Irish government was faced with a *fait accompli*. They were told that if they persisted in seeking a major show trial the British would be forced to defend its actions in Ireland by revealing details about politicians in the Republic who were closely associated with both wings of the IRA, and other matters which could prove highly embarrassing to the Dublin government. The Irish government, so goes the theory, opted for caution and safety and for better Anglo-Irish relations.

When Littlejohn realised he was facing extradition, he asked that Lord Carrington, Geoffrey Johnson-Smith, Lady Pamela Onslow, Douglas Smythe and Oliver be served with summonses to appear on his behalf at Bow Street Court. The summonses were not issued and the charges against Christine Littlejohn were dropped, leaving Kenneth, Keith and Robert Stockman in the dock. Littlejohn claims, plausibly enough in view of the inter-governmental deal, that he was told that, if he admitted to involvement in the robbery at Smethwick in 1970, he would not be extradited but would be sentenced to fourteen years in prison for handling stolen goods: 'Inspector Parker said to me that if I managed to beat the extradition rap he had been ordered to charge me with handling stolen goods and the maximum sentence was fourteen years. I thought, if I admit it I am leaving everyone else in stook. So I didn't admit to the robbery. If I had done then we couldn't have been extradited, but it was the threat of the handling charge that kept me quiet.'

Littlejohn apparently felt that if he faced extradition he had a better chance of surviving because he could rely on blackmailing British intelligence or presenting a defence to an Irish court that he was working for the SIS; he never imagined that he would ever be extradited or that he could go to prison. He also possessed a bizarre sense of honour. He knew that if he wished he could force the police to charge him with the Smethwick robbery by claiming that he was involved in it. This course of action would, however, leave his younger brother and his friend, Robert Stockman, to face extradition without him. It was easy for others to manoeuvre Kenneth Littlejohn towards an extradition hearing. It was held in camera before Lord Widgery at Bow Street. The nineteenth-century law which was invoked to allow the hearing to be conducted in secret was part of a ploy by the government through its agent, the Attorney-General, to limit the scope of the Littlejohns to embarrass Lord Carrington and others by claiming that they committed the Dublin robbery while working for British intelligence. The British government needed to have Wyman back safely in England before allegations of spying surfaced in the newspapers. The Irish Attorney-General, Colin Condon, had given an assurance that the Littlejohns would be tried in Ireland only for criminal and not for political offences. Lord Widgery ruled that they be extradited. As they were flown to Dublin, Wyman and Crinion were placed on a specially guarded flight to London. Within several months Robert Stockman was freed from Portaloise prison and charges against him were dropped.

Kenneth Littlejohn decided that his appearance in a Dublin court was an indication that he was being sacrificed for something but he did not know that the 'something' was Douglas Smythe. Littlejohn reckoned that he would 'have his day' in court but that he would also reveal the details of his connection with British intelligence. In the course of the trial in August 1973 he attempted to paint a picture of how he worked as a British agent within the IRA, but his story did not have the desired impact, because the trial centred on the Grafton Street robbery, and only when Kenneth Littlejohn himself was giving evidence was he free to give an outline of his time as a self-confessed British spy.

There were moments during his testimony when he exhibited the bravado which was his trademark. When asked about the use of guns in the robbery and the threat to human life, he replied: 'The only people who were in danger were the men who actually took part in the robbery. If anybody got hurt I might have shot them out of hand.' He told the court that he would not reveal the supplier of the gun he carried, and as for the other guns used by his accomplices 'there were a lot of guns and ammunition in Ireland already'. He attempted to convince the court that he did not rob the bank for personal gain, stating that he had left £11,000 in a flat in Dublin and taken £2000 with him to England, that £67,000 was a lot of money and very tempting but no use to him personally. The money, he said, was to be used to set up and equip a splinter group in the IRA which he intended to lead and train. When asked what happened to the bulk of the money, since only the £11,000 sum was recovered, he replied that it might have found its way into IRA funds, but he could not be sure because he was not an accountant. When it was put to him that the robbery was a crime he answered: 'In my view I was saving the lives of a lot of people.'

On the afternoon of 3 August 1973 Mr Justice Finlay addressed a crowded courtroom at the Special Criminal Court in Dublin. He stated that Kenneth and Keith Littlejohn were now convicted of the crime with which they had been charged and the offence carried a maximum penalty of penal servitude for life. The robbery had been carefully planned and involved taking a young wife and her children as hostages and ruthlessly putting them in terror not only of their own lives but also of Mr Curran's. The court was satisfied that in the preparation and execution of the crime Kenneth Littlejohn was the leader and Keith took an important, if somewhat subservient, role. Regardless of the motives or mixture of motives which led to the commission of the offences, the least sentence the court could impose on Kenneth Littlejohn was twenty years' penal servitude; Keith Littlejohn was sentenced to fifteen years. As the brothers were ushered from the dock to begin their sentences in Mountjoy Prison, Kenneth Littlejohn turned towards the public gallery and said: 'Thank you, England. Ask Carrington what he thinks of that.'

For several days after the trial there was speculation about the Littlejohns' claim that they worked for British intelligence. Only newspapers in the Irish Republic paid much attention to the trial and the allegations that surfaced from Kenneth Littlejohn's testimony. However, the Irish government and particularly the former Taoiseach, Jack Lynch, were embarrassed by the Littlejohn saga because great emphasis was placed on whether a deal had been done to release Wyman and Crinion and whether Lynch had been informed at an early stage by his London ambassador that the Littlejohns were working for British intelligence.

In the weeks following the trial, the only point at which the British government felt the need to say anything about political affairs in Ireland was when Jack Lynch was reported in newspapers as having 'a suspicion' that the bombings in Dublin on 2 December 1972, which killed two people and injured seventy-four, were the work of British intelligence agents. This assertion attributed to a former Taoiseach, added to mutterings of a similar nature within Dail Eireann, threatened to cause a serious rift in Anglo-Irish relations. In London, Lord Wigg, who had been responsible for security under the previous Harold Wilson administration, called for the resignation of Lord Carrington, arguing that the Littlejohn affair demanded a public inquiry and that relations between Britain and the Irish Republic were in serious decline. The British government did not react officially to Jack Lynch's statement but made it clear through unofficial channels that they placed little reliance on a claim based merely on 'suspicion'. However, the impact of Jack Lynch's allegation was to be lasting and will be dealt with later in this book.

By the end of August 1973 it seemed the Littlejohn affair was relegated to the history books. Brian Mathers was eventually convicted for his part in the robbery and sentenced to ten years' imprisonment. In January 1974 Robert Stockman, who described himself as a thirty-five-year-old clothing production manager of Wellington Street, London, appeared before the Special Criminal Court in Dublin charged with the robbery of £1141 from the Hillgrove Hotel at Latlorcan in County Monaghan in the Irish Republic on 8 October 1972, and of being armed with an offensive weapon and in the company of another person. Prosecuting counsel told the court that Stockman had held up the hotel receptionist at pistol point and snatched the money, which was the proceeds of a dance. Stockman, outlining his history to the court, said that he had been arrested by Scotland Yard detectives on 19 October 1972 and charged together with the Littlejohn brothers. After he had been extradited to the Republic, the charge relating to the Grafton Street bank robbery was dropped. A further charge of harbouring one of the brothers in London was also dropped. He denied ever having been in Monaghan and claimed he was in London when the hotel robbery was committed. He told the court that he had planned to buy a restaurant in Torquay with Kenneth Littlejohn and, when questioned about this, volunteered the statement that the deposit for the restaurant was not part of the £67,000 stolen from the Allied Irish Bank. The Criminal Court judge, Mr Justice Ryan, acquitted Stockman of all charges relating to the Monaghan robbery, observing that the identification parade from which Stockman had been picked out after the crime was 'open to comment'.

So, in January 1974, it seemed as though the Littlejohns would be forgotten and would languish in Mountjoy Prison until the late 1980s. That was not how Kenneth Littlejohn intended it to be.

From the moment the Littlejohns entered Mountjoy Prison they were kept in solitary confinement. Since their admission in August 1973 that they were British agents placed them in danger from other political prisoners, they were kept in B-Basement, an area reserved for prisoners undergoing punishment for breaches of discipline. B-Basement was capable of holding thirty-five inmates, and after a riot in the prison in October 1973 the Littlejohns, who had until then been the only prisoners in B-Basement, had the opportunity to converse with other inmates who were leaders of the October riot. Aside from this they experienced little contact with the outside world, though they received several visits from friends in Britain and two visits from a British Embassy official. It was rumoured in the prison that the brothers negotiated a truce with IRA prisoners, mostly Provisionals, after Keith was beaten up by several Republican inmates.

However, all their time in custody, the Littlejohns were planning an escape. At 7.20 pm on 11 March 1974, while other prisoners were watching television, Kenneth and Keith left B wing through a gate and door at the northern end of that block and made their way across the prison grounds to the south-east corner of the outside wall. In order to reach the wall they were obliged to pass the ends of C and D wings, where guards were normally on duty. On this occasion there were no guards, and when the Littlejohns reached the outside wall there were four planks of wood, each measuring 17ft by 9ins by 3ins, placed against the 20-foot-high wall. Conveniently, or by arrangement, the planks were positioned in such a way that the brothers were quickly able to assemble a makeshift ramp. The police who patrol outside the wall must have been otherwise engaged, because the brothers managed to clamber on to the wall and make their way towards a small tower. As they reached the tower they were spotted by a prison warder, who raised the alarm. They both leapt from the wall to make good their escape but Keith landed awkwardly, injuring his ankle, and gesticulated to his older brother to hurry away.

Kenneth made his way into Dublin and, despite exhaustive searches in the city and throughout the Irish Republic at airports and ports, he was not found. He surfaced in Amsterdam and for the next two years he held clandestine meetings with journalists and continued to point the finger at British intelligence. The most detailed interviews were carried in the

London magazine *Time Out,* which gave Littlejohn a platform for brazenly describing his exploits and recounting how he was 'sold out' by his spymasters. The *Time Out* articles were, however, valuable in placing firmly on the record the thoughts of a self-confessed spy. One paragraph in the *Time Out* interview struck me as characteristic of a man who had begun to believe his own lies:

I wouldn't actually have taken up arms against the British.... I was continually meeting the relatives of people who had been murdered or who died in some way or other. Some of them were very, very tragic, particularly those who were victims of execution squads and other bloody psychopaths that were around, doing the work I was doing. I thought in some small measure that I was doing something to stop, not the genuine Republican lads, but the horrible maniacs that were running about. I felt that the only way you could stop them was that you needed someone who could play it dirty, like me. Maybe this was tilting at windmills, maybe it was an absurd idea, but I just felt that if you ever stopped people like this, you needed someone who was just as bad and maybe I could help to do it.

I think that, finally, Littlejohn was, in his own words, 'tilting at windmills'.

Two years later he was again extradited to Dublin, given the opportunity, once again, to stand in front of a Dublin court, this time on an escape charge, and reiterate his allegations. By 1976, however, people were tired of the Littlejohn saga. His escape and his tendency to embellish his story while on the run from prison only served to discredit if not debase his original claims. His account of his prison escape was as fantastic as everything else about his life. He told a *Time Out* reporter how he hid in Dublin, slept on a beach, 'got his bearings' and hitched a ride on a train, reached Drogheda, walked thirty miles, took a train to Belfast and—well, no one knows how he left Northern Ireland. In fact Littlejohn never revealed how he managed to get to Europe. His escape from Mountjoy Prison raised serious questions about security at the prison and whether Littlejohn had 'inside help'. If British intelligence knew Kenneth Littlejohn as well as I believe they did, it is only natural to speculate that it was in their interest to assist him to escape, because in so doing he damaged his credibility. Had he remained in Mountjoy Prison, a forgotten man and a victim of circumstance, the mythology, doubt and suspicion might have led enquiring minds to use his story to damaging effect. Kenneth Littlejohn was returned to prison in 1976 and, with his brother, was released in 1981. The Dublin government explained the early release as being on health grounds. This was interpreted as a case of leniency, perhaps with British collusion; after all, the Littlejohns did not provide a service. There was also a theory that the time they spent in solitary confinement damaged their health, thus demanding a compassionate response from the Irish government.

On their release, little notice was taken of their thoughts or dated allegations. They returned to Britain to live in hiding, meanwhile threatening that they would further embarrass the British government by writing
a book which would reveal the 'whole truth' about their time in Ireland.
That never materialised. Within one year of his release, Kenneth was
gaoled for six years for armed robbery. Littlejohn's counsel, attempting to
explain why his client was in possession of a gun, said that Kenneth
owned a weapon because he feared an IRA reprisal attack. Littlejohn told
the court he planned to make a living as a writer and added: 'I tried to
bury Kenneth Littlejohn ten years ago. On this occasion it was as if we
were caught up in something we could not stop.' His form of expression
even in 1982 was redolent of a man who devoured the more pompous
lines of cheap novels. Mr Justice Drake remarked: 'Yours is a very unusual background. You still have the opportunity to make an extremely good
life out of writing.'

The judge may have detected something in the character of Kenneth
Littlejohn which few observed. Essentially, he was a man who enjoyed
danger, loved the high-life, but was not willing to work honestly and was
unscrupulous in his dealings with others. One must ask whether British
intelligence recognised and appreciated these qualities in a man they
were prepared to recruit. If so, in a democracy, one must inevitably question not simply the wisdom but the morality of such a decision. It leads
to an erosion of confidence in the law and a dark suspicion that anything
can be contemplated in pursuit of the defeat of terrorism. Equally, the
sanctioning of the use of the Littlejohns in another country is open to the
accusation that MI6 were irresponsible in selecting them as agents of Her
Majesty's Government overseas. Moreover, there will always remain suspicion that the whole story contains dangerous revelations and that the
Littlejohns were *agents provocateurs.* For example, it has been argued by
reputable journalists that the Littlejohns were involved in several bank
raids. They were by their own admission participants in petrol-bomb
attacks on Gardai stations which, at the time, served to reinforce a view
that the Provisional IRA was posing an increasing threat to the stability of
the Irish Republic and that harsh measures were required to deal with
them. Within the mythology which bedevils Irish life, the Littlejohn saga
served only to reinforce the concept of 'Perfidious Albion'.

Only those who have access to the index cards in Century House and
the file on John Wyman, alias Douglas Smythe, know the true story. There
is little doubt that Wyman/Smythe was masterminding operations much
more important than those undertaken by the Littlejohns.

Self-confessed mercenary recruiter, Leslie Aspin, who sent British
mercenaries to Angola in 1976, claims to have taken money to Kenneth
Littlejohn when the brothers were living near the border. Aspin says that

on one occasion he went to the town of Newry and delivered money from 'his bosses', whom he says were British intelligence: 'The Littlejohns were petty criminals who were blackmailed into working for British intelligence. Once they found themselves in the big time, they panicked and blew their cover. I worked for the British in Northern Ireland and my job was to take over from the Littlejohns but my cover was blown after Irish intelligence tipped off a newspaper.'

The last mention of the Littlejohns occurred in 1982, when the Provisional IRA sent a parcel bomb to the Kensington home of Lady Onslow. Fortunately a detonator failed to explode the 2lb bomb hidden in a book.

While the Littlejohn brothers were operating in 1972, another episode occurred which, with retrospective analysis, illustrates how lucky the brothers were to survive their period in Ireland, and how events in a dirty war often leave so many unanswered questions.

In the early hours of Sunday, 6 February 1972, a pop group was travelling home along the South Armagh border when the group's van driver spotted a body lying by the roadside. As the van slowed almost to a standstill, it became apparent that the body was not that of a road-accident victim. It was a dead man lying in a foetal position. However, what suggested that the dead man was another victim of the war was the grotesque death-mask which almost covered his features. His face was hidden from the nose upwards by surgical tape, broken by a series of holes. The pop group drove to Dundalk and reported their grim discovery to the Gardai, who in turn informed the RUC. When policemen from both forces reached the murder scene, they discovered that the body was ten yards on the Northern Ireland side of the border at Culloville—which meant that the body was the responsibility of the RUC. The IRA always ensured that it never came into conflict with the Southern Irish security forces because it saw the Republic as a haven where its position would be compromised if it forced the Gardai to investigate its activities. For this reason bodies were left north of the border as if to indicate subtly that the conflict was only in Northern Ireland. Both wings of the IRA were therefore able to operate with impunity in the South because they were not being sought for crimes within the Irish Republic. The RUC officers standing in the cold mist at Culloville on 6 February knew instinctively that they were looking at a crime that could well have taken place fifteen yards from them on the other side of the border but they were powerless to operate. The situation was reminiscent of the American Wild West in the nineteenth century where gunfighters such as John Wesley Harding remained at liberty for a long time because they were free to cross state borders and thereby escape prosecution.

The scene on the border on that cold morning was a familiar one and was to be repeated with great regularity. The RUC sealed off the area and began a painstaking search for clues. It soon became apparent that the victim, who appeared to be a man in his mid-thirties, had been shot elsewhere. His hands were tied behind his back with sash-cord and the five holes in the surgical-tape mask were bullet holes, but there were no empty bullet cartridges in the vicinity and no visible signs of a struggle. Forensic experts quickly concluded that the body had probably been taken from a car and dumped at the roadside. The body was removed to Newry mortuary, where a post-mortem confirmed that five bullets from a .38 revolver had entered the back of the victim's skull killing him instantly.

A sharp-eyed detective who saw the body being carried into the mortuary observed that the victim bore a striking resemblance to a man who had been the central figure in an IRA propaganda exercise four months earlier. This hunch was followed up: Scotland Yard checked the victim's fingerprints on its files and came up with the name Barry Barber, alias Hans Kruger, alias David Seaman. The name Barry Barber did not immediately conjure up an IRA connection, but David Seaman was a name which was firmly fixed in the minds and files of the RUC and British Army. On 23 October 1971 the Official IRA, through the auspices of their Sinn Fein HQ at Gardiner Street in Dublin, had presented David Seaman to the world at a hastily prepared press conference. Seaman, who gave his address as Anglesea Avenue, Manchester, and his age as thirty-one, told assembled journalists that he was a deserter from the SAS and had 'gone over to the Official IRA' because of what the British Army was doing in Northern Ireland. He said he had been to Belfast with other British agents to cause explosions in pubs, hotels and police stations in order to maim or kill civilians and to discredit the IRA.

Seaman claimed that he and a fellow SAS operative had bombed the Four Steps Inn on the Shankill Road in Belfast, killing two people. He also told the pressmen that he had been trained by British intelligence in silent killing, espionage, safe-blowing and other techniques for special warfare, and that he had defected because the work he was being asked to undertake was a crime against humanity. The chubby little Englishman augmented his allegations by reading a lengthy personal statement outlining how he had worked in Ireland as a British agent on three other occasions. Once in 1968 he had posed as an American Army deserter, but his story was not believed and he was sent back to England. On another occasion he and another agent had been dropped by parachute on to Howth Heath outside Dublin, as part of a training exercise, but his colleagues had been arrested for being drunk and disorderly and the mission ended. Finally he had been parachuted on to Bray Head, also outside Dublin, but had been arrested by the police and returned to England.

Recently he had been forced to take part in two missions in Belfast in return for a promise of money and the return of his son who was being cared for by welfare authorities in Suffolk. His statement included an admission that he had a criminal record for assault in England.

The immediate impact of the press conference was sensational coverage of his revelations in Irish newspapers and a more guarded reflection in the British press. Initially it appeared as though the IRA had won a propaganda coup, though the Provisionals and a few members of the Official IRA privately indicated that caution was required. Within twenty-four hours, leading newspapers in Britain were carrying detailed stories about David Seaman. One might question how so much detail could have been so readily available, but that is only one of many unanswered questions. Suddenly David Seaman was really Barry Barber, a 'Walter Mitty figure' regarded by neighbours as a fool and a hoaxer, according to the British press, and the IRA was beginning to experience negative effects from its propaganda exercise; in fact the IRA was being made to 'look very foolish'. Seaman quickly shunned the limelight and retired to Morans Hotel in Dublin to join his girlfriend, Norma Grindrod, and her two young sons. Within a week he returned to Manchester and continued to issue statements claiming he was a spy, but adding that his defection to the IRA was really a ploy to discredit them. Some people believed him but the sensational newspaper coverage had ineradicably damaged his reputation.

The Ministry of Defence in London rejected his story as a 'fabrication' and 'utter nonsense'. A ministry official told enquiring journalists that Seaman had served only seven months in the Army and was never in the SAS.

The *Guardian* on 25 October reported:

In Manchester, former neighbours were amused by his claim. They knew him as a 'Walter Mitty' always telling fantastic stories about exploits from his past, like fighting in the Burma Campaign, pearl diving in Honolulu, flying Red Arrow planes and being an undercover agent. They said that he had worn an identity bracelet inscribed 'David Seaman, Special Air Service', but it had been bought and inscribed at a local market.

Seaman reacted to this denunciation by telling Irish journalists that he expected such a reaction.

An *Irish Independent* reporter wrote the following on 25 October:

Last night Seaman, who is in Dublin with a woman friend and her two sons, said he was afraid an attempt would be made to rub him out. He said: 'I know what can be done. I myself was personally responsible for the deaths of twelve terrorists in Aden.' He also claimed that under the name Hans Kruger he worked for a month on a Howth trawler, sending back radio messages to London every night from Howth Head. But the boat on which he worked—The Wind Rise—sank some time ago and its skipper, a Lithuanian refugee, George Kivis (also know as George Volvo), died last week. He said his body was found in Howth Harbour. Seaman demonstrated his ability to speak French, German and four Scandinavian languages and says he is an expert in karate and judo. He refused to reveal who is paying for his stay in Dublin but said he had been promised a job in an architect's office in Dublin by the Official IRA.

So who were David Seaman and Hans Kruger? They were Barry Barber, who grew up in a working-class family in Manchester. His parents detected at an early stage their son's inability to make friends and his tendency to spend too much time in his own company. At school he continued to be a loner and showed little aptitude for learning, but had a talent for creating stories in which he played the central role, that of the hero. However, he was afforded the opportunity to be a real hero at the age of thirteen, when, according to a local newspaper report, he fought a blaze in his home to prevent it spreading and engulfing other houses. In this instance the hero, it later transpired, had started the fire. In 1956, aged only fifteen, he left school and began a succession of jobs, none of which lasted very long. He worked as a trainee milkman, a miner and a seaman. After a year he enlisted in the Parachute Regiment as Private Barber, 23511300, but within a month was in trouble with his superiors. In December 1957 he was arrested for joy-riding and being unlawfully in possession of a signals pistol and cartridges. This ended his career in the Parachute Regiment, which had apparently been unaware that prior to joining the young Barry Barber had been fined for knifing a youth in a pub in his home town of Manchester.

Barber was again in trouble with the law in April 1958 after an escapade at an RAF base in Leeming, Yorkshire, when he broke into the base, climbed into a trainer plane and fired a signals rocket, causing considerable damage to the plane and its control panel. He told police he was suffering from memory loss, but they knew he was drunk. He was placed on probation but this failed to control him and he spent one year in Borstal. His fondness for military camps led to his being arrested while in possession of a commando knife outside Castlemartins Camp in Pembrokeshire in October 1961 and once again he claimed he was suffering from loss of memory. When arrested he gave a false name and presented the police with a choice of stories, including statements that he was a deserter from the Parachute Regiment and, alternatively, that he was a major drugs smuggler; he was sent back to Borstal and remained in custody for four months. His next misdemeanour surprised not only his family and friends but also the police. In May 1962 he was arrested by police in Dublin and told them he was Hans Kruger, a German national and a Russian spy. They soon uncovered his real identity and returned him to England to face trial on a charge of acting with intent to rob. Accompanied by a prostitute, he had hitched a lift, threatened the driver with a pistol and told him to 'keep driving'. Barber told the court that he suffered from amnesia and was not in possession of his senses at the time of the incident. The court accepted his plea and acquitted him.

His trip to the Irish Republic seems to have triggered off an obsession with that country. In November 1962 Irish police received a telephone call informing them 'that a man was seen with a parachute at Bray Head outside Dublin'. When two constables arrived at Bray they searched the area and found Barry Barber, who told them he was a British agent on a training mission. He was taken into custody, where he again offered police an alternative version of events: he said he had bought the parachute in his home town and travelled to Ireland on the Holyhead to Dun Laoghaire ferry. This time he was returned to England without being charged with an offence. In the spring of 1963 he was imprisoned for six months for stealing money from his parents. One year later he was back in Dublin claiming to be Hans Kruger, an East German agent. He was in possession of a stolen radio transmitter, was charged with larceny and was given a three-month prison sentence.

Towards the end of 1964 he returned to England and tried to join the Army. He was accepted but was quickly discharged when it was discovered that he had omitted to outline his previous service and dishonourable discharge.

After this he remained within the law and was married in 1968 to a divorcee with three children. She bore him a son but the marriage collapsed. Again he joined the British Army and re-enlisted with the Parachute Regiment; seemingly his previous history in the Army and his criminal record did not come to light. The Paras soon found him unsuitable and transferred him to another regiment, which made a similar judgement, and he was permitted to buy himself out of the services. In total his career as a soldier amounted to seven months: two months in 1957, twelve days with the Royal Fusiliers in 1965 and five months with the Paras and Royal Anglian Regiment in 1969. In September 1971 he met Nora Grindrod, who was separated from her husband and had custody of her two young sons. She fell in love with him and within one month joined him on a trip to Ireland which would finally lead to his death somewhere along the Irish border.

As we know, as David Seaman he held a press conference with the assistance of the Official IRA towards the end of October and returned to Manchester. However, what did not become known at the time was that the IRA sent several of its men to England to talk to him. This was done because IRA leaders were confused as much as anyone else about the manner in which Seaman had discredited them. They wished to know whether he was simply a crank, a deliberate 'plant', or a fool who had been used against them. On 26 January 1972 he went to stay with a male friend at Howth on the outskirts of Dublin. His girlfriend remained at home, unaware of his decision to leave Manchester, and was certainly not told by Seaman that he was returning to Ireland. The following day he was seen in the company of a stranger in the Gresham Hotel in Dublin's O'Connell Street. Witnesses recalled that the stranger was conspicuous because he was tall, wore a trilby and an expensive overcoat, that both men talked for over an hour and that Seaman behaved 'excitedly'. Police investigations later revealed that a hotel on the Irish border had a booking for that night in the name of David Seaman but he failed to appear. On 29 January he was back in Howth claiming, according to his friends, that he had been in Northern Ireland for a meeting with an SAS contact. David Seaman disappeared for the next eight days. No one has ever reported having seen him during that period, so we must assume that he was in the hands of his killers. The Provisionals say they did not kill him and the Official IRA did not comment on his murder, though all the evidence points in their direction. The Official IRA had a motive: he embarrassed them publicly at a time when they were vulnerable—when the Provisionals were undermining their power base, the Irish government saw them as a threat and MI6 was trying to infiltrate their ranks to discredit them. Since David Seaman's public claims did considerable damage to the IRA, there were many journalists, as well as members of the Republican movement, who wondered whether he was really a British agent as well as a crank.

A report in the *Irish Independent* illustrates the dilemma faced by journalists as well as the IRA. Weeks after Seaman was discredited the reporter met him in a hotel and wrote the following account:

As he planned to leave the country, Seaman revealed: 'My mission in Ireland is finished. I was sent to discredit the IRA and I have done so. The whole story was concocted by them and I was told by London to go along with it until now. I infiltrated the IRA in Belfast and convinced them I was prepared to defect. They then made up a story that I was disgusted with British tactics in the North and I was briefed on it. I was driven to Dublin and stayed for a few days with a couple on the North Side who are Members of the Officials. I was then moved to a City Hotel two days before the news conference.

Asked why he was revealing his mission, he replied that it was his instruction to blow sky-high the IRA story. Then in my presence, Seaman backed up his claims. He phoned the Admiralty in London. In James Bond fashion he asked for the Radio Room and then the Duty Officer. When the Officer came on the line, Seaman said tersely: 'Has one of your stations gone off the air?' The Officer replied: 'No.' Seaman then said: 'This is David O'Brien, I'm coming home tonight. Please pass on this message to Major Jago.' The London voice answered: 'You have been on before. We will pass the message to Security.'

Then Seaman told me to contact a Cork telephone number where he claimed a British Intelligence Operator could be contacted. He told me to give the password, 'Roses are red in Lancashire', to which the reply should be, 'I thought the roses were white in Lancashire'.

We rang the number and gave the password. We received the correct reply. We then told the person (pretending it was Seaman) that he had to get out quickly. He said he would contact London. He rang back saying a call had already been made (Seaman's earlier call to the Admiralty building in Whitehall).

Whatever the truth of the Seaman/Barber/Kruger claim, the self-confessed spy demonstrated that he had abilities and personality traits which tend to make espionage successful, but for amateurs, ultimately dangerous. If Barry Barber, alias David Seaman, had never returned to Ireland he could have lived off the one story which was unassailably a fact: the damage he inflicted on the IRA at a news conference in October 1971. The fate of Barry Barber also serves to illustrate how lucky the Littlejohns were to survive their foray into the dirty war and how each of the protagonists in the conflict sought to deceive each other irrespective of the cost to human life. In this instance, the Official IRA murdered a man whom they had exploited, simply because they were unable to separate fact from fantasy—which is often the central thrust of espionage. In its eagerness to damage the reputation of the British Army, the IRA showed itself incapable of assessing the character of one small, fat, balding Englishman whose person did not even suggest that he was capable of being a spy.

5

The Pitchfork Killings

Many killings of the early 1970s remain shrouded in mystery, and the passage of time and continued violence make it likely that until the perpetrators are brought to justice doubt and suspicion will centre on many organisations including the British Army, which is known to have been involved in lawful and unlawful killing. The fact that soldiers were involved in MRF-related killings is sufficient evidence, though circumstantial, for some nationalists and certainly many Republicans to conclude that the Army sanctioned assassination in Northern Ireland. On that premise the Army's detractors point at certain mystery murders and accuse the Army of being responsible. Thorough investigation is required in the case of killings for which no one has been tried and where suspicion of military involvement has arisen. That involvement may well turn out to be the result not of Army policy but of soldiers exacting revenge for the killing of colleagues by the IRA.

The largest number of unsolved murders in any period of the war occurred in 1972 after the abolition of the Stormont government and the imposition of direct rule from Westminster. Loyalist paramilitaries reacted to the fall of their government by venting their wrath and hatred on innocent Catholics. They saw the Catholic population as the defender and harbourer of the IRA, whom they believed forced the British through terror to destroy the major bastion and symbol of Unionist rule and domination, Stormont. The Loyalists began a campaign of terror which led to some of the worst excesses of brutality and bestiality during the conflict. Innocent people were tortured with knives and in some instances branded with red-hot irons before being killed. It was a period of extreme lawlessness, when the security forces found themselves unable to cope and when the IRA was bombing the heart out of the towns and cities of Ulster. During this time there were a number of unsolved murders of Catholics in border areas.

Nationalist politicians pointed the accusing finger at the Ulster Defence Regiment, which patrolled border districts in support of the British Army. The UDR was a newly formed regiment which had replaced the B Specials. Most of its members were Protestants, and the regiment was prepared to allow dual membership with the UDA, the massive Loyalist paramilitary organisation. This was later to prove a major error and a serious threat to the security and credibility of the UDR. However, in 1972 no one in security circles was concerned that the regiment drew the majority of its members from one community and that many of them were also members of Loyalist paramilitary groups who believed themselves to be in a war in which they were busy killing innocent Catholics. Be that as it may, the accusations were made against the UDR and not the British Army, which was equally active in border areas in a security role. Later events suggested that maybe the accusing finger had pointed once too often in the wrong direction.

The killings which are the subject of this chapter represent one of the most complex episodes in the history of the war and might never have been understood if one man had not suffered from pangs of conscience. The story begins in 1972 near the Irish border in the lush and scenic countryside of County Fermanagh. At 4.20 pm on 23 October, Mary Ann Murray was sitting in her home at Kerrykenny near Newtownbutler when a tractor drove to the side of her house. She looked out to see her son, Andrew, unloading firewood from a trailer which was tethered to the tractor. Alongside him was his employer, thirty-one-year-old Michael Naan, who owned a farm in the townland of Aughnahinch several miles from the Murray home. Andrew Murray was twenty-four, the second youngest in a family of three boys and three girls. He was a dutiful son and was known as a quiet, inoffensive young man. He had been two months in the employ of Michael Naan and had persuaded him to use his tractor and trailer to supply the Murray family with firewood out of Naan's land. Mrs Murray did not speak to her son or Michael Naan but remembers hearing the tractor leave and seeing Michael Naan driving the tractor and Andrew sitting on the trailer. She noted the time as 4.40 pm and knew that Andrew would be home within a few hours. He never stayed overnight at the Naan farm, though he could do so if he wished.

At 5.15 pm John James McCaffrey, who was working in his saw mill at Clonaree, looked towards the road to Newtownbutler and saw Naan and Murray travelling on the tractor and trailer towards Naan's farm. That was the last sighting of the two men alive. At 6.05 pm the following day, 24 October, John Patrick Hanna, a representative for a fuel company, was on his way to collect an account from Michael Naan. As he drove off the main road into a laneway leading to the farm he noticed a tractor and trailer at the entrance to the farmyard. He was unable to drive his Austin pickup van past the tractor and decided to make his way on foot to the farmhouse. As he approached the tractor his attention was drawn involuntarily to an area of swamp to the right of the lane. When he edged towards the swamp his worst fears were confirmed—that an object sticking out of the swamp was in fact a hand and that a body lay just beneath the surface. Hanna rushed to his van and drove to Newtownbutler police station, arriving there at 6.15.

A police report confirms that Sergeant Cecil Brown, Constable McBrien and Assistant Constable Beattie reacted speedily to Hanna's information and arrived at the Naan farm before 6.30 pm. Sergeant Brown sealed off the murder scene and began to search the surrounding area and farm buildings. In a byre he found the body of Michael Naan lying beside a cow and her calf. He was lying face upwards and there was a considerable amount of blood around his face and mouth and particularly in the area of his chest. A search of the laneway revealed grass which was 'saturated in blood'.

In the days following the gruesome find, news reports referred to the murders as the 'pitchfork killings' or 'pitchfork murders'. Since both men were Catholics, there was speculation that their deaths were the result of sectarian violence; indeed 1972 was the worst year for sectarian assassinations throughout Northern Ireland. Another theory which seemed equally credible within the nationalist population was that the two had been killed by members of the Ulster Defence Regiment in retaliation for the murder of one of its members in the Newtownbutler locality on 21 October. At that time the UDR, which was acting in support of the British Army, was a relatively new regiment and was believed by many nationalists to be a re-shaped version of the anti-Catholic B Specials.

Newspaper coverage of the murders tended to reflect either one or the other theory, but the one element on which all seemed to agree was that Naan and Murray had been brutally killed with a pitchfork. It is reasonable to suppose that, for so many reports to make this assertion, someone at an official or unofficial level must have encouraged journalists to believe that the murders were committed in this way.

Journalists at that time were unaware that autopsies carried out on the bodies on 25 October ruled out the use of a pitchfork; this information did not become available until an inquest hearing in 1973. I raise this matter because it is one of the most central and confusing issues concerning the double murder. I was one of the journalists who covered this story and later referred to it in a Penguin Special, *Political Murder in Northern Ireland,* published in 1973. My co-author, Denis Lehane, and I contested the pitchfork theory and asserted that both men were killed with a dagger.

On 25 October an RUC inspector searched the Naan farm, in the company of members of other specialist police branches (photography, fingerprinting, mapping and scenes of crime), and later made the following observations:

There was a heavy concentration of blood over a small area of grass convenient to the trailer. Opposite this was a marsh area or partially dried up slurry pit. There was a track in this marsh about thirteen yards from where the blood was found. From my knowledge of the crime I was aware that this track was where the body of Andrew Murray was found. There was also blood on the floor inside a nearby byre in the farmyard. A long period of dry weather had prevailed at the time with the result that the farmyard and adjacent area were dry. I do not recall noticing any graips, pitchforks or other such implements at the scene and certainly none to which I associated any significance in so far as the murders were concerned. Michael Naan's dwelling house in the farmyard was examined. It was found to be intact—no windows were broken or doors forced. On a table in the living-room was found the remnants of where tea had been partaken of by two persons—suggesting an afternoon snack. I took part in an organised search for the murder weapon along with Inspector McGuinness, Detective Sergeant Harrison, Constables Milne, McFadden, Sheering and other police. This search was in the fields to the Newtownbutler side of the farmyard towards a lough and to the right of the lane leading from the dwelling house to the Newtownbutler road. Nothing was found. On the following day at the request of the police, water was pumped from a pond at the side of the lane (on the Newtownbutler road side) in a search for the murder weapon without result. On October 28, I again visited the scene to conduct a search and on November 3 I returned with Scenes of Crime Department Constables and made a further examination.

From all accounts the RUC conducted thorough searches. It must have appeared unusual to Inspector Gilligan that a farmyard should not contain a pitchfork or similar implement, much less the murder weapon. Gilligan knew from the autopsies that the murder weapon was 'most likely a double-edged dagger'. Why, one must ask, were there no pitchforks or similar tools, when Naan was known to use them for mucking out the byre and other farmyard chores? Why would a murderer or murderers remove such implements as pitchforks when the murder weapon was a dagger? The received wisdom in public and journalistic circles remained that Naan and Murray were killed with a pitchfork, yet the autopsies conducted by the Deputy State Pathologist, Dr Derek Carson, on 25 October, two days after the murders, proved otherwise. Dr Carson was in no doubt about his findings, as he revealed in this statement about the murder of Michael Naan:

The wounds could not have been caused by a pitchfork or graip. Some of the wounds had run together, giving the false impression of a larger weapon having been used. All the wounds, at least seventeen in number, had apparently been caused by the same weapon. It must have been sharp, pointed and probably double-edged, although one end of each wound was more sharply pointed than the other. The most likely weapon would be a double-edged dagger, with a blade up to one inch wide and at least 5½ inches long.

Dr Carson made similar observations in his report on Andrew Murray and concluded that they were both probably killed with the same weapon. So why should a story persist that the murder weapon was a pitchfork and who would benefit from such a story? I should like readers to bear these questions in mind as the story unfolds.

Dr Carson's post-mortem reports were revealing about other aspects of the killings. Naan's chest contained a group of multiple stab wounds concentrated mainly on the left side and centre of the front of the upper chest. There were seventeen wounds in all, with the uppermost wound occurring just below the throat. A group of seven wounds, some of which were possibly made by two or more thrusts, gave the impression that a larger weapon had been used. Superficial wounds below the neck were shallow incisions indicating that a knife had been drawn slowly across the throat. Death was due to wounds which had pierced the chest cavity: the left lung and heart were extensively damaged to the extent that massive bleeding would have rapidly caused his death. An interesting observation by Dr Carson was that 'the absence of significant injuries about the hands and forearms of Naan' suggests that the deceased had made little effort at resistance, or had been prevented from doing so.

His findings in respect of Andrew Murray bore striking similarities to the Naan autopsy: 'The man was of slim build and measured 5' 6" in height. He was healthy. There was no natural disease to cause or accelerate death or to cause collapse. There were multiple stab wounds distributed over the front and back of the chest. In all there were at least thirteen stab wounds.' The pathologist also noticed that some wounds were grouped together, superimposed as though several thrusts had contributed to each wound. Many of the wounds had penetrated the chest cavity, damaging the lungs, heart and the major artery, the aorta. There was bruising to the scalp which suggested blows intended possibly to incapacitate the victim. Unlike Naan, however, Murray had been stabbed in both the chest and the back. Both reports encouraged police to the view that they were looking for more than one murderer.

Inspector Gilligan interviewed 'numerous persons in the Newtownbutler area' and made 'enquiries across the border in the Republic'. The latter course of action would imply that he was considering an IRA connection, perhaps the notion that the murders were part of an IRA feud, though from the evidence at the time this would not seem to make a great deal of sense; however, one would, I suppose, expect every possible avenue of inquiry, suspicion and theory to be fully exhausted by police. No one then or now within the nationalist or Republican community has sought to identify Naan or Murray with the IRA, and the RUC at no time intimated that they suspected either man of having paramilitary connections. The IRA will as a rule claim its dead, except in circumstances where it has secretly buried its own men (as illustrated in chapter 2). On rare occasions the IRA has conceded to requests from families of dead IRA men not to make public their IRA membership. There has never been conclusive evidence that Naan was in the IRA; if he was and the IRA had a reason in 1972 to conceal his affiliations, one would have expected his name in an IRA roll of honour at a later time. I make this point because another murder occurred in the Newtownbutler area at that time. The victim was Louis Leonard and he was believed to have been killed by Loyalists. Two years after his death, his membership of the Provisionals was made known at an IRA Easter commemoration ceremony. The revelation appeared after a large financial award had been made to Leonard's wife and family by the government. If his membership of the IRA had been known beforehand, the sum of money awarded would have been minimal. Since Naan had no immediate dependants, there would have been no conceivable gain for the IRA in remaining silent if he had indeed been a Provo. In any event 1972 ended with an inconclusive murder inquiry.

By January 1973 the RUC was, however, pursuing a new line of thinking as a result of observations conveyed to them by two local people who were in the vicinity of the Naan farm on 23 October. Police knew that 23 October was a crucial date because the pathologist had confirmed that that was the day on which Naan and Murray died. New information gained by the police, though it did not point to the killers, at least added to what was a sparse file on the murders. The first witness was Oliver Melarkey, a lorry driver, who told police that he drove along the Newtownbutler road on 23 October and at 6.45 passed the lane entrance to Naan's farm:

I saw on the road in front of me what I thought was cattle. I then put on my head-lights and I saw the figures were soldiers or, to be more correct, persons in military uniform. I saw four such persons in all and there were two on each side of the road. Their uniform was green with patches of brown. They had guns across their arms which appeared to be rifles. One of the men on the right side of the road had a walkie-talkie set with an aerial. They all wore black berets on the sides of their heads.

From this account it would have been reasonable for police to infer that the 'persons in military uniform' could well have been IRA, especially since they wore 'black berets', but the witness added a qualification: the berets were of the 'Glengarry type', a form of headdress worn by Scots soldiers. Oliver Melarkey had, however, noticed behaviour which he considered unusual and not in keeping with his experience of soldiers on duty:

They were all on foot and there was no sign of any vehicle. The two on my left [i.e. Naan's lane side] were standing with their backs to me facing Newtownbutler. They were actually on the Wattlebridge side of Naan's lane whilst the two on the other side of the road were directly opposite Naan's lane and looking towards it. They took no notice whatsoever of me. I was surprised to see soldiers on foot out on this road at this time and this was the first time I had ever seen soldiers on foot on this road. At other times I saw soldiers but they always had military vehicles with them. It also struck me as strange that they did not turn towards me when I came along as soldiers always do. I am definite that it was 6.45 pm because I went straight home and the time was between 6.55 and 7.00 pm when I arrived there.

These observations were written down by police but were not, at that time, made part of a formally prepared statement because Oliver Melarkey said he did not wish to place his wife and children in danger.

The other person who travelled past the entrance to the Naan farm on 23 October was Dympna Brady, and she recorded the time as 7.30 pm. She saw a black Morris Minor car 'sitting on the roadway' facing Newtownbutler. The car's rear red lights were switched on and she saw two occupants in the vehicle. As she drove towards the parked car, she dipped her headlights (the custom when one is approaching a military roadcheck to prevent soldiers being illuminated and presented as targets to terrorists), and then saw three men standing beside the parked car. She 'took them to be Army':

They were along the side of the car and one or two of them was talking into it. I slowed down as I expected to be stopped, but the parked car moved off slowly. The three men on the road were dressed in military uniform and as I slowed down they shouted: 'Move on, keep going, keep going.' I could not say what kind of accent the person had but it was not an English accent. I did not notice guns with the men but I think they were wearing black berets. I drove behind the Morris Minor car towards Newtownbutler and it turned left at the chapel out the Galoon Island road.

Dympna Brady and Oliver Melarkey's reports of seeing men in military uniform with black berets sounded all too familiar in border areas. Detectives knew the group of men could well have been an IRA patrol, but one piece of detail suggested it might have been a British Army patrol making a routine check of the neighbourhood. That piece of detail was Melarkey's description of the berets as being of the 'Glengarry type'. The Glengarry is a Scots Highlander's woollen cap, generally rising to a point in front with ribbons hanging down behind. Police knew that such caps were worn by members of the Argyll and Sutherland Highlanders Regiment, but the caps were not black unless the soldiers were wearing cap comforters, which were part of their winter kit.

Detectives assigned to the murder inquiry decided that they were obliged to examine the Army. Security files confirmed that 13 Platoon of Delta Company, Argyll and Sutherland Highlanders, had been billeted in a field adjacent to the Naan farm for several days prior to the murder and had moved camp on 24 October, the day the bodies were discovered. The RUC contacted the Army and asked that the matter be checked out with the officers in charge of 13 Platoon in October 1972. Officers from the Army's Special Investigation Branch (SIB) visited the Argyll and Sutherland Highlanders' Ritchie Camp at Kirknewton in Scotland in January 1973 and interviewed thirty-one-year-old Major John Jeremy George McKenzie, who was in charge of Delta Company in the Newtownbutler area between 20 and 27 October 1972, on attachment from the Queen's Own Highlanders.

On an MOD form marked 'Case No. 15549/3', Major McKenzie stated that on 23 October 13 Platoon had searched an island on Lough Erne and had sent a liaison patrol to Crom Castle, the home of Lord Erne. He also reported that he had no troops within two miles of the Naan farm until 1400 hours on 24 October, at which time he placed three roadblocks to cover the funeral procession of UDR Private Bell, who was murdered by the IRA. McKenzie said all these men wore combat kit and Glengarry hats, and weapons carried included self-loading rifles; each 'sub-unit' had a IXA41 radio. In his statement, which was brief and was carried on two A4 forms 266A/266E, he also gave the following information: 'The other military organisation in the area belonged to Lord Erne and are about 8 strong based at Crom Castle. It is further believed that they have military-style uniforms and are armed. They might have had radios but this was not confirmed.'

On reading Major McKenzie's statement one is obliged to invent questions which must have been put to him to elicit the information. The obvious conclusion is that he answered queries relating to points, suspicions or the need for clarification arising from the information provided by Oliver Melarkey and Dympna Brady. In the text of his statement to the SIB he says little about the activities of 13 Platoon on 23/24 October, thus giving the impression that to his knowledge there was nothing untoward about the platoon's movements on those days. Is it fair to ask whether he was also implying that if 13 Platoon was in the vicinity of the farm during the period specified in his statement this was not with his consent and was something which was not conveyed to him?

His description of the kit worn by his men, their weapons and the presence of a radio operator with each 'sub-unit' would indicate that he was answering questions which emanated from points made by the witnesses about the men 'in military uniforms' who were observed in the vicinity of the Naan farm on the evening of 23 October. However, McKenzie adds detail which could not have related to anything contained in the statements of Melarkey and Brady. He talks of another 'military organisation' based at Crom Castle and 'further believed' to have 'military-style uniforms' and to be armed. Why should he proffer this information? Why does he not name the other 'military organisation'? Had it been the UDR unit he would not have been so vague in his language. Had it been officially a British Army unit he would have named it. Even if this reference merely related to a question from the SIB, he would have known the nature of this 'other organisation' because according to his statement he was a visitor to Crom Castle and 13 Platoon sent a liaison patrol to the castle on 23 October. Was he or were the SIB investigators seeking to establish whether this 'other organisation' of eight men should be suspects? As this story will illustrate, there is no evidence that the group at Crom Castle were involved in the double murder, nor is there any other official record indicating that such a group existed, nor is there evidence to suggest that RUC detectives interviewed members of this anonymous organisation which, according to McKenzie, had a military capability and military-style uniforms. McKenzie's statement that his men were not, from his knowledge of their movements, in the area at the time of the murders, and that there was another organisation in the vicinity, ended the line of inquiry which sought to investigate the possibility of military involvement in the double murder.

As far as the records show, the SIB investigation went unnoticed within the lower ranks of the Argyll and Sutherland Highlanders but for one exception. Lieutenant Andrew Malcolm Burlton Snowball, commander of 13 Platoon, Delta Company, later confirmed that he was aware that his senior officer had been interviewed. One might well deduce that other members of Delta Company and, in particular, 13 Platoon also learned of the brief investigation.

However, there the matter rested and would have remained an unsolved incident except for one man. In 1978 a man in his mid-twenties walked into a city-centre police station in Glasgow. He said he wished to talk to detectives because he had vital information but would not divulge its nature until he spoke to someone in authority in CID. Once he had been led to the CID office and asked by a senior detective to reveal his information, the young man began to explain why he felt the need to talk to the police. He said he believed he knew the identity of the man known as the 'Yorkshire Ripper'.

The detective looked at the young man in front of him not only in wonderment but with a degree of scepticism. There were people, mainly cranks, constantly claiming they knew the identity of murderers, but this young man did not look like a crank, though his claim seemed fantastic. The 'Yorkshire Ripper' police inquiry, one of the biggest ever, had been in progress since 1976, but it was the first time this Glasgow detective had ever personally been faced with someone claiming to know the 'Ripper'.

The young man went on to explain that he had been reading newspaper reports and listening to broadcasts about the 'Ripper'; and he felt that a man with whom he had worked was the person being sought by the West Yorkshire Police. What was it about this man that suggested he was the 'Ripper', the detective asked. 'He had killed people with a dagger in Northern Ireland,' the young man replied.

The detective suddenly realised that he was about to hear startling information and he sent for several colleagues. In the next hour the young man described how he had served with the Argyll and Sutherland Highlanders in Northern Ireland in the autumn of 1972 and how he had learned that one of the men in his platoon had 'butchered' two innocent people with a dagger and 'enjoyed the killing'. He added that the killings were known as the 'pitchfork murders'. This young man, whose identity has since remained a secret, and whom I shall call 'Mr A' for the purpose of this story, told of the killing of Naan and Murray and named the murderer as Sergeant Stanley Alexander Hathaway of 13 Platoon, Delta Company. Mr A said the matter had been 'on his conscience' for six years but the pleas for assistance to find the 'Yorkshire Ripper' made him realise that it was his duty to reveal his secret if he was to prevent more killings.

Glasgow detectives contacted the RUC and discovered that there were indeed 'pitchfork murders' in 1972 which remained unsolved. Both police forces co-operated in examining Mr A's claims and, with the assistance of the Army's Special Investigation Branch, established that Sergeant Hathaway's service record indicated that he was out of the country during the 'Ripper' killings and could therefore be ruled out of the inquiry. However, what interested the RUC were the murders of Naan and Murray. Painstakingly, RUC detectives examined the 'pitchfork murders' file to discover that the Argyll and Sutherland Highlanders Delta Company had been the subject of a line of inquiry in 1973 which had ended with the statement taken from Major McKenzie at Ritchie Camp in Kirknewton. Suddenly the spotlight was switched again to Delta Company, and Mr A provided not only his own experiences of the platoon's movements on 23/24 October but hearsay evidence which at such an early stage in the investigation was valuable in the process of unravelling the sequence of events on those two days.

Mr A affirmed that Hathaway had been seen in the company of other men on the night of 23 October. He named these men as Sergeant John McFayden Byrne and Lance-Corporal Iain Fletcher Chestnut but was unable to state with any certainty whether they were involved in the killings; however, he added that he believed the platoon commander, Lieutenant Snowball, knew about the killings. The RUC and Scottish police began an exhaustive investigation assisted by the Army. Their primary task was to test Mr A's allegations by interviewing Hathaway and Byrne, who were with the Army in Germany. Both men were flown to Northern Ireland before Christmas 1978 and denied that they or any members of 13 Platoon murdered Naan and Murray. Lance-Corporal Chestnut had left the Army, was working on a North Sea oil rig and was not easily contactable.

The RUC inquiry once again reached a cul-de-sac, the only hope being that Chestnut might provide information to corroborate Mr A's testimony. The team now assigned to the case consisted of two RUC officers, Detective Inspectors Scott and McBurney, and two SIB officers, Sergeant Robert Stronach and Sergeant Malcolm Denton. From the outset they operated professionally and with due deference to each other's roles: the civil power and the armed forces. On 8 February 1979 Iain Fletcher Chestnut was brought to Aberdeen police headquarters from his home in the city. Detective Inspector William McBurney from Gough Barracks in Armagh and Sergeant Malcolm Denton of SIB met Chestnut, and explained to him that they were investigating the killings of Naan and Murray and that they wished to 'elicit his duties and that of his platoon' in October 1972.

Chestnut agreed after caution to make a statement, which began with a résumé of his life and military career: 'I reside at Provost Rust Drive with my wife and two children. I joined the Army in 1964 and served with the 1st Argyll and Sutherland Highlanders in Borneo, Aden, Germany, N. Ireland and the United Kingdom. In April/May 1973 I was dismissed or dishonourably discharged from the Army over an escapade involving an air rifle during a tour of duty with "D" Company which began in July 1972 and finished in November 1972.' Chestnut illustrates here that his memory is flawed, though one should not be inclined to believe that a man with his Army experience could not remember whether he was dismissed or dishonourably discharged. He omitted to tell the investigators that he lost a stripe while serving with the Army in Newry. His crime was putting nuts and bolts into a rubber-bullet gun—which converted it into a lethal weapon rather than a gun designed for riot purposes. He later claimed that he was a 'scapegoat' and was punished as an example to other soldiers who were using a similar technique. However, if one is to believe this claim one must first examine Chestnut's dealings with the police in the 'pitchfork inquiry', during which his behaviour was not always that of a man of integrity. An example of his tendency to be 'economical' with the truth is to be found in his statement of 8 February 1979. After outlining his military career he added the following:

The 13 Platoon moved to a new camping position but I can't say if we moved very far and all I can remember of the site was that it was on top of a small wooded hill beside an old ruined building. I have a vague recollection of either seeing a funeral or being told there was a funeral on. I believe it was the funeral of a UDR man but I can't remember when it was. On the day that we moved from this second location, I remember seeing police and military vehicles at a farm and on stopping being told that two bodies had been found. Mr Snowball who was leading the platoon went up to the farm but returned almost immediately and told us that there had been a couple of bodies discovered at the farm. I believe our Company Commander, Major McKenzie, was there and I assumed from what I heard that the bodies were still at the farm. I am quite sure that this was early in the morning.

The statement continued with an outline of Chestnut's responsibilities in the days that followed. Then he returned to the subject-matter which interested the police and Army investigators:

While we were doing a vehicle checkpoint after leaving the farmhouse where the bodies had been found we began to wonder why we had not heard the shots at the farmhouse as we could not have been camped very far away the previous night. Some time later the word got round that the guys had been pitchforked, which explained why we had not heard any shots. There was also speculation as to whether the murders had been carried out by the UDA or UDR. The general opinion was that it was the UDR in revenge for that chap that was killed. I never heard any talk or rumours as to who was actually responsible for the killings and I never heard exactly how they had been killed or where they had been found though I had heard as I have said that they had been found on the farm. I have never heard any talk alleging that members of the Regiment were responsible for the deaths, prior to reading a report in the Daily Record during December of 1978 to the effect that two men from the Regiment were accompanying police back to Northern Ireland. I suppose I believed that two men were going back to Northern Ireland and I tried to figure out what tour of duty the murders occurred on as I could not mind having gone to Fermanagh. I had only been on one tour of N. Ireland with the Argyll and Sutherland Highlanders, though I had been on one tour prior to that with the Royal Scots. It was not until after I had spoken to CID today that I remembered that I had been on a short spell of duty in Fermanagh.

Chestnut omitted to point out at this juncture in his statement that 13 Platoon's tour of Fermanagh had been very brief, ending a short time after the murders. He went on to outline the regulations in relation to patrolling and then turned his mind to the crucial question of his association with Sergeant Hathaway:

You were not allowed to carry a sheath knife or any other type of personal weapon. At no time did I ever go out on a reccy patrol with Sgt Hathaway or other members of the Regiment during which anything unusual occurred apart from one patrol in Armagh when Corporal McCullough got shot. At no time was I ever detailed to carry out a reconnaissance patrol round the Naan farm and I am positive I never heard of him until after he was killed. I have never carried a Bowie knife in Northern Ireland though I did have a sheath knife in Aden, nor did I ever have any discussion about throwing away or losing a knife, with any members of the Regiment. I owned and carried a clasp knife when on duty in Northern Ireland.

So ended Chestnut's statement. His comment about knives derived from questions put to him prior to the statement. The police phrased the questions to protect their source, Mr A, who had informed them that Chestnut did carry a Bowie knife while on duty in Fermanagh. After the interview and statement, a search was conducted at Provost Rust Drive to determine whether such a knife was still in Chestnut's possession, but no Bowie knife was discovered, and Chestnut, who was present at the search, was unable to find his clasp knife, which he claimed he had with him in Fermanagh. He was allowed to go free.

However, the RUC and Army investigators were not impressed by the manner in which he had delivered his evidence and his tendency to be vague about his stay in Northern Ireland. A month after the Chestnut interview, Sergeant John McFayden Byrne was flown to Army HQ at Lisburn in Northern Ireland and was interviewed vigorously by both SIB and RUC personnel in an effort to break down his claim that he was not involved in the murders and knew little about them. As he had said before, he told the detectives that he believed 14 Platoon found the bodies and 13 Platoon was camped in the grounds of Crom Castle. This time, however, Byrne added a detail which was to become a central feature of the investigation: he told his interrogators that he had a 'vague recollection' that the name of one of the murdered men had been on an 'intelligence brief'. He added that 13 Platoon did not place a cordon round the Naan farm or arrange to search it.

When asked if he had ever taken part in a reconnaissance patrol with Hathaway, Chestnut and Privates MacGuire and Clarke, he replied that he might have done but it would have been unlikely for Chestnut to have been present, since although Chestnut was indeed in 13 Platoon he was not in his section. However, if such a patrol had gone out it would have been normal for it to have reported to the platoon commander, Lieutenant Snowball, on its return to base. Byrne also volunteered the information that he had heard stories about the murders, particularly how they were carried out: 'After the bodies were found we heard that they had a pretty gruesome death and I think pitchforks were mentioned. Later, after we got back to our main base at Bessbrook in Co. Fermanagh there were reports in the news media that the Army were involved in the murders, but that was just laughed off.'

Byrne's statement did not take the inquiry much further, and the investigating officers decided it was imperative that they talk to Lieutenant Snowball, who by this time was Captain Snowball and stationed at Warminster Military Camp. Detective Inspector McBurney recorded meeting Snowball on 6 April at Warminster and informing him of the nature of his inquiries. Snowball replied that he was aware of the investigations and of recent publicity in relation to the murders, but he could not 'visualise any of the men under his command having been involved because after such a long time and the way soldiers talk he would have heard of it'. He added that he had never heard any rumours to suggest that military personnel were involved.

Snowball agreed to make a statement, which was witnessed by McBurney and Sergeant Denton of the SIB. In his statement he recalled his trip to County Fermanagh, being billeted on Crom Castle estate and having drinks with the earl (Lord Erne). He could not remember exactly who told him about the double murder or when he heard about it, though he could have heard about it at an 'O' Group (intelligence) meeting at Lisnaskea. He also mentioned using 'Q' vans while he was with Delta Company in Fermanagh. This seemed like a curious piece of detail when I first read his statement, but it proved significant, as I shall later illustrate. Suffice it to say at this stage that when Snowball referred to 'Q' vans in his 6 April statement he was alluding to the use of unmarked Bedford vans to transport platoon commanders from the field to 'O' Group meetings, which would have been held in Newtownbutler or Lisnaskea; it was a means of moving senior personnel from one place to another safely, because terrorists expected soldiers to travel in military vehicles and convoys and not in civilian-type vans. Snowball's statement ended with the following observations:

After those murders I did not hear any rumours suggesting that the Company may have been involved. However, in 1973 I heard that the SIB had been to the Battalion and interviewed Major McKenzie in relation to a suggestion that troops had been in the area at the time of the murder. I must point out that I believe I may have been involved, together with my Platoon, in that search where the torch and balaclava were found. I knew that there was a possibility of Naan being involved in the Republican Movement but I did not know to what extent. I probably would have learned of Naan's suspected involvement at an Intelligence Briefing. I am not aware of persons in my Platoon carrying a substantial type of knife. They may have carried clasp knives. We always wore normal combat kit with the Glengarry. I cannot recall any incident in Fermanagh where four persons were stopped by a patrol and then released. I am not aware that there was ever a possibility of searching Naan's home or of a reconnaissance for a possible search of the house by night.

Several remarks in Snowball's statement require elucidation. First, he mentions that a military torch and balaclava were found during the search of a farm in the Newtownbutler area but does not indicate which farm it was. I fail to understand why the matter should be referred to, because there is no account of such a find in the RUC documents that later became part of court proceedings, and the only mention of such a find is in Snowball's statement. Maybe the matter was raised as a peripheral issue by the investigators and he felt he had to respond, though its significance is not established. Further, his choice of language in respect of Naan's 'suspected involvement' with the Republican movement exemplifies a vagueness one would not expect from an officer who was in charge of a platoon covering the area of Naan's farm and who attended intelligence 'O' Group meetings designed to provide commanders with detailed assessments of suspects. Finally, Snowball says he 'cannot recall any incidents in Fermanagh where four persons were stopped by a patrol and then released'. I suspect that Snowball made this comment in response to questions put to him by Denton and McBurney, who had information from Mr A that after the murders a vehicle containing four men in overalls was allowed access to Naan's farm by military personnel from

13 Platoon with clearance from company HQ at Lisnaskea. Denton and McBurney were convinced that the vehicle was at the farm on the night of 23 October or the early hours of 24 October, a considerable time before the RUC learned of the murder. This element in the story, though peripheral, will be of significance to the reader in assessing one of the most vital elements of what to this day remains a mystery.

McBurney and Denton left Warminster on 6 April without the crucial pieces they needed for putting together a complex murder puzzle. On 5 June Detective Sergeant Brian Taylor, from Gough Barracks in County Armagh, accompanied Detective Inspector McBurney to Celle Military Camp in West Germany, where they were met by their opposite numbers in the SIB, Sergeants Denton and Stronach. The four men analysed their progress in the murder inquiry in preparation for the interrogation of Sergeant Hathaway, who was stationed in the camp with the 1st Armoured Division Engineer Regiment. The interrogation began at 2.00 pm and ended at 4.00 pm. Hathaway revealed nothing of significance but the detectives agreed that they should conduct a prolonged interrogation the following day. At 11.00 am on 6 June the two SIB sergeants began the questioning, and Sergeant Denton proved a very able investigator, as shown in his notes:

Denton:	A witness has said that troops were seen on the road on the night of the 23rd by Naan's farm. Could that have been you and a half-section?
Hathaway:	It must have been.
Denton:	Did you visit Naan's farm?
Hathaway:	Not to my knowledge.
Denton:	Where was your bivvie area that night?
Hathaway:	I don't know. It must have been close by the farm and the roadway you are talking about.
Denton:	What time did this patrol take place?
Hathaway:	We went out, I think, about eight. I can't be sure. It could have been earlier or later.
Denton:	How long were you out on patrol?
Hathaway:	Maximum time to patrol is two hours, so it would have been a bit less than that.
Denton:	Was it dark?
Hathaway:	Yes, it would have been.
Denton:	What were you wearing?
Hathaway:	Combats. After dark we wore Tam O'Shanters or Glengarrys outside-in.
Denton:	Who were the members of the half-section?
Hathaway:	I can't remember.
Denton:	Did you call at Naan's farm?
Hathaway:	I can't remember.
Denton:	Were any of the other farmers reported dead?

Hathaway:	No.
Denton:	What about the UDR man, Bell?
Hathaway:	I don't know anything about him.
Denton:	There were two incidents while you were in Fermanagh that you knew nothing about. You couldn't have been a good Platoon Sergeant, could you?
Hathaway:	Maybe not.

As the interview proceeded, Hathaway continued to be unable to remember the exact location of 13 Platoon at various times, the types of vehicles used by them or relevant dates.

Denton:	You saw a situation report about people being killed, where were you when you saw this document?
Hathaway:	At the castle.
Denton:	At what time of day?
Hathaway:	Early evening.
Denton:	And the previous evening you were out patrolling by Naan's farm?
Hathaway:	Yes. When I saw the report I realised that was the area we had been patrolling.
Denton:	When you were out patrolling you would have had a Section Corporal with you. Which one?
Hathaway:	I don't know.
Denton:	Look Hathaway, you were out and about intelligence gathering, weren't you?
Hathaway:	Yes.
Denton:	So you would have taken whichever Section Corporal was switched on, so who was it?
Hathaway:	Well, Byrne was switched on.
Denton:	Then I put it to you that Byrne was with you?
Hathaway:	I expect so.

In a game of cat and mouse, Denton eventually established that the half-section which had patrolled near the Naan farm on the night of 23 October comprised Hathaway, Byrne, Chestnut and a radio operator, Private John Brennan McGuire.

Denton:	Were you going to search Naan's farm?
Hathaway:	I don't know, maybe.
Denton:	I put it to you that you were going to search Naan's farm early the next morning and that night you were doing a recce around the farm.
Hathaway:	No.
Denton:	Did you have information that Naan was suspected of being involved with the IRA.
Hathaway:	No, but we had a list of suspects and he could have been on that.

Denton:	Was he?
Hathaway:	I can't remember. All I remember is that there were 6 names.
Denton:	Did your Platoon not pick up information that Naan was a suspect and that was why he was on the list?
Hathaway:	I can't remember.
Denton:	Out of the people we have seen there are only three with bad memories. You are one of them. This is a very serious matter and we have been fair to you. But let me tell you how things stand. You and your Merry Band were on that roadway. Therefore you would have visited Naan's farm. Naan's name was known to you. Either you found the two dead bodies there and said nothing, or you or one of your men killed Naan and Murray. The Pathologist puts the time of death as the evening of Oct. 23 and you were there. Throughout this enquiry, of the people we have seen, the ones who could remember anything, said we should go and speak to you.
Hathaway:	Why should they say that?
Denton:	It's come all the way down the line from the OC to Snowball to you.
Hathaway:	I didn't see any dead bodies. I didn't kill anyone nor did my buddies. None of my buddies were capable of anything like that. Christ I couldn't kill anyone.
Denton:	Hathaway, as far as we're concerned, it was you or one of your men and I want you to tell me about it.

Hathaway burst into tears at this stage and said: 'I suppose I have been trying to put it out of my mind. I did it. I did the killings. I killed them and they just wouldn't stop screaming. Oh my God. I have been having nightmares about it. That bloody dog at the farm must have found the bodies and kept howling when we got back to the location. I have been hearing that dog ever since. My God I didn't want to kill anyone.'

Hathaway completely broke down after delivering his confession and was unable to be questioned for almost an hour. When the interrogation resumed, he began by telling Denton that the confession was 'a weight off' his mind and that he never intended to kill anyone. He asked what would happen to him and whether his wife and children would suffer for his crime. Denton pursued his questioning about how the killings happened:

Hathaway:	We were out intelligence gathering and came to this bloke Naan's farm and started looking around and came across Naan in this stable place. We started asking him questions about who he was and where he had been in the last two or three hours. He wouldn't

answer the questions. I told him I knew who he was. He was on our list as being an IRA Quartermaster or something.

Denton: Who all was there?

Hathaway: Self, Byrne, Chestnut and McGuire.

Denton: Anyone else?

Hathaway: There may have been someone else.

Denton: Who?

Hathaway: I don't know.

Denton: Who found Naan in the stable?

Hathaway: Me and Byrne. The others were outside looking around. He started getting stroppy with us. He said that we couldn't pin anything on him, that he had been lifted before and got away scot free because there was nothing on him.

Denton: Is that when you put the knife in his throat?

Hathaway: I don't remember doing that. He said he knew us and that he was going to get the IRA boys on to us. He knew people who were quite capable of knocking off troops. He knew where we were and could get quite a few of them to cause us trouble. He continued to be abusive and knew we couldn't harm him or lift him. I can't remember if he went for me. Byrne said; 'Do him in', or something like that. I had the knife in my pocket. I'd taken it off one of the Platoon who had it on his belt. I got it out and struck him in the stomach. He started screaming: 'I'll get the boys on you.' He was still standing up. I must have carried on stabbing him. He was shouting for someone else. He tried to run out of the stable. Byrne blocked the door. I went after him to keep him quiet. He was shouting at someone to get the boys. He stopped screaming. He must have died on me.

Denton's notes show Hathaway further admitting to the killing of Murray and returning to base camp where he washed himself beside a Saracen armoured vehicle. Hathaway continued:

I was covered in the stuff, must have been blood. It was close to Naan's farm and I could hear that bloody dog. Snowball was there. He said: 'What's happened?' Somebody said what had happened. I can't remember what Snowball said at first but he then said, 'It'll be alright.' He then took the knife from me and said, 'We must get rid of this.' I don't know what happened to it. I think it was chucked away in the water the next day. We were moved out after 2 or 3 hours, it was still dark, to the castle. The OC was there. That's it.

Denton: Why did you move location?

Hathaway: The Major came to the location to tell Snowball to get us out.

Denton:	What caused the nicks on Naan's neck? Had you been questioning him with a knife at his throat?
Hathaway:	I don't know. I must have done at the start when I was questioning him about his whereabouts. Then he made a grab for me and I struck him. He may have had a pitchfork because he was mucking out a cow. The knife was a dagger with a crossed pattern on the shaft with a finger guard on the side.
Denton	What was Snowball's attitude?
Hathaway:	Just that things were to be covered up and he told everybody never to ever mention anything about this to anyone.

At this point Sergeant Denton put it to Hathaway that he had been ordered to be rough with Naan, not to kill him, but to upset him enough for him to arrange for members of the IRA to be called in to retaliate. The interrogation ended with Hathaway telling Denton and Stronach that he felt better after confessing to the murders because the 'howling dog' had haunted him.

Hathaway's revelations to the SIB detectives placed the RUC and Army's murder inquiry on a new footing: their task was now to find corroborating evidence, to test Hathaway's assertions and to analyse some of the points he had raised.

The analysis centred first on Hathaway's claim that Snowball knew of the crime. Secondly, Hathaway's reference to his having heard a dog howling all night tended to lend credence to an SIB theory, put to Hathaway, that a search of the farm had been planned for the morning after the murders. Naan did not have a dog, but military searches used sniffer-dogs to detect explosives. According to the military record for 23/24 October, a sniffer-dog was required for a search of premises on the 24th, but the premises were not identified in military documents relating to the duties assigned to 13 Platoon on those dates.

The RUC and SIB officers decided to fly Hathaway and Byrne to Northern Ireland for further questioning, to arrange for Chestnut to be arrested in Aberdeen, and to charge them with murder. Although the evidence pointed conclusively to the involvement of these three men, no decision was taken about McGuire, since even Hathaway had tended not to implicate him. By contrast, a case could be made against Chestnut in respect of the murder of Murray: Mr A had alleged that the knife used in the murders belonged to Chestnut, and the four officers felt that Chestnut was basically a liar.

On Saturday 9 June, Sergeant Denton and Detective Sergeant Taylor questioned McFayden Byrne in Interview Room BF13 at Castlereagh RUC station. Byrne told the officers that Company Sergeant-Major

Higgins had mentioned the murders to him in 1973 when the inquiries were being made at Ritchie Camp, Kirknewton, and prior to that at Bessbrook, where they were eventually based after the murders. Snowball told him that he hoped the matter would be 'kept quiet'.

Byrne's account of the killings differed from Hathaway's: 'I was outside the barn when a scuffle started. I ran in and saw Hathaway stabbing Naan two or three times. Naan fell. When we got back to the bivvy area the whole platoon was there and Hathaway and I went to wash the blood off. Snowball appeared when we were washing the blood off. He said it would have to be kept quiet.' This version of Naan's murder tended to place all the blame firmly on Hathaway; yet the post-mortem evidence suggested that Naan either put up no resistance or was restrained while being stabbed—and that would have required at least two persons. Byrne also appeared to be indicating that the whole platoon had witnessed their blood-spattered return from the farm. However, he was unable to provide information about the whereabouts of the murder weapon, but merely claimed that someone had thrown it away. Unlike Hathaway, he did not name that someone as Lieutenant Snowball. Byrne did, however, provide a graphic account of the killing of Murray: 'We decided we could not let him go. I had the knife and tried to stab him but couldn't. Hathaway took the knife off me and stabbed him.' Byrne added that he and Chestnut held Murray while he was being stabbed; that McGuire was physically sick and was told to leave the scene; and that he helped Hathaway and Chestnut to throw Murray's body into a slurry pit at the side of the lane.

When Byrne was questioned about whether there was an observation post on the farm, he denied that one existed. He was also asked if Snowball was present during the killings and he replied emphatically that the lieutenant was not with the patrol at the farm.

The investigators turned their attention to Iain Fletcher Chestnut, who had been flown from Aberdeen on 11 June and presented for questioning at Castlereagh RUC station on the 12th. When it was put to him that Byrne and Hathaway were implicating him in the murder of Murray, he offered his version of events. He said that Byrne and Hathaway were in the barn while he was in the laneway with McGuire. He stopped Murray, who was walking along the lane, and made him lie face down on the ground. While this was happening noises were coming from the barn. He held Murray down until Byrne and Hathaway returned.

I grabbed his heels, and Byrne took one of his arms. Hathaway was kneeling at his head. The next thing Hathaway stabbed the guy on the back and that's when the sudden shock of it hit me.

Chestnut agreed with the detectives that the patrol led by Hathaway was irregular because it contained a member from each section of 13 Platoon, when a patrol normally comprised members from just one section; the 'odd nature' of the patrol convinced him that 'it was organised from even further up the line than Sergeant Hathaway'. He added that when he was discharged from the Army he considered revealing everything about the murders but was frightened because he believed the killings were 'Army orientated' and anything he said would be 'twisted by the Army'.

This latter claim is convenient for a man who seeks to imply that his guilt related to orders: one could deduce that by trying to implicate people at a higher level he was trying to minimise the role played by Hathaway, Byrne and himself. When asked if he thought Hathaway had entered the farm with the intention of killing Naan, he replied that Hathaway was a good soldier who went by the book. It did not seem to occur to him that a good soldier does not kill innocent people with a dagger.

Chestnut agreed to make a formal statement giving a detailed account of the events of 23 October 1972. According to this statement, the camp established by 13 Platoon almost overlooked the Naan farm. At 9.00 pm that day the patrol went towards the farm because it was believed that Naan was a recruiting officer for the Provisional IRA. It became apparent to Chestnut that he was not on a normal patrol, because they simply walked up to the farm, whereas the usual procedure was for them to 'snoop about'. Chestnut produced a grisly description of how Hathaway stabbed Murray, then turned him over and continued to stab him until he stopped 'gurgling'. However, he said the murder weapon was thrown away immediately after the murders and was not given to Snowball, as Hathaway alleged. When the patrol returned to the camp, Chestnut suddenly realised that Hathaway was covered in blood, and Snowball witnessed that fact:

Just prior to getting into camp, Hathaway I think it was told us all to keep it quiet or words to that effect. There was no more talk of the killings that night. I assumed that the orders had been given higher up because Hathaway had come back into camp and washed himself openly in front of the Platoon Commander under the light of a torch. The following morning early we broke camp and moved to a new location later in the day. Later after I returned to Bessbrook I heard speculation and it was generally believed that it was another sectarian killing.

This statement once again raised in the minds of investigating officers the possibility that there had been a cover-up, and the allegations about 'D' Company officers required investigation. There were other vexed questions: the time at which the murders occurred, who knew about them, and why it was not until 6.05 pm on 24 October that the bodies were found and the RUC informed.

The detectives turned to Captain Snowball in the hope that he could clarify the sequence of duties of 13 Platoon on 23/24 October 1972. On 12 June 1979 Detective Chief Inspector Scott and Sergeant Denton met Snowball and informed him that a number of people who had been under his command were assisting with the murder inquiry. Snowball is reported to have reacted with the words 'Are they?' As the interview continued, the detectives asked whether he had sought advice from Major McKenzie at the time of the murders, since he was then a young and inexperienced officer. He replied that he did not but that for nine months he was the youngest serving officer in the British Army and was twenty years old when the murders took place. When Chief Inspector Scott enquired whether he had discussed 'the matter under investigation' with anyone, he answered that he had discussed it with his father and 'the General'; he did not identify 'the General'. Snowball admitted that Chestnut phoned him after newspaper reports in December 1978 and that he gave Chestnut his father's telephone number. He also 'ran into Chestnut' on several occasions while serving in Aberdeen.

At this point in the interview Detective Superintendent Ernest Drew appealed to Snowball to assist the inquiry and delivered a homily on guilt:

I informed Capt. Snowball that other soldiers found the enormous pressure of guilt so unbearable that they had decided to be completely frank and tell the truth in written statements. I continued by saying that very often the fear of detection filled the consciousness but when detection came the pressure was relieved and the deep sense of relief made confession a satisfaction. I went on by referring to different cases where men found it necessary to surrender to the police after committing crimes because of the simple fact that the load of the deed done was so heavy they could carry it no longer and had to unburden themselves. The Captain sat for a moment or two without speaking and then asked if it would be possible to speak to Staff Sgt. Denton of the SIB alone. I agreed and Chief Inspector Scott and I withdrew from the room.

Denton emerged from the room twenty minutes later, and what followed is contained in a statement later made by Detective Superintendent Drew:

On returning to the interview room I told Snowball that I understood he now wished to tell us about the double murder. He informed us that contrary to what he had previously said, he had in fact been aware that some members of his Platoon had been responsible for the murders. Mr Snowball agreed to make a written statement and during this time he stopped and muttered, 'I never thought they would do it.' When Chief Inspector Scott asked what he meant he informed us that they were always joking in the camp as to what they would do with McGuinness [IRA and Sinn Fein leader] or someone like that but it had never crossed his mind that they would ever carry it out.

Snowball's written statement outlined his duties on the day of the murder and subsequent events. I am reproducing much of it here because it is an aid to understanding some of the inconsistencies present in the whole of the police case, even after the interviews with Chestnut, Byrne and Hathaway:

After our arrival in Fermanagh, we camped for a couple of days down on the Border by a salient. We then moved to another site somewhat nearer to Newtownbutler and just off the main road from Wattlebridge to Newtownbutler. After our arrival at the site, I became aware that a nearby farm was occupied by a man named Naan who was on our suspect list. Though it was known by my men that Naan was a Provisional no instructions were ever issued by myself in relation to sightseeing or action to be taken in the event of meeting him. As it was known that he was involved in everything that went down there, his name was discussed on occasions. A day or two after we got to our last site, I went to an 'O' Group at Lisnaskea around 1800 hrs and it was attended by the Company Commander and Platoon Commanders. Before leaving for the 'O' Group I gave instructions to my Platoon Sergeant, Sgt Hathaway, that a patrol should go out sometime in the evening within the local area. On the evening referred to I went to the 'O' Group in a 'Q' Van which was sent out from Lisnaskea. After the meeting I returned to my area in a 'Q' Van. On my return to base I went straight to the command post and confirmed that a patrol was on the ground. About half an hour later the door of the Saracen was opened and someone said the patrol was back. I can't remember who that was. About five minutes later I went out and saw jerry cans of water being poured over soldiers. I can't remember who was there but I remember Sgt Hathaway was one of them. It was dark at the time and there was a torch being used for light. This was taking place within an old shed and I just stuck my nose in and then went back to the command post. When I looked into the shed I saw one of the men was cleaning a knife, which I am sure was a folding knife. After spending a few moments in the command post, I made my way towards my basher which was in the trees close by. As I was moving back to my basher either Sgt Hathaway or Byrne spoke to me and I asked what had happened when they were out on patrol as I suspected in my own mind that they could possibly have killed somebody. I can't remember the exact details of what they said but it was along the lines that they had killed two men at Naan's farm. I went to my basher where I mulled the whole thing over in my mind and decided that for the good of the Army and the Regiment it must never go any further. I have never discussed the matter with any other officer except when investigations started and Army barristers. I was asked about the possibilities of our involvement, to which I replied, 'I suppose it is feasible but I cannot see how it would happen.' About two years ago while serving in Germany, Sgt Byrne mentioned it to me in passing but there was no discussion about it. Sometime after the first reports appeared in the papers, an ex-member called Chestnut contacted me by phone while I was serving in Edinburgh. He expressed some anxiety but I told him not to worry. He contacted me again by phone sometime after he had been seen by police and the reports had appeared in the papers but I just said don't do anything stupid. Though I had my suspicions that Chestnut would have been on the patrol I never was actually aware that he was on it. I knew that Sgt Hathaway was on it, but I never actually knew who else was on it though I always had my suspicions.

Staff Sergeant Denton recorded the details of his twenty-minute interview. Snowball had admitted that Hathaway and the other members of the patrol had worn their kit turned inside-out on the night of the killings. He denied that he had ever spoken to Major McKenzie or Sergeant-Major Higgins about the crime and supported their contention that they had not been in an observation post overlooking the farm on the night in question. He was unable, however, to remember whether a search had been planned for the Naan farm on 24 October although he accepted that a search had taken place that day at a sawmill premises adjacent to the farm. Snowball admitted that he might have sent a patrol to cordon off the farm after the killings but added that he 'could not honestly remember'.

Since there were still many anomalies within the evidence, on 11 August RUC detectives McBurney and Scott went to Ritchie Camp at Kirknewton to ask Major McKenzie if he could enlarge on the information they had received to date. In particular they wanted to discover whether Naan was a leading IRA suspect, whether 'Q' vans were used and whether a search was planned for Naan's farm on 24 October. Major McKenzie made the following statement:

Before every operation i.e. search, we would have held an 'O' Group. This would have been during the evening of the day before and at the 'O' Group we would have allocated a search team and dogs if necessary and I would have given the Platoon Commander orders as to what I wanted done. If we had decided to search Naan's farm the above procedure would have been carried out. I do not specifically remember an 'O' Group for the Naan farm search but if I had decided to search the farm I would have done so after an 'O' Group as above. The procedure for selecting a particular house was as follows. The Platoon Commander would produce a series of names that he believed to be of interest as a result of his normal patrolling. I would compare these with any names I had received from Army/RUC/UDR and if a name appeared on my list as well, we would plan a search or observe that house. I am not happy about the apparent procedure concerning the stated search on Naan's farm. The anomalies are as follows. If we had wanted to search the house of a suspected terrorist as opposed to a routine search we would have mounted a formal Company search. I would not have allowed any visits to the house by a patrol before the search. I also would have done a daylight recce with the Platoon Commander and the Company Sgt Major. I would also have probably sent the search team back with the Platoon Commander to be ready for an early search next morning. If a search had been called off

because the Platoon Commander felt that it was compromised he would himself
have returned to tell me. As I have said before I was not aware of us having a 'Q'
Van. We used normal military vehicles to travel everywhere. I would like to add that
I do not believe that we had planned to search Naan's farm at any time. I may well
have been given his name but if I had been told that he was an IRA Quartermaster
and therefore likely to have weapons and explosives in his possession, I would
have planned a more thorough and large-scale operation. At that time there was
virtually no information available and I instructed the Platoon Commanders to get
out and find out as much as they could. They were able to select their own Platoon
bases as they saw fit. They need only inform me of their locations once they had
selected them. They were given an area of operation and each could move around
within their areas as they liked. Their duties entailed chat-up patrols to every
house in their area and vehicle checkpoints to monitor the traffic. Once they felt
that an area or house needed searching we would arrange this at the next 'O'
Group. During this period, Naan was a nonentity. However, after his murder there
was much discussion in the Company about the fact that this was an IRA man. I
believe that as a result of this the personnel in the Platoon have misinterpreted
the importance of Naan and that he in our minds at that time assumed an importance after his death which was not apparent before it. I do recall a vehicle was
stopped which contained four men and which was subsequently released and that
this we felt at the time was probably a mistake as these men were of interest.
This information was given to me some time after the vehicle was released but I
cannot say precisely at what stage I got this information or precisely when the vehicle was stopped.

McKenzie's statement ended with an assertion that he had not been
informed of the killings and found it difficult to understand why
Snowball had kept the matter hidden from him for seven years. He
added that early in 1979 Snowball had phoned him to indicate that the
Fermanagh 'incident' had raised concern in the Argyll and Sutherland
Highlanders and that he would like to speak to him. McKenzie had
invited him to dinner that following week, but no discussion of the
incident had taken place until after dinner, when he had walked
Snowball to his car. Snowball had asked what he thought of a report
that the Army were involved in the murders. McKenzie said he told
Snowball not to worry, since police would 'get all the facts and it
would turn out to be an IRA smear against the security forces', and
Snowball left without mentioning that his soldiers had been involved
in the murders.

When one examines McKenzie's statement in detail, it is obvious
that his views on central issues conflict sharply with statements made
by Snowball. For example, Snowball talks about travelling in a 'Q' van
but McKenzie says there was none available to his company.
McKenzie describes Naan as a 'nonentity', which is contrary to
Snowball's belief that Naan was a Provisional and on a suspect list.
McKenzie's statement also refers to a vehicle with four men in it, yet

in a statement made in 1979 he said specifically that he had 'no knowledge' of the group left at the farm stopping a van with four wanted persons in it.

I was puzzled when I began to examine the reference to a vehicle. I wondered at first whether it was the car mentioned by Dympna Brady who said she saw soldiers talking to two people in a black Morris Minor near the entrance to Naan's farm at 7.30 pm on 23 October. However, I rule this out because other evidence had led me to identify another vehicle as the one which was at the farm after the killings. The existence of a civilian vehicle in the vicinity of the farm was confirmed when detectives interviewed other members of 13 Platoon. These soldiers, six in all, agreed that a cordon was thrown round the Naan farm after the killings. One of those interviewed was Sergeant Joseph Lawrence Burke, who was a corporal in 1972, and his evidence is fascinating because he claims that the decision to seal off the farm was taken at an 'O' Group meeting—which would have been held at Lisnaskea or base camp—and that this decision was made in the knowledge that Naan and Murray were dead. His evidence about a vehicle also demands scrutiny:

I remember the day we were asked at the 'O' Group to go to a farm to seal off the area until the RUC arrived. Mr Snowball briefed me at the 'O' Group. Prior to being called to the 'O' Group I was in my basher. I don't know who called me from my basher to go to the 'O' Group. Lieutenant Snowball, Stan Hathaway, Corporal Campbell and Healey were at the 'O' Group. After the briefing at the 'O' Group I went out and got my patrol together, who were Clark, Carson, Birnie and one other. I believe that my patrol walked down to the laneway leading to the farm, we checked the farmyard to ensure that there were no vehicles there. We then walked about halfway down the lane leading from the farm to the main road and stayed there all night. I had briefed my patrol prior to leaving the base camp. I told them that we were to seal off the lane leading to the farm as two persons had been murdered at the farm and we had to stop any persons entering the farm until the arrival of the RUC. Sometime during the night I stopped and checked a shooting-brake coming up the laneway towards the farm. There were four male occupants of the shooting-brake, they were dressed in light overalls and said they were from Clones. The particulars were circulated to Company HQ and I was informed to allow them to proceed to the farm. The shooting-brake left the farm again after about 10/15 minutes. I stopped and searched the occupants and vehicle before allowing it to leave the area. At first light we were withdrawn back to base camp. Later on that day Chestnut who shared my bivvy told me that he had gone with Byrne, Hathaway and McGuire to the farm the previous evening and murdered people there. He said that they had knocked on the door of the farmhouse and it was opened by Naan who did not tell them anything. Chestnut said that Naan was the local Quartermaster of the Provisionals and the reason he had done it was in revenge for some of our own lads being killed.

I assume that the shooting-brake with four men in it was the vehicle which McKenzie claims contained four wanted men. In his statement of August 1979 he says it was a mistake to allow the four men to the farm. Is it believable that men who came from Clones in the Irish Republic and were dressed in overalls would be permitted by company headquarters to proceed on their merry way after spending ten to fifteen minutes at the farm where the owner was apparently not present?

Lance-Corporal Frederick Clarke, who later became a sergeant, was guarding the farm with Burke, but his recollection of the vehicle and its occupants is different: 'I didn't search the people in the car but I did recognise them. I don't seem to remember if the vehicle was searched at all. I don't remember if I spoke to any of the men in the vehicle. The vehicle stayed long enough for Corporal Burke to 'P'-check the occupants and then it was released. A 'P' check means to take all the personal particulars and send them by radio to Newtownbutler police station.' Although Clark claims he knew the occupants of the car, he does not identify them. He also says the information was relayed to the police. A 'P' check in 1972 could have taken five minutes or an hour.

So who were the occupants of this car? I am not inclined to the view that they were wanted men—in other words, members of the IRA. The fact that each of them was dressed in overalls suggests that each worked in a similar profession or were dressed for a collective task.

If they were military personnel, what precise task could they have been given? Let us imagine that a cover-up is in progress. Two men have been murdered and a cordon has been thrown round the farm to prevent access. Would other military or security forces personnel be permitted access? Consider the title 'pitchfork killings' and the fact that for seven years the murders were commonly believed to have been committed with a pitchfork. Yet no such implement was found on the farm by RUC investigators, nor was there any fingerprint evidence; in fact, there was no evidence available to police. If at first the view within military circles was that the murders were committed with a pitchfork or similar implements, is it not possible that in the heat of the moment four men in overalls (men whom one soldier recognised) were sent in to clean up and remove any incriminating evidence? The answer lies in the realm of conjecture but, I suggest, reasonable conjecture.

Burke also claims that the area was sealed off to allow for an investigation by the RUC; but according to the statement of Inspector Gilligan the RUC did not arrive until 6.20 pm on 24 October after the body of Murray was found by a civilian, John Patrick Hanna, and according to Burke's evidence he and his men were withdrawn from the farm at first light.

When RUC detectives began to interview Burke and the others they were puzzled by the fact that each soldier had a different impression of the time-scale of events on 23 October. Corporal Frederick Clarke told police that Naan's farm was kept 'under constant observation' and that late on the night of 23 October or very early on the 24th he was awoken by soldiers 'talking, laughing and carrying on'. He heard words like 'stabbed', 'blood', 'killed', 'wash me down', and so on. Clarke's description differs from that of Snowball, though it is confirmed by some of his colleagues: 'I looked out of the tent and saw four persons being washed down at the back of a four-ton lorry. I saw two of them with a jerry can which was sitting on the tailgate of the lorry and they were dipping water over themselves. I saw another man standing in a large metal pot being washed by another man. I would say altogether that there was between 12 and 15 people at the back of the lorry.' This scene of jollity is alleged to have taken place 'late at night or early the next morning'—which conflicts with Lieutenant Snowball's concept of the timing of events. Sergeant William Campbell told police he remembered Hathaway's patrol returning from duty before midnight. The question raised by those men who talked of Hathaway and his patrol returning late at night was whether the patrol went out before or after an 'O' Group meeting. Snowball was certain that when he returned from the 'O' Group the killings had already taken place.

In attempting to unravel the conflicting assessments about time, one must consider a statement made to the police by Lance-Corporal Robert Turnbull Hogan: 'I remember one night I was detailed for duty as sentry in the camp. My duty was keeping observation of the camp and surrounding area from a position overlooking the camp with "Noddy" which was a night sight. I was told to keep my eyes open for a patrol coming in between 2.00 am and 3.00 am. I saw four soldiers enter the camp and I heard a lot of shouting and heard voices shouting "keep the noise down".' Which patrol was the one referred to in this statement? That question has never been answered. If it was Hathaway's patrol, then once again one would place the killing after the 'O' Group meeting. Turnbull also revealed that he was using a night observation device, or NOD. Since Major McKenzie told police that there was one night observation device and that was located at company HQ, one must assume he was unaware of the presence of the device at 13 Platoon's base. He told police that he might have used a NOD on a routine reconnaissance task on 23 October so was there at least one other device available to 'D' Company?

Turnbull Hogan provided an additional piece of enlightening information for the RUC detectives. He said that in February 1973 he was in the company of Chestnut and McGuire when Chestnut mentioned the 'pitchfork murders': 'He told me the patrol had posed as an IRA assassination team by altering their uniforms by turning their jackets inside-out and by wearing cap-comforters on their heads and by not wearing puttees on their trousers. Chestnut said they went into the barn on the farm and one of the men, thinking the patrol was an IRA patrol, said, "I didn't tell them nothing." The patrol then killed the two men by stabbing them.' This account suggests a premeditated ploy which led to murder. If the patrol dressed to look like an IRA team, one needs to ask whether such a ploy would have been decided on the spur of the moment. Could these have been the three men dressed in 'military uniform' whom Dympna Brady saw. She 'took them to be Army', but thought they were wearing black berets. Oliver Melarkey saw a similar group of four men forty-five minutes earlier but he described the black berets as 'the Glengarry type'. Do these descriptions fit a patrol with cap-comforters on their heads and their uniforms turned inside-out? That is another dimension to the story which remains to this day unanswered.

Another question which constantly emerged but remained a mystery was whether the cordon search ordered for the farm took place on 23 or 24 October. Sergeant James Healey of 13 Platoon informed police that at a briefing on 23 October he was told there was to be a cordon search. He said he was detailed to remain and guard the base camp with four others—which implies that most of the platoon was engaged in the cordon search. Healey believed that Hathaway's group was a reconnaissance patrol which would have gone to the farm in advance of a search if procedures were being followed.

Either Sgt Hathaway or Byrne ordered me to go and inspect my sentries. I did this and finished duty and went to bed. My relief was L/Corporal Burke. I did not see any of the recce patrol before going to bed. I only either saw Hathaway or Byrne and there was nothing abnormal about him at that time. Sometime later I was awakened, at which time the cordon search operation began, leaving myself and three or four others at the bivvy area. I cannot say what time this was but normally it would have been an hour before first light.

Like much of the evidence, Healey's estimate of time is confusing. His reference to first light raises the possibility that the cordon search that was about to take place was the one Snowball and McKenzie said happened at a saw-mill adjacent to Naan's farm. One might, however, deduce from his timings that the killings occurred while he was asleep and that this would have been night-time and not early evening.

Despite so many inconsistencies and unanswered questions, the RUC proceeded with charges against four members of 13 Platoon: Hathaway, Byrne, Chestnut and Snowball. Hathaway and Byrne were charged with murdering Naan and Murray; Chestnut was charged with the killing of Murray; and Snowball faced a charge that, knowing that offences had been committed, he withheld that information from the police. The Army provided legal assistance for Hathaway, Byrne and Snowball, but denied it to Chestnut.

The case of the 'pitchfork murders' is one of the most complex I have encountered as a writer and journalist. There are many aspects which I find disturbing. It seems that a cover-up was sustained for a long period of time. The farm was apparently sealed off after the killings to allow for a 'cleaning-up' operation: no pitchfork or similar implement was found, despite the fact that Naan would have possessed such normal farm implements, and despite the belief that a pitchfork or pitchforks were used in the killings. Police investigations revealed that a considerable number of soldiers knew about the involvement of members of 13 Platoon but were content to conceal the facts. If there was indeed a clean-up operation, at what level was it ordered. Can any credence be placed on the claim that the vehicle on the farm after the killing contained four wanted men and the Army mistakenly allowed it to be present on the farm for ten to fifteen minutes and leave without hindrance? One is therefore left with nagging doubts. Was there a large operation? Staff Sergeants Denton and Stronach during interrogations suggested that Hathaway went to the farm to 'rough up' Naan but not to kill him. One either accepts that or believes that the two men were killed in revenge for the murder of Private McCullough of the 1st Argyll and Sutherland Highlanders, and that Hathaway and his patrol dressed in an unusual fashion that night so that if they were seen it would be thought they were IRA.

The scenes of jollity, the washing-off of blood and the general atmosphere in the camp are an appalling indictment of the members of 13 Platoon, their training or their understanding of the nature of their role in Northern Ireland. We shall never know what really happened, and that alone is a sad reflection not just on Hathaway, Byrne and Chestnut but on the whole of 13 Platoon if not 'D' Company and the 1st Argyll and Sutherland Highlanders Regiment.

In January 1981 the law did, however, deal with the central characters in the case. Hathaway and Byrne eventually pleaded guilty and were sentenced to life imprisonment, both of them electing to serve their sentence in Britain. During the trial Hathaway was severely tested under cross-examination and was emotionally weakened. Chestnut pleaded guilty to the lesser charge of manslaughter and was given four years' imprisonment. He had spent two years (1979–81) in custody and was released after the trial because of the 50 per cent remission rule in Northern Ireland, which allows for convicted terrorists to serve only half a stipulated sentence. He left Northern Ireland and I am led to understand that he changed his name. Captain Snowball received a one-year suspended sentence for withholding information. In April 1981 the

Army made it known that Snowball had resigned his commission.

While the 'pitchfork' inquiry was at its zenith, on 11 June 1979, a brief news report written by a highly respected freelance journalist, Ivan McMichael, appeared in BBC news bulletins. It stated that three members of the Argyll and Sutherland Highlanders were being interviewed at Castlereagh police station in Belfast in connection with the murder of a Fermanagh butcher, Louis Leonard, in December 1972. Leonard had been stabbed and shot five times and his body had been found in a fridge in his butchery shop. The report was correct, but the matter was never resolved. To this day, the killing of Leonard, who like Naan and Murray was a Catholic, has remained a bizarre mystery. When Leonard's body was found two nationalist MPs sought to blame the Army but without evidence.

Twenty-six-year-old Louis Leonard was married with a young son and was regarded as a respectable member of the community in Derrylin village in South Fermanagh. The fact that he was also an experienced terrorist remained a well-guarded secret until four years after his death.

On 15 December 1972 he was working late in his shop preparing Christmas orders. At 10.40 pm he was visited by his brother Barry, who was the last person to admit seeing him alive. At 11 pm Louis Leonard's wife Betty arrived outside the shop and found it locked. Leaving the van with the keys in the ignition in an alleyway separating the butcher's premises from another shop, she made her way to a local hotel and enquired if anyone had seen her husband. She was informed that people had been at the shop earlier. Betty Leonard went home to Lisnaskea believing, she claimed, that her husband would find the van and drive it to their house. The following morning she phoned the police and told them her husband was missing. At lunchtime friends of the Leonard family forced entry to the butcher's shop and found Louis's body in a large walk-in fridge. He had been shot five times in the head and chest with .45 and .38 calibre weapons, which would undoubtedly have been handguns, either revolvers or pistols.

Police began to piece together Leonard's movements on the night of 15 December, in particular to discover whether he had been seen after 10.40 pm. According to an eyewitness account, a 'large expensive-looking car' had stopped outside Leonard's shop some time between 10.40 and 11 pm. The eyewitness, a woman, was sitting in a car parked outside a hotel opposite Leonard's shop when she saw a well-dressed man approach the shop and furtively look through a side-window. He then went to his car and drove off after several minutes. Some ten minutes later the car returned and two men stepped out, one of them the same well-dressed man. The eyewitness told police that he constantly rubbed his hands together as if to ward off the coldness of the night; his companion was wearing overalls. The stranger walked to the front door of the shop and the eyewitness remembered having seen them in the company of Louis Leonard and assumed they were friends. She saw the car leave and noticed that the lights in the shop were extinguished. Another female witness also saw a dark-coloured car and two men fitting a similar description. The second witness told police that she saw a man aged about forty who appeared to be working at one of the car wheels because he adopted a 'squatting position' as he approached. His companion, who was in his thirties, walked from Leonard's shop, placed an object in his pocket, locked the door and got into the car. The other man, who was over six foot tall, joined him and the vehicle drove away. This evidence led investigating detectives to the view that Leonard was killed before the two mystery men left the shop.

In March 1973 the police case assumed a more intriguing character with the evidence of new witnesses, some of whom saw lights on in Leonard's shop at 1.30 am on 16 December. This conflicted with earlier evidence from one of the female witnesses who saw the shop in darkness before 11 pm and from Betty Leonard who arrived at the premises at exactly 11 pm to find it locked and with no lights on. One witness testified that a Morris 1100 van matching the description of Louis Leonard's was parked outside the shop at approximately 1.45 am. This was also a curious detail because police found the van in the alleyway on the morning of 16 December in exactly the spot where Betty Leonard said she had left it. Another witness alleged that three men, one of them in a white coat of the type worn by a butcher, were standing in front of Leonard's shop between 1.00 and 1.30 am.

Even though Leonard's father reported that soldiers had photographed Leonard in his shop one week before his death, the case remained a mystery. At the time of the inquest, the one important piece of information about the secret life of Louis Leonard was missing: his membership of the Provisional IRA.

The photographing of Leonard by soldiers is certainly irregular, and may well have been intended as a threat or a warning, or else devised to force him to run, to 'come into the open' and reveal his contacts. As the 'pitchfork inquiry' proved, there were many unanswered questions about military tactics. On the other hand, it could have been a sectarian killing. Post-mortem evidence suggested that Leonard did not struggle, and if the IRA was settling a score Leonard would not have been given an opportunity to resist. However, the IRA theory is a weak one, because the Provos commemorated Leonard after waiting four years to allow for his widow to receive £20,000 compensation from the British government for the unlawful killing of an 'innocent man'.

Since the IRA has never been known to honour someone executed by them, one may speculate that the killers were either Loyalists or soldiers. The Loyalist paramilitaries, the UVF and UDA, never claimed responsibility for the killing, but that would not rule out their involvement. In many instances, they neglect to admit responsibility either to confuse investigating agencies or to shift responsibility, if only temporarily, towards others. The dark-coloured car seen outside Leonard's shop that night was never traced, though there were suggestions that it had a Belfast registration number. There was no hard evidence against the UVF or UDA. However, as I will show later in this book, Loyalist paramilitaries, particularly the UVF, were capable of identifying and executing people such as Leonard.

6

Robert Nairac
Hero or Villain?

The organisation whose activities in Northern Ireland are always shrouded in secrecy and controversy is the Special Air Service Regiment. In the early years of the conflict 10 Downing Street issued frequent denials that the SAS had a role in Northern Ireland, in response to constant accusations by nationalist and Republican politicians that the SAS was secretly stationed in the province with the aim of conducting an assassination campaign. These accusations became part of the IRA propaganda war as the IRA claimed that unsolved murders were the work of SAS patrols. The SAS image of stealth, firepower, aggression and efficient killing power was such that successive British governments were reluctant to admit that the SAS played any role in Northern Ireland for fear that such an admission would tend to support IRA allegations or give added impetus to the criticism of the SAS by nationalist and Republican politicians. It is unthinkable that the SAS should not have been deployed in some capacity in the early 1970s for the simple reason that the British Army found itself fighting a serious urban guerrilla war and a dangerous conflict in border areas such as South Armagh for which regular soldiers were not adequately trained or equipped. The plain fact is that the SAS did have a limited role in Northern Ireland from the early 1970s, and Kitson used SAS personnel to train MRF units. However, after increased violence in 1975 the public clamour in the United Kingdom was so vociferous that the government felt justified in publicly announcing the deployment of the SAS on 7 January 1976. The events of 1975 which strengthened British resolve to use the SAS included a bombing campaign in Britain, the murder in South Armagh of members of a Catholic pop group by the UVF and members of the UDR, and a new campaign of terror by Loyalist paramilitaries in the border area. In January 1976 two incidents finally moved the decision on the SAS to the top of the political agenda: the killing of five Catholics on 4 January and the murder of ten Protestant workmen the following day. These cases of mass murder by paramilitaries on both sides finally convinced the Prime Minister, Harold Wilson, that South Armagh needed to be subdued and the one regiment capable of seeking out the perpetrators of such crimes was the SAS.

Initially only eleven members of the SAS were available to be deployed, but within two months there were sixty SAS soldiers in South Armagh. Their presence in Northern Ireland determined the need for accurate intelligence and, as with all SAS operations, their work was to remain secret. Special intelligence units responsible only to MI5 were established to provide hard information for the SAS. One person who was quickly recognised as someone capable of working with them in South Armagh was a young man with experience in that region as an intelligence operative liaising between military intelligence and Special Branch.

Robert Nairac was born in 1948 and was the youngest of four children to Maurice and Barbara Nairac. Maurice Nairac was a general practitioner and later became an eye surgeon. It would later appear ironic that Maurice was Catholic and his wife Protestant, a division which was mirrored in a society where their son would later become famous and infamous. The family lived initially in the north of England and enjoyed a comfortable middle-class lifestyle. At the age of ten Robert was sent to Gilling Castle preparatory school and one year later to the leading Roman Catholic boarding-school, Ampleforth College, which was presided over by Basil Hume (later Cardinal Hume). In his years at preparatory school and at Ampleforth, Robert Nairac excelled at sports including rugby and boxing and enjoyed outdoor pursuits such as fishing and wildfowling. At Ampleforth he was regarded as a romantic, always acting out a part, perhaps the role of a historical figure with whom he was enamoured at a particular time. One of his tutors felt that young Nairac was insecure, concerned always to 'prove himself' and measure up to figures like T. E. Lawrence. This same tutor later remarked: 'I always expected him to come to a sad end because I always saw a sad end to his nature.'

He tried to excel at all sports but at flyfishing he was a perfectionist. By the time he left Ampleforth for Oxford he was the epitome of the successful schoolboy. At Lincoln College, Oxford, he studied medieval and military history, but created sufficient time away from his studies to enjoy his outdoor pursuits, to the extent that he kept a hawk in his room and occasionally used it for hunting. During his periods at home he tended his collection of animals and birds which included a polecat, ferret, buzzard, kestrel and goshawk.

At Oxford he resurrected the almost defunct boxing club and became a boxing blue; he was also good with his fists outside the ring and enjoyed a 'good punch-up'. Nairac shied away from women, preferring his own company and pursuits or the companionship of men. While at Oxford he joined the Grenadier Guards and completed his finals, not in cap and gown, but in his Army uniform. One of his tutors felt that Robert Nairac showed little sympathy for much in the modern world and believed the Army would engage and realise his romanticism.

After Oxford he undertook a postgraduate course at Sandhurst. During this time he took part in an exercise where he was given a platoon and told to take a hill which was being held by the Gurkhas—who knew from experience to expect an attack from a particular direction. Nairac impressed his superiors by choosing an unorthodox route for a successful attack which involved taking his men through arduous terrain, and proving that he was not foolhardy but took only calculated risks.

In 1973 Lieutenant Robert Nairac was on the streets of Northern Ireland, learning at first hand about a conflict between Catholics and Protestants. Because of his own background, he found it difficult to understand that people of different religions could kill each other. He was a devout Catholic who regularly attended mass as a child and teenager and also, though less frequently, as an adult. When he returned home on leave his parents detected that he was shocked by the bitterness and hatred he encountered in Northern Ireland and the dreadful social conditions in Catholic ghettos such as Ardoyne in North Belfast. Whatever disillusionment he may have felt, his first taste of duty in Belfast did not deter him from seeking out a more daring role in the Irish conflict. He did not need to plead for a change in status because his immediate grasp of the complexities of Northern Ireland and his intellectual and soldiering abilities made him an obvious candidate for undercover work. There has and probably always will be controversy and conflicting claims about the organisation he joined in 1973, after his first six-month tour of duty, but suffice it to record at this stage that it was not regular Army. He was sent to Kenya, where he underwent a lengthy survival course; on his return he told his parents that he had been forced to live off whatever he shot. His mother was convinced that her son was undertaking a military role which was best suited to his talents and ambitions. A colleague who knew him at that time has remarked that the survival course was an ideal test, since Nairac was always looking for ways of assessing himself.

After Kenya he attended a course at Warminster on psychological operations. Finally he was sent to Hereford, now Stirling Lines, where he was trained by members of the SAS in intelligence gathering and 'field-work'. Nairac also spent some time in the Army intelligence wing of the School of Service Intelligence, where he learned about the methods and techniques for collecting information, particularly surveillance, which provides most of the combat intelligence available to commanders in the field.

In April 1975 he received a tankard as a gift from Special Branch colleagues in Armagh; this is the only indication that after his six months as a regular soldier in Belfast he was working with Special Branch. The only members of the forces who worked closely with Special Branch were military intelligence operatives, the SAS and a new grouping, the 14th Intelligence, which was an SAS-trained organisation whose task was to conduct covert operations in certain defined areas of Northern Ireland. The 14th Intelligence comprised 50–100 operatives and was divided into smaller units which used as their cover the bases of regular Army regiments. Robert Nairac was attached to 4 Field Survey Troop of the Royal Engineers stationed at Castledillon in County Armagh. Castledillon is an estate which in 1974 was the base for the Royal Engineers, but there is no official record of 4 Field Survey Troop. However, Roger Freeman, the Parliamentary Under-Secretary of State for the Armed Forces, admitted in 1988 that this survey troop did exist, was formed early in 1973 and was disbanded in late 1975. Freeman also admitted that 4 Field Survey Troop was stationed at Castledillon in 1974–5 but that all documents relating to that period have, as a matter of normal procedure, been destroyed. When Roger Freeman was asked in Parliament for additional information about this survey troop, his reply served only to explain the nature of a normal RE survey troop—namely that its role was to provide or process aerial photographs, ground surveys and maps for the Army as required—and did not answer the specific question about a survey troop which does not appear on the Royal Engineers' list for 1973–5. In fact, smaller units from 14th Intelligence were so disguised solely because of their secretive role and (what has never been admitted) because their operations were run and controlled from London.

A member of RUC Special Branch who met Robert Nairac in 1974–5 observed: 'Robert was a professional and in no respect could he be considered naïve. He was working for a secret organisation which was based in several parts of Northern Ireland. Even on the Castledillon base, he and fellow operatives were housed in separate quarters and no one, I mean no one, was allowed access to their work. They remained apart from ordinary members of the security forces.' This Special Branch officer also described a meeting with Nairac and 'an old man from London', whom I assumed to be Maurice Oldfield or Peter Wright. He said Nairac and this man sought information on the whereabouts of a large IRA explosives dump.

The old man simply stressed the importance of the operation and left. I never saw him again. Robert wanted me to use my major informer even though it might put him at risk. Robert was interested in identifying the dump and booby-trapping it. I told him my informer might just be one of the guys who was sent to take something from the dump. Robert didn't care but I told him to fuck off. I was prepared to do my best to find the dump because we all knew that a lot of stuff had come into Ireland, but if it meant finding the particular dump in my district and risking an informer who had long-term potential, there was no way I was going to do that. Having said that, I had a great respect for Robert's ability, and people who say he was naïve didn't know him. He was good.

Whether Nairac was working for 14th Intelligence or SAS, he was undertaking dangerous tasks, operating in the most violent and potentially risky parts of Northern Ireland in what was known as the 'bandit country' of South Armagh. He spent much of his time out in the field and also liaised with Special Branch personnel and military intelligence operatives. Captain Fred Holroyd, who was a military intelligence agent, met Nairac in South Armagh and was convinced that he was an SAS member. It was not until 1975 that the British government admitted that the SAS were being posted to Northern Ireland. For the previous six years, both Tory and Labour administrations had denied that SAS troops were being deployed in the province. From 1969 onwards nationalist politicians, the nationalist population and the Irish government attributed killings to the SAS, and the 'image of that regiment was of a gung-ho organisation'. It would have been difficult at any time until 1975, when major sectarian atrocities occurred, to justify the use of the SAS in the conflict. After 1975 an admission that SAS personnel had served in Northern Ireland before 1975 would have been tantamount to saying that successive governments had lied. There is no reason why the SAS should not have been used for six years in other guises, such as the Military Reconnaissance Force or 4 Field Survey Troop or, for that matter, the organisation revealed in 1988 to be 14th Intelligence. In some respects, the organisation to which Robert Nairac belonged is irrelevant, in that it is sufficient to recognise that he was an undercover operative. Although Nairac's version of the story is not known, some of his undercover work now seems absurd. He frequented bars in the Republican stronghold of Crossmaglen village in the company of regular Army patrols, though he often carried a double-barrelled shotgun, which was not a normal military weapon. One naturally asks why he sought to draw so much attention to himself. He talked to bar customers and encouraged many of them to believe he was Irish. For example, he told an elderly lady from

Crossmaglen that he was born in Spiddle in Connemara on the west coast of Ireland. Since she herself was born in Connemara, she questioned the young soldier about Spiddle, and he satisfied her curiosity by describing a derelict cottage in a townland known to her. He told another resident that he was from West Meath. In Paddy Short's pub in Crossmaglen he adopted a Belfast accent which fooled many of the customers. Short remembers thinking there was 'something devious' about the young soldier whom he later discovered was Robert Nairac. He also recalls that Nairac claimed to be from the Ardoyne area of North Belfast. Nairac was not averse to singing Republican ballads in the pubs and earned himself the nickname 'Danny Boy'.

Many people have found this dimension to his work particularly risky if not silly. However, in the light of information conveyed to me, I am convinced that Nairac was behaving so differently from other soldiers for a deliberate purpose. By expressing an empathy with everything Irish (such as music), showing a knowledge of the counties, claiming an Irish birthplace and through his singing, he was establishing a political and cultural identity in the hope that disaffected Republicans or Provisionals would recognise him as someone with whom they could communicate. The role he was playing also made him more acceptable in a volatile anti-British area. His period in Crossmaglen afforded him the time and opportunity to talk to people and assess their strengths and weaknesses, and his play-acting made it possible for a British soldier, albeit an intelligence officer (he was now Captain Nairac), to converse with Republicans. It is difficult for those who have not been to areas such as Crossmaglen and other parts of South Armagh to understand that Nairac was subtly and cleverly interrogating people, assessing their potential as informers and possibly providing cover for other spies. Some people in Crossmaglen may have thought him devious but they did not consider him to be an intelligence officer. When he was seen talking to an informer, therefore, it was in the guise of 'Danny Boy' who sings Irish songs and lies about his Irish ancestry. To some extent, Nairac was theatrical and suspended disbelief sufficiently to allow himself space to operate—but at a price. When working outside Crossmaglen he had to be sure that his disguises were professionally applied.

In 1977 Nairac was stationed at Bessbrook Mill, the base for the 1st Battalion of the Worcestershire and Foresters Regiment. His duties were still to provide intelligence for combat forces such as the SAS. His area of operation remained South Armagh, but of particular interest was the district surrounding Drumintee, a hamlet several miles north of the border with the Irish Republic and halfway between the troubled towns of Jonesboro and Forkhill which, with Crossmaglen nearby, represented the most dangerous area for troops, whether they were on foot, in the air or in armoured convoys. It was and remains a part of Northern Ireland where strangers, including journalists, are regarded with suspicion, and where the IRA runs its operations without referral to the Army Council in Dublin or the leadership in Belfast. As one high-ranking Provisional put it: 'In South Armagh they [the IRA] do their own thing. Those guys don't like anyone, including the media. They don't concern themselves with the niceties of politics or propaganda. In fact, they are dangerous and professional. They know their neighbourhood and they run their own war down there.'

The Provisionals in South Armagh possessed some of the most expert bomb-makers within the IRA, and active service units who knew the landscape because they lived there. Their intimacy with the countryside and their support from local people ensured their protection and receipt of information regarding the movements of soldiers and vehicles. According to security forces assessments, the Provisionals regularly carried out spectacular operations within a three-mile radius of Drumintee. These included a landmine explosion which killed four soldiers, two other landmines which killed an Army explosives expert, Captain Gleeson, and a private, and the shooting of a police constable and rifleman.

Captain Robert Nairac was given an intelligence briefing on this area and informed that the Three Steps Inn, which held music sessions, much like Short's pub in Crossmaglen, was a well-known meeting-place for IRA men and sympathisers. Nairac was asked if he could infiltrate the premises—become a regular customer, identify known members of the Provisionals and seek to develop contacts. It was a dangerous mission, but considered to be worth the risk. Unlike other intelligence operatives, Nairac would be working alone. He was capable of mimicking a Portadown accent which could be readily recognised and accepted: he knew the area and was able to voice the sentiments and songs identified with Republicanism. Having practised the techniques in Crossmaglen, he was now more experienced, self-assured and knowledgeable. If he could identify any of the faces in the pub from photographic records of known Provisionals, it would help construct a picture of Drumintee and its inhabitants, including those who were being sheltered.

Nairac's manner of working differed greatly from that of military intelligence operatives in other parts of Northern Ireland. Normally an operative would enter premises such as the Three Steps only if he knew that three days earlier a small back-up team had 'dug in' nearby and that another agent was also on the premises to provide a distraction or immediate protection in the event of danger. However, this method was not suited to South Armagh, where the local population was forever vigilant and supportive of the IRA and more than one stranger in a pub was likely to attract too much attention. Another reason why Nairac worked alone is that his information was used not for regular Army operations but for the SAS, and there were not enough similar operatives available to provide the cover he would normally have required. As with every SAS operation, secrecy is of paramount importance and success depends on few people knowing of plans and objectives. For this reason, Nairac's contacts with Special Branch and military intelligence were kept to a level which required liaison but they were never developed operationally.

At 9.00 pm on Saturday 14 May 1977, Robert Laurence Nairac was in his quarters at Bessbrook Mill preparing for a trip to Drumintee. He put on a shoulder holster, placed his 9mm Browning pistol in it and lifted two magazines. Then he informed Captain David Allan Collett, who was on duty, that he was leaving the base. Collett says Nairac was dressed in civilian clothes and before he left he checked out his Browning pistol and the two magazines. Nairac said he was going to the Three Steps Inn but did not offer an explanation for his visit to the pub, though he said he would return to base at 11.30 pm.

Nairac left Bessbrook Mill at 9.25 pm in a red Triumph car, registration CIB 4253. Twenty-three minutes later he used his radio telephone and his call-sign '48 Oscar' to inform the base operations room that he was en route to Drumintee. Two other calls were received from him at 9.52 and 9.56. At 9.58 he made his last call to indicate that he was closing communications and was at his destination. Did the operations personnel know that this was his second visit to the Three Steps Inn in forty-eight hours? That has never been made clear, but a Drumintee housewife, Kathleen Johnston, saw Nairac in the Three Steps 'on Friday, May 13':

At around 9.00 pm my husband Patrick and I went down to the Three Steps for a drink. A neighbour had a drink too many and kept coming back and forward to us. I have seen a photograph of a man [she identified it as Nairac] and he was sitting on the other side of the steps to the balcony watching the television and his attention was drawn to us because of the actions of this drunken neighbour. The man smiled over at us. Later this man was still at the bar. I saw him go over to the counter. He was acting as if he had lost something. I spoke to him asking if he had mislaid anything and he told me he had lost his cigarettes. He went back and sat down. My husband and I left the pub at about 10.00 pm. As we were leaving the man in the photograph was also leaving. He smiled at us and walked up to his car which was parked at the top of the car park. I saw him open the door of his car but that is all I saw.

Kathleen Johnston saw Nairac twenty-four hours later and recalls that he was singing with the band in the Three Steps.

On the Saturday night the owner of the Three Steps, Desmond McCreesh, was sitting in his Mercedes in the pub car park. He was acting as a security guard and ensuring that patrons parked their vehicles in a proper fashion. He saw a red Triumph Toledo being driven off the

Jonesboro Road and into the top of the car park. The driver parked the car so that it was facing the main road. He then got out of the vehicle and walked into the bar. McCreesh later recalled that the man was dressed in dark clothes, had bushy hair and a moustache. From this description, which was confirmed by other witnesses, Nairac was different in appearance from the man seen in Short's pub in Crossmaglen. McCreesh was so suspicious of strangers because of the risk of car bombs and the fact that licensed premises were targets that he examined Nairac's car.

After this person went into the bar I went up and looked at his car as when I saw it coming into the car park I noticed something unusual about the number plates. When I examined them I discovered that some of the numbers were covered in cement. I looked inside the car and saw a number of cigarette packets lying on the back seat. Both the car and the person driving it were strangers to me. At about 11.30 or so I was sitting in my car listening to the radio when I saw three people go up past my car heading towards the top of the car park. Although it was pretty dark at the time I am fairly sure that these three men were three strangers whom I had seen earlier: that is two boys who got out of a grey-coloured Ford Escort and the person I now know to be the soldier. As they walked past my view, the soldier was slightly in front of the other two, about a couple of feet or so. I sat in my car for another ten minutes or so and I heard or saw nothing outside.

Before considering McCreesh's description of what appears to be a normal scene in a car park, it is necessary also to examine events in the pub before Nairac was witnessed leaving, two or three feet ahead of two strangers. Malachy Locke, who was employed by McCreesh as a farm labourer and part-time barman, later told police he had seen Nairac standing in the middle of the bar, and also remembered serving two strangers. Music was being provided by John Murphy's band from Creggan, Crossmaglen, and a member of the band, Edmund Murphy, vividly recalled Nairac: 'He was in the company of some people. There might have been four or six involved. He went to the toilet about three times. At 11.15 when he was coming out of the toilet, he asked me if a Belfast man could sing a song. I told him to write it down on a piece of paper. He said "no" and I was just to call it out. He gave his name as Danny McElean.' Ten minutes later, Charlie Quinn, another member of the Murphy band, told the assembled drinkers that there was a special request for Danny McElean who had come 'the whole way from Belfast'. Both Quinn and Edmund Murphy were aware that 'Danny McElean' spoke with a Belfast accent. He sang not one but two Republican songs, one of them a favourite in Republican pubs, 'The Broad Black Brimmer'. McElean told the band the key in which he intended to sing and impressed them with his singing ability. After the songs, Nairac, alias Danny McElean, was seen to return to the bar and the company he was with earlier.

The spelling of the name 'McElean' derives from police notes of interviews with several people who were in the Three Steps on 14 May. However, since there is no Catholic name spelt in this way, I believe that the name was probably McErlean and that Robert Nairac was unable to introduce an 'r' sound into his speech sufficiently to imitate the Belfast accent. The tendency of an English person would be almost to erase the 'r' sound in McErlean.

When the band stopped playing, Edmund Murphy accidentally struck Nairac on the head with his guitar and immediately apologised. The incident is important because it establishes that Nairac was in the bar at 11.35, the time remembered by Murphy before he packed up his gear, put it in his van and returned to the bar to be paid by McCreesh. He did not see Nairac but noticed two young men standing outside the bar and they appeared to be 'waiting for someone'. As Murphy was getting into his van several minutes later he heard a scuffle at the top of the car park. There were four or five people involved and he assumed it was an 'ordinary brawl'. McCreesh's account to the police that he saw Nairac leave ahead of two strangers conflicts with Murphy's evidence, since Murphy was in the bar just before midnight being paid by McCreesh and (as I shall reveal later) the brawl at the top of the car park and the two strangers were connected. It is possible that McCreesh was confused about time and perhaps events.

Nairac did not return to Bessbrook Mill at his prearranged time of 11.30, and at 12.05 am Captain David Collett informed his commanding officer that he was concerned for Nairac's safety. This resulted in a secret course of action which involved the use of SAS personnel, and it is likely it entailed an immediate reconnaissance of the Three Steps including the sending of an agent into the pub, which did not lock up until almost 1.00 am. Soldiers were drafted into Drumintee to conduct a search, but the RUC was not informed of the captain's disappearance until 5.45 am. I do not understand the reason for such a delay in communicating the problem to the police, who were equally if not more familiar with the territory. Perhaps there was a wish to conceal the nature of Nairac's work in the expectation that he would arrive back at base within a few hours.

At daylight a search of the car park at the Three Steps revealed Captain Nairac's car. It had a broken mirror and there were bloodstains on the roadway, suggesting that a struggle had taken place. Security forces in the Irish Republic were alerted, and an extensive search was carried out by police and soldiers. On Monday 16 May, the Provisional IRA issued a statement claiming they had executed Captain Nairac: 'We arrested him on Saturday night and executed him after interrogation in which he admitted he was an SAS man. Our intelligence had a number of photographs of him and he was recognised from them.' The IRA statement did not remove the Army's suspicion that Robert Nairac could still be alive and undergoing torture. It was uncharacteristic for the IRA not to leave a corpse on a roadside or at the scene of a shooting as a warning or for propaganda.

The hunt for the captain took a dramatic turn on 18 May, when a Gardai patrol was stopped by two local men a short distance from the Newry/Dundalk border. They handed the Gardai two bullet cases and led them to where they had found them—at a bridge over the river Flurry in Ravensdale Forest. Police found bloodstains in the corner of a field bordering the river and under the parapet of the bridge. There were bloodstains on the grass, silver and copper coins and signs that there had been a struggle.

From this moment co-operation was stepped up by the security authorities on both sides of the border. On 21 May, a week after the captain's disappearance, the Provisionals' newspaper *Republican News* carried a front-page story with the headline 'SAS Captain Executed' and alongside it a photograph of Robert Nairac in his Guards uniform.

The elimination of Nairac is an obvious breakthrough in the war against the Special Air Service. Sources close to the IRA refuse to say how much detailed knowledge they now have of the SAS but they are obviously highly pleased with what Nairac has either given them or confirmed. IRA sources have revealed that Capt. Nairac was a high-ranking SAS officer. When arrested he had in his possession a Browning automatic with two magazines. He pretended he had been in Canada and brought the gun home with him. When arrested, he gave as his identity that of a Republican Clubs' Member; this Stick ['Stick' or 'Stickie' was a term given to a member of the Official IRA by the Provos] identity was broken almost immediately by an IRA Officer. SAS morale must now be shattered as one of their most highranking officers has been arrested, interrogated, executed and has disappeared without a trace.

The IRA were playing a game of nerves, and Nairac's intelligence colleagues had to consider seriously the prospect that he was alive. The absence of a body also forced a decision to halt and even abandon certain operations because of the risk that they were compromised. Those who knew Robert Nairac felt certain that he would not break under torture but the intelligence services had to be sure. Was the IRA hiding the body to create paranoia and force the Army to abandon some of its operations, or did the IRA have in its possession vital information extracted from Captain Nairac? Answers to those questions were required quickly. Meanwhile the Army was busy confusing the media about Captain Nairac's professional role, though Brigadier David Woodford of 3 Infantry Brigade, which covered the South Armagh area, was more forthright, saying that Nairac worked occasionally with the SAS.

Some of the questions were answered towards the end of May with the arrest of twenty-four-year-old Liam Patrick Townson, from Meigh outside

Newry. Townson, the son of an English civil servant, was living in Dundalk and was known to be a Provisional. He was on a security forces suspects list in Northern Ireland and it was as a result of information from Northern Ireland sources that the Gardai picked him up as he sat in a car at a roadblock near the border. Townson was charged with the murder within a matter of days, and on 8 November 1977, with no body on which to base the charge, three judges sitting without a jury in Dublin's Special Criminal Court found Townson guilty of murdering Captain Robert Laurence Nairac. It was only the third recorded case in the Republic's history where no body was found. The conviction was made on the basis of two statements which Townson denied making. In all he made seven statements, but only two were considered admissible as evidence. He was sentenced to penal servitude for life.

The case proved complex, but little was revealed about the life or activities of the victim. Captain Collett told the court that he saw Nairac leave Bessbrook Mill with his Browning pistol and that the pistol (patent no. IT7774) had been specially modified by Nairac. It had a filed-down butt and the normal safety catch had been replaced with a larger one. The holster was of a type designed to allow the weapon to hang under the armpit. Captain Nairac also possessed a personal pistol, which was found in his room after his disappearance. Captain Collett accepted that one was indeed a personal weapon but could not express an opinion about the Browning because service weapon numbers were not disclosed for security reasons. In the Triumph car a powerful microphone was hidden under the seat, the normal radio was adapted for sophisticated communication, and a button on the dashboard was designed to act as an emergency signal for assistance.

The court also heard that Townson had taken Gardai detectives to Ravensdale and in one place had indicated a concealed package containing two guns, one the modified Browning and the other a weapon belonging to himself. At another spot he pointed out a plastic bag containing clothing which he said belonged to Nairac's killers. Among the clothing was a pullover owned by Townson, and under an armpit forensic experts found a strand of hair which matched hairs on a brush belonging to Nairac. There was also blood on the pullover, and the court accepted it as Nairac's blood even though the Army had no record of his blood group.

The defence case was based on the contention that six of the statements had been made under duress and that one was not even in the accused's handwriting. The judges ruled five of the statements inadmissible on the grounds that Townson had been denied constitutional rights during the periods of interrogation. However, what was acceptable was damning and disgusting and helped to resolve some of the awful mystery

surrounding the soldier's disappearance. Townson admitted the murder in
these terms.

I shot the British Captain. He never told us anything. He was a great soldier. I had
been drinking in a pub in Dundalk. Danny O'Rourke came in. He told me to get a bit
of hardware and there was a job to be done. We went down the road in Kevin Crilly's
car. I got my gun, a .32 revolver. I went to the bridge near the road at Ravensdale. I
fired a shot from the gun on the way out to test it. They were all there when I got there
but I don't think young McCoy was there. I had a lot of drink taken. I asked the
Captain who he was and he said he was a stickie. I asked him who he knew and he
said Seamus Murphy from Drumintee. I told him I didn't believe him, that he was a
British Soldier and I had to kill him. I hit him on the head with my fist and then the
butt of my gun. He said: 'You're going to kill me, can I have a Priest?' He was in a
bad state. I aimed at his head. I only put one in him. The gun misfired a few times. I
left the body there and went home across the fields. I don't know where the body is
and that's the truth.

Townson did not have a proper relationship with the truth, and it is
doubtful if his admission fully explains the dirty nature of the final span
of Robert Nairac's life or the whereabouts of his body.

But Townson was only part of the story. North of the border the RUC
relentlessly pursued their inquiries, and one year later five South
Armagh men appeared in court in Belfast charged in connection with the
murder. The case made legal history because it was the first time people
had been tried in a UK court for an offence committed in the Irish
Republic. Three of the men, twenty-one-year-old Gerard Fearon, eighteen-year-old Thomas Morgan and thirty-three-year-old Daniel O'Rourke,
were jointly charged with murder. Michael McCoy, aged twenty, was
charged with kidnapping and Owen Rocks, aged twenty-two, with the
crime of withholding information about the kidnapping of Nairac.

Owen Rocks made a statement which mentioned people who have
been sought by police but never apprehended. He described a conversation with Pat Maguire, Terry McCormick, Kevin Crilly (the man mentioned by Townson as the driver) and O'Rourke. McCormick, according
to Rocks, said: 'We think that fellow at the bar is an SAS man. We're
going to take him outside and give him a good hiding.' Rocks said he
would assist. Ten minutes later Nairac left the bar followed by
McCormick and Maguire and about thirty seconds later by Crilly. Rocks
stated that he knew they were going to take Nairac away in a car. This has
a more serious implication than his initial use of the colloquialism 'hiding', which means a beating. He told police he took no part in what happened and instead accepted a lift from McCoy. On their way home they
overtook a bronze-coloured Cortina which contained about five men and was
travelling slowly. The Cortina was being driven by Crilly, and Townson was
sitting in the front passenger seat:

I think Pat Maguire was in the back because I think I heard his voice. Somebody in the back of the Cortina spoke to McCoy. I didn't hear what was said. I had a good idea what they were up to when I saw Townson with them. I heard someone in the back of the Cortina say to Michael McCoy: 'Do you think this fellow is SAS?' McCoy said he couldn't tell. McCoy then drove off to the Fairways Hotel in Dundalk.

According to Rocks, Townson's appearance alerted him to the intentions of the occupants of the other car, yet he and McCoy were content to go to a hotel for a late-night drink knowing a man was about to be killed.

McCoy told the police he remembered Nairac in the Three Steps because he had black shaggy hair, a moustache and a long black coat. However, McCoy did not subscribe to the 'hiding' or beating theory. He said Rocks instructed him that McCormick and others were going to remove 'the SAS man for questioning' and not to get involved. McCoy remarked that he saw Nairac being beaten by Maguire and McCormick in the car park: 'The man struggled to get up and staggered. I caught hold of him and Maguire and McCormick took him off me. Just then a fellow called Crilly pulled alongside the car park and Maguire and McCormick put him into Crilly's orange-coloured Cortina.' McCoy sought to diminish his role in the abduction of Nairac and offered a curious time-scale, similar to the one claimed by Rocks. McCoy argued that after the abduction he returned to the bar, finished a drink, begged a lift home to Forkhill, where he arrived at his father's home at 11.45 and collected the family car, drove back to the Three Steps, bought petrol and with Rocks aboard headed for Dundalk. On the way there, they passed Crilly's Cortina. Townson was in it and someone in a rear seat said: 'Is that a good job that was done?' McCoy replied: 'It's not a bad job.' He maintained he knew they were referring to the killing of Nairac.

Thomas Morgan, who was accused of murder, implicated not only Rocks and Crilly in the abduction but many others:

The dance band was loading up and about five minutes later I saw McCormick go over to the SAS man and say something to him. The SAS man then walked out of the pub and through the front door, McCormick followed him out. Paddy Maguire followed McCormick. I walked out after McCormick and Maguire and Fearon came with me. Danny O'Rourke and Michael McCoy went out too. Owen Rocks came out with us and Kevin Crilly left the pub too. I knew all these boys were in on it. When I got out I noticed that Paddy Maguire was blocking the space between the Band's mini-bus and the front door so that no one else could get out of the pub. I could see McCormick over at his car taking a red and black scarf and putting it over his face. At this time the SAS man was at the top of the car park. I want to tell you that I didn't scout the road down to the border the way I said before this statement. That was lies. I saw McCormick walk up the car park after the SAS man and after a short time I heard a scuffle and McCormick shouted on us to come up.

In the ensuing fight Captain Nairac dropped his revolver. McCormick warned the others of its existence and searched for it while the majority of the men crowded round the soldier, beat him and restrained him. McCormick found the modified Browning and placed it against the soldier's head with the warning: 'Don't move you fucker or I'll shoot you.' Crilly and Morgan were both told to fetch their cars and, according to Morgan, as he walked towards his car he glimpsed some of the men kicking Nairac and pulling him by the hair. Nairac was eventually forced into Crilly's car with the Browning jammed between his shoulder blades. Two cars left the Three Steps car park. Crilly's bronze Cortina drove off with O'Rourke in the front passenger seat and Nairac in the rear with McCormick and Maguire at either side of him. Morgan followed in his car accompanied by Gerard Fearon. Both vehicles drove to Ravensdale Forest as though by prearrangement and stopped beside the bridge over the river Flurry. Nairac was forced out of the car, and Crilly left with O'Rourke to fetch 'Townson or some of the boys'. This last phrase, used by Morgan during police interrogation, implies that the hit-men, senior IRA figures or what a leading Provisional has since called 'the real IRA', were being summoned, and that Morgan and the others were not Provisionals; the evidence indicates that they were certainly not senior members.

The phrase 'Townson or some of the boys' could also be interpreted to mean that Townson was not one of 'the boys', not a Provisional, since the phrase when used in this context in Ireland invariably means IRA. Though it is a puzzling phrase, my research proved that Townson was in the IRA. One is therefore obliged to conclude that the phrase was intended to indicate a wish that Townson be contacted but that if he was not available some of the other 'boys' in the neighbourhood be summoned. Of all those legally held to be connected with either the abduction or death of Nairac, only Fearon and Townson admitted to IRA membership. My research confirmed that only these two were in the IRA, though I was unable to determine whether Crilly, Maguire and McCormick, who have never been charged, were anything more than Republican sympathisers. There is no evidence that they were in the IRA, and Fearon, who named the other members of the IRA in his area when questioned by police, did not seek to name Crilly, Maguire or McCormick as IRA members, even though they were with him on that night. In the course of examining the death of Nairac I spoke to a high-ranking Provisional; it was he who used the phrase 'the real IRA' and when one contextualises the phrase one is obliged to look closely at those involved in the tragic episode and the manner in which they behaved. The leading Provisional to whom I spoke said: 'It may well be that, after Nairac was executed, the real IRA moved in and took over. They then analysed what happened and dealt with the removal of the body.' This person offered no information aside from this brief comment, which is none the less an interesting remark. The phrase 'real IRA' suggests to me that the abduction and murder of Nairac was not an operation planned by the IRA, even though, as we know, at least two members of the IRA were involved.

McCormick and Maguire appeared always to be in control, and this suggests that they were not merely Republican sympathisers, but it is odd that they sent for Townson, unless they were seeking orders on what course of action to take. If they believed they were in possession of a member of the SAS, then they would have understood his value to the IRA and the requirement to refer the matter upwards. However, while they waited for the arrival of Townson and possibly others, Maguire and McCormick began to question Nairac brutally. Morgan gave an account of what happened: 'I went down into the field and down the side of the bridge. The soldier was sitting on his bottom with his back and head against the wall. He had his hands over his face as if he was trying to save his face. His mouth and nose were bleeding. McCormick was down on one knee beside the SAS man and was asking a lot of questions about who he was and all of that. Fearon and Maguire were standing up and Maguire was pointing the gun at him.'

According to Morgan, Nairac kept telling them he was a member of the Official IRA and offered them a Belfast telephone number which they could use to authenticate his claim. When Maguire took out a cigarette box to write down the number, Nairac seized the opportunity to catch him off-guard. As the soldier struggled to his feet, weak from the beatings, he was again set upon. Morgan told police he 'kicked him in the balls' and when he fell he kicked him repeatedly. Maguire warned Nairac that if he again attempted to escape he would shoot him.

McCormick continued the interrogation. Morgan estimates that by this time they had been in the field beside the bridge for ten minutes and, despite the punishment he received, Nairac 'still had his senses about him'. Morgan told police that he was asked by Maguire to drive Fearon to the Three Steps, pick up Fearon's 3.5 litre Rover, park it outside the Border Inn at Jonesboro and return to Ravensdale. No explanation was ever offered, but from all accounts it took place and when they returned to the bridge they discovered that Nairac had been moved into the middle of the field and Townson was present. He had a gun and was hitting Nairac over the head with it and asking him what he knew of the Official IRA in Dundalk. Because Nairac was claiming to be a member of the Officials from Belfast, Townson insisted that if he was a 'stickie' he would know 'stickies in Dundalk'. Nairac was lying on the ground on his side. Townson was kneeling beside him and kept laughing as he struck the soldier five or six times. Nairac's only defence was to place his hands over his head. The beating continued for over five minutes. Then

Townson got to his feet and told the others he was going to 'take this fella over the fields and shoot him'. He dragged Nairac to his feet and began marching him away from the group. They had only gone a few yards when Townson screamed that the soldier had the gun. Nairac's attempt to escape was futile. He stumbled as he grabbed his pistol but was laid low with a vicious blow from Townson. Maguire picked up a heavy piece of dead wood and beat him over the head. When Maguire stopped hitting him Morgan noticed that Nairac's face and head were saturated with blood. As he lay on the ground Townson pointed the pistol at him. Nairac knew he was about to die and asked that he be allowed the service of a priest to make a final confession. Townson callously told him he had only one minute to ask for absolution and say a prayer. As Nairac mumbled an act of contrition through his battered lips, Townson pointed the gun at his head and pulled the trigger.

As though it was not enough that a man should suffer as Robert Nairac had done, his death was to be much more horrifying. The Browning pistol simply clicked. Townson in a rage shouted at his victim: 'Fuck you, it's only blanks.' He placed the gun closer to Nairac's head and pulled the trigger until it fired, at the fourth attempt. Maguire asked if the soldier was dead and Townson, who remained for a short time looking at his grisly handiwork, replied that he could 'tell by the soldier's eyes' that he was dead.

Civilised people will find it bizarre that Morgan went home and the following morning attended mass at ten o'clock in Dundalk and at eleven in Jonesboro.

O'Rourke admitted accompanying Crilly to Dundalk to bring Nairac's executioner to Ravensdale. He also told police that during a struggle with Nairac in the field McCormick was accidentally shot by Maguire. It was a detail which confirmed the panic that set in each time the injured soldier tried to escape. It also showed how brave and determined Robert Nairac was.

When the police were building their case against the five South Armagh men, they sensed that of all of them Gerald Fearon would prove the most difficult to 'crack'. His initial reaction to the murder inquiry was: 'I know fuck all about it.' However, Detective Sergeant Alan Simpson and Detective Constable Peter Dalton of Crime Squad HQ in Belfast were able interrogators. At first Fearon denied any knowledge of the murder during persistent questioning; then, under pressure, he decided to offer the detectives a small piece of information in an effort to give himself time to think and re-evaluate his dilemma. He said he was with Morgan at the Three Steps on 14 May around closing time and that they took a car and 'scouted the roads to see if the Army was in the area' because someone was going to be 'picked up' at the inn.

Twenty-four hours after this interrogation session had begun, Fearon became more helpful and described the abduction and events in Ravensdale. Unlike his co-accused, he said that Nairac was questioned repeatedly about the SAS despite his maintaining that he was a member of the Official IRA. Nairac's driving licence contained his photograph and an address in the Ardoyne area of Belfast; since McCormick knew Belfast well, he questioned Nairac in detail and decided that he did not know the Ardoyne district as well as he should if he really lived there.

Fearon told his interrogators that he met O'Rourke, Crilly and McCormick in the Border Inn the following day to discuss the killing. They agreed that the victim was either 'an Army man' or a member of the Loyalist Ulster Volunteer Force, but they 'were nearly 100% sure that he was a soldier'. The one detail which puzzled the RUC as well as all the security groupings was the disappearance of the body. Fearon revealed that the meeting at the Border Inn included a discussion about the body.

Detective Sergeant Simpson recorded the following:

We asked Fearon why they had not conveyed the body back into the North directly after the killing and he said they were too afraid of running into Garda or Army Patrols at that time of night. He said that a couple of days later he had again seen either Maguire or McCormick in Jonesboro, he couldn't remember which one it had been, but whichever one it had been, told him that the body had been taken care of. We asked Fearon what he meant by that remark and he said he did not ask the person who had told him this but he assumed that they had meant that the body had been dumped back over in the North. When asked by us, Fearon said he honestly had no idea where the body was but felt it would be somewhere on the Northern side.

Fearon was the only one of the five who admitted and was charged with membership of the IRA as well as with murder. He gave his interrogators the names of other people within his unit, which was within the Provisionals' 3rd Battalion in South Armagh. When asked if he had been involved in bombings and shootings, he smiled, and claimed he had spent only six months in the IRA.

The detectives pressed him about the disappearance of the body and appealed to him to reveal its whereabouts for the sake of the deceased's family. After repeating the conversation in the Border Inn, Fearon remarked that a week later he had heard a rumour that the body had been dumped near Forkhill, where the SAS had shot IRA Staff Captain Peter Cleary, in April 1976.

At the trial of the five men, Fearon and Morgan were convicted of murder and sentenced to withholding information.

To this day the body of Robert Nairac has never been found, and the mystery has generated an abundance of theories. During Townson's trial, his lawyer, Patrick McEntee, the leading criminal advocate in the Republic, argued that Captain Nairac could have been going south to assassinate someone on the night of his abduction or to pay informers: 'Could it be that after the fracas, Captain Nairac made his way back, to be spirited away to safety? There was also the consideration that Townson was drunk, that his gun misfired and he put only one bullet in the victim. Could it have been that they left him there for dead and he stayed there lying dodo?' McEntee's theorising could be forgiven were it not preposterous in the light of the evidence of Townson and the others; Fearon, for example, admits he was told that the body had been 'taken care of'.

I believe the IRA leadership ordered the body to be removed to draw the Army into a game of nerves. Initially it was not known when Nairac died or what information he might have divulged. IRA intelligence decided to sit back and watch how their counterparts in the undercover war reacted, to discover whether any informers in South Armagh would seek protection when they realised their cover could be blown.

That does not answer the question of what happened to the body. Rumours circulated that it had been put through a meat-processing plant, that it had been fed to livestock on a border farm. One theory was that the Provisionals could not reveal the whereabouts of the body because of the appalling injuries to Captain Nairac, since this would be used against them in the propaganda war. Although it is only conjecture, there is every likelihood that initially the body was destroyed, and that this made it impossible for the IRA not only to admit to having moved the body but to reveal its whereabouts to the Nairac family. Because of its Catholic history the IRA were embarrassed by the condemnation of priests who insisted that the Guardsman was entitled to a Christian burial. Considering the manner in which he was executed and the disappearance of the body, the IRA achieved only notoriety by the killing. Many people within the Catholic community who passively supported the IRA felt degraded by the unchristian treatment of the young soldier and of his grieving relatives. Perhaps some day the truth will come out and Robert Nairac will be given the burial he would have wished and his family needs.

A number of factors may have contributed to his death. Primarily, working alone, undercover, in such a small, closely knit community was hazardous. The IRA claimed that they planned his abduction, and various writers have described the murderers and accomplices as members of an IRA unit, but the evidence suggests otherwise. The IRA needed to convince its members in Ireland that it was capable of undermining the enemy and capturing an SAS officer. However, the facts indicate that it was not professionally planned. Police sources in Northern Ireland admit that aside from Fearon, who was an IRA 'lightweight', and Townson, who had to be summoned and who was a hit-man, that Morgan, O'Rourke, Rocks and McCoy were merely Republican sympathisers. The men who were not before the courts, such as McCormick, Crilly and Maguire, were involved with the Provisionals but at that time were on the periphery of the organisation. Someone in the bar that night or the previous night probably recognised 'Danny Boy', as he was known in Crossmaglen. Maybe McCormick sensed something strange about Nairac. It was McCormick who whispered something to Nairac in the bar and who masterminded the abduction. What did McCormick know or suspect, and what was said that enticed Nairac to what appeared to be a meeting in the car park? Did McCormick offer him information and thus trap him, or was it something much more simple such as an invitation to a local house for late-night drinks and good music? We may have an answer to that if McCormick is tracked down, or we may never know. One factor is not in doubt: Nairac's courage and tenacity and, before his death, his simplicity of belief and his acceptance of his death.

Over the years many journalists have described Nairac as naïve. I do not believe he was. I am convinced he was following orders, and any criticism of the events which led to his capture and death must be directed towards the intelligence hierarchy. Many questions need to be answered. Why was Nairac encouraged or permitted to enter a Provo area with an alias which was that of a member of the Official IRA? There was so much enmity between the two organisations that he would have been regarded with suspicion. Why was he allowed to visit a pub whose customers came from a catchment area which included Crossmaglen, where Nairac was known? Surely long hair and a moustache would not have changed the features of a man whom people in Crossmaglen had undoubtedly scrutinised with a view to remembering him. The Three Steps Inn was in a remote part of South Armagh and was not a place where strangers would have gone for a drink. Why allow a good operative to risk life and limb with a weak alias, with no back-up and with a knowledge of Belfast that did not fool his captors? The fact that people thought his name was McElean indicates that he could not pronounce the 'r' in the name McErlean; that would have been noticeable to Republicans suspicious of a stranger who claimed to be from Belfast. In an area so closely knit as South Armagh, most people in the bar on that fateful night would have viewed any outsider with suspicion and hostility. Finally, what was so important that he should have risked his life, or was taking risks his way of seeking exhilaration?

Robert Nairac's mother said the survival course in Kenya was suited to his ambitions and interests. It seems that so also was South Armagh, 'bandit county' as it is termed in the tabloid press. To some his violent death was inevitable. An Oxford don, who was fond of him, also saw another side of his character: 'He was accident prone and when I learned of the nature of his work in Northern Ireland I had a sense of impending tragedy.' Perhaps the most poignant comment about him was made by one of the monks who tutored him at Ampleforth College: 'He would not have been drawn to a conventional war. He was really the SAS-type with fatal flaws and these were his tendency to get emotionally involved and over-recklessness.'

In 1979 he was posthumously awarded the George Cross, and many people thought they had heard the last of the Nairac case, but it was not to be so.

Thomas Morgan was released from prison in 1986, having served nine years of a life sentence. His release was part of a Northern Ireland Office policy to free a number of lifers, though most life sentences in Northern Ireland do not extend much beyond ten to twelve years because of the 50 per cent remission rule which halves all sentences and also reduces life sentences where a judge has not stipulated that life should mean life. One year after his release Morgan was killed when his Vauxhall car was in collision with a concrete mixer on the main Newry to Belfast road.

Gerard Fearon was also freed in accordance with the lifer-release policy in 1985. The terms of his release stipulated that he could be recalled to prison to continue his life sentence if the security forces believed him to be associating with undesirable elements or if he committed a misdemeanour. Daniel O'Rourke served his sentence and was released in 1982. Michael McCoy was freed in December 1979, having served half his sentence, and Rocks was the first of the five to be set free in January 1979.

Kevin Crilly and Pat Maguire have been 'on the run' in the Irish Republic since the murder, and no attempt has been made to have them extradited. Terry McCormick fled to the United States and was last heard of in New Jersey, where he was in trouble with the law for breaking the jaw of a patrolman. Since McCormick, Crilly and Maguire were never interviewed about the abduction and murder, the British authorities have felt that an extradition plea would prove futile. Should any of them return to the United Kingdom, warrants will be issued for their arrest.

Townson has appealed against his sentence without success. Unlike the others, he took part in the murder of a British soldier not merely through IRA involvement but because of a much more deep-seated inadequacy. Townson lived at Meigh, a townland between Newry, Forkhill and Jonesboro. His father was a former British soldier, an Englishman who had spent a tour of duty in Northern Ireland during the war and, like many young soldiers, married a local girl. He liked the place so much that he decided to settle down at Meigh in South Armagh, where he worked as a sanitary inspector for the Department of Health. He was regarded as a respectable family man with a strict and very English attitude to life. Neighbours remember his expressing the view that children were taught too much religion at school, which he felt was intended merely for academic study. Liam Townson grew up with a peer group which, at the beginning of the conflict in 1968–9, would have regarded him as the son of an Englishman. He, for his part, would have been obliged to over-compensate, to express an even greater hatred for everything British than the average Provisional. It would have been a prerequisite to full acceptance by his peers that he denied everything British including the obvious and personal aspects of his life—his father's nationality and history in the British Army. Townson's expression of hatred was fully realised in the brutal torture and execution of an English soldier.

Finally, I believe it is worth returning to the statement I quoted earlier in this chapter that 'the real IRA' appeared on the scene after the murder of Captain Nairac, since I feel it is crucial to an understanding of what happened. With that statement in mind I sought out a leading Provisional in an attempt to clarify further the phrase 'real IRA', and to establish why the IRA had not tried to kidnap and interrogate Nairac in a well-planned operation and whether the IRA believed, as some have alleged, that he was a hit-man. The member of the IRA to whom I spoke offered the following explanation which, if credible, may help to unravel part of the mystery.

Nairac was out in the open. IRA intelligence reckoned that he was possibly a decoy and was there to entice would-be informers to approach him or to draw attention away from someone more important than himself who was operating in the same area. There was also a recognised possibility that he genuinely believed he was in deep cover and that his cover was good enough to fool people. IRA intelligence was content to wait and watch. By the time of the Three Steps Inn episode he was someone who knew the neighbourhood and many of its occupants but he had changed his image from the guy who was seen around Crossmaglen. That would not have fooled the IRA, but he might well have thought that it would. If he was in the business of gathering intelligence, which seems his more likely role, he would have appeared in pubs as he did in the Three Steps and maybe have left a cigarette packet on a table, bar counter or in an ashtray for someone to pick up. Such a cigarette packet would carry information or details of a meeting arranged for him and his contact or informer. On the other hand his informer might meet him in the bar or toilet and pass on a message or leave a cigarette packet or box of matches with intelligence about the IRA contained in it. The fact that he appeared in the pub the night before he was killed and again on the night of his death means that he was meeting someone or being pass information. If there was intelligence on his person that is one reason why the IRA would have moved in to search the body after Townson and the others left the scene. On the night of his death those involved were drinking and were not in possession of the whole picture. They didn't know what IRA intelligence knew, nor did they behave in a manner which would have suggested that they knew his significance. A real intelligence operation would have necessitated Nairac being taken to a safehouse to be interrogated by people who would have been in a position to know what to ask him and how to extract it from him. While Nairac was alive the IRA was content to leave him in the open where they could see him and know what he was up to. He was no use dead. They were not able to watch him every day but would depend on people to let them know where he was seen and who he was talking to. It is a cat-and-mouse game. The real IRA job would not have happened in the way it did at the Three Steps. Those involved didn't know the importance of the person they were abducting. They may have suspected that he was a Brit or maybe a member of the UVF but that was about it. It is likely that when the local IRA intelligence learned what happened and analysed it and examined the body, they realised the identity of the dead man. Maybe they found intelligence material from an informer on the body. They would have known from his Browning pistol that he was SAS-related. It was a special type of weapon that would only be carried by someone special. The IRA probably decided to capitalise on a killing which they had not sanctioned by pretending that he was alive. They couldn't leave the body around indefinitely, so at the outset it was probably decided that if they were going to use the ploy that he might still be alive it was safer to get rid of the body entirely. Only IRA intelligence in that area will know what happened to the body—no one else.

There's been a lot of talk about Nairac but little about the way he operated. He worked in the way SAS people are trained to behave. He was involved, it seems, in an unusual method of intelligence gathering. It follows that he probably had his own contacts and gathered information on which only the SAS acted. The guys who do hits, do hits, but he was someone who probably provided the intelligence on which hits or ambushes of IRA personnel are planned. The only thing which suggests that he may also have been required to shoot people is the presence in his quarters of a personal weapon. That suggests that he was required to do unattributable work, otherwise service-issue weapons would be sufficient. However, his activities bear all the hallmarks of someone engaged in intelligence gathering. He operated with more freedom than Special Branch or Army intelligence would allow. The IRA knows that in the mid-1970s small intelligence-gathering units were established to provide specialist information for the SAS. Nairac worked for one of those units and as such was not responsible to Army intelligence proper but to MI5. He was permitted to operate alone, and the intelligence he acquired did not go through the normal Special Branch/military intelligence channels. The reason is that everything connected with the SAS is highly sensitive and secret and is handled outside normal security channels. That was also the reason why he did not have the back-up which Special Branch or military intelligence officers would require and, as a rule, be given. Therefore, because no one was entitled to know what the SAS were doing, Nairac was operating on the edge without proper back-up protection. Now, that implies that what the SAS were doing, as the IRA knows, was not within the law. The SAS depends on accurate intelligence and people like Nairac were being sent out alone to acquire it. The only thing even the IRA will admit is that he was a brave soldier.

It is noticeable that the comments from that member of the IRA are cautiously interspersed with a number of qualifications. However, two pieces of information appear to break through: that Nairac in the course of gathering intelligence was compromised by a group of people who recognised him as a threat but never fully learned his real identity; and that the IRA became officially involved only after his death. They knew he was involved in intelligence gathering and were prepared to wait and watch. Had they believed he was directly involved in the killing of their members, there was every opportunity before his death for them to have killed him. The IRA never claimed that he was a killer. That allegation was left to a former member of military intelligence.

7

Dirty Tricks and Conspiracies
Holroyd and Wallace

One result of the dirty war has been the emergence of conspiracy theories which have become an integral part of the propaganda war and have been used to great effect by the IRA and other paramilitaries. Ironically those who have shaped the major conspiracy theories have not always been within the ranks of terrorism, and in this chapter I shall be dealing with one such set of theories, how they arose and how much emphasis should be placed on them.

The memory of Captain Nairac remained untarnished until 1984, when a former undercover soldier who knew the murdered captain began to tell his story of events in Northern Ireland in 1974–5. The 'whistle-blower' was Captain Frederick John Holroyd and his story was that Nairac was involved in assassination and sectarian murder. The allegations came to the attention of the investigative journalist Duncan Campbell, who spent six months examining them and discovered that the RUC had conducted an inquiry and produced a 900-page report, which included an analysis of Holroyd's claims. The report was with the Director of Public Prosecutions when Campbell began researching Holroyd's military career in Northern Ireland. He soon discovered that in 1983 the Ministry of Defence had also ordered a secret inquiry into accusations about the dirty war. Campbell's research led to the first public awareness of Holroyd and his allegations, when he published a series of articles in the *New Statesman* magazine dealing with claims of British

Army dirty tricks including kidnap, plots, assassination, forgery and political psychiatry.

Central to the published material was Holroyd's assertion that Nairac had executed a leading IRA man in the Irish Republic. The victim was twenty-seven-year-old John Francis Green, who was, according to Holroyd, a commander of a Provisional IRA battalion in North Armagh. I have spoken to Holroyd, and the story he told Campbell in 1984 has not changed significantly. He says that he met Nairac at the British Army's Mahon Road base in Portadown in County Armagh in January or February 1975. Holroyd was serving as a military intelligence officer attached to J Division of Portadown Special Branch and knew Nairac was working for the SAS. According to Holroyd, Nairac visited him in his quarters and they discussed the murder of Green, whose body was found at a remote farmhouse in the Irish Republic on 10 January 1975. Green was renowned as one of the few IRA personnel to have escaped from Long Kesh (the internment camp later known as the Maze) in 1973. In January 1975 he was on the run from the security forces and in hiding at a farmhouse owned by an elderly Republican sympathiser, Gerry Carville. Although Green was a prominent IRA man, he was not, as some people suggested, an IRA battalion commander.

Holroyd says Nairac told him that he and two SAS colleagues knew where Green was in hiding and travelled one evening to Carville's farm. Nairac and a sergeant-major crept up to the farmhouse and watched Green through an uncurtained window. Then they kicked open the door and shot him repeatedly. When Holroyd expressed amazement at this account of the killing, Nairac responded by producing a polaroid photograph of Green's body. The photograph showed Green lying on his back, blood-spattered. Holroyd adds that Nairac allowed him to keep the photograph and it remained in his possession until 1982, when he gave it to Detective Superintendent George Caskey, who was leading the RUC inquiry into British Army dirty tricks in Northern Ireland. According to Holroyd the RUC later told him that the polaroid photo was taken by Gardai who inspected the murder scene.

Duncan Campbell dismisses this by maintaining he was told by a 'very senior Garda source' that no officer 'had either the equipment or official reason to take such a picture' and that the morning after the murder Gardai photographers took pictures using standard black and white film. Campbell's treatment of Holroyd's allegation implies that details he discovered during his research supported the claim:

Nairac's account of the killing, as provided to Holroyd, is chillingly exact. Irish police investigations produced reports of an unknown vehicle in the area at the time of the killing—a white Mercedes or Audi—which eyewitnesses thought contained three men. Farmer Gerry Carville has told us that for more than a month he had left his farm at the same time each evening to tend to a neighbour's cow…. Garda investigation of the killing confirmed many aspects of Nairac's account. The room in which John Francis Green was shot dead was indeed uncurtained at the time. The front door frame was kicked in and still bears the cracks. Forensic experts, whose reports we have also seen, later established that two guns were used to shoot Green; one is thought to be a Luger, the other a Spanish-made Star pistol.

However, the RUC offered Campbell an alternative theory: that Green was killed by a 'deranged Protestant called Elliott', who believed his brother had been killed by the IRA on Carville's farm and went to the farm with an accomplice to kill Carville, not Green. (Elliott has since died.)

From 1984 onwards there has been a great journalistic debate about these allegations. If one accepts Holroyd had a conversation with Nairac in which they discussed the Green killing, one could validly argue that Nairac might well have been in possession of a considerable amount of detail about the murder, and much of this would have come from forensic examinations and the postmortem report. Army contacts have encouraged journalists to accept that Nairac may have boasted about the killing purely on information he received, and in order to impress Holroyd. Much of the debate has centred on Holroyd's claim that Nairac possessed a polaroid photograph. Campbell believes the photo could only have been taken before the arrival of the police and was most probably taken by the murderer. In fact Nairac may well have given Holroyd a photograph, but one which was taken after police arrived at the murder scene.

When Holroyd first made public his allegations, the polaroid photograph was not available and the RUC were refusing to confirm or deny that they had received one from him. He told selected journalists that the photograph would show a window in the murder room and darkness outside—proving it had been taken at night. Duncan Campbell's argument that the Gardai would not have taken a polaroid does not take account of the way in which professional photographers operate. A professional photographer will take a polaroid photograph of a room to determine the required lighting. In the case of a murder scene, a polaroid may ultimately be valuable evidence if the conventional cameras should be defective. Therefore the Gardai photographers may have taken a series of photographs to ensure a record of the scene should they return to Dublin with film which proved unsatisfactory. If any polaroid photographs were handed over to the RUC, one of them may have found its way into the hands of Robert Nairac.

In September 1987 the journalist David McKittrick, who years earlier had been supportive of Holroyd's claim, wrote in the *Independent* newspaper that he now found inaccuracies in the allegations about Nairac. He turned his attention to the issue of the polaroid:

Mr Holroyd originally said the photograph was not available for inspection, but the Royal Ulster Constabulary obtained it from his ex-wife in Zimbabwe. The Independent has examined the original photograph and obtained a copy. It does not match Mr Holroyd's description of it. There is no window in the picture, and since flash was used, it is unclear whether it was taken in daylight or at night. But it is clear that the photograph was taken many hours after Mr Green's death and not by his killers. The large amount of blood on and around the body is obviously not fresh but congealed. Forensic science evidence indicates that the photograph was taken about 18 hours after the victim's death.

McKittrick added that the Gardai Technical Bureau's photographers had taken the polaroid and circulated it to border Gardai stations, and that a copy had later been sent to the RUC. Holroyd's allegation centred on Nairac, but privately he indicated that one of the two men who accompanied Nairac to the farmhouse was Tony Ball, his superior officer, who has since died.

While researching this book I came across new information which revealed that the real murderers of Green were Loyalists and not Nairac. One of them is a UVF hit-man and the other a senior member of the UDA. Both men are from Portadown and would have been known to Fred Holroyd in 1974–5. One of the killers was involved in the planning of the Miami Showband massacre in 1975 and in numerous sectarian murders. I shall return to them in the next chapter, but suffice it now to record that J Division of the RUC Special Branch and Fred Holroyd had these men under surveillance in 1974–5.

From the moment that Duncan Campbell published Holroyd's allegations until now, the debate has widened and gained momentum. The *Independent* carried a full page of articles aimed at 'unravelling the truth in Ulster's dirty war'. Another article, also written by David McKittrick, dealt with the second major allegation about Captain Nairac, namely that he had been involved in the Miami Showband massacre. Duncan Campbell's research in 1984 established a tenuous connection between Nairac and the Miami Showband murders on the basis that Nairac had killed Green and that bullets taken from Green's body matched bullets removed from a Miami Showband victim. However, Nairac was not involved in either crime, and I shall demonstrate in the next chapter that both crimes had a connection but it was not an Army captain named Nairac. Holroyd should have been in receipt of sufficient hard intelligence to know that the Miami Showband killings were Loyalist-inspired, with an input from several people within the Ulster Defence Regiment.

So why did Holroyd make his allegations about Nairac? Was he encouraged to do so by others, or did his initial claims lead to journalistic overkill which in turn took him on a course from which there was no return? In order to find an answer, one must first ask who is Fred Holroyd and what was his role in Northern Ireland?

Holroyd left Harrogate Grammar School in 1959 and in 1961 became a private in the Royal Horse Artillery. From this lowly status he rose through the ranks and undertook courses in a variety of disciplines such as diving, parachuting, navigation and helicopter handling. He represented to his colleagues the archetypal image of the man who enjoyed soldiering and studying warfare techniques. As the Northern Ireland conflict developed, he was selected for training at the Joint Services Intelligence School at Ashford in Kent. In 1974 he was posted to Northern Ireland and assigned as a captain of a special military intelligence unit to J Division of RUC Special Branch, based in Portadown. His task was initially to maintain surveillance on known members of the IRA and set up contacts within the organisation with a view to recruiting agents (informers), and later to organise surveillance on Loyalist paramilitaries in Portadown and its environs.

Holroyd was an able officer and a fine operative, as evidenced from this citation from RUC Assistant Chief Constable Charles Rodgers:

I found him to be a man of unquestionable loyalty, outstanding courage, with devotion to duty that one looks for but rarely finds today. During the two years he was attached to the RUC, the Force enjoyed a success record against terrorists in my area of Portadown which has not been equalled before or since. It is my considered opinion that the part Capt. Holroyd played made a very significant contribution to our success. His leadership qualities and dedication inspired the men around him. From my long years of experience of dealing with terrorists, I can say that he is exceptionally well-equipped for any Command Position that requires loyalty, courage, dedication and anti-terrorist know-how.

This testimony was repeated on many occasions; the collective wisdom in Special Branch circles was that Captain Holroyd was a man of impeccable judgement and commitment. However, that did not appear to be the Army's opinion of him in May 1975 when he was removed from Northern Ireland with four months of his tour of duty remaining to be served. Holroyd claims he was removed without warning. First he was given a medical examination at Musgrave Park Hospital in Belfast and then he was told to report to an Army hospital in Netley outside Southampton, where he spent a month undergoing psychiatric evaluations. He says he was told his removal from Ulster resulted from complaints made by his wife and her doctor, who made it clear that unless he was sent to an

Army psychiatric unit they would apply legally to have him committed. He maintains he was also told that his wife alleged that he was threatening her with a 'hidden gun', meaning an unattributable personal weapon. Holroyd says he only kept an extra barrel for his service weapon at home.

Duncan Campbell claims he spoke to the woman who was then Holroyd's wife, and she denied having demanded he be committed:

Holroyd's ex-wife and her GP deny the MOD claim that they requested that he be certified. Holroyd's ex-wife says that she merely told another Army wife that her husband was under too much strain in his job and had wanted to return to England with her and their children for a month, to avoid further pressure on their marriage. She had not been threatened with a gun but had merely told his Army Colleagues that he kept his 'unattributable' gun (in fact merely a spare barrel) in the house.

After his stay in the Army hospital, he was told he would not be returning to Northern Ireland. He was offered a job which would not affect his rank or salary and was assured that his record would bear no reference to his mental condition at the time of his departure from Northern Ireland. A Board of Inquiry examined his case at his request, but it failed to recommend that he be allowed to return to active service in Ulster. In 1978 he left the United Kingdom a disillusioned and embittered man who felt the British Army had betrayed him. He was unable to recognise stress in himself and saw the psychiatric evaluation which ended his tour in Northern Ireland as a denial of his ability and of his contribution to the undercover war.

By his own admission, when Holroyd was being moved from Musgrave Park Hospital to the Army's psychiatric unit at Netley he heard someone remark that he was a dangerous man, and he claims he was held under armed guard in Musgrave—much to his disquiet. He believes this period in his life and his departure from the province were part of a conspiracy to remove him from duty in Northern Ireland because he was caught in a conflict between the various arms of security. Holroyd makes a more serious allegation that an attempt was made to ambush him and that it was organised by MI5. This is what he says in his book *War Without Honour* (1989):

The more I thought about it, the more I thought that something strange was going on. Those half joking threats from Brigade; the Brigadier's own personal distaste for me; the conflict of loyalties between the Army and the police, with the Secret Intelligence Service (MI6) acting independently and often against their will...it all seemed to point to some kind of conspiracy. But I realised if I was going to get through this I was going to have to look at it more rationally. I would have to pinpoint how exactly I had left myself open to this treatment and why I should have been targeted. What I wasn't aware of in Musgrave Park was just how far an altogether different body might have been responsible. I just didn't know how ruthless MI5 were prepared to be in their quest to take over the Ulster operation. Certainly an ambush had been set up for Bunny [Dearsley] and myself out at Kilwilkie.

The central point made in this statement by Holroyd is that, while he was working for Army intelligence and MI6, MI5 was taking over in Ulster and prepared not only to have him committed to a psychiatric hospital but to ambush him. Kilwilkie is the name of an estate at Lurgan. Holroyd claims another ambush was planned for him and his colleague but it failed, and further alleges that members of the Army and MI5 conspired to subject him to what he calls 'political psychiatry'. He names so many high-ranking people as part of this conspiracy that one is left with the impression that he must have been a major threat to MI5 interests in Ireland, or was seriously in need of psychiatric treatment. One wonders whether he was also claiming at that time that Nairac was involved in the Green murder and Miami ambush.

The fact that neither the Army nor the intelligence agencies have responded to Holroyd's claims has created a situation where the only way in which many people have been able to assess his allegations is by examining what he has said about himself. If I had not sought to discover that the killers of Green were Loyalists and that Nairac was not involved in the Miami massacre, I too would be left in a situation in which I would be assessing Holroyd's story on the basis of his own statements. It has to be said that the RUC were obviously pleased with his work, though it may also be true that they did not know the exact nature of his work within the Army and whether he was fulfilling his duties in respect of the allegiances he claims to have had. The only evidence that there was a conflict of interest between MI5 and MI6 at the time comes from Holroyd, Colin Wallace and Peter Wright. Even if there was such a conflict, would MI5 have sought to ambush MI6 operatives or single Holroyd out for 'political psychiatry'? There are no obvious answers to any of these questions. Holroyd was, from RUC accounts, a good officer, but he admits that he was under considerable strain in 1974–5. His mother had died of cancer and his father, who also had cancer, spent the remaining months of his life in Northern Ireland under his son's care. Holroyd says it was tragic to watch his father die. If one places both tragedies in the context of his professional life as an undercover soldier, one is obliged to assume that Fred Holroyd must have been under extreme pressure. After his father's death, his marriage began to fall apart and he says that both he and his wife were taking Valium. During the period when all these events were conspiring to place so much strain on his life, he met Nairac. One wonders whether he recognised that the younger man was being groomed to take over from him and whether this later turned to a resentment which culminated in Nairac's becoming part of his bitterness towards the Army and MI5.

His own observations about those last months in Northern Ireland are interesting because they tell us something about the man who was later to destroy Nairac's image:

Through the spring our marriage deteriorated. But just as it had done with dad's illness, this made me throw myself into my work with an even greater commitment, and this of course simply strengthened the downward spiral. By now I was handling the agent known as The Badger in the Republic, liaising with the Special Branch and continuing to provide information to Mr Smellie (MI6) at Lisburn. Whatever happened with my wife, Fiona, I was determined that my work should not be affected. But it was not to be. I came home one night early in May and discovered that I had gone off in the morning without checking if I was being followed and adopting the usual techniques to ensure personal safety. My private life had at last intruded where it did not belong. I had been racking my brains to find some way through the endless bitterness and recrimination and only two days before had gone to a travel agent in Portadown and arranged a break for the whole family in Canada. Afterwards I had visited a jeweller's and bought Fiona a ring. But any peace between us was shortlived. Now I saw that my domestic problems might lead to my actually being killed if I did not act decisively to do something about them. I went in and told Fiona that I could no longer go on as we were and she would have to go home and base herself in England for the rest of my tour. This would not interfere with the Canadian trip but would make sure that the long saga of unhappiness was finally settled. Inevitably a row ensued. We were both at our wits' end.

Holroyd says he and his wife slept in separate rooms that night. The following morning he discovered his wife and children had left the house. At 11.30 a brigade major arrived and, according to Holroyd, said that Fiona was making 'extraordinary allegations' against him: 'The worst implied that I had threatened her and the children with a gun I was keeping in the house. F asked me where the unattributable weapon was and I said there was no such weapon. I had had various weapons there in the past which I had borrowed from the SAS armoury for certain operations but the only gun I had now was my Army issue Walther PPK.' It was after this exchange that Holroyd was taken to Musgrave Park Hospital. Before leaving his house, Holroyd says he was told that his wife's doctor had made a statement that he had threatened Fiona and the children with a gun.

When one examines what subsequently happened to Holroyd, such as his removal from Northern Ireland and his incarceration at Netley, one is easily encouraged to see that he was a man likely to become embittered. As he freely admits, the journey from the battlefield of Ulster to Netley cost him everything he had achieved in his Army career. I believe that in trying to find reasons beyond his obvious suffering from severe stress he was obliged to construct the conspiracy which eventually placed Nairac at the centre of it. Nairac was the man who took over many of Holroyd's duties. Did Nairac try to impress Holroyd when they first met by producing the photograph of Green to indicate how much he knew about the killing and how good his sources were in that part of Northern Ireland? Was that attempt to convince the experienced, hardbitten veteran something that became a twisted memory which served another purpose when Holroyd subsequently embarked on a crusade to clear his name by damning others? In placing before the reader some of these questions, I feel it only right to point out also that Holroyd was a tough veteran and that I do not dismiss everything he has said or written about Northern Ireland but am obliged to look for reasons for his statements about Nairac in the light of new information about the Green murder.

In 1978 Fred Holroyd joined the Rhodesian Army and served for three years, returning to the United Kingdom in 1981 to take up a post with the firm Group 4 (Total Security). Then in 1982 he became security superintendent for Marks & Spencer at Oxford Street in London and remained with the company for a year. By 1983 he was very unsettled. On his return from Rhodesia he worked in several jobs, not remaining in any of them for more than a year. He felt his life could have been much better if he had not been forced to leave the undercover role at which he undoubtedly excelled.

In 1983 allegations were beginning to surface, quietly at first, that Northern Ireland was a theatre for dirty tricks and for factional fighting between MI5 and MI6 in the early to mid-seventies. The source of these allegations was Colin Wallace, a native of Northern Ireland, who was employed by the Ministry of Defence as an information officer when the Army arrived in the province in 1969. Because of his intimate knowledge of Ulster he became an adviser to intelligence chiefs and was constantly sought out by undercover operatives. His work fitted into Kitson's development of counter-insurgency policy, since the gathering of information, its analysis and dissemination, misinformation and black propaganda are essential to psychological operations (psychops) or what used to be termed psychological warfare. Wallace became a central figure in the Army's Information Policy Unit—a bland description of what was essentially part of a psychops unit. In Wallace's own words, in recorded interviews with me, his duties in Northern Ireland included the following activities:

Information Policy activities were carried out at three levels of consciousness. To the press it was a liaison section that provided a link between the Operations Network and the Press Room. At certain levels within the security forces it was seen as a counter-propaganda organisation dealing in white information. It did have a third and totally undeniable role in which black operations popularly known as dirty tricks were used. Being the only unit of its kind in the province, the Information Policy section undertook assignments for other agencies such as the Northern Ireland Office, the RUC, etc., though these organisations were often quite unaware of the fact. The relationship between Information Policy and the other intelligence organisations was quite different in that they were to a great extent conscious of the nature of the unit's work if not of specific activities. Very few members of the intelligence community, other than those directly involved in a particular project, would be told of Information Policy involvement...the relevant activity could then be totally denied if something went wrong. Indeed, the need to know principle was taken to such lengths that I frequently found Information Policy disinformation appearing in intelligence summaries and graded as A 1. As the only indigenous member of Psychological Operations in Northern Ireland I was involved in a wide range of activities and a multitude of disguises.

Wallace claims that he pretended he was a barrister and appeared at the sittings of the Widgery Tribunal which investigated the shooting dead of thirteen civilians by paratroopers in 1972 in what later became known as Bloody Sunday. Holroyd remembers meeting Wallace in Northern Ireland and says Wallace was dressed in a UDR uniform. Holroyd did not talk to him, on the basis that he did not trust the UDR. Wallace says his disguises—his 'covers'—were highly successful:

It is perhaps worth recording that the covers used in connection with Information Policy were highly successful in that almost all of the dirty tricks attributed to the Psy Ops unit by the terrorists and their supporters had nothing whatsoever to do with us. Most of the activities uncovered were freelance or cowboy activities carried out by the brigades or over-enthusiastic individuals without proper clearance or expertise. Basically the main tasks of the Psy Ops unit were:

A. undertake operations which would act as a cohesive factor between the various elements of the security forces and the public...in both Northern Ireland and the rest of the United Kingdom.

B. undertake operations to discredit the paramilitaries and their supporters.

C. undertake operations to cause dissension within the ranks of the terrorists and their supporters.

D. undertake operations which would discredit organisations and individuals who, by their activities, were hindering the work of the security forces.

Wallace rightly says that in the early 1970s intelligence quickly became a growth industry. The result was a great deal of rivalry, confusion and conflict which produced the unlikely situation in which MI6 and MI5, who normally do different jobs, each saw Northern Ireland as their territory. Wallace contends that political events in Britain in 1974 led to the two groupings finding expression in activities which he considered unlawful. Wallace points the finger at MI5 and not the Secret Intelligence Service, MI6, for which he worked:

In the aftermath of the three-day week and the fall of the Heath government various individuals and organisations in Whitehall and its environs became very concerned by what they saw as a growing threat from the left wing of the labour movement. Plans were drawn up to take counter-measures should further industrial unrest or disruption occur. Various key members of the intelligence community past and present, assisted by influential figures in the public service, politics and commerce, produced a series of political and psychological warfare projects.

Those projects, according to Wallace, were designed to prevent the election and re-election of a Labour government, to prevent any coalition between Labour and the Liberals, to collate and disseminate black information which could be used to discredit or control those politicians who were known to hold power behind the scenes in the three major parties and to remove Heath as leader of the Tory Party and replace him with someone who held a harder view on how to cope with political and industrial unrest:

Quite a number of political figures were highly vulnerable on account of their sexual, social or financial activities. The introduction by Labour of the Sexual Offences legislation relating to homosexual offences had, to some extent, reduced the risk of exposure of some Westminster MPs but the changes in the law did not apply to Northern Ireland. The Kincora Boys' Home situation was just one of a number of areas where Ulster politicians were highly vulnerable to exposure and it provided a suitable base from which a disinformation campaign could be mounted. I would stress that the wider concept of this strategy did not become apparent until late 1974 or early 1975 and after I had refused to undertake a project designed to discredit several MPs. It is also true to say that the various Army officers who directed psychological operations in the province from 1969 to 1974 had no knowledge or part of this campaign or at least I have no evidence that they did. The campaign involved a number of activities:

A. information leaked to the press to embarrass the Labour government or to create public hostility to the Labour Party in the run-up to the 1974 general election.

B. the manufacture of false intelligence to influence political policies.

C. the planting of manufactured intelligence to show links between Soviet and other communist agencies and the terrorists.

D. compiling information which could be presented to show that the government's policies were not only hindering the work of the security forces but also putting the lives of troops and police at risk.

Wallace's claims about the use of dirty tricks in Northern Ireland have been accepted by many journalists who were fed false information. I was one of those journalists, and while writing about the overall conflict in the early 1970s, I accepted a story from the Army Press desk which I later discovered was manufactured to discredit the IRA. I did not realise for some time that I had been used. However, Wallace says that, aside from the use of black propaganda to damage the terrorists, the reputations of politicians in Northern Ireland and Great Britain were in danger of being compromised. This allegation is one which is believed by some journalists but dismissed by others.

Wallace also claims that MI5 were aware of a homosexual vice ring operating within the Kincora Boys' Home in East Belfast. He says he was sufficiently concerned about Kincora that he reported the matter to a member of the intelligence staff at Army HQ in Lisburn but it was not dealt with because Kincora was part of an MI5 operation. Wallace says this was cynical manipulation which resulted in the ill-treatment and continued sexual abuse of young boys. The boys' home was run by William McGrath, a notorious homosexual who was the leader of a shadowy paramilitary organisation, Tara. Tara was strongly anti-communist but, ironically, anti-UVF. McGrath was a member of the Orange Order and also a member of Ian Paisley's Free Presbyterian Church. He may well have been in the employ of MI5 from the mid 1960s. He had access to the Loyalist community, and as such was a mine of knowledge about Loyalism and Unionism. He was later prosecuted for homosexual offences at Kincora.

Others who were said to be part of the homosexual ring are now dead. One of them was John McKeague who ran another Loyalist paramilitary organisation, the Red Hand Commandos, which was involved in many sectarian killings. McKeague's organisation attracted many teenage recruits. He was shot and wounded, it is said by the INLA, and was not available to be interviewed about the Kincora affair. Another prominent member of Belfast society, Joss Cardwell, was interviewed but committed suicide in 1983 before the Kincora inquiry was held.

The inquiry concluded that there was no evidence that civil servants, military intelligence or RUC personnel were involved in homosexual activities at the Home or in suppressing information about the happenings in Kincora. Many journalists who covered the inquiry and were aware of the background to it were not convinced by its findings. Colin Wallace was not at the inquiry. He says the Kincora affair was part of another, larger project on which he was asked to work:

Officer A asked me to undertake a project which I later discovered was designed to cause major dissension within the Loyalist leadership and thus avert the Ulster Workers' Council Strike which was being threatened as a means of bringing down the power-sharing executive. I was given a file containing extracts from intelligence reports and other documents from which I was to construct and write in the Ulster idiom two or three personal accounts by non-existent people giving details of the homosexual activities of well-known political figures and to link these activities to other political figures in London. The technique was quite simple in that accurate intelligence was to be reconstructed and collated in such a way that it would appear to be the personal experiences of individuals. The object of the project was to put pressure on key people who might play a vital role in the unrest, particularly those whom intelligence believed had influence or control over the Loyalist paramilitaries. I carried out some work on the project, codenamed Clockwork Orange 2, but after a short time Officer A told me to stop because London had a change of mind and wanted the Ulster Workers' Council Strike to succeed. I later discovered that this new strategy was part of the overall policy to discredit Harold Wilson in that the Sunningdale Agreement was a Conservative initiative and was now being seen to fail under Labour. Also it became clear that during the strike false intelligence assessments were being given to the government so that incorrect decisions were made.

As someone who has studied the events of 1974, I believe the allegations made by Wallace provide a compelling argument to explain the reasons why the strike was allowed to proceed and the power-sharing executive collapsed. The Army was reluctant to intervene when the province was virtually taken over by Loyalist paramilitary organisations such as the UDA. The Cabinet was informed at one stage that the Army was not prepared to remove the barricades or to take over the power stations. The province was brought to a standstill and there was a complete breakdown of law and order, yet the Army, which was there in support of the civil power, did not exercise its muscle. I was told by a high-ranking officer that assessments were presented to Downing Street which suggested that if the Army intervened there would be a situation in which they could not cope, and that they would be left facing two enemies, the IRA and the Loyalists. That, I believe, was not sufficient reason for allowing a takeover of the state and the collapse of the only experiment in the sharing of political power between Catholics and Protestants. There is a suspicion that there may well have been a hidden agenda of which the Wilson government was unaware. Wallace says he became concerned about the work he was being requested to undertake for Clockwork Orange 2 in respect of the two personal accounts he was being asked to produce:

I was supplied with further information which I was to add to the narrative and I was also to produce a third personal account which I was to attribute to a prominent but unidentified political personality. The tone of the new project was very different from that of the previous one in that it was much more political in content and involved a number of Westminster MPs. Kincora featured prominently not because of its importance but because it provided a local story link which could be quickly substantiated by any investigative journalist. Amongst the new information I received was a report from the RUC which indicated that various people associated with Ian Paisley were involved in or aware of the Kincora situation. This report listed a wide range of Loyalist politicians and other personalities and key figures in the Orange Order.

Wallace says he recognised that he was being asked to undertake a black operation without political clearance and that it was directed at elected

Members of Parliament. He claims he was asked by a senior officer to leak the contents of 'another document' about Kincora so that the press would investigate the matter. He refused to continue with Clockwork Orange 2 but leaked 'other Kincora material' which was given to him by an officer at Army HQ.

He told a person whom he refers to as 'Officer A' that he could not continue with the Clockwork Orange project unless he got some form of very high political clearance. Wallace claims that he returned the file on Clockwork Orange and that his refusal to proceed was resented:

Officer A contacted me saying that his superiors were furious that I had refused to go ahead with the project, and said it could be regarded by some that I had withdrawn from the scheme because I was pro-Loyalist and therefore a security risk.

Wallace says another colleague told him that his official telephone was being tapped and that the 'Northern Ireland Office lot were after his blood'.

A few days before Christmas 1975 he was told that he was being moved from Northern Ireland because there was a threat to his life. Wallace was not inclined to accept this; he believed the threat to his life had been a constant one and there was no reason to consider it had increased.

On the day he was due to leave Northern Ireland to take up a posting in Preston he placed a restricted document in the letter-box of *Times* journalist Robert Fisk. He was under surveillance at the time and was later questioned about this leaking of a classified document. In February 1975 he was suspended from duty.

Wallace says MI5 had decided to remove him from Ulster because they could not rely on him to do their dirty work and they were putting their own people into the key jobs in Information Policy.

In June 1975 he was dismissed from the Ministry of Defence and in November of that year he briefed his solicitor about his allegation that he has a scapegoat who was caught in a conflict between the intelligence agencies. In 1976 he wrote to Harold Wilson telling him about dirty tricks and how in 1974 they had been aimed at the Labour government. In 1980 he was sentenced to ten years' imprisonment for the killing of a Sussex antiques dealer, Jonathan Lewis. The court was told that Wallace was infatuated with the victim's wife. Wallace consistently pleaded his innocence.

What Wallace has to say about his time in Northern Ireland is now high on the political agenda throughout Britain and Ireland; it has also created two camps, one which believes that Wallace is telling the truth and that he is a victim of MI5 dirty tricks and the other which says that he has a 'credibility problem'. Wallace admits that his conviction for manslaughter creates such a problem. His detractors also say that anyone

who worked in an intelligence role in Northern Ireland should not necessarily be believed. I personally feel that much of what Wallace says
about the use of dirty tricks is very credible, but that does not mean that
everything he says stands up to scrutiny. Maybe he will be proved right.
Only time and a great deal more investigative work by journalists and
politicians will finally determine how much reliance should be placed
on his claims. If one believes them in part or in their entirety there is
every reason to worry about the ways in which democracy is also compromised by those who should be upholding it. It also serves to illustrate
how a dirty war generates strategies of a dubious nature. In his close association with Holroyd Wallace not only has tended to support Holroy's
allegations but has provided supportive information. It is in this area that
Wallace's credibility may also be tested, though he may seek to distance
himself from Fred Holroyd's claims in the coming year. The parliamentary interest in what Wallace has to say is not extended to the same
degree to Holroyd, who has never had the type of evidence which
Wallace has been able to present. It is on those issues where they overlap
in their testimony that one tends to find discrepancies.

Holroyd and Wallace claim, for instance, that in one week ten grade-
one agents were wiped out by the IRA because of internecine squabbles
generated by MI5. As I revealed in an earlier chapter, a number of agents
including Heatherington and McGrogan were killed by the IRA—but not
ten, and not in one week. The story about the loss of agents initially
struck me as wild exaggeration. The loss of ten agents, I deduced, could
have been related to military intelligence gossip which Holroyd heard
while serving in Portadown. How could ten agents be murdered in one
week, apparently at some time in 1974–5, and escape media attention? I
contacted Holroyd and asked him for exact dates of these killings, but he
was unable to expand the basic claim that this had happened. Other journalists who had read about it have dismissed it or ignored it on the
grounds that the Army would never reveal such a loss of personnel, even
of agents or informers.

I was further intrigued when I discovered the 'sting' which ultimately
led to the execution of Heatherington, McGrogan and others, and I wondered whether those deaths might have resulted in gossip within military
intelligence circles which Holroyd and Wallace translated into a 'loss of
ten grade-one agents'. This seemed possible, since the two events were
connected (albeit loosely): Heatherington and the others were killed during Holroyd's period of service. If I am right—that gossip about the loss
of *some* agents became 'ten'—then there is every reason to examine carefully other claims by both men, because they may have been misled by
just such gossip. I was initially inclined to believe that Holroyd was the

source of this story about the ten agents but Wallace, in a personal account of his time in Northern Ireland, says he was also told by a colleague about these agents. One would expect that both these men, with their wide experience of military matters, would be able to define when and where such a major loss occurred, particularly in one week. I defy them to prove it, because there has never been any evidence to show that such an event occurred.

I think Holroyd did hear about many secret matters but never fully understood their significance. I believe the explanation for the story of the loss of agents is to be found in a related matter which illustrates how Holroyd pieced together information to create conspiracies.

While Holroyd was in Portadown he undoubtedly heard of a teenager, Columba McVeigh, who disappeared in 1975 and has not been seen since. Holroyd told Duncan Campbell what he believed happened to McVeigh, and Campbell investigated the case and wrote about it in the *New Statesman:*

Another of Holroyd's accounts concerns a plan to discover the IRA's major escape route from Belfast for wounded and wanted men. The plan went wrong, resulting in two, and possibly five deaths. Sgt Tony Poole of the Intelligence Corps who worked as a Field Intelligence NCO at the RUC station at Dungannon set up the plan in 1974 and explained it to Holroyd. Poole planned to use a Catholic youth, who had recently been questioned by the Army, as his infiltrator. The hope was that he might finish up at an IRA training camp in the Irish Republic. But Poole's choice of agent was ludicrous. The operation quickly went wrong and his operative, Columba McVeigh, a woolly-headed 17-year-old, went to jail for four months. In February '75 an innocent Protestant man was killed almost certainly as a result of the bungled operation. Three Catholics are believed to have been shot in a tit-for-tat revenge killing.

According to Holroyd's account, Sergeant Poole decided that McVeigh should be encouraged to plant ammunition in his home. The Army would be told to raid the house and find the ammunition, but in advance of the raid McVeigh would escape and seek sanctuary from the IRA. Holroyd says Poole and his fellow operatives were keen to compromise a priest whom they believed was the organiser of an escape route for IRA men fleeing Northern Ireland. McVeigh was given the ammunition and told to conceal it in his bedroom. The house was searched in an early-morning raid, but Columba McVeigh had left the house during the night. When the ammunition was found a warrant was issued for the arrest of the seventeen-year-old.

Holroyd says Poole told him that McVeigh responded to orders and sought shelter from the priest but was rejected. After several days on the run from the police and Army the teenager visited Dungannon RUC station and asked for Poole but was turned away. Within one week of the arms discovery, McVeigh was arrested, charged with possession of ammunition and confined, on remand, to Crumlin Road prison. It was noticeable that at his court hearing he refused to recognise the court in a manner indicative of a member of the IRA.

When Duncan Campbell investigated Holroyd's story, he wrote the following:

The IRA knew that McVeigh had not joined. Inside Crumlin Road he was beaten up by the Provisionals and accused of being a stool pigeon. He confessed his involvement and agreed to give the IRA complete details of his dealings with the Security Forces and a list of names of people working with them. This information was sent out of Crumlin Road in a coded letter. The Army specialists decoded it and showed the list of names to Holroyd. The list the IRA had obtained from McVeigh was nonsense, fabricated in order to escape further beating. At the head of the list of Catholics supposed to be collaborating with the British was a well respected local solicitor and an SDLP politician. At the top of the list of Protestants was the McVeigh family's milkman, a Protestant who lived in the same area as the family. We have also spoken to a public figure in Dungannon who saw the list after it had been sent out and he confirmed that he saw the same names as Holroyd.

In February 1975 a milkman doing relief work on behalf of the McVeigh family's regular milkman was shot dead. Holroyd says that immediately after the event he made an insertion in his notebook indicating that the murder was a case of mistaken identity and that the intended victim was the regular milkman who was at the top of McVeigh's list of Protestant agents.

McVeigh was released from prison several weeks before the shooting. His punishment for possessing ammunition was a suspended prison sentence. Since this did not reflect the seriousness of the offence, the obvious leniency of the sentence was a signal to the IRA that Columba McVeigh had 'friends in high places'. The teenager did not remain in the Dungannon area and left his home in Donaghmore for Dublin, where he lived with his brother. Before the year ended he disappeared, and until now no one has known of his fate. I can reveal that he suffered a similar fate to that of Seamus Wright and Kevin McKee. He was executed and buried secretly in the Irish countryside.

The story told by Holroyd has features of which he was unaware. In Crumlin Road prison McVeigh fell foul of the Heatherington/McGrogan plan which led to paranoia and the mass interrogation of IRA men. McVeigh arrived in prison at a dangerous time and, when questioned repeatedly about the ammunition and how it came to be in his possession, he broke down and revealed his connection with military intelligence. However, for some time after his release the IRA took no action against him because the 'sting' discredited many confessions extracted in the prison. Columba McVeigh probably thought he was safe, as did others. He was not: when the discredited IRA men returned to the streets and reasserted themselves, McVeigh was one of those agents whose death warrant was signed.

Although Holroyd was correct in stating that the IRA assassinated Army agents, the death toll was not ten, and not all of them were 'grade-one' agents, as McVeigh's behaviour clearly shows. He was an IRA volunteer, and according to the IRA his execution was held in secret to spare his family 'public embarrassment'. Holroyd also claimed that McVeigh was part of a plan to discover an IRA escape route and that when the plan backfired this caused the deaths of agents.

In his published account of his life Holroyd again refers to the loss of agents by MI5 and says he was told by an SAS officer who was working for the intelligence services at Lisburn that an NCO in the Intelligence Corps had been running ten different sources in the IRA and had seen them all murdered within a few days of MI5 taking over operations. The officer had responded by going into a bunker and shooting himself in the head because he was made distraught by the news.

Holroyd uses this anecdote to illustrate the alleged incompetence of MI5 in losing ten agents. There is no evidence that ten agents were ever wiped out by the IRA within such a short space of time, and the IRA told me that they regarded this claim with derision. Since Holroyd maintains he was given this information by an SAS officer, one is obliged to ask whether Holroyd was being lied to by a source. On the other hand is it a claim he would have manufactured to reinforce his story about the incompetence of MI5? Or did Holroyd mishear what was being said to him by the SAS officer whom he names in his book? However one chooses to answer these questions, the fact remains that the IRA has never been in a position to wipe out ten agents in such a short period. Such an achievement is not something the IRA would have chosen to hide, since it would have rivalled the killing of a large number of British agents in Dublin by the famous IRA leader, Michael Collins, and his hit-squads in 1920. One is left with the feeling that Holroyd is either capable of rewriting history to support his conspiracy theory concerning his departure from Northern Ireland, or unable to determine when colleagues were telling him the truth, or else unwilling in this instance to recognise that the statement he says was made by the SAS officer does not stand up to scrutiny.

I feel that Holroyd was indeed a man who was highly respected for his undercover work but who may well have been unable to cope with all the other problems in his life at the same time as dealing with terrorism and constantly placing his life on the line. The RUC were impressed with his soldierly qualities, but they were not in a position to recognise the other stresses. It may also be true that once the Army recognised that someone with access to highly classified information was in need of help the decision was taken to remove him from an area where a minor mistake could have cost him and possibly others their lives. I am convinced that his period in Netley and his inability to return to the war front where he believed he functioned best added to his feeling of resentment and isolation. Unlike Colin Wallace, he was in the unique position of not having a criminal record and of being in the front line of a dirty war. It is my contention that Wallace saw the value of having Holroyd as a fellow traveller in seeking to attract media attention to his cause. Holroyd was in a position to reveal much about the intelligence agencies' role in the war. However, he was only one person in the war and therefore unable to offer a 'global' view of it. Holroyd I see as a man who collected scraps of information which he did not always understand and which he often misunderstood. The subsequent dissemination of those scraps in his association with Colin Wallace served to make the dirty war murkier, though it must also be recognised that what they both had to say encouraged a greater scrutiny of particular events and helped indirectly to clarify certain aspects of the conflict.

8

Killers in the Ranks
Loyalist Terror Groups and the Security Forces

The communal violence which tore asunder an already deeply divided society in 1969 exposed the difficulties faced by those responsible for the policing of Northern Ireland. In 1968–9 men within both the RUC and the B Specials not only demonstrated a hatred of the nationalist community but showed exactly where their loyalties lay. This was no more clearly illustrated than in West Belfast, where Loyalist mobs were allowed and even assisted by some members of the RUC and B Specials to burn Catholic homes and loot shops. I remember as a journalist watching policemen stand idly by while Loyalists set alight Catholic-owned business premises in North Belfast. When one makes these observations, people tend to assume one is criticising the entire RUC or B Specials. The degree to which members of both forces colluded with mobs is difficult to quantify. I would say that available evidence indicates there was a small percentage of individuals within both forces who were willing to allow and encourage Loyalist violence and others who were too terrified to be perceived as preventing it. The reason why there has always been a problem is that the RUC, like the B Specials, is essentially composed of men and women from the Protestant community. That is not to say that the force is sectarian but simply that Catholics refuse to join the RUC because they will be immediate and easy IRA targets. There has also been a historical reluctance on the part of Catholics or nationalists to join the RUC, and I am not aware of any number of nationalists ever having joined the B Specials. The RUC has always been a target for Loyalist terrorists in that some seek to join the force; and members of the force, because they originate in the Loyalist community, by default or by design supply Loyalist paramilitaries with information about the other community. Throughout the Troubles members of the RUC have been known to frequent Loyalist clubs and pubs. Other policemen have passed on information about Republicans and members of the IRA to Loyalists in order to seek revenge for the killing of fellow policemen. In a number of instances, as this chapter will show, there have been Loyalist killers in the ranks of the RUC.

The other organisation which has been seriously penetrated by Loyalist terror groups is the Ulster Defence Regiment. Like its predecessor, the B Specials, the UDR comprises men and women from the Protestant community; and like the RUC it has consistently failed to attract more than a small percentage of Catholics because of IRA threats and because of the regiment's reputation as the B Specials under a different name. In 1989 it became clear that the UDR was like a sieve and that intelligence was being leaked by some of its members to Loyalist paramilitaries. The UDR gave Loyalist paramilitaries the opportunity to exploit its intelligence, to obtain military training through membership, and to have greater freedom of movement under the guise of acting in the capacity of members of the security forces. From its birth the UDR did not introduce tight enough controls to ensure that prospective recruits were not members of paramilitary groupings, and the problem was further compounded by the fact that dual membership of the UDR and UDA was acceptable to the military authorities. The UVF, which throughout much of the Troubles has been an illegal organisation, has also exploited membership of the UDR and its potential for widely circulating intelligence files on the nationalist community throughout its ranks.

The history of the UDR is littered with the names of members who have been engaged in terrorism: this alone illustrates how easy it has been for Loyalists to gain access to the regiment. While the RUC does not possess such a history, it has also exercised greater control over its members and stricter security, and has changed its image since 1969. Within the Loyalist community the RUC is now seen as a force which has been used to suppress Loyalist protest, whereas the UDR is regarded by Loyalists as a Protestant force whose purpose is to defend Ulster against the IRA and invasion from the Republic. This Loyalist perception of the UDR is strongly held in areas where Protestants are living close to the

border and where many of them (a large perccentage being members of
the UDR) have been murdered by the IRA. In those areas Protestants will
join the UDR to defend Ulster as though it were a historical duty and to
gain the necessary weaponry to protect their families and homes, since
members of the UDR are entitled to carry personal weapons for their protection because of their military role. However, the UDR is not simply a
full-time force but has a large part-time reserve, and Loyalist groups such
as the UDA and UVF have actively encouraged their members to become
part-timers in the UDR. In this way they obtain weapons, training and
access to files on the nationalist community and IRA, which the
UDA/UVF regard as the greatest threat to Ulster. Membership in turn
guarantees for Loyalist paramilitaries up-to-date knowledge of the whereabouts of security force patrols in areas where the UDA or UVF may want
to transport arms or carry out the murder of Catholics.

In South Armagh the UDA and UVF operate jointly and have made
great use of having members within the Ulster Defence Regiment. The
UVF and UDA believe the real war is being waged in South Armagh
because the Army is under the most intense pressure there. The IRA uses
the border to escape into the Irish Republic, and some of the most experienced IRA bombers and active service volunteers operate in South
Armagh, particularly in the countryside near Crossmaglen, Forkhill and
Newry. Since the UDR has suffered its greatest onslaught in South
Armagh, where Protestants live in small, tightly knit communities and
justifiably feel constantly under threat, this has also created a deep
hatred of the Catholic community which harbours the IRA. Both the outlawed UVF and the legally constituted UDA have used their base in
Portadown to co-ordinate attacks from South Armagh on towns in the
Republic including Dublin itself. The fact that there were killers in the ranks
of both the RUC and the UDR made it possible for them to operate more
effectively within South Armagh and in bombing the centre of Dublin.

On 7 July 1987 Ken Livingstone, the newly elected Labour MP for Brent
East, told a packed House of Commons 'it was likely' that Captain Robert
Nairac organised the killing of three members of the pop group, the
Miami Showband, in 1975. The left-wing MP said the gun used to kill
John Francis Green was also used in the Miami Showband massacre.
Livingstone was basing his allegation on claims made by Fred Holroyd,
and though both these men were making false assertions they did, by
default, draw attention to the murders of the pop group, an event which
fits perfectly into what I regard as the dirty war. The 'Miami massacre',
as it became known in the press, is one example of collusion between
Loyalist paramilitaries and members of the security forces, namely the

Ulster Defence Regiment. Such collusion has frequently been misinterpreted and has led to a widely held belief in the nationalist community
that Loyalist-inspired violence is often masterminded by British military
intelligence in liaison with RUC Special Branch. However, the Miami
massacre best illustrates the degree to which Loyalist terror often
depends on co-operation from dissident UDR personnel and not from
British military intelligence or Special Branch.

In the early hours of 31 July 1975 a minibus containing five musicians
and their equipment made its way out of the mainly Protestant town of
Banbridge in County Down and took the road for Dublin. The musicians
were members of the Miami Showband, which was proving, after thirteen years in showbusiness, that it could still attract large audiences and
stay at the top of the Irish charts. The band comprised six members, but
one of them had left Banbridge in his own car to travel to his home in
Antrim. At a time when the violence in Northern Ireland was severely
limiting the social life of the population, the Miami Showband refused to
be restricted and travelled to the most difficult areas. All the members
were Catholics, some from the Republic of Ireland, where the band was
based. The religious persuasion of the band did not deter them from playing in dance halls in predominantly Protestant towns such as Banbridge,
and for their obvious tolerance and courage the Miami musicians were
highly respected throughout Ireland. The Banbridge gig in the town's
Castle Ballroom was the Miami's first appearance there for over four
years. As the minibus left the town the trumpeter, Brian McCoy, who was
driving the minibus, remarked that it was marvellous to receive such a
warm reception from the Banbridge audience and it illustrated that
Northern dance halls provided the best gigs in Ireland. The band was
tired but knew the journey to Dublin would be swift because of the
absence of traffic on the road.

As the minibus approached Loughbrickland, a few miles from
Banbridge, McCoy noticed a red torch being moved in a circular motion
on the roadway fifty yards ahead of him. As he slowed his vehicle a man
in military uniform used the torch to direct him to park the minibus in a
layby. Believing they were being stopped at a military roadcheck, McCoy
produced his driving licence as a means of identification, but the band were
ordered to leave the minibus and line up with their backs to the side of the
vehicle so that they faced a ditch at the edge of the road.

At this stage ten men in uniform were in the vicinity of the vehicle.
Des McAlea, the band's saxophonist, thought it was a joint UDR/British
Army patrol because he heard an English voice and local accents. The
soldiers were armed with self-loading rifles and sub-machine-guns. Some
wore berets and some did not. McAlea saw a man with a moustache who

was wearing dark glasses and appeared to be the leader of the military patrol. This man demanded that each member of the band give his name and date of birth. McAlea became suspicious because the request was not one he associated with a regular military roadcheck.

McAlea would remember the leader's face because of his aggressiveness and his annoyance with members of his unit who were talking to some of the musicians about the success of the Banbridge gig. Stephen Travers, a guitarist who had joined the band six weeks earlier, was frightened when the band members were asked to place their hands on their heads. He stepped out of the line-up and walked to the rear of the minibus to ensure that several soldiers who were about to search the vehicle did not damage his guitar. He was asked if there were valuables in his guitar case and when he replied that it contained his guitar he received a punch in the back and was told to return to the line-up. The band members were facing the ditch and therefore unable to observe the search of their vehicle.

Then Travers heard a large bang and experienced a searing heat. He felt himself propelled, as if in slow motion, into the ditch. Suddenly events changed and he had a sensation of tremendous speed as he rolled through the ditch. He heard machine-gun fire and someone say: 'C'mon, those bastards are dead. I got them with dum-dums.' He thought dum-dums were blanks because he felt no pain. In fact he had been hit by several bullets, one of them a dum-dum which struck his hip, exploded inside him and exited through his left arm.

Des McAlea was fortunate in escaping such serious injury:

There was an explosion which lifted me off the ground and flung me into the ditch. Then there was a burst of automatic fire. I realised we were in trouble and I stayed as close into the ditch as I could. I remember calling out the names of some of our lads but there was a second burst of fire. I was unconscious for a while and when I came round the wagon was on fire and so was the ditch. The fire was getting so close to me that I had to move. I rolled out on to the grass. I saw Brian McCoy's body and he was dead.

McAlea ran down the main road towards Newry and hitched a lift to the town's police station. When police arrived at the murder scene they were shocked by what they saw. The Miami's lead singer, twenty-nine-year-old Francis 'Fran' O'Toole, was lying over twenty feet from the roadside. His body was riddled with twenty bullets and a pathologist later confirmed that he had probably been shot as he lay on the ground face upwards. Brian McCoy lay dead nearby as did Tony Geraghty, the band's youngest musician, aged twenty-two. He had been shot from behind, some of the wounds indicating that he had also been shot as he collapsed.

His body contained eight bullets. Stephen Travers was found to be alive and was rushed to hospital, where he recovered several months later.

Fifty feet from the front of the burned-out wreck of the minibus police found a man's body blown in two and bearing extensive burn marks. Ninety feet from the rear of the vehicle was another body in a similar condition. Debris from the minibus was scattered over a 100-yard radius and a careful search of the area revealed a sub-machine-gun, a magazine containing .32 rounds, another with 9mm rounds, a .38 pistol, three green berets, a human arm tattooed with the inscription 'UVF Portadown' and a pair of spectacles.

Identification of the mutilated corpses proved easier than police expected. Within twelve hours of the killings, the UVF issued a statement that two of its members, Major Horace Boyle and Lieutenant Wesley Sommerville, had been killed while on patrol:

A UVF patrol led by Major Boyle was suspicious of two vehicles, a minibus and a car parked near the border. Major Boyle ordered his patrol to apprehend the occupants for questioning. As they were being questioned, Major Boyle and Lt Sommerville began to search the minibus. As they began to enter the vehicle, a bomb was detonated and both men were killed outright. At the precise moment of the explosion the patrol came under intense automatic fire from the occupants of the other vehicle. The patrol sergeant immediately ordered fire to be returned. Using self-loading rifles and sub-machine-guns, the patrol returned fire killing three of their attackers and wounding another. The patrol later recovered two Armalite rifles and a pistol. The UVF maintains regular border patrols due to the continued activity of the Provisional IRA. The Mid-Ulster Battalion had been assisting the South Down–South Armagh units since the IRA's Forkhill boobytrap which killed four British soldiers.

Three UVF members are being treated for gunshot wounds after last night but not in hospital.

The UVF statement was cleverly designed to offset public condemnation. It also illustrated a deeper knowledge of the movements of the Miami Showband than might have appeared on a first reading. There were indeed two vehicles on the fateful night. The band's manager left Banbridge ahead of the minibus. That was known to the killers. However, he never stopped his vehicle at any point between Banbridge and Newry. The UVF quickly issued its statement in the knowledge that the bodies of Sommerville and Boyle would indicate that both men were close to the detonation of the explosion which killed them. The statement provided a story which would have fooled many people at a time when the police were in possession of only circumstantial evidence to connect Sommerville and Boyle to the cause of the explosion.

However, police files soon confirmed that Sommerville was a terrorist suspect in 1974, when he was acquitted of being involved in an attack on a Catholic housing estate. The offence involved holding bakery workers captive and driving their bread van packed with explosives into an estate at Coalisland in County Tyrone. What was not immediately apparent to the public in July 1975, though it was to the RUC, was that Sommerville and Boyle were part-time members of the Ulster Defence Regiment, and this equated with the discovery of berets at the murder scene as well as McAlea's eyewitness account of men in military uniform. While Travers recovered slowly in hospital, McAlea provided a description of the leader of the UVF patrol which was circulated to police stations throughout the Portadown/Armagh area. However, it was the seemingly trivial discovery of spectacles at the scene which was to prove crucial. Police asked an optician to examine them in the hope that there might be something about them which would identify their owner. The optician told police that he had 10,000 patients on his files and that this type of spectacles was worn by only one in 500,000.

That provided the breakthrough: a check of the files of opticians in South Armagh turned up a twenty-nine-year-old optical worker, James McDowell. His description fitted that of the man with the moustache and dark glasses whom McAlea believed was the leader of the patrol. On the basis of a tip-off police also arrested twenty-five-year-old Thomas Crozier, who, like McDowell, hailed from the town of Lurgan.

Both men were members of the Ulster Defence Regiment. Under police questioning they refused to reveal the identity of their accomplices but admitted that the explosion was caused by a bomb being planted in the minibus by Sommerville and Boyle. Crozier, a lance-corporal in the 11th Battalion of the UDR stationed at Lurgan, said that on the night of the murders he drove to the grounds of a school in Lurgan and picked up two other men. He then drove to a layby on the Newry-Banbridge dual carriageway and joined five others who were in uniform. They set up a roadblock with all the trappings of a regular military checkpoint. Crozier told police and later a court that he did not play a prominent part in the massacre and he could not reveal the names of his accomplices because to do so would endanger the lives of his family. When asked if he did not regard membership of the UVF and UDR as incompatible, he replied that both were legal organisations. In that respect he was correct, because a ban on the UVF had been lifted early in 1975 by the Secretary of State, Merlyn Rees, and was not reimposed until November 1975. However, membership of the UDR and the other Loyalist terror group, the UDA, has never been declared incompatible: the UDA is not an illegal organisation and joint membership of it and the UDR was declared to be acceptable by a UDR commander, Denis Omerod, in 1972.

The trial of McDowell and Crozier did not reveal the extent of

UVF/UDR liaison, the planning which took place before the Miami massacre or why the band was targeted. In fact the murder of the Miami
Showband was planned weeks before in a house in Portadown. The man
who assumed overall responsibility for the operation was once in the
UDR but is a free man and for legal reasons I shall refer to him as Mr A.
He is known to the security forces and has been questioned about numerous murders and bombings. I can reveal from sources within the UVF
that his reason for choosing the Miami was to use them as a means of getting a bomb into the Republic. The plan was to stop the minibus at the
roadblock and, while the musicians were being questioned with their
backs to the vehicle, for Boyle and Sommerville to plant a bomb under
the driver's seat. The bomb was a 15lb gelignite device with a clock-timer
and was concealed in a briefcase which Mr A knew would slide under
the driver's seat. Should the van be stopped by Irish customs, the bomb
would be sufficiently concealed. The device would be set to explode after
the vehicle crossed the border. Mr A's intention was that not only would
the band members be killed but they would be judged to have been transporting explosives. The result would be tighter controls over all persons
crossing the Irish border and the UVF would have secretly succeeded in
bombing the Irish Republic. Should it ever be discovered that the van had
been stopped at a military checkpoint, the IRA and nationalist politicians
would blame it on the British and not the UVF. The plan went wrong: as
Boyle and Sommerville were priming the device it exploded. McDowell
then gave orders to leave no witnesses. Like his companions, he was not wearing a disguise because the van was to be blown to pieces en route to Dublin.

Another reason for choosing the Miami as a target was the band's high
profile within the community that the UVF wished to discredit. For the
sake of conjecture it is worth examining what is likely to have been said
if the UVF plan had succeeded. Since there were no witnesses to the
roadblock, the immediate conclusion would have been that the bomb had
been placed on board by the band. In England a bomb exploding on a pop
group's van would be immediately understood to be an act of sabotage,
but in Northern Ireland people would conclude that the explosives were
in transit and detonated prematurely because of a faulty timing device or
an uneven road surface. At the time of the massacre, the UVF/UDA were
trying to illustrate that the border was not secure and that explosives
could be easily transported. If the bomb had indeed exploded before the
van reached the border, in a town like Newry people would have speculated about a likely target—for example, an Army post. The suspicion
that a band was 'carrying' the explosives would have led Unionists to feel
justified in arguing that all nationalists were potential terrorists, and it
would have embarrassed the Irish government because the Miami

Showband lived and were based in the Republic. It would also have illustrated the failure of the government of the Republic to recognise that its border was being used by the most unlikely groupings. The deaths of all the band members would also have served as a blow against the Catholic population. It might have led to greater security on the border because of the shockwaves such a deduction would have created. The plan to kill the pop group was a military-style operation which failed because of one error.

Aside from the presence of the four members of the UDR already mentioned there were several other UDR men and at least one non-member of the regiment, thirty-one-year-old James Joseph Sommerville, the brother of the UDR/UVF man who died in the massacre. McDowell, Crozier and James Sommerville were each sentenced to over thirty years' imprisonment for their part in the crime.

Mr A was questioned by the RUC's 'A' Squad of detectives set up to track down the ten-man gang. He was ruled out of the police inquiry because of insufficient evidence and because he was not a man to weaken under police interrogation. Mr A was angry about his arrest and was convinced that there was an informer within UVF ranks. Having decided that the informer was not in the team which formed the bogus roadblock, he turned his attention to those who were involved peripherally with the massacre. In January 1976 he singled out Samuel Fulton Neill from the town of Lurgan, whose car had been used by some of the UVF unit travelling to the checkpoint on the night of the murders. Although he had been interviewed by police, no charges had been preferred; he had told detectives that his car had been stolen—when in fact he had lent it to Crozier knowing that it was to be used in a UVF operation. Mr A ordered his execution in the belief that it was he who had given Crozier's name to the police. As Neill left a pub in Portadown on 25 January, he was shot five times in the head and died instantly.

Another killing connected with the Miami murders was that of a forty-five-year-old part-time UDR captain, Billy Hanna, who had won the Military Medal while serving with the British forces in Korea, and later joined the B Specials and, on their disbandment, the UDR. On the night of 26 July 1975 he drove home from a function in a British Legion Club in Lurgan. As he stepped from his car outside his house two young men walked up to him. He asked: 'What are you playing at?' One of the men produced a pistol, held it to Hanna's temple and pulled the trigger. As Hanna lay on the ground, the gunman acted like a professional assassin, and fired a second bullet into the back of his head. The killer was Mr A and his companion was Horace Boyle. Hanna's wife watched the killing but has been too distressed since then to identify the assassin and his accomplice. Prior to his death, Hanna was under surveillance by members of RUC Special Branch and by the military intelligence officer who replaced Fred Holroyd. It was believed that Hanna was closely connected with UVF operations in South Armagh and that he was intricately involved in assisting the UDA/UVF to plan and co-ordinate the bombing of Dublin and Monaghan in 1974. By 1975 both the UVF and UDA, which often carried out joint operations, were concerned that there was an informer in their midst. Suspicion centred on Hanna, who was trying to distance himself from his terrorist connections. A week before the Miami massacre, Mr A decided that Hanna was a security risk: because a large number of UDR/UVF personnel were to be used in the Miami job, Hanna was in a position to know that the operation was being planned. A decision was therefore made to eradicate the risk by killing him.

The connection between members of the UDR and Loyalism owes much to the history of North Armagh, which cradles Lurgan and Portadown, two towns as tribal, extreme and sectarian in character as any nationalist or Loyalist district of Belfast. North Armagh was one of the first areas after Belfast to see the terrifying results of sectarian conflict between the Catholic and Protestant communities. A carefully planned UVF/UDA raid on the UDR's 11th Battalion barracks in Lurgan on 10 October 1972—when an estimated eighty-three self-loading rifles and twenty-one machine-guns were stolen—provided Loyalist groups with the means to wage armed conflict.

From the outset of the troubles the UVF and UDA encouraged their members to join the UDR not only to acquire weapons training, intelligence about Republicans, and the ability to set up roadblocks which could be used to check constantly on the movements of IRA suspects. They also had another motive: assassination. The intensity of hatred arising from the historical divisions, the proximity of the border and the obvious strength of the IRA in the south of the county made for a bloody conflict. The frequent murders of local Protestant members of the UDR served to fuel sectarianism. On the one hand the IRA tried to justify the murder of UDR men by maintaining they were part of the 'war machine'. On the other hand the Loyalist paramilitaries claimed the murder of innocent Catholics was part of a self-righteous policy of revenge. It is not surprising that the UDR was easily infiltrated when dual membership of a terror group such as the UDA and the UDR was acceptable to the regiment's leadership.

The UDR battalions in County Armagh, the 11th and 8th, were the major infiltration targets for the UVF and UDA, and the result was sectarian murder. Thomas Leonard, a member of the 8th Battalion of the UDR, machine-gunned an elderly Catholic couple on their farm near Cong in County Tyrone. Three weeks after the Miami massacre another bogus roadblock claimed the lives of two Catholics, Sean Farmer and Colum McCartney. The roadblock remained in place on the main Newtownhamilton-Castleblaney road outside Armagh for over an hour. A plain-clothes police patrol passed through it after presenting RUC identity passes. Farmer and McCartney were stopped and shot dead. The area where the shooting took place was within the responsibility of UDR. Crimes connected with the UDR have spanned the whole of Northern Ireland: over 100 members of the regiment have been convicted of serious offences including murder, attempted murder, causing explosions and having explosive substances. Five months after the Miami massacre, Alexander Irwin of the 8th Battalion was gaoled for three years for possession of fuse wire and ammunition—an offence mirrored elsewhere in the province. Another constant problem facing the British Army and RUC were thefts of weapons from UDR bases and from UDR men's homes. It was, however, the involvement of members of the regiment in shootings and cross-border bombings which led to many of the conspiracy theories concerning military intelligence or security services involvement in terrorism. It may also be the case that the evidence that an English accent had been heard at the roadblock before the Miami killings, coupled with the fact that a Star pistol was used in both the Miami and Green murders, led Holroyd and some journalists to conclude that Robert Nairac was present not only at the Carville farm where Green was killed but also at the bogus roadblock where the musicians lost their lives.

It is important to clarify at this juncture some of the controversy surrounding the Star pistol and how this and the hearing of an English accent at the scene of the massacre were later used to connect Nairac, wrongly I contend, to both the Green and the Miami murders. The Star pistol used to kill Brian McCoy at the Miami massacre was the same weapon as that used to shoot Green. Forensic tests established without doubt that this was the case. Mr A used the pistol to shoot Green, and after the murder it was returned to a UVF weapons dump in Portadown. When the Miami murders were planned, weapons were taken from the same dump and one of them was the Star pistol. Its presence at the scene of the Miami killings is significant only in that it connects Mr A with both the execution of Green and the planning of the Miami massacre. Like all terrorist weapons the pistol belonged to a particular unit and was kept within an area controlled by the unit. As such it was available when required unless a battalion commander in the area requested weapons to be transferred from one unit to another. When Holroyd and Wallace began developing the theory that Nairac killed Green, they were later obliged to conclude that he must also have killed McCoy in the Miami massacre. Their reasoning was not simply loose but wrong. Although the

Star pistol was used in both crimes and in the Miami massacre an English accent was heard, it is, to say the least, highly dubious if not absurd to conclude from such superficial factors that Nairac was present at the Miami murders. I was told by a source close to Mr A and another Loyalist hit-man that Nairac was not present at either murder. The source I regard as impeccable, and the other hit-man is in a position to know exactly who was involved in both episodes. He will be referred to later in this chapter as Mr B; he has no reason to protect or damage the image of Robert Nairac and has been accurate about other events which took place in the South Armagh area. For reasons which should be obvious to the reader I am not prepared to name the source, who is known to Mr B but is not a terrorist. Mr B was involved in the murder of Green but says that Mr A pulled the trigger. The arguments of Holroyd and Wallace, irrespective of what I have learned while researching this book, remain unconvincing when one considers the fact that they connect Nairac with the Miami massacre because of an English voice at the scene of the massacre and the Star pistol. I have been unable to discover the identity of the person with the English accent; I am informed, I believe reliably, that it was not a member of the UDR, but that is as much as my source is willing to say on the matter.

If the reader accepts my evidence of the execution of Green it is much easier to understand how such a man could professionally execute Captain Billy Hanna. Mr A maintained control over the majority of major Loyalist terror attacks in South Armagh, forged close links with the UDA in Portadown and was willing to act as a hit-man when he saw fit. He did not confine his activities solely to County Armagh but was prepared to undertake and plan operations in County Antrim. Not only was he in command of men who were members of the UDR; he was also linked to dissidents within the RUC who believed in terrorism. Two other leading UVF officers, C and D, had a contact within the RUC: twenty-five-year-old Constable William McCaughey, a member of the RUC's frontline Special Patrol Group (SPG).

William McCaughey came from a strict Presbyterian background and was raised in a townland close to the village of Ahoghill in County Antrim. His father, Alexander, was an elder in the local Trinity Presbyterian church and, though he was a pillar of respectability, he harboured a deep-seated hatred of Catholics. William inherited his father's bitterness and was known as 'the Protestant boy', a nickname that spanned his youth and adulthood. When he joined the RUC he was obliged to leave home because of his range of duties. In 1975 he was posted to South Armagh. That year he married his wife Angela, they bought a house at Woodlane in Lurgan and had their first child. McCaughey therefore found himself in Lurgan at a time when Mr A was planning a resurgence of Loyalist violence.

He had been in Lurgan only one year when he came into contact with C, who lived in nearby Portadown, and whose history of violence would have been apparent to members of the Special Patrol Group, since they were in the front line in the war against terrorism. McCaughey, however, was riddled with prejudice and saw terrorism as the violence of only one of the communities in Northern Ireland. It was inevitable, therefore, that through mutual contacts in the world of Presbyterianism and Orangeism C and McCaughey should meet and agree that they could serve each other in a joint cause: revenge and retaliation against Catholics for crimes committed by the IRA. The self-righteous, introverted McCaughey saw himself as a politically motivated idealist prepared to kill for God and Ulster. His narrow and intense religious upbringing, allied to his confirmed belief in the righteousness of Protestant Unionism, created a walking time-bomb with all the ingredients which shape terror. To the world at large and his colleagues in the RUC, however, he was a dedicated policeman committed to law and order and the defeat of terrorism. His decision to reside in Lurgan was also significant, because Lurgan and its sister town of Portadown were centres for the planning and execution of Loyalist violence and their proximity to IRA strongholds in the south of County Armagh heightened tension. McCaughey was also working in an area of Northern Ireland which held the greatest risk for soldiers and policeman and generated constant stress in the daily lives of members of the security forces. Members of the SPG were obliged to drive over roads which were constantly mined by the IRA, and this daily confrontation with danger, the deaths and injury of friends and colleagues coalesced to produce a case for retribution in the view of McCaughey and ultimately some of his colleagues.

On 19 April 1977 McCaughey decided to take the law into his own hands after being told about an IRA attack on the police station in his home town of Ahoghill. Although the assault on the station failed, one policeman sustained a gunshot wound to his ankle. McCaughey was incensed that the IRA should choose his birthplace, quickly made enquiries about the incident and was informed of rumours in circulation. Ahoghill being a predominantly Protestant and staunchly Loyalist place, the townspeople had immediately sought a scapegoat. Irrespective of who started the rumour, it suddenly became common currency that the IRA attack had been planned and co-ordinated with the assistance of a local Catholic shopkeeper. Respectable people in Ahoghill did not stop to think that the person who was being singled out for malicious gossip was a man who had lived alongside them for thirteen years. He was William Strathearne, a thirty-nine-year-old father of eight children; this quiet, respectable and inoffensive man was certainly not the type of person to have ever expressed political sentiments which the majority Unionist population in the town would have deemed offensive. McCaughey was told that Strathearne had hidden the IRA gang's guns after the attack and that scarring on his face was due to a premature explosion which had happened while he was a bomb-maker in an earlier IRA campaign.

William Strathearne ran the local VG grocery store and it was a successful business. He was deeply involved in community projects and was a member of the Village Association. He hailed from Bellaghy in County Londonderry and was a well-known Gaelic footballer in his youth. The scarring on his face, which served to heighten rumour after the IRA attack, was caused by an accident sixteen years earlier: while he was working at a car, the petrol tank exploded, killing his brother and leaving him seriously injured for a long time. It was this accident which cut short a promising football career and terminated his ambition to run and own a garage and workshop.

McCaughey knew Strathearne and like other people in Ahoghill he should have been aware that the sudden campaign against him was a tissue of lies. However, he made no attempt to dispel the vicious rumours and instead decided coolly and clinically that Strathearne should be killed. Within twenty-four hours of the Ahoghill incident he sat down with a friend and fellow member of the Special Patrol Group, Sergeant John Oliver Weir, and planned Strathearne's death. Sergeant Weir, aged twenty-nine, was an officer with seven years' experience and five commendations for police work. On the evening of 19 April both policemen met in a pub in Armagh city and McCaughey explained that Strathearne should be killed in revenge for the attack on Ahoghill RUC station. No mention was made of the rumours about Strathearne; McCaughey said that this was to be a sectarian murder as a form of retribution, and that a friend in the UVF who was an experienced assassin would do the actual killing. He had no difficulty in encouraging Weir to be a partner in crime. McCaughey assured his accomplice that there was little risk, since he knew the area around Ahoghill and could ensure that they were not stopped by security forces' patrols.

McCaughey drove Weir to a house in Lurgan to meet C. According to Weir, McCaughey insisted that he remain outside the house until C allowed him to enter the premises. Once in the house Weir discovered that C and McCaughey were not alone. There was a fourth man, whom for legal reasons I shall refer to as D. Although Weir, I believe, knew that D was a UDA leader from Portadown, what he may not have known is that C and D were connected with the killers of John Francis Green and that C was the organiser of many terror operations for the UVF including the Miami massacre.

C and McCaughey agreed that the killing should be carried out that night, and McCaughey outlined his plan. The two policeman and the two known terrorists would travel in separate vehicles, one of them a lorry, to a meeting-place close to Ahoghill. McCaughey said a phone call to certain people, whom he refused to identify, would provide him with the necessary information about security movements in the Ahoghill district. His intention was that the two vehicles would meet at a prearranged time at a roundabout near the town of Moira. McCaughey would then drive behind the lorry to a point about one mile outside Ahoghill. From there he would transport C and D to the village by car and show them where Strathearne lived. After the murder he would return them to their lorry. McCaughey reckoned that by accompanying them to the village he would ensure that, if his car was stopped with Messrs C and D inside, the vehicle and its occupants would not be scrutinised because of his membership of the RUC. He also insisted that Weir should be a passenger in the car so that the presence of two policemen would further establish the car and its occupants as respectable people.

C agreed that the plan was excellent but for one item—the murder weapon. He pointed out that if he and D were to get to Ahoghill and home safely they could not risk carrying the weapon except while in the presence of McCaughey and Weir. McCaughey said that he had an unattributable .45 pistol which was 'clean' and could not be traced. As experienced terrorists Messrs C and D knew exactly what was being conveyed to them by the word 'clean'. The pistol had, in other words, no history of use in terrorist crimes. Forensic examination of bullets removed from the body of a murder victim can determine not only the type of gun used but also whether that gun has been used in previous killings. Accordingly any suspect charged with a murder involving a gun that police know has been employed in previous killings can face charges relating to other crimes. Moreover, when bullets from the victim of an apparently motiveless murder match those used in a crime known to be the work of a particular terrorist organisation, police can attribute responsibility to that organisation. Messrs C and D were therefore reassured by McCaughey's intention to use a clean pistol, which he said he kept at home.

Weir drove McCaughey to his Lurgan home to pick up the gun and then they travelled to the Moira roundabout. Messrs C and D were waiting there in the lorry and transferred to the car, where C was handed the weapon. As they made their way towards the village, McCaughey explained that Messrs C and D would be taken to within 200 yards of Strathearne's home above his grocery store. He would remain with Weir in the car and they would listen to the police radio for any signs of a problem. It was suggested that C should first ring Strathearne's doorbell but be prepared that he might not open the door because it was 2.00 am. In that event, C was to open fire on the door and hurry back to the car. C replied that he would rather 'do the job properly'. He would ring the doorbell and if Strathearne did not appear he would shout to him that his child was sick and he urgently required aspirin for her. C's ploy worked. When he and D rang the doorbell, William Strathearne opened a window above his shop and looked into the street. As soon as they told him they needed aspirin for a sick child, he rushed downstairs and opened the shop door to his killers. C shot him twice in the chest at point-blank range.

Weir and McCaughey drove Messrs C and D to their lorry at the Moira roundabout and waited until the two terrorists had driven off towards Lurgan. The two policemen travelled to the McCaughey farm and disposed of the murder weapon.

On 5 June 1978 McCaughey was again on the trail of revenge and retaliation, this time in County Armagh. That evening the Rock Bar in the predominantly Catholic village of Keady in South Armagh was the target. A bomb was placed against the door of the bar, shots were fired through the windows, and a customer who tried to leave the bar was shot twice in the stomach by McCaughey. The reason why shots were fired through the windows was to keep customers in the bar while the bomb was being detonated so that the explosion could cause maximum damage to the bar and the people trapped inside. Fortunately the bomb, which was composed of 10lb of gelignite, failed to explode, though the detonator ignited.

McCaughey escaped in a car which was later abandoned and set alight. The gun he used in the attack was left in the burning car. What was disturbing about the bomb attack was that McCaughey's accomplices were three members of the RUC's Special Patrol Group stationed in Armagh. They used an official police car to scan the Keady area before and after the attack and with the benefit of a police radio were able to give themselves ample warning of the presence of Army or RUC patrols.

The three were Reserve Constable Laurence McClure, Constable Ian Mitchell and Constable David Wilson. They were later given suspended prison sentences. In an unusual judgement the Lord Chief Justice, Lord Lowry, said he recognised the motive for the attack on the bar and felt the three policemen were misguided, wrong-headed and, above all, unfortunate. Their actions, he said, sprang from a feeling of frustration that ordinary police methods had proved relatively ineffective for combating terrorism in Armagh and elsewhere. However, it should not be thought that he looked lightly on offences committed by members of the RUC. Lord Lowry certainly expected too much from certain nationalist politicians who felt that his remarks tended to detract from what could have been a ghastly massacre at the Rock Bar. They expressed the view that the Lord Chief Justice's comments eroded the seriousness of the crime and exonerated those involved by suggesting that their motivation was one of frustration and not naked prejudice or revenge. Was Lord Lowry more in touch with the records of McClure, Wilson and Mitchell? They, like McCaughey, were highly decorated policemen, and there was no evidence to imply that they had been involved in any other terrorist acts.

Twelve days after the abortive bombing of the Rock Bar, the IRA unleashed a murderous attack on two policemen in South Armagh. One of the policemen, Constable McConnell, was killed instantly but his companion, Constable Turbett, was wounded and taken captive by his attackers. When McCaughey heard that a fellow policeman was being held captive, he felt that the only way of forcing the IRA to release Constable Turbett was to find a means of bargaining with them. He decided to kidnap a well-known Catholic priest and hold him hostage, while making it public that, if the IRA killed their captive, the priest would be executed. McCaughey required an accomplice, and he found one in twenty-five-year-old Sergeant Gary Armstrong of the RUC's Special Patrol Group in South Armagh. McCaughey suggested they kidnap the parish priest in Ahoghill, Father Hugh Murphy, an elderly member of the village community who was highly respected by Protestants. His war record as a padre was common knowledge, and unusually for a Catholic he was a prominent member of the Royal British Legion.

At 7.30 am on 18 June Father Murphy, dressed in pyjamas and dressing-gown, responded to a knocking on the door of the parochial house. He opened the door and was confronted by a man wearing a balaclava mask and carrying a gun. A second man, similarly dressed but without a gun, arrived on the scene and blindfolded Father Murphy before forcing him into the rear seat of a waiting car.

The priest was driven by his kidnappers, McCaughey and Armstrong, to the McCaughey farm, where a hood was placed over his head and he was led into an outhouse. His hands were bound and he was tied to a ring which hung from the wall and was used for shackling cattle. For twenty-four hours McCaughey, with the knowledge of his parents, issued public statements warning of the fate that would befall the priest if Constable Turbett was not released. A massive security forces operation followed the kidnapping of Father Murphy, and the McCaughey farm was one of many in that neighbourhood visited by police and soldiers.

McCaughey senior persuaded his son to let the priest go free. Within forty-eight hours and after numerous public appeals for the release of both the priest and the policeman, Father Murphy was driven from the McCaughey farm, still blindfolded, and released near the house of one of his parishioners. His ordeal was terrifying, but nothing compared to the plight of Constable Turbett, whose bullet-riddled body was found in a derelict farmhouse one week later.

On the basis of excellent detective work, McCaughey and Weir were brought to justice and sentenced to life imprisonment for the murder of Strathearne. Messrs C and D escaped the police net and remain free men. It is unlikely they will ever be charged with the Strathearne murder because Weir and McCaughey will not testify against them and they have not been known to break under interrogation. Sergeant Gary Armstrong walked free from court with a two-year sentence suspended for three years for falsely imprisoning the priest and possessing a gun with intent to kidnap.

Lord Lowry told McCaughey and Armstrong that he understood 'the harrowing compulsion which made them carry out the crime'. They had, he said, been trying to secure the safe return of their colleague, Constable Turbett. Sixty-year-old Alexander McCaughey was also able to walk from the court to freedom with a suspended sentence after he pleaded guilty to hiding the weapon used in the killing of Strathearne and to his involvement in the kidnapping. Lord Lowry told him he understood why he committed the crimes: 'Your real punishment has been to find out what terrible deeds were done and to have first the apprehension and then the grief of knowing the situation in which your son had put himself. I am satisfied you are most unlikely to do this again, that your punishment is greater than anything I could impose on you and that you yielded to the natural temptations that would beset any father in the same position.'

McCaughey went to prison, I believe, with the knowledge of more crimes than those with which he was charged. I say that because of his close association with Mr A, because he was able to acquire guns, explosives and accomplices from within the RUC, and because of an attempt to poison him while he was awaiting trial.

During this time he was also encountering domestic difficulties. His wife, Angela, decided to divorce him after he was arrested in 1978. She said he had assaulted her while she was seven months pregnant with their third child. McCaughey took to reading the Bible while awaiting trial and in 1980 he became a prominent born-again Christian. His wife spoke out publicly in condemnation of him in August 1980, when Cullybackey Apprentice Boys (an Orange institution) unfurled a banner presented to them by the convicted murderer. She told journalists she was disgusted with her husband and with the Apprentice Boys' Cullybackey branch for publicly honouring a man who had murdered an innocent shopkeeper. Angela McCaughey also announced her intention to change her name and those of her children by deed poll. She asked the prison authorities to prevent her husband writing to her and confirmed that he claimed to be reconverted to Christianity and regarded himself as a political prisoner rather than a criminal.

McCaughey, Weir and their accomplices damaged not only their own lives and those of others but the reputation of the RUC and particularly the Special Patrol Group in the minds of nationalists and Republicans. I think it is important to emphasise that this story is about a group of men (and maybe there were others), not about the RUC. After all, it was the RUC which unflinchingly detached them from its midst and prosecuted them. Equally, an analysis of the story of McCaughey and his accomplices dispels certain myths such as those concerning Captain Robert Nairac. However, the damage is incalculable, because McCaughey proved that he could operate with impunity for years. One might ask, for example, how much intelligence he passed to the UVF and UDA.

In 1989 new evidence of collusion between members of the security forces and Loyalist terror groups emerged. It became clear that hundreds of files on members of the IRA, Sinn Fein and people suspected of involvement with both groupings were being given to the UDA and UVF by soldiers, policemen and, particularly, members of the UDR. The UDR appeared to be the organisation most involved, though there were suspicions in journalistic circles that there were probably as many leaks from within the RUC, but, since the police were investigating leaks of intelligence documents, it was in their interests to ensure that the UDR shouldered much of the blame. I do not necessarily subscribe to such a theory but I do accept that it was within the UDR that the UDA and UVF had the majority of their contacts. It was clear by the autumn of 1989, when Deputy Chief Constable Stevens was investigating the security forces in Northern Ireland, that Loyalist terror groups had benefited over the years from help within security forces' ranks. In this realm of the dirty war there is no need for conspiracy theories to explain this aspect of the war. Clearly Loyalist attacks throughout the conflict have been organised in some instances with the assistance of security forces personnel rather than security forces leadership. The fact that such instances can be proven leads to the suspicion at the very least that there may well be other similar incidents which have not yet come to light and at worst leads to a hardening of historical attitudes towards the security forces from within the nationalist community. What is not in dispute is that it was the RUC that investigated and provided the basis for prosecutions in the cases I have outlined. In a dirty war that may not be enough to prevent the inevitable conspiracy theories from emerging.

9

Honeytraps

The arrival of the Provisionals on the scene in 1970 transformed the situation on the streets and ended the honeymoon for British troops who had arrived in August 1969 as defenders of the Catholic population. Events in 1970 changed the manner in which the troops operated and heralded the difficulties they would face in later years. It was in 1970 that the Provisionals began preparing for a war with the British Army— planning arms shipments, training volunteers and moulding their organisation into an urban guerrilla force. The Provisionals' Chief of Staff, Sean MacStiofan, told other members of the Army Council that once units were equipped with modern weaponry the war with the traditional enemy, the British, would begin in earnest. What he really meant was that when the time was right the IRA would start killing soldiers on the streets of Northern Ireland. The IRA campaign in 1970 amounted to bombing commercial targets and the killing of two policemen in a booby-trap explosion close to the border. While the Provisionals busied themselves devising a political language of revolution through the IRA newspaper *Republican News,* a series of events on the streets coalesced to harden attitudes within the Catholic community towards the British Army and to ignite the traditional Republican methods espoused by the Provisionals.

In May the Conservative administration of Edward Heath replaced the Labour government at Westminster and led to a change in military strategy in Northern Ireland. Encouraged by the presence of the Tories in power, the British Army believed the new government would support a change of Army policy from the peacekeeping role to a more assertive one of seeking out the troublemakers in both communities. In June the Army illustrated its willingness to adopt an aggressive posture by dealing harshly with rioters and seeking out IRA weapons. As a result of a tip-off, soldiers entered the Lower Falls area of Belfast on 3 July and in a house search they uncovered a quantity of pistols, a sub-machine-gun and explosives; the weapons belonged to the Official IRA. The seizure led to crowd reaction and within a short time a full-scale riot was in progress. The area was an Official IRA stronghold, and at the height of the disturbance the Provisionals pulled their men out and left the Officials to face the full force of the British Army. In this way the Provos avoided losing what few weapons they had in a confrontation which could only end in disaster. As the Officials engaged the troops, the narrow streets of the Lower Falls became a battleground, with guns being fired and grenades thrown. The rioting began at 6.00 pm and within four hours, as the area was shrouded in CS gas, the Army general, Sir Ian Freeland, placed a curfew on the area. The general later explained it was not in fact a curfew but merely a 'movement restriction on the population of that area for their own safety and the safety of the soldiers'. His decision also had the effect of clearing the area of the media. Those few journalists who were unable to avoid the imposition of the curfew were arrested and charged with breaking the curfew order, though the charges were later dropped. However, without the media there to observe their activities soldiers undertook a search operation which went beyond the rules of normal Army conduct. Hundreds of homes were damaged and several pubs and business premises were looted. The search did yield a massive quantity of weapons, ammunition and explosives, but it also allowed soldiers to behave with reckless abandon and thereby served to signal a change in Army strategy. Four people were shot dead, one man was killed when he was hit by an armoured personnel carrier, and sixty people were injured, fifteen of them soldiers. The Army were judged by many nationalist politicians to have overreacted. The quantity of CS gas, 1600 canisters, was considered to be excessive in a small area which housed a lot of elderly people and children.

The Provisionals, who were suspected of starting much of the trouble, benefited from the outcome. That episode and others where the Provisionals were the instigators in 1970 fuelled a resentment towards the Army within Catholic areas and reinforced the Provisional IRA philosophy that the soldiers were the traditional enemies of the nationalist population. Some observers saw the Army's developing role of aggression as a policy of attrition in keeping with the thoughts of Brigadier Frank Kitson, who believed that riots provided the ideal opportunity for seeking out and arresting the extremists. By the end of 1970 the Provisionals were ready for their own war of attrition. As the Army was announcing that rioters were liable to be shot, the Provisionals were planning to kill soldiers but not during riots. The Provisionals had learned one important lesson from the Lower Falls curfew: that the British Army was a formidable enemy in open warfare. Some IRA members decided that other methods were required to kill soldiers. Those Provisionals who decided to devise new and what would eventually be considered dirty tactics were influenced in their thinking by the volunteers in Cumann na mBann, the female wing of the IRA.

The role of women in the shadowy world of espionage and terror has been depicted in novels and movies as glamorous and deadly. In reality that imagery holds certain truths, but in the world of terrorism women tend to be more deadly than glamorous. Exceptions to the rule have been the Irish terrorist Maria Maguire, who was in the headlines in the early 1970s as a pretty, miniskirted gunrunner, and Leila Khaled, the first female hijacker, whose smouldering attractiveness made her a Palestinian pin-up.

The IRA always recognised the deadly capabilities of its female members but traditionally refused to permit girls and women to play a prominent role in the expression and execution of terror. The supportive role of women in IRA history until 1971 mirrored the role of women in Irish society. The male adopted the dominant, overt role, while the female was subservient. Women were only allowed to act as couriers or to help move guns and explosives. It was unthinkable to the IRA that women should be in the front line of the war killing soldiers. The image of Leila Khaled hijacking a plane over London on 6 September 1970 may well have been a signal to the Provisionals that the time had come for women to play a prominent role in guerrilla warfare. It was also a time when well-educated young women such as the Price sisters were joining the Provisionals and asserting their right to be at the forefront of the conflict. It was younger women within the IRA who recognised that the 'honeytrap', the use of sexual entrapment, was a way of luring soldiers to their deaths. Such a tactic would never have been contemplated by the IRA in other decades, but by the end of 1970 and the beginning of 1971 there were younger IRA commanders who were prepared to consider any tactic which would deliver soldiers to their deaths. These younger elements were not rooted in the old Catholic IRA tradition and their hatred of the British Army was so intense that it disposed of previous IRA principles and tactics. A new type of war was taking shape. There was a great deal of bitterness within the minds of many young people—resentment of a system which the British had kept in place for fifty years, anger against soldiers who were behaving with heavy-handedness towards the Catholic population, and a general feeling that the Provisionals were right in maintaining that the Army was in place to deal with only one section of the population, the nationalists. The Provisionals opened up old historical wounds, and no one in military or political circles had the foresight to realise what was happening or to seek to develop a different military or political strategy to counter the rise of romantic nationalism. Kitson did recognise one of the difficulties facing the Army: that the Protestant population was always 'leaning on us' to do something about the Republicans.

In this atmosphere the IRA began planning the murder of off-duty soldiers. The British Army had failed to learn the lessons of Palestine and allowed young soldiers to drink while off-duty in pubs in Belfast city centre and in town centres such as Lisburn. Cumann na mBann argued that soldiers were easily identified because of their regular Army hairstyles and they were vulnerable because they were unarmed. The proposal made to the IRA was that the soldiers could be lured from bars by the offer of sex, and then taken to a convenient place and shot.

On 9 March 1971 three young Scotsmen from the Royal Highland Fusiliers decided to spend an off-duty day in Belfast city centre. Two of the soldiers, seventeen-year-old John McCaig and his brother Joseph, aged eighteen, were new to Army life and on their first tour of duty. They knew little of the background to the conflict in Northern Ireland and did not regard themselves as being at risk. Another member of their unit, twenty-three-year-old Dougald McCaughey, agreed to join them on a pub crawl to alleviate their boredom and to seek out female companionship. At that time the city centre had not yet become a target for bombers and a nightly haunt of sectarian assassins, and it was regarded as a neutral area of Belfast which offered a lively nightlife. The three young Scotsmen were based at Girdwood Barracks on Belfast's Antrim Road, half a mile from the city's main shopping precinct.

On 9 March the McCaig brothers from Ayr and McCaughey from Glasgow travelled into town in much the same way as they did in their home towns. They were casually dressed, and aside from their accents and short hairstyles they did not appear at first sight to be off-duty soldiers. They visited several bars in the vicinity of High Street and Royal Avenue and in one of them they were singled out for attention by two female IRA volunteers in their early twenties who were searching bars for soldiers. On that day there were many off-duty soldiers in town, and one can only speculate that the youth and demeanour of the teenage McCaigs suggested that they were vulnerable. Until now it was always believed that IRA men apprehended the three soldiers, but that is not true. The female terrorists followed the three soldiers to Mooney's Bar in Cornmarket and befriended them there; doubtless they chose their moment to approach the soldiers after a considerable quantity of alcohol had been consumed. At some stage in the evening, one of the women made a prearranged phone call to an IRA safe-house in Ardoyne and confirmed that a car and assistance were required. A short time later, three men from the IRA's 3rd Battalion arrived in Mooney's. The two women welcomed them as friends and introduced them to the soldiers. The three IRA men were from Ardoyne. One of them was Paddy McAdorey, who was shot dead by the Army later that year. Another man, whom I cannot name for legal reasons, is, I believe, living in the Irish Republic and was known as a professional killer who bragged about his exploits. However, to the young soldiers the IRA men must have appeared pleasant and friendly.

As the evening progressed, the soldiers became intoxicated and the IRA women invited them to a party which they said was being held on the outskirts of Belfast. The IRA men said they had two cars and they would drive everyone there. As closing time approached the IRA team and the soldiers left the bar. McCaughey and the McCaig brothers followed, carrying their pint beer glasses, and walked to a nearby street where the IRA team had left two cars. The IRA leader and the two women got into one car and the other IRA men and the three soldiers climbed into the other. The vehicle carrying the women contained two weapons. It was driven towards North Belfast and the Crumlin Road while the other car travelled behind at a short distance. Both cars proceeded countrywards and left the city limits. On the Hightown Road the first vehicle came to a halt when the car behind sounded its horn. The IRA leader left his vehicle and was told by his accomplices that the three Scotsmen needed to urinate. The soldiers left the car, each of them with a beer glass in one hand, and began to urinate at a ditch by the roadside. At this stage the IRA men took the guns from the first vehicle. Joseph McCaig was shot three times through the back of the head. His brother was struck with the butt of a pistol and shot twice in the head. McCaughey was shot once through the back of the head.

It was a professional execution which shocked Catholics as well as Protestants in Ireland. To the Army it was a warning that was not fully heeded. Since it was believed that the soldiers had been picked up by IRA men, the IRA could use the same ploy again. No one was ever charged with the killings. The IRA leader was one of the toughest and most infamous IRA men in the Ardoyne district, and regarded by the Army as a hardened terrorist. His accomplices left Northern Ireland for the safety of the Irish Republic in the mid-seventies. One of them was a ruthless killer who enjoyed killing at close quarters and who shot a policeman at point-blank range with a carbine before fleeing to the Republic. As I mentioned in chapter 2, the names of the three killers were made known to the Army in 1972 by the SDLP councillor Paddy Wilson; his revelation was made to a masseuse in an Antrim Road massage parlour and tape-recorded by Army intelligence, who were running their own honeytrap as part of the MRF operations.

The Army's failure to discover the role of IRA women in the soldiers' deaths and their reluctance to curtail the off-duty activities of soldiers was to have fatal consequences. As a result of the killing of the three Fusiliers, Belfast city centre was made out of bounds to off-duty soldiers, but this policy served to encourage soldiers to frequent pubs and hotels on the periphery of the city and near the town of Lisburn, which was predominantly Protestant and the site of Army headquarters. The change of habit did not go unnoticed in IRA circles, particularly in Ardoyne, where Martin Meehan was in control of the 3rd Battalion and on the Belfast Brigade Staff. The Brigade Staff were told that it was possible to lure soldiers from a well-known hotel near Lisburn and that the 3rd Battalion could handle such an operation, since they had proved their ability to do so by killing the Scots soldiers. The Provisionals' Belfast Brigade gave permission for a similar operation, even though it might well take place within an area covered by the 1st Battalion, whose responsibility extended outwards towards Finaghy and Lisburn. As with the Four-Square Laundry operation the Brigade Staff were consulted because of the IRA's strict rule that volunteers or active service units should operate only in those areas defined for their units, companies and battalions. If the Belfast Brigade were prepared to bend the rules, that implies that the 3rd Battalion was offering to use the same team as in the murder of the Scottish soldiers. I do not know if the same team was indeed used, but I leave the reader to make a judgment based on the facts.

During March 1973 two IRA women paid daily visits to the lounge bar of the Woodlands Hotel outside Lisburn. It was a favourite drinking haunt for off-duty soldiers from Army HQ and was deemed to be a safe haven. The two women introduced themselves to soldiers as Jean and Pat, names which would not have appeared to be Catholic and therefore did not arouse suspicion about their origins. They appeared to be aged between eighteen and twenty-two. One of them was of slim build with thin features and shoulder-length mid-brown hair. Her companion was well built and attractive, with a small upturned nose and dark wavy hair. Both were smartly dressed and about 5ft 7ins tall. By 24 March they had made friends with five NCOs from Army HQ. On that day the soldiers met the women at the Woodlands and were invited to a party in their flat on Belfast's Antrim Road, in a part of the road which the girls said was safe. As an enticement the two terrorists told the soldiers they would be inviting other female friends, that the flat was already prepared for a party and food had been cooked for the occasion. One of the NCOs decided for personal reasons not to go, but his four colleagues were keen to enjoy an evening with attractive women who were making their flat available for what appeared to be an interesting party restricted to eight people.

One of the NCOs, Staff Sergeant Penrose, phoned his wife from the hotel to say he was planning to have a quiet drink in the mess and watch television. Instead he accompanied the girls and his three colleagues in a car which took them to no. 358 Antrim Road. The IRA women led the soldiers to a ground-floor flat. Inside a fire was lit and food and drinks were laid out on a table. As the soldiers poured themselves a drink one of the women said she would drive to a house nearby and pick up two friends. While the unsuspecting soldiers were making themselves comfortable, two gunmen burst into the flat, frogmarched the soldiers into a bedroom and ordered them to lie face downward on a bed. The gunmen then opened fire, raking the bed and its occupants. Two soldiers died instantly and a third died later from his wounds. One soldier survived, possibly because he moved as soon as the first shot was fired. Nevertheless he was shot in the neck and part of his tongue was blown away. After the gunmen fled, he managed to crawl out of the flat and was seen by a young girl in an upstairs flat who raised the alarm.

The soldiers who died were Michael Muldoon, aged twenty-five, Barrington Foster, twenty-eight, and Thomas William Penrose, also twenty-eight. The soldier who survived was never named on the grounds that he might some day be called to identify the killers and until then he remains a target as the only witness of the savagery.

The Army was quoted as saying that it was reviewing its policy about the movement and conduct of off-duty soldiers. A military source was reported to have remarked that the dead soldiers had been based at Army HQ for some time and were aware of the risks. In fact they had been allowed to be exposed to an unforeseen risk. The IRA had hired the Antrim Road flat some time prior to the murders and left it vacant until the moment when the two female terrorists knew they were ready to lure soldiers to it.

The NCO who had declined the invitation to the flat was able to provide detailed descriptions of the women and within days photofit pictures were on the front pages of many newspapers. Journalists speculated about the incident, and Simon Hoggart, writing in the *Guardian,* claimed the Army reckoned the killers were 'members of the Provisionals acting with or without authority from the Belfast Brigade'. Within seventy-two hours of the murders Army and police raids took place in the Antrim Road and New Lodge Road areas. Five days after the killings, morning newspapers carried a photograph of a woman whom police said they were seeking to interview in connection with the murders. Although they were not prepared to name her, the police did tell journalists that she was known to them in connection with militant Republican activities. The photograph was of Roisin McLaughlin, a thirty-year-old housewife from Clifton Drive, about a quarter of a mile from the scene of the murders. What journalists did not know was that police had raided the McLaughlin home the day before and removed the photograph from Mrs McLaughlin's bedroom.

Roisin McLaughlin was not at home, but her husband, William, was arrested and taken to Glenravel Street police station where he was interviewed by Chief Inspector Abbott. William McLaughlin told Abbott that the murders had nothing to do with him. Abbott replied: 'They have plenty to do with your wife.' A member of military intelligence who was present said: 'Look, McLaughlin, you are not helping yourself or your cause by adopting your attitude that you don't know anything. We know that your wife is involved in IRA intelligence and is a party to these murders.' McLaughlin replied that Roisin was primarily a housewife but also did voluntary work for the Northern Ireland Civil Rights Association and the Association for Legal Justice. The English intelligence officer retorted: 'You must be bloody naive to think that we believe that. We know about her work in the IRA and the part she has played in these killings.' McLaughlin pointed out that neither he nor his wife was involved in any conflict with the police or Army. He was told he was free to leave the police station.

Two months later, Roisin McLaughlin was arrested in Cork in the Irish Republic, 300 miles from her home in Belfast from which she had vanished after 24 March, the day of the murders. Gardai swooped on a car in which she was a passenger. Her companions were her husband and Matt Fitzpatrick, who was due to appear in court to answer a charge of membership of the IRA. Mrs McLaughlin was no longer a brunette and had dyed her hair blonde. She was wearing brown trousers and a white coat. Later that day she appeared in a district courthouse looking very composed. An extradition warrant was granted and she was remanded in custody with the right to appeal against the court's decision at the Dublin High Court. On 30 May she appeared before Mr Justice Finlay in Dublin and was granted bail after arguing that she was the mother of a twelve-year-old boy and she believed her incarceration was having a 'deleterious effect on his welfare'.

Roisin McLaughlin was again before the Dublin High Court on 19 December 1974, and it was expected that the matter of her extradition would be finally resolved. Detective Inspector Matchett of the Royal Ulster Constabulary told the court that he had led the inquiry, and that he believed that Mrs McLaughlin was involved in the murder of the soldiers and that she was the woman who left the flat and returned with the gunmen. Detective Inspector Matchett's evidence was ably expressed, but some of his statements indicated that he was aware that the extradition warrant was being contested on the basis of unconstitutionality and the assertion that Mrs McLaughlin was being sought for a political offence which the Irish judiciary was unlikely to deem sufficient for extradition. Matchett said there was no reason to believe Mrs McLaughlin was a member of the IRA or that she was associated with any group engaged in political activity intended to effect a change of government in Northern Ireland. He was assuring the court that if she was returned to Northern Ireland she would be charged only with offences relating to this particular incident and that those offences would be concerned with murder and attempted murder. RUC headquarters, he maintained, had confirmed that she would not be either interned or detained.

This aspect of Matchett's evidence was clearly designed to circumvent a situation in which people who claimed they were involved in politically motivated events were able to avoid extradition from the Irish Republic. That situation has since been relaxed rather than changed, but in 1974 Matchett was fighting a losing battle, and his statements that Roisin McLaughlin's alleged involvement was not political and that the RUC did not believe her to be a member of the IRA represented half-truths. His evidence conflicted with the media reports which followed the murder of the soldiers and the statements being made privately to journalists by both the RUC and the Army.

William McLaughlin also gave evidence and was asked by Counsel for the State if he had ever been a member of the IRA. The judge instructed McLaughlin that he was not obliged to answer the question and could simply say that he did not wish to reply. McLaughlin took Mr Justice Finlay's advice. He was also asked if he believed his wife was a member of the IRA and he replied that he could not 'state that'.

Counsel for Mrs McLaughlin told the court that he was unwilling to call her to give evidence because he might expose her to the risk of incriminating herself either in respect of the offence of murder as charged in the extradition warrant or in respect of some other offence in 'this jurisdiction or the jurisdiction of Northern Ireland'. The judge remarked that he could not in this case, any more than in others, have regard to the reasons for not calling a party to give evidence, nor could he fill any gap arising from the absence of such evidence.

Reviewing Detective Inspector Matchett's assertion that he had an open mind about whether the crime was motivated and carried out by the IRA because they had not claimed responsibility for it, Mr Justice Finlay declared it was most unlikely that the murders resulted from personal revenge, robbery or crime of passion. With regard to what constituted a political offence, the judge stressed that if such a murder as that of the soldiers was carried out by or on behalf of an organisation which by such methods sought to overthrow the government, then there could be no doubt that it was political. He added that in relying on Matchett's evidence he was obliged to conclude that the murders of unarmed soldiers were part of a paramilitary organisation's aim to overthrow the government of Northern Ireland. It was, in his opinion, a matter of probability that the offence named in the warrant was a political one, and on that basis he was refusing to order Mrs McLaughlin's extradition. Finally, Mr Justice Finlay pronounced that, in view of the fact that Roisin McLaughlin did not give evidence on the grounds that she might incriminate herself, he would not allow her to claim for the cost of her legal defence.

Roisin McLaughlin walked from the court to freedom in the Irish Republic knowing that if she ever sets foot on British soil she will be arrested and charged. An unnamed soldier remains a witness to the Antrim Road massacre and he may some day face her across a courtroom, though that is unlikely to happen while extradition remains a political issue. Roisin McLaughlin is only one of hundreds who are sought by the British authorities.

The Antrim Road killings forced the Army radically to review the activities and freedom of movement of off-duty soldiers. However, as in all wars, it is virtually impossible to guard constantly against terrorism. In 1981 the IRA learned that soldiers were regularly frequenting a disco at the Robin's Nest pub adjacent to the railway station in the town of Lisburn. Once again they prepared a honeytrap, a device they had not used successfully for eight years. When I was researching the role of female terrorists, I was told that on several occasions between 1973 and 1978 efforts were made to lure soldiers from licensed premises in the Lisburn area, but all attempts failed because previous murders such as the Antrim Road killings had generated fear and caution among off-duty members of the military. The IRA say they abandoned several honeytrap operations 'at the last moment'. Lisburn was the ideal place for the IRA to seek out soldiers who were out on the town looking for easy sex, for girls who were willing to invite them to parties or to their flats. The women of the IRA knew exactly what some soldiers had in mind and were prepared to offer sex to lure soldiers to a place where they could be murdered. Lisburn was regarded as a relatively safe area for soldiers because the majority of its inhabitants are Protestants and it is close to Thiepval Barracks (Army HQ). However, these reasons for assuming it to be safe did not deter the IRA in 1973. I believe the Army authorities, for the sake of expediency and to create an element of normality in the lives of serving soldiers, were prepared to take a calculated risk by not declaring Lisburn pubs out of bounds. A similar policy was applied to other towns with a majority Protestant population such as Holywood, but events indicate that the risks for off-duty soldiers in a dirty war may be too high.

They certainly were too high on 4 September 1981, when two privates, twenty-year-old Sohan Singh Virdee and twenty-one-year-old John Lunt, both of the Royal Pioneer Corps, decided to spend the evening in Lisburn town centre. After visiting two pubs they made their way to the Robin's Nest, where they knew there would be a disco and the opportunity for picking up females, and in a short time they were joined by two young women who engaged them in conversation.

The women asked Virdee and Lunt if they were soldiers, but both replied that they were not in any way connected with the military, and they gave their names as Fred and Wally. The women said they were nurses and lived in a flat in the Stranmillis area of Belfast, a quiet, middle-class neighbourhood adjacent to the Malone Road. It was they who bought the first round of drinks, and Virdee and Lunt began to feel so much at ease that each indicated to the other without words which of the women he wished to make his 'pick-up' for the evening. Considering the history of the Northern Ireland conflict, it is astonishing that neither Virdee nor Lunt—who were willing to disguise their true identity—was suspicious of two women who were prepared to lead the conversation, buy the first round of drinks and enquire if 'Fred and Wally' were soldiers. Perhaps it is a measure of the male ego, sexual demands or the vulnerability of men in stressful jobs that security can so easily be eroded, particularly in pubs and after drinking alcohol. Eventually Virdee and Lunt's female companions suggested that they should all return for late-night drinks to the Stranmillis flat. When the girls explained that they did not have a car, 'Fred and Wally' replied that they could supply one.

The four left the Robin's Nest and walked to Lunt's car. Initially the car would not start and Virdee and the girls proceeded to push it. A patrol of military police appeared on the scene and asked Lunt what was happening. He informed them of his identity and told them that he was giving the girls a lift to their flat. The military police accepted the explanation and left. Their role at that time was to patrol Lisburn to ensure that soldiers were safe and were not disturbing the peace. As Lunt drove towards Belfast he had to stop at a filling station to buy petrol. One of the women handed him money and asked him to buy some bread for making sandwiches at the flat. This further reassured the soldiers of the normality of the situation. When the four arrived at the flat, which was on the first floor of a large terraced house in Stranmillis Park, the girls told Virdee and Lunt to make themselves comfortable. Lunt informed police of his reaction on entering the flat:

As I walked up the hall I could see Fred sitting on the settee in a room to my left. The girl with me told me to go in and sit down and she would join me soon. I sat beside Fred. I can't remember where the girl went at that stage and I did not see the girl Fred had been with. I was sat on the right-hand side of the two-seater settee. Fred had just spoken a few words of conversation to me when two dark figures burst through the door in front of us. I could see that both of these persons had hand-guns and were holding them in a two-handed grip and pointing them directly at us. The next thing I knew there was a burst of shots, not automatic shots but single shots in quick succession. I would say five to six shots were fired. Both of us slumped over the settee. I remember feeling pain in my arms. I got the impression the figures were masked, were wearing dark clothes and were not very big. These two figures rushed out of the door from which I had come in and, at the same time, I saw a third gunman emerge from the door in front me. He was slightly bigger than the two previous ones and was dressed in a lightish cream-coloured suit. He carried a revolver in a two-handed grip similar to the first two gunmen. At that stage I had got up on my feet in front of this man who fired approximately three to four shots at me, some of which struck me. I collapsed to the floor. As this man ran out the door the girl I had been with appeared in the doorway. She screamed or shouted something at me before running out of the room in the same direction as the gunmen—that was into the hall and out the front door. My mate Fred was lying slumped on the settee, motionless. I remember I got up and walked around a bit but I'm not quite sure to where. The next thing I knew, a lady came into the room and said, 'Oh, my God'. She went to get an ambulance. I was shot in both arms, left shoulder and right leg.

His companion was not so lucky. He was found to be dead on arrival at hospital. Fortunately Lunt was able to provide police with descriptions of the girls who lured him and his colleague to the flat.

The one to whom I was speaking was mid-twenties and about 5ft 8ins. She had a nice figure, medium build, shoulder-length hair parted in the middle, ginger to blonde; pale face with freckles, clean, straight teeth, eye shadow and thin oval face. She spoke with a quiet pleasant voice and on occasions used phrases such as 'here's me' and 'so am I'. She was wearing a lightish-coloured blouse buttoned down the front but opened at the neck to such an extent that one could see part of her breasts.

He also remarked to police that the other girl's breasts were large and she had a 'rounded sort of big backside'.

His description of both women shows plainly their physical attractions for him and, presumably, his unfortunate friend. He indicated that they were dressed in a provocative manner and that they talked to the soldiers about sharing supper and possibly breakfast, thereby creating the impression that both girls were available for the night. This ensured that Lunt and Virdee were more interested in sexual enticements than their safety. Lunt was unable to tell police the names of the girls, though he mentioned that they only used Christian names and that one of them 'had a daft name like Ethel'.

Investigating detectives were particularly interested in one piece of detail about the woman who accompanied Virdee. Lunt remembered that she had tattoos on her right forearm. They were smallish, and it was his impression that one was a 'short name' and the other was composed of dots in the shape of lines.

Within less than a year the RUC arrested two young women on the evidence of a supergrass and charged them with the murder of Private Sohan Singh Virdee. They were twenty-one-year-old Alice Martha Taylor from Broadway in the Falls area of Belfast and Maureen O'Neill, aged twenty-four, from Joy Street in the Markets area close to Belfast city centre.

At an identification parade Lunt picked out O'Neill but not Taylor. When the trial began, the case against Taylor was based on a statement she made to police within one hour of her arrest in May 1982, but she denied that she had voluntarily made the statement. O'Neill argued in court that she was in Kerry in the Irish Republic when the murder took place and had a range of people to confirm her alibi. The Crown argued that hair found in Lunt's car matched hers but produced no forensic evidence to substantiate the claim. The Crown case against O'Neill was also based on Lunt's identification and on the fact that she had tattoos on her arm. However, her counsel argued that the tattoos were typical of those sported by many girls of her age. O'Neill, he added, had the tattoos painted on her arm while at school and the defence could produce nine other girls with similar markings.

The case against O'Neill collapsed not only on the issue of the tattoos but when Alice Taylor was judged to be guilty by the Diplock court. At that point defence counsel saw an opportunity to damage the Crown case. O'Neill's lawyer pointed out that Lunt's identification evidence against her was weakened by the fact that he was unable to select Taylor at an identification parade, and yet it was alleged that Taylor was the woman with whom he had spent most time on the night of the murder.

Mr Justice McDermott accepted O'Neill's defence because, he stated, there was a reasonable doubt that she was not the person described in court as 'Virdee's girl' and Lunt had identified her not by visual recognition but by a heart-shaped tattoo on her arm. 'As a reasonable number of girls are tattooed this leaves me less than satisfied that Private Lunt's identification is sound,' the judge remarked. He did not, however, accept her alibi that she was in Kerry.

As for Alice Martha Taylor, Mr Justice MacDermott gaoled her for life. She had actively aided the gunmen and the judge was in no doubt that she possessed the necessary intent, as well as being aware of the nature

of what she was doing in 'bringing the Brits to the flat'. The judge depart-
ed from rebuking Taylor only to remark that he felt she had shown
remorse since the murder.

Taylor's statement was legally an admission of guilt, though she
attempted to suggest that she was an unwilling accomplice; that the operation was haphazard; and that she did not realise that the soldiers were
to be shot. She also failed to name her accomplices. However, it is an
example of the ease with which murder can be committed when women
are used as bait:

Sometime around the end of May 1981 I was asked by a man to check to see if there
were any Security Forces between Beechmount and the Springfield Road. I assumed
this was a member of the IRA and the arrangement was that I was to walk in front of
him and if there were any police or army about, I was to bend down and he would
know to turn back. I only knew this man to see. I did this for him and there was no
one about. The man went on up to Kashmir. I was going to my cousin's house on the
Kashmir Road at the time. About the end of June 1981 the same man approached
me in the Iveagh Club which is off Broadway. I was there with a friend at a dance. He
came over to me and asked me outside to speak to him. When I went out he asked
me to do a job and I said I would. He told me he would see me later and make
arrangements. A couple of days later he called at my house at 43 Broadway. There
was no one in the house but me and I asked him in. He told me that he wanted me
to go along with another girl to bring a couple of Brits back to a flat. I asked him when
he wanted me to do this. He told me some time in the near future and he would be
in touch with me some time in August. The same man came back to my house, picked
me up in a car and drove me over to Stranmillis. He parked the car in Stranmillis Park
and described the flat to me. He explained that I would meet another girl in the bus
station at the back of the Europa Hotel. He would tell me later when we would be
going on the job and it would be a Friday night. He also told me we would be going to
a pub in Lisburn to pick up Brits and bring them back to the flat about midnight. This
man called back at my house. I'm not sure whether it was the Friday we brought the
Brits back or the day before. He told me the job was on that Friday night and that I
was to meet the other girl as planned. I think it was just after eight o'clock when I
went to the bus station. I was approached by a girl. I knew her face but I don't wish
to mention her name. We got on the bus to Lisburn and got off at Lisburn's railway
station. On the journey we talked about the pub we were going to and that it was full
of Brits. The girl seemed to know it well and told me it was the Robin's Nest.

Taylor added that she and her friend talked to several soldiers until
they were joined by Lunt and Virdee; her friend bought most of the
drinks. She did not tell police that she and her accomplice talked of supper and breakfast. At the end of her statement she declared that she
allowed her friend and the soldiers to enter the flat, closed the door
behind them, then walked into the street and heard shots coming from
the flat: 'I'm glad I wasn't in the flat when the Brits were shot and I'm
sorry it ever happened at all. I knew I was bringing these Brits to the flat
for the IRA but I didn't think they were going to be shot.'

Taylor's attempt to abdicate responsibility for her actions was absurd and impossible to believe, since she was a member of the IRA's female wing, Cumann na mBann, a grouping much more secretive than any other within the IRA. She was not chosen at random for such an operation and she knew her associates. Members of Cumann na mBann have included the Price sisters, Mairead Farrell and many others who were central to the planning and execution of major operations. Their most successful roles have been in luring soldiers to their deaths and in accompanying IRA operatives abroad to create an image of young couples on holiday. Unlike the IRA, Cumann na mBann does not give interviews and its members are rarely observed in action, but it is no less an effective terrorist grouping. One can only guess at the number of soldiers who ignored the charms of provocative females in Northern Ireland pubs or turned down offers of supper and breakfast.

10

Secret Liaisons
The Security Forces and the UDA

A t the beginning of 1972 the Home Secretary, Reginald Maudling, declared that if there was a concerted effort by both communities a lasting solution could be found to the problems of Northern Ireland. His view was not shared by the SDLP's Austin Currie, who told an anti-internment rally in Belfast that within six months the Unionist Prime Minister, Brian Faulkner, and his 'rotten Unionist system' would be smashed: 'To Maudling, I say: why should we talk to you? We are winning and you are not.' For his part, Brian Faulkner saw the continued use of internment as the way of solving the problem. To him the defeat of the IRA was the sole issue in Ulster and he stood implacably opposed to any dialogue with Catholics which would question or interfere with Unionist political domination. Maudling's hopes after three years of street demonstrations, rioting and the shooting of soldiers by the Provisionals sounded hollow.

There were those in the Protestant community who were beginning to assert that violence achieved change for nationalists and it could also halt the erosion of the Protestant way of life in Ulster. Advocates of such a policy of violence from the Protestant and Loyalist community were to be found not only in the UDA and UVF but also within political circles on the fringes of the Unionist Party. In the Catholic community there was constant reiteration of an ominous warning that at any time there might be a 'Protestant backlash'. The use of this term was not restricted to Catholics but was often used by Loyalists as a reminder to everyone that, if events began to slide from Unionist control, Protestants would rise up and the subsequent 'backlash' would engulf Northern Ireland in a civil war; Catholics would be killed in their thousands and would be unable to defend themselves against the formidable weaponry available to Protestants through gun clubs, the police and the UDR. The communities were more polarised than in 1969. In the minds of Loyalists all Catholics supported the IRA. This assumption was readily made because of the overwhelming nationalist opposition to internment and the feelings expressed by Currie that Unionism was going to be smashed. Catholics were fifth-columnists and in the eyes of the majority of Unionists were undermining the Protestant heritage and way of life in order to achieve the IRA aim of creating a united Ireland.

A Loyalist newssheet in August 1971 contained a letter which illustrated the bitterness, resentment and naked hatred which was welling up in Loyalist circles:

I want to remind Protestants that these animals are crawling into Ulster, hitting vital points like the RUC stations etc. The ugly thing is that the bastards are getting away with it. Then the question arises, what the hell is the UVF doing about it? You've got to fight fire with fire, and personally I don't think they've enough fire to make the animals sweat.

In the same period, after internment, the UDA was born and the following statement in the news-sheet, *Loyalist News*, signalled not only its birth but the way in which it was to be shaped:

Being convinced that the enemies of the Faith and Freedom are determined to destroy the State of Northern Ireland and thereby enslave the people of God, we call on all members of our loyal institutions, and other responsible citizens, to organise themselves immediately into platoons of twenty under the command of someone capable of acting as sergeant. Every effort must be made to arm these platoons with whatever weapons are available. The first duty of each platoon will be to formulate a plan for the defence of its own street or road in co-operation with platoons in adjoining areas. A structure of command is already in existence and the various platoons will eventually be linked in a co-ordinated effort.

Those statements make it obvious that by the beginning of 1972 preparations were being made within Loyalist areas to arm the UDA, and the UVF was being called upon to adopt a more violent stance towards the nationalists.

In February the former Stormont cabinet minister, William Craig, arrived in the town of Lisburn for a rally. He was escorted through a waiting crowd by leather-jacketed young men on motorcycles and was announced to those assembled before him as 'The Leader'. Craig told the crowd: 'We are determined, ladies and gentlemen, to preserve our British traditions and our way of life, and God help those who get in our way.' There were many who placed a sinister interpretation on the implied threat, and it was exactly what was required by those people who were writing letters to the *Loyalist News* and the edition of the UDA newssheet *Bulletin* of that same month:

I have reached the stage where I have no longer any compassion for any nationalist man, woman or child. After years of destruction, murder, intimidation, I have been driven against my better feelings to the decision—it's them or us. What I want to know is where the hell are the men in our community? Have they any pride? Have they any guts? Why are they not organised in, not defence, but commando groups? Why have they not started to hit back in the only way these nationalist bastards understand? That is...ruthless indiscriminate killing. If I had a flame thrower I would roast the slimy excreta that pass for human beings. Also I'm sick and tired of you yellow-backed Prods who are not prepared to fight for your own street, let alone your own loyalist people. When civil war breaks out, and God forgive me but I hope its soon, I at least will shoot you along with the Fenian scum.

The leader writer of the UDA *Bulletin* responded to this letter, which was supposedly from a female subscriber, by agreeing with her sentiments and suggesting that others who felt like her should direct their energies towards support for the UDA.

There was no immediate response from the UDA to the demand that killing should begin, though the UVF shot a Catholic in the Woodvale area in February. Other events taking place in Northern Ireland were producing the ingredients which would create a Protestant backlash and unleash the 'commando groups' referred to in the *Bulletin* letter. On 26 February, William Craig again resorted to strong words, and there was little ambiguity in the message he spelled out at a rally in the County Fermanagh town of Enniskillen:

We feel the time for talk is over. We want the Ulster Loyalists to commit themselves to a course of action. We are finished with all this wishy-washy approach to the menace which threatens our province, and by the time we all come together in an all-Ulster rally in Belfast on 18 March every part of the world will know where the Ulster Loyalists stand and will know that the Ulster Loyalist is capable of doing more than talk. Late as the hour is, and it is jolly late, I can say with confidence we are going to win this struggle. We are going to beat the conspiracy into the ground and we make no accommodation with the enemies of this country, the enemies of democracy.

There were those in the Loyalist paramilitary organisations who were not going to wait to hear what Craig or anyone else was going to say at the proposed rally in March. Two nights after his speech in Enniskillen, two innocent Catholics were shot but survived. Republicans claimed that plain-clothes soldiers were involved in one of the attacks. There was no evidence to support this allegation, but the fact that it was made was indicative of a feeling in the Catholic community that when Catholics were murdered or shot, in this case by unidentified men operating from a moving car, the gunmen were undercover soldiers. This attitude also showed a lack of knowledge of the intentions or capabilities of the UDA or UVF at that stage in 1972. Retrospective analysis of both shootings indicated that they were the work of Loyalists who were flexing their military might and experimenting with a form of indiscriminate violence which within several months would claim the lives of several hundred innocent people, the majority of them Catholics. However, intense resentment of British soldiers and the tendency of nationalists to attribute every act of violence against Catholics to the Army was later to have more serious consequences in the way in which sectarian assassinations were generally assessed.

At the beginning of March the IRA exploded a bomb in the Abercorn restaurant in the centre of Belfast. Three people were killed and scores seriously injured. The carnage and the indiscriminate nature of the attack convinced many Loyalists that the IRA was a ruthless enemy which was willing to kill women and children in no-warning bomb attacks. The British government was becoming increasingly disillusioned with its attempts to find a solution to the problems of Northern Ireland. The Unionists wished to maintain majority rule and the nationalists wished to be rid of Stormont. On 24 March 1972 the unthinkable occurred: the British government suspended Stormont and imposed direct rule. Six days earlier Craig had told a Loyalist rally in Belfast that any attempt to interfere with Unionist rule would be confronted and Protestants would fight, if necessary. He also sounded an ominous warning to the 75,000 people who had gathered to hear him: 'A sophisticated intelligence service will be established and if the politicians fail it will be our job to liquidate the enemy.' Two days later he clarified the use of the words 'liquidate' and 'enemy' by saying that he was referring to the IRA, who should be 'put down'. He warned that the situation in Northern Ireland was moving towards war. The introduction of direct rule did not bring about war as most people would understand the word, but it did unleash a backlash. Within a short time people were indeed being liquidated and they were innocent Catholics. What Craig failed to understand was that Loyalist paramilitaries did not know how to distinguish between a Catholic and an IRA volunteer and, like the woman who wrote to the Loyalist news-sheet, they did not have any compassion for Catholics, whom they viewed as either members of the IRA or the people who supported and harboured them.

The UDA soon showed its numerical strength by holding huge parades in Belfast with men hooded and dressed in combat gear. The sight of such large numbers of paramilitaries marching openly on the streets without hindrance from the police or Army served to frighten Catholics and convince them that the security forces were either afraid to confront the UDA or prepared to allow them to act as the policing agent in Protestant areas. Assassinations of Catholics continued in April and May; but if one event, aside from direct rule, can be described as the catalyst which pushed the situation over the edge in 1972 and unleashed the Protestant backlash with unparalleled ferocity it was the truce negotiated between the Provisional IRA and the British government. It came into force on 25 June and, following the imposition of direct rule, finally convinced many Loyalists that the British government was prepared to capitulate to IRA violence and that as a consequence Northern Ireland would find itself in a united Ireland. The UDA and UVF began a major campaign of sectarian killings. The IRA responded, but not in the same proportions. In the months that followed the truce some of the most gruesome murders ever committed in Northern Ireland were carried out by members of the UDA/UVF. The IRA truce lasted until 9 July, and during it William Whitelaw held secret talks in London with IRA leaders who were flown over to meet him.

During the truce there was one killing each day, and by the end of July the number of sectarian killings totalled thirty-six. This death toll illustrated a significant change in events when one considers that the violence from the 1969 riots until the truce had claimed thirty-one lives. In the remaining months of 1972 the killings continued unabated. That can be attributed to the fact that the UDA in particular, because of its overwhelming numbers, controlled major routes and areas of Belfast where most of the murders took place. The UDA had set up what they termed 'no-go areas' throughout Northern Ireland on 1 July following the IRA truce. Their control of these areas went unchallenged by the police and Army; they patrolled the districts dressed in combat gear and stopped anyone they considered to be a stranger. They also took strangers or Catholics snatched by UDA hit-squads to UDA clubs or pubs under their control. Most of the killings in 1972 took place in the heavily populated areas of North and East

Belfast where the UDA was firmly in control. Some observers are of the opinion that the UDA was not challenged in the same way as the IRA because it did not pose a threat to the established order. It was not formed to kill soldiers or policemen, and therefore the enemy the security forces were required to oppose was the IRA.

Irrespective of whether such a view has ultimate validity, events of 1972 show that the UDA remained relatively unchallenged by the security forces. The RUC did bring a number of UDA members before the courts, but the majority of the murders from that period have to this day gone unsolved. One can only speculate about the reasons for that, though one is obliged to acknowledge several factors which offer an insight into the difficulties facing investigating agencies such as CID at that time. The RUC found itself operating in areas where the UDA was in control of policing and therefore it did not have the freedom to act as events demanded. The sheer number of killings made it difficult for the RUC to work with the efficiency one would expect in a murder investigation elsewhere in the United Kingdom. Finally, it is clear that many policemen compromised their neutrality by continuing to frequent and socialise in premises controlled by the paramilitaries. In the Shankill area the UDA often killed people in illegal drinking clubs and were not concerned about leaving traces of the victim's blood on the floor or walls. The police knew such places were being used for murder, but as one policeman explained to me: 'There was little we could do. It was a difficult time. The clubs were illegal [shebeens], so there was no way of knowing the identities of those who controlled them. We were understaffed at the time and there were so many killings.' While researching the first part of this trilogy, *The Shankill Butchers,* I uncovered evidence that as late as 1975 policemen in the Shankill area were drinking in pubs which were the haunts of UDA and UVF units; in one instance, policemen from C Division (Tennent Street, Shankill Road) regularly frequented a bar knowing that the outlawed UVF held meetings above the premises. At the same time policemen knew that to enter some UDA or UVF premises for the purposes of searching them would have required, in the words of one RUC officer, 'a British Army regiment'.

Until September 1972 the Army appeared unwilling to deal with the UDA because of a reluctance to fight a war on both fronts. However, the Parachute Regiment dealt with rioters on the Shankill on 7 September much as it would have dealt with Republican troublemakers. The UDA engaged the paratroopers with guns and several civilians were killed. A similar confrontation took place in East Belfast the following month and again the Army won the exchange. Apart from these two exchanges the authority of the UDA in Loyalist areas did not lessen, though the gun battles served as a reminder from the Army that the UDA was not invincible.

By the end of 1972 there had been over a hundred sectarian killings; the vast majority of the victims were Catholics, and the west and east of the city were the major killing grounds. Some of the victims were tortured and branded with red-hot pokers. In the Catholic community the presence of the MRF and the shootings attributed to plain-clothes soldiers also served to fuel speculation that many of the sectarian killings were either the work of the Army or being permitted by the Army. According to one theory, the indiscriminate killing of Catholics was intended to alienate the nationalist population from the IRA because the IRA was incapable of realising its primary objective of being the defender of nationalists; as support had been withdrawn from the Official IRA for its failure to provide defence in 1969, the constant killing of Catholics in 1972 would generate a similar reaction and deprive the Provos of support. A similar theory concluded that the sectarian assassination campaign was convenient for the security forces because it involved the Provisionals in a sectarian war and detached them from their purpose of waging a guerrilla war against the Army. The proponents of both theories were to argue in late 1972 and much more forcibly in 1973 that it was Kitson's policy that sectarian killings should continue to divert the Provos from their real aim and entangle them in a dirty little war with the Loyalist paramilitaries which would lead to their being easily discredited. Not unnaturally, much of this type of theorising was Provisional IRA propaganda, though it must be said that they did not become engaged in an all-out sectarian war like their counterparts in the Loyalist community. The fact that 90 per cent of the victims of the assassination campaign of 1972 and 1973 were Catholics testifies that the Provisionals maintained their role as an organisation involved in a war with the British Army, UDR and RUC. If there was an attempt to immerse them fully in a sectarian war, it failed. The theorising did, however, have other proponents such as the Northern Ireland Civil Rights Association, which advised people in June 1973 how to behave in the event of being shot by 'assassins':

A Civil Rights team has devised some advice for civilians shot by SAS/MRF squads. Provided you are alive when the shooting stops, pretend to be dead until the squad moves away, otherwise they might try to finish the job. If there is an Army post nearby do not worry. It will not be manned or if it is the occupants will be busy writing a press statement saying that no military personnel were involved in the shooting. Shout for help and get yourself carted off to hospital; the police will take a statement and investigate. Revealed evidence suggests that they may find within a few hours that you were shot by the SAS/MRF. However, you may not have proof of this fact until many months later and only then if you can get someone into court.

By the time this statement appeared, the Northern Ireland Civil Rights Association was firmly entrenched in a Provisional philosophy, but the statement none the less articulated a widely held belief among Catholics that the Army was involved in assassination and, by inference, in the sectarian killings which by the autumn of 1973 had claimed the lives of nearly 200 innocent people.

The theorising eventually became part of the political currency of the Provisional IRA, though it was also believed by many nationalist politicians and priests. In later years, when it became clear that the MRF squads were made up of Republican and, particularly, Loyalist paramilitaries, the suspicion of Army or security forces involvement in political assassination was given greater credence, but there was still little hard evidence. In the late 1970s a Loyalist killer, Albert Walker Baker, claimed that he had worked for the security forces. Journalists took little notice of his allegation on the grounds that Baker was a killer and should not be believed. In 1973 I had written in the book *Political Murder in Northern Ireland* that there was a paucity of evidence that the Army was directly engaged in the assassination campaign, and I declared that the case against the Army was unproven. That remained so and was unchallenged until the arrival on the scene of Colin Wallace and Fred Holroyd.

Once Wallace and Holroyd began to tell the public that the British Army and the security services were involved in dirty tricks, the search for evidence began in earnest. Duncan Campbell, a renowned investigative journalist, and politicians such as Ken Livingstone and Dale Campbell-Savours listened to Wallace and Holroyd and began searching for other evidence. Ken Livingstone and the *Daily Mirror* journalist Paul Foot became interested in the case of Albert Walker Baker. From his cell in Frankland Prison he was leaking information damaging to the RUC and British intelligence. Before I assess Walker Baker's claims, it is essential to examine the nature and history of the man.

Albert Walker Baker was twenty-two years old when he went absent without leave from the Royal Irish Rangers and returned to his parents' home in Belfast. The only feature that distinguished him from his Belfast roots was the English accent he had acquired in his time away from the city. It was June 1972, a period when Ulster was in turmoil and sectarian murder was on the increase. Baker's military training made him an ideal recruit for the largest Loyalist paramilitary army, the legally constituted Ulster Defence Association. He joined the UDA and strutted around the streets of his native East Belfast with a swagger and assuredness lacking in other paramilitary men who did not have an army training. After only a month at home he walked into the Vulcan Bar on the Newtownards Road in East Belfast, produced a .45 pistol and stole £821. He was assisted in the robbery by three other members of the UDA. They committed the crime for pocket money, and the robbery was the first of eleven which Baker would commit in the ensuing twelve months. Baker quickly came to the attention of the UDA leader in East Belfast, Tommy Herron, a ruthless, uncompromising and criminally inspired individual. In recognition of Baker's training and his potential for violence, Herron appointed him as a bodyguard for members of the UDA's ruling body, the Inner Council, which held its meetings in an East Belfast hotel. Baker patrolled the hotel armed whenever the Inner Council was in session. In August 1972, two months after his arrival in Belfast, Baker was ordered by Herron to kill a waiter who worked at the Girton Lodge hotel in East Belfast. He was told the waiter was a Catholic and that he might have overheard matters being discussed by the Inner Council. The waiter was nineteen-year-old Philip Anthony Fay, who lived with a Protestant friend, Andrew Baxter, at 83 Island Street in East Belfast. Fay seemed unaware of the risks of living and working in a staunchly Loyalist neighbourhood. He was regarded as friendly and inoffensive, he never talked of politics or religion and was extremely industrious. Unfortunately, the Girton Lodge was one of two hotels frequented by the UDA leadership and he obviously came to the attention of Tommy Herron. On 12 August 1972 he was interviewed for a job at a more plush hotel, the Stormont, and was asked to start work there on 21 August.

However, on 17 August, Albert Walker Baker was given the following instructions by a leading member of the UDA: 'Go to 83 Island Street. There are two blokes living in the house. You'll know Fay because he's the one with the black curly hair and moustache. Make sure you do him right. Shoot him through the back of the head so that if he is still living his brain will be damaged and he will not be able to identify you.'

Baker did not question the instructions. Taking a .32 pistol and five rounds of ammunition from a UDA arms dump, he made his way to Island Street in the early hours of 18 August, hammered with his fist on the door of no. 83 and waited for a considerable time until Fay opened the door. Baker recognised him and held him at gunpoint. He asked him if he was a Catholic and Fay said he was. Then he told Fay to turn round and shot him once through the back of the head. As Fay lay on the ground, Baker crouched over him and fired three shots into the side of his head, behind his left ear. It was a killing carried out in the style of a clinical and ruthless assassin. Baker proceeded to kick the body into the hallway, closed the door and walked casually along Island Street to a rendezvous with a UDA leader, who asked if Fay was dead. Baker replied that he was, and his companion commented: 'He'd better be.'

Andrew Baxter was in the house that night, and said that Fay talked to him of his new job prospects and they retired to bed at 12.45. He maintained he did not hear the shooting because he was a deep sleeper and only learned of the murder when he woke at 7.30 am.

One month later, Baker and the UDA leader whom he met after the Fay murder were patrolling the Newtownards Road after midnight when, according to Baker, someone said that a 'Taig [Catholic] was coming down the road'. After a few minutes Baker went to the UDA leader's house, which for legal reasons I cannot identify because it would also identify him. In the house was a middle-aged man, who appeared to be drunk. In response to questions from Baker and others who were present, the man told them his name was Paul McCartan and he was a Catholic. Baker, the UDA leader and others bundled McCartan into a car and took him to nearby waste-ground, where Baker shot him three times through the head at point-blank range. The weapon used was the .32 pistol which killed Fay.

Paul McCartan was a barman who lived in East Belfast and was obviously spotted by someone who knew him to be a 'Taig'. He might well not have died that night had he taken the advice of a police sergeant, who was in a patrol from Mountpottinger police station when McCartan was walking down the Newtownards Road. The policemen saw him fall, and they stopped and assisted him to his feet. The sergeant said McCartan was not incapable and was 'able to stand fairly steady'. (McCartan's alcohol level according to a post-mortem report was 290mg/100ml in a blood sample, 371mg/100ml in a urine sample.) Stallard also said he asked McCartan if he wished a 'lift home but he refused saying he would rather walk'. McCartan was not shot until two hours later; in the meantime he had been badly beaten in the UDA leader's house while being questioned about his religion and identity.

Within several months of his arrival in Belfast, Baker had a considerable reputation in Loyalist paramilitary circles and was a member of what was termed within the UDA the No. 1 Assassination Team. Baker's potential for savagery is best illustrated by a murder which took place one week after the killing of Paul McCartan.

On 3 October twenty-one-year-old James Patrick McCartan from the town of Holywood travelled to Belfast with friends, including twenty-year-old John Jamison, who was to be married the following day. They were joined by Jamison's bride-to-be, Geraldine McCausland, two of her girlfriends, Patricia and June, and Robert McCamley. The group first had drinks in the Toby Jug bar and then went to the Park Avenue Hotel in East Belfast where a disco was in progress. Unknown to James McCartan and his friends, the Park Avenue was a meeting place for UDA leaders. John Jamison gave police the following account of that night:

Jimmy McCartan, Robert and I went to the toilet and as we were returning, Jimmy asked a fellow for a light. This fellow seemed to be a bouncer or somebody who had something to do with the hall. He said we were strangers and that they were funny about strangers but we would be all right. While we were talking to this fellow, another fellow came over and said: 'Don't you call you McCartan?' Jimmy said 'no' and this fellow said: 'It's Rice, isn't it?' Jimmy again said 'no'. A few others had joined us at this time and this fellow turned to one of them and said: 'Are you sure this person is a McCartan?' The person he spoke to was positive. We walked away and sat down with the girls.

James McCartan (no relative of Baker's previous victim) was from a well-known Catholic family in Holywood and also had an uncle named Rice from the same town. Holywood is only two miles from East Belfast and, being a predominantly Protestant area, it has close social ties with the Newtownards/Holywood Road district of East Belfast. Since the Park Avenue Hotel was on the route to Holywood from the Newtownards Road, McCartan would have been readily identified. John Jamison continued:

The bouncer warned those who were questioning Jimmy not to cause trouble. We decided to go, though June and Patricia opted to stay. I asked my fiancée to remain in the disco for a few minutes in case of trouble and I accompanied Jimmy and Robert out of the disco. I saw a fuzzy-haired fellow and about six others standing outside. I walked on; Jimmy walked on but Robert seemed to have turned back. These fellows stopped me and Jimmy and one of them said that Jimmy was called McCartan but I replied that it was not so. I said he was okay and I knew him. This fellow said: 'I don't care, he's going for a ride with us.' Geraldine had joined us just as they began dragging Jimmy away. Geraldine started shouting that they 'were not going to shoot him'. One of them said in an English accent: 'He's a fenian bastard.' Geraldine rushed forward and this guy punched her in the eye. I went for this fellow and grabbed him and one of his mates grabbed me. They put me on the ground and gave me a few kicks and thumps.

The brave attempts by McCartan's Protestant friends, John Jamison and Geraldine McCausland, were not sufficient to prevent his being kidnapped.

The man whom Jamison identified as having an English accent was Albert Walker Baker. He and his accomplices, whom I cannot name because they have not been convicted of this crime, drove McCartan to the house of the leader of the No. 1 Assassination Team. They dragged him by the hair into an upstairs room and ordered him to stand with his hands against the wall. He was asked his name and replied that he was James McCartan from Holywood. Meanwhile, in another room, some of McCartan's captors discussed whether they should transport him to another building or shoot him and dump the body nearby. One of them returned to where Baker was holding McCartan at gunpoint with a .32 pistol and said it was decided that they would take McCartan to Jones Club at Claremont Lane (also in East Belfast). They took McCartan in a car and when they arrived at the club they removed his coat and brown boots and began questioning him about the Provisional IRA. Nine members of the No. 1 Assassination Team were present, and each of them punched and kicked McCartan. Baker struck McCartan repeatedly on the back with a wooden pickshaft until it broke in two. Then McCartan was lifted from a kneeling position and held with his arms outstretched. Baker produced a dagger and stabbed McCartan twice through the palm of his left hand and once through the palm of his right hand. They loosened the belt of his trousers, dropped them to his ankles, and someone suggested 'cutting the balls off him'. Baker ran the knife up his left buttock, opening up a long shallow incision. They tied a rope round one hand and another round his ankles, held him by the ankles, swung him round and dropped him on the concrete floor on his head.

According to Baker, McCartan was 'in a bad way'. Several of those present decided it was time to shoot their victim, and they took him to a car and drove him to Connswater Bridge off the Newtownards Road. McCartan was frogmarched to a stretch of waste-ground and a green cloth hood was placed over his head. Baker shot him with the .32 pistol once through the back of the head and as he fell to the ground he crouched over him and shot him twice through the right ear.

Between September 1972 and May 1973 Walker Baker committed a series of robberies, and he claims he was not involved in any more sectarian killings until February 1973. On that morning, along with three other members of the No. 1 Team, he left UDA headquarters on the Newtownards Road, where they had spent the night, and made their way towards the Cherryvalley district, off the Upper Newtownards Road. They travelled in two cars, one a legally owned vehicle which was to be a getaway car, the other a car which had been stolen the previous night. Baker was armed with a Mills grenade, and the target was a bus which transported some twenty Catholic workmen each morning from Belfast to a school in Cherryvalley which was under construction.

The UDA plan was approved by Herron and another member of the

Inner Council, who for legal reasons cannot be named here. One of the team was to throw a tin of paint at the bus windscreen to force the driver to stop. Another UDA volunteer would smash a rear window with a hammer and Baker would toss the grenade into the vehicle. The fourth UDA man would be waiting nearby in the legally owned car. The plan proceeded as intended and the grenade exploded, killing forty-six-year-old Eugene Patrick Heenan and injuring many of his workmates. Baker and his accomplices visited UDA headquarters later that day. They were complimented for the success of their mission, and a member of the Inner Council gave them each £10, a sum which had been promised and which in effect was the price of a murder. What Baker did not understand was that, if human life was so cheap, then his own might have little value if he ever crossed his associates.

In the spring of 1973 there were violent confrontations between the UDA and the British Army. I was told by a former UDA leader that although Baker showed himself willing to shoot Catholics he was not willing to shoot soldiers: 'The thing about Albert was that he was one of the best operators I had ever seen. He was well trained as a soldier. It made us suspicious that he wasn't able to deliver when we found ourselves in a gun battle with the Army in East Belfast. We expected great things of him but he didn't deliver.' Baker's failure to 'deliver' aroused suspicion, in particular because the UDA knew in 1973 of the presence of the Military Reconnaissance Force. When the UDA leadership, through contacts within the Provos and as a result of media stories, learned of the MRF, it began to examine those within its ranks who might well have other allegiances. Attention turned to Walker Baker. Questions were asked about his sudden appearance in East Belfast and why, if he was absent without leave, the Army and particularly the RUC had not arrested him. The UDA was of the opinion that Walker Baker's presence in East Belfast was known to the RUC's CID and Special Branch in Mountpottinger station. When Baker discovered he was suspected of being an agent, he ran for cover to England. He returned to his regiment and was court-martialled for being absent without leave.

At 1.55 pm on 31 May 1973 he walked into Warminster county police station and told the duty sergeant, Anthony Godley, that he wished to confess to four murders and eleven armed robberies. Godley was flabbergasted, and asked why anyone should wish to make such an admission. Baker replied that he had taken to reading the Bible and he could no longer 'bear the thoughts' of what he had done. However, he told Godley he would never reveal who was with him during the four murders because to do so would place his family in grave danger. He admitted killing Fay, and claimed that Fay was an IRA intelligence operative. He said he shot Paul McCartan because he 'was shouting about being a Catholic'. The reason he gave for killing James McCartan was that 'he was a wanted IRA man who was pointed out to us at a dance'. He told Sergeant Godley, 'I slit him up his right side', and demonstrated this by holding up his right leg and indicating a point midway between his kneecap and thigh. 'I must have broke his spine with a pickshaft.'

The manner in which Baker graphically described his actions did not resemble that of a man who had been converted to Bible reading. He appeared to revel in the narration, sparing no effort to provide the minutiae of his killing techniques, to the extent that he felt obliged to point out that it was not an ordinary grenade which he used to kill Heenan but a 'Mills grenade'.

Baker was also interviewed by Detective Michael Bridewell on 31 May. At this stage, I believe, he revealed his real reason for walking into the police station—which had nothing to do with Bible reading: 'Baker asked if I could keep his statements out of the newspapers. I told him I didn't deal with the Press. Baker said that if he could stay in England he would tell me the names and places where arms, ammunition and bodies could be found. I told him I could not make such a decision but I would be in touch with the proper authorities. He admitted belonging to the UDA.'

Baker was later removed to Salisbury police station, where he was again interviewed by Detective Bridewell: 'Baker told me that he was going to walk into a river to finish it all but decided instead that his story had to be told. He said: "What I have told you I expect our Special Branch already know." I asked if he meant about the UDA and he replied: "Of course, some of them are with us."' On 2 June Baker told Detective Inspector Hamilton that if he was allowed to serve a prison term in England he would 'give him all the hits in the East End, Derry and all Belfast'.

It appeared from Walker Baker's contact with investigating officers that he wanted to do a deal, but it was convenient to explain his motives for making a confession on the basis that he was reformed, was suffering remorse and had turned to religion for comfort.

Walker Baker was returned to Northern Ireland in secret and further interrogated. He appeared before the Lord Chief Justice, Sir Robert Lowry, in October 1973 and was sentenced to life imprisonment with a recommendation that he serve a minimum of twenty-five years. No mention was made of the fact that an agreement had been reached that Baker would serve his sentence in an English prison. His lawyer, Michael Lavery QC, told the court that Baker went absent from the

Army after a drinking spree, arrived in Belfast, was tempted by the lure of money within the UDA, joined the organisation and trained its members. Counsel added that Baker found that UDA methods ranged from mutilation to murder and he became sickened by the murders and robberies he carried out. He returned to England to make 'a new start in life'. 'He has made attempts to atone for the terrible things he has done. He gave valuable assistance to police and enabled them to break up assassination groups.'

As behoves counsel in such cases, Michael Lavery, a brilliant lawyer, used all his persuasiveness to extract from the court any leniency available to his client but in vain. Baker himself was hoping for a deal, and I am convinced that he could have been charged with many more murders had he chosen to admit them. He was, in effect, the first supergrass, but he was clever and like many mass murderers he was prepared to reveal only some of his crimes. If, as he told the police, he knew of all the hits in Belfast and elsewhere and the where-abouts of bodies, he had been at the centre of Loyalist violence. Knowing he was already at risk from the UDA and perhaps all Loyalist paramilitaries, Baker possibly believed he could bargain for immunity if he offered the authorities his knowledge of the UDA. As a bodyguard for the Inner Council he would have been privy to the planning of many murders, abductions, robberies and explosions. However, he did not manage to extract a deal from the authorities, aside from an agreement that he serve his sentence in England.

One year later he was back in Northern Ireland as a Crown witness against some of his accomplices, but his evidence was not sufficient to secure convictions of all the members of the No. 1 Assassination Team. The UDA has denied Baker was a member:

Some of his friends may have been members but we would not have an Army deserter in our ranks. It would be a security risk. Baker is talking nonsense and is receiving some form of leniency for implicating this organisation. We happen to be the whipping boys. We collect money by holding raffles and ballots. We do not take part in armed robberies. We have never denied we are at war with the IRA and we use whatever means necessary against them but these were sectarian murders and we would have nothing to do with them.

Throughout the 1970s and early 1980s there were few references in the media to Walker Baker, though his mother tried to attract interest in her son's case. She told journalists that he had been working for the Army while in the UDA. It was an easy claim to make, and it was the only defence left. It was a claim which many Republicans, Loyalists and left-wingers were willing to believe, and also seemed to fit the pattern of MRF activities in that period. In the mid-1980s Walker Baker began to agitate from prison for a review of his case. Father Denis Faul, who has campaigned on issues of social justice for twenty years, visited Baker in Frankland Prison to examine his allegations about British military involvement in the killing of Catholics. With the emergence of Holroyd and Wallace's revelations, Walker Baker renewed his claims but now appeared to be willing to name names. I believe this was initially a tactic to force the authorities to give him an early release. However, Baker was indicating privately that his information was primarily concerned with police and not Army indiscretions and of police involvement with Loyalist paramilitaries. When I met Wallace and Holroyd in 1988 they indicated that if I was investigating dirty tricks by the security services and RUC Special Branch I should examine the Walker Baker case. I soon discovered that Baker had attracted the interest not only of former Army officers, but also Ken Livingstone MP, Paul Foot, the *Daily Mirror* columnist, who had visited Baker, and journalists in Ireland, who had written articles suggesting that the former soldier and UDA hit-man had devastating evidence of British intelligence involvement in assassination. Suddenly Walker Baker was in the news and conspiracy theories were developing.

To illustrate what he had to say, I provide extracts from a conversation between Baker and Ken Livingstone in Frankland Prison in August 1988. For legal reasons I am obliged to omit some of the people named by both men:

Livingstone: I am convinced that MI5 was acting or individuals with MI5 and the security services were looking after and helping to operate all the UDA and some of the IRA.

Baker: I have never mentioned it to anyone before but, as far as I was concerned, we were operating for the UDA but we had close links with the intelligence services: — who lived in Fraser Street. He's living in the Sandy Row district of Belfast at the moment.

Livingstone: Do you mean MI5 or is it just always the intelligence services?

Baker: All we knew was that — was an operator. He was working for the British intelligence services.

Livingstone: What makes you so certain of that?

Baker: Tommy Herron, the vice-chairman, who was assassinated, told myself and a couple of others to contact the British intelligence controller who was — and we were in contact with a man named Bunty by phone. We only knew his name as Bunty but the other one was —. [He mentions the name of the man he says now lives in Sandy Row—a Loyalist area on the periphery of Belfast city centre.]

Livingstone: Did you ever meet either of them?

Baker: I met — [the Sandy Row operative]. I used to go from East Belfast into the centre of Belfast, then to York Street to a telephone kiosk. — phoned Bunty, the controller, and he gave us the telephone number, and later other officers of the Inner Council contacted Bunty, and the arms we were getting to do the assassinations were coming from the Royal Ulster Constabulary.

This opening sequence from Livingstone's interview represents an attempt to discern whether Baker has any evidence of security services involvement with the UDA. In my opinion, Baker provides none. Baker is still unable to substantiate his allegation of MI5 involvement with the UDA. The man whom he refers to as living in Sandy Row was a member of the UDA's ruling body in the early seventies. The opening sequence of the interview contained leading questions which, in my opinion, were not properly designed to establish the truth of Baker's claims.

Livingstone proceeded to ask Walker Baker if he could name members of the RUC who were involved with the UDA, and he replied:

Whitelaw set up a group of twenty-one top detectives—otherwise called the Inner Circle Murder Squad—and the man in it that we were in contact with was —. He was the man passing all the information to the UDA. He was the deep-penetration officer, the UDA officer who was also a member of CID. And one other policeman who was handing over the weapons was in uniform. He was handing over Sterling sub-machine-guns, pistols, revolvers, ammunition and magazines.

When I was examining Baker's allegations I made private inquiries from a contact within the RUC, who informed me that two Sterling sub-machine-guns disappeared from Mountpottinger station in 1972 and that their disappearance was not discovered for a considerable period of time. RUC Special Branch believes these guns were used by the UDA to make similar sub-machine-guns which were employed in many sectarian killings. However, Baker claims that other weapons were also given to the UDA:

Livingstone: And presumably the RUC officers were all members of the Orange Lodge and some were members of the UDA?

Baker: We were led to believe that those officers handing over the weapons were getting their orders from higher authority. But you see the public did not know that weapons were going missing from RUC stations. The station where I lived was Mountpottinger. Ammunition was coming to UDA HQ or down to —'s house in — Street and he was handing the weapons over to us and we were using them for assassinations. When they came to raid —'s house they got a .45 revolver but it was never

ever brought out in court that it was a police weapon. He got twelve months for having an illegal weapon in his house but it was never established that the weapon belonged to the RUC.

Livingstone: When were you first aware that there was more than just the UDA acting with elements in the RUC?

Baker: When I met — [he mentions the name of the man he says now lives in Sandy Row].

Livingstone: Presumably there had been talk and general gossip in the UDA?

Baker: I was the bodyguard for the Inner Circle. I knew Tommy Herron, Andy Tyrie, Ned McCleary, the whole lot of them. I was their bodyguard. I used to go with them to the hotel where this man, young Fay, was assassinated. That's where the UDA would hold their meetings. I was told to go and assassinate him because he was a Catholic and he was picking up information.

Livingstone began to question Baker about an incident at the Red Lion pub in the centre of Belfast involving the UDA and a member of the 'Inner Circle' Murder Squad, an incident that livingstone said he had heard about from Republicans. Baker responded:

— of the Inner Circle Murder Squad was involved in that. The UDA went over to do an assassination at the Red Lion which is beside the Albert Clock in Belfast city centre, but a police Landrover came round the corner and — [he refers to the same detective] was parked in the car park just beside the Albert Clock. The assassination didn't come off because the Landrover came round the corner, so the guns were put in the detective's car and he drove them back through police and Army checkpoints to East Belfast and handed them back over to us. But the assassination was carried out later with police guns and machine-guns -Sterling sub-machine-guns.

When Livingstone asked Baker about the killing of Fay, the version he gave differed slightly from those given to police in England and subsequently in Belfast:

I was sitting —, you see I used to have to do security on the whole territory and there was me, —, — and a few others who were also doing security at the hotel. We'd move into the hotel and fake the waiters' coats and things. We'd be armed and we'd be walking through the hotel and down the lobbies and corridors underneath. So the Inner Council was in this room and Fay came with drinks. They ordered drinks and he came up with the drinks and Tommy Herron — . I don't know where he got the information—but he found out the geezer was a Catholic. He ordered his assassination in case he overheard anything and I went down to Island Street and assassinated him.

When Baker was admitting his part in the murder to police in Belfast and in England he did not describe his role in the hotel or how Fay entered the room where the Inner Council was meeting. It may be that at the time he did not wish to identify himself too closely with the Inner Council or them too closely with Fay. It could be he was worried about risking the safety of his family by implicating, even indirectly, such high-ranking figures as Inner Council members. On the other hand one has to ask whether Baker was bragging to Livingstone to convince him of his closeness to the Inner Council.

In his use of language Baker betrays himself as a cold, clinical killer lacking in emotion, who deals with the subject of murder in such a matter-of-fact way that he describes the young man he so cruelly executed as a 'geezer'. Is this the man who walked into a police station suffering from remorse? Does he sound like someone who should be believed, or is he the calculating mass murderer plotting to distance himself from the decision-making process, absurdly believing that this will lead to an early release? Or is he a man seeking to revenge himself on a system which punished him with a life sentence? Equally, could some of his claims remotely relate to the truth?

Livingstone sought to discover whether Unionist politicians attended Inner Council meetings of the UDA. Baker replied that they were careful never to appear in places where the UDA leadership were known to meet, since they were likely to be under police surveillance. The UDA leaders would hire the upper room of the Bunch of Grapes pub on the Beersbridge Road in East Belfast for meetings with Unionist politicians. Baker emphasised that although Unionist politicians were not involved in UDA operations some would have known what was taking place owing to their contact with the UDA leadership. He then informed Livingstone that he had spoken to the RUC Corruption Squad but had not told them all he knew, and he offered an explanation of why he believed he might now be a target and, ironically, why he wished to return to serve his sentence in Northern Ireland:

I believe if I expose the RUC, the weapons and so forth and the British intelligence involvement that I'll be found dead in my cell. I am presently taking legal action against the British government to get repatriated back to Northern Ireland because they say I am not unsuitable to go back. I was only under the impression I came to this country for two years. They've got a special unit in Northern Ireland for converted terrorists. Well, one of the points I am bringing out in this judicial review is the RUC arms going missing. If this fails, I've only got one option left and that's to publicly petition Charles Haughey to ask the Gardai to investigate the RUC. I know it will cause a stink in Parliament but it's the only option left open to me. If they do not under any circumstances move me back to Northern Ireland I will publicly petition Haughey and I will give the Gardai all the details. Under the Anglo-Irish Agreement, section 'D', paragraph 'F', it states that they can intervene. I never thought the RUC would be charged anyway because the Kincora file [Kincora was a boys' home where a homosexual ring operated involving prominent

Loyalists and several English civil servants working at the Northern Ireland Office; the home was situated in East Belfast, less than half a mile from UDA HQ] went missing from RUC HQ at Brooklyn [also in East Belfast] and the RUC's a tightly knit family and everything that goes in does not come out. All the information they receive is kept and the Kincora file was kept. Now if they were to charge the RUC officers, it's my belief that the Kincora file would reappear somewhere.

The above statement reveals that Baker had spent much time studying the Anglo-Irish Agreement, searching for ways of manoeuvring himself from obscurity into the limelight of Northern Ireland where, as part of a group of terrorists 'converted' to Christianity, his case would be more favourably examined by the Life Review Board. Conversion is a classic terrorist symptom in Northern Ireland. In some cases it has been a genuine reaction to solitary confinement and has had a beneficial effect. Several judges have responded favourably to a plea of conversion, and so has the Life Review Board, which constantly examines lifers for release or parole. Interestingly the conversions have taken place among Loyalist paramilitaries and not Republicans. The reason may be that Republican ideology has historically been supported by Catholicism in Ireland. Loyalist terror lacks that politico-religious imperative, so although Loyalists claim to be fighting for God and Ulster there may well be a subconscious lack of conviction that their type of God would approve of their forms of terror. However, many examples of conversion have been short-lived psychological reactions to imprisonment and others have been deliberately fabricated to seek leniency in court. Baker's comments about Kincora, aside from being an attempt to discredit the RUC, are laced with assumption, gossip and a single element of truth—namely that documents relating to the Kincora scandal did disappear from RUC files. He would have learned that from Colin Wallace or Ken Livingstone or from an intricate examination of certain press reports. Regarding the UDA's knowledge of Kincora, Baker observed: 'The whole Inner Council knew about it but there was no Inner Council members involved in it. There was politicians and senior Northern Ireland Office officials involved in it. I know one who's in the House of Commons. He's one of your own men.'

Livingstone: What was the attitude of the UDA? Presumably, pretty contemptuous of the Kincora people?

Baker: Well, as far as they were concerned they were being organised by the British intelligence and they kept away from that. They knew the intelligence services were running it.

Once Baker had mentioned Kincora to Livingstone, the interview centred on this topic, with Baker alleging that a senior political figure had been sexually involved with the young boys in care in the Kincora Boys' Home. However, Baker's replies to questions from the Labour MP were riddled with conjecture and generalisation. As far as his comments about the security services were concerned, he provided no evidence, although he claimed the UDA took photographs of Unionist politicians entering and leaving the Kincora building. Baker then led the interview back to his favourite topic, the RUC:

I was present when — [the uniformed policeman from Mountpottinger] walked into UDA HQ and handed over a Sterling sub-machine-gun. I was also present in a house in Diamond Street when he walked in. I was reassembling a self-loading rifle belonging to the UDR. It was handed to the Shankill UDA and they sent it to us. We even took a .38 pistol off a policeman at a roadblock. The next day — [the uniformed police officer] came down and said he wanted the pistol back and there were going to be raids. He gave us the names of the houses to be raided and we gave him the pistol. Everything that was in those houses was cleared out. I was also sitting at the bar in the Templemore when — [Inner Circle detective] walked in. I had two holdalls with about twelve guns in each. I was with —, —, sorting the guns out and swapping pistols, ammunition and magazines. — [detective] was sitting beside us.

He also told Livingstone that he gave the RUC the names of UDA bombers who had attacked the town of St Johnston in the Irish Republic in 1972. He said he believed this information was never conveyed to the Irish police because it would have compromised relations between Heath and Lynch, who were due to meet. Baker was asked about the 1972 bombing of Dublin, which the Provos say was the work of British intelligence and which Jack Lynch also reportedly linked to the British, albeit tentatively:

The cross-border activities were operated by one man, —. He was a member of the Inner Council from Derry. He was in charge of all cross-border operations and he had a link to a policeman in a police station in Derry's Waterside. You know the attacks on bars in Donegal—I told the RUC about that. — did them for his operators and two of our bombers from Belfast. It was coming up to Christmas 1972. There was St Johnston and shooting incidents in Donegal—machine-gunning bars. I think those bombs in Monaghan and Dublin were operated by British intelligence.

This aspect of Baker's evidence is of particular interest. The Dublin bombing in December 1972, which claimed so many lives, is still a mystery and should therefore be examined in the light of Baker's remarks. He indicated the UDA's ability to undertake a cross-border campaign in that year. Aside from the targets mentioned by him, it would be fair to assume that the obvious target for Loyalists would have been Dublin. Baker may well have known that the UDA bombed

Dublin, but he preferred to lend weight to a well-publicised theory that the Dublin attack was the work of British intelligence, in order to stress his view that British intelligence was not averse to engaging in murder. His account also confirmed what his interviewer, Ken Livingstone, believed. On the other hand, the eventual scale of damage to human life in Dublin and public reaction would have discouraged the UDA from publicly admitting its involvement. It was a legal organisation; it did not publicly claim responsibility for murder, and it even disassociated itself from Baker once he was convicted of brutal slayings. In fact, it was not until June 1973 that the UDA created the label of convenience, the Ulster Freedom Fighters (UFF), to claim responsibility for violence. By revealing what he knew about the UDA's ability to bomb cross-border targets in 1972, Walker Baker may well have provided a case for arguing that it was UDA/UVF members who bombed Dublin before Christmas in 1972 and not anyone connected with the security services. If the former Taoiseach, Jack Lynch, and other prominent Irish politicians had carefully examined the evidence in the context of what I have outlined, I believe they would not have hinted at British intelligence involvement.

In a separate part of the document which records his conversation with Livingstone, Baker alleges that the police colluded in the death of Paul McCartan: 'This man, McCartan, we picked him up at the corner of Finmore Street. He was let out of the RUC police Landrover about 50 yards from where we picked him up. He was actually let out of the police Landrover and we were standing waiting for him. The RUC picked him up and let him out about 150, about 100, yards from where we were. They knew we were there.' He added that police knew who was responsible for the murders in East Belfast and that by allowing McCartan to walk past Baker and the others the police were condemning him to death. Baker's evidence conflicts with that of the policeman who claims he offered McCartan a lift to his home. Although his accusation is based on supposition, I think the police were irresponsible in allowing McCartan to walk through a dangerous neighbourhood. The RUC patrol was morally and professionally obliged to insist on accompanying McCartan to his home. According to the police evidence, he was seen to fall, though he was 'fairly steady' when asked to reveal his name and address. His name would have indicated his religion, and his alcohol level would have suggested a degree of drunkenness. In the political climate of Northern Ireland, at 12.30 am, with hard men standing on street corners, the police patrol should have taken McCartan home, if necessary against his will. In not doing so, they provided Baker with an opportunity to point an accusing finger at them.

However, Baker gave Livingstone a different reason for the murder of Paul McCartan from the one he gave to police in England and later in Belfast before his court appearance. He told Livingstone that McCartan was a 'nobody' who was killed to 'keep the pot boiling' and to 'frighten the IRA and the Catholic community'. I firmly believe that the majority of killings by Loyalists then and in later years were carried out for such motives. The killing of Catholic 'nobodies' was a form of indiscriminate terror intended to frighten the Catholic population into rejecting the IRA, which claimed to be the defender of the nationalist population yet was unable to prevent such open terror. Ironically, the Loyalist tactic of attempting to demonstrate the IRA's inadequacy only forced nationalists further into a tribal ghetto and into the arms of the Provisionals.

Baker also told Livingstone that the 'Inner Circle' detective regularly provided the UDA leadership with RUC files on Republicans and people suspected of being involved with Republicans. These files were, according to Baker, like decks of cards and contained photographs. As I shall seek to demonstrate later in this book, this accusation does not surprise me, because the Loyalist paramilitaries received a large number of such files from disaffected members of the RUC and UDR in the 1970s. However, Baker makes 'a much more serious allegation':

Half the assassinations in Northern Ireland in the early seventies wouldn't have been committed if there hadn't been RUC backing. Half the people who died in those assassinations would have been living today, or more, if the RUC hadn't supported the assassination teams. The RUC knew who were the assassination teams. Every single one of them. For instance when I came forward, a policeman known as 'Paisley's friend' [nickname] sat at a table and gave me a book of photographs of everybody I operated with. The photographs were taken at different places and he gave me a book of photographs of everyone who belonged to the assassination teams in East Belfast. He said: 'There you are, Albert, have a look at them and tell us who you know and who you don't know.' I picked up the book, looked at it and I just couldn't believe it because they had every single member of the assassination teams down there—every single UDA man in the city centre, Dundonald, Ballybeen, getting off the bus, going to work, getting out of cars. So, if they didn't know who was on the assassination teams, what were the photographs for?

Baker further claims that when he was returned to Northern Ireland he found himself in the presence of the 'Inner Circle' Murder Squad detective, and that he told other policemen the detective was connected with the UDA: 'I said to them that he was in the UDA and the assassinations and he's handed over pictures and photographs of

Republicans and so forth. I was told: "Don't say anything about it." I told them that he was one of us but they said to say nothing. That night they went up to see my mother and father and told them not to say anything about this and not to do anything.'

One of the comments made by Baker in the course of his meeting with Ken Livingstone was that he was in contact with Republicans in prison. I believe this is how some of his allegations made their way to the outside world. Republicans would have been keen to circulate his claims; in turn those claims circulated by the Provisionals reached Ken Livingstone and were put as genuine questions to Baker. When the theory came full circle, it was being addressed to Baker as though the allegations were not his and he was being asked to corroborate them. As a result, when someone not sufficiently acquainted with Baker's claims reads the transcript of the interview with Ken Livingstone, Baker appears to be confirming widely held suspicions or allegations which have their origins elsewhere, when in fact the prime mover or prime conspirator all along was Albert Walker Baker.

Part of his evidence which I believe demands scrutiny is that there was at least one disaffected police officer in Mountpottinger station who was supplying the UDA with weapons and information. The RUC know—though they have not made a public admission—that weapons disappeared from Mountpottinger station in 1972-3. In the light of Baker's claim, I believe there is a need for investigation of those whom Baker is prepared to name. Equally, I think, it is important that other aspects of his story should be treated with scepticism.

There is, however, one piece of evidence I uncovered in preparing this book which demands answers, otherwise some of what Baker has said to Ken Livingstone may require a revised analysis. It is a hitherto unknown aspect of the Walker Baker story which may one day surface in his own account of events; and it concerns a secret trip he made while in custody in Northern Ireland in 1973. An inspector of prisons accompanied him on a journey to England where he was interviewed in a prison by MI6 investigators. The entire trip took less than twenty-four hours, and Baker was returned to his cell in Crumlin Road prison in Belfast without arousing suspicion. It was kept secret from the Royal Ulster Constabulary and to this day they have not been official-ly informed about it. I discovered that details of the trip were placed on a prison record, but it did not reveal the nature of the discussions which took place between the Loyalist assassin and MI6 personnel. The fact that an inspector of prisons accompanied Baker indicates that the journey was unusual and serious and that it had to be kept secret from all but a very few people. The orthodox procedure would have been to send two prison officers with him, but I am informed that this was considered unsatisfactory and a security risk. It was believed that some prison officers were not entirely 'trustworthy' and, as I illustrated in my book *The Shankill Butchers,* even the RUC regarded certain prison staff with a degree of suspicion on the grounds that they could easily be compromised and had Loyalist sympathies.

Since his conviction and the agreement to allow him to serve his sentence in England, Baker has campaigned for an early release, claiming that he was offered a deal when arrested in return for not revealing that he worked for British intelligence and that members of the RUC assisted UDA murder squads. RUC files show that while he was in custody in Belfast he privately hinted that he was in possession of explosive information about police officers. He was visited in prison by Assistant Chief Constable Meharg on the orders of the Chief Constable, Kenneth Newman, and was told that there would be no deal. I am also reliably informed that Newman ordered an internal inquiry which reported that Baker's allegations about the RUC were unfounded.

That leaves the 'unofficial' trip. Why did it take place and why was the RUC not informed? Did MI6 not trust the RUC, or were they concerned to conduct a private investigation into suggestions that he worked for them? Were they worried that they had a rogue operative who used Baker, or were they interested in Baker's allegations about police officers? I am inclined to believe that they were perturbed about Baker for reasons which concerned them alone. So why has Baker never made known the trip to England? Surely it would be in his interest to extend his revelations? It could be that Baker has withheld information about this episode because it is the only bargaining weapon left to him. The 'unofficial' trip and the fact that it has been kept as a secret prison record serves to muddy the waters somewhat. Like so many happenings in the dirty war, it leaves many questions unanswered and implies that MI6 and Baker were connected. It is for MI6 or those in authority in government to reveal the nature of that connection, to state whether Baker was an agent and informer, or whether an intelligence agency was merely seeking to determine the veracity of allegations about the British intelligence community. If clarification is not forthcoming there will always remain a suspicion that Baker was not only an assassin but part of a conspiracy.

What is unfortunate for both the Army and the RUC is that in 1972 the security forces' effort was aimed at the IRA, to the extent that the UDA and UVF, if not ignored, were at least perceived by some within military and police ranks as being the 'good guys'. When a bomb exploded at McGurk's Bar in North Queen Street killing fifteen people in 1972, the Army said it was an IRA 'own goal' and that the bomb was in the centre of the bar when it went off. That view was contrary to the evidence of a boy who saw the bomb being planted and to the forensic evidence, which showed that the seat of the explosion was the doorway of the bar. UDA men were later found guilty of the attack. Journalists were also told that another bomb, which exploded at Kelly's Bar on the Whiterock Road, was an IRA own goal. However, a secret Army observation post allowed soldiers to record the registration number of a car used in the bombing which exploded outside the bar. The Army said its occupants left the car and went into the bar for a drink, and a bomb in the car exploded prematurely. The registration number of the car would have indicated that it had been stolen earlier in a Protestant area. No one left the car and walked into the bar just before it exploded. The vehicle was abandoned by members of the UVF who left the vicinity of the bar as soon as the car bomb was in place. Again the explosion occurred in 1972, when it seemed the only terrorists were the IRA.

There was a closeness between some members of the Army and Protestant paramilitaries. In response to a *Sunday Times* revelation that the UVF was in possession of security forces files, the journalist Kevin Myers observed:

The fact that files on visitors to Republican prisoners in Long Kesh and on IRA suspects in the Catholic ghettoes have been leaked to a Protestant paramilitary organisation should not have surprised anyone....The fact that there has been a steady flow of information from the Security Forces to Loyalist paramilitary organisations has been common knowledge for some years now. Early in '73 I was shown some of the UVF files on the IRA. They were massively documented and many of them were officially listed 'Restricted'. I was shown a street map of Ligoniel, a northern outskirt of Belfast, which had been drawn up for British Army patrols; every house where a suspected IRA man was either occasionally billeted or lived was listed with some photographs attached. It was a formidable collection which formed only part of the UVF files. The UDA too have been receiving official files, often containing information not known to local British Army Battalion Intelligence and reserved to Army HQ at Lisburn. For example a leading UDA man was able to tell me within hours that a victim of a random assassination by the UVF was once a member of a certain IRA Unit.

Myers did point out that this did not mean that the Army was 'hand in glove' with terrorists but that a number of men in the security forces were sympathetic to the Loyalist cause. 'Jim Hanna of the UVF told me that a British Army patrol assisted him and two other UVF men into Corry's Timber Yard which overlooks the Catholic Ballymurphy area and were present when one of the three shot a young Catholic. He said that an Army Major discovered what was going on but did not arrest the UVF men.' Reliable Loyalist sources admit that in 1972 an Army officer approached a Loyalist paramilitary group and asked them whether they would be prepared to kill Ann Walsh, a Provisional from the Lower Falls. The officer, a major with an infantry regiment, offered safe conduct to the assassination team. A hit-squad undertook the mission but it was abandoned at the last minute because of unforeseen difficulties.

Myers argues that the intelligence files in Loyalist hands were piling up in 1972 because of disgruntled RUC men and members of the UDR, and he singles out an Army Officer, based in North Belfast, who was passing information about his patch to the UVF. The reason why security files were readily available to a wide range of security personnel was that the situation had to a degree developed out of control. Unfortunately some of the files contained information about suspects who were in fact innocent of any paramilitary involvement. So many people were being screened, particularly in nationalist areas, that files being handed to Loyalists contained the names and photographs of people who had merely been seen in the company of known Republicans.

Jim Hanna, the senior UVF commander in 1973, named among his close associates four Army officers, all attached to 39 Brigade intelligence at Lisburn HQ which was close to Hanna's home; for legal reasons they cannot be named here. Soldier A was an unknown quantity, but was believed to be a member of the SAS in a liaison role with 39 Infantry Brigade, one of a group brought into Northern Ireland by Brigadier Frank Kitson. Soldiers A and B spent a lot of time in Hanna's company, socialising and discussing politics. Hanna once told Kevin Myers that the Army officers often talked to him about his involvement in the UVF and went drinking and hunting with him. At the time Hanna was masterminding a bombing and shooting campaign. Hanna was later shot in a UVF feud. Within hours of his death police removed a series of photographs of Hanna and his Army associates. However, Kevin Myers acquired one photograph from a UVF source and published it. It portrayed Soldiers A and B in Hanna's home. Soldier B was pointing a revolver at the camera, and Soldier A an automatic rifle. They were both smiling.

Myers speculated that the Army officers 'milked' Hanna for information but did not hinder his military operations, though the relationship was not typical of the Army's overall attitude to Loyalist paramilitaries. I would concur with Myers's conclusion because the Army targeted increased intelligence on the Loyalist terror groups from 1973 onwards—and successfully so. However, the liaisons between members of the security forces and Loyalist paramilitaries were not appropriate to a democracy. Those liaisons such as were formed with Hanna only served to lay the groundwork for other conspiracy theories and the suspicion that the malaise lay deeper.

11

Airey Neave and the INLA
The Unseen Hand?

In October 1986 Enoch Powell, the Unionist MP for South Down, claimed the Americans were responsible for the murder of Tory MP Airey Neave seven years earlier. Powell's allegation was made in a speech to the Federation of Conservative Students at a rally in Birmingham. He placed the murder in the context of a conspiracy, which he said began twenty years earlier and involved the British Foreign Office, British military intelligence and the United States, in particular the CIA. The aim of the conspiracy was to create a United Ireland within the NATO Alliance, and the immediate objective was to get rid of the Northern Ireland Unionist government which was an obstacle to the creation of a united Ireland. Powell told the students that MI6 and its friends 'proved equal to the job' but the Americans became alarmed when they realised that the new Tory leader, Margaret Thatcher, and her chief aide, Airey Neave, were not going 'to play ball'. 'The roadblock was cleared by eliminating Airey Neave on the verge of his taking office as Secretary of State for Northern Ireland and events were moved along the timetable path. Mrs Thatcher was then taken along the road signposted towards the next stage of the conspiracy—the Anglo-Irish Agreement.'

Many Tory MPs including the Prime Minister, Margaret Thatcher, condemned Powell for making such a claim, and Dame Jill Knight strongly suggested that the time was long past when people respected the logic of

Mr Powell. From 1986 onwards Powell has continued to reiterate his claim, but has never provided the supporting evidence which should be available when a politician decides to utter such a major allegation. I contend there is no evidence whatsoever to link the CIA or any other official body with Neave's death. However, the subsequent killings of some of those who planned his murder produced other theories—namely that there was a revenge motive which led to British involvement in planning the execution of the leaders of the terror group which assassinated him. The murderers of Neave were members of the Irish National Liberation Army (INLA), and the origins of that organisation are important to an understanding of why they selected a major British politician for assassination and how their decision bore no relation to Powell's theory that his death was part of a 'dirty tricks' policy to further a British-American conspiracy.

The INLA was born in 1974. On 8 December that year the rambling hotel known as the Spa in Lucan, County Dublin, was the venue for a meeting of eight Republicans and socialists. The Republicans, who were in the majority, were members of the Official IRA who were disillusioned with the policies of their organisation. They felt that the Official IRA had failed to provide a coherent policy on the national question after its split with the Provisionals, that its violence lacked direction, and that its understanding of socialism was not sufficiently radical.

Hence the meeting in the Spa brought together Republicans who considered that force was necessary in the immediate objective of forcing the British out of Ireland and as a preliminary stage in creating a workers' republic in the spirit of James Connolly and his Citizen Army of the pre-1916 period. The socialists had come to accept the physical-force thesis and the necessity to seek accommodation with a Republican strategy which would deliver the preliminary goal of British withdrawal. The central figure uniting these political groupings was Seamus Costello, who had joined the IRA as a teenager and fought in the campaign of violence in the 1950s, earning for himself the nickname 'The Boy General'. He was a committed Republican who perceived himself to be in the tradition of the man he considered the real hero of the 1916 revolution, James Connolly. After the 1970 split he became disenchanted with the Official IRA as he saw it move towards a policy of uniting Catholic and Protestant in Northern Ireland at the expense of fighting to remove the British on the road to a socialist republic. The Official IRA was indeed redefining its philosophy, and this would lead to its jettisoning its claim to have a military wing, its Republican label and its aim of a United Ireland in favour of a more modest policy of uniting workers; the result was eventually the emergence of the Workers' Party and the apparent disappearance of the Official IRA.

At the Spa hotel the delegates, with Costello in the chair, formed the Irish Republican Socialist Party (IRSP). Many delegates then left the hotel with the aim of spending succeeding months in marshalling support for the new party. Those who stayed held a secret meeting, with the Boy General again in the chair. Costello, who was in an IRA Flying Column in the 1950s and subsequently played leading roles at senior military levels of the IRA, announced the formation of a military wing of the new political party. He told those present that an initial sum of £50,000 was available for the purchase of weapons. Sitting alongside Costello was twenty-seven-year-old Ronnie Bunting, a Protestant who had converted to Republicanism—though his father, Major Ronald Bunting, was a staunch Loyalist and had been Ian Paisley's leading henchman in the early years of the Troubles. Bunting Junior was a product of the Queen's University People's Democracy organisation, which forced the civil rights struggle into a violent stance in 1969 and whose members included Bernadette Devlin, Eamonn McCann and many other radicals.

Costello told his gathering that he intended to name the new party's military wing the Irish National Liberation Army. Some present argued successfully that the name and existence of the organisation should be kept secret until such time as a major operation was planned and successfully executed, and that if a need arose to resort to the use of the military wing it would be called the People's Liberation Army. This eventually occurred much sooner than anticipated. The Official IRA reacted aggressively to the emergence of the IRSP, and when members of the military wing began to take arms from Official IRA arms dumps a feud developed.

The first fatality was on 20 February 1975. He was Hugh Ferguson, a defector from the Official IRA. The new terror group reacted quickly and shot dead the Official IRA's quartermaster in Belfast, Sean Fox. As the feud continued there were more deaths and seventy people were wounded. Clergy and trade-union officials attempted to mediate but failed. On 28 April a teenage recruit to the IRSP killed the Belfast leader of the Official IRA, Liam McMillen, as he walked through the Lower Falls area. McMillen was a Republican of long standing, and highly respected for his knowledge of politics and history. His death temporarily ended the feud. The bloody baptism of the IRSP and the sudden emergence of its military wing made it clear that the military wing was dictating events and was likely to take control of the party. Bernadette McAliskey (formerly Devlin) and others on the party executive argued unsuccessfully that the IRSP and not the INLA should be the dominant force. When a debate on this issue ensued and a vote was taken, Costello, the chairman of the IRSP but also Chief of Staff of the INLA/PLA, placed his casting vote in favour of the INLA's retaining ultimate control of the military and political direction of the movement. Bernadette McAliskey and ten others resigned; she later said that her departure was related to differences over the IRSP's balance between Republicanism and socialism. Costello maintained that the problem within the new party had arisen because the INLA had been forced to surface much too early under the guise of the People's Liberation Army in order to protect its members from the Official IRA. He did not admit that the dispute was related to a battle for the Marxist line that the party should control the military. Costello quickly established a military structure for the INLA which was very similar to that of the IRA. He set up an Army Council with a General Headquarters Staff to provide logistical support for several brigades, which in turn had units based on a cell system.

Ronnie Bunting was given the role of director of intelligence on the GHQ and adjutant of the Belfast Brigade. He was ideally suited to the intelligence role, since he was a clever, well-educated man with an experience of terrorism. His career in the IRA had developed in the early 1970s and he was an associate of Joe McCann, a well-known member of the Official IRA who held radical views and was involved in the first major political assassination attempt in Northern Ireland. (The target was the then Unionist Minister for Home Affairs, John Taylor. McCann was later shot by soldiers as he ran unarmed through the Markets area of Belfast.) By profession Bunting was a schoolteacher, but the Catholic Church in West Belfast denied him a job because of his religious background, though it was said by one clergyman that there was an additional reason—Bunting's claim to be an agnostic. One of his associates told me that Bunting was never fully accepted within the Catholic community: 'Ronnie was a dedicated Republican and socialist but people saw him as the son of Major Bunting. He tried hard to prove to people that he was genuine but he faced considerable prejudice. People saw him as a Prod and never fully trusted him. Those of us who were his comrades knew differently.' Bunting found work in the Medical Records Department of the Royal Victoria Hospital in Belfast and acquired a house for himself and his wife Susan in the Turf Lodge district, a staunchly Republican estate in the heart of West Belfast. His job would have given him access to the addresses of thousands of people, presumably including members of the security forces. His colleagues in the INLA were amazed that he was given security clearance to work in the Medical Records Department since Bunting was known to the RUC and Army and had been interned.

The initial problem facing the INLA was the acquisition of weapons and explosives. Costello pointed out to his men that the Provisionals would not tolerate any attempt to interfere with their Transatlantic arms-smuggling operations, and in any case Irish Americans would not support a grouping with obvious left-wing objectives such as the IRSP/INLA. The only alternative was to forge links with other organisations of the left in Europe and the Middle East and to purchase arms in both regions, since the PLO and other groups were often content to supply small amounts but required payment for large consignments because they too needed money. Accordingly Bunting set up meetings with 'anti-imperialist' groups in France and Germany to establish contacts, start a dialogue with the PLO and develop an arms-smuggling route. The initial meetings in Germany were arranged through contacts with students and journalists who visited Northern Ireland and through channels which had previously been established by members of the Official IRA. Bunting attended a secret meeting with members of Rote Armee Fraktion (Red Army Faction), also known as the Baader-Meinhof group, who provided him with a liaison with the Movement Second June, the PLO and 'safe contacts' in Paris. Subsequent meetings led to an arms deal with the PLO.

Two INLA volunteers, Seamus Ruddy and Phelim Lally, were sent to Paris. Initially they arranged for small quantities of pistols and AK47 Kalashnikov rifles to be transported to Ireland. These were smuggled to Ireland in cars using continental ferry routes. Then a larger arms deal was negotiated with the PLO and money was required. The INLA robbed a security van in Limerick and acquired £250,000, half of which was the payment for arms which would be smuggled into Ireland over a prolonged period. Lally and Ruddy travelled to the Middle East to pick up the first part of the consignment, which consisted of Soviet 71 grenades, plastic explosives and assault rifles. While crossing the border from Turkey into Greece in a mobile caravan Lally and Ruddy were arrested and the arms seized. Costello was obliged to pay a large sum of money to have Lally and Ruddy released, but his major worry was that their capture compromised relations with the PLO. Now that the PLO were publicly accepted as the group which supplied the weapons, the intelligence services began to scrutinise the PLO's European contacts and operations.

In 1977 Costello, who had survived an assassination attempt after the killing of McMillen, was shot dead as he sat in his car in a Dublin street. His assassin, Jimmy Flynn, used a sawn-off shotgun. He walked alongside Costello's car, watched his victim reading a newspaper and then fired four rounds through the car window. Flynn was later murdered by the INLA. Costello's departure robbed the INLA of an experienced leader and left younger radicals such as Bunting in charge of military operations. Bunting continued with others to develop international contacts. One of his associates from that period remembers how he operated:

After Costello was shot, the security services and forces were always probing to discover who was emerging. I attended a conference in 1978 in Germany with the Red Army Faction and other groups that are as close as Sinn Fein is to the IRA. Deals were done and the PLO also proved helpful. Contacts in Rome proved instrumental in setting up arms deals. Ronnie was not essentially a gunman. He was intelligent and efficient and argued a lot that our policy should be to do more political hits instead of shooting members of the security forces. He believed that once you started to hit those with political control you began to damage the edifice of power and force change.

Bunting's strategy also included what Costello from the outset believed was essential to launch the INLA—a major operation. In Bunting's view that necessitated the killing of a leading political figure, preferably someone whose death would symbolise 'a popular hit' in Ireland. He chose the one man in British politics who was unequivocal in his denunciation of terrorism and his suggested methods for combating it: Airey Neave. In the Republic of Ireland in 1978 Neave, as the Tory shadow spokesman for Northern Ireland, was labelled 'an Ireland basher'. His criticism was levelled not just at the Irish but at the Labour Secretary of State for Northern Ireland, Roy Mason. On 18 March 1978 he stated: 'We recognise that the Irish Government have taken a number of steps to counter terrorism but if they want to seem credible and sincere in their condemnation of coldblooded murder in the North further action is required. Despite joint legislation on fugitive offenders, there are far too many people skulking in the Republic who are wanted by the RUC for terrorist crimes in the North.'

Airey Neave had escaped from the Nazi prison camp at Colditz and later recorded his escape and other Second World War exploits in a book entitled *They Have Their Exits.* However, throughout the 1970s he was a colourless politician with a low profile on Ireland issues. His political prominence developed during the late 1970s and must be seen in the context of his political affinities and his closeness to Margaret Thatcher. He masterminded her rise to the leadership of the Conservative Party, and this served to elevate him to a more defined political role and overshadowed his history of political anonymity. Though he represented Tory fundamentalism throughout his political life, he had been ignored by successive Tory leaderships. In 1975, with his sixtieth birthday looming, political success was finally on the horizon. Margaret Thatcher rewarded him with the shadow brief for Northern Ireland, and he also served as her chief adviser. His loyalty was greatly appreciated because he brought to his work not only a dogged determination but two decades of political experience. Most political observers were convinced by 1978 that the next government would be Tory and that Airey Neave would assume the role of Secretary of State for Northern Ireland. This concerned the Dublin government, the Catholic Social Democratic and Labour Party and senior members of the British Labour Party. Ulster Unionists, however, saw his views on terrorism as akin to theirs, though they were refusing to talk to him in the autumn of 1977, partly because Enoch Powell was encouraging Unionist MPs to help prolong the life of the Callaghan Labour government in the hope of extracting concessions.

Neave relentlessly pursued the security issue, demanding that the Labour government introduce internment, full-scale deployment of the SAS and the arrest on sight of known Republicans whether or not there was evidence against them. The SDLP and other nationalist groupings in Ireland feared that Neave as Secretary of State would exacerbate the conflict by adopting draconian measures such as internment which had previously failed and left a legacy of bitterness. They also perceived Neave as a majority-rule Unionist, who did not believe in the prospect of power-sharing in Northern Ireland and saw a devolved government as the way forward. Some nationalists interpreted this to mean the return of Unionist majority rule in a Stormont parliament. The SDLP argued that this would represent a retrograde step and return the province to the situation before 1969, to greater alienation within the Catholic community and to increased support for terrorism. It is doubtful if Airey Neave would ever have been in a position to implement any of his ideas, though he would undoubtedly have introduced a harsher security policy. The INLA were not prepared to wait to discover whether Airey Neave would defeat terrorism with stricter methods and so change history. They saw him as the 'popular hit'.

We chose Neave not because of the threat that he posed. The Provos would eliminate a political figure if he was a threat or, like Paisley, they will not hit him because his extremism furthers their cause by damaging Unionism and therefore confronts the British in another way. They will also hit a leading politician in revenge for what that person has done to them. The Brighton Hotel bomb was a revenge attack and was probably related more to that than ultimately changing the course of British history. We hit Neave because of what he represented and we knew that nationalists, Republicans and socialists would understand and so it would be a popular hit. He represented oppression. His language was riddled with it. He had to go.

Although these remarks partly symbolise INLA/European terrorist thinking, they also express another important factor. The INLA was determined to launch itself on the terrorist scene with an assassination which would strike at the heart of the British establishment and bring itself to prominence. They were in competition with not only the Provisionals but other organisations throughout Ireland, and they were determined to prove that they could be as ruthless and daring. The planned assassination was, I believe, as much a callous stunt as it was a politically motivated act.

In January 1979 a member of the INLA from North Armagh, who is a free man at the time of writing, developed a detonator which later became known as the mercury tilt-switch device. The switch in itself was harmless and could be purchased through a radio spares catalogue. However, the bomb-maker, who spent much of his leisure time tampering with mechanical devices, soon recognised that the mercury tilt-switch advertised in the catalogues would allow a bomb to be detonated without the use of radio signals which enable it to be detected or exploded prematurely by Army scanning machines. He ordered several switches and experimented with them until he produced a prototype bomb, which he demonstrated for the INLA leadership. It was a simple mechanism. A tiny bomb was attached with magnets to the underside of an empty car, which was dragged by a tow-rope from another vehicle at a considerable distance. When the car containing the bomb mounted a small incline, the bomb exploded. The tilting caused water in the switch to be mixed with mercury, and this in turn set off an electrical current and detonated the bomb. The bomb-maker explained that the switch could be applied to a vehicle when it was stationary with little risk to the bomber. However, once the car was tilted, the chain reaction would begin.

The INLA leadership including Bunting demanded that, if such a device were to be used for a major hit such as Neave, it had to be tested 'for real'. A victim was chosen in the bomb-maker's home town of Portadown. He was Robert McAnally, a twenty-year-old lance-corporal in the Ulster Defence Regiment. On 6 March 1979 McAnally drove his Morris Marina estate car out of a car park at West Street in Portadown. As the car left the car park it went over a small ramp and an explosion ripped through the vehicle mutilating the lower half of the driver's body. He died one week later after several operations including the amputation of his legs. Police investigating the murder tried to trace his movements to discover when the bomb had been placed under the driver's side of the car. Since they did not know that it had been placed and primed in the car park, they wondered if it had been put under the vehicle earlier in the day and wired with a timing device. Only one newspaper, the *Belfast Newsletter*, suggested that a mercury tilt-switch might have been used. I assume that someone within the police or Army had informed a reporter of indications from forensic tests. The *Newsletter* offered the following possible explanations: 'One theory is that the booby-trap was fixed to the British Leyland Marina overnight at his home. Another is that a magnetic bomb with a mercury tilt-switch was slipped under the car as it sat in the car park.'

Little attention was paid to the latter theory by the media or seemingly by the security forces until several weeks later. The killing of McAnally sealed the fate of Airey Neave. A unit of four INLA men led by a man from West Belfast was tasked with the assassination. The unit tracked

Neave's movements to and from the underground car park at the House of Commons each day. They attached the bomb with two magnets to the underside of Airey Neave's blue Vauxhall car. The bomb included a wristwatch set to prime the bomb at a time when the terrorists knew the car would be in the underground car park at the House of Commons, and a mercury tilt-switch was attached to it so that once the bomb was primed it would explode when the car was accelerating or going up an incline. The terrorists knew that even if the car was travelling slowly it had to be driven up a ramp from the Commons car park, and it was then that the bomb went off. After the explosion a policeman ran to the car to discover that Airey Neave was still alive, though his legs had been blown off. Half an hour later he died in the hospital. The House of Commons was shocked. Lord Fitt, who was standing beside Margaret Thatcher when news reached her of the terrible end to the life of her friend and colleague, said she was shocked and unable properly to convey her grief.

The assassination placed the INLA firmly on the stage of international terror and led to demands that the perpetrators be found. Unfortunately the security services and the police and Army in Northern Ireland knew little about the INLA. The INLA informed reporters that the killing was the 'operation of the decade': 'We blew him to bits inside the impregnable Palace of Westminster.' A leading member of the INLA told *Magill* magazine in Ireland that Neave was killed because he was a militarist and because he was demanding greater use of the SAS and the strengthening of the UDR: 'It is time that Westminster armchair-militarists suffer directly the consequences of their policies.' No mention was made of the fact that Airey Neave was an easy target, a 'popular hit'. The *Magill* reporter asked how the bomb had been planted and was told, incorrectly, that it had been placed under the driver's seat while the car was parked under the House of Commons. The designer of the bomb which killed Airey Neave claims to have set up a demonstration of the device for the Provisionals and in return they gave him several rifles and pump-action shotguns. During 1979 the INLA continued to develop its terrorist campaign and a select group of volunteers were given training at a PLO camp in Lebanon.

Meanwhile the IRSP was becoming involved in prisoners' action committees and translating IRSP political philosophy into foreign languages so that it could be exported to a wider audience. In particular they were keen to export their analysis of the 'dirty protests' taking place in the H-Blocks. The term H-Block derived from the shape of the cells which held terrorist prisoners, the majority of them IRA, at the Maze prison outside Belfast. The Maze was originally known as Long Kesh, which was in essence a concentration camp housing Republicans and Loyalists during the internment phase. At that time Long Kesh was divided into compounds controlled by the various terrorist organisations. The internees drilled and the camp was run along the lines of what people associate with movie images of Colditz, except that prisoners held in Long Kesh were regularly given political and military lectures to prepare them for the war when they were released. This behaviour was permitted under an order by William Whitelaw in 1972 which accorded special-category status to not only internees but those sentenced to more than nine months for offences related to civil disturbances. This granted prisoners the right to wear their own clothes, have extra visits and food parcels. They were not obliged to work. By December 1974 there were 1200 prisoners in Northern Ireland enjoying special-category status. It gave the paramilitaries a prisoner-of-war status which the government began to recognise as causing a total breakdown of discipline within the prisons. As a propaganda weapon it was used, particularly by the IRA, to embarrass the British government. The IRA were adept at telling the world that the British government kept political prisoners in its gaols.

As a result of a report by Lord Gardiner, special-category status was abolished for anyone convicted of an offence after 1 March 1976. This had the effect of reducing the number of special-category prisoners and thus weakening the influence of the paramilitaries in the prison. Long Kesh, which remained the IRA symbol of government repression because of its compounds, was renamed the Maze prison. New cell blocks were put into operation to house terrorist prisoners convicted after 1 March. Those cell blocks were constructed in the shape of an H and were designed so that each block held 100 prisoners. The H-Blocks had probably the most modern facilities in any prison within the United Kingdom, each block being linked to workshops and recreational areas and facilities. The IRA recognised that erosion of political-prisoner status deprived it of much-needed propaganda and was a way for the British government of criminalising terrorists. Republicans, both Provisional IRA and INLA, refused to co-operate with the new system. In March 1978, 300 prisoners began to refuse to wear prison clothing or to do prison work. They used their cell blankets as a form of clothing and smashed the furniture in their cells. As the protest escalated more prisoners became involved and the tactics became more extreme. They refused to use the washing or toilet facilities and smeared the walls of their cells with excreta. This latter tactic gave the action the title 'dirty protest' and the world's press soon became acquainted with what was going on in the Maze prison in particular, though the protest was not restricted to that prison. Nationalist politicians and the Catholic Bishop of Armagh, later to be Cardinal O'Fiaach, called for the British government to negotiate with those engaged in the protest and to do something about the 'inhuman conditions in the Maze'. In order to focus attention on the protest in Europe and the United States, an organisation known as the National H-Blocks/Armagh Committee was formed. The government soon realised that the H-Blocks Committee was making steady progress in orchestrating support for the 'dirty protest', particularly among Irish Americans in the United States. Many people in the Protestant community saw the committee as an organisation promoting IRA demands and at worst a front organisation for Republican terrorists. The British government for its part was keen to support such a view as a means of discrediting the committee. The committee was heavily laden with Republican figures, as well as people on the political left who saw it as a human rights issue. Those Republicans who were prominent in the H-Blocks leadership were from within the Provisional IRA/Sinn Fein, the INLA and the Irish Republican Socialist Party.

One of the leading figures in the IRSP was Miriam Daly, a fifty-two-year-old lecturer in political studies at Queen's University. Aside from her role as a political strategist within the IRSP/INLA she was also a key member of the National H-Blocks/Armagh Committee. Miriam Daly was a formidable campaigner, but secretly she was giving political lectures not to university students but to students of terrorism. During the mid-sixties she had worked in Camden Town in London and helped newly arrived Irish immigrants. With the emergence of a civil rights campaign in Northern Ireland in 1968, she returned to Belfast, where she became intricately involved in the campaign and for a short period was a member of the Social Democratic and Labour Party. Her politics, fiery and colourfully expressed, were more suited to a harder tradition, and it was to Republicanism that she turned her attention. Although she devoted much of her time to campaigning on behalf of prisoner welfare groups, essentially she was a new breed of radical who was ideally suited to INLA/IRSP politics. Like Costello she dreamed of uniting all 'anti-imperialist' groupings in Ireland and was also prepared to sanction the use of terror. Fifteen months after the murder of Airey Neave, she met an equally brutal fate in mysterious circumstances.

On the morning of 26 June 1980 Miriam Daly's husband James, who was in Dublin, phoned his home in the predominantly Catholic Andersonstown area of West Belfast. He was pleased to discover that 'Miriam was at home and was in excellent form'. Some time between 2.30 and 3.15 in the afternoon she was seen buying a cake in a local bakery shop. At 3.20 her ten-year-old daughter arrived home from school to find her mother lying dead in the hallway, her hands and feet bound, and a considerable amount of blood on the floor. A scenes-of-crime officer who arrived an hour later reported: 'Mrs Daly's body was face downwards on the floor. A large area of the hall was covered in blood. Four spent cartridges and two bullets were nearby. Her hands and legs were tied. It seemed to me that an execution had taken place.' Several feet from the body was a cushion which the killer had used to deaden the sound of the six fatal shots fired into Miriam Daly's head from a 9mm semi-automatic pistol. Detective Sergeant Clarke, who undertook to lead the murder investigation, was puzzled by the use of this particular weapon: as he pointed out at an inquest: 'Only one weapon was used—a 9mm pistol. It is the first time that this particular type of weapon has come to the attention of the police. And the phone was cut.'

No organisation claimed responsibility for the murder, and detectives were puzzled by the fact that it had been professionally executed in the middle of the Andersonstown area in daylight. There was no evidence to suggest that Loyalist murder squads had ever shown such professionalism or daring. The result of uncertainty as to the identity of the killers fuelled speculation, as reported in *Hibernia:*

The most likely explanation is that a Loyalist group was responsible but another theory is that she was the victim of an SAS undercover squad. Her killers carried out a clinical and professional murder. The phone was silenced inside the house but gave the impression to several incoming callers that it was ringing unanswered....

Another factor is the clear determination of practically every branch of the British Secret Service to deliver up those members of INLA responsible for Airey Neave's assassination. A special Cabinet sub-committee, orginally set up to deal with emergencies such as the 1974 miners' strike, gave carte blanche—including unlimited financial resources and promises of commendations—to those Anti-Terrorist Squad officers who produced convictions for Airey Neave's assassination. Other groups, such as MI5, MI6 and the little-known Security and Intelligence Group which is attached to the Territorial Army and comprises SAS members, have also made their enquiries. As the months went by with little or no results, other more ominous noises began to emanate from the same agencies. If there were no convictions, the messages ran, then there would be satisfaction of another sort; even if it meant killing non-military members of the IRSP such as Miriam Daly.

This *Hibernia* article also concluded that the most likely culprits were Loyalist paramilitaries, yet it carried the theories which pointed to an unseen hand, namely that of the British military. This demonstrated one rule in the dirty war: when in doubt, blame the British; it's good for propaganda. The press officer of People's Democracy issued a statement condemning the murder and alleged British complicity: 'We believe that the conception of this campaign of assassination and the detailed planning and intelligence necessary are beyond the capacity of any of the Loyalist groups. Theirs may be the hand on the trigger but the brain is that of British Military Intelligence.'

Two months after the killing David McKittrick wrote an article for the *Irish Times* claiming that Loyalists were the killers but their target was James Daly, and adding that the killers were probably members of the Ulster Defence Association. McKittrick based his story on security forces' sources. In the immediate aftermath of the murder there were numerous press reports that the killers were in the Daly home for several hours and that only highly trained assassins would undertake such daring. Journalists were unaware that Miriam Daly had been seen in a bakery between 2.30 and 3.15, that she left her home shortly before 2.30 and that her body was discovered at 3.20. Their assumption that the killers had spent part of the day in the house led to the speculation that they had been waiting for James Daly to return from Dublin and that he was the intended target. This is borne out by David McKittrick's report on 14 August 1980: 'As yet no evidence has appeared to suggest that members of the security forces were instrumental in the death of Mrs Daly. The fact that Loyalist gunmen had coolly remained in her home for a time in a hardline Republican area has been pointed to by Republican sources as evidence of security force collusion in the incident.' While David McKittrick was printing an inaccuracy about the time the killers spent in the Daly home, he was also expressing the theory that only SAS-type operatives could so 'coolly remain in the Daly home and finally execute Miriam Daly'.

What few people knew at the time was that UDA leader John McMichael (later assassinated by the Provisional IRA) had set up a number of hit-squads. McMichael privately confided to associates that the squads were professionally trained and had access to good intelligence, and that he had contacts within the UDR and RUC who kept him informed of the whereabouts of targets and when necessary would provide information about security forces' movements in areas prior to and following an assassination. I met McMichael on numerous occasions and formed the opinion that he was a clever and ruthless enemy of Republicanism. On one level he was a man who sought to give working-class Loyalism a political ethos which was not simply rooted in the Unionist tradition but capable of being moulded to take Northern Ireland along an independent route or towards a degree of shared-responsibility government with Catholics. Behind the political rhetoric, however, he was also a leader of the UDA's military wing, the Ulster Freedom Fighters. He shaped the UFF into a militarily more capable force than previously, and a former soldier who had been discharged from the UDR helped to train a new grouping of men into assassination teams. Like Bunting, McMichael decided to go for 'political hits'.

Gerry Adams was placed at the top of the hit-list. The plan was to kill him as he travelled to the annual Republican commemoration at Bodenstown in the Irish Republic. A bogus UDR roadblock would be set up on the route that Adams would take and he would be killed on the spot. McMichael was certain he could acquire up-to-the-minute intelligence on Adams's route on the relevant day. However, the plan was finally abandoned in favour of other assassinations including the killing of

Miriam Daly. The target for the killers was not James Daly but his wife, who was regarded as one of the leaders of the INLA. There is every reason to assume that the killers did have what McMichael claimed to possess, up-to-the-minute intelligence from dissident members of either the UDR or the RUC, because such was the professionalism of the killing that planning would have required accurate information owing to the geographical location of the Daly home and the need for close surveillance to establish that Miriam Daly was in her house. The killers may have entered the premises while she was at the bakery shop, but all the evidence indicates that they spent little time in carrying out their appointed task. The fact that the pistol was a military-issue weapon rarely if ever used by terrorists remains a puzzle, but it may well have been stolen from the security forces or borrowed from someone in a security role. However, in the context of Northern Ireland, such a weapon could have been a 'one-off' in a consignment of other weapons purchased abroad.

If the murder of Miriam Daly created speculation that an 'unseen hand' or, in Republican parlance, 'British intelligence' was involved in assassinations, then a double murder several months later served to fuel such suspicions.

At 3.30 am on 15 October 1980 gunmen wearing khaki pullovers and ski masks burst into a house in the Andersonstown area and shot dead two men. One of the men was the INLA leader, Ronnie Bunting. His wife was also shot but survived. After the double murder, Paddy Devlin, a former SDLP chief whip and cabinet minister, blamed the SAS and to this day is convinced that an 'SAS-type' unit was responsible. Once again the finger pointed at the British because of the manner in which the assassins behaved. Yet in this instance there was reason—not properly articulated at the time—to believe an 'unseen hand' was behind the murders.

Ronnie Bunting's wife Susan observed that the killers were cool and calm, 'like animals with no fear': 'They had no smell of fear about them.' The man who was shot with Bunting was a significant figure in the IRSP/INLA, Noel Lyttle. His death received little scrutiny because he was less prominent than Bunting. However, unknown to the public he was a political strategist who had assumed Miriam Daly's role and responsibilities within the terror group. He was a central figure in the H-Blocks campaign and exported anti-British propaganda. Until 1.00 am on that morning Lyttle and Bunting had sat discussing their organisation's future strategy. Susan Bunting says her husband joined her in bed at 1.30 and Noel Lyttle was given a bed in a room where the Buntings' fourteen-month-old son was sleeping. Two other children, aged three and seven, were in another bedroom. Susan Bunting's recollection of the killings provides an insight into the professionalism of the hit-squad.

At 3.30 we heard banging downstairs. We both jumped out of bed but, by the time we

got up, the men were already pushing in the bedroom door. We tried to force the bedroom door closed but the shooting started and I fell back on the bed. The next
moment two men were in the room and started shooting Ronnie.

Susan Bunting jumped on the back of one of the men but he continued
to fire. She was shot three times in the side, back and one hand.

While I struggled with one of the men, the other left, casual-like, without a care. As
he walked downstairs he shouted something like: 'Come on Geordie or Georgie.' The
other man then left and as he walked to the stairs he shot me in the mouth. I turned
and saw Ronnie. I knew he was dead. His eyes were wide and just staring. Noel, I
think, was still alive because I could hear him breathing.

Noel Lyttle was shot as he tried to get out of bed and died from his
injuries on the way to hospital. Susan Bunting sent her seven-year-old
daughter Fiona to summon help. When neighbours arrived they found
Susan Bunting still alive, sitting looking at her husband's body. She was
taken to intensive care in the Royal Victoria Hospital. She was unable to
furnish police with exact details of the murders until she recovered, and
then she revealed interesting observations. The killers wore ski-type
masks which covered their faces but provided holes for their eyes. They
were dressed in green ribbed pullovers with suede patches on the shoulders. While they were leaving the house they covered each other with
handguns in a military-style routine.

The car used by the killers was never traced, despite eyewitness
descriptions of it. This appeared highly unusual, because stolen cars
used in Loyalist killings are normally found abandoned or burned out.
Nor were the killers ever traced. The Protestant Task Force, an organisation which was only heard of in 1974 and has not been known since,
claimed responsibility for the murders. All that is known about this
grouping is that it issued a statement in 1974 saying its members were
former British Army soldiers. The statement bore the hallmarks of the
UDA, which created several labels, 'flags of convenience' to allow them
to claim responsibility for acts of violence. The Bunting/Lyttle murders,
I am informed from sources within the UDA, were carried out by the
squad that murdered Miriam Daly, and the killers were provided with the
necessary intelligence to enable them to get in and out of Andersonstown
safely and to gain entry to the Bunting home. Lyttle's presence was
regarded by some journalists as merely a 'bonus' to the killers. It is my
information, however, that they knew he was there. I am prepared to
believe the source of my information.

The facts themselves indicate that the gunmen behaved as though they
knew that their exit from the murder scene was guaranteed. They used a
sledge-hammer to batter down the door and they knew where to find not
only Bunting but Lyttle. Since Bunting's home was searched on numer-

ous occasions, security forces' files contained detailed notes on the lay-
out of his house and the sleeping arrangements. The killers would have
been concerned with escape and evasion. In wearing military-style
pullovers, they might have been permitted through a roadcheck, provided they had bogus identification. On the other hand, if they were assured
of safe passage from the murder scene, they might have worn military-
style gear to create paranoia in Republican ranks. Whatever the truth,
they were not amateur terrorists, and they acted with an assuredness
which, I contend, derived from a knowledge that their escape route was
clear. The INLA claims to have evidence that the killers were allowed to
pass unhindered through a UDR roadcheck after the killing. McMichael
later boasted that his 'people' carried out the murders and that they had
valuable assistance from people in the UDR who were sympathetic to the
aims of the UDA. As I demonstrated in an earlier chapter, the UDA and
UVF in North Armagh were able to operate successfully because of collusion by disaffected members of the police and UDR. I believe from the
information I have received and from what has already been published
that McMichael exploited this type of liaison to effect in 1980. The RUC
were puzzled by the Daly and Bunting episodes because of the behaviour
of the killers and their ability to penetrate an area under constant security surveillance. In RUC minds there was the suspicion that the gunmen
were acting on excellent information which could not have come from
intelligence gathered simply by the killers.

The final irony in the history of Ronnie Bunting was that his remains
were taken for burial from a funeral parlour opposite UDA headquarters
in East Belfast. As the cortege left the funeral premises a Loyalist flag was
raised in the UDA building. Major Ronald Bunting, the rabid Loyalist and
one-time associate of Ian Paisley, later told an inquest jury that he
believed his son had been killed because he fought for social justice. He
said that though he and his son were far apart politically they agreed on
fundamental issues. He saw him as a virtuous and high-minded man who
fought oppression and injustice whenever he found it, and was unwilling to accept that his son was a terrorist. Major Bunting's comments
reflected the absurdity of the situation in Northern Ireland. The Bunting
family saga epitomised the ironies of a society where father and son could
support opposite political extremes of the two tribes. In the case of Bunting
Junior, conversion proved, as in so many cases, that Protestant Republicans
tend to be more extreme than Catholic Republicans—as Catholic Loyalists
inevitably are more Loyalist than Protestants born in the tradition.

These strange dimensions to Irish/British life went unnoticed at the
inquest. Susan Bunting created the headline 'SAS killed my husband and
Noel'. That placed the killings predictably in the mythological realm of
dirty tricks.

1980 was a productive year for the UDA's revamped assassination squads within its military wing, the UFF. If observers had taken a closer look at particular events they would have become aware that the claim by nationalist politicians such as Paddy Devlin that SAS hit-teams were at work was a nonsense. The UDA's hit-list was composed mainly of members of the IRSP/INLA who also happened to be involved in the National H-Blocks Committee. Equally all of those on that committee were judged by the UDA to be members of the INLA, though such was not the case. Three weeks before the Daly killing a UDA hit-squad assassinated a member of the committee who did not belong to the INLA, and the manner in which the killing was planned should have indicated the true capability of the UFF.

The victim was John Turnly, aged forty-four, a member of the SDLP who later joined the Irish Independence Party. Like Ronnie Bunting, he was a Protestant converted to Republicanism and therefore loathed by Loyalists, who saw his political conversion to the other side as betrayal. Turnly was born into an old landed Protestant family and his father was a leading member of the Unionist Party. He was a teacher by profession but as a young man worked in Far-Eastern tea plantations before living in Japan and marrying a Japanese girl. In 1973 he returned to his native Carnlough in County Antrim and settled down. When he joined the SDLP, his father reacted by trying to disinherit him. After his father's death in the late 1970s, John Turnly, now a leading member of the Irish Independence Party, lived on his family's 300-acre estate with his wife and two children. His politics made him prominent because he lived in an Ian-Paisley-dominated constituency comprising towns such as Larne which were centres of rabid Loyalism. After trying three times to win a seat on Larne Council, in 1977 he became the council's only non-Unionist member. In 1979 he stood against Ian Paisley in the Westminster election. His politics, like those of Bunting, were extreme, and this incensed Loyalists. Since he was a member of the National H-Blocks Committee, the UDA viewed him as a closet terrorist, though his overt Republicanism and his 'act of betrayal' would alone have been sufficient to mark him down for assassination in the violent climate of Northern Ireland. His killers later claimed he was murdered because he was a member of INLA, but I am sceptical about such a motive. The killers belonged to the UFF, and they would have known that Turnly was neither IRSP nor INLA and was associated with Bunting and Daly merely through membership of the National H-Blocks Committee. The killing of Turnly, however, was to have a bearing on the Daly and Bunting murders when the members of the hit-squad were sentenced by a court in 1982. The killing, its planning and allegations made by one of the murderers had the effect of encouraging some people to re-examine the murders of the INLA leaders; and the suspicion of an unseen hand, if not the actual involvement of the SAS, surfaced again.

The men who killed Turnly were members of a UFF cell based in the town of Larne. The cell consisted of the following men: Robert McConnell (aged twenty-five), his brother Eric (aged nineteen), William 'Junior' McClelland (thirty-two), William McFetridge (thirty-two), David Hastings (twenty-six) and Matthew Martin (twenty-six), who was described in court in 1982 as a former sergeant in the Ulster Defence Regiment. Hastings and Martin, though members of the terrorist cell, were not charged with Turnly's murder. The former was sentenced to seven years' imprisonment in 1982 for stealing guns and wounding a police constable, and Martin was given five years for an attempted bombing, throwing an unlit petrol bomb and making pipe bombs in 1974. Matthew Martin's presence in the UDA's military wing, his long history of terrorism and his membership of the UDR illustrate once again how the UDA has so often been in a position to exploit the military and intelligence benefits of a wing of the security forces, namely the Ulster Defence Regiment.

The Larne UFF unit took its orders from the UDA leadership in Belfast. In April 1980 Robert McConnell, deputy leader of the cell, received instructions from Belfast to build a dossier on 'John Turnly from Carnlough'. According to McConnell, two high-ranking UDA officers told him that Turnly was 'a leading man in the INLA'. McConnell was instructed to discover where the target lived, the places he visited and 'whether he had any connections with any known INLA terrorists'. Since McConnell was a fish salesman, he decided to use his job and his boss's vehicle as a cover in assembling information on Turnly:

We found that he lived out at Carnlough and one evening I went out to sell fish to make sure it was the right house. I remember selling fish to Mrs Turnly at the big house where they lived. While I was there I saw their car sitting so I took the number. It was a Datsun estate, a metallic wine colour. I drove my Ford Escort van from the house but on the way down their avenue I stopped and took a lot of photographs of the house and other places on the estate. Me and two other boys came back to the estate on a lot of other occasions after this and watched the house for Mr Turnly to see when he was coming and going. We were also watching to see who was going to the house to find out if there were any INLA men visiting him.

From McConnell's account to the police this seems to have been a highly planned surveillance operation, though one wonders how they would have known whether a particular visitor to the Turnly home would have been an INLA member unless McConnell was taking photographs which the UDA could check against intelligence files on that organisation. If the UDA was in a position to check photographs of visitors to the Turnly home, they must have had access to security forces files. However, if one member of the cell had an obvious connection with the UDR, such checking might well have been possible.

McConnell claimed that after he gave the UDA leadership his dossier of photographs and written observations they contacted him some time later and informed him that Turnly was indeed 'a leading man in the INLA'. 'We were given orders to shoot him,' he stated:

The three of us [Robert and Eric McConnell and William McClelland] worked out the best way this could be done without endangering his wife and children. We found out that Turnly didn't drive his car and his wife usually drove him about. We didn't want to shoot him in his car as that would have meant his wife and children would have got hit as well. It was decided that the best way to shoot John Turnly was when his wife was leaving him off at a public meeting in Carnlough. We knew the meeting was organised by Larne Council for June 4 to discuss development in the town and he was due to attend it. On the Monday before we planned to shoot John Turnly one of the boys went to Carrickfergus and collected a stolen car, a blue Ford Cortina, and brought it back and parked it at Riverdale Flats in Larne. I had information that a top Provisional IRA man in Belfast had a blue Ford Cortina, the exact same as the one which had been stolen for us. I got number plates made up the same as the Provo's car number and I put these on the stolen car. The next night, Tuesday, we done a dummy run in the stolen Cortina.

This part of McConnell's testimony is significant because he indicates that the killers intended to imply that the murder of Turnly was committed by the Provisional IRA by using a number plate which could be traced to a member of the Provos. This leads one to wonder whether the killing of Bunting and Lyttle was also deliberately styled to give the impression that military-type personnel were involved. McConnell's mind-set suggests a sophistication which, if placed against many terrorist episodes in Northern Ireland, encourages the view that many things are not as they seem or as they are portrayed.

The day after the false plates were fitted, McConnell took his brother and McClelland in the stolen car and drove along the route from Turnly's home to Larne to decide where the murder would be committed. They obviously felt it was safe to drive around in a car with number plates which if checked by a police or UDR patrol could, through the normal computerised link at vehicle checkpoints, have indicated an IRA connection. There is no evidence that they possessed prior knowledge that the route would be free of vehicle checks, so they must have been prepared to accept an element of risk. Their reconnaissance led to the decision to shoot John Turnly as he alighted from his car in Carnlough to attend the public meeting.

The following day, Wednesday, 4 June, Robert McConnell finished work at 5.00 pm and went to the Bodega Bar in Larne, where he met his younger brother and McClelland. Ironically the leader of the cell was not Robert McClelland but Eric, whose career in terrorism began at the age of fourteen when he joined the Young Citizens Volunteers, the junior wing of the Ulster Volunteer Force. Initially membership involved drilling and playing football. The drill sessions took place in the Protestant Hall in Larne and were organised by Jackie —. He left because he 'didn't like the UVF's attitudes', and joined the UDA. Two brothers (whom I am not prepared to name for legal reasons), who were friends of his girlfriend, in turn introduced him to Colin —, the UDA Provost-Marshal in Larne, who took him into the UDA.

Before Eric McConnell set up the active service unit or cell in Larne, he received the following communication from 'S.G. and B.K.' of the UDA's Strategic Defence Administration:

It has been suggested that you are suitable for Active Service Cell membership within your area of which you have agreed to join. You will be required to adhere to the following rules which are essential for the secure operations of any Cell:

1   Absolute secrecy about Cell membership, structure, strength and movements.

2   Cells can only operate efficiently by mutual co-operation and agreement therefore Cell operatives will only communicate and be answerable to the Cell Commander who will also be Military Commander of you local unit. Apart from the Commander there shall be no rank held by any members of the Cell.

3   All rumours or any enquiries relating to any aspect of Cell operations and movements no matter how trivial they seem must be reported immediately to the Cell Commander.

4   A Provost Squad is operating and is equipped to protect the security and welfare of Cells. It is essential that Cell Members do not retaliate against any harassment no matter how severe the provocation may be as this would seriously threaten internal security.

It has been proved that during training a mutual trust, respect and understanding develops between Cell Members and their Commander. We, as architects of many existing Cells, have no knowledge of the identities of individual Cell Members. This we believe has been ample safeguard against the drawbacks of infiltration, egotism and power struggles possessed by other organisations. This has been reinforced by the fact that no members of an existing Cell have been picked up for questioning. We welcome you as a member of this existing and growing weapon against subversive gangsterism and thuggery which is at present destroying the social fabric of Ulster and we wish you and your colleagues every success in the tasks which lie ahead of you.

Yours sincerely,
Strategic Defence Admin.

It was in the spirit of the above letter that Eric McConnell began selecting UDA men for an active service unit. At the time of the Turnly murder
he had hand-picked twenty men, though only six of them were within
the cell structure at that time. When he recruited one of the cell members
for active service he boasted that the twenty men were ready to operate:

> He said that things would be different and that intelligence on targets would be 100
> per cent before any action was taken. He said they were looking for prestige targets
> to regain public support as they had lost it during the last number of years because
> of the way they operated doing innocent people. I asked him what innocent targets
> they hit but he would not say except that there were quite a few.

Eric McConnell's decision to set up an active service cell was accomplished in an unusual fashion because he was not commander of the
UDA in Larne and he set up the cell independently of the Larne leadership. However, in order to ensure that he did not transgress against the
Larne bosses he endeared himself to the Larne commander and involved
him in the cell. That man was William McFetridge. His role in the killing
of Turnly was restricted to the initial planning and to the search for documents revealing the whereabouts of the Turnly home. Eric McConnell
was known as a tough young man who was prepared to kill, and Robert,
with less terrorist experience, was understood to be easily influenced by
his younger brother.

In his testimony McFetridge later played down his role in the killing
of Turnly: 'I went to the Highways Hotel and made some enquiries about
Turnly. A couple of days later I met Junior McClelland and went with
him to look up newspapers in the Library to see reports on the local elections and get information relating to Turnly.' They failed to get relevant
data, and McClelland asked McFetridge if there was another method of
acquiring details about their target. McFetridge replied that he knew a
Miss—who worked in the *East Antrim Times* office. Accordingly they
went to the newspaper office and with scissors removed press clippings
which contained details of John Turnly and his family. McFetridge later
admitted that he knew Turnly was 'for the chop'. It is interesting that the
local commander was subservient to the cell commander and that the
rules outlined by the Strategic Defence Administration communiqué—
that the local should also be the cell commander—were not strictly
applied. This may have been due to the fact that McFetridge was a weak
man who was not prepared to be an assassin. On the other hand
McConnell may have exploited McFetridge's unwillingness to exercise
his authority as local commander and have insisted that he himself be
placed in control of the cell. Eric McConnell established his own rules:

he conferred the title of deputy leader on his brother, and designated 'Junior' McClelland as intelligence officer. McConnell's rule-breaking represented a serious breach of security for a UFF cell. He also kept in his house notes of financial dealings: 'Eric £5; Cud £2; Lefty £3; Page £3; Brownlee £3; Nat £5; McKay £5; McKee £5; Hunter £3; Craig £3; McDowell £3; Jocks £2; Spence £2: Total £44.' Documents of this nature later proved invaluable in helping his associates to be tracked down. The exact nature of the financial transactions was not revealed, but they were understood to be payments or contributions.

On 4 June 1980 at the Bodega Bar, Eric McConnell joined his brother and McClelland for a few drinks while they went through a final check-list of their plans and post-murder tactics. Eric told his accomplices there were three guns in the Cortina, which was parked near the Bodega. After the killing they would destroy the Cortina and return home in the Ford Escort van. He stressed that after the shooting they would wash their faces and hands with paraffin to remove any lead residue resulting from the weapons being discharged. Eric McConnell, the young but experienced terrorist, was leaving little to chance. His brother Robert later confessed how they killed John Turnly but was careful not to name Eric or McClelland; I have added the names where necessary:

One of the boys [Eric] went and got the Cortina. I took the other boy [McClelland] with me in my Ford Escort van and I drove down the coast through Glenarm and just before you come to Carnlough I took the Ballymena road on the left. I drove up that road about a mile and parked the van at the side of the road. The boy [Eric] with the stolen car arrived with the guns we were to use. I forgot to say that my van had all its transfers removed. I got into the Cortina and the guns were handed out. The boy in the front [Eric] had a sub-machine-gun, I had a .25 Mauser semi-automatic and the other boy [McClelland] had a Walther 9mm. I put my gun under my leg on the seat. We all had blue nylon overalls and green woollen masks. We put the overalls on and I took over the driving of the car and we drove down the Coast Road through Carnlough and out past the gate lodge at the entrance to the Turnly Estate. I turned the car and pulled into a lay-by just after the entrance to the Turnly's. We sat there half an hour or so and an 1100 car came out of his Estate and turned up the backroad into Carnlough. We thought that maybe Turnly was in this car and I followed it. I caught up with it and when I saw an old man was in it I drove back to the lay-by. After a short time I spotted Turnly's Datsun estate car coming down the avenue. It drove past where we were parked and I saw Turnly's wife driving and he was sitting beside her. I waited and then followed. I kept a good distance behind Turnly's car and when we got to within 20 yards of Smyth's [the venue for the public meeting] we all pulled on our masks. We were all wearing pink rubber household gloves. I saw Turnly's car park at Smyth's and I pulled the Cortina slightly in front of it. The two boys with me got out with their guns and I looked back and saw John Turnly get out of his car. The boys started shooting and I looked across at the other side of the road and I saw people standing. I was worried in case some of these people would do something stupid so I held my gun out of the window and fired four shots in the air. This was to stop anybody from coming over the road and into the way of the shooting. When I looked around the windscreen of the Datsun was shattered and I heard a woman screaming. The two boys jumped back into the car and I drove off. I drove to the Ford Escort van. The boy in the front [Eric] got out and into the van and followed us up the road, we all got out, put the guns into a green holdall and put them over a hedge. We drove the car up a lane and got our overalls, gloves and masks and threw them into the car. One of the boys [Eric] took a plastic container of petrol from the car and poured it over the Cortina and threw a lighted match inside. The car went up in flames and we returned to the van. When I was about to get into the van two cars passed on the Coast Road. I saw one of these cars slowing up and the driver looking over. I stood in front of the number plate so that he wouldn't get the number. We got into the van and headed for Ballymena.

The killers drove to the car park of the Battery Inn at Ballymena and, using paraffin from a container in the van, they washed their hands and faces with the liquid and dried themselves with a towel. They entered the Inn, washed in hot water in the toilets and drank beer. On their way back to Larne they were flagged down at a UDR vehicle checkpoint on the dual carriageway outside Larne. The van was searched and they were taken to the town's police station where they were questioned but released after twenty minutes. That decision was fatal: the McConnells killed a Catholic in Larne six weeks later.

It was not until September 1980 that RUC detectives interviewed the McConnell brothers, McClelland and McFetridge. The RUC team was a formidable array of tried interrogators: Croy, McGarry, Richardson, Kilfedder, Thomson, McBrien, Johnston and Cousins, most of them members of the Regional Crime Squad from Castlereagh. Their break-through came when they penetrated the defences of Robert McConnell. It took a week to break his younger brother, Eric. When Robert McConnell made his confession he also told police where to find the cell's arms, which included the guns used in the Turnly murder.

I find Robert McConnell's reference to the use of a 9mm Walther pistol an interesting detail. Such a weapon was used in the Miriam Daly killing, but police at her inquest seemed unaware that a gun of this type had previously been used by Loyalists. That was probably an oversight on the part of the detective who gave evidence at the Daly inquest. Perhaps he was unaware of the use of such a weapon by the Larne cell, or perhaps the RUC did not ballistically compare the 9mm pistol which police later found and traced to the McConnells with the bullets taken from the body of Miriam Daly. The detail is interesting, however, because it confirms that this type of weapon was in Loyalist hands and therefore tends to add weight to the theory that Loyalists murdered Miriam Daly.

On 11 March 1982 Lord Justice Gibson gaoled the McConnells and

McClelland for life for murder. McFetridge admitted the lesser office of manslaughter and was sentenced to twelve years in prison. After the judge delivered the sentences and made a forthright condemnation of the killers, Robert McConnell produced a verbal bombshell:

In or around the month of April 1980 I was working as a fish salesman in the Larne area. At that time, although not a member, I had links with a Loyalist para-military organisation. I was stopped one day near Cushendall by a van containing a number of men. I became satisfied subsequently that these were all members of the SAS and I had dealings with them on that and a number of subsequent occasions through their leaders who were Sergeant Tom Aiken and Corporal McGow. Aiken had just returned from duty in Hong Kong and he drove a red Opel car with a dent near the front driver's headlight and McGow drove a green Audi. Aiken had a well-spoken Scots accent. On the occasion when I first stopped and after they had satisfied me who they were they asked me to place a listening device in a bar in Cushendall where they said Gerry Adams and another man were waiting to meet with some others. I went into the bar and fixed the device to the underside of a stool near where Adams was sitting doing a crossword. After I left the barmaid came out and bought 50p-worth of brown fish from me in what I was satisfied was an attempt to discover if I was a genuine fish salesman. She asked me if I knew who the man in the bar was and I said: 'Who? Gerry! I think I've seen him before. Did he ever work in GEC?' When I returned I was stopped by the man in the van and I was offered money in an envelope which I refused. I agreed to meet them again and do things like that again if the need arose. They knew that in the course of my business I was going in and out of Republican areas and during a series of subsequent meetings with me they discussed with me Republican leaders and, in particular, Turnly, Miriam Daly and Bernadette McAliskey. They said they had information that over a two-year period the Republicans had a plan to escalate tension in the Province by civil disorder, large-scale importation of arms and explosives and by certain actions which would arouse the sympathy of Republican people with the ultimate objective of starting a civil war. We realise now that this involved the Hunger Strikes. We were told by Sergeant Aiken that Turnly was important in this regard because of his experience of imports and exports and because of his experience of dealings with the East—he having spent time in Laos and Cambodia. During this period weapons, uniforms and information on how to obtain intelligence-gathering equipment was supplied by Sergeant Aiken who would contact me by telephone and arrange for me to pick up various items on lonely roads at the dead of night. I am making this statement so that the Court and the public will be aware that information concerning Turnly and the others was fed through me by British Intelligence Services and this information was of the nature I have already described.

McConnell made his statement after he was sentenced, so it was not intended as a ploy to encourage the judge to regard it as a mitigating factor. One is obliged to ask serious questions about it. Why would McConnell seek to blacken the image of security services or the SAS? What did he have to gain? Was this claim of a military connection McConnell's way of punishing his military contacts because they did not protect him from a life sentence? Is McConnell, who is a self-confessed murderer, someone to be believed? Since this claim was not made during the police interrogation in 1980, McConnell had two years in which to concoct such a story. During two years in custody he made no effort to convey such allegations to either the RUC or the media. If one believes that McConnell deliberately devised a fantastic story of a military connection in his life, what could possibly have been his motive? Could he have wished to disassociate himself from the crime in the hopes that at some point in the future a Life Review Board might view his request for parole in a lenient fashion? Was he seeking to protect himself from IRA or INLA revenge?

I offer one explanation which, in respect of the activities of the UDA, might appear to have substance. The UDA is a legal organisation and in 1982 it was developing a political strategy in the hope that it could eventually emulate the political success of Sinn Fein. That strategy demanded that the UDA constantly use convenient labels such as UFF to distance itself from acts of violence committed by its members, so that its overt political image did not become tarnished to an extent that the British government might feel obliged to proscribe the organisation. McConnell, by implicating the UDA leadership and not the UFF in the murder of Turnly, who had no terrorist connections, was placing the UDA firmly in the role of a body which was orchestrating political killings. It is a curious element of Northern Ireland life that everyone knows that the UFF is the military wing of the UDA, and the UDA's survival as a legal grouping depends upon a tacit acceptance that the UFF is a different organisation. Similarly the acceptance of Sinn Fein as a legal grouping demands blindness to the historical reality that it is an integral part of the armed struggle and therefore of the Irish Republican Army. For reasons of political manoeuvring and expediency, successive British governments have sought to ignore the truth.

The terrorists play the rules of the political game to ensure they remain in the game. McConnell's statement that the UDA leadership demanded the death of Turnly implied that they may also have ordered the deaths of Daly, Bunting and Lyttle, since there was an apparent political connection between all of those people through their membership of the H-Blocks Committee and the UDA's apparent willingness to believe they were all members of the INLA. Robert McConnell's confession to police was disturbing the equilibrium of the political game by making public the UDA leadership's direct intervention in terrorism and implying that they had ordered other political assassinations. Therefore there is a distinct possibility that the UDA encouraged McConnell to shift attention to the SAS to obscure UDA involvement and a subsequent public examination of the UDA's role.

On the other hand, the progress being made by the National H-Blocks Committee from 1978 onwards was considerable in terms of its propaganda for the IRA and to a lesser extent for the INLA. McConnell made his statement about the H-Blocks campaign retrospectively, but it is worth reflecting on the events which took place while McConnell was in prison for two years awaiting trial. Those events may indicate that the UDA did indeed regard as grave the activities of the H-Blocks Committee in view of their consequences. In 1980 Republican prisoners at the Maze went on hunger strike to draw more attention to their demands. The government announced that it would look at the issue of clothing but there would be no return to special status. The government also made it clear that although it was prepared to consider civilian-type clothing for male prisoners it would be clothing 'officially' provided. Many people sympathetic to the government position saw this use of the word 'official' as stupid and unnecessary when it was just as easy to concede the clothing issue by allowing the prisoners to wear their own clothes. On 18 December the hunger strike was called off amid speculation that the IRA had abandoned it in confusion after the Secretary of State, Humphrey Atkins, presented the prisoners with a lengthy document as the basis for discussion of their demands. One prisoner in particular viewed the IRA position as an untenable one—twenty-six-year-old Bobby Sands. He advocated a hunger strike which would continue until death if necessary, and he began the first stage of such a hunger strike on 1 March 1981, the fifth anniversary of the phasing out of special-category status. The hunger strike would claim the lives of ten Republicans and during it Sands, while dying, would be elected MP for Fermanagh/South Tyrone in April. He died after sixty-six days refusing food, and his death and that of the other hunger strikers represented a major propaganda coup for the IRA. The hunger strike campaign lasted until August of that year. During it there was considerable violence and tension between both communities. The presence of 70,000 people at Sands's funeral was seen within the Loyalist community as a conviction that the IRA and, in particular, the H-Blocks Committee had achieved the objective of raising IRA fortunes. After the deaths of some of the hunger strikers, Cardinal O'Fiaach warned that the British government could well face the 'wrath of the nationalist population' if it persisted with its stance and allowed young men to die. On the streets of Northern Ireland terrorist violence claimed the lives of over sixty people, seventeen of them members of the security forces. As far as Loyalists were concerned, and in particular the UDA, they were justified in their opposition to the H-Blocks Committee. Maybe they were in a position as early as 1979–80 to recognise the events which would flow from the activities of the committee.

The other possibility is that McConnell was telling the truth and that military personnel were indirectly controlling a UDA active service cell. If that were true, McConnell might have made his statement because his 'controllers' had failed to protect him from a life sentence. Moreover, if British intelligence services were indeed involved in these murders, one must speculate on their motives. One might wonder whether the death of Airey Neave led to a search for revenge. Alternatively, as McConnell's statement suggests, the British government may have been concerned that the advent of the H-Blocks protests, and the powerful propaganda being disseminated worldwide by a range of politically astute people, represented a change in IRA fortunes and a significant threat to political stability. The National H-Blocks Committee comprised a range of radicals—such as Daly, Turnly, Lyttle, Bunting and McAliskey—who were agitating for political status for terrorists and who were arguably the most articulate political activists of that period. They made excellent use of the international media, and their campaign led directly to the major hunger strike of 1981 which galvanised support for the IRA on an unprecedented scale. Could the British government have foreseen that and attempted to prevent it by encouraging one of its agencies, the UDA, to assassinate the political activists on the National H-Blocks Committee? McConnell's statement from the dock implies that such a plan existed. However, he had two years in prison to make such an allegation or to have a statement prepared for him by the UDA leadership.

Whatever the truth, in January 1981 one other member of that H-Blocks Committee, Bernadette McAliskey, almost lost her life to a UDA hit-squad, and mystery shrouds that event too.

An SAS team was dug in around her house, without her knowledge. They had cut telephone communication to the house and their presence was not even known to the local army commander. Although they saw the UDA hit-team arrive, they did not apprehend them. The gunmen went into McAliskey's home and shot her several times. They were arrested as they left the property. A member of the SAS team discovered Mrs McAliskey was alive after the shooting and gave her first aid until medical support arrived. His actions saved her life. Why were the terrorists allowed to enter the house? Was the SAS squad in place around the house because of information that Bernadette McAliskey was about to be murdered?

Answers to these questions have never been forthcoming. That fact along with others served to indicate to some people either that there was an 'unseen hand' or that the intelligence community knew the UDA were engaged in an assassination campaign and no effort was made to prevent it happening because the targets were people who were themselves regarded as a threat to the stability of the state. In a dirty war everything is possible, but one is forced to ask whether in this case it is likely that there was a connection between all the events other than what was, according to known facts, a campaign of political assassination by a revamped UFF.

12

Agents, Informers and Double Agents

I n the shadowy areas of the dirty war, the use of people as informers, agents and *agents provocateurs* not only creates controversy but raises serious issues for a democracy. The police, Army and intelligence agencies never admit that they 'employ' people to spy on their behalf or that they tolerate the fact that some of those people act in a criminal fashion or are encouraged to do so to enhance their standing within terrorist organisations. The use of informers is vital to operational intelligence, which determines the way in which the security forces combat terrorism. It is said that informers supply over two-thirds of all intelligence and they do so for a range of motives including money, threats, blackmail, revenge, or even the thrill, and occasionally the desire to defeat terrorism. In seeking accurately to define terms such as 'informer' or 'agent' one can turn to the definitions provided for aspiring intelligence officers by the School of Service Intelligence, Army intelligence wing:

a. *A Source:* A person, thing or activity from which intelligence information is obtained.

b. *An Agency:* is an individual or specialised organisation used in collecting and or processing information.

c. *An Agent:* in intelligence usage, is one who is authorised or instructed to obtain or to assist in obtaining information for intelligence or counter-intelligence purposes.

d. *An Informant:* is any individual who gives information. The term is generally

used to describe a casual or undirected source as distinct from
an informer, who is normally connected with criminal activities,
can be directed and receives payment for his services.

Those definitions seem to indicate that an agent is someone who
does the work of an informer but is not connected with criminal activities—in other words, the employee of an arm of the security services
—though it could equally apply to someone who is not a member of a
terrorist organisation but receives large sums of money for providing
intelligence on that organisation or becoming involved in its workings.
I believe the definitions offer meagre scope either for truly assessing
the roles of people within those military categories or for judging the
legality or ethical nature of this dimension to the war. When an
informer is caught by the paramilitaries and executed, the police,
Army, MI5 or MI6 never admit the person was working for them. In
fact they do not admit to the use of those operatives as described in the
School of Service Intelligence document. It is a generally accepted
principle that the use of agents and informers is a necessary, if not
essential, means of defeating terrorism. However, since the risks for
those who undertake such work are enormous, one may assume that
the majority of informers do not volunteer for the work. I think it is fair
to say that an agent is an employee of government who contracts out
work to people who are then defined as informers. It is my contention
that both are employees, but the informers take the greater risks
because they operate at the cutting edge of terrorism. Some agents do
take frightening risks but in a more calculated fashion.

If informers survive there are no medals. However, if they have been
supplying high-grade intelligence, they may have been well enough
paid to retire outside Ireland, provided their handlers allow them such
a luxury. It is believed that many people who have told friends and relatives they were leaving Ireland to escape the Troubles, or give their
children a new life, were 'retiring' as informers, having secreted their
money in banks outside Ireland. What happens to those who are paid
meagre sums and who cannot afford to escape the eventual risk of a
terrorist punishment? Informers are rarely pardoned by paramilitary
organisations. The IRA has cleverly offered amnesties to encourage
informers to repent and in some instances they have imposed exile on
informers rather than a death sentence to encourage other informers to
reveal themselves.

An example of exile being used as a punishment for a self-confessed
informer occurred in 1975. The informer was a teenager from Drumary
Park in Armagh, the area controlled by the Provisional IRA's 2nd

Battalion of the North Armagh Brigade. He told the IRA that he began informing after he was caught stealing from parked cars outside a cinema in Armagh city. He claimed police told him they would not press charges against him if he supplied them with information on known Republicans. They assured him that there would be no risk, that he would be given money and told what to do. I checked this story with relatives of the young man and they confirmed that he was indeed an informer. Most of the work he undertook was simple surveillance on men in his neighbourhood who were known to be Provisionals. On some occasions he met his contact, a Special Branch inspector, at the town dumps, passed information and received a payment of £10 or £15. He had at least fifty meetings with his contact, and on one occasion he informed an Army patrol of the presence of two armed IRA men, Jake McGerrigan and John Nixon. The patrol set up an ambush and when the IRA men came into view the soldiers opened fire, killing one man and wounding the other. After the young man's confession the IRA showed leniency towards him for behaviour which in their view merited execution, because they hoped to encourage other informers to reveal themselves. This young man was one of the fortunate few. Since the IRA knew their organisation in Armagh was deeply penetrated, they felt it was worth setting aside the death penalty for informers in an effort to stem the flood of information from other spies in their midst.

When terrorists murder someone they claim is an informer they sometimes issue a statement asserting that the person admitted this while 'under interrogation'. The latter phrase demands careful scrutiny of the claims, because violence and torture are used to extract 'confessions', and such tactics call into question anything said by people unfortunate enough to find themselves interrogated by terrorists. That is what happened to forty-three-year-old Eric Dale, a minor figure in the INLA who had been close to the Provisional IRA in the early 1970s and was interviewed about terrorism on several occasions. In April 1983 he was remanded on bail by the Central Criminal Court in Dublin, where he faced charges relating to possession of detonators. A native of County Down, he had moved to Portadown in County Armagh but left his wife and family and in May 1983 was living in Monaghan with Claire McMahon and her three young children. On 3 May at 9.00 pm Eric Dale heard a knocking on the door of his house. Before opening the door he peered through a window and saw several armed men outside his home. Telling Claire McMahon of their presence, he instructed her to go to the sitting-room. She later described the events: 'As Eric opened the door a masked man entered and came into the sitting-room. I was shaking and trembling and the masked man told me everything was all right and not to panic. The only people in the sitting-room were me and the three children.'

Claire McMahon was unaware that the face behind the mask was that of Dominic McGlinchey, the most wanted man in Ireland, and the operations officer on the General Headquarters Staff of the INLA; a man who had killed at least thirty people, civilians as well as members of the police, Army and UDR. McGlinchey's balaclava had slits for his eyes and stretched below his chin; he wore a combat jacket, and a shoulder holster resting on his chest contained a .44 magnum revolver. His right hand was positioned near the gun butt and his left held the holster.

In the only recorded interview with McGlinchey, published in the *Sunday Tribune* in November 1983, he told the Dublin journalist and editor Vincent Browne that he preferred to 'get in close' to his victim:

It's usually a matter of who gets in first and by getting in first you minimise the risk to yourself and put your man down first. It has worked for me down the years. I wouldn't be as good as they are shooting it out over distances because I don't get the opportunity for weapons and target training like they do. So I believe in getting in close. On the Cookstown job a while ago I went up to the bunker outside the police station and just opened up on the policeman in the bunker.

While Claire McMahon was facing McGlinchey she was unaware of events in the hallway. She was 'kept reassured' by McGlinchey, who told her everything would be fine and allowed her to take her eight-year-old son Edward to the toilet. As she crossed the hallway she saw Eric Dale lying face down with his head towards the door. At least six men dressed in masks and combat jackets surrounded him. 'As I came back from the toilet with Edward I noticed that the first masked man had moved from the sitting-room to the hallway. I asked what was going on and he said they only wanted to question Eric about guns or something that was missing. At this stage Eric was standing up and was being held up on either side by a masked man, each one holding him by the arm.'

As she looked at Dale, he turned his head towards her and said: 'I never harmed anybody.' Then he was marched out of the door, and McGlinchey told his men to 'tell Dale's missus what was going on'. One of the terrorists approached her and said that if Eric was not home by morning she was to travel to Culloville in South Armagh where she would be contacted. Another terrorist asked Eric Dale where he kept his car keys. Dale replied that they were in the car. Claire McMahon, realising that the car was about to be stolen, asked how she was expected to travel to Culloville without the vehicle. The terrorist told her she would be contacted 'somehow'. She subsequently overheard Dale's captors ordering him to climb into the boot of his car and Dale replying that it was not possible. However, his captors unloaded the spare wheel and other items and pushed him into the boot. Claire McMahon never saw him alive again.

On 7 May, four days after the abduction, a body bound and wrapped in plastic was dumped by the roadside near the border at Killeen between Newry and Dundalk. It was Eric Dale. A post-mortem revealed that he had been shot in the head, and his body bore signs of torture and severe beating. The discovery of the corpse was followed by a statement from the INLA that Eric Dale had 'admitted under interrogation' that he had supplied security forces with details of the movements of Seamus Grew and Roddy Carroll, who had been shot dead by members of the RUC in December 1982. (The deaths of Grew and Carroll were later the subject of part of the Stalker inquiry.) The INLA also claimed that he had provided information that led to a number of arrests and the seizure of weapons, ammunition and explosives belonging to the INLA, and that prior to his death he had been making inquiries about the whereabouts of Dominic McGlinchey, who the statement said was an 'alleged INLA man wanted on both sides of the border'. Eric Dale's twenty-three-year-old daughter reacted angrily to the INLA statement, pointing out the use of the word 'interrogation':

There is not a shred of truth in what the INLA have alleged. My father was beaten and tortured by his murderers. They claimed he admitted giving information under interrogation but nobody could withstand the terrible torture inflicted on him. My father was a dedicated Republican and gave the last eleven years of his life to the Republican cause. These people who did the dastardly deed are worse than animals. They cannot call themselves Irishmen and are nothing but gangsters.

McGlinchey had a personal interest in the abduction, interrogation and murder of Dale or, for that matter, anyone he suspected of having been involved in the Grew and Carroll killings. They were shot by members of the RUC's E4 branch, who claimed that they believed Ireland's most wanted man, Dominic McGlinchey, was travelling in the car in which Grew and Carroll were shot. Using several cars, the E4 team trailed the three INLA terrorists from the Irish Republic, even though it was outside the RUC's jurisdiction. Stalker was unaware of this and subsequent events on the night of the Grew and Carroll shooting. The E4 operatives were in two cars, one behind the vehicle carrying the terrorists and one in front. On the Northern Ireland side of the border E4 operatives were positioned in a car in a laneway, waiting for a signal from the E4 car trailing behind the terrorists, when they would ram the INLA men's car, thus ensuring that there were armed E4 men coming from behind and in front. The vehicle travelling ahead of the target car was to pass the laneway and then return quickly, so that when the terrorists' car was rammed there would be considerable fire-power to deal with McGlinchey and his associates. It has never been revealed that the E4 operatives in the trailing car lost contact with the target car, with the result that the INLA men's car was not rammed. As soon as the error was discovered, a radio communication to other E4 units up ahead set in motion another ambush, but when the terrorists' car was attacked McGlinchey was not inside it. He had left the vehicle at some point between the intended and the final ambush point.

After the deaths of his fellow terrorists, McGlinchey sought to dis-cover who had revealed his whereabouts. The E4 operation was launched after someone passed on information that McGlinchey was scheduled to travel into Northern Ireland on that night. McGlinchey, though unaware that he had been under surveillance before he left the Irish Republic, knew that his movements and travel arrangements were known to only a few people. Unfortunately Eric Dale was one of those people. Terrorists often restrict knowledge of their travel arrangements to a defined number of their associates so that if some-thing goes wrong they are able to isolate those with the relevant knowledge. The E4 units who watched McGlinchey in what was a for-eign country were in breach of Irish sovereignty, but they were pre-pared to take the risk of causing an international incident to trap an INLA leader who was a mass murderer and one of the security forces' most dangerous adversaries. They undertook the mission as a result of information about McGlinchey's whereabouts. E4 was responsible for the surveillance, but firepower was provided by a special support unit whose men were trained in SAS tactics at Aldershot. Dale knew of McGlinchey's whereabouts, and it has never been admitted officially that members of E4 were operating within the Irish Republic. However, Dale was not the only person with information about the INLA leader.

A man who was eventually discovered to be a major spy within the Provisionals—George Poyntz—was also aware of McGlinchey's specif-ic travel plans. Poyntz was later spirited out of South Armagh by his Army handlers. I was told that he was a contact for many terrorists who, when crossing the border, required assistance such as a safe-house in which to hide or information about the safest routes. Poyntz knew about McGlinchey. Was it Poyntz or Dale who informed, or was Dale a man who was willing to admit to anything under torture? We shall never know. During the course of my research I also learned that

Poyntz met the UDA leader Jim Craig, who was murdered in 1988 by members of his own organisation. The UDA claimed Craig was involved in 'setting up' John McMichael, the UDA/UFF leader killed by the Provisionals in 1988. Craig told a close associate that he met with Poyntz at the latter's instigation. Poyntz offered to provide information on known Provisionals and determine a time and place whereby a UDA hit-team could 'wipe them out'. Craig is said to have remarked of this offer when relating it to a colleague: 'I knew what that fucker Poyntz was about. We would send a hit-squad in. They would do the job and on the way out the SAS would do our boys—just like killing two birds with one stone. I knew that if Poyntz was setting up his own people he had to be working for the Army and the ploy to get the Provos was also one to expose us.' Poyntz's offer to Craig came at a time when the UDA was capable of killing Bunting, Daly and others.

The use of agents or informers is often an intricate affair. In 1989 the Provisional IRA executed a man to whom it attributed the designation 'British agent' rather than 'informer', the IRA's traditional label for people whom it believes have betrayed its secrets. The 'British agent' was thirty-five-year-old Joe Fenton, a father of four from Andersonstown in West Belfast. On the night of 26 January he was found in an alley in the Lenadoon housing estate not far from his home. His killers had fired four bullets into his head before they sped away in a stolen car. By morning the Provisional IRA had issued a statement saying they had killed him because he was a 'British agent'. In most instances the families of those branded with informing have angrily denied IRA claims. Within two days of Joe Fenton's death a different pattern emerged. In accordance with standard police policy, the RUC stated that the dead man had no connection with the security forces. However, his father, Patrick Fenton, told journalists that 'RUC pressure led directly' to his son's death. He said he was making this known after reading his son's written statement to the IRA about his activities as an informer: 'Having seen and read evidence which was presented to me I accept his death and wish to say that the position in which he was placed, due to pressures brought to bear on him by the Special Branch, led directly to the death of my son.' This was an unusual statement from a man with moderate views and no paramilitary connections.

At the funeral the local priest Father Tom Toner, who is an outspoken critic of the IRA, expressed his revulsion about the Fenton affair:

The IRA is not the only secret, death-dealing agent in our midst. Secret agents of the state have a veneer of respectability on its dark deeds which disguises its work of corruption. They work secretly in dark places, unseen, seeking little victims like Joe whom they can crush and manipulate for their own purposes. Their actions too corrupt the cause they purport to serve.

Father Toner reserved his most bitter comments for the IRA, who he said disgraced everything Irish and everything Republican. He said the Irish were left feeling unclean not because of the British presence, Unionist discrimination, harassment or murder.

To you the IRA and all who support you or defend you, we have to say that we feel dirty today. Foul and dirty deeds by Irishmen are making Ireland a foul and dirty place, for it is things done by Irishmen that make us unclean. What the British could never do, what the Unionists could never do, you have done. You have made us bow our heads in shame and that is a dirty feeling. The IRA is like a cancer in the body of Ireland, spreading death, killing and corruption. It is the unrelenting enemy of life and the community is afraid because it cannot see or identify it. We want the cancer of the IRA removed from our midst but not by means that will leave the moral fibre of society damaged and the system unclean. Fighting evil by corrupt means kills pawns like Joe and leaves every one of us vulnerable and afraid. And it allows Joe's killers to draw a sickening veneer of respectability over cold-blooded murder and to wash their hands like Pontius Pilate.

Father Toner's funeral oration eloquently attacked the dirty war and that part of it which makes use of informers or agents. Some people might see his views as naïve, particularly in respect of the tactics required to remove the cancer which he refers to as 'spreading death, killing and corruption'. Some might argue that all those things he identifies as being fatal to the development of society cannot be removed by mere condemnation, but by strong, if necessary unorthodox, action. Others might argue, as he does, that violence cannot be defeated by violence. In the Fenton episode, however, violence was not used to confront the IRA: according to the available evidence Fenton was working within the IRA to destroy it. One might then ask whether he was operating within the law or outside it at the behest of his controllers. If someone is coerced into acting as an informer and is engaged in criminal activity, is this morally justified in war? Do matters of general morality need to be put aside in the cause of destroying the enemy? The answers will differ from person to person, but society may have to decide for its own future whether a dirty war can be won by using unethical tactics.

The life of Joe Fenton as an agent/informer is not in doubt to those who knew him, such as his father and Father Toner, and the story they have accepted is as follows.

In 1980-1 Fenton was asked by the IRA to undertake a task for them which would be regarded as 'a favour'. The term 'favour' was used by the IRA to indicate that he would not be compelled to do more than one task—moving a quantity of explosives from a dump to a safe-house. Fenton accomplished this but was shocked when approached privately by members of Special Branch who told him they were aware of his work for the IRA and, in particular, the transporting of a quantity of explosives. They convinced Fenton that they could bring charges against him and establish his guilt but that if he did a little work for them the matter would be forgotten. He was also offered financial inducement for any information he could provide.

One might think that it should have been easy for Fenton to say no to the Special Branch suggestion, but one has to understand the complexities of life in Northern Ireland. Fenton would have suspected that someone in the IRA was an informer who had compromised him. Since he was not a member of the IRA, if he had wished to tell the IRA of the Special Branch approach, there was no one to whom he could have spoken in the certain knowledge that he was not talking to an informer. Fenton therefore agreed to work for Special Branch, and a date was set for a meeting at which his handlers would discuss the details of his relationship with them, what they required from him and some of the techniques he would need to learn to keep himself alive.

However, Fenton had no desire to keep the appointment. After returning to his wife and children he planned a new life in Australia, and he did not appear for the scheduled meeting with his Special Branch handlers; but his plans were dashed when the Australian High Commission Consulate in Edinburgh rejected his application for immigration status for himself and his family. The Australian authorities will not comment on this on the grounds that it is improper to discuss such issues. The Special Branch and MI5 may well have had an intricate plan which specifically required someone like Joe Fenton. According to the IRA, he told them that the Special Branch and MI5 had informed the Australian authorities that he was a suspected terrorist.

When Fenton's plans failed he found himself once again in a shadowy world where he was being addressed by a Special Branch sergeant and an Englishman named Don. I have been told by a source within the security forces that 'Don' is one of a number of MI5 liaison officers who oversee Special Branch operations or devise operations which are run by Special Branch operatives. Major operations are discussed within the Task Co-ordinating Group, which comprises operatives from Special Branch, MI5, E4, Army intelligence (plain clothes) and the SAS.

The IRA says that Fenton told them he was drawn into the 'world of spying' by threats and blandishments. He regularly met his handlers, and they gave him a phone number whose arrangement of digits indicates that it was located in East Belfast, an area housing RUC head-quarters and other security complexes where police and Army operations are planned and run.

According to the IRA, Fenton was an ordinary working man who assisted them with a 'favour'. In his employment as a van driver he was not in a position to improve his lifestyle. Then his career changed rapidly: he became a salesman for an estate agency and within a short time set up his own business, Ideal Homes, on the Falls Road. Fenton, say the IRA, was given £15,000 to finance his business and subsequently received supplementary payments of over £2000. As an estate agent he was able to offer the IRA big 'favours'—the use of empty houses on his 'for sale' lists as safe-houses, temporary arms dumps or meeting places for IRA leaders and active service units. Fenton also let the IRA know when properties which would be suitable for meetings were about to come on the market. According to the IRA, Fenton was encouraged by his handlers to assist the IRA in this fashion. The security forces could bug properties in the knowledge that Joe Fenton would keep them on a 'for sale' list and allow the IRA to use them. Although the IRA will not admit the extent of the damage caused to their operations in Belfast, as one IRA leader put it to me: 'We are talking about a major penetration, the loss of active service people, bombing units and a knowledge of our workings and thinking. When something like this happens it is impossible to assess the extent of the damage or to remember every property he provided or what happened or was discussed on those premises.' Another IRA man, well known to the security forces, told me that on his release from prison he was approached by Joe Fenton and offered temporary accommodation in one of the many properties listed for sale by Ideal Homes. The IRA say Fenton also used his business as a front for hiring cars for transporting arms, explosives and men, and that these cars were kept under surveillance.

Fenton had changed from the man who did a favour to being intricately involved in the world of terrorism. As an affable family man who was not politically committed to a Republican ideology, he did not fit the image of the terrorist. Those who knew him well believe that his first 'favour' for the IRA was undertaken out of fear, and that it was a similar motive which led him into the hands of Special Branch and MI5. None the less his role as an informer enabled the police and Army to apprehend several IRA bombing teams as they travelled to targets and to arrest over twenty members of active service teams in possession of guns.

Yet time was running out for Joe Fenton. In 1988 the IRA established a mortar bomb factory in the Andersonstown area, in a house provided by Fenton, the use of which was limited to a few people. The house was raided by the security forces and four men were arrested. IRA intelligence began to examine Fenton and eventually concluded there was a link between security forces' successes over a long period and properties provided by Ideal Homes. When they investigated the history of Joe Fenton's professional life, they uncovered his sudden ability in 1982–3 to set up an estate agency business. That was the major flaw in Joe Fenton's past. Until 1988 his business was a success story mirrored by one of the symbols of new-found wealth, a BMW car, but in 1988 he appeared to adopt a casual approach to his business and rarely appeared in Ideal Homes premises. In July 1988 he was arrested and questioned by police on suspicion of laundering money for the IRA. This may have been a ploy to distract attention from his real work, unless the RUC officers who arrested him were unaware that Fenton was an important informer. In fact he did launder money and was able to use his legitimate business to disguise the passage of IRA rackets-monies from one business to another.

According to the IRA, his arrest by police was an integral part of a policy to provide the authorities with increased powers to investigate a range of businesses. The IRA maintains that there were organised leaks that protection money was being laundered through estate agencies and when businessmen like Fenton were arrested the public were encouraged to believe that all businesses, including estate agencies, required investigation. I feel this explanation is an attempt by the IRA to make propaganda out of an incident which may well have happened simply because Fenton was indeed laundering money for them.

Joe Fenton was doomed to be one of life's failures. His business began to crumble—though it might be fair to suppose that a man under such enormous pressure did not have the potential or application to take control of his life and eradicate the problems. It is impossible to estimate how much the constant threat of discovery affected his conduct. Some of his friends detected a noticeable decline in his ability to apply himself to the running of Ideal Homes. As it began to slide towards bankruptcy, Joe Fenton could not find the means, primarily financial, to resurrect his business. He was under suspicion by the IRA and he no longer played a major role in their operations. Towards the end of 1988 he was driving a taxi to supplement his income. At the beginning of 1989 the Ideal Homes premises were closed by its landlord, who decided there was little to be gained in pleading with Fenton to pay back rent on the building.

The IRA concede that Fenton was not in a position to cause them damage for a considerable time before his death, since they took steps to limit his access to secrets once suspicion centred on him. They believe that, once he was unable to supply information of the calibre which led to so many arrests, his handlers withdrew their financial subsidy. According to them, Fenton told them that his handlers refused to believe that he was not in a position to help them and claimed that he was trying to extricate himself from the 'partnership' with them.

Joe Fenton's death was a sad ending to the life of a naïve man who was easily manipulated. The IRA exploited him from the outset and left him exposed, and other nameless people were equally willing to place him in jeopardy. In killing him the IRA saw itself as omnipotent— an element to the tragedy that was instantly recognised by Father Toner.

Before I completed this book I returned to an investigation of the Fenton story because I was intrigued by the fact that both Father Toner and Joe Fenton's father, while condemning the IRA for the killing, were adamant that the security forces were also to blame for his death and accepted that Joe Fenton was, as the IRA claimed, an informer. It seemed to me that the IRA must have been able to offer Fenton's father and the priest ample information to indicate that the role of the security forces was of a dubious nature. I sought out contacts in the IRA to no avail, because I was told the material was much too sensitive to be revealed to me. With a writer's persistence I contacted a senior member of the IRA and was finally given what is a startling account not only of Fenton's career as an informer but also of the fashion in which, according to the IRA, he was sacrificed, as well as claims that other people were also sacrificed to keep him in place as an informer. The information shocked me. I believe that it was conveyed to Father Toner and Fenton's father in some form. They may well have been given the type of account which I am about to record for the reader, or they may have been presented with written evidence. Existing evidence in respect of courts martial by the IRA is contained in written notes. During the course of writing this book I learned that the IRA tends to be methodical about its court-martial procedures because of the requirements of the IRA's General Army Orders (see the Appendix). A detailed note of what is said by the 'accused' at a court martial is kept as a written record so that it can be studied by IRA intelligence analysts. In addition the IRA sees itself as an organisation with a history which is recorded not so much for posterity as for those who join and wish to learn about the past. Courts-martial papers are kept in secret dumps and are restricted even within the IRA.

The account of my meeting with the senior member of the IRA whom I believe was in a position to know about the Fenton case is recorded here in the form of questions and answers because I feel that this will best illustrate the aspects which most confused and troubled me.

Author:	How important was Fenton as an informer?
IRA leader:	It is difficult to estimate the full extent of the damage. He had access not only to information but also to people. He provided safe-houses. We know that more than one such house was bugged because we later discovered the devices. That means that we cannot fully determine exactly what was said by volunteers who were in those houses and felt they were free to talk about operations. We know what he did compromise and we are not prepared to talk about that because of ongoing inquiries. He also provided transport for active service units and the movement of weapons. Now like all well-placed informers not all of his information would have been acted on because it would have placed him in jeopardy.
Author:	When did suspicion fall on Fenton?
IRA leader:	Several people whom he allegedly assisted were suspicious of him. When I say that, I mean people for whom he provided transport or lodgings. Those suspicions were conveyed to senior figures.
Author:	Why were they not acted upon?
IRA leader:	That is where the matter becomes complex and interesting. Fenton was not simply active in providing safe-houses and transport. He was also providing information to a senior figure in the organisation.
Author:	Surely, if a number of people doubted his loyalty, that would have been a sufficient motive for people in authority at brigade level initiating an inquiry or placing him under surveillance.
IRA leader:	That is why I say it is complex. Fenton was giving information to a senior member of the IRA. Now if one is a senior member of the IRA and one has an informant who is providing reliable, accurate and exciting material, are you going to listen to others who are saying that your informant is a tout? You are going to ward off the criticism because this man is enhancing your position within the organisation by providing you with information which makes you look good.
Author:	Are you saying that Fenton was in possession of information about the very people you say he was working for?
IRA leader:	Exactly.
Author:	Was the man in the IRA to whom he was giving the information aware that he was being conned but happy to have good information to guarantee his stature within the IRA?
IRA leader:	No, he did not know, and neither would anyone if they were in his position and being fed the calibre of information which Fenton was giving him.
Author:	Did he not ask where Fenton was acquiring this information?
IRA leader:	No. One's instinct is to be content to receive highly sensitive information without querying its source. After all, Fenton was an estate agent. He was trusted by his IRA guardian, who probably believed that Fenton was right to protect his sources. That is a simplification of the issue. Not everyone behaves in the fashion in which the IRA officer was behaving. However, when you realise

the nature of the information he was being given it is natural to recognise that it was hardly the type of information which one would instantly believe was coming from the security forces.

Author: What type of information?

IRA leader: He was providing his IRA protector with names, addresses and vehicle registrations of uniformed policemen and members of CID. Now you would hardly think that this was the type of information you would be given by a tout. Remember that Fenton was crucial. He was operating at the highest level within the Belfast Brigade. He was exactly where his handlers wished him to be.

Author: Was he being run by Special Branch?

IRA leader: He was much too important to be simply the property of Special Branch. He was being run by Special Branch in conjunction with MI5. He told us that. He was so important that we now realise just how much they were willing to sacrifice to keep him in place. They were prepared to give us the lives of ordinary cops to keep suspicion away from Fenton. They knew he was under suspicion. They learned that not simply through the bugging of safe-houses but because his IRA protector would have been obliged to convey to him the fact that suspicion was being directed at him from several people. Those who suspected him were kept at bay because of the nature of his information. However, suspicion grew, and there were those within the movement who were not prepared to let the matter rest and sought to pursue it at the highest level.

Author: Was there a body of evidence presented to a higher authority?

IRA leader: Yes.

Author: Was that not a signal to the IRA that he should be interrogated in the fashion to which suspected informers are subjected?

IRA leader: In normal circumstances the answer would be yes, but other people were advising him, namely his handlers, and as with previous occasions when he was close to being caught they offered him a lifeline.

Author: What kind of lifeline? Did they advise him to leave Northern Ireland?

IRA leader: Fenton took the heat off himself by providing the IRA, through the officer who was protecting him, information which the IRA was quick to recognise as vital. He offered the names of two informers who were operating within the brigade area. They were a husband-and-wife team, Gerard and Catherine Mahon, who were in their twenties. IRA intelligence acted on the information and placed surveillance on the couple. Their house was used as a dump on occasions and it was wired by British intelligence. We learned that later. They also tampered with IRA explosives devices which were occasionally stored in their home. They were interrogated, admitted their guilt and were court-martialled. They did not mention Fenton because they did not know of his treachery but he knew them. We now know through the interrogation of Fenton that he was told to give us Gerard and Catherine Mahon to remove suspicion from himself.

When a guy is supplying information of that calibre, the tendency is to regard him as valuable and not to suspect him. As time went on, however, and the Belfast Brigade lost men and weapons and eventually a mortar factory, the suspicion heightened and it pointed towards Fenton. A weight of evidence was assembled which suggested that at the very least he should be interrogated. Fenton knew that time was running out and he bolted. The IRA thought it had lost him but he returned to Belfast within a short time. He claimed he had gone to England to watch a big fight. The dates of his absence coincided with a big fight but that did not halt the demands for an inquiry. When he was finally court-martialled he told us that his MI5/Special Branch handlers told him to return to Belfast after he bolted. They told him to say that he was at a big fight. They must have known that we would not accept that kind of reasoning.

Author: Why did they send him back?

IRA leader: Before I answer that let me tell you what is the final twist to this story because it also explains the way British intelligence operates. They were willing to sacrifice Fenton for a purpose. The reason we know why they were prepared to sacrifice him is that after we shot him we uncovered an extremely sophisticated bug in a house which Joe Fenton had provided as a safe-house. In that house members of the IRA discussed Fenton's fate and the evidence against him. Therefore, his handlers knew that IRA suspicion was so great that he was likely to be found guilty and executed. They were still prepared to send him back. They sent him back to cover their tracks because they had someone equally important in place. They expected the IRA to be preoccupied with Fenton and to believe that Fenton was alone. That is always the way the Brits operate. Fenton was only a pawn to them. By sending him back they were allowing us to think that we had our man. The IRA had one informer in the Belfast area. The IRA also realises that, by placing so much effort into examining the Fenton case, other matters concerning another possible informer could be so easily obscured. Fenton was not the first and he will not be the last.

The killing of Gerard and Catherine Mahon took place in September 1985, just over three years before the murder of Fenton. They were shot in an alleyway in the Turf Lodge area of West Belfast. Gerard Mahon was shot first and as his wife broke free from the execution squad she was also mortally wounded. It is believed that she found the strength temporarily to escape from the killers after she was forced to watch her husband being shot in the head. As she ran down the alley she was shot in the back. The Mahon house was sealed off for several days and thoroughly searched. The manner in which the search operation was conducted suggested that Gerard and Catherine Mahon were no ordinary couple.

While examining the case of Joe Fenton, I encountered an equally bizarre story of an informer who was caught by the IRA and 'encouraged' to reveal the details of how he met his handler. The informer said that every week his handler picked him up in a car at Kennedy Way on the edge of the Andersonstown area and 'took him for a drive' through Belfast. The trip lasted fifteen minutes and during it they discussed the information which the informer had acquired.

After the interrogation, the IRA told the informer they would give him immunity if he participated in a plan to capture his handler. The informer agreed, and the IRA decided that, when the handler stopped his car at Kennedy Way on the return leg of one of the weekly trips round Belfast, the informer would spray an acid substance in his face. An IRA squad would be positioned nearby to rush to the car and abduct him. On the appointed day, the informer was armed with a small spray the size of a perfume bottle, containing a substance which caused temporary blindness when in contact with the eyes. The informer played his intended role until the final moment when he withdrew the spray from his pocket. As soon as he saw the informer's hand reach towards him, the handler knocked the spray sideways and the acid substance was spattered on the windscreen. The IRA patrol had no time to act as the handler opened the front passenger door, pushed the informer out of the car, and drove the vehicle at high speed from the scene.

Within twenty-four hours the informer was arrested and taken to the police station close to Milltown cemetery. After being questioned about his attempt to compromise his handler, he was released, but told that he would probably be killed by the IRA because it would be leaked that he had only pretended to spray the acid at his handler. On his release, the IRA, as predicted, abducted him and subjected him to further questioning. Having decided that maybe he had not fully played his part in the attempted kidnapping of his handler—and if he was willing to betray one set of controllers he was likely to have been turned again—they questioned him about his arrest after the abortive kidnap. He told them about the prediction the police had made. While the interrogation was taking place, the premises were raided by an Army patrol; the informer was rescued but the IRA interrogators escaped. The informer was never seen again. According to the IRA analysis of the episode, the informer was released either because it was hoped the IRA would kill him (and that would be retribution for his betrayal of his handler) or to 'see where he would run'. To support the latter theory, they point out that his release almost led to the capture of a team of IRA interrogators.

As far as I am concerned the one certainty is that the informer would have been assassinated by the IRA. Beyond that point one can only guess at motives of the handlers. The story epitomises the games that are played: they are riddled with deceit, double-dealing, contrived and genuine moves, and sometimes simple methods which are assumed to be complex. Those who are caught between the two sets of players will never know when the rules are being changed or the true nature of the game.

The most controversial story of an agent-handler relationship began in 1971 and lasted nine years before ending in a bizarre twist. The agent was listed on RUC Special Branch files as Agent 294, and his handler was SB Sergeant Charlie McCormick, the intelligence operative who was a constant presence in the life of Agent 294 but not his only master. Agent 294 was Anthony O'Doherty. He was born in the village of Portglenone in County Antrim in 1949. Twenty years later O'Doherty was steeped in the Republican tradition but was not a member of the IRA. He enjoyed being seen at Republican marches and commemoration ceremonies, and it was at such a ceremony in 1970 that he came to the attention of Detective Sergeant Charles McCormick. O'Doherty was selling copies of a Republican pamphlet, *The United Irishman*, when McCormick approached him and exchanged pleasantries. On that occasion McCormick, along with uniformed police, was on duty observing the commemoration of Roger Casement. The venue was the windswept hilltop overlooking the spectacular scenery of Murlough Bay on the North Antrim coast. McCormick made a mental note of many of the Republicans present but was drawn to the fresh-faced O'Doherty because his profile had not previously appeared on Special Branch files. He was vigilant to any opportunity to detect the presence of a newcomer to the Republican fold, and someone who might eventually prove to be a useful contact. The young man was on the periphery of the Republican gathering, and his behaviour and demeanour struck the experienced detective as being the traits of a naïve individual. McCormick's intuition and judgement on that day encouraged him to suspect that O'Doherty was approachable, unlike the majority of Republicans present, who were antagonistic and unwilling to be engaged in conversation by a plain-clothes policeman. His hunch was correct. He employed a favourite technique of overt friendliness and suggested empathy with the historic commemoration. O'Doherty was impressed by a policeman taking an interest in him, a mere pamphlet-seller, and by the policeman's affable manner. The policeman's lack of the expected invective lulled the young man into a conversation during which he revealed his name and where he lived. He was unaware that everything he said was being mentally recorded by an astute Special Branch operator. That was their only meeting until the morning internment without trial was imposed in August 1971. Anthony O'Doherty was arrested on the orders of the Special Branch and, in particular, on the advice of McCormick, even though it was questionable whether O'Doherty was actively connected with terrorism. Once in custody, O'Doherty discovered that the police-man interviewing him was the affable plain-clothes cop who had talked to him at Murlough Bay.

O'Doherty was at his most vulnerable when arrested. He had been taken from his home in the early hours of the morning and treated roughly. The experience had unnerved him and filled him with fear. It was a happening which bore no relation to the role-playing that he associated with selling Republican propaganda. McCormick reassured O'Doherty that he should not be anxious. At the same time he pointed out that he was being held without trial and there was the possibility that he could be incarcerated and the key thrown away. However, O'Doherty had the opportunity to walk to freedom if he was prepared to consider a deal. O'Doherty faced a classic dilemma: he could be imprisoned indefinitely; he could agree to a deal but fail to comply with McCormick's demands, but that would lead to his rearrest, against which he could not legally object; or he could do a deal and be guaranteed freedom. His options were stark, but for O'Doherty there was no doubt which one suited him. He was prepared to accept the offer of freedom at a price. In this early stage of a blossoming profes-sional relationship one may observe the shrewd tactician McCormick and the young, impressionable but equally shrewd O'Doherty. The lat-ter was about to embark on a career as Agent 294. Within O'Doherty's psyche was a desire for danger which he was prepared to accept from any quarter. However, McCormick offered two other major entice-ments, aside from the prospect of freedom. One was money, lots of it. The other was protection for O'Doherty's family, at a time when sec-tarianism was a fatal dimension to the situation in Northern Ireland. In his interview with O'Doherty that morning McCormick had estab-lished that the young man was concerned that his family in the divid-ed city of Derry were at risk from Loyalists, so he allayed this fear by offering protection in the event of threats to the O'Doherty family.

Anthony O'Doherty left police custody with a handshake from McCormick, who arranged a further meeting to discuss the finer details of their professional contract. At their next meeting O'Doherty was encouraged to join the Official IRA, since it was the grouping with which he had been loosely connected at the Murlough Bay ceremony.

He was also introduced to another member of the Special Branch, Ivan Johnston, who he was told might occasionally require his services. O'Doherty was informed that he would receive a basic financial retainer but additional payments would be made to him for information he supplied. The size of the payments would vary according to how effective the information proved. For example, as a result of information the seizure of a rifle would yield more money than the discovery of a revolver; an IRA explosives dump would guarantee a substantial payment, as would the arrest of active service volunteers; whereas hearsay information would be paid at the rate of only £5 or, at most, £10.

O'Doherty did not prove to be a highly competent agent. In 1972 he was rearrested after an armed robbery at a shirt factory in Derry. He was not charged with any offence, but was detained without trial on a Second World War naval vessel, HMS *Maidstone,* which was moored in Belfast harbour and housed a large number of Republican internees. O'Doherty's incarceration in the midst of active Republicans allowed him to be privy to gossip which was of interest to Special Branch. He was held for four months on the ship and was 'visited' on four occasions by McCormick and another member of Special Branch. They questioned him about conversations among Republicans on the subject of future strategy, the ongoing conflict and those who were central to it. After four months, on McCormick's orders, Agent 294 was moved to the main internment camp, Long Kesh (now the Maze). O'Doherty's detention on HMS *Maidstone* almost ensured his acceptance in Long Kesh, which held some of the most prominent members of both wings of the IRA. After six weeks there he was released and told that Special Branch had revised its plans for him. McCormick said it was vital that he 'got in on the Provie scene'. He and his colleagues were beginning to recognise that the Provisionals and not the Officials posed the major threat.

O'Doherty accordingly began associating with people connected with the Provisionals. He says he provided good information, but McCormick was preoccupied with marital problems and money was not forthcoming in exchange for information. As a result O'Doherty devoted himself exclusively to Ivan Johnston, who became his handler. That relationship ended in October 1973, when Johnston resigned from the RUC to set up a road haulage business. His decision to leave at the early age of thirty-four was due to the risks incurred by his job and the stress on his wife Elsie and their three children. O'Doherty resumed his working relationship with McCormick, and they reactivated their financial 'contract'—money for information graded in accordance with its substance.

Meanwhile Ivan Johnston was working hard to provide a new and more prosperous life for his family. On 10 December 1973 he was cruelly reminded of the risk facing policemen when a Special Branch detective with whom he had worked earlier that year was the victim of a booby-trap bomb concealed in his car outside his home. Johnston was shocked and expressed fears to colleagues that the IRA might target him. His fears were well founded. Two days later he was abducted at gunpoint from his lorry at a border crossing between the counties of Armagh and Monaghan. As the lorry came to a standstill at a customs clearance post, masked and armed IRA men dragged Ivan Johnston from the vehicle and bundled him into a waiting car. A male employee of Johnston's haulage firm, who was a native of Mayo in the Irish Republic, was unharmed by the terrorists and permitted to leave. The kidnappers drove off with Ivan Johnston in the general direction of Monaghan town in the Irish Republic. Johnston showed naïvety in travelling in a border region and from someone with considerable security experience it was a strange decision. It was not his first business trip to the Irish Republic, and the fact that it took place two days after the assassination of his former colleague, Detective Constable Maurice Rolston, illustrated a careless if not foolhardy mentality. A massive search for Johnston was mounted on both sides of the Irish border, but to no avail. Elsie Johnston and the Church of Ireland Primate, Dr George Simms, made separate appeals to the terrorists to spare the life of their hostage. The terrorists, as always, proved impervious to public opinion or the pleas of a distraught wife and mother. Forty-eight hours after the abduction a body was discovered beside a hedgerow in a remote part of the South Armagh countryside, a short distance from the border. The victim, a male, was bound and gagged and there was a bullet hole in the back of his head. While Elsie Johnston waited for the body to be identified, she told detectives who were consoling her that the IRA had no right to take Ivan because he had harmed no one.

Before the body on the border was officially identified as the missing ex-policeman, the Mid-Ulster Brigade of the Provisional IRA issued a statement saying they 'executed Ivan Johnston and that when they kidnapped him he was in possession of photographs of IRA men who were on the run'. They said he also had two police identification cards which permitted him to carry out undercover work in the Irish Republic. They justified the murder on the grounds that Ivan Johnston admitted 'under interrogation' that he was involved in 'brutalising' Republican suspects during interrogation sessions at Ballykelly Army base. 'He was executed only after it had been positively established that he was deeply involved in undercover activities for the forces of occupation. He admitted that his identification cards had given him free passage for his undercover activities in the Free State.'

Is it possible that Ivan Johnston was engaged in Special Branch work, using his haulage business as a cover, or that he was doing freelance surveillance for his former employers in RUC Special Branch? The RUC say there was no question of Johnston's being involved in security duties after his retirement:

It is not our normal practice to reply to the purported public statements of murderers. It has, however, been reported that Mr Johnston, a former police officer, was in some way still acting as a police officer and this was the reason for his death. Mr Johnston resigned from the RUC two months ago, and in doing so, he ceased to have any connection whatsoever with the RUC. He was a civilian involved in the purely civilian business of earning his living as a husband and father. For the IRA to attempt to justify his murder with an outright lie is a cruel and cynical exercise typical of that organisation.

Ivan Johnston's murder was cruel and sadistic. His body bore marks of torture, and post-mortem evidence revealed that burns on his body indicated that he could well have been lowered into a bath of scalding water.

In the aftermath of his death, the Special Branch tried to estimate how much he might have revealed under torture about security forces operations, particularly the agents he ran. They probably also wondered whether one of those agents/informers had betrayed Rolston and Johnston to their IRA assassins. According to O'Doherty, Johnston compromised him to the IRA while under torture. O'Doherty claims that after Johnston's murder he was asked by the Provisionals to attend a meeting at the Four Seasons Hotel at Drogheda. As he entered the building he saw four IRA men and he 'smelled a rat'. He tried to leave the building and they seized him. He fought, freed himself from their clutches, rushed to his car and drove to Monaghan Gardai station, where he made contact with a member of Irish Special Branch, and was then escorted safely across the border.

On a subsequent occasion, according to O'Doherty, IRA men abducted him while he was drinking in a pub in Swatragh in County Londonderry. They bundled him into a waiting car and held him at gunpoint. He produced a pistol which had been concealed in one of his boots, disarmed his kidnappers and forced them to drive him to Swatragh town square, where he alighted from the car and made good an escape. He spent the following eighteen months constantly moving from place to place, living in haysheds and forests. Several times a week he met McCormick and his senior officer, Inspector Jimmy Blair.

O'Doherty's role as Agent 294 might never have come to light if he had not been arrested by Belfast CID and held for questioning for seven days in September 1977. In the course of interrogation he implicated himself and alleged that his handler, McCormick, was involved with him in armed robberies. He admitted possession of firearms including a pistol, a rifle and a sub-machine-gun. In what may well have been a dangerous precedent (though no less dangerous, I contend, than the continued use of Agent 294), the police released O'Doherty after he gave them 'several undertakings'. The 'undertakings' have never been revealed, but according to a Special Branch inspector it was felt O'Doherty was 'touching on something much deeper' and the authorities felt it was in their interests to free him. The Special Branch inspector who negotiated Agent 294's release from CID was Jimmy Blair. He had a vested interest in ensuring that O'Doherty did not reveal too much about the unorthodox if not illegal activities of the Special Branch and their highly unethical use of agents.

At the time of his release, what did the RUC have on file about Anthony O'Doherty? When arrested in September 1977 he was interviewed by Detective Inspector Alan Simpson of Regional Crime Squad Headquarters. Simpson was a member of an interrogation team within Regional Crime which became known to terrorists as the 'A Squad' because of its success in questioning suspects and the knowledge its members displayed when interrogating suspects. Other names in the A Squad team were Mooney, French, Donnelly, Newell, Hall and Rea. These men helped to damage the INLA through their police work and as a result became terrorist targets. When Detective Inspector Simpson interviewed O'Doherty he took the following notes, which later formed part of the Crown case against O'Doherty:

I am a Det. Inspector attached to HQ Crime Squad based at Knock, Belfast. On September 29 1977, accompanied by Det. Constable Dalton, we carried out an interview with Anthony O'Doherty at Castlereagh Police Office, Belfast. On September 30 between 1.20 and 2.25 pm I interviewed O'Doherty by myself at Castlereagh Police Office. The essence of both these interviews was repeated and embodied in the notes of a lengthy interview with O'Doherty which took place on September 30. This particular interview commenced at 1.35 and Det. Constable Dalton was present. I explained to O'Doherty that throughout the preceding six days whilst at Castlereagh he had been interviewed by several police officers and during the course of those interviews he had spoken about his involvement in the campaign of violence. We then had a lengthy discussion about his background and his personal and political views.

Detective Inspector Simpson then quoted the following statement from O'Doherty:

In 1975 I knew that a particular person did a robbery at the Northern Bank in Cushendall. Around £3500/£4000 was taken. The main recipient of the money received £3000. He also conveyed the person who did the robbery from the scene. I also know that on that day the Army were kept well clear of Cushendall and the Military Intelligence Officer was taken away to fish that day. This was to delay the arrival of helicopters in the area as they had to be tasked by the Military Intelligence Officer. The person who did the robbery received about £800 and to my knowledge it was spent on drink and other social activities. The person who received the bulk of the money used it to pay outstanding bills. I heard that friends of his received expensive presents and among the proceeds were a lot of Bank of Scotland notes. I believe he went to Scotland on a holiday to dispense of these notes to avoid arousing suspicion. When the robbery was done the money was taken to the other person's flat directly where it lay dormant for 5/6 months and was doled out gradually. In January 1977 I know that these two persons did a robbery at Martinstown Post Office. From the intelligence in my possession, the previous recipient of the money drove the car and the person who carried out the robbery walked across the fields. It was dark at the time and was timed to happen about three minutes before closing time. Everything went smoothly. I don't know how much was taken as the person who did the robbery did not have a chance to count the money. The recipient who was waiting at the car for the arrival of the person who did the robbery took the money at once. These two persons drove directly to the flat in Ballymena.

The money was taken to the field but it was not counted in the presence of the person who did the robbery as it was best they parted company as soon as possible. The person who did the robbery did not receive a single cold shilling of the money.

At the flat the money was placed inside a triangular corner unit. The money from this robbery was to be used by the recipient to buy a new car. About six weeks later the Martinstown Post Office was robbed again by the same two persons. It was a replica of the first robbery. A similar sum of money was taken and the person who did the robbery went back across the fields and got into the waiting car. They then drove to Ballymena and went to the flat again. On arrival at the flat they both went inside but parted again shortly afterwards as the driver had to go on duty. I know that the person who did the robbery was given clear indication not to fire the weapon used in the robbery as it previously had been test-fired and shells were available for comparison. The person who did the robbery on this occasion received about £125 three days later. The person who did these robberies did it partly for the proceeds and partly for friendship. There were also slight hints of blackmail. The person who received the proceeds was in deep financial trouble and facing losing his job because he could have gone to gaol as he was required to pay £40 per week maintenance. Also he had a large mortgage to meet. It was pure depression on his part. On occasions he sobbed about his financial trouble. These three robberies were the only ones done by these two men.

Before making the statement, O'Doherty insisted he could not reveal the name of the recipient but indicated that he was a policeman. He told one of his interviewers, Detective Constable William Allister: 'God, I can't tell you. I did the robberies on my own and not for any organisation.' At the time of making this statement, O'Doherty refused to name the policeman, whom he claimed had been 'good to him'. His case was that he had committed the robberies on his own initiative to help this policeman because he was in financial difficulty.

Despite O'Doherty's admission of criminal offences, he was released. Was it because the detectives were keen to discover the identity of the policeman whom O'Doherty was accusing, or was it because O'Doherty was being clever? The latter thesis is worth examining in the light of other matters which O'Doherty discussed with his interrogators. He went on to offer them information which related to them and pointed to the fact that members of the INLA were aware of their identities and were targeting them. One is obliged to ask whether indeed O'Doherty offered this information to make himself valuable to his A Squad interrogators and to buy himself freedom. Why else would detectives release a man who by his own admission was a criminal? In offering them such information O'Doherty showed that he was more than willing to compromise his own brother, John Joe. There is therefore a sense, one feels, that O'Doherty was buying himself freedom with the following revelations:

The person who received the bulk of the proceeds of the robberies found out that Denis Murray [policeman] had reported his suspicions about those two persons being involved in robberies to RUC Headquarters. About seven months ago the same person told me that Malachy Close had been arrested and had cracked. He said that Close had told the CID that I done all the robberies around the Cushendall, North Antrim area generally. He told me that the RUC's 'A' Squad would probably be interrogating me and to watch out for Kenny French as he was as sharp as a lance. He said that if I did any talking, he would be sitting there whistling and he would get John Joe to get a piper to take me to Aughnacloy graveyard. He described Kenny French as being a flashy dresser with dirty-fair hair in a teddy-boy style. He said he was about 5ft 9ins with a very sharp face. He said he dressed better than the usual type of person and was about 35 years of age. That's all he told me about him. At the same time I asked him who ran 'A' Squad. He told me it was Billy Mooney who used to be a Special Branch man in Lisburn. He said that Mooney was over 6 ft tall, dressed sober, strong full features with a Roman nose and grey/blue eyes. His hair was parted and swept back. His hair was black. He said he was elderly, about 48 to 50. I want to stress that when he told me about French and Mooney, it was not to set them up but merely that they were the opposition at Castlereagh.

O'Doherty referred to the discovery of a bomb under McCormick's car outside a fellow policeman's house. The bomb exploded while it was being defused by the Army. O'Doherty later alleged that McCormick put it there to indicate that he was being targeted by the Provos because he was a serious threat to them.

O'Doherty's statement ended with a further mention of his brother and a claim that both of them were present during discussions about murders:

About two weeks ago I was in Killybegs in the company of Peter Pringle [Killybegs native], Vinty Fegan, Frank Gallagher, John Eddie McNicholl, Joe Kelly [Dungiven] and Bernie McAteer. Pringle said we would have to do something with 'A' Squad as they were destroying the organisations. Gallagher said that plans were in hand but it was hard to plan such a big operation and keep it tight. He said that it only takes one grasser to destroy this operation. He asked John Joe if there had been any intelligence on it. John Joe said that a fair bit had been done. Gallagher said that each Company Officer Commanding should be left to look after the fuckers who were harassing them. Pringle said that this was another of these operations which was half planned and never carried through. Gallagher said that wasn't it right that White had Donnelly/Hall/Rea [author's note: members of A Squad] sewn-up. White is the OC of the IRSP in Derry. Gallagher suggested throwing ten-pound bombs into the ground-floor windows of the 'A' Squad members' houses. Cahal Maguigan was lifted by police in connection with the Ballymena bombs. John Joe told me that hard man Maguigan had been out in an Army helicopter and pin-pointed the house where the bombs were made outside Toomebridge at the Clady 'dump' which was a field near Beechland Park. I said to John Joe that Maguigan would not do that.

Even after this statement, the latter part of which places O'Doherty by his own admission in a conversation about the mass murder of A Squad detectives, the RUC authorities were prepared to release him. O'Doherty was indicating that his paramilitary connections extended beyond the Provisionals. He was prepared to compromise his brother and name a large number of people as accomplices to conspiracy to murder. One must ask whether O'Doherty gave police the story about the planned murder of A Squad members in order to keep himself out of prison and to emphasise his abilities as an informer/agent. Surely on the basis of the whole statement Detective Sergeant McCormick was entitled to know that Agent 294 was accusing a policeman of complicity in three robberies and accepting money from a man alleged to be the OC of the Provisionals in South Antrim. Were A Squad not aware that O'Doherty was a police/Army agent? Since there is no indication that the A Squad detectives knew O'Doherty's alias as Agent 294, this suggests that Special Branch was a law unto itself. However, they must have recognised that he was a self-confessed criminal who led a bizarre and dangerous lifestyle; he was a practised liar and a confidant of terrorists. Surely, therefore, he would have told them he was an agent in order to gain freedom. If the RUC did know he was Agent 294, did they not think it necessary to inform McCormick that his agent alleged he was providing a 'recipient' policeman with the proceeds of robberies? McCormick was not told anything, and O'Doherty was released and subsequently worked for McCormick for a further three years. Did he give A Squad some kind of undertaking that he would work for them, if they released him? One is, I feel, entitled to ask this question. If such an undertaking was given, O'Doherty had suddenly acquired additional handlers without McCormick's knowledge. Yet there is no evidence that he reached any agreements with A Squad to achieve his release.

However, I was told by a Special Branch source that Inspector Jimmy Blair was made aware of O'Doherty's dealings with A Squad. This source added that Blair was told that O'Doherty would also be providing information for A Squad. That arrangement may well have suited Blair, who was also one of O'Doherty's handlers. It was not in Blair's interests that A Squad examine too closely the activities of Agent 294. As events will show, Blair was not averse to allowing agents including O'Doherty to commit criminal acts, and I believe he was content to maintain a professional connection which did not generate too much scrutiny.

Until August 1980 O'Doherty operated with McCormick and Special Branch, though on 16 March 1978 he attended a prearranged meeting with members of A Squad, namely Detective Constables French, Newell and Dalton and Detective Inspector Alan Simpson. They drove him 'by arrangement' to Portglenone and from there O'Doherty directed them to Garvaghy Road on the outskirts of the village. Detective Inspector Simpson recorded the event:

O'Doherty told us to stop the vehicle. He disappeared across the fields and returned approximately 30 minutes later. He handed us a Webley and Scott double-barrelled shotgun and cartridge belt with cartridges. O'Doherty told me that the weapon was one of a pair of shotguns stolen by Benedict McAteer from the home of Charles Connolly outside Portglenone. O'Doherty added that he had discovered where McAteer had concealed one of the shotguns and he was handing it to me. He undertook to try to locate the second shotgun.

Again Agent 294 went his merry way working for A Squad as well as Special Branch. McCormick remained oblivious of the allegations about a 'recipient' policeman. Inspector Jimmy Blair continued to make use of O'Doherty, who was serving several masters. O'Doherty revealed in court two years later he was also working for Army intelligence. According to O'Doherty, the Army trained him in surveillance techniques which included the mounting of observation posts, the use of photographic and tape-recording equipment and unarmed combat.

In fact, McCormick said that for long periods he did not meet with O'Doherty but was aware that his agent was living rough in the countryside. It is McCormick's contention that O'Doherty was able to do this only because of his training with the Army. There is every reason to assume that the ability to live in such a fashion indicated not simply Army training but specialised training by one of the Army's elite units such as the SAS. On the other hand, O'Doherty by his own admission was also associating with terrorists—which would have necessitated meeting in rural areas with active service units of men who were on the run and hiding out in forested areas in North Antrim. O'Doherty was, it appears, working for several organisations. His movements were always erratic. Special Branch, as McCormick told me, did not always expect to see O'Doherty on a regular basis. After all, he was a self-confessed terrorist who was wanted by Provisionals (so he claimed), was capable of associating with the INLA because of family connections and was also playing the role of an agent. From all accounts he was a man with a busy schedule. The Army for its part has never admitted that O'Doherty worked for them, but by tradition they would not do so even if O'Doherty was being truthful about the matter. No evidence came to light at the time to prove a connection with the Army, though I am told that such a connection existed. McCormick knew there was such a relationship between his agent and the Army but refuses to talk about it. A Special Branch source told me that O'Doherty worked for a special Army unit and was given training by them.

O'Doherty was not arrested again until June 1980, at a time when the Chief Constable, Sir John Hermon, was tightening controls on the activities of Special Branch. O'Doherty made further admissions about his life as Agent 294 but was again released. However, during his interrogation he was made aware of police interest in Detective Sergeant McCormick. On 3 August 1980 O'Doherty was rearrested and charged with over forty offences including attempted murder, blackmail and possession of weapons and explosives. One wonders why it should have taken nearly three years and what was the precise motive for such a decision. He was arrested under Section 12 of the Prevention of Terrorism (Temporary Provisions) Act and conveyed to Castlereagh, which police refer to as 'police office' but which in fact is a sophisticated centre for conducting interrogations and is sometimes known as a 'holding centre'. He was then driven by Simpson, French and Newell to Ballymena and en route they told him they believed he was responsible for a shooting at the home of a police constable, Eugene Kearney, in 1974. O'Doherty admitted that he was, though he said he had not intended to harm Kearney, whom he knew from schooldays, but had fired shots over Kearney's house to gain favour with the Provisional IRA.

On 4 August Simpson and Dalton interviewed O'Doherty at

Castlereagh police office and informed him that they were making inquiries into serious crimes in the Portglenone and Cushendall areas of County Antrim over a number of years. They told him their 'interest' was in robberies, the blackmailing of a bank manager, explosions and shootings. After being cautioned, O'Doherty agreed 'to tell all he knew about such crimes'. Simpson told him 'some of the ground' had been covered at their interviews in 1977, but O'Doherty said he required his memory of those interviews to be 'refreshed', so Simpson quoted from notes of the 1977 interrogation sessions and asked O'Doherty to repeat his allegations to establish the truth of what had been said three years earlier. He recorded the following statement by O'Doherty which was tendered in evidence at O'Doherty's trial:

Neither McCormick or me had any money. He could not even afford to give me the retainer of £10 or £12 a week that he was getting for me so he decided if he cleared all the army or police from the Cushendall area would I rob the bank. I had earlier said to Charlie McCormick that I was going to Scotland to get a job. He said not to go as I was the only half-decent contact he had. He said: 'John-Joe will clear you in the long run with the Provos. If we can pull a wean of bum shootings like the one at Constable Eugene Kearney's that will put you back on the map.' I agreed to do the bank in Cushendall and about a fortnight before the robbery Charlie took me down to Cushendall and showed me the area. I did not know the Glens of Antrim at all and so he was going to show me where to go and where not to go. We used a van. We had a look at the bank and Charlie said if I could hold up six people the money problem was solved and we'd have ten grand so we came back again to Ballymena. Two or three days later we took a handgun and a hand-grenade down to a spot near Cushendall and hid them in a hedge. We went back to Ballymena. The day before the robbery, it was in the evening, Charlie ran me down to Lisnahunchian and I hijacked a car. I used a red light and was dressed like a soldier. I stopped a mini car with a woman in it. I told her I needed the car and she said it was all right and got out of it. I got into the mini car but could not find the starter. I found out later that the starter was on the floor. I told her to get back into the car and she drove off. As I was talking to her another car stopped as the driver thought it was a proper roadcheck. I went over to the driver and told him to get out as I was taking his car. He just got out. I think it was a Cortina. I took the car and drove down the Glens to a quarry. I parked the car in a quarry and stayed there all night. I could not even sleep as it was cold and snowing. Charlie had told me to do it at 11.30 in the morning. I stayed in the quarry until 11.30 or so. I had no watch so it might have been earlier. I drove to Cushendall to see if there were any UDR or police about and then went out and picked up the gun and hand-grenade. I drove back to the bank and parked outside. I put on a mask and went into the bank. I just demanded the money. There were two or three customers in the bank and the staff. I just said 'hand over or else' or something like that. They did. I passed a pillowcase through the counter and said I did not want any change. A man took it and filled it with banknotes. I went back out and got into the car. I drove off about four miles out of the town in the Ballycastle direction. I parked the car and walked over fields for about three miles. At times I lay down in the whin bushes. I eventually came to the road near a chapel where

Charlie was to pick me up at 6.30 pm. He was an hour and a half late and he came about 8.00 pm in the van. I forgot to include that just after I done the bank I drove straight to Cushendun. I parked outside the Post Office, I went in and the Post Office was empty. The woman shouted to 'hold on' as she would be downstairs in a minute. She came downstairs and I said: 'I'm here for the money.' She said 'that's all right' and handed me a brown envelope with the money in it. I went outside and sailed away in the car. It was then I parked the car and took to the fields. After he picked me up in the van, we went to his house. He took the money and the gun and left them in the van. He then gave me a change of clothes and I slept that night in his house. Charlie bought me a Ford Escort out of the proceeds which cost £950. He gave me £20 a week for six months and took me to Bangor and bought me a coat and a pair of trousers. We went to the 'Town and Country' in Newtownards for a meal. Charlie told me that if he gave me too much money I would make a mouth of myself around the town. Over the next few months I heard again that the Provos were out to kill me. I then met Benny McAteer and he told me that Dan Kearney was carrying a lot of money. We got toy guns and masks and went across the fields to his farm. Dan was in the yard talking to some other man. I can't remember which one of us had the gun but one of us said to Dan to hand over his money. He gave us the money out of his pockets which wasn't even £30, I think. I then did a raid on a furniture store but because I didn't get much money out of it Charlie said we would have to visit Cushendall again. I said I was not going into the bank again on my own. Charlie said I could hardly expect him to go in with me. I must have talked him into going as he agreed to go. He ran me out to the Michelin car park. We had agreed that we could steal a car there. I stole a Cortina by using a bunch of keys I had. I hid the car in Parkmore Forest. Charlie picked me up and drove me back into Ballymena and got my car which I think was the Datsun 100A which I think I had at the time. I drove the car down the Glens and parked it on a laneway which leads down to the river. Charlie picked me up and we went home again to Ballymena. He said he would have trouble getting away the next morning but would make an excuse out. The next morning about 9.30 or so, I'm not sure, but we met on the Doury Road. Charlie was in his own car. We then drove to the stolen car at Parkmore Forest. We put everything on and kept the masks rolled up in the caps. We had combat jackets, guns and masks stored away in the Forest. We got into the stolen car and drove to Cushendall village. We parked the car outside the bank and went inside. Charlie said he did not want to do any talking. We had the masks pulled down. It was nearly the same procedure as the time I had done it on my own. The man behind the counter filled the pillowcase. I took the pillowcase with the money and we both went back into the car. Charlie drove it. We headed off and he nearly lost it on a bend. We headed towards Ballymena for a couple of miles and abandoned the car. We walked across the fields to where my car was parked. We got into my car and drove along the Ballymena scenic route to Parkmore Forest. We threw all the money and guns into the boot of Charlie's car and I went back in my own car to Ballymena. We got around £3000. I got paid every week for a year about £20.

By contrast to the 1977 revelations, in this statement Agent 294 is suddenly naming McCormick. Was he being encouraged to be direct, or was this part of an ongoing strategy? On 5 August, O'Doherty continued his revelations, again naming McCormick and accusing him of serious offences involving shootings at policemen. It was O'Doherty's claim that shootings were 'staged' by McCormick so that he could pretend to investigate them, accuse IRA men and in doing so illustrate his ability to solve crimes quickly and so enhance his professional standing (which was not very high). O'Doherty also alleged that shootings were 'staged' to allow him to prove to people in paramilitary organisations that he was a real terrorist and not, as was the generally held belief within the Provos, an informer. O'Doherty also claimed that his handler had a personal interest in one shooting, that of Police Constable Kearney:

Charlie said: 'You can have a go at that big cunt Eugene Kearney.' Charlie said he had asked Constable Kearney to square a motoring case but he had refused to do so. I said I was not getting involved in any shootings along the Bann at 3 o'clock in the evening. Charlie said: 'I can tell you about Kearney. He is going with a bird down and around Rossnashane and he is easy meat.' I said I knew nothing about it other than that she was called McAleese. Charlie said that if I could have a go at his house or down at Rossnashane he would give me a few quid. Charlie said he thought he was on the way out. I asked him what made him think that. Charlie said they were forming Regional Crime Squads and Harry and the rest of the boys were in on them. He said: 'I have produced nothing and the next thing I will be a sergeant in Bessbrook.' Charlie said there was a conspiracy against him and he needed results and needed them quick. I think it was around that time that things did go bad for him as I could not do anything as I had a bad back. Charlie had the Sten gun and rifle stashed away. I said I could tell him how I could get Kearney any Saturday night. Charlie said he was not telling me to do it but there was the Sten and Kearney was home on a Saturday night. He said: 'One in the leg will not do him a bit of harm because he wouldn't square a motoring offence.' I said that if I did that I would only have 400 yards to go to the Bann River and he did expect me to swim it or run around in circles about Gortgole. He said: 'I'll tell you what we'll do. I'll sit down at Milltown and lift you.' We decided to do it and Charlie took me out in the Celica car with the Sten and he supplied the ammo. He dropped me off along the Milltown Road and I crossed the fields with the Sten to the back of Kearney's house. It was about 1.30 in the morning and Eugene Kearney came home. He came to the back door of his house, parked the car and locked it. He opened the door of the house and went in. He put on an inside light. I think it was in the scullery. About five minutes later the light went out and one went on upstairs in a bedroom or on a landing. I just opened fire on the car. I don't know how many rounds were fired. The car was a Marina. I ran down the fields and got into a car where Charlie was waiting for me. He said to me: 'Did you get him?' I said: 'Naw.' He said: 'It's just as well.' I told Charlie that the finger would be pointing straight at me. I said this as we drove along the back roads. Charlie said: 'I have a young fellow named Quinn who is an Agent in the Millquarter area. I will tell him to put in a report that Grant and McIlroy were responsible for the shooting. You put in the same report.' This was to keep me right and Charlie right.

I then got involved in trying to get 'Farmer' Kane out of Internment so that he and I could be the two top men in County Derry. It was believed I was responsible for putting him inside so his release would put me in favour again. Sometime after this I got involved in shootings at Portglenone Police Station. I used a .303 rifle—I had no ammunition but Charlie got me some. The first two times Charlie dropped me off up the Garvaghy Road. He gave me two boxes of .303 ammunition with fifty rounds in each box. He also gave me a bandolier which held clips. The first time I walked across a field about 80 yards and because of the security lights I could see the silhouette of the station. I fired about six shots and picked up the shells. Charlie didn't wait for me but headed off into Ballymena because he wanted to come back out to investigate it.

Weeks afterwards I did a replica with Charlie and fired about the same number of shots. After some months me and him started working together again. My back was bad at the time but he took me for the odd day out fishing and shooting. I think it was around 1975. Sometime around then Charlie ran me out to Portglenone. We were coming down past McClellandstown Orange Hall where we saw a lot of activity. I think there was a dance on. We knew there was always a lot of trouble at it and that a police car would be there to check the dance. I said to Charlie that it would be a good time to have a go at the police car. Charlie said he would rather that I didn't bother. I asked why. He told me there were a lot of Special Patrol Group personnel running around Portglenone. He said: 'Fuck you. If you are going to do it fire wide and high.'

I had the Sten gun with me. He dropped me off about 500 yards below the Orange Hall. I went up to a corner on the road and got into a hedge on the right-hand side of the road going towards the Orange Hall. There were cars going up and down the road and I saw the police car coming from the direction of Portglenone. I let it go past me. It was doing about 25 m.p.h. I fired and the bullets bounced off the road. What actually happened was that as I was cocking the Sten it went off before I intended it to. I emptied the magazine which held about 22 or 24 rounds. I ran off through the trees and the police started firing back. I hid the Sten in a hedge near Ahoghill and me and Charlie picked it up two days later. Charlie told me to get rid of the Sten as it was far too hot and to drop it into the River Bann. I gave it to our John-Joe for two Walkie-talkie radios.

O'Doherty was, in police parlance, 'singing', and on 5 August he was asked about a bomb which was found under McCormick's car during their ill-fated relationship.

Charlie told me he went to Moody's home at Ballylummin between Portglenone and Ahoghill for tea every Sunday and I was to plant the bomb. Charlie supplied the material for the bomb. He produced 2lbs of gelignite which was a funny shape and not in sticks like big candles. It was about seven inches long and sort of twisted. Charlie also produced two detonators and we made up the bomb. I got a clothes-peg, put two staples through it and connected two wires to it. The battery was an Ever-Ready, a bit broader than a cigarette packet. We connected the wires to the battery but broke the circuit with a big brass switch, smaller than a house switch but like one which you would find in an old bread van. I think the switch was taped to the battery and marked on and off on a bit of paper which was stuck to the switch. We arranged that when the switch was in the position marked 'off' it was actually 'on' and vice versa. The jaws of the clothes-peg were kept open with a piece of plastic which is on a shirt collar when it is new. The plastic was attached to a piece of fishing line with a fish hook on the end of it. All this was arranged round the explosives but the detonator was kept out of it. This was all made up on a Friday and taken to within a mile of Moody's house and hidden under whin bushes. I was to go on Sunday night between 9.30 pm and 9.45 pm and leave it under Charlie's car where it could be easily seen. I did go out that Sunday night, picked up the bomb and went across fields to Moody's house. I saw Charlie's brown Celica car parked at the door at the back of the house. I put the bomb under the car where it could be easily seen. I tried to hook the fishing hook to the front tyre but the hook caught in my gloves. When I got the hook out I just threw it on the ground. I just left and went in my own car back home. I met Jimmy Blair the next day and he said to me that me and McCormick were going well when we decided to blow-up his own car. A few days later I met Charlie and he was driving an old Vauxhall Viva and he was as pleased as punch. He had some stuff left over from making up the bomb for under his car. He asked if I knew any Reserve Police around Portglenone that we could hit. I said the only one I knew was Marks. Charlie and me made up another bomb. We had about ½ lb of explosive left. It was a replica of the bomb under Charlie's car but I can't remember if it had a brass switch. It had a switch of some sort. Me and him went and had a look the night before the attack in his wife's Vauxhall Viva. We left the bomb in a hen-house and fired a couple of shots. The people in the house fired back. There was nothing about the bomb on the news so I phoned the police in Ballymena and tipped them off about it. I heard on the news later that day that the bomb exploded injuring a policeman in the foot. I done it to boost my morale, that's all. There was no intention on my part or Charlie's to cause any harm. I was arrested shortly after this and brought to Castlereagh but later released.

O'Doherty was clearly not content to confine his version of events to his relationship with McCormick as an agent; he also provided them with an account of his part in an attempted murder of policemen which by his own admission did not involve his handler:

I knew Willie Lees on and off for about ten years through Republican Clubs things. He sent for me and asked if I knew Dessie Grew who was looking for a boy called Poland who was a policeman from around Ballymena. I said I knew Poland and he drinks in the Adair Arms in Ballymena. Lees told me that Grew and Stephen King had stayed about Lees' mother's looking for John Poland and had actually seen him. They had guns and all staked out to do Poland. Lees said Grew wanted to see me. I said I was not terribly interested in Grew as I was sure he only wanted to see me through the sights of a rifle. Lees told me that they had now moved to Mulvenna's at Glenarm. I said if there was something going on I would have to make a phone call first. I phoned the IRSP office in Dublin where my sister Patricia worked. I told her a hound dog was looking for me and was he after me. She said no that it should be all right. I then met Grew in Lees' house the same week. I went in and he was sitting there. Grew got up, shook hands with me and said: 'Tony how are you? Willie probably explained to you why we are here'. I said he did. I said if anything happens to Poland or Blair around the town he may shoot me as it would be blamed on me right away. Grew said we have the stuff here and we don't want to take it away again. He meant gelly and guns. Grew asked me did I know if he went to school or chapel. I said I was having fuck all to do with it. Willie Lees then said we should put a hoax bomb outside the town and put a real bomb where the police and army would take up a position to deal with it. They had by this time gone off the idea of shooting or bombing John Poland. I did not agree with the hoax bomb that Lees talked about. Grew said he had a better idea. He said we should break into an unoccupied house and leave a bomb and phone the police. That was shot down as well so they then settled for a booby trap. He [Lees] said Archie Mans had a lot of old Volkswagens near Carninny. He said there was a moss across the road from him that had two or three old derelict cars and that would be the spot. William Lees agreed to gather up bits and pieces and I supplied the two shifting spanners which came with my Colt car. Nothing was done that night. I went round to Lees' house the next night which was Monday. Grew was sitting in Lees' at the time but was heading back down to Larne. Grew came to Lees' house with a brand new socket set. Grew also brought with him two gallons of paint. William Lees had an old tank of gas. He gave me back the two shifting spanners as Colt or Mitsubishi were written on them and could be traced. Grew and William Lees went out to Wilsons' estate and came back with three or four pounds of gelignite or some type of explosive. It was wrapped in clear plastic. Grew got a tin, heated it up and burned a hole in the face of a watch. The watch would not go after it so Willie Lees gave Grew his own personal watch. Grew burned a hole in this watch with a pin. He stuck the bare end of a piece of wire in and stuck it with superglue. Grew then stuck the watch to the piece of board about 6" long and about 2" wide. He stuck it with superglue. He also had a clear plastic tube taped to the board and a small square transistor radio battery taped between the watch and the tube. He then soldered wires coming out of the watch, the battery and the plastic tube. He tested the circuit with a bulb. He left it in such a way that the wire only had to be connected up to the detonator and then placed in the explosive. There was mercury inside the clear plastic tube. They tried to find ball bearings but could not, to include in the bomb. Grew's car was parked outside so he went out to it and lifted out the back seat and placed the made-up bomb under the back seat. He also put the explosive in, but kept it separate. He put the back seat on again. Willie said there was no point. I said I would go on home. Lees and Grew got into Grew's old Fiat car and followed me as far as Dunvale. He also took the old tank of gas and the socket set and the paint tins. I knew that they were going to set the bomb inside one of the paint tins and when it was lifted it would go off. I went to my work the next morning and heard on the news that three policemen had been injured at derelict cars outside Ballymena. I knew that our job was going to plan. About a week later I met William Lees and he told me that if the bastard had lifted enough explosives the three policemen would have been dead.

O'Doherty also admitted extorting a large sum of money from a bank manager through blackmail and claimed he committed the crime to assist people he knew in the IRSP/INLA.

He also made allegations that McCormick, in collusion with him, carried out the murder of a police officer, Sergeant Joseph Campbell, in Cushendall in County Antrim on 25 February 1977. O'Doherty alleged that McCormick had carried out the murder because Campbell was aware of McCormick's participation in crime with O'Doherty. Ultimately, as a result of these allegations and further statements by O'Doherty, McCormick had to face charges which included armed robbery and the murder of Sergeant Campbell. The evidence against McCormick, however, consisted essentially of O'Doherty's statements, which were uncorroborated evidence of an accomplice, and Justice Murray, sitting in Belfast, dismissed all the charges with the exception of the charge of armed robbery. He sentenced McCormick to twenty years' imprisonment. McCormick subsequently succeeded in having the conviction overturned by the Court of Criminal Appeal. In January 1984 Lord Lowry, the presiding Appeal Court judge, remarked that the evidence against McCormick was inadequate for such a conviction. He said the trial judge misdirected himself in law as to the credit-worthiness of O'Doherty and was wrong to find O'Doherty's evidence against McCormick capable of being believed.

In the context of what happened in the various court cases it is interesting to note what Detective Sergeant Charlie McCormick said when arrested: 'I, Charles McCormick, didn't kill Sergeant Campbell. I never arranged to get a gun or anything. There is no way Joe Campbell is in his grave because of me.' When it was put to McCormick that he had used methods beyond normal policing and killed Campbell because the policeman had discovered this, McCormick replied: 'Before God I didn't.'

When he was informed that O'Doherty was the source of these allegations, he reacted by describing his agent as a Walter Mitty character whose job had 'got beyond him': 'I did my job and it wasn't accepted. I didn't do Joe Campbell and I didn't do any of these things. O'Doherty must have been asked to bring down a Special Branch man. He must have been interrogated by the Provos. He is a snivelling bastard. I friggin' well never did any of these things. I am completely innocent. How could you take the word of that lying bastard.' McCormick told his interrogators that O'Doherty had named to him the killers of Joe Campbell: 'O'Doherty told me it was a dirty one and no one wanted to know about it.' He added that he could account for his movements on the night of the murder.

When asked about O'Doherty's claim that the booby-trap bomb which was found under his car was a 'staged operation', he replied that this was nonsense and named those he believed were responsible for what he knew to be an attempt on his life. He said it was 'daft' to suggest he knew about the bomb. Such a suggestion, he said, was 'pure shit'. He was hated in Toomebridge and a gang from that area planted the bomb. After the incident he was advised by his doctor to spend a fortnight away from work. He also denied O'Doherty's allegations that he was involved in robberies.

He told his interrogators that O'Doherty as a source was 'hard to handle' and was dangerous, though he had turned up 'good gear'. He was paid retainers of £5 or £10 per week, with £200 for results and £300 for seizures, and McCormick was often out of pocket because of payments to his agent. As a result of information from Agent 294 he had uncovered an arms dump in Cushendall, a mortar-bomb factory and rocket launchers. The agent had also given him information about the killing of Lord Louis Mountbatten to the effect that his murderers were either from the Markets area of Belfast or from the town of Castlewellan. A chief inspector who interviewed McCormick recorded that the accused sergeant admitted knowing that O'Doherty possessed guns but claimed that other officers were also aware of this.

The result of the interrogation of Charles McCormick was that this Special Branch sergeant—who once guarded the Queen when she visited Northern Ireland—was, as I have recounted, charged with the Campbell murder as well as twenty-six other offences including those of armed robbery, making bombs and causing an explosion.

While he was being held in custody in Crumlin Road prison, he said that the prison authorities discovered a plot to kill him and stopped it 'just in time'.

In the same prison, Anthony O'Doherty was being held, for his own safety, in solitary confinement for twenty-three hours a day. On 25 August he was visited by A Squad detectives.

I believe that, when he made his allegations about McCormick, O'Doherty was fully aware that there was the prospect of a deal with the authorities. I believe he was part of a developing strategy which became known as the 'supergrass' system. In 1981 O'Doherty pleaded guilty to the charges against him and received sentences totalling eighteen years' imprisonment. This paved the way for him to become the first supergrass—in the trial, in March 1982, of the only policeman to be charged on the basis of supergrass evidence. It had taken the authorities several years to act on O'Doherty's claims. The trial of McCormick, based as it was on the evidence of an informer/agent (O'Doherty), is a fine example of the problems facing judge, prosecutor and defence council alike in an age of terrorism where the informer may be expected to be a star witness.

At the trial of McCormick, O'Doherty went into the witness box and offered an account of life as an agent. He said he lived on a knife-edge: leading a double life was a dangerous game in which one slip would mean a death sentence. O'Doherty argued that he chose such a life for humanitarian reasons and not because of money or freedom. He agreed with defence counsel that he had been paid £1000 for a blackmail offence, that he had carried out a robbery merely for kicks, and that he had given terrorists the address of an Army intelligence operator.

In cross-examination, McCormick's defence counsel, Desmond Boal QC, one of the most astute and experienced members of the Northern Ireland Bar, asked O'Doherty how he could be court-martialled by the IRA when he had constantly denied being a member of that organisation. O'Doherty replied that his brother told him he had been court-martialled and sentenced to death by the Provisionals. Boal put it to him that maybe he had reconciled himself with the Provos. O'Doherty answered: 'It wouldn't matter if I killed the whole British Cabinet. Charlie McCormick showed me a book of IRA Standing Rules which says that a death sentence cannot be retracted. It stands for evermore— Amen.' He declined to comment on a suggestion by defence counsel that he finally defected to the IRA to have his death sentence commuted. He also denied that he persuaded the Provisionals that he was more useful to them as a double agent than as a dead agent. When asked how someone known as an informer could obtain information valuable to the security forces, O'Doherty replied that the 'staged' shoot-outs had had the desired effect of re-establishing him in Republican circles.

Explaining his motives for working as an informer/agent, he stated: 'For the first six months after I was released from Internment I was under a subtle form of blackmail. Afterwards I worked partly for humanitarian reasons, partly for excitement. These men were handing me out guns. They were hardly going to turn round and intern me. It was a normal working relationship. I put myself at a great deal of risk.' The verbal exchanges in court between Desmond Boal and O'Doherty contained the elements of a fencing match with thrust and counter-thrust:

Boal:	Is it true that you became a practised liar?
O'Doherty:	Up to a point.
Boal:	Therefore you are a practised liar!
O'Doherty:	Certainly, when I was doing my job.
Boal:	To you, lying was like riding a bicycle—a facility you never lose.
O'Doherty:	You are twisting my words.

O'Doherty admitted receiving money for information but said the role of agent cost him money, whereas he could have chosen a job of work which would have given him a Friday-night wage packet and no problems.

Counsel suggested to him that his loyalty to the IRA was illustrated by the fact that on many occasions he supplied the police with enough information to ingratiate himself with them, but not enough seriously to damage the IRA's operations. O'Doherty said this was a ridiculous allegation and he could name sixty occasions when his tip-offs to police were successful.

Counsel pressed O'Doherty to reveal how many agencies employed him. Did he work for CID, Special Branch, the Army, IRA and IRSP? O'Doherty agreed this was correct 'up to a point'. 'So you worked for five agencies. You were prepared to sell yourself to five agencies,' said counsel. 'I was getting no money out of it,' replied O'Doherty. Counsel suggested that the payment he was receiving was his freedom or his life.

O'Doherty told the court he was armed 'from the start'. He was given a .38 revolver, then a .32 revolver, a .303 rifle, a .45 revolver and a Sten gun which had belonged to the Provisionals.

Counsel turned his attention towards an offence of blackmail to which O'Doherty had pleaded guilty. O'Doherty admitted that he, his brother and another man obtained £8000 by blackmailing a Cushendall bank manager. He said the money was obtained by making a threat of death on behalf of the IRSP, but he was not a member of that organisation: 'I was asked to do the thing and I did it. That doesn't make me a member of the IRSP.' Desmond Boal said there was evidence that Sergeant Joe Campbell had investigated the blackmail in February 1977.

Boal:	His death came about because of enquiries he made into the blackmail and what he learned about it.
O'Doherty:	No.
Boal:	And if we are to look for the murderer of Sergeant Campbell, we look to you, your brother or...
O'Doherty:	That's lies. McCormick shot Campbell. I believe Campbell may have suspected that it was me and McCormick who were behind the blackmail.

Boal hounded O'Doherty, constantly analysing and chipping away at his evidence. The result was that O'Doherty said he had no evidence that McCormick was involved in committing robberies. He also named a person, not McCormick, who he said killed Campbell. 'I want to make it clear', he told counsel, 'that I did not tell any policeman about Charlie McCormick being involved in armed robberies nor did I kill anyone. At no time have McCormick or myself been involved in criminal activities.' Under further cross-examination, he said those were his words to RUC investigators in 1978. Counsel pointed out that those admissions were completely different from other statements he made to the court. O'Doherty agreed, turned to the judge and said that in 1978 he was 'covering up' but at his final arrest in 1980 he broke down.

Counsel put it to O'Doherty that police were suggesting to him that Mccormick was involved in crime.

Boal: I am saying to you that you were prepared to admit that
               Sergeant McCormick was involved in crime whether you knew it
               or not.
O'Doherty: I knew it was true because Sergeant McCormick was always
               along with me.

Counsel's constant questioning of O'Doherty was naturally directed at his credibility but O'Doherty remained remarkably firm. Much to the consternation of defence counsel, he admitted that he had regularly received prison visits from the detective in charge of the Crown investigations against McCormick and he had, in his cell, copies of statements he made to police in 1980. He denied that he and the detective were conspiring against McCormick or that they 'contrived' their evidence 'along certain lines'. Boal suggested that O'Doherty's evidence was a tissue of lies concocted with the purpose of getting McCormick convicted and thereby gaining a remission of sentence for the witness. O'Doherty's initial reply was that counsel was the first person to make such a suggestion. He then paused and added: 'You are one of the first—other people have suggested the same thing.' The words 'other people', he said, referred to other prisoners.

Defence counsel completed his cross-examination and then addressed the court, pleading that his client had no case to answer. He told the judge, who was sitting without a jury, that it was the defence submission that it would be dangerous to convict on the uncorroborated evidence of an accomplice 'who is an informer and by his own admission was playing a double game'. Mr Boal argued that there was a distinct possibility that O'Doherty was a double agent:

He is a man living on his wits. He is a man who has lied and lied—a man who is a practised liar and has given various accounts of the matters at issue. If there is to be any force or significance to the proposition that it is dangerous to convict on the uncorroborated evidence of an accomplice, then surely this must be it. Having heard this man in the witness box and observed him, having heard the admissions that have flowed from his own mouth, this is not a man who can be relied upon, particularly beyond a reasonable doubt. His evidence is flimsy and almost irrelevant. In practical terms, as well as in legal terms, before your Lordship can convict, your Lordship must believe that man. I submit that nobody having listened to that man over the last few days can put his hand on his heart and say he is satisfied he is telling the truth.

Mr Boal's eloquent submission was rejected by the judge and the case continued.

The most revealing evidence about Special Branch operations came during the appearance in the witness box of Inspector Jimmy Blair. He admitted working with O'Doherty and added that he and another 'officer' were working with him in 1981. This was the period when O'Doherty was in prison. Blair refused to reveal the name of the other officer for security reasons, nor did he say whether he was from Special Branch or Army intelligence. So, even while O'Doherty was in prison, he was in the employ of at least one agency. Of course in the run-up to McCormick's trial he was held in a specially constructed area of Crumlin Road prison which later housed other supergrasses. While there he was possibly being debriefed or briefed.

Blair admitted that during his career with Special Branch O'Doherty worked for a number of Special Branch officers and an Army intelligence officer, and that this was unsatisfactory. 'Did you ever have suspicions that he received weapons from a special unit of the Army?' asked Desmond Boal. Blair replied that he had but it was not his duty to ask questions about it. 'Did you not think this was a matter which should excite police interest?' enquired Boal. 'Not at that time. It came to my notice that Detective Sergeant McCormick and O'Doherty were working with that unit and they had taken him away and trained him,' Inspector Blair answered. This statement by Blair was lost to the media in the coverage of the McCormick case and it is something to which I shall return later in this chapter.

Blair said he was aware that members of O'Doherty's family were connected with the IRSP and INLA and although it was possible in view of this that O'Doherty was a double agent he had no difficulty assuring himself that this was not the case.

At this point in the trial, Blair found himself seriously compromised legally by questions from defence counsel concerning the workings of Special Branch. In the coverage of the trial this episode received little attention, yet it is crucial to an understanding of the values of such an agency and how those values pose grave questions for a democracy. Desmond Boal asked Blair if he had ever encouraged persons other than policemen to shoot in unwarranted circumstances. Blair replied that he did not wish to answer the question. When pressed further by defence counsel, Blair said he could not answer for reasons of security. He then paused and added that he could not reply on the grounds that he might incriminate himself. This was a most useful and, I feel, disturbing statement by a senior Special Branch officer. As a result the court was adjourned for ten minutes. When the trial resumed the judge directed that he was according the witness privilege. Inspector Blair did not have to answer the question.

However, the court heard information which perhaps throws light on Blair's reluctance to 'incriminate' himself. Another Special Branch officer gave the following version of events during the McCormick trial:

In February 1974 O'Doherty gave information that a wanted terrorist was in the area. O'Doherty was under pressure from other terrorists. At that time he wanted to establish himself and make it known he was not working for the police. The information was that this terrorist was on the wanted list and could be found at a certain house and O'Doherty thought that if he staged the firing of some shots in the air that would give us an excuse to search the area and find the wanted person. Subsequently that took place. We fired some shots in the air in the vicinity of a UDR patrol. The police however did not find the wanted man.

Mr Boal pointed out that 'firing some shots in the air' was an inadequate description of what happened. He put it to the superintendent that O'Doherty would say there was a heavy exchange of fire on both sides, that the place where O'Doherty ambushed the patrol was riddled, and that two UDR soldiers were wounded. The superintendent accepted that there was heavy firing but said only one UDR man was wounded, not seriously, when a fellow soldier's gun accidentally discharged in a Landrover that was supposedly under fire.

When questioned about O'Doherty's reliability as an agent, the superintendent said that before 1974 his information yielded results but after that year he did not come up with important data: 'Before 1974 he was producing results that saved a considerable amount of lives in the community. In my opinion he seemed genuinely concerned to combat violence and did everything he could to prevent incidents taking place.' That is an inadequate description of a man who was at the time serving an eighteen-month sentence for over forty terrorist offences including the attempted murder of three policemen. The superintendent completed his evidence by accepting a proposition from Desmond Boal that if O'Doherty was a successful double agent Special Branch would have remained unaware that he had been turned by the IRA.

Before McCormick took the witness stand the court was given an indication of the manner in which he had been treated when first interviewed by colleagues. A superintendent said he put it to McCormick that the RUC considered him to be worse than the Provisional IRA. Mr Boal described the statement as vulgar abuse of the accused and the judge said it was unnecessary. Then McCormick walked into the witness box and, head bowed, told the court that he was a teenager when he joined the police force in 1958. He was stationed in County Fermanagh, in the village of Kesh, but moved to Ballymena in 1961. He worked on a part-time basis for CID and became a detective constable in 1969.

McCormick stated that when he became involved with O'Doherty he was aware that the agent had another handler but this was not unusual. It ensured that if a handler died or was murdered an agent or 'tout' was not lost to memory. O'Doherty told him about arms dumps and the command structure of the Provisional IRA in South Derry. 'We knew that his own family and especially his brother, John Joe, were involved with the Provos and that John Joe was the main man at the time.' After Ivan Johnston was murdered, McCormick said that O'Doherty was concerned that the former Special Branch officer might have revealed under torture O'Doherty's status as an agent. He told the court that he and his agent were friends and it was unprofessional to give informers the impression that one was using them.

McCormick said he first became suspicious that O'Doherty was involved in acts of terrorism when the agent failed to appear at a rendezvous in March 1976 and a Cushendall bank was robbed that day. Although he continued to use him as a source, he reported to the authorities that he believed he 'had a criminal on his hands'. It was the witness's view that O'Doherty turned against him because he was being used by the Provisional IRA.

When asked about his knowledge of Sergeant Campbell, who was a pillar of the Ballycastle community, McCormick told the court that he suspected the station sergeant of leaking Special Branch intelligence to the IRA. The RUC Chief Constable, Sir John Hermon, later took the unusual step of referring to a court case and condemned the allegations as a slur on an innocent man who was a fine policeman. McCormick at his trial denied all O'Doherty's allegations, including that which related to a bomb under his car: 'Whoever placed that bomb had only one intention. That was to take my life and that of whoever was with me.' He described how he discovered the bomb and phoned Inspector Blair to inform him about it. They both examined the bomb and Blair pulled a fishing hook out of the car. McCormick urged Blair to let go of it and to think of his youngsters and wife at home.

Towards the conclusion of McCormick's evidence to the court, he was asked whether there were times a 'blind eye would be turned' on the activities of an agent. He replied: 'Many's a time a blind eye was turned in relation to incidents but I can assure you that O'Doherty did not get authority from me or anybody else to carry out the attack on Sergeant Campbell nor was he assisted by me.' When the presiding judge asked if Special Branch was required to decide whether to prosecute a source who was known to be guilty of a crime, McCormick replied that such a decision would not be a Special Branch matter and added: 'A report would be submitted. Our superiors knew the type of job we were involved in and they understood the difficulties.' It was a less than satisfactory answer, but it indicated the dilemmas facing the Special Branch in their use of an agent.

In his summing up, defence counsel Desmond Boal returned to the substance of an earlier submission and stressed the dangers arising from placing any reliance on the evidence of an accomplice:

An accomplice is nine times out of ten able to talk with plausibility because he was there. That plausibility gives an impression of truthfulness which may be carried on to a jury deciding that he is truthful in everything he says. It is because of that, that the courts have said it is dangerous to convict on the evidence of an accomplice. O'Doherty is far from an ordinary accomplice. He is a liar because he says he is a liar. Not only is he a liar but a practised liar. It must be perilous to rely on the uncorroborated evidence of a practised liar. He has lived by lies, he has survived by lies and owes his life to lies. He agreed with me that for a period of years he lived a lie and that implies so very much. If he had dropped his guard at any time he was a dead man. It is frightening to think of the errors that would be created if courts convicted on this type of evidence. As a miscreant he should not be believed. He is defective morally. He has been involved in crime ranging from burglary to attempted murder. O'Doherty is a killer and a hypocrite. One cannot imagine a more vile creature being put into the witness box of this land.

Mr Boal suggested that O'Doherty believed he would walk free from prison at an earlier time than the law ordained. The self-confessed agent was an active and dangerous Republican. Defence counsel also illustrated that O'Doherty's demeanour was, in his view, typical of someone with a love for drama and the theatrical, a sense of vanity and a desire to be 'centre-stage'. He perceived O'Doherty as intelligent but dangerous because of his cunning and intrinsic subtlety.

Charles McCormick, who had been suspended on full pay during his trial, had spent almost four years in prison. His next move, he said, was to sue for wrongful dismissal and to sue for wrongful arrest; he is still waiting for the outcome of legal proceedings against the RUC. He says the RUC knows who killed Campbell and he wants the culprits to be charged.

McCormick lives in Ballymena; in his spare time he drinks with former colleagues and other policemen, and enjoys gardening and fishing. He gives the impression that he has a devastating story to tell but will not tell it if the RUC accedes to his request that the murderers of Joseph Campbell are publicly charged and compensation is paid for wrongful arrest and dismissal. It may be that the question of financial compensation is secondary, but I was left with the feeling that it is none the less an issue. The dispute between McCormick and his previous employers remains unresolved. I conducted a lengthy conversation with him in the presence of another journalist. He was affable, served us excellent whiskey, but was cautious with words. It seemed that if McCormick ever decided to reveal the details of his life as a

Special Branch officer there would be many people interested in what he had to say, but that perhaps his story would be prevented by his former employers, who might use the Official Secrets Act against him.

I was told by a Special Branch source that McCormick had led 'an interesting life' and that he worked for a time with a special Army unit based at Castledillon in County Armagh. Robert Nairac and Tony Ball were members of the same unit, which was concerned with terrorist operations, both Republican and Loyalist, stretching from Armagh into the north and north-west of the province. Blair confirmed that both McCormick and O'Doherty worked for a special unit of the Army. His use of the words 'special unit' is, in itself, significant. Is it possible that O'Doherty was trained in Castledillon? He was trained by the Army, but the Castledillon unit, according to my source, was one of several in Northern Ireland which were responsible to London and not Army authorities in Northern Ireland. These units communicated with each other and there was one in South Derry which probably trained O'Doherty and liaised with McCormick. According to my sources he came into contact with Nairac through the special unit operating on his patch.

Inspector Jimmy Blair was retired from the RUC after the trial; he committed suicide in April 1989. The McCormick trial, and particularly the evidence of Special Branch officers who talked of staged shoot-outs and confirmed that O'Doherty was supplied with an arsenal of weapons, conveyed images of a dirty war in which the rules were being loosely interpreted and even broken. Jimmy Blair's refusal to answer a question on the grounds that he might incriminate himself left him open to speculation that he had authorised agents to use weapons. One allegation which did not emerge at the trial was that O'Doherty had regularly removed IRA weapons from dumps and given them to McCormick, who had them fired so that bullets could be retained for forensic examination to determine if the weapons were used in assassinations or ambushes; O'Doherty had then returned the weapons to the dumps.

Another matter which did not come to light during the McCormick trial was that a chief inspector of Special Branch who was scheduled to give evidence for the Crown disappeared from his home for several days, approximately a week before the trial began. He went to court to give evidence but his bout of amnesia left him distressed and he was not considered to be in a fit state to give evidence. He later went on extended sick leave due to ill-health and eventually retired from the RUC to become a security officer for a firm in Northern Ireland.

The trial and the bizarre story which unfolded left many questions unanswered. McCormick says he was framed. His lawyer claimed that Agent 294 was turned into a double agent by the Provos and that meanwhile he was also working for a special unit of the Army. The Army escaped scrutiny in the trial, so one can only wonder what role was performed for them by Anthony O'Doherty—man prepared to denounce everyone around him, even members of his family, when his own freedom was at stake.

Four months after McCormick's conviction was quashed, O'Doherty was told that the Secretary of State for Northern Ireland, James Prior, recommended that the Royal Prerogative be used to remit eight years of his sentence. This ensured that he became a free man because of the 50 per cent rule applying to determinate sentences for terrorism in Northern Ireland. O'Doherty was quietly moved to safety. After his release an unsuccessful murder attempt was made by the IRA on his brother, John Joe.

O'Doherty was conveyed to another part of the United Kingdom where he was given a new identity and a weekly sum of money. Within a fortnight he was back in his old stamping ground of Ballymena. The police soon discovered his whereabouts and returned him to his new living quarters across the Irish Sea. Several months later, O'Doherty was again back in Ballymena. This time the police were obliged to snatch him from a sidewalk and return him to the safety of his hideaway. He told them he could not cope with living away from home. I believe that by that stage he knew he was not at risk from the Provisionals. Maybe he had, in IRA parlance, done them 'a favour'. I have also learned that when McCormick and O'Doherty were operating together they would have violent arguments which were then quickly forgotten. Theirs was a strange relationship, and it is possible that O'Doherty may have wished to be in Ballymena close to the man he betrayed. The only other relationship he seemed able to sustain was, for a time, with a young woman who was separated with five children. A journalist told me that O'Doherty was observed in a shop in Ballymena in May 1989. The information about the sighting had come from another journalist; and the claim did not appear any more bizarre than O'Doherty's lifestyle.

However, he was a survivor in a dirty war in which he played an integral part. Desmond Boal, McCormick's lawyer, denounced him as a killer, yet several agencies had been prepared to employ him. McCormick would argue that terrorism is dirty and as such requires dirty or unconventional tactics. If such methods are indeed necessary for winning a dirty little war, then the use of people like O'Doherty could be widespread, and that creates problems for a democratic society.

Although O'Doherty was a survivor, others were not so fortunate. Several months after the killing of Joe Fenton in 1989 another Catholic businessman lost his life at the hands of the IRA. The victim was forty-eight-year-old John McAnulty from the town of Warrenpoint outside Newry. Aspects of his life and the events leading to his death are reminiscent of the Fenton case. McAnulty lived a flamboyant lifestyle, drove expensive cars and was regarded as an affable, amiable extrovert who enjoyed displaying his wealth by buying expensive rounds of drinks for acquaintances in bars. He married when he was in his late teens but the marriage lasted only a year. He left for England, where he worked on building sites and drove lorries for building contractors, but did not settle in one job. At the start of the Troubles he returned to Northern Ireland and bought a garage business in Meigh, the townland outside Newry where Robert Nairac's murderer, Townson, lived. The business was well supported by locals. Aside from providing a mechanical service it also bought and sold second-hand vehicles. Republican sources in South Armagh say that in 1970–1 John McAnulty allowed vehicles which were for sale at his garage to be used by both wings of the IRA to transport weapons across the border and to ferry men 'on the run' from Northern Ireland to safe-houses in the Republic. The sources are adamant that McAnulty was not a member of either wing of the IRA but was a sympathiser who was willing to perform favours when asked, mostly by the Provisionals. He remarried, though maintained friendly terms with his first wife Peggy, who lives at Camlough, a village on the outskirts of Newry.

In the early 1980s he established a haulage business with six lorries and employed about a dozen drivers working on shifts. His firm, Cambrook Farm Feeds, dealt in grain. McAnulty was known to be unscrupulous about the restrictions imposed on people transporting goods across the border from one part of the island to the other. In accordance with EEC regulations, exchange-rate subsidies were paid for goods which crossed the Irish border, and McAnulty was prepared to send cargoes of grain to criss-cross the border, earning several subsidies on the same shipment. He was also not averse to allowing his vehicles to be used for smuggling livestock and other goods. This brought him into contact with a subculture which feeds on fraud and lives off the border. By the mid-1980s the authorities in both parts of Ireland were exercising strict controls in an attempt to eradicate smuggling. Those who were engaged in this criminal pursuit not only required IRA sanction to pass through certain territories but, according to the security forces, were also forced to pay the IRA 'subsidies', otherwise known as protection money. The IRA's knowledge of the border—

where it could be crossed at any time without risk from police, Army or customs—was vital to successful smuggling. When the British government clamped down on subsidies, haulage firms such as McAnulty's began to face economic hardship. His response was to wind up his business, but the assets were insufficient to pay debts he owed on both sides of the border. In May 1989 he and other hauliers were arrested and held for questioning by customs investigators—much as Fenton and some estate agents were subjected to scrutiny and brief interrogation about money-laundering for paramilitaries. Although McAnulty and the others were freed after questioning, it was clear from documentation seized from his premises that the investigation would continue.

On Sunday 16 July, he drove with his first wife to a pub on the outskirts of Dundalk in the Irish Republic. After midnight six masked and armed men forced their way into the premises and seized him. They dragged him into the car park and in an ensuing struggle he was beaten and blood was spilled on the ground. He was bundled into a car. Twenty-four hours later his body, naked from the waist up, his feet bare, his hands bound and a towel wrapped loosely round his head, was found by the roadside at Culloville in South Armagh.

The Provisionals' South Armagh Brigade issued a statement that they had killed him because he was an informer. They claimed he was guilty of passing information to the RUC from 1972 and he regularly met 'his handler' in the Downshire Arms Hotel in Banbridge, a predominantly Protestant town between Belfast and Newry. The IRA said McAnulty's brief was to frequent pubs along the border and maintain surveillance on certain Republicans. The information he supplied, according to the IRA, led to raids on dozens of homes and placed the lives of IRA men at risk.

The murder led to media speculation that McAnulty had been killed because he owed protection money to the IRA, or that a debtor had paid for his assassination. Privately the RUC said that he was not an informer, but that would have been a predictable response. The Gardai were also sceptical about the claim that he was an informer; however, like the RUC they have a policy of making no public comment in such circumstances except for condemnation of the murder. One other theory surfaced in the *Sunday World* newspaper:

The abduction and murder of wealthy Warrenpoint importer, John McAnulty, may have been a panic reaction by the IRA following the smashing of their top European hit squad by French Anti-terrorist Police. Sources in South Armagh say McAnulty may have been involved in bringing weapons into Ireland in grain shipments from France. The sources say the dead man visited France earlier this month and his wide-ranging contacts there would have been useful to the IRA. Intelligence experts say

that France was a safe haven for IRA units involved in attacks on British Army targets in Germany and the Netherlands. But the French connection began to fall apart.

The Sunday World's investigative reporter, Martin O'Hagan,
believes he was held captive by the IRA unit which killed McAnulty.
O'Hagan was abducted in South Armagh some time before the
McAnulty killing:

I went into South Armagh after receiving a communication that local Republicans
wished to talk to me. Like most journalists you understand the risks of the job and
one of them is to talk to sources you know or who request to speak to you. I was
given details of a rendezvous and drove there but when I arrived, I was confronted by masked men in combat jackets, carrying walkie-talkie radios and battered-
looking AR15 Armalite rifles. I was hooded and bundled into a car and driven to a
house which I believe was probably on the Southern side of the border.

Martin O'Hagan was interrogated by two IRA men about *Sunday World*
staff and the newspaper's contacts in the Republican movement.
During the interrogation, which lasted twelve hours, the reporter was
told that his name had been found on documents taken from two RUC
undercover detectives who had been shot months earlier by the IRA in
South Armagh. The policemen had been returning to their base after
meeting with their counterparts in Dundalk. Unfortunately their
deaths left security forces uncertain of what the IRA might have taken
from the bodies and car of the two policemen. There was no way of
determining which files, personal documents or address books both
men were carrying when killed. Their meeting in Dundalk had been
arranged to discuss cross-border security. Intelligence chiefs recognised that there was every risk that the Provisionals had come into
possession of important intelligence.

Martin O'Hagan was told by his interrogators that documents taken
from the murdered policemen named a *Sunday World* reporter as
someone who met regularly with a Republican contact in County
Armagh. O'Hagan said his interrogators demanded the name of the
Republican contact but he replied that he had no knowledge of such a
person. They also told him that information on top-security files taken
from the policemen pinpointed police informers and that roads
around the border would soon be 'littered with touts'.

According to O'Hagan, the IRA men threatened to drug him to make
him talk. One of them remarked that forty-year-old David McVeigh,
whom they shot as an informer in September 1986, went to his death
protesting his innocence. McVeigh, whose two brothers are serving
long prison terms for IRA-related offences, was lured to his death after

being told he was being sent to an IRA training camp in the Irish Republic; he left his wife and children at his Lurgan home and was found several days later dead on a border laneway. O'Hagan was frightened and constantly expected to be killed: 'I sat on the edge of my seat and my heart was pumping. I thought that this was the end for me. I remember the feelings of anger I felt that these people, whom I didn't even know, had the power of life or death over me.' Fortunately, Martin O'Hagan was driven back to his car and released: 'When they were letting me go I was again bundled into a car which had the rear seat removed. I panicked and shouted: "You bastards are going to kill me." Someone in the darkness shouted back. "We're not but there are a lot of others who lay where you are lying and who were shot.'

Those final words to Martin O'Hagan were chilling, and one can only speculate on what John McAnulty's killers must have said to him. They not only shot him but prefaced his death with torture; his body bore the marks of a beating and cigarette burns. There was media speculation from 'security forces sources' that McAnulty had been abducted and taken to a house on the northern side of the border. The likelihood is that he was tortured in a house in the Republic not far from where he was seized. Martin O'Hagan may well have been taken to the same premises.

Father Denis Faul, the headmaster of a Dungannon school and an outspoken critic of violence, knows of a 'house of torture' near Dundalk which has been used by the IRA for the 'interrogation, torture and execution' of a large number of the thirty-three people whom the IRA has killed as informers since September 1973. Father Faul talked to me about this house and said that examples of torture included cigarette burns and the use of electric shocks. Many people tortured there were not executed, and this confirmed for Father Faul the presence of such a 'house of torture'.

The IRA indulges in moral indignation when a rioter is struck with a plastic bullet. It constantly alleges that its members are 'roughed up' during interrogation. It cites the techniques of torture used on selected people at the outset of internment which caused the British government to be censured by the Court of Human Rights in Strasbourg. How can it make such condemnations when it treats human beings so cruelly, when it expresses such disdain for the sanctity of human life and so sadistically prepares victims for the summary extinction of life? No one can ever know the suffering endured by someone such as John McAnulty or Ivan Johnston in those long hours before a bullet brings a grotesque form of relief. As someone who has written about and investigated this dirty war, I am left without the words to describe accurately the sickening dimension to the violence which is the torture of helpless people. No cause justifies it, and any cause will be for ever tainted and destroyed by it, because no cause morally succeeds by dispensing with the human being's dignity and unalienable right to justice and to life.

In the world of agents and informers, those agencies which regard democracy, the law and justice as sacred should also consider whether dignity, justice and the law require to be upheld and that a dirty war is not always won with dirty tactics. A government must ask itself whether a self-confessed terrorist such as O'Doherty, who pleads guilty to over forty offences including attempted murder, is entitled to a Royal Prerogative. Such a decision by Jim Prior as Secretary of State for Northern Ireland can easily signal double standards which may well damage the very fabric of the judicial system. The professionalism of the security agencies is vital in a dirty war in which the rules can become obscured or blurred. The question inevitably is whether such distortion is deliberate.

13

A Dead Man's Revenge
IRA Informers and Arms Discoveries

In the undercover war Special Branch and military intelligence constantly watch for the opportunity to turn a terrorist into an informer or simply for someone who is willing to work as an agent for a financial retainer. Where money is not a sufficient incentive for a terrorist to forsake his or her allegiances, other methods are used such as coercion or blackmail. One story I investigated provides a fascinating and disturbing insight into the way in which terrorists are 'turned' and has an ending which would appeal to any writer of crime stories.

In the early 1970s while the Provisional IRA was swelling its ranks with young men and bombing the heart out of the major centres of commerce in Northern Ireland, it was also recruiting people well away from prying eyes in rural areas and also in the unlikely towns which are dotted around the province. In 1974 in Portaferry, a picturesque fishing village on the mouth of Strangford Lough, thirty-two-year-old James Young took the IRA oath of allegiance and for a short time was only obliged to play a minor role in the ranks of the Republican movement. In 1975 his life took on a much more dangerous character when he was asked by the officer commanding his unit to take part in a robbery to raise funds for the purchase of weapons and the support of prisoners' dependants.

The plan was for Young and two other volunteers, one of them an eighteen-year-old youth, to rob Structural Ceramics, a company based in the village of Killough in County Down. Young was told that the robbery would take place when the firm's payroll was on the premises. For several weeks in August and early September 1975, Young and his accomplices placed surveillance on the company premises, planned an escape route and discussed the fashion in which they would enter the place. A decision was reached that Young would dress as a woman, and that would enable him and his companions to pass through the security at the entrance to Structural Ceramics without attracting undue attention. On 19 September the three men entered the building, produced guns and made the staff lie on the floor. They ripped out telephones and made their getaway with £2700 in cash. What was not apparent at the time was that Young's gun was an imitation firearm because his unit did not have a plentiful supply of weapons.

The proceeds of the robbery were handed to the unit OC, and Young and his accomplices were ordered to 'lie low' until they were contacted by the IRA. Young spent a quiet Christmas with his wife and children and was not contacted by the IRA until January 1976. He was invited to a meeting with his OC and several other IRA officers, who told him that a plan was being laid which would ensure that numerous commercial areas in County Down would be rased to the ground, not with conventional tactics such as car bombs or bombs placed in holdalls, but with small incendiary devices that could be easily concealed. In February he was ordered to place an incendiary bomb in a clothes shop in the centre of the town of Downpatrick. He travelled to the target area with two others but they all panicked because there was tight security in the neighbourhood of the shop. Young decided not only to abandon the mission but to rid himself of the incendiary device because of the risk of being apprehended with it on the return journey to his home town of Portaferry, a considerable distance from Downpatrick.

James Young's life as a terrorist was soon to end. Before the summer of 1976 he was in police custody charged with membership of the IRA, robbing the ceramics factory and possessing incendiary devices. Under police interrogation he did not prove to be a difficult person and he readily admitted his crimes; in any case he was not in a position to pretend to be innocent because an informer had provided his interrogators with details of his activities. On 11 November he appeared before Belfast City Commission and was sentenced to eight years' imprisonment.

Within four years he was released from prison custody, having served the recommended 50 per cent of his sentence. On his release he resumed his family role at his home in Beechwood Avenue, Portaferry, aware that if police believed he was consorting with terrorists he could be summarily returned to custody to serve the remainder of the eight-year prison term. Young cautiously maintained links with members of the IRA but was not an active participant in terrorism. In August 1981 he was involved in a car accident on the road between Newtownards and Portaferry and the matter was referred to police in Newtownards. Young was judged to be responsible for the accident, to have been driving dangerously and without proper documentation. He was obliged to report the matter to his local police station but although he did so it was not immediately resolved. The constable who dealt with him visited his home several weeks later and told him to make an appearance at the police station within a week.

Young went to the station believing he would be required to make a statement about the car accident in accordance with normal police procedures. However, he found himself in the presence of two men dressed in plain clothes, who appeared to be detectives. Although they did not discuss the fine detail about the car accident, they did make a point of stressing that it was a dangerous business and could result in Young's being returned to prison to serve the remainder of his sentence. They added that such a course of action would remain at the discretion of the police. Young was terrified that he would once again be obliged to leave his wife and children, and as the conversation developed it became obvious that the two men in front of him were aware of his fears. Finally they offered him an opportunity to avoid returning to prison and facing any charges relating to the car accident: he could work for them. It was a classic situation. The two policemen who were dealing with him were members of the RUC Special Branch. I was told that Young was occasionally under surveillance on his release from prison but the decision to attempt to turn him was taken only after his local police station put his name through the police computer to check his identity and background as a result of the car accident. When it was realised that he was a former terrorist who had possibly transgressed even in a minor way, the matter was referred to Special Branch on the basis that Young appeared to be in a dilemma which might be turned to the advantage of the security forces. The two Special Branch officers informed Young that if he worked for them he could be a paid agent, and outlined the type of sums he could earn—which would supplement his earnings from labouring jobs. They specified that he could earn as much as £100 per month, with larger sums being available if he provided knowledge of the whereabouts of terrorist leaders, weapons or explosives. As an agent he could either receive a monthly retainer or alternatively rely simply on payments for information he provided. In essence they were offering him the role either of paid agent or of informer receiving money for whatever knowledge he was prepared or willing to sell. As a paid agent he would be in their employ and constantly at their bidding.

Young was not concerned about money; he was worried about being returned to prison and being separated from his family. When he requested time to reflect on what had been put to him, he was told that once he had decided on a course of action he should phone a Newtownards number and ask to speak to Denis. (It is now the number of a dental surgery.) According to the IRA it was almost a month before Young, unknown to them, contacted Denis and as a result of their telephone conversation went to a prearranged spot on the road from Portaferry to Newtownards to meet Denis. From the time of this meeting Young became an agent. However, he refused to accept money, perhaps as a way of suggesting that he was undertaking the role out of fear and duress and not for financial advantage. The date was November 1981, and from that time Young was under orders, not simply from Special Branch but also from military intelligence, who were keenly interested in the IRA's operations in County Down. Denis introduced Young to another man whom Young came to know as David Fletcher. Young now had two handlers, a necessary ploy in security forces' dealings with agents or informers. The use of two handlers ensures that there is always one available to attend meetings; that two minds are constantly assessing the behaviour and value of an agent or informer; and that in the dangerous climate of Northern Ireland the untimely death of one handler does not mean that intimate knowledge of an agent or informer is lost. A Special Branch operative explained it to me in the following way:

When there are two handlers it may be a case that two agencies are involved. I would be representing Special Branch and the second handler might be representing the 'London Calling' boys [MI5? MI6?] or military intelligence. It will depend on the nature of the informer or agent and what he has to offer or the area of operations to which he has access. The decision on who will be involved apart from me would be taken by the Task Co-ordinating Group which represents all the interested parties. Even in circumstances where it is merely a Special Branch matter the rules are that two handlers be involved. There is so much which is never committed to paper for security reasons or because the job we do is about maintaining your own contacts, hence the need for two handlers. If I am bumped off by the IRA the other handler will know who I was running. If there was not another handler and I was wiped out, an agent or informer who was under my control might read about my death in a newspaper and think it was his lucky day and he could just go away and never think about it again in the knowledge that only one handler knew about him. No, informers and agents don't get away that easily...there's too much at stake in this game. You see, you never know just what they're thinking. Some may do it for the money and keep doing it for the money. Others do it because we've made sure they've no choice and once they're in then the more they give us the deeper they're in the game. The advantage of two handlers is also that you need all the time to be watching your back and assessing what they're thinking. If they can be turned once, they can be turned again, depending on the stakes.

Once Young was 'in the game' he was under orders to become more actively involved with the IRA than he had been in 1975-6. The IRA were not suspicious about Young's enthusiasm for active service duties but were glad to have an addition to their ranks. The fact that he had served time for the Republican cause almost guaranteed his immediate acceptance into active service and dispelled any doubts about the suddenness of an interest which had not been apparent on his release from prison. Over the next three years Young operated as an active service volunteer while serving his handlers in the security forces. No one is ever likely to know all the information he gave to his handlers. The IRA says he passed on details of a co-ordinated bombing campaign in County Down which resulted in the security forces setting up stake-outs close to the intended IRA targets. The IRA adds that most of the 'bombing strikes' and many other operations were abandoned. They claim that Young took part in one abortive bombing mission, and that he compromised numerous shootings as well as bombings, which led to the imprisonment and death of IRA members.

By the end of 1983 the IRA were aware that many of its operations were known to the security forces, and suspicion centred on units that had been involved in the planning of the abortive bombing strikes. As with many IRA operations, prior knowledge is restricted to a definable range of people and by December 1983 a secret inquiry was under way to find a 'major informer' in the ranks of those who were privy to information about the bombing campaign. James Young's period as a valuable agent was almost at an end. IRA intelligence was busy narrowing the field of suspects to those who knew about individual operations which were compromised over a period of two years. By the end of the first week of February 1984 they believed the culprit was James Young. They interviewed other volunteers who were acquainted with him and those who had accepted him into active service in 1981. The issue of the car accident was raised as the only example of any contact Young was known to have had with police after his release from prison. IRA intelligence realised that if Young was an informer he had not been recruited by the security forces in prison but after his release. They enquired about the car accident and learned that police never proceeded with the matter. This sealed Young's fate. From experience the IRA knew that Special Branch were adept at using minor criminal indiscretions by paramilitaries as means of inducing them to inform.

By the end of January the IRA say their net was closing but they decided they had to find a way of persuading Young to leave his home town without arousing a suspicion that he was being singled out as an informer, and a way of getting him to South Armagh without having to kidnap him in County Down and transport him towards the border. IRA reasoning was based on a set of principles which has applied in the majority of episodes of this kind. Firstly, the skilled interrogators and executioners of informers are based in an area of South Armagh which spans both sides of the Irish border. Secondly, in South Armagh, which is traditionally known as 'bandit country', it is easy to conduct the interrogation and execution of informers because the area is not fully under the control of the security forces and is difficult terrain in which to conduct large-scale searches. In Belfast, Portaferry or other centres of population the security forces are extremely capable of conducting large-scale searches of a particular area. Away from observation in the lonely countryside of South Armagh or in remote areas outside the Irish Republic town of Dundalk, the IRA can detain and interrogate an informer for days without risk of capture of the informer and his kidnappers.

Young was told he was required to attend a reorganisational meeting of the IRA. He was not given the date, time or place but was informed that shortly before the meeting he would be contacted and accompanied to the meeting by another volunteer. The IRA were taking no chances. They reckoned that Young would probably tell his handlers that he was scheduled to go to a secret meeting, but the fact that he did not know the date or time ensured that if his handlers were suspicious they would not be in a position to follow him. The IRA were also convinced that Young's handlers would be interested in his attending such a meeting on the basis that it would provide up-to-date intelligence.

Young informed his handlers that an IRA meeting was planned and gave them his limited knowledge of it. They were concerned that he might be walking into an IRA trap but none the less they did not prevent him from doing so. They gave him two phone numbers, one of which he was to use before he left home for the IRA meeting, the other being his contact number once the meeting ended. The IRA never gave Young the chance to make contact with his handlers but moved swiftly. Young was informed about the supposed meeting in the presence of two volunteers who ensured that he had no opportunity to use a telephone. They travelled with him by car to South Armagh, where he was handed over to the IRA's special interrogation and execution unit.

Young was taken to a house, stripped to his underpants and at gunpoint was questioned for three days. He was continually threatened and denied sleep but was not subjected to the kind of torture which would have left its imprint on his body. According to the IRA, he admitted working as an agent and apart from passing information about the 'bombing strikes' he also gave his handlers details of other operations: 'He gave details of a co-ordinated bombing strike in County Down. After this he complained to his handlers that he could have been killed as he was on one of the operations. He was assured that he was in no danger and ordered to carry out bombing operations as before.'

The IRA claim Young confessed that he was told by his handlers to interfere with explosives charges set by IRA bomb engineers in such a way as to ensure the bombs would not detonate. They also say he passed Special Branch information about a weapons camp which he attended in June 1983, and in October 1983 gave information on the movement of weapons (which was fortuitously abandoned). Young's IRA interrogators were particularly interested in his handling of weapons and in whether he passed information about the movement of guns and where they were stored. They knew that at the beginning of January 1984 they had asked him to transport a sub-machine-gun to Belfast and told him the gun was intended for an arms dump outside the city without giving him the location of the dump.

His interrogators had good reason to question him about the weapons because in 1984 the IRA were aware that informers were being used to place bugging or tracing devices in weapons so that arms dumps could be located by the security forces or active service teams intercepted as they left a dump to carry out an atrocity. Young told his interrogators that he did inform his handlers that he was asked by the IRA to transport a weapon to Belfast. His reason for doing so, he told them, was that he was frightened that he would be caught in possession of the gun at a security forces' roadblock. He gave the gun to his handlers the night before his planned journey to Belfast. They escorted him from Portaferry to Belfast the following day to ensure that he was not detained at a roadblock, and even travelled into West Belfast, where he was required to hand over the gun. They had the gun in their possession throughout the journey, and gave it to him shortly before the handover. Young then made his way to a house in the Andersonstown estate and left the gun with another member of the IRA. Unknown to Young, that gun was to have a significance in events after his departure from West Belfast. According to the IRA, on 7 January, several days after the weapon transfer, Young met his handlers and gave them information about the identities of IRA volunteers in County Down.

Five days after the kidnap, Young's clothed body was found lying face down by a stone wall on a roadside near Crossmaglen in South Armagh. He had been shot once in the head. A rug was draped across the upper part of his body. Young left a wife and four children and his death was described by the deputy leader of the SDLP, Seamus Mallon, as an example of the hypocrisy of the Provisionals, 'who claim for themselves the right to a fair trial while denying others the most basic civil right of all...the right to life'. The IRA issued a statement that if Young had come forward at any time within the previous thirty months and admitted that he was 'an RUC agent' his court martial would have taken a more lenient view. There are those in authority who would interpret that statement as indicating that if Young had done so he would either have been used by the IRA as a double agent or have been shot much earlier than 14 February 1984.

There is little doubt that Young damaged the IRA in County Down. A member of Special Branch told me that he was one of their most valuable agents. When I enquired why he was permitted to attend the so-called meeting, he replied, 'There is no way you can plan for every eventuality. Young was informed that it might be a trap but that was based on supposition. If there had indeed been a meeting he would have been in a position to find out a lot about the Provos. In this game everything is a risk. The IRA plays its games, we play ours. We don't execute the IRA when they're caught but they execute our people. There's a lot at stake, we have to take the risks and of course it means a loss of life.'

As Young went to his grave the IRA began analysing what it knew about him, in particular the circumstances relating to the transportation of the gun to Belfast. Why did his handlers become so intricately involved in the moving of a weapon? They could easily have arranged safe passage for the car which the IRA gave him. Why were the handlers so concerned personally to ensure that this particular weapon reached Belfast? The IRA concluded that the handlers must have bugged the gun. The Belfast Brigade was contacted and asked to trace the sub-machine-gun. They revealed that it had been moved through Belfast to County Antrim and was in an arms dump close to a housing estate at the hamlet of Carness, just outside Dunloy.

Meanwhile the security forces were preparing a sting for the IRA. They were pleased they had not informed Young that a bug and tracing device had been planted inside the butt of the sub-machine-gun. Both devices had been fitted inside the weapon the night before it was moved to Belfast. It had also been forensically tested and proved to be a weapon used in the killing of several members of the security forces. While Young was being interrogated by the IRA, Special Branch, with the assistance of military intelligence, were keeping a trace on the sub-machine-gun. By the time of Young's death they knew it was in the arms cache near Dunloy. However, they were faced with the possibility that the IRA, as a consequence of interrogating Young, might suspect that the gun was bugged and have set up their own sting. The dominant view within security circles was that, since Young was never told about the bugging devices, the IRA could only guess about whether someone had tampered with the weapon. On the other hand, the IRA might not even consider such an eventuality.

The IRA believed that if the weapon was bugged an SAS team or an

RUC special support unit would be placed close to the arms dump to effect an ambush. The IRA ordered surveillance on the arms dump and the task was given to the Provisionals' North Antrim Battalion. Two volunteers were selected to form an active service unit to be used in the event of an SAS team being discovered in the vicinity of Dunloy or Carness. One of the volunteers was twenty-one-year-old Henry Hogan, who lived at Carness, and the other was eighteen-year-old Declan Martin from Dunloy. These two were armed with an Armalite rifle and a sawn-off 12-bore shotgun.

While the IRA made its plans a two-man SAS team was chosen to 'dig in' at Carness. In the team was twenty-six-year-old Sergeant Paul Oram, from Gomersal in West Yorkshire, whose parent regiment was 9/12 Royal Lancers attached to 9 Infantry Brigade in Derry. Oram was married with a five-month-old daughter and was an extremely competent soldier; he had told his family he was 'doing a job for Maggie' in Northern Ireland. In 1983 he was awarded the Military Medal after shooting a member of the INLA in Derry. Two men armed with a rifle and handgun had accosted him on the street in Derry and as they tried to kidnap him he opened fire. One of the men, Neil McGonigle, was shot through the head and died instantly; the other terrorist was wounded in the shoulder. With this kind of experience behind him, Oram was chosen to lead the two-man SAS surveillance team that security chiefs hoped would identify IRA active service volunteers when they approached or attempted to leave the arms dump. For its part the IRA had chosen two experienced terrorists with a personal knowledge of Dunloy and particularly the housing complex at Carness where the arms dump was sited.

On 19 February Oram and a fellow SAS man set up a covert observation post in a field overlooking Henry Hogan's home at Carness. Oram's orders were to maintain surveillance on the surrounding area. He was also told that the Hogans were a Republican family. At the time Henry Hogan's brother Michael was serving a prison sentence in Portaloise gaol in the Irish Republic for IRA offences, while Henry was suspected of IRA membership. If Henry Hogan or any other member of the IRA was seen approaching the arms dump or spotted in the vicinity of the housing complex at Carness, Oram was to radio that information to back-up SAS teams. Two cars containing members of the SAS were on the outskirts of Dunloy waiting for orders. They were so well briefed about the arms dump and the geography of Carness that they knew every yard of the target area.

So did Henry Hogan and Declan Martin. The IRA hoped that by maintaining a low-level presence in the area, they would not arouse suspicion. From experience they had learned that an SAS surveillance stake-out would normally involve only two men and that Hogan and Martin could operate quickly, kill the soldiers and fade into a countryside they knew well. The plan was to identify the SAS post and wipe it out before SAS back-up teams could be alerted. Hogan and Martin were aware that if the SAS had placed an observation team on the periphery of the arms dump the site chosen would be a nearby field. The IRA team also set up a covert post overlooking a field. They were dressed in combat gear and balaclavas and were armed.

On 21 February the IRA volunteers saw movement, perhaps only slight, in the field overlooking the Hogan home. They radioed to a third volunteer who was nearby that they had spotted members of the SAS and from the amount of camouflage it was evident that there were two men in the team. Hogan asked for instructions and was told that he should move against the SAS hide-out under cover of darkness.

At 8 pm Hogan and Martin crept stealthily down the field and approached the covert post. Yards from it they rose to their feet and walked slowly to the edge of the hide-out. They pointed their guns towards Oram and his companion and ordered them to stand up. The two SAS soldiers, realising they were in mortal danger, swung round to fire, but Oram was shot dead and his companion wounded. Hogan and Martin believed they had succeeded in killing the SAS men and ran for cover. The fact that they did not 'wipe out' the SAS men was to be their undoing. Oram's companion pressed a radio signal which alerted the waiting SAS teams. They sped into Carness in two unmarked cars. Patrick Robb, a resident of Carness, was resting on a sofa in his home when he heard bursts of gunfire. Other residents also heard shooting, and saw two cars arrive and armed men wearing hoods run in a pincer movement towards the field. The cars contained four SAS men, most of them armed with what residents described as 'small, compact machine-guns'; these were sub-machine-guns used only by the SAS in Northern Ireland. One resident heard a man shouting for help. It may have been Oram's companion.

Perhaps the best eyewitness account was later given by eighteen-year-old Dominic McMullen, who was working at his car outside his home close to the Hogan house. He heard English voices but also saw the two IRA men run towards a chain-link fence, jump over it and run about ten yards. He heard shots and saw them fall: 'There were Englishmen running and they jumped over the fence and ran over to them. One of the boys must have still been living and an Englishman just pointed the gun down at the ground and all I heard were the shots coming and the sparks. It was definitely a soldier firing into a body on the ground.'

This evidence (of a type later given in respect of SAS shootings in Gibraltar) bore a ring of truth. The subsequent inquest tended to bear out McMullen's testimony. A soldier identified only as 'A' gave evidence to the inquest that he shot one of the IRA men as he lay on the ground. The soldier said he saw two armed men, at whom he fired four shots. When he approached to remove their weapons he noticed that one of them was still moving and he fired two more shots into him. A forensic scientist told the inquest that the person who was shot on the ground was Declan Martin and that bullets were found embedded in the ground underneath his body.

The killing of the two IRA men finally ended the saga of the informer James Young and was in a way a dead man's revenge, but a costly revenge.

The morning after the shooting many newspapers reported that the security forces were hunting a third IRA man, who had escaped. The police offered journalists a 'photo opportunity' to record the fact that three guns had been found in the field where the shoot-out took place. Two of the guns were an Armalite and a sawn-off shotgun, the weapons used by Hogan and Martin, and the third was a 9mm sub-machine-gun of continental origin with a handgrip. Was there a third IRA man? And was this the gun that was bugged? Neither the IRA nor the security forces are willing to answer such questions. The IRA has never admitted the exact whereabouts of the arms dump. It may have been a hole in the ground, or it may have been a concealed space in a house in Carness. If it was the latter the IRA would not comment, because to identify a house as an arms dump would place the owner or occupier in a criminal context. The IRA may never answer the two final questions which would complete the story of Young and the bugged sub-machine-gun. One is left to speculate on whether the sub-machine-gun shown to journalists belonged to a third IRA man or whether it was the weapon that Young transported to Belfast. Since the security forces knew the location of the dump, they could well have removed the bugged weapon after the killing of Oram and the two IRA men. The story of a third IRA man not only was supported by the discovery of a third weapon but had the effect of permitting the security forces to carry out large-scale searches of the North Antrim area for several days. Many of the searches inconvenienced the local population and some were carried out in a heavy-handed fashion. However, they were perceived to be justified and beyond criticism because of the claim that a third IRA gunman was on the loose. The way in which the story ended satisfied both sides involved in the intrigue.

The participants in the undercover war, as this story illustrated at the time, were content to maintain a posture which served to protect each other's secrets and ways of playing the game. If anyone had implied that the shooting at Carness was the result of an elaborate plot, both sides would have refused comment. It is one of the complex ironies of the dirty war which I sought to unravel: the tendency of both sides to pretend that it does not exist, as if they are players in a game which they prefer to keep secret even to its spectators. It is as though they say to themselves that if anything is revealed about such a war they are both compromised. There is a terrible absurdity about it, and yet a curious logic, as expressed to me by a member of the IRA:

Public comment about the details of an operation is dangerous because it may reveal what we know about them. The moment that they become aware that we know the techniques or way in which they think or operate, they will change the rules and vice versa. This is a war that has to be played in the shadows because of its nature and the need for double-think and deception.

No matter what each side may say or do, it seems the best-laid plans may be wrecked. That was evidence in one story which I researched as a result of a tip-off from a fellow journalist about an IRA volunteer who was shot dead in July 1988. The volunteer was thirty-three-year-old Brendan Davison, who lived at Friendly Way in the Markets area of Belfast. In the 1970s he was imprisoned for attempted murder and possession of weapons and was released from prison in 1980. Like many IRA men of that period he became prominent in Sinn Fein and undertook electioneering work. He maintained contact with the IRA, was not a major activist but was aware of terrorist operations. In June 1987 he was shot as he stood outside a bookmaker's shop near his home. He was not seriously wounded and was quickly back on the streets after a short stay in hospital. Those responsible for shooting him were members of the Ulster Volunteer Force. On the evening of 25 July 1988 Davison was at home in his ground-floor flat having breakfast when there was a knocking at his front door. A neighbour heard him enquire who was outside and he was told it was 'the peelers' (police). As he peered through a spyhole in the door, nine shots were fired through the door and he was killed.

A postal worker who was in the vicinity saw the killers before the shooting. They were in a Vauxhall car and were dressed in police uniforms. He did not believe they were policemen because the car was not armour-plated. A police Landrover passed him twice as he observed the Vauxhall car. Residents of the area saw the bogus policemen arrive outside Davison's home. One of them stepped from the car armed with a rifle, hammered on the door to Davison's flat and then fired a burst of rounds into the door.

The rifle used in the murder was a Czech-made weapon, and forensic examination of bullets found at the scene indicated no previous history of use in terrorist operations. At the time of writing there is no evidence that the rifle was ever again used. The police Landrover which was in the area at the time of the shooting was in no way involved, and the driver later told an inquest that he did not see the Vauxhall car. There is every likelihood, however, that he did pass it at some point on his travels through the Markets district, but his failure to observe it was probably due to inefficiency or because he was preoccupied.

What did not come to light is that Davison was a police informer. That was not the IRA view because they gave him a military-style funeral in keeping with his membership of the IRA. I found the story of his shooting puzzling, since my source confirmed that a member of Special Branch, on learning of Davison's death, commented: 'Stupid bastards, the Prods. They took the best informant in the city out of the frame.' If that is in fact what happened—and I have no reason to doubt the source of my information—even the best-laid plans can be disrupted. Equally, if he was indeed one of the best informants in the city there was no way in which he could have been protected. His killers' elaborate plan also indicated that they believed him to be an important figure in the IRA and that they possessed the kind of intelligence which enabled them to target him in the right place at the right time. All in all he was a wanted man. If he was indeed a leading informer, it is likely that he would sooner or later have been killed, if not by bogus policemen, certainly by members of the IRA's execution and interrogation squad in South Armagh. The RUC say he was killed by Loyalists. An important informer, he was undoubtedly replaced because irrespective of setbacks or unforeseen circumstances the game has unlimited moves.

He would have been a grade one informer because of the role he played in the IRA. I learned from an impeccable source that he was an experienced interrogator who presided at many courts martial. According to a priest who had reason to learn about him, he was present at interrogation sessions in a house outside the town of Dundalk where informers and those suspected of informing spent the remaining hours of their lives. Another priest, Father Denis Faul, investigated the alleged use of a house by the IRA near Dundalk and told me the premises were 'a place of torture' where electric shock treatment and other degrading and inhuman practices were applied. As an informer himself, Davison was uniquely placed to learn what other informers divulged to the IRA before they were shot. Such intelligence would have been invaluable to Special Branch in their assessment of what the IRA knew about them and whether, before his death, an informer divulged the full extent of his treachery and those IRA secrets he betrayed to Special Branch. Knowledge of how much the other side is aware of the degree to which it has been penetrated, and of how far its secrets and the identity of its personnel has been compromised, can mean the difference between life or death, success or failure. A disturbing dimension to this story may well be that Davison's role as an IRA interrogator, and the information he was extracting from people about to die, was more important to his handlers than the lives of those unfortunate people and the possibility that a scrap of information about their predicament might have saved their lives. Maybe that is an idealistic and unrealistic view in a war which is not fought on a conventional battlefield and where the compromising of one source may lead to the deaths of many or the saving of the lives of hundreds.

The fact is, most informers have a limited life-span, though a few have remained in place for a considerable period of time. In some instances the few informers who were operative within the IRA for over five years outlived their usefulness by providing information which was of such significance that it had to be acted on immediately by the security forces, thereby compromising the informers and so leading to their deaths. It is worth noting that the use of informers has related mainly to the IRA because it is the organisation which the authorities regard as the greatest threat to stability and to the very existence of the Northern Ireland state. It is considered so dangerous because it would have changed the course of European history this century if the bomb at the Royal Hotel in Brighton had wiped out the entire Tory cabinet. The use of informers in Loyalist organisations has, I contend, not been regarded with the same kind of critical appreciation. This is due in part to the fact that as far as the British government is concerned the Loyalists do not pose such a serious threat as the IRA. Secondly, the authorities find it much easier to acquire information on Loyalist groupings because historically the security forces draw most of their members from the Loyalist Unionist community. Loyalist groups have been penetrated with greater ease by the intelligence agencies, since many of their members owe allegiance to the Crown and are therefore much more easily encouraged to work for the state. In recent years Loyalist terror groups have sought to finance international arms shipments, and that has made them more of a target for Special Branch and MI6, but the IRA still remains the major enemy and the group to which most intelligence resources are directed.

Since the early 1980s until the present time the constant worry within security circles has been the IRA's potential to rearm and equip itself with modern and sophisticated weaponry from Middle Eastern sources. Security chiefs have known that, if the IRA could achieve one massive arms shipment, the war in Ireland would be in place for another decade. They are worried that if the Provisionals could acquire surface-to-air missiles such as the American Stinger, which was used by the Afghan rebels against the might of the Russian helicopter and fighter force, they could make the movement of troops in Ireland an impossibility and change the course of the conflict by elevating it to a new and much more dangerous level. The presence of such a weapon in IRA hands would threaten all Northern Ireland ministers, if not the Prime Minister herself.

It was with such fears in mind that all intelligence efforts were directed towards finding and creating an informer within the IRA's Quartermaster area of operations related to the storing and movement of weapons in Northern Ireland. Intelligence chiefs knew that if such a person worked at Quartermaster level within the Belfast or Derry brigade he would have access to knowledge of the movement of arms from the Republic for use in the conflict in the north of the island. Such a person would be able to provide details of the type of weapons being moved, whether new weapons were being made available to active service units and whether the IRA was receiving new arms shipments.

In 1980 Special Branch informed MI5 that a former member of the Provisionals, thirty-nine-year-old Frank Hegarty, bore all the signs of being the type of person who might be vulnerable to an approach by Special Branch. Hegarty was from the Rosemount area of Derry and his links with the IRA had been severed years earlier. He had not officially left the organisation but had drifted away from a terrorist lifestyle. Special Branch were sensitive to any trait exhibited by a terrorist or former terrorist in the city of Derry which might suggest that he could be 'turned'. Frank 'Franko' Hegarty was a heavy gambler who was constantly spending money on horse and greyhound racing. He lived in the Shantallow area of the city with a woman and her five children.

According to the IRA, Hegarty later told them that Special Branch first approached him with an offer of £400 in cash as an initial payment, to be followed by a retainer of £25 per week if he provided them with titbits of information. The weekly retainer was paid by his two handlers, whom he met at prearranged spots in Limavady or the Waterside area of Derry; one of them belonged to Special Branch, the other was a member of MI5. Like many informers before him, Hegarty may have thought that he would not be required to provide sensitive information, since he was no longer active in the Provisionals, and that he could always offer low-level or useless material.

Before long, however, Hegarty was encouraged to rejoin the IRA. Special Branch files indicated that his previous role in the Provisional IRA was in the Quartermaster's department, and that was where they required him to work now. Hegarty, I am told, offered himself to the IRA for active service and was readily accepted because his record showed that he was trustworthy. As a result of his previous period with the organisation, he was highly knowledgeable about the smuggling and storage of weapons and explosives. Hegarty's reinstatement as a terrorist was gradual. Whatever information he supplied did not jeopardise his role as an informer or create suspicion about his loyalty, and he continued to meet his handlers.

In 1985 it was apparent to the intelligence agencies that the IRA had acquired a massive arms shipment from the Middle East on a scale which shocked even security chiefs, who were already aware that a large quantity of weapons was likely to find its way into IRA hands. Hegarty and other highly placed informers, men like Joe Fenton, were suggesting that the 'big one' had arrived from Libya, been brought in by ship and offloaded on the south-west coast of Ireland. Their information indicated that the shipment was so large that quantities of Russian-made weapons were being stored in purpose-built underground bunkers in the Irish Republic. Staff from the Quartermaster departments of the Belfast and Derry brigades were involved in the movement of parts of the shipment. Guns and explosives were being moved by its Quartermaster staff to parts of the border close to the lines of supply used by the Derry Brigade's active service units. Hegarty was now in a position which was vital to his handlers.

In January 1986 he suddenly disappeared from his home in Derry. That month, Gardai acting on information from the security authorities in Northern Ireland uncovered a massive quantity of Russian-made AK47 rifles and ammunition at Carrowreagh in Roscommon and at two sites near Sligo. While the IRA reeled from the discovery of the largest arms dumps ever found in the Irish Republic, Frank Hegarty was in England, in a house at Sittingbourne in Kent, under guard from members of Special Branch acting on orders from MI5. The IRA did not immediately suspect Hegarty but ordered an internal inquiry to determine how many people possessed information about the arms dumps. While this was taking place, Hegarty's girlfriend visited him in Kent. She was not involved in any of his activities and assumed he had gone to Sittingbourne because he wanted to work and reside in England, away from the stress of Derry. She returned home leaving Hegarty with his minders. According to the IRA, he later confessed that while in Kent he was provided with money for placing bets on races he watched on television. He lived alone, but at least six heavily armed minders were positioned in an adjoining property.

It has been said that he became homesick and decided to return to Derry in the belief that he could convince the IRA that he was not responsible for the arms finds. However, the IRA reckoned that he 'had bolted' before the arms discovery and they waited. Experience told them that informers often returned through homesickness or because their handlers wished them to do so in order to confuse the IRA about the number of informers in existence. 'Franko' Hegarty returned to his native city. His family and girlfriend welcomed him home; throughout his period in England he had regularly phoned them, indicating that he was working and obviously giving no hint that he was hiding from the IRA.

It has been suggested that he was lured home by the IRA with an offer of immunity because they were terrified that he would become a supergrass. The IRA denies that any such offer of immunity was conveyed to him, though they admit that they suspected him of having been responsible for compromising their arms-smuggling operations. I am not inclined to believe the IRA. They knew he had been in the Quartermaster's department which dealt with smuggling, and that he had disappeared to England in the days prior to the arms finds if not on 26 January, the very day of the Gardai discoveries. I am told they had means of contacting Hegarty in England. A promise of immunity might well explain why MI5 allowed him to return.

It is possible that he returned because he was homesick, as the IRA claimed, since that was apparently the case with Anthony O'Doherty. Homesickness would not, I believe, have been sufficient incentive to a man who knew he would surely die—so perhaps the IRA were offering immunity or maybe his handlers were encouraging him to believe he could persuade the IRA of his innocence. I am inclined to the view that the IRA lured him home. Once he was back they acted carefully and moved against him only after he had been living for two weeks in Derry. When I asked the IRA about Hegarty I was told the following:

He'd damaged our organisation. He was trusted and was good at what he was asked to do by us. He was involved in transporting arms and there was no suspicion about him until we began to examine the people associated with the captured weapons - those on our side who knew of their existence and where they were being stored. His disappearance was a major indication but we waited patiently. We knew where he was and that he was probably well guarded. He told us at his court martial that money and gambling lured him into acting as an informer. He was picked up by MI5 agents on the M2 motorway on the day of the arms finds and flown by private plane to Kent, where he was debriefed by MI5. Hegarty didn't know that the information he gave about the arms dumps was to be acted on, and that is why he was suddenly seized while driving along the M2. They had told him that the guns and ammunition would only be lifted once they were broken down and moved into smaller dumps. He knew himself that if they were seized while in large dumps IRA intelligence would eventually narrow down the number of people in possession of information about the location of the big dumps. They sacrificed him because it was important to keep the Anglo-Irish Agreement alive at a time when it was falling apart. The fact that joint security operations were leading to such massive arms seizures was a way of reinforcing the very nature and basis of the Agreement—security cooperation. Hegarty came home because he was homesick. Maybe his handlers wanted him home. Maybe there was another mole and they wanted us to believe that he was the only one. We are fully aware that such things happen in this kind of war. However, the reality is that we shot an informer. They know it but will never admit to it publicly because they prefer to make people believe that they do not exploit people like Hegarty and finally sacrifice them.

There is little doubt that Hegarty was held in a house in Sittingbourne. In November 1985 two houses in the village were taken over by members of Special Branch under the control of members of MI5. I believe this was done because they did not know the moment when they would be required to act on Hegarty's information. Six months later, on 25 May 1986, Gardai informed the RUC of the presence of a body near Castlederg in County Tyrone. It was Frank Hegarty. His hands were tied behind his back, tape covered his eyes, and he had a bullet wound to the head.

A member of RUC Special Branch commented to me that Hegarty had died saving other people's lives because the 120 rifles and 18,000 rounds of ammunition found by the Gardai would surely have killed a lot of innocent people. The SDLP leader, Seamus Mallon, described the killing of Hegarty as the IRA's shoot-to-kill policy, while Martin McGuinness of Sinn Fein argued that he regarded criticism by the SDLP and clergymen as pathetic and that Special Branch and British intelligence placed people in a position in which they were forced into acting as informers and subsequently lost their lives. The RUC said publicly that its policy was to offer no comment or denial on specific claims by the IRA: 'In the past attention has often wrongly centred on whether a person was giving information to the police rather than on the fact that they were brutally murdered by self-appointed executioners. No inference or conclusion should be drawn from the RUC's silence in particular cases.'

Father Michael Canny, who officiated at the funeral mass for Frank Hegarty, said that while the IRA offered an excuse for the murder it was no justification for what was a cruel, unjust and brutal killing. Probably no one in the church was aware that, irrespective of the condemnation, the undercover war was claiming the lives of many more people who worked in the shadowy world of espionage.

According to the IRA, Hegarty told his interrogators that his handlers said he was working for 'Maggie' and that the information he was providing was being conveyed directly to 10 Downing Street; Hegarty, they claim, believed that this was the case. If it was indeed Hegarty who provided the intelligence which led to the big arms finds, one is inclined to believe that he was indeed working for 'Maggie'. Information which led to the seizure of part of the Libyan arms shipment would have been conveyed to the cabinet, if not the Prime Minister, who takes a personal interest in the war against the IRA.

14

Treachery and Special Branch Spies

In the perilous world in which informers and the Special Branch operate, the treachery of just one person within the security forces can lead to the unmasking and subsequent assassination of valuable informers or agents. In 1978–9 one police officer's treachery led to the destruction by the IRA of an entire Special Branch spy network in Belfast. The incident also provided an insight into the workings of the intelligence-gathering agency and raises many questions about its methods.

Special Branch, which perceives its operations as central to the defeat of terrorism, is extremely protective of its need for secrecy, and its members are always carefully vetted. Within the organisation, information is restricted to those who need to know. CID often finds it difficult to extract necessary information from Special Branch officers, and there is often mistrust and resentment between the groupings. Special Branch's handling of informers/agents is kept secret from the most senior officers in other branches of the RUC. It is believed that, by restricting knowledge of particular operations to individual Special Branch officers, in the event of a security leak those in possession of specific information can be easily identified. This may help to limit damage, but it can never prevent or eradicate treachery.

In 1978 a member of the RUC reserve asked his superiors if he could apply for a post with Special Branch. He was told that he would not be considered for such a job because the rules stipulated that only full-time police staff were considered eligible, and membership of Special Branch was not easily achieved. Police officers were selected for Special Branch duties only at the invitation of the organisation and not as a result of an application. It was pointed out to the reserve officer that, even if a person was selected for Special Branch work, a final decision on suitability was made after exhaustive vetting procedures to ensure that the prospective 'candidate' was trustworthy.

The reserve officer, whom I am obliged to refer to as Officer A for legal and security reasons, was angered by the attitude of his superiors. However, they knew from his file that he had made repeated requests to be considered for Special Branch duties. In fact his file also bore testimony to his considerable experience in providing back-up support for undercover police and Army teams in Belfast. He was a member of an elite squad known as the Bronze Section, which was attached to the Special Patrol Group. He revelled in his back-up role and harboured an ambition to be 'running spies'. A former colleague of Officer A has this to say of his behaviour in 1978: 'He was overweight and overstressed and looked a lot older than his thirty-five years. He showed all the signs of someone living on the edge of life.' To placate him and in recognition of his services he was given the job of collator assisting Special Branch. However, he still regarded himself as capable of operating as a fully fledged Special Branch officer; no one was sufficiently aware of his inner bitterness or his obsessive ambition.

Officer A's job of collator placed him in a unique position. He was constantly viewing and filing information. To understand the significance of his role one may examine the following comments of another policeman who worked close to him at that time:

He was essentially a cipher for a wide range of information. Now he would not have known how to connect it. Much of the information would have related to payments to informers or records of conversations, the movement of suspects, etc. Ironically, he was essentially privy to a range of material which was not known to the average member of Special Branch. He was dealing mainly with material relating to Belfast operations. Much of it would, however, have been in a coded form or would have referred to incidents without actual names being included. Therefore, without a more detailed knowledge of events his work as a collator restricted his knowledge of the more intricate workings of Special Branch. For instance, a document might have passed across his desk relating to information from an informer within an IRA unit in F Company of a particular battalion. Now — [Officer A] would not have known the identity of the informer. The only way he could ever have discovered it was if he was told by the relevant Special Branch operative or by the IRA. The IRA would know which of their men was in possession of information about an operation and by their own means of intelligence narrow the leak to one person. So — [Officer A] was working with material which offered him little information on informers and their handlers, but was potentially damaging if given to terrorists.

Officer A's ambition to play a more integral part in the intrigue of Special Branch activities led him to devise a plan to convince his superiors that his value was not being recognised. He aimed to establish contact with a leading member of the Provisional IRA and thereby begin an association which he hoped would enable him to set up a spy network. Once he had made contact, he believed he could offer his newly created source low-grade information on police operations. This would lead him closer to the IRA and make it easier for him to 'turn' IRA members.

His first step was undertaken with the naïvety which was to characterise many of the subsequent events in his life. He wrote a letter to Martin Meehan, one of the best-known IRA leaders in Belfast. Meehan was from the Ardoyne area of North Belfast and was responsible for many IRA operations throughout the 1970s. Officer A obviously believed that a letter written to such a prominent figure would not be discovered by those within the intelligence community who are responsible for mail interception, much of which takes place within the main sorting building in downtown Belfast. Ironically, the letter to Meehan, which was posted through the open mail, got through the security-checking system. It was apparently mailed to an address which Officer A had discovered on Meehan's Special Branch file. It was not his home address but a house which he was believed to frequent occasionally and which was owned by a person with Republican rather than IRA connections. The letter indicated a disillusionment on the part of Officer A and his willingness to assist the Republican cause. I am told that Officer A's letter outlined a means by which the IRA leader and the police officer could meet.

The first meeting was brief and merely established contact between the two men. It is believed to have taken place in a large open area of Belfast's Antrim Road known as the Waterworks, which contains two disused reservoirs surrounded by landscaped walks. Traditionally this stretch of land has been a place where people walk their dogs or feed the many swans which nest there each year. During subsequent meetings other members of the IRA were present. I am told that one of the IRA men later became prominent as a Sinn Fein councillor. Officer A was given another contact, thirty-three-year-old Peter Valente, a father of four from Unity Flats in North Belfast. This arrangement enabled Officer A to meet publicly and frequently with a member of the IRA who was less prominent than Martin Meehan, and enabled Meehan to retain control over Officer A through the North Belfast 1st Battalion.

Suddenly Officer A, unknown to his superiors, was achieving his primary goal of establishing contact with the IRA. Although Officer A was pleased with his success, he soon found that the IRA expected him to prove his value as a spy by providing them with information on which they could act. He began by passing on the type of coded information which crossed his desk, believing, stupidly, that it would appear valuable but would lead nowhere. Events soon began to change. In July 1979 Martin Meehan was arrested and questioned about the abduction and imprisonment of a seventeen-year-old informer, Stephen McWilliams, who worked for the Special Branch and military intelligence.

Stephen McWilliams worked in a staunchly Republican club, the Felons, in the New Lodge district. He became an informer early in 1979 after being caught breaking and entering the Central Bar in Belfast city centre. Between committing this crime and appearing in Belfast Juvenile Court he was recruited to spy on the IRA in North Belfast. He pleaded guilty to the burglary and was ordered to pay £365 to the owners of the bar in compensation for the damage caused. His recruitment as an informer may have been based on coercion, the prospect of an easy sentence in the Juvenile Court or the promise of money for information. Whatever the reason, he subsequently met his handlers at the Grand Central Army base in Belfast's Royal Avenue on a regular basis. The fine imposed by the court was convenient for those trying to recruit him because they could offer him money to enable him to pay it. McWilliams was valuable to them because his job at the Felons Club placed him daily in the company of Republicans. He reported regularly on the movements of known Republicans and later admitted that his handlers showed him a photograph of Meehan within a short time of his recruitment. He reckoned that occurred in January 1979. On 11 July McWilliams was kidnapped at the Felons Club and over four days he was moved between four IRA safe-houses where he was interrogated and beaten. He told his captors that he was a British Army informer and revealed the nature of the information he passed to the security forces. McWilliams would have been another fatality in the Northern Ireland Troubles but for the intervention of the Army. Four days after he was abducted, an Army patrol raided the house where he was being held. They captured one of the kidnappers and took the seventeen-year-old to the Grand Central base to meet his handlers. The result of that meeting was the arrest of Martin Meehan and four others, bringing the total in custody to six men. Meehan was charged with conspiracy to kidnap McWilliams and with participating in his imprisonment.

The security forces were jubilant to have such a high-ranking and dangerous Provisional behind bars. Meehan was held in custody until April 1980, when he was gaoled for twelve years with five other men receiving varying sentences for their part in the McWilliams episode. McWilliams's evidence identifying Meehan was described by the judge as of 'poor quality', but the presence of Meehan's car in Oakfield Street where the rescue of McWilliams took place corroborated the 'poor quality' evidence. The identification supplied by McWilliams was based upon his allegation that when he was being transferred from one of the four safe-houses he caught a fleeting glimpse of Meehan, whom he claimed was driving a car which was surveying the route ahead for the other kidnappers. McWilliams told cross-examining counsel that he did not know Meehan 'to see' but recognised him as the 'spotter car' driver when he saw him in an identity parade the day after the rescue. However, he admitted to being shown a head-and-shoulders photograph of Meehan in January that year. The investigative journalist Ed Moloney made the following observation about the case:

McWilliams' evidence was proved to be false, resulting in the acquittal of Kevin Mulgrew from the New Lodge area. In the end it came down to the judge choosing between Meehan who was a convicted Provo whose only defence was that he had spent the day at the Folk Museum near Bangor with his girlfriend and children and then spent the rest of the night at home and a 17-year-old boy engaged as an informer in dangerous work. Inevitably the judge chose McWilliams and there are some who would say that in Northern Ireland it couldn't have been otherwise.

Whatever the merits of the case, Meehan, a man capable of acting in such a fashion, was taken off the streets and a teenager escaped death to begin a life of exile from the IRA.

What fascinates me about the arrest of Meehan is that prior to his arrest Special Branch filmed him meeting Officer A. I am reliably informed that Meehan was filmed entering the upper end of the Waterworks at its Cavehill Road entrance and Officer A from the Antrim Road exit. Officer A was walking his dog, and they appeared to meet casually at a point between the disused reservoirs. This was never made known and was certainly not mentioned at Meehan's trial in 1980. However, the sequence becomes interesting when one considers the following questions. Officer A was meeting Meehan and Valente prior to Meehan's arrest. Did he convey to Meehan the fact that he was being spied on by McWilliams? Was the McWilliams evidence merely a means of getting to Meehan and removing him from circulation once it was discovered that he was 'handling' a Special Branch collator, namely Officer A? Was Meehan simply caught in a terrorist act, or could it be that once McWilliams was rescued Special Branch suddenly perceived a means of using an informer to testify against Meehan and remove him from the streets? The truth may never be known but it lies somewhere within the scope of those questions.

My reason for making that assertion is rooted in subsequent events. On 26 October 1980 Officer A was finally arrested and found to be in possession of the names, addresses and vehicle registration numbers of

senior figures in Special Branch. Under questioning he admitted his dealings with the IRA. When he was confronted with the film of his meeting
with Meehan and photographs of meetings with Valente and a leading
member of Sinn Fein, he revealed that his initial intention was to establish his own spy network but confessed that the Provisionals succeeded
in 'turning' him, by paying him substantial sums of money. The immediate problem for Special Branch was to determine the amount and types
of information which he supplied to the IRA. A deal was struck with
Officer A: no charges would be preferred against him and he would be
permitted to leave the country if he co-operated with Special Branch
investigators. The deal was sanctioned by the Attorney-General on the
grounds that a court case would make public information which could be
damaging to national security. This reasoning was spurious, but it was a
convenient way of providing Special Branch with the freedom to examine
in miniature every dealing Officer A conducted with the IRA.

Meanwhile Special Branch acted quickly to turn one of Officer A's IRA
contacts, Peter Valente. Knowing of his dealings with Officer A, they
were in a position to confront him with the possibility that A might give
evidence against him. It is not known exactly how Valente was recruited,
but he became an informer after the public arrest of Officer A. I am led to
believe that, by the time Officer A was arrested, Special Branch had firmly established the nature of his relationship with the IRA and felt that the
matter was too serious to allow it to proceed any further. It may well be
that through watching Officer A, Meehan, Valente and others they
learned a great deal about the workings of the IRA in North Belfast. Their
major concern was what Officer A had passed to his IRA contacts before
they discovered his treachery. I have reason to believe that it was in the
spring of 1979 that they realised information was being leaked to the
Provisionals. A Special Branch contact told me that information crossing
Officer A's desk was thoroughly vetted after his treasonable behaviour
came to light. A cynical view might be that this was a bit like closing the
stable door after the horse had bolted. The Officer A episode was to have
a number of repercussions.

On 12 November 1980 Peter Valente disappeared. Forty-eight hours
later he was shot dead in an alleyway in the predominantly Protestant
Highfield estate which is sandwiched between West and North Belfast.
The killing was publicly deemed to be the work of Loyalist assassins, in
particular the Ulster Defence Association. The RUC, especially Special
Branch, knew differently. Valente's killers had pressed a new, crisp £20
note into his hand as he died. It was a private message to Special Branch
from the Provisionals. Although the RUC, according to their official policy, do not comment directly on the motives for murder, Chris Ryder

recognised the nature of this murder in his book *The RUC: A Force under Fire* (1989): 'In the unwritten protocol of IRA–RUC relationships, the money—"thirty pieces of silver", one detective called it—was an unmistakable pointer to the true motive for his death.'

Since the IRA were not prepared to admit publicly to the murder of Valente, they devised a private message to their adversaries in Special Branch. The IRA's reluctance to be associated with a so-called execution was because Valente was active in a current campaign to end the H-Blocks in the Maze prison. Significantly his brother Jim was a prominent IRA prisoner conducting the 'blanket' protest against the wearing of prison clothes, which the IRA contended was part of a policy to criminalise IRA inmates and to eliminate their status as political prisoners. Peter Valente was active in the street campaign and the marches throughout Ireland aimed at highlighting a prison protest which was being given attention by the international media. The IRA were concerned that, if they acknowledged they had murdered a leading anti-H-Blocks activist, this would be exploited to damage public support for the 'blanket' protest. However, the IRA have privately confessed that they informed Jim Valente that they had shot his brother. Jim Valente was granted compassionate leave from the prison to attend his brother's funeral.

The IRA interrogation of Peter Valente helped them to put together missing pieces from what amounted to a jigsaw puzzle of information passed to them during their dealings with Officer A. On 20 January 1981, twenty-three-year-old Maurice Gilvarry was found dead on the South Armagh border. His hands and feet were bound and his death bore the hallmarks of an IRA execution. Within twenty-four hours the IRA issued a statement admitting they killed him and describing him as a volunteer with the Belfast Brigade. They said he had given information to the police about IRA operations, the movement of weapons and the use of safe-houses. Gilvarry was a member of the 3rd Battalion of the Provisional IRA and lived at Butler Street in the Ardoyne area of North Belfast. Chris Ryder believes there was a 'domino effect' which began with Valente but can be traced back to Officer A. The killing of two other informers followed in quick succession. On 2 February, Patrick Trainor, who had been an informer for several years, was shot in West Belfast. On 27 June, Vincent Robinson was shot and his body dumped in a garbage chute at Divis Flats in the Lower Falls district of West Belfast. The 'domino effect' ended on 27 September 1981, when twenty-two-year-old Anthony Braniff was murdered. His family later claimed that he had been tortured, and the IRA replied that marks found on his body were powder burns caused by the discharge of a weapon close to the body. The Braniff killing signalled the end of an episode which began with one man's treachery.

In January 1982 the IRA finally admitted killing Peter Valente. It also released a statement announcing a two-week amnesty for informers 'to admit their crimes' and declaring that informers who were 'banished' from Ireland were free to return to the country to have their cases reviewed. This ploy indicated that the IRA knew the elimination of one spy network did not mean the eradication of all the informers within its ranks. Three months later the IRA left a body at the South Armagh border. The victim was twenty-four-year-old Seamus Morgan from Belfast. The Provisionals said he was an informer, but his family vehemently denied the claim. The truth may be locked in Special Branch files, or the murder may have resulted from IRA paranoia. What is not in doubt is that many young people recruited by Special Branch and other intelligence agencies are the frontline soldiers and not the men who manipulate or control them. The policeman who was turned by the Provisionals was not prosecuted. I am informed that this policeman has 'found God' and has devoted his time to evangelising. There are those who believe that 'finding God' is an expedient choice after crimes have been committed. One of his colleagues wryly suggested that it would have been preferable if he had 'found God' before he found the Provisionals and they found Valente and the other agents.

In the months following the unmasking of Officer A a further inquiry took place within the RUC to uncover another mole. This time the inquiry was related to the fact that Chris Ryder, in an article for the *Sunday Times*, revealed that several men, including Valente and Gilvarry, were informers. In the aftermath of the Officer A affair, the Chief Constable, John Hermon, was incensed at the possibility that someone in a sensitive area of police operations was leaking secret information to the media. Hermon was obsessed about secrecy and distrustful of the media; likewise many journalists were not particularly enamoured with his treatment of the media. However, he was in control of the police and he decided that security within his force was under threat. Accordingly he invited Joe Mounsey, an Assistant Chief Constable from the Lancashire constabulary, to investigate the source of the leak to Ryder. Hermon, it is said, believed it had originated within Special Branch. Mounsey, who was often credited with bringing Myra Hindley and Ian Brady to justice for the Moors Murders, approached the task of finding Ryder's mole with dogged determination. A policeman who worked in Special Branch at that time says that the inquiry was seen as a witch-hunt and was unnecessary, since those named were dead, and the IRA knew they were informers—as did Special Branch and even the public.

In Special Branch we regarded the witch-hunt as counter-productive. However, I suppose Hermon was paranoid about leaks following the — [Officer A] episode. On the other hand Hermon had an intense mistrust of the media and was concerned about the management of news-related material. He didn't want people willy-nilly giving off-the-record stories. He wanted to be in control of what the public was told.

Chris Ryder sardonically comments in his book that Mounsey spent nine months preparing confidential guidelines for keeping the media at arm's length but the morning after the guidelines document was circulated within the RUC its contents were published on the front page of a morning newspaper. However, Mounsey did not simply prepare guidelines; he identified the source of Ryder's information as a Special Branch officer, whom Hermon quickly transferred to other duties.

In putting together this story, which began in 1981 when Chris Ryder revealed that the IRA was uncovering a spy network, I painstakingly examined all the details of this episode and uncovered an additional dimension which I believe the IRA never discovered and which Special Branch is unlikely to admit. It concerns Maurice Gilvarry, who was 'executed' by the IRA two months after Valente. When Gilvarry was murdered the IRA issued a lengthy statement indicating the seriousness with which they regarded his informer role:

We are extremely reluctant to execute volunteers, realising the methods and duress, the physical and psychological pressures used by the RUC to solicit information. But this was no simple case of a volunteer being arrested and breaking down and then reporting the matter to his unit. Maurice Gilvarry admitted to a court martial of his peers that he had passed on information on an ongoing basis for years.

However, the IRA did not know the full extent of Gilvarry's dealings with Special Branch. Chris Ryder says Gilvarry provided information which led to the SAS killing three IRA men in an ambush in North Belfast. The IRA refuse to confirm this, and one needs to be wary of such claims. Special Branch may well have conveyed this to Chris Ryder to disguise the fact that the person who made possible the SAS ambush was still in place as an informer. On the other hand the IRA may hold a similar view and deliberately appear confused about the matter. Whatever the truth, while acting as a Special Branch informer Gilvarry was an IRA active service volunteer and a hit-man who was involved in a double murder.

On the evening of 3 February 1980, sixty-year-old Patrick Mackin and his fifty-eight-year-old wife Violet settled down to watch television. Their home was at 568 Oldpark Road, an area of Belfast renowned for civil strife and bordered by Loyalist and IRA strongholds. Patrick Mackin was a Catholic who felt safe living in North Belfast, even though he was a retired prison officer. Before his retirement he had been responsible for training prison officers at a special unit outside Belfast. Prison officers have been targets for terrorists during the Troubles, but never on the same scale as police and soldiers, and this may have been the reason why Patrick Mackin remained in Oldpark. According to his friends, he saw his retirement as ending his concerns about being on a terrorist hit-list.

Some time after 7.00 pm that night, gunmen burst into his home and shot him several times as he sat in an armchair. His wife was also shot while she was sitting. They both died instantly. When detectives arrived on the scene, the television was on and there were drinks on a table in front of the dead couple. Within twenty-four hours, Special Branch contacted CID and told them they knew the culprits. They named three men whom they said were members of the provisional IRA. Special Branch said that after the shooting the killers walked into a drinking club in Ardoyne and boasted about the shooting of the elderly couple. The detailed account of this alleged episode in the Ardoyne club contained some curious elements. Special Branch claimed that one of the trio, to whom I shall refer henceforth as Mr B, described to people in the club what the people were wearing when they were shot. A detective constable who listened to the Special Branch account remembers the crucial elements:

The Special Branch officers said that — [Mr B] described in detail to other members of the IRA what Violet Mackin wore, right down to the colour of her clothes and slippers, and also described Patrick Mackin's clothes. Now myself and my colleagues thought this was highly unusual if not bizarre. Killers, from my experience, don't take much interest, particularly detailed interest, in the way their victims are dressed. For an IRA man to immediately go to a drinking club and spend his time giving intimate details to people of the way his victims dressed was not something which happened as far as we knew. Special Branch, of course, said they knew all of this from a source whom they would not divulge. They insisted we arrest the culprits whom they named. Now we knew that two of those named were bad boys, capable of murder, but — [Mr B] was not. We told Special Branch that there was no way — [Mr B] was involved but they insisted that their information was correct.

Mr B was picked up with two others for prolonged questioning and confirmed CID suspicions that not only was he innocent but he was being 'fitted' for a double murder he did not commit. Mr B was a relative of the Provisional IRA leader Martin Meehan. He was shot by the Army in the early 1970s but not a member of the IRA, though he associated with people on the fringes of Republicanism. Investigating officers from CID insisted that he was innocent and eventually released him. His co-accused were found guilty of the murders.

The person who supplied Special Branch with their information on the double murder was Maurice Gilvarry, yet Gilvarry was the man who killed the Mackins. It was he who actually pulled the trigger. By trying to get an innocent man 'fitted' for the crime, he remained for a time an active terrorist in whom the IRA had confidence. The murders demonstrated his commitment to the IRA and he was also able to remain secretly in the employ of Special Branch. One is obliged to ask whether Special Branch knew that he murdered the Mackins. Surely Special Branch officers could have made an observation similar to that which immediately occurred to CID officers—that killers do not pay much attention to how victims are dressed—unless they were too preoccupied with finding the culprits to pay much attention to Gilvarry's evidence. He told them he was in the club and presumably they believed him. If by chance they suspected that he was the trigger man, would they have sacrificed a useful informer? This raises questions about the use of active terrorists as informers. Were Special Branch prepared to allow him to commit murder on behalf of the IRA, to keep him in place as an agent? Did he give them the names of his accomplices but not reveal his own part in the crime?

The source who confirmed this story placed me in contact with another member of the RUC, since retired, who corroborated the detail and who was later very disturbed when he discovered the connection between Gilvarry and Special Branch. If one should contend that Special Branch firmly believed Gilvarry, and that such contacts and liaisons are necessary in the defeat of terrorism in a dirty war, one is still left with a lingering suspicion. In this instance one might ask whether the informer was more important to Special Branch than his guilt—providing, of course, that they knew about his involvement. This creates a corollary—namely, that in such an event the informer survives only if he acts as a terrorist, and therefore the rules applied to informers are different from those applied to 'other terrorists'.

I found this story disturbing and quickly detected the apprehension in the retired police officer who had been faced with Special Branch insistence that they knew the culprits. His instinct told him that someone was being deliberately 'fitted' for a crime. The question that remains unanswered is whether Gilvarry acted independently of Special Branch to protect himself by pointing the finger at an innocent man, or whether Special Branch acted in collusion with him and were content to unmask two of the culprits while sacrificing an innocent person to keep their agent in place.

15

The Technology of Surveillance

I n May 1984 the English policeman, John Stalker, was asked to conduct an inquiry into an alleged shoot-to-kill policy by the RUC. Part of his investigation centred on the activities of a police department known at the time as E4. It was a specialist department assigned to the task of spying on IRA suspects and known terrorists. The department was subdivided into areas of expertise: E4A, which most concerned Stalker, dealt with man-to-man surveillance; E4B comprised the department's technicians who were adept at planting and concealing bugs, phone-tapping and the use of other electronic gadgetry; E4C and E4D specialised in photographic surveillance such as the use of hidden cameras, miniaturised cameras designed for concealment in cars, suitcases and other items. These experts also used hidden video cameras to record events in known terrorist haunts or to maintain surveillance of an identified arms dump. Prior to the Stalker inquiry the technicians in E4B did not possess the expertise of their counterparts in MI5, who were also active in intelligence duties in the province. However, because the activities of E4 were supervised by Special Branch and were ultimately under the control of MI5, technicians from MI5 often carried out tasks as part of E4 operations. This happened frequently and was not always due to the fact that MI5 operatives possessed better equipment and greater knowledge but because the intelligence agency wished to control a particular operation. In such a circumstance MI5 technicians planted the necessary bugging equipment and supervised its use. An Army base would be used as the nerve centre to record all intelligence data picked up by the bug, with the result that MI5 controlled not only the operation but also the intelligence and the tapes on which it was recorded. This involvement of MI5 was to have controversial significance in the Stalker inquiry.

However, E4 overall and E4A in particular were given the most dangerous and secretive of roles within the RUC, with overall supervision accorded to Special Branch and, ultimately, the Chief Constable. E4A operatives were provided with back-up cover from teams known as special support units, whose members received SAS training in a centre at Aldershot, and whose brief was to provide, if necessary, 'firepower, speed and aggression'—a phrase which some believe referred to ambush techniques. E4A operatives were regularly engaged in following suspects or known members of the IRA. Often they were required to 'dig in' close to where their quarry lived or was hiding; sometimes they had to conceal themselves in bushes or remain for days in specially prepared holes in the ground or in derelict buildings. Occasionally they would 'dig in' for several days close to an IRA arms or explosives dump to record the movement of IRA volunteers so that they could be apprehended or ambushed. Aside from 'human-eyes' surveillance, E4A also provided technical services such as filming or photographing members of the IRA and suspects.

John Stalker found that the most frustrating part of his investigation related to a shooting in a hayshed on 24 November 1982 in which a teenager, Michael Tighe, was shot dead and Martin McAuley was seriously wounded. Both were in the hayshed when shot, and Stalker later discovered that the building was bugged. However, he was never allowed access to the tape-recording of the events in the barn. Stalker was determined to verify whether a warning was shouted before police opened fire and whether Tighe and McAuley were, as police alleged, cocking antiquated rifles which were found in the shed.

The bug was concealed in a rafter in the building. Not only was it capable of transmitting conversations live but its electronic signal was powerful, and a recording of events in the hayshed was made at Mahon Road Army base in Portadown. This advanced bugging equipment ensured that the hayshed was constantly under surveillance without operatives being required to 'dig in' near the building and risk being discovered and killed. After the shooting the bug was removed from the barn by two leading members of the RUC. Prior to that incident the hayshed had, on a separate occasion, also been bugged by MI5 at the request of E4A. A quantity of explosives were known to be concealed on the premises. MI5 personnel placed a tracking device within the explosives which was designed to set off a signal at Mahon Road Army base as soon as the IRA moved them. The intention was to alert the special support units so that an IRA bombing team could be intercepted, ambushed and, if possible, apprehended en route to a bombing target. The security forces did not wish the IRA to know that a highly placed informer had told them of the presence of the explosives. By placing a tracking bug in the explosives and only acting when the bombing team was in transit, E4A hoped to deceive the IRA into believing that the bomb-team had been apprehended by chance. The informer would be protected, and both the explosives and an IRA team would be taken out of circulation. Unfortunately the tracking device failed to operate at the moment the explosives were moved. This cost the life of two policemen, who were killed when those explosives were converted into a landmine and detonated at Kinnego in South Armagh.

A tracking device and bug were also used in another incident investigated by Stalker, but he remained unaware of the events surrounding the operation. The BBC reporter, Chris Moore, who especially well knows the precise nature of the Stalker inquiry and what was hidden from Stalker, revealed the details of this controversial bugging in a television broadcast in 1988 that went virtually unnoticed:

> The BBC has been told that MI5/MI6 electronically bugged a car being used by three IRA men in Armagh in 1982. The three men, Eugene Tonan, Sean Burns and Gervais McKerr, were shot dead by the RUC's anti-terrorist unit. We've been told John Stalker was never made aware of this bugging operation. What he did not know was that MI5, MI6 and the RUC combined forces in an electronic bugging operation. We've been told that the car in which Burns, McKerr and Tonan were shot dead was bugged. We've been given to understand that the security forces involved in the covert surveillance operation were able to listen to the conversation going on in the car.

Moore was correct, and the last movements of the three IRA men were recorded on a tape which John Stalker did not even know existed. The bug was placed inside the IRA men's car about an hour before they were shot dead. According to Moore, the bug convinced E4A operatives that McKerr and his companions were on their way to murder a UDR man:

> Our sources say the three IRA men were planning a murder attack on a member of the security forces. At the time of the shooting, we've been told, it was thought the IRA men were on their way to the home of their intended victim to complete their operation. It was only afterwards, when no weapon was found in the car, that the security services involved realised that the journey was what our sources describe as a 'dry run'. What was heard of the conversation in the car apparently increased the security forces' belief that the attack was imminent.

What Moore did not reveal was that the bug was taped to the underside of the car at the instigation of British intelligence operatives and not E4A, though it was E4 special support personnel who fired almost a hundred bullets into the car. The bug would have provided a clear broadcast of the conversation in the car which Moore says, according to his sources, was misunderstood. In addition a tracking device was also placed alongside the bug, so that if the bug failed to function the tracking device would alert the technical operatives at Mahon Road Army base that the car was being moved. One wonders whether Stalker's investigation and his subsequent book might not have been more controversial if he had known about this other tape or the details of Chris Moore's investigations into the episodes examined by him.

The use of tracking devices has led to numerous incidents in which IRA volunteers have been apprehended on their way to bomb targets. The IRA is aware of the damage caused to their operations by such means.

We know that we have lost men because of tracking devices. Two years ago one of our units in Derry lifted ten pounds of explosives from a sealed dump and made it into a bomb. The target was chosen and the bomb team left a safe-house, but on their way to the target, they were forced to abort the mission because of heavy security. They returned to the safe-house and the bomb was replaced, timer intact, in the dump. It was decided that the same target would be hit one week later. Twenty-four hours before the second attempt, a decision was taken to divide the ten-pound bomb into two five-pound devices. The ten-pounder was taken out of the dump into the safe-house. As the lads split it, they discovered a tracking device in it. They knew they were probably under surveillance and about to be hit. That bomb team escaped from the safe-house with minutes to spare. We also believe that the Brits have not only used tracking devices but have also booby-trapped our bombs—with the result that some of our people have been killed on bombing missions.

The IRA have described how tracking devices (also known as radio tagging devices), bugs and other minute gadgets have been placed by the police and Army inside IRA weapons:

We discovered that they were bugging weapons. They would find an arms dump, preferably what we call a sealed dump. That is one which has been carefully sealed to be used only when authorised, unlike other dumps, which might be a cupboard in a house or an area under floorboards. The latter dumps are for weapons in constant use. The sealed dump is designed for special occasions. When a consignment of guns or explosives is brought into an area as surplus gear, they are placed in a sealed dump. Now if the Brits discover a sealed dump they have the technology to open it and reseal it. We know this because they have done it to our cost. If they get into a sealed weapons dump they can place a small tracking device or a bug inside a rifle butt or in a rifle barrel. They can also booby-trap guns so that they will explode when fired. We caught one of our people who bugged weapons for them. We did not know the extent of his role until we captured him. We know he was an informer so we set an elaborate trap for him. We designed a bogus roadblock and stopped him as he was driving along a road close to his home. At the roadblock he was threatened and told he was about to be shot. He was told the roadblock was manned by members of the SAS. The guy panicked and said he was an agent. When we interrogated him he told us how he bugged rifles in a sealed dump. We executed him and buried him. His wife knows about it but because she is Republican we will not reveal his name to avoid embarrassing her. To combat bugging we have anti-bugging gear, but to be sure we now have a strict policy about arms and explosives dumps. Before weapons go into a dump, they are carefully examined and cleaned. Before they are used, they are again examined. Of course, there is no sure method, though we now employ techniques to ensure that we limit the extent to which people have access to dumps.

An example of how police plans can go wrong occurred in 1988 and has until now remained secret. Police operatives discovered the whereabouts of an IRA explosives haul in the form of a large bomb, and they replaced the Cortex fuse with one which would not work. They then allowed an IRA team to transport the bomb and place it outside premises in Belfast city centre. Police and Army believed that by replacing the Cortex they were protecting the city centre, preventing loss of life and also safeguarding their source, since capture of the bomb-team and the explosives would have led the IRA to the informer. However, no one informed the Army's bomb-disposal experts. When the bomb was discovered outside the taxation office, the surrounding area was sealed off. Army bomb experts, unaware that a dud fuse had been placed in the bomb, used a small explosives charge to defuse it. Unfortunately this served to trigger the bomb, which exploded, causing considerable damage. If the bomb-disposal officer had known about the dud fuse, he could have removed it and thus defused the bomb; the IRA would have assumed that his expertise had won the day. That operation was carried out by operatives of what was previously E4A.

After the controversy caused by the Stalker investigation and the publication of his book, the RUC changed the name of the surveillance department's units to E41/E42. The operatives who have expertise in the use of technology are known as E4B/C/D etc. One other change that has occurred is the reduced role of MI5 technical specialists; E4's technical experts now plant their own bugging and tracking devices. There is considerable ill-feeling between the RUC and MI5 because MI5 apparently 'walked away' from the hayshed inquiry, pretending that their involvement was minimal. According to RUC sources, MI5 always tended to interfere and demand a role in E4 operations, but when controversy reigned, as with the Stalker investigation, the intelligence service 'ran for cover' and was deliberately obstructive, referring all enquiries to RUC personnel and suggesting that the culprits could be found in police ranks.

It is in the field of human surveillance that RUC and Army operatives are at great risk. Robert Nairac's death was a testimony to the dangers facing intelligence operatives who are required to be physically close to the terrorists. Unlike Nairac, several Army intelligence men have had narrow escapes.

On 8 July 1975 Staff Captain C. E. Eldred was on a mission in the Falls area, dressed casually and driving a yellow Datsun car. However, members of the IRA observed that he was making repeated trips along the Lower Falls and they set a trap for him. Only his judgement and reflexes saved him. As he made one of his numerous passes of Clonard Street he became aware of a number of IRA men following him in a car. He realised he was about to be rammed, but in his haste to escape them he almost fell into their trap. Ahead he saw a group of people on a street corner and understood that, once he had been rammed, they would descend on him. He swung his car to turn into Sevastopol Street but crashed the vehicle. Although he could have used firepower to hold off his attackers, he fled on foot to Springfield Road police and Army post. Inside the vehicle the IRA found an identity card with his photograph and other details: height, 5 foot 10 inches; eyes, green; hair, brown; serial number, 24126906. The Army issued a public statement saying that he was engaged on routine military duties. However, the car and its contents indicated the nature of Eldred's work. There were scores of photographs of known members of the IRA and of people suspected of IRA involvement; there were also documents detailing the movements and backgrounds of terrorists, maps and a sub-machine-gun of a type issued only to the SAS. Eldred took a considerable risk in travelling alone. His task was undoubtedly to shadow and report on the movement of IRA personnel. In his car was a transmitter linking him to his base so that once he spotted a wanted terrorist that information could be quickly relayed to uniformed troops in the Lower Falls district.

Two years later in West Belfast another intelligence operative on a similar mission was not so fortunate. He was Paul Harman, who was using a false name, Hugill. The IRA later showed selected press men some of the documents recovered from Paul Harman's car after he was shot dead. They also issued the following statement which the Army privately accepts, containing some accurate information in respect of the codes Harman used to communicate with his base:

His complete intelligence data, personal firearm and a slim transistor-like set of flares were uncovered. Had our Volunteers hesitated, Harman at the press of a flare button could have immediately alerted British Army patrols. In the files were discovered the miniaturised photographs of 73 Republicans. Around the photographs of veteran Republicans, Billy McKee, Gerry Adams and Advice Centre Worker, Mary Kennedy, were circles, which we suspect at this stage of our research, were singled out for possible assassination, as symbolic levels, to weird Brit thinking, of Republican organisation. Five weeks ago a black taxi was fired at from a passing car in West Belfast. The number of this civilian vehicle, as well as a long, long list of others, was among the spy's files. Much of the information and a few photographs were of non-Republican civilians. The codes were as follows: buildings were named after fruits, e.g. Grape meant a church, Pear, a taxi, Apple, a pub. Towns and Republican areas throughout the six counties were named supposedly after English football teams, e.g. Derry was Oxford, Dromore in Co. Down was Celtic and Crossmaglen was Notts. Other premises which the Brits associated with other independent sections of the Republican Movement were named after planets: 85B Falls Road was Sun.

Inside a grubby copy of the 5th January 1977 edition of *Amateur Photographer* were intelligence maps of Belfast and its environs. The routes which the Brit spies use in their plain-clothes vehicles and seemingly other spy routes, were plotted out.

The statement was typical of the IRA's policy of exploiting a situation for propaganda purposes. Its author was obviously not aware that Celtic is not an English football club. However, the use of codes as outlined was correct. Contrary to what the IRA might say, the Army maintained that Harman was performing a task for the protection of the Catholic population, and the suggestion that he was an assassin was absurd.

One year later, in 1978, an undercover squad was almost caught unawares in North Belfast. At that time there had been many sectarian killings in the area, and it is likely they were operating to counter the activities of travelling killer-squads. The discovery by local people of the Army undercover team came four days after the murder of fifty-two-year-old William Smyth, chairman of the local Catholic Ex-Servicemen's Club. Smyth was shot once in the head outside his house as he returned home from the pub. It may well have been in response to this killing that four undercover soldiers set up a secret observation post in a former shop at 199 Oldpark Road. The premises offered a view of any vehicles or people moving along what was a busy and troubled area of the city. The day after Smyth was murdered, the owner of no. 199 discovered that a side-door to the building was open. He was concerned because the premises were used to store materials for a building company, and his first thought was that a burglary had taken place. When he examined the ground floor where the materials were kept, he was pleased to discover that nothing was missing. The following day he returned to no. 199 and to his consternation found a padlock on the side-door had been forced to permit entry. He again inspected the stored materials but they were all in place.

Two days later, a resident who lived in a house adjoining no. 199 told the owner that he had heard noises coming from no. 199 the previous night. Both decided to investigate. After searching the ground floor they decided to examine the upstairs area, which was vacant. They climbed the staircase and made a cursory inspection upstairs. As they turned to go back down, a voice screamed at them from above: 'Don't move or I'll blow your heads off.' Above them the trapdoor to the attic was open and a large figure loomed in the darkness with a pistol aimed at them. In a split second the dark figure plummeted towards them and, as if with a rugby tackle, brought them both crashing to the floorboards. As they recovered from their fall, three more men descended swiftly from the attic. The four strangers, all of them dressed in light military clothing, had heavy stubble and smelled of human excrement. They radioed for assistance and within a short time an Army vehicle arrived. The owner of no. 199 was released. His companion was held for questioning for an hour at a nearby Army base before he too was freed.

The IRA later claimed that the soldiers were seen removing a parcel from the house which they attempted to conceal from a small crowd of local residents who gathered at no. 199 when they realised that something untoward was happening. According to the IRA, the parcel was partially unveiled as undercover soldiers climbed into an armoured personnel carrier, and it contained a jacket similar to that worn by the person observed shooting William Smyth. Responsibility for his killing had been claimed by the Irish Freedom Fighters, a previously unheard-of grouping. The IRA suggested the IFF did not exist but was a British counter-insurgency ploy to cause confusion within Republican ranks. They maintained that local people believed that one of the undercover soldiers resembled a description of Smyth's killer. Although the IRA could not justify its claims they suited its purpose of attempting to discredit the security forces.

The incident illustrated how undercover soldiers were required to exist for days in a hostile environment, probably using the attic as an observation post. The Army procedure in such circumstances would be to remove or slightly dislodge one or two slates to permit a view of the surrounding neighbourhood. At night infra-red sighting would be used to scour the area, to note the movement of people and particularly cars, from which most sectarian killer-squads operated.

The use of undercover teams in this way has narrowed the scope of terrorist organisations in Belfast. Through their observations such teams enable the intelligence community to track the movements of the majority of known subversives. All of this information is constantly being fed into a computer by intelligence analysts. When a dangerous terrorist does not appear on surveillance lists over a given period, alarm bells start to ring, and the police and Army begin to believe that something unusual is being planned. The discovery of the Gibraltar bombers was the result of what is known as man-to-man surveillance. Once Danny McCann or Mairead Farrell disappeared from surveillance lists, suspicion arose that they were engaged in a special mission.

While researching this book I was told by the IRA that the intelligence services' priority in Ireland is surveillance geared towards the England Department. This was the first use of the term 'England Department' that I encountered. When I enquired what was the 'England Department' I was told the following:

The England Department is an entity kept separate from all other IRA operations. The Brits know that. It is their major target. The England Department is the most closely guarded cell structure within the IRA. It is the most tightly formed unit, with cells within cells. Even the IRA leadership is restricted with regard to knowledge of this department. The Brits put all their efforts into trying to get close to this department. They know that if they can get one breakthrough they are in business. We know that they expend so much effort and resources on man-to-man surveillance. They do that because they know that we have learned a great deal. We also have technology. We are careful about the means by which we communicate. Therefore it all comes back to what may seem the simplest method but which, if successful, is the most devastating. For example—if, say, the Brits uncovered an operation like Gibraltar, it could happen this way. McCann, Savage or Farrell [the Gibraltar trio] are not where the Brits expect them to be. If they do not appear on surveillance reports over a given period, the Brits become suspicious. The Brits devote every available effort into finding at least one of them. Word goes out to all their operatives and informers or to the Gardai and Irish Special Branch to find them. If they find one, they will concentrate on that person in the hope that he or she will lead them to the others and possibly a planned operation.

An account of how surveillance teams operate and how terrorists react to them was given to me by a leading member of the Irish People's Liberation Organisation, a breakaway group from the INLA:

When driving from place to place I know I am probably under surveillance. If I am stopped at a roadblock, the likelihood is that I have lost those trailing me. They will have alerted the security forces with orders to detain me at the roadblock. Once those watching me are back in place I will be allowed to proceed on my journey. If I am going anywhere that requires special methods whereby I am certain that I am not being watched I will restrict details of my movements and my intended destination to one, perhaps two people. In the event of me being apprehended, I am able to narrow the number of suspects who have possibly betrayed me. When someone is arrested, interrogated and released, he or she is debriefed by the PLO. Debriefing is very important. It helps us build a dossier on interrogators, their techniques, mannerisms and, maybe, even dress sense because that may reveal something which may be of value at a later date. Debriefing also seeks to establish what the enemy knows about us or about the individual who was interrogated. For instance the type of questions asked by the interrogator may reveal interesting details. We ask our people to remember the questions they are asked. An interrogator has a lot of information in his head. He may betray himself because he is trying to be clever or boastful. I was once debriefed and the questions I had been asked were analysed and we narrowed down to two the number of people who could have betrayed information about certain matters. When they place surveillance on you they are thorough. It is not like the movies. We discovered by deliberately placing our own surveillance on a leading activist in our organisation whom we knew was being watched that they will use a large number of people and they will even operate in several cars. They are good. Most of the time you will never know unless they want you to know. They may want you to know to panic you or to suggest that someone is betraying your movements or to unnerve you and wear you down.

An intelligence expert who has written extensively about the CIA told me that Belfast is similar to Berlin during the Second World War and is the ideal city for training operatives in man-to-man marking. The cars used by surveillance teams, particularly E4, are constantly resprayed at a plant designed specifically for this purpose at RUC headquarters in Belfast.

The science of intelligence-gathering is very precise and can best be illustrated by definitions provided by the School of Service Intelligence, Army intelligence wing, which names three types of sources and agencies from which intelligence can be obtained:

1   Those which are Directed i.e. ones which can be tasked by an Intelligence officer to provide answers to his questions.
2   Those which are Undirected in that they provide information but an Intelligence Officer has no control over them. This category is limited to permanent or semi-permanent sources such as newspapers published by an enemy, or regular news bulletins put out on radio or television by hostile Governments or forces.
3   Those which are casual, that is those which may or may not be known to exist and which provide useful information unexpectedly.
4   In making a collection plan Intelligence Staffs will normally rely on Directed Agencies and Sources to obtain their critical Intelligence requirements within a specified time limit. Information from Undirected Sources will normally be received in the form of Intelligence summaries from higher formations, or reports from specialist agencies, and is of value in preparing assessments or Intelligence Estimates. Information from Casual Sources is unpredictable and in the absence of collateral or confirmation from a reliable source, it is difficult to establish its authenticity and ensure that it is not part of an enemy deception plan.

The principal 'directed sources' available to intelligence staff are Army and police observation posts, foot patrols, armoured reconnaissance patrols, aircraft, and devices and sensors, both ground and airborne. Observation posts constantly relay information on vehicles and pedestrians. In the larger posts, such as the one established on top of Divis Flats in West Belfast, there are several observers continuously scanning the streets of the Lower Falls area using high-powered binoculars and, at night, infra-red sights. The information collected is fed into a central computer for evaluation but it is also available for immediate analysis and action. Police and Army foot patrols constantly study the faces of all pedestrians with a view to maintaining a permanent watch on known and suspected subversives. Helicopters hover above troubled areas carrying a range of sophisticated photographic equipment capable of constantly broadcasting live pictures to a ground base. Other types of aircraft regularly photograph the Northern Ireland countryside and have permission to overfly the Irish border. Again, such aircraft are fitted with infra-red and thermal sensors to detect the presence of landmines and arms dumps, and to determine convenient areas in which to deposit under-cover soldiers who will spend several days in dugouts in areas such as South Armagh. Ground sensors are also placed in strategic parts of the countryside on both sides of the Irish border. These are small electronic devices which can be hidden in the ground, in tree trunks or in hedgerows and emit signals indicating the presence of humans. Sensors are vital for undercover teams who need to know whether there is an IRA patrol in the vicinity of a dugout.

Military and police intelligence staffs are not normally involved in the use and exploitation of 'undirected sources'. This task is usually under-taken by specialists from the Defence Intelligence Staff. However, the School of Service Intelligence considers that military intelligence per-sonnel in Ireland should recognise potential undirected sources, which they define as a new publication or broadcast on a new wavelength, and should arrange for the recording and reporting of such information through the correct channels, so that the source can be exploited.

The School of Service Intelligence states that, in general, undirected sources consist of all types of written material and radio or television broadcasts which may contain useful information. These would include not only all IRA publications but also academic assessments and all writ-ten material about the conflict, including books such as this one. Intelligence personnel constantly scrutinise all journalistic comment, because journalists often provide detailed information deriving from sources close to terrorism. Likewise film documentaries may unknow-ingly lead the security forces to the source of a terrorist act by indicating the area in which it was planned. Investigative journalism is always under scrutiny, and, according to an intelligence expert to whom I spoke, journalists often unwittingly reveal their source: 'Journalists know their phones are tapped but they need to use them and the immediacy of their jobs determines that they tend to carelessness for the sake of expediency. Equally, they talk in public places to other journalists about their suc-cesses and failures. They are also easily followed.'

The area in which the intelligence staffs always hope to be in advance of the terrorists is that of technical development. Nowadays the wide range of technology is, according to the military, capable of providing systematic observation, by day and night, in all weather and in condi-tions of adverse visibility. Imagery and sensor equipment is used for ground-to-air surveillance by covering troops, for patrol observation posts and for air-to-ground surveillance by reconnaissance aircraft. In border areas surveillance teams on the ground are equipped with manu-ally operated imagery and sensor systems, but the soldiers' eyes and ears are regarded as the most formidable surveillance devices. Soldiers in this role are given image-intensifying night observation sensors, which harness and enhance whatever radiation, whether invisible or infra-red, is available even on the darkest nights. These devices can be in the form of an individual weapon-sight or an NOD (night observation device). All weapon-sights can be used for surveillance purposes and can detect any active *near*-infra-red devices such as vehicle headlights. (The word 'near' in the context of infra-red has nothing to do with the range of the electromagnetic spectrum. 'Near-infra-red' denotes those wavelengths which are nearest in magnitude to those of visible light.)

However, all image intensifiers suffer from fog, rain and smoke, which scatter the existing light. They cause eyestrain through prolonged usage, and the narrow field of view restricts the ability to cover a designated area. While 'near-infra-red' devices are used for night viewing and photography, 'far-infra-red' devices are used for detecting objects from the heat emanating from them. The infra-red night-viewing equipment uses an infra-red sensor in conjunction with an infra-red lamp. Its range depends on the power of the infra-red source and the type of objects on which the equipment can be used: sniper-scopes on individual weapons have a range of up to 600 metres, binoculars used with vehicle headlights for night driving have a range of 80 metres, and sights/searchlights on armoured vehicles have ranges of up to 1200 metres.

In the air the intelligence task is to search out areas on the ground where the IRA are storing arms or building a hide from which a military or police patrol can be ambushed. For this purpose near-infra-red photography is employed. Objects seen against a background of vegetation may match the background when seen by visible light, but they are differentiated when seen by infra-red sensors. Although this phenomenon is revealed by night-viewing devices, it is, according to military experts, more commonly exploited by photography. All that is required for taking photographs using infra-red light is a special film and a filter for the camera, and the main purpose of the photographs is to detect objects camouflaged against ordinary visual observation.

One of the most important surveillance developments in Northern Ireland has been the thermal imager known as T1. All objects are known to have what is described as a 'discrete' or individually distinct temperature of their own. This can be measured accurately by detecting the 'far-infra-red' radiation they emit, and, as a result, heat pictures or thermal images can be produced on a screen. Thermal images can penetrate fog, rain, foliage and even camouflage. Permanent thermal photographs can be taken by using an airborne sensor. These can indicate what is beneath camouflage or underneath a trapdoor to an IRA arms bunker. However, the easiest targets to detect, according to military watchers, are vehicle engines, cooking equipment and the barrels of recently fired weapons.

One of the most unusual airborne devices used in the Ireland conflict has been the unmanned drone. This is a small device powered for short flight and launched from a plane or helicopter. Since 1972 many people living in border areas have probably heard strange sounds in the air during the hours of darkness, unaware of what was flying above them. Drones provide short-range reconnaissance both by day and by night, using optical and infra-red sensors. They are tasked by intelligence staffs. In 1972 the British Army acquired what was known as the AN/USD or Midge, a drone with a speed of 410 knots and a maximum travel effectiveness of 60 kilometres. It flew at 300 to 600 metres above ground level, and it carried recording equipment which in daylight conditions, flying at a height of 600 metres, could produce a 70 per cent stereo overlap with vertical cover of a strip of ground 600 metres wide and 30 kilometres long. It also had oblique coverage over a distance of 1750 metres on either side of the vertical. When it was equipped with infra-red sensors it had an all-weather capability. Its limitations were that its flight path was pre-set and the maximum flight distance was 120 kilometres with an average of 100 kilometres. The maximum flight duration was nine minutes. There was no in-flight transmission and the time taken to retrieve the data collected was at least eighty minutes. Consider how the world has changed technologically since 1972, and one can only wonder at the sophisticated drone available for use in Ireland today.

However, the advances in technology often prove useful for only limited periods. Success generates scrutiny and, once the terrorists become aware that a particular device is being used against them, they alter their tactics. The Provos, aware of the sophisticated nature of aerial photography, say they have learned how to construct bunkers which are not easily detectable from the air. An example of the failure of technology was the construction of large military watchtowers along the border. In April 1987 Judge Gibson was blown to pieces within range of some of these watchtowers, and another attack intended for a member of the judiciary killed a family along a stretch of road covered by the towers. Frank Doherty, a journalist who has an acute knowledge of technology and has written extensively on this aspect of the war, discussed counter-measures used by the IRA in an article in *Phoenix* magazine in September 1988:

Two of the most hush-hush weapons used by the British, aerial remote-sensing and radio-tagging, have been turned back on the British and now give the Provos considerable advantage. Remote-sensing is the system which allows the British to detect hidden weapons, command wires and landmines from the air, using a combination of thermal imaging, side-scan radar and multi-spectral photography. Having put up with the effects of remote-sensing for years, which meant that many of their operations were detected in advance, the Provos have learned the art of electronic camouflage. For example, their footprints crossing fields en-route to an ambush site can be spotted by taking infra-red pictures from low-flying spotter planes on routine surveillance. The Provos have also learned to cross the countryside by moving along the perimeter of fields, where hedges provide cover for their footprints from the air, or alternatively they use cattle to cover their tracks if they are moving around a culvert where they have set a landmine. They have also become adept at using various weather conditions to out-wit aerial observers and those in the static observation posts which dot the border. The favourite time for the Provos to go on the move is when it is wet and windy. Various British devices which operate on the 'doppler-shift effect' are useless then. Doppler-shift devices detect movement using electronic beams. If the trees and hedges around them are moving in high wind they are ineffective. Heavy rain and thick mist also variously effect electronic-viewing devices which normally see in the dark.

Similarly the Army and police are constantly studying the IRA's technological developments, particularly in the field of bomb-making. Military strategists admit that the IRA has proved adept at devising new types of detonation devices and methods of delay-timing explosions. It is in the latter field that the IRA has created the greatest worry for the security forces. It was the Provisional IRA that devised a delay mechanism whereby a bomb could be secreted in a building with a timing device set to explode it months or even a year later. In terms of bomb-making techniques the war will always favour the terrorist until the security forces find a means of combating a particular bomb-maker's methods. The IRA also now possess bugging equipment and devices for detecting bugs. While I was writing this book, I was informed by a contact that the Provos discovered a miniature bug in the ceiling of a house in Belfast and were amazed at both its size and its capability. It was the tiniest device they had ever encountered but could relay conversations across several rooms in a house.

The most controversial dimensions to the dirty war occur in the fields of phone-tapping and computerisation. Phone-tapping has been taking place since the beginning of the present conflict. In 1969 it was organised on a small scale and was carried out by attaching small listening devices to individual telephone lines in telephone (then Post Office) exchanges. Telephone engineers ignored the presence of tapping devices because their employment involved signing the Official Secrets Act. When enquiries were made by engineers about phone-taps, dark-suited men arrived at an exchange and reminded the staff of the precise nature and scope of the Official Secrets Act. As the need for phone-tapping increased, selected members of Post Office engineering staffs, mostly at a managerial level, were employed in an extra-curricular listening role; at night they secretly entered telephone exchanges, often accompanied by military personnel, and listened to selected lines as well as identifying individual lines which were marked for permanent tapping. Eventually, a more sophisticated means of tapping was established in Belfast city centre, and in recent years massive amounts of cable have been installed to link Army premises at Lisburn to the entire phone network which is based in Belfast. This has raised suspicions that phone-tapping is more widespread than officially indicated. The journalist David McKittrick addressed this issue in the *Irish Times*:

The Special Branch appears to tap only with Ministerial authority but the other three Agencies [Army, MI5 and MI6] regularly break the law. Reliable sources say the illegal taps have often run into hundreds. Specific figures are difficult to obtain because none of the three agencies involved tell each other what they are up to. Tapping targets have in the past included the Rev. Ian Paisley, John Hume, William Craig, Paddy Devlin, although sources say there now appears to be less eavesdropping on politicians. Other targets include Provisional Sinn Fein and Ulster Defence Association, callboxes in pubs frequented by paramilitaries, newspaper offices and the Europa Hotel, principally because of the large number of journalists who use the hotel. Reliable sources say that phone-tapping is very wasteful in manpower, in that listening to the conversations takes so much time. And different sources agree that for all the time put into it, telephone intercepts produce very little information of any real value. The Army has always paid a great deal of attention to journalists' phones. Again, it is difficult to imagine that much hard intelligence could be gleaned from them.

Modern technology has made the phone-tapping exercise less dependent on human resources. Through the use of computers recording equipment can be activated by voice-imprint or by the speaking of selected words. The word-activated system is very useful, though there is undoubtedly still a need for manpower to evaluate the phone conversations. Tapping can take place anywhere between an exchange and the target's home or centrally in Belfast. A journalist who once worked as a telephone engineer provided an interesting insight into telephone-tapping in an article in *Phoenix* magazine in 1983. The journalist, under the pseudonym Nicky Tam, referred to the use of a telephone-intercept system known as Pusher (an acronym for Programmable Ultra and Super High Frequency Reception). At the British embassy in Dublin, he claimed that Pusher 'listened' on microwave radio channels which carried phone and telex signals from major communication centres in Dublin to all parts of Ireland.

A former Army officer told me about one method of listening to conversations in buildings that was used in Northern Ireland in the early 1970s. A device monitored the vibrations on a window and analysed them to reproduce a conversation taking place in a room. This former officer recounted one such incident with a degree of mirth:

In 1974, as the Ulster Workers' Council strike was in progress, there was considerable instability. No one was quite sure how certain political figures would react to events. We were concerned about the pressure being placed on the power-sharing executive, and particularly the nationalist representatives, namely the SDLP, who were sharing the governing of the province for the first time. We had to know which way they would turn in order to assess with clarity the future of the executive. At one point Gerry Fitt was at Westminster and was communicating by phone with his party's chief whip, Paddy Devlin. We knew that they probably reckoned their phones were tapped and would be careful about what they said to each other. However, we judged that once off the phone Paddy Devlin, whose house was being used as a meeting place, would be free to talk. We also believed that whatever code he was using with Fitt would be revealed in the privacy of his house. We bounced microwaves off windows of his home and recorded the conversations in his living-room. It was very valuable.

It was, however, the use of what *Time Out* magazine dubbed 'terminal surveillance' that generated controversy, speculation and, at times, over-reaction. In the early 1970s, when most intelligence data were still stored on index cards, stories appeared in newspapers and journals that the Army was in possession of a computer which had files on the majority of the population. The reports claimed that the computer files contained detailed and personal information on individuals. Evidence since then tends to support the view that no such computer existed until 1978-9. On 12 April 1981 the *Sunday Tribune* published excerpts from documents detailing the use of an Army computer codenamed 'Vengeful'. The *Tribune* claimed that British military intelligence operated an espionage network under a number of 'secret guidelines':

'Farmer's Daughter' is an espionage system which details all features of households in clearly-defined cross-border areas. The 'Borderlist' is a programmed section on the Operation Vengeful computer which includes vehicles from the South or those seen travelling in border areas. And 'Border Crosser' is a system which monitors all traffic which crosses from the South into the North and traces its every move.

The documents on which the *Sunday Tribune* based its article came from the School of Service Intelligence's military wing and indicated that the computer, 'Vengeful', had fifty terminals in Northern Ireland, which assisted soldiers who fed into it car registration numbers and sought details on vehicle occupants and drivers. As the *Tribune* rightly pointed out, it included a 'Border List' of vehicles which travelled to Northern Ireland from the Republic, and under a subsection, 'Farmer's Daughter', the computer contained 'minute details' on houses and their occupants on both sides of the border. The *Tribune* revealed much that would not at the time have appeared in media publications in Great Britain. It reproduced photostatted excerpts from the secret documents showing that British military intelligence areas of responsibility were not merely confined to British soil in Ireland:

Besides the information stored on vehicles and persons the computer data banks also include precise details of organisations which in an introductory list of abbreviations are listed as 'Republican and Left Wing'. These include associations like the Association for Legal Justice, the Ancient Order of Hibernians, Irish Civil Rights Association, Irish Republican Army and Irish Republican Socialist Party. But also on file are the Gaelic Athletic Association, the Falls Taxi Association and others. Details on these organisations include the 'Aims and Policy' which give an indication as to the direction that organisation may take or what attitude they may adopt towards a given situation.

The documents which were the basis for the *Tribune* article were genuine, and Duncan Campbell of the *New Statesman* has also seen them. 'Vengeful' existed in 1974 as a computerised system for registering every vehicle in Northern Ireland and assisting soldiers at road checkpoints. However, according to Duncan Campbell's source, it did not initially provide useful information. From 1978 onwards a smaller but more sophisticated computer undertook 'Operation Vengeful', creating what the *Tribune* described as a 'highly sophisticated espionage' operation in Ireland.

Computers with their attendant images of a society constantly under scrutiny have been a major source of intelligence. Department of Health and Social Services computer files have provided the basis for assembling a much larger profile of the Northern Ireland population. In addition, bank accounts have been examined, telexes have been tapped and mail has been surreptitiously opened. It is all part of a war, and it often happens at a level where most people are unaware of it. The age of technology has provided the security forces and agencies with additional means to combat terrorism, but even the most sophisticated of devices require time, money, manpower and hours upon hours of analysis. The most successful means of intelligence gathering still appears to be the traditional one—the use of informers, who are closer to terrorists than computers and thermal imagery and, unlike bugs, can move independently.

16

Money, Qadhafi, Guns

I n the decades prior to 1969 IRA violence was financed by subscriptions from sympathisers in Ireland and from Irish-American organisations in the United States. The American dimension was not significant in previous campaigns, though it was from the United States that the IRA acquired the Thompson sub-machine-gun which was its trademark until the arrival in the early 1970s of modern weaponry such as the Armalite rifle. As far as cash was concerned, before 1969 the IRA was embarrassed about having readily available funds and frowned on the idea of making money. Its reluctance to acquire money by criminal means was evidenced by its treatment of two volunteers who robbed a bookmaker's shop in Berry Street, Belfast, in 1941. When the two culprits arrived in prison they were ostracised and regarded as common criminals by Republican prisoners. The attitude that robbery was anathema to Republicans remained in place until the commencement of the 'dirty war' in 1969.

The communal violence which signalled the campaign of terrorism led immediately to the erection of barricades in many towns and cities. In the major centres of Belfast and Derry, where the barricades became a feature of life so did crime. Barricades were formed by hijacking lorries. The goods on hijacked vehicles were often removed by mobs, but there was one particular commodity that could easily be converted into profit—alcohol. Although the IRA soon realised that brewery lorries provided a ready source of capital, as yet they had no outlet for selling the goods. While the IRA (initially the Official IRA) examined ways of selling hijacked alcohol, suppliers were concerned that their business was being seriously damaged because the paramilitaries controlled the areas behind the barricades and would not permit brewery lorries to deliver goods to those pubs which had not been destroyed in the August 1969 rioting. One brewery encouraged one of its representatives to approach the IRA leadership to negotiate a way round the impasse. The IRA agreed to allow access to Republican areas if the brewery was willing to pay a 'price'. The deal which was struck was that the brewery would provide one lorry-load of alcohol free to the IRA each week; in return, access would be guaranteed to lorries from only that brewery. Illegal drinking clubs were being set up in many areas to replace burned-out bars, and these became the outlets for the lorry-loads of 'free' alcohol. Once other breweries learned that a deal could be struck with the IRA, they agreed to similar terms. Suddenly, the Official IRA and the Provisionals were receiving income from illegal drinking clubs, many of which were later licensed by government. The pattern in Republican neighbourhoods was duplicated by Loyalist paramilitaries. Profits accruing from this scam provided paramilitary groups with a means to pay volunteers and prisoners' dependants and create a fund for the purchase of weapons. However, the sudden change in IRA policy generated its own form of abuse, and individuals used some of the money to finance flamboyant lifestyles. This happened more frequently on the Loyalist side, and in the 1980s led to a purge within the UDA of men who were seen as 'Godfathers'. Some of them were assassinated.

In 1969-70 the Provisionals, as part of a deal with a brewery, insisted that one of its leading figures be placed on the brewery payroll to oversee their business dealings with the company. This was agreed because business was booming and those clubs under the Provisionals' control conducted all their trade through that brewery. The Provos also appointed an accountant to handle all their business with the brewery and to negotiate prices for the alcohol sold to IRA-controlled outlets. All paramilitary groupings benefited from similar arrangements.

Paddy Devlin, the former SDLP chief whip, who was a member of the IRA in the 1950s but is today a writer and broadcaster, believes the barricades were crucial in allowing the paramilitaries the freedom to shape a dimension to the dirty war which we now define as the 'rackets'. His views are based on a close observation of the events through his experience as a leading member of the Central Citizens Defence Committee:

The barricades brought an influx of criminal and low-life types into so-called defence organisations which evolved into the Provisional IRA. It was a tribal thing which brought monies, even state monies from government agencies in Dublin, into the

North for Catholic aid. Collections were being set up and were received by area leaders who got used to handling money which led to the setting-up of full-time leaders and their staff. They evolved into the Godfathers who sustained their own existence and position with funds generated on the same basis as the New York Mafia families. They allowed for the hijacking of cars and trade vehicles. If you were a trader you were permitted to trade if you paid to the funds for the so-called poor and homeless.

The violence also affected public transport: whenever barricades were being built, buses belonging to the city were set alight. Some enterprising people saw an opportunity to profit from the need for an alternative form of transport. Black London-type cabs were bought and travelled through Republican areas of Belfast providing a service at prices which undercut bus fares. This caused unfair competition with the buses. As the number of cabs increased, the drivers paid into a central fund. On several occasions this fund was looted, and in the absence of a police force the IRA were summoned to deal with the culprits. Since the IRA recognised the potential revenue from this service, they took payment from the central fund. After the IRA became involved, a great many more buses were burned. When the authorities attempted to end what became known as the black taxi service, the IRA prevented buses from entering Republican areas, and the authorities backed down. In time, like the illegal drinking clubs, the taxi service became an accepted part of the way of life in certain areas of Belfast. The Loyalists, as with the alcohol rackets, also set up a black taxi service.

Nothing was immune from extortion, not even banking. Several banks in Belfast paid the Provisionals and, in turn, were provided with paramilitary watchers who identified hold-up men. The IRA recovered the stolen money, returned it to the banks and punished the robbers either by kneecapping or banishing them from Ireland.

Businessmen knew that the safest way of remaining solvent was to pay for protection. A well-known joke in Belfast was that, if a group of businessmen were in a room and only one denied that he paid protection, he was likely to be the person supplying it. The expansion of paramilitary interests created wealth which was in turn invested. As the major terrorist organisation the Provisionals had the biggest share and their racketeering activities created the greatest wealth. However, the Provos' spending on weapons devoured much of their income, whereas other groupings such as the Official IRA and Loyalist paramilitaries invested in businesses by buying pubs and shops and their leading figures developed expensive tastes and better lifestyles.

In border areas the IRA raised money for the 'cause' by extracting payment from smugglers—men such as John McAnulty who were involved in the transfer of vehicles, grain, livestock and other products to the Irish

Republic. Alcohol was and has remained a favourite product for smuggling because its price in the Irish Republic is often double that in Northern Ireland. Customs officers often ignored the illegal passage of goods out of fear or because of direct threats.

In some instances the IRA was deemed to be responsible for robberies which were in fact carried out by criminals not connected to paramilitaries. In a society where law and order breaks down, crime in general tends to thrive. There were also individual terrorists who used their organisations as a front for their own freelance robberies and extortion.

When massage parlours opened in Belfast in the early 1970s they all paid protection money. Sometimes a massage parlour paid money to several organisations or to people claiming to represent a terrorist group. Once it was known that Northern Ireland society was riddled with racketeering, criminals of all kinds took advantage of the fact that a businessman could easily be conned into believing that he was paying his money to paramilitaries. One businessman who paid money for years put it like this:

When you set up a branch of your business in an area and lads come round and demand a weekly payment, you could not ask them for proof that they were IRA or UDA. They didn't carry identity cards. You just paid up. They could have been common criminals or, on the other hand, they could have been the real thing. I paid two groups of people for two months in an area, until one day, two guys came in and told me they were UVF. I told them politely that I was already paying to the UVF, and I added as an aside that I was also paying the UDA. One of these guys looked at me, reached inside his pocket and withdrew a pistol. He told me he was UVF and it was their area and that the UDA would not be demanding money. I never saw the bogus paramilitaries again but I was required to pay the real guys the money I was paying to the other two groups of extortionists. The real guys told me that my premises would be protected. Several years later in another part of Belfast I was offered protection from a security firm which was a front for the UDA. It was like living in one of those American cities you see in movies except that it's for real and these guys don't mess about.

At the beginning of 1970 one man started a business which involved leasing equipment to illegal drinking clubs that were gradually being taken over by the Provisionals. The business quickly began to thrive and became a lucrative operation. This did not go unnoticed in the ranks of the Provisional IRA who decided to divest the businessman of his leasing arrangements. The bussinessman was persuaded to sell his franchise for the equipment. The Provos recognised the potential in his business and took over the entire operation.

The major racket which was devised by the Official IRA and became a feature of the financial dealings of all paramilitary organisations was the extortion of monies from building sites. The most cunning aspect of this form of racketeering concerned the use of tax-exemption certificates. This is how it was explained to me by a politician who investigated it:

In normal circumstances a contractor who has a £20 million job employs sub-contractors to undertake the work. Now if the job is a massive housing development the contractor may employ several sub-contractors. A sub-contractor will in turn employ a labour force and will agree a sum of money for the job which will be paid to him by the main contractor. The sub-contractor acquires a tax-exemption certificate from the Inland Revenue on the basis that he has a bona-fide business. The sub-contractor hands the certificate to the contractor. The contractor pays the sub-contractor e.g. £20,000 per week but is not required to pay the tax of those being employed by the sub-contractor.

The sub-contractor pays the wages from the £20,000 he receives from the contractor and deducts a percentage for the Inland Revenue. The sub-contractor makes the tax deduction each week and, at the end of a finanical year, he hands over a large sum of money to the Inland Revenue. The exemption certificate, in effect, exempts the contractor from paying the tax and places the onus on the sub-contractor.

The paramilitaries cleverly saw an advantage in the abuse of this system. For example, a paramilitary sets up a business and calls his business the Boardroom Backers. He is in effect a sub-contractor. He acquires a tax-exemption certificate by criminal means or has one forged. He gives it to the contractor who is offering him £20,000 for a year on a housing job. The sub-contractor deducts £2000 each week for tax. The job is done in the year and the contractor is happy. The sub-contractor and his company Boardroom Backers disappears, never to be seen again, and so does £100,000 into paramilitary coffers. Well, it is more lucrative than that and the scam is much more clever.

The sub-contractor employs people who are receiving unemployment benefit and who are willing to accept lower wages because they could be easily compromised or are willing to make a weekly financial contribution to the 'cause'. The £100,000 could easily be £150,000.

The Official IRA devised this racket with the help of one of their men who was working in Birmingham and who illustrated for them that it was easy to acquire real tax-exemption certificates or forge them. This man later accused the Provisionals of initiating the scheme as a means of protecting the Official IRA, which had taken on a respectable image as the Workers' Party. A Belfast city centre accountant provided the IRA with advice on how to run this racket and he also did the paperwork on the setting up of bogus companies. In situations where a sub-contractor was a bona-fide operator, the paramilitaries ensured that the middle-man who provided the labour force for the sub-contractor was one of their men. My informant put it this way:

When a sub-contractor was genuine, he would hand the tax-exemption certificate to the contractor and undertake the legally required responsibility of collecting the necessary income tax. However, he would need to hire a workforce. The paramilitaries might have a company named Exit Pay which could provide carpenters, bricklayers, etc., for the job. This company would employ men on the double, pay them lower than normal wages or ask them to pay a weekly sum to the cause. No matter what way it worked the paramilitaries had a way of siphoning money from the system.

Trade unions were unaware of the way in which labour was being manipulated and workers paid. Bogus companies often sent fifty weekly contributions to the union office to indicate that the workers were happy and working normally. The paramilitaries feared that if UCATT, the building workers' union in Belfast, discovered the racket they would expose it. By the late 1970s every paramilitary organisation was involved in this, and Belfast, for example, was carved up geographically by the terrorists. According to my informant:

The paramilitaries, Republican and Loyalist, met occasionally in a pub off the Antrim Road in North Belfast. The city was divided so that an area, even though it contained Catholic and Protestant areas, was defined as IRA, UDA, UVF, Official IRA or INLA. In this way they ensured that no one encroached on another's territory. It was in all their interests. I know of examples where a job needed to be completed quickly and it was on a site in a Protestant area. Roofers were required and the UDA approached the INLA and asked for assistance. A squad of Catholic roofers was escorted every day to this UDA-controlled site and their protection was ensured. The reverse also happened. This is a dirty business and the public is blind to what is really going on.

In the area of housing development, it was the Northern Ireland Housing Executive, a government-controlled body, which suffered from racketeering. They dealt with main contractors, not sub-contractors. However, in areas where violence was rife, contractors charged an extra 25 per cent on top of their tender for a housing project, to take account of the prospect of having to pay extortion monies to paramilitaries. The Housing Executive would have been aware that tenders for work in troubled areas differed by 25 per cent from tenders offered by contractors for work in districts where there was no obvious paramilitary presence. Paddy Devlin, who was on the Housing Executive's board, believes that a few contractors with paramilitary connections were given information by a member of the executive staff which enabled them to devise tenders at a price which would be acceptable to the housing body. It is reckoned that over a ten-year period the paramilitaries benefited by several million pounds from operating their swindle against the Housing Executive.

While I was investigating the history of racketeering, I discovered that until 1988 businessmen were permitted to claim income tax relief for having to pay extortion monies to the paramilitaries. This was not made public either because the government did not wish to encourage extortion or because it preferred only a limited number of businessmen to be aware that such a tax relief facility existed.

Public disquiet about the swindling of Housing Executive funds led to newspaper reports accusing the IRA of a large-scale fraud; Chris Ryder, who was the *Sunday Times* correspondent in Northern Ireland, published articles pointing to a major fraud of this kind. Several politicians in Northern Ireland claimed that the IRA had benefited by a sum of £1 million to £3 million. A former lord mayor of Belfast, John Carson, said the figure was probably closer to £15 million. The damage to public confidence in the Housing Executive led to an Investigatory Commission led by His Honour, Judge R. T. Roland. He presented a written report in 1979 which cost £224,000, excluding the salaries of permanent officials involved in the investigation. The report's findings did not support the press speculation but nevertheless confirmed the existence of racketeering. In its coverage of racketeering in West Belfast the report stated:

A considerable amount of money went astray. We find this to have been a substantially correct allegation. The Northern Ireland Housing Executive paid out considerably more money on the contracts than was warranted and it is clear they did not obtain value for money. We estimate that in relation to Moyard and Turf Lodge more satisfactory contractual conditions and arrangements could have saved £800,000 and there is also a strong presumption that the work at Whiterock and Springhill cost more than it should have done. During our consideration of the allegations, we were aware that various figures had been put forward by those making allegations as to the amount purportedly lost by the NIHE. Some put the figure as high as £3, £4 or even £10 million. We are satisfied that these figures grossly overstate the extent of the excess cost and have no basis in fact.

Building firms controlled by the members of the IRA were set up to carry out the work and charged exorbitant rates is another allegation. This allegation cannot be positively substantiated. The firms engaged on these contracts employed ex-detainees and Andersonstown Co-Operative was formed by detainees. All of the firms were probably subject to paramilitary influences, but there is no evidence that they were set up to carry out the work and charge exorbitant rates....

It was the loose nature of the contracts and the lack of close supervision which was responsible for the loss of money.

The report ruled out misconduct by Housing Executive employees, admitted that one company, under pressure, paid the IRA £5000, but was unable to deal conclusively with allegations that the workforce regularly paid the IRA:

There is no direct evidence of direct payments of individual workers to the IRA but there is evidence of such payments being made. It is established that regular deductions, generally £1 per week, were made from the worker's wages as contributions to the Green Cross Fund (a fund apparently established to give financial aid to the families of prisoners, detainees and those on remand) but we have no evidence that any of this money reached the IRA.

Paddy Devlin believes that Judge Rowland's report was inadequate because the police at the time were not organised to investigate fraud and the police input was therefore minimal. A vital witness left the jurisdiction before his role in the racketeering could be examined. This witness was under pressure from both the Provisional IRA and the Official IRA because he knew the intimate dealings which enabled these groups to manipulate the funding for housing redevelopment and rehabilitation. Devlin says the Rowland report reduced the fraud for a period of three years; then gangs appeared on building sites with weapons and ordered bona-fide contractors and sub-contractors to vacate sites in favour of businesses willing to deal with paramilitaries.

The Provisional IRA was perhaps the only organisation which devoted the bulk of its money to the financing of war, despite reports to the contrary. The Provo campaign required finances on three fronts: first, the purchase of weapons on the international arms market; secondly, the salaries of active service volunteers and contributions to the families of prisoners and of deceased members; thirdly, the purchase of propaganda materials and the cost of running the ballot-box strategy. From time to time there have been well-planned reports in the media, emanating from the intelligence community, and claiming that the IRA uses its funds to finance extravagant lifestyles for its members. Such reports have little basis in fact and are designed to portray the IRA as a Mafia-type organisation rather than an ideologically motivated army. Like most writers and journalists I have not encountered IRA men who lead flamboyant and expensively tailored lives. I have, however, met a few former UDA leaders who made no effort to disguise the wealth acquired from racketeering. Nowadays all the paramilitary organisations ensure that any opulence is not evident, since it only serves to damage the public image of terrorism.

The Provisional IRA has always been the major banker, because for many years it received support from people not only in the whole of Ireland but also in America, Canada, and, of course, in the large Irish community in Britain. The Provisional IRA's major priority after its formation in January 1970 was to equip its rapidly expanding army. Initially money was used in the United States to purchase small quantities of weapons which could be easily concealed as Aer Lingus freight or on ships' cargoes. The IRA was fortunate at that time in having the sympathy of many people in the Republic, notably in the crucial area of customs. It had sympathisers at Kennedy airport who loaded weapons on to Aer Lingus planes. Merchant seamen also smuggled guns and ammunition into Britain or directly to Ireland. At first the importation of arms was haphazard, and weapons of different design, manufacture and calibre found their way on to the streets of Belfast and other centres of conflict. In early 1970 the IRA suddenly received a batch of Mark 1 carbines—short, semi-automatic rifles weighing less than 6 lb and ideal for quick concealment and street fighting. The Mark 1 carbine was the weapon best suited for urban guerrilla warfare; it originated in the Second World War and the Korean war, and millions were manufactured by the USA. (The RUC were later equipped with them and they remain in use by the police.) The carbines replaced IRA weapons of an older vintage such as the .303 Lee Enfield rifle, which was heavy, bolt-loaded and delivered a muzzle-flash which betrayed the location of its user. From the American market in 1970 the IRA also received Second World War sub-machine-guns known as 'Grease' guns. They were an improvement on the Thompson sub-machine-gun which the IRA made famous in Ireland. The Thompson, first invented in the 1920s, was cumbersome and heavy; it fired .45 ammunition, was not designed for accuracy but produced a frightening rattle and was an excellent weapon for 'riot conditions'. The Garand rifle, ideal for sniping and used by US servicemen in Korea, also found its way into IRA dumps.

The Provos quickly recognised that the American arms route would never provide massive shipments of guns needed for a developing war with the British. Only small consignments could be shipped, because British intelligence was aware of the American connection, was constantly harassing IRA sympathisers and was forever watchful for a mistake which would lead to the arrest of the smugglers; the FBI too was vigilant. With this concentrated scrutiny the Provos decided to develop another arms route closer to home, one which would provide larger shipments of weapons and explosives. In any case, although the United States could easily be exploited for weapons because of its gun laws, it did, ironically, have tight controls on the use, sale and availability of plastic explosives.

The Provisionals made their entry into the European arms market with the aim of acquiring one large shipment of modern weapons of high-velocity calibre, so that guns and ammunition could be standardised throughout the IRA units and training more efficiently devised. In 1970 IRA volunteers were required to know the workings and individual peculiarities of a wide range of weaponry and therefore were not professionally adept with any single weapon but merely capable of firing many. The IRA's desperation to buy weapons led to their dealing with an American named Freeman, who walked into Sinn Fein offices in Dublin, announced that he was an arms dealer and offered his services. Freeman went to Europe to set up an arms deal with the Czechoslovakian manufacturer, Omnipol, and liaised in Dublin with Daithi (David) O'Connell, a member of the Provisionals' Army Council. Joe Cahill, another IRA leader, began encouraging sympathetic businessmen in the Irish Republic to raise £20,000 in cash for Freeman to make a down-payment on the weaponry.

While Freeman was in Europe, O'Connell decided to fly to the continent to meet him to finalise preparations for the purchase and transportation of the weapons. O'Connell behaved amateurishly. Maria Maguire, a twenty-three-year-old unemployed graduate, was infatuated with O'Connell. Although he was a married man O'Connell allowed her to spend a lot of time in his company and invited her to accompany him on his arms-trafficking trip. According to Maguire, who later wrote about her exploits, O'Connell gave her a .38 automatic before the two of them left for Paris, armed, but carrying passports in their own names. Maria Maguire's account reads like a soap opera involving two lovers engaged in a daring exploit. For several days O'Connell and his pretty companion travelled across Europe carrying a large sum of money and two pistols. Maria Maguire claimed the IRA leadership were worried that the 'Irish people' would discover that they had negotiated an arms deal with a communist country. She also reckoned that the IRA leader was anxious because he paced up and down in his hotel room and chain-smoked: 'Dave tried to relax. He drank a lot of Scotch, as he always did when he was trying to calm his nerves.' Maguire returned to Dublin, acquired more funds, conducted conversations on the phone with O'Connell and returned to the continent.

Joe Cahill arranged for a warehouse to be provided for the storage of the arms in Amsterdam. He placed a Cork businessman in charge of this part of the operation and devised a plan to ship the weaponry from Rotterdam to Derry. Considering the failure of the arms-smuggling operation in 1970, it was perhaps foolish for the Provisionals to attempt to repeat the exercise with only a few variations in tactics. O'Connell inspected the Czech arms at the Omnipol factory and was supplied with the company catalogue—obviously an attempt by Omnipol to encourage future sales. O'Connell later claimed that he was followed from Czechoslovakia by Czech or Russian agents. However, he was also convinced that British secret service agents were also watching him. Since the Cork businessman proved inept at providing a warehouse in Amsterdam, O'Connell made alternative arrangements. Maria Maguire and another IRA helper, who arrived in Amsterdam to provide bureaucratic assistance, made preparations for shipping the Czech consignment from Rotterdam. Maguire was not informed how the weapons would be disguised to pass Dutch customs' regulations, but this information was not deliberately concealed from her, since it would have been obvious that a false description of the IRA cargo would be needed for the ship's manifest.

While O'Connell and Maguire were in a hotel room recovering from a hangover, they glanced at a copy of the *Daily Telegraph* and learned from a short paragraph that the IRA Chief of Staff was on the continent in search of arms. Both Maguire and O'Connell were astounded—yet their journeying through Europe was sufficient to have attracted considerable attention from many authorities. Maguire later claimed that they were followed throughout Amsterdam that day and in the evening they learned that the Czech arms consignment had been seized at Schiphol airport. The consignment of 166 crates contained rocket launchers, grenades, sub-machine-guns, rifles, pistols, hand grenades, ammunition and plastic explosives.

While O'Connell and Maguire began to seek an escape route from Holland to Dublin, the IRA Army Council agreed a plan to kidnap the Dutch ambassador in Dublin in the event that the couple were arrested by Dutch police, to hold him hostage and to bargain for the release of the two Provos. The plan was not put into effect because O'Connell and his companion travelled to France and flew to Cork. So ended the first major arms-trafficking, as well as the sexual affair between an IRA leader and a woman who was later described as 'a terrorist groupie'. Maria Maguire, who some Provisionals later believed was a British agent, fled Ireland with the aid of an *Observer* journalist and wrote her account of the year she spent in the IRA. The book, *To Take Arms,* was a poorly written, naïve and sensational account of her infatuation with O'Connell and Republicanism. In her absense she was court-martialled, and to this day the Provisionals say she will be executed if she is ever located. As she admitted at the end of the book, there were few places left for her.

After O'Connell's failure, the IRA began again to negotiate a deal with the Czechs but on a smaller scale, and this resulted in the purchase of a batch of pistols. In 1972, however, the American arms market provided a new dimension to the war, one which represented a chilling warning of the danger created when the IRA acquired modern weaponry, and which illustrated what could have happened if the Czech consignment had reached the streets of Northern Ireland. The American contribution was a batch of rifles much more reliable than any previously used by the IRA. These were AR180 rifles, 3 foot 8 inches long, with a folding butt which made them easy to conceal; they were light, easily cleaned and simple to operate; and they fired .223 high-velocity bullets, with devastating effect. They became publicly known as Armalites and in IRA parlance as 'widow makers'. The first batch of Armalites originated from the Howa Machinery Company in Japan and were part of a limited edition of this particular weapon which fired tungsten-tipped bullets capable of piercing armour. Since few of these weapons were manufactured, the IRA supply dried up, but in 1974-5 the American dealers substituted another Armalite: the AR15, the sporting version of the American military M16.

However, although the Provos retained their interest in the European arms market, there was a slight change of events from early 1971 onwards. During that period Northern Ireland became the focus of attention for many 'observers' and 'students' of conflict: ideologically committed left-wing people from other European countries, some of whom had not experienced armed conflict in their own societies and others who had already travelled elsewhere to observe conflict. Among those people whom I shall call the 'conflict travellers' were a few who had personal experience of warfare in the Middle East and were closely related to the Palestinian cause. What has never been revealed in any of the studies of this period is how contacts were established between the 'conflict travellers' and the IRA, and how those contacts led to the Middle East and what some people have termed the Libyan connection.

Much has been written about IRA contacts, so-called allegiances and the appearance of representatives of other terrorist groups from the Middle East at IRA conventions. This has led to wild speculation and inadequate reporting of the real links established by the Provos and of the fact that most of their arms deals with Middle-Eastern contacts have been conducted in the usual way—money for guns. Since all terrorist groups need both weapons and money, they will exchange guns for money or money for guns, depending on what they require at any given time. There are exceptions to the rule; for example, guns or money may be made available to another organisation as part of a package deal which might require one organisation to carry out acts of terror on behalf of another or provide safe-houses, guns and explosives for a hit-team from another country. The IRA refuses to carry out terrorist acts for other organisations. I am informed that in 1988 Gerry Adams went to Tehran to discuss the release of a Belfast man, Brian Keenan, who was being held in Beirut. While he was there IRA representatives attended a meeting with members of the Hezbollah in Beirut. The IRA delegation offered fake Irish passports in return for Keenan's release, which they estimated would give them a major propaganda coup. Although the Hezbollah regarded the offer of passports with derision, they were keen to seek an arrangement with the IRA, and Hezbollah representatives offered to release Keenan on condition that the IRA provided assistance to active service teams in Britain. A leading member of the Provisionals confirmed to me that such a meeting took place and that no agreement was reached because the IRA was not prepared to undertake operations for any other grouping, to be associated with their aim or to become involved in their operations by supplying weapons, safe-houses, or any kind of practical assistance. One can only speculate about the type of deal being offered by the Hezbollah and the outcome of such a liaison if agreement had ever been reached on joint operations. However, the IRA knows that such a partnership would damage the IRA's reputation in Ireland and annoy sympathisers in Britain and the United States.

I have been told that the crucial contacts were initially made with the Basque separatist movement ETA, which already had a well-established arms-supply route to the Middle East. A small grouping of 'conflict travellers' set up a significant range of contacts leading directly to the Middle East and to Algeria. It was through Algeria that the Provisionals established relations with both the PLO and, through them, Libya. The Basque connection was recognised by the Australian lecturer, Michael McKinley, in an essay in the book *Terrorism in Ireland* edited by Yonah Alexander and Alan O'Day. McKinley did not know how the contact was made, but he nevertheless dated it to 1972. However, like many observers he lapsed into a political analysis as if to indicate that the Basques and the IRA shared a common ideology, broadly based on a socialist thesis. The IRA contact with the Basques, like many others, was forged on the much simpler basis of convenience. It suited the IRA to take up an offer from the Basques for a dialogue to discover how they could assist the IRA, whom they regarded as political fellow travellers. The IRA, McKinley states, 'were reported' to have signed a political agreement with the Basques in 1972. There is no evidence that this occurred, and people close to the Provisionals at that time deny that any agreement was signed between the two organisations. McKinley, to his credit, recognises that there was a mutual understanding about weaponry, but he interprets this to mean that they 'reciprocated with firearms and technical [explosives] expertise'. He bases this upon claims made by Maria Maguire that Sean MacStiofan met leaders of ETA, who in exchange for explosives training of Basque terrorists by the IRA supplied the Provos with fifty revolvers.

As her book indicates, Maria Maguire was familiar with the use of speculation and hearsay. MacStiofan never made such a deal, according to those close to him. Since the Basques were nearer to the Middle East, they would not have required explosives training. It is conceivable that in the late 1970s the IRA and the Basques attempted to share their technical knowledge, though I suspect it would not have been necessary. Once the IRA established their Middle Eastern contacts they no longer required the Basques except for the movement of small quantities of weapons. Michael McKinley accepts that explosives and the technical knowledge needed for their use were both easily obtained, and that the IRA would not have been required to train ETA operatives on a continuing basis in the field of terrorism, as one observer claimed. He also agrees that after the early 1970s the relationship between the IRA and ETA was reduced to the exchanging of delegates to political conferences. However, the initial relationship was undoubtedly significant because it also led to contacts with other terrorist networks and sympathisers of terrorism in France, Germany and Holland.

By the summer of 1972 the IRA had negotiated a deal for a consignment of RPG 7 rocket launchers from Algeria, one of the PLO's backers. This had been organised with the assistance of the PLO and the small group of 'conflict travellers' who set up the Basque/Middle East connection for the Provos. While the RPG transportation was being arranged, a much more significant relationship was being formed between the Provisionals and the Libyan leader Mu'ammar al-Qadhafi (Gaddafy). Like the other Middle-Eastern relations, the Libyan contact was rooted in events of 1971, though it was eventually the PLO and Algerians who introduced the Provisionals to a man who saw their struggle as a nationalist revolution with an anti-colonialist dynamic. Qadhafi's admiration of the IRA was made public in a radio speech on 11 June 1972: 'At present we support the revolutionaries of Ireland who oppose Britain and are motivated by nationalism and religion. The Libyan Arab Republic has stood by the revolutionaries of Ireland their arms and their support for the revolutionaries of Ireland.'

This speech was made—contrary to subsequent reports, some of them believed to be from British intelligence sources—before any Provisionals formally met Qadhafi or his official representatives. It has been written that the Provos were in Tripoli in January or February 1972, whereas the Provos privately argue that they did not visit Tripoli until a formal trip had been organised. The arrangements were made in the Libyan Delegations Offices in Warsaw in August 1972. Joe Cahill, accompanied by a leading Provisional who has never been named, met senior Libyan officials who discussed how their President's support for the IRA could best be realised. The Provisionals bluntly conveyed their need for weapons and pointed out that their finances were low, since they had lost money on the O'Connell arms deal and had used much of their funds to buy arms in America and pistols from the Czechs, as well as supporting the families of a large number of men who were interned. The Libyans stressed that, if the Provisionals wished to be aided substantially, they would be obliged to visit Tripoli and convey their requests to the President. Having gone to Warsaw with a veritable weapons' shopping list, the Provos were disappointed but were prepared to proceed further with the Libyan connection.

It is now widely accepted that members of the Provisional IRA went to Libya at the end of August 1973 posing as schoolteachers. At that time legitimate advertisements were appearing in Irish papers seeking teachers of English for educational establishments in Libya. According to the freelance journalist Ed Moloney, two teachers, one from County Monaghan and the other from County Down, were interviewed for posts in Libya by members of a little-known society in Dublin. Moloney says a Libyan member of this society was told by the Libyan authorities to recruit these men in the knowledge that they were Provos. A third person who went to Libya on behalf of the Provos was recruited by the Libyan delegation in London. Some of those who left Ireland to teach in

Libya between 1972 and 1974 ended up teaching English to members of the Libyan Army. During the autumn of 1972 the Provos in Tripoli negotiated a large arms consignment and were also promised financial assistance. The Libyans, though prepared to provide weapons, made it clear that the IRA would be responsible for the transportation of the weaponry, which would include heavy machine-guns, AK47 assault rifles, submachine-guns, pistols, grenades, rocket launchers, warheads and ammunition. There would also be £2 million in cash.

In January 1973 Joe Cahill, who was known for his organising ability, travelled to Tripoli. Libyan intelligence provided him with advice on how to move the weapons by sea from Tripoli to Ireland. They recommended a contact: Günter Leinhauser, convicted in 1967 for trying to smuggle a large consignment of guns and explosives to Kurdish insurgents in Iraq. Leinhauser and his wife Marlene held a 90 per cent share in a German shipping company called Giromar. In Cyprus they registered a boat, the *Claudia*, for the purpose of transporting the Libyan 'gifts' to Ireland. Contrary to speculation, the *Claudia* was only ever loaded with one shipment of IRA weapons, and this took place at Tripoli docks.

In darkness, on the County Waterford coastline at Helvic Head on 28 March 1973, the Irish Navy boarded the *Claudia* and found five tons of weapons. Joe Cahill and five other men on board were arrested. At the time there was speculation that documents or possibly money had been dumped overboard. Subsequent reports also claimed that Qadhafi had paid millions into Irish bank accounts for the Provisionals. When writing this book I asked a member of the Provisional leadership about these reports. He told me that almost £2 million in cash was on board the *Claudia* and it was the only item which was worth saving and could be cleared away in time. He said that no one was later prepared to admit to this because it was deemed to be publicly acceptable to take weapons from anyone, but to allow so-called communists to finance an IRA campaign would have been thought shocking and, if made known, would have damaged the IRA profile. If the money was sealed in containers, dumped overboard and later recovered, that would explain how the IRA continued to wage its campaign through the mid- to late 1970s. £2 million would be worth ten times that amount today—which indicates the buying power that Qadhafi may well have given to the IRA. I see no reason to disbelieve this report considering its origin.

The capture of the *Claudia* could be attributed to several factors. The intelligence service which seems to know most about the episode is the Mossad, the Israeli service, and they privately admit that they tipped off the British, who had a minimal presence in Tripoli. The British, on the other hand, might have traced Joe Cahill's movements out of Ireland and been waiting for something to develop in the Middle East. Before the *Claudia* even reached Ireland, radio listeners in Tripoli would have been aware of the presence of IRA men in their midst because several Provos delivered anti-British broadcasts with a triumphal tone. There would have been no better way of signalling to the intelligence community, particularly the Mossad, that something was about to happen. At any rate the Mossad may well have known by then the nature of the IRA deal. The *Claudia* made considerable efforts to conceal its intended route by constantly retracking, but its eventual capture suggests that before it left Tripoli British intelligence, the Royal Navy and finally the Irish Navy were aware of its destination. One theory in IRA circles is that the Irish Navy stumbled on the ship, but that seems like wishful-thinking and is distinctly lacking in imagination, given all the intrigue that surrounded the arms deal.

The *Claudia* saga once again demonstrated to the IRA the futility of organising large shipments of arms over huge distances without proper planning. According to the IRA the *Claudia* deal was organised in a haphazard fashion, too many people knew about it, and Qadhafi's public pronouncement of support before the shipment left Tripoli turned the spotlight on Libya as an arms source. The failure of the operation provided the IRA with a lesson about their benefactor: his egotism knew no bounds, and he was not prepared to hide his support for them.

In twelve months following the capture of the *Claudia*, the IRA acquired small quantities of weapons in the Middle East which were shipped to Spain, sent overland to France and by boat to Ireland. During that period Qadhafi is rumoured to have offered them an opportunity to become involved in an import-export business by trading Irish goods to Libya, which imported the majority of its luxury goods. The IRA says this was not an offer which appeared on their agenda and they were 'too busy running a war to pose as businessmen'.

They did soon discover that the Libyan leader could be fickle and was easily disposed to revising his political views. In the summer of 1974 Loyalist paramilitary organisations aided by people on the fringes of the Unionist political parties organised what became known as the Ulster Workers' Council strike, a modern rebellion without much violence but with widespread intimidation. It led to the collapse of the power-sharing executive government in Northern Ireland and verged on a unilateral declaration of independence. For several weeks a Loyalist body, the Ulster Workers' Council, resembled a political cabinet and held the British government to ransom. The Chief of the General Staff told the British Prime Minister, Harold Wilson, that the British Army did not wish and was ill prepared to face workers on barricades. International media coverage of the UWC strike was based on the premise that it was a workers' strike. Qadhafi saw it as a workers' rebellion. He was impressed but also confused. Suddenly he was faced with a crisis of allegiance. The workers were Protestant and engaged in a form of revolution which in part equated to Qadhafi's political ethos but their message was not that of the IRA, which Libya supported. Further confusion reigned when Qadhafi's requested a meeting with the Loyalist paramilitary Ulster Defence Association, which policed the 'strike'. Believing they were, like the IRA, opposed to British imperialism, he felt they were entitled to his support. For its part the UDA wished to dissuade Qadhafi from helping the IRA. They also had a hidden agenda: they too needed weapons and they saw Libya as a potential supplier. The request for a meeting came from Libya through its London delegation and the auspices of a Unionist MP at Westminster. Qadhafi was later quoted as having viewed the 'strike' as a 'valid mechanism which reminded him of his own non-violent coup of September 1969'.

The UDA was invited to send a delegation to Tripoli on 1 November 1974 to participate in a seminar intended to find a solution to the problems of Ireland. However, that was not the publicly stated aim of the seminar: it was arranged in conjunction with the previously unheard-of Development of Irish Resources Organisation, which claimed to be politically non-aligned and to be interested simply in the development of Ireland's offshore oil and gas resources. Several days after the UDA delegation arrived in Tripoli, a group representing the Provisional IRA flew into the capital and booked into the same hotel as the UDA men. The situation proved farcical, and little was resolved in the talks which subsequently took place. However, the UDA returned home in November convinced that they had persuaded Qadhafi that the Provos were not freedom fighters and that the resolution to the problem lay along the political road to an independent Northern Ireland.

Many commentators believe that, from the arrival of the UDA in Tripoli, Qadhafi's relations with the IRA deteriorated until they were virtually non-existent. In December 1974 both the Libyan President and his Prime Minister, Major Abdul Jalloud, made private statements that their country's aid to the Provisonals had amounted to £5 million, a figure which included the £2 million in cash, the five tons of weapons on board the *Claudia*, the purchase of the vessel and payment for Leinhauser's services.

Qadhafi's association with the UDA resulted in a meeting in September 1975, when UDA delegates discussed with Libyan government representatives the prospect for Libyan financial involvement in an independent Northern Ireland. His brief flirtation with the UDA was embarrassing to the British and created the potential for further confusion and conflict. However, contrary to popular belief, Qadhafi did not lose admiration for the Provos but privately maintained contact with them, while being careful not to make the public pronouncements which were reminiscent of 1973 and the *Claudia* débâcle. In the mid- to late 1970s the Libyan government found itself under diplomatic pressure from the Irish government to desist from supporting the IRA. Qadhafi responded by indicating that his country had severed ties with the IRA. This was untrue. Qadhafi and the IRA knew the folly of organising large arms shipments from Libyan soil, so he was arranging contacts for the Provos with others in the Middle East who were willing to sell arms.

In 1979 a former paratrooper and member of the IRA, Peter McMullen, claimed that the Provos had received seven tons of weapons from Libya including surface-to-air missiles. He told a reporter that the major obstacle to the use of the missiles was the fact that the instructions which arrived with them were in Russian. McMullen was 'spinning a tale'. At the time he made this claim he had fled Ireland and was in an American prison cell contesting an extradition request from the British authorities. McMullen was known to be capable of telling marvellous tales, and this one was intended to convince people of his inside knowledge of the IRA, because the basis for his plea against extradition was that he had been a member of the IRA and was a political offender. He knew the American judiciary were not keen to extradite Irish political offenders, particularly members of the IRA, to Britain.

Qadhafi's contribution to the Provisionals was to find them sources of weapons which could not be traced to his country. The contacts were Palestinians based in three terrorist training camps in Libya. In 1976 Tripoli became a meeting place for the Provisionals and representatives of the PLO, who knew where to acquire a ready supply of weapons: Lebanon. It was to be a straightforward deal—Western currency in exchange for weapons and plastic explosives. The PLO had a surplus of arms and needed money, while the Provisionals required weapons and were prepared to pay with hard currency. Once again the Provisionals decided to attempt to buy a large quantity of guns and explosives at a cost of almost £400,000, but this time they devised an elaborate plan to ensure that few people knew of their intentions.

In April 1977 a company named Progress Electro was established, with offices in Dublin rented by a middle-aged man with a Liverpudlian accent calling himself Robert Kingsley. Unknown to the authorities he held a new Irish passport in the name of John O'Neill, but his real name was Seamus McCollum, and John O'Neill was a long-dead Dubliner. The offices of Progress Electro at Middle Abbey Street in Dublin's city centre were shabby, but were merely an address of convenience. Seamus McCollum (alias John O'Neill, alias Robert Kingsley) was a 'sleeper' whom the IRA had reactivated after a long period when he lived in Liverpool as a respectable member of society.

Although he had a Republican past, the IRA believed it was long forgotten. In 1954 he was caught ferrying explosives from Liverpool to London and was gaoled for five years. On his release he went back to Ireland, where the IRA border campaign was ending, but was interned at the Curragh camp. Eventually he returned to Liverpool, where he worked as a shipping clerk. He maintained contact with friends in the Republic but was not regarded as someone connected with the IRA. When the present campaign of violence began he made no effort to become involved in IRA activities or politics. According to associates, he was confused about the split which led to the creation of the Provisionals, but after events such as internment and 'Bloody Sunday' he became sympathetic to the Provos. Accordingly he offered his services to members of the Army Council who had known him during the 1950s campaign. They recognised that as a shipping clerk he could be valuable in helping with the smuggling of weapons. At first they encouraged him to maintain a low profile until they were ready to make use of his services. As one IRA man put it to me: 'Aside from a few services he provided, it was decided that he should remain clean until the moment when he was needed to perform the big one.'

In April 1977 Progress Electro purchased two large electrical transformers at a cost of £30,000. The transformers were then officially shipped to Limassol in Cyprus, where their innards were removed and replaced with over 700 lb of explosives (half of it plastic), mortars, assault rifles, grenades, rocket launchers, machine-guns, machine-pistols, ammunition and rocket-propelled grenades. This consignment of a considerable range of weaponry and explosives with deadly potential had been moved to Cyprus by the PLO and was handled at Limassol by members of the IRA who had spent several months in the city preparing for the operation. PLO contacts there helped them pack the consignment into the transformers, which were in turn loaded in crates marked 'defective'.

The plan was devised by the former shipping clerk and overseen at every stage by Seamus Twoomey, McCollum's main IRA contact. The transformers were to be shipped back to Ireland in the belief that customs would recognise the returning machines and not search them because they had been examined on their outward journey. A glance at them would not have revealed anything untoward, though McCollum and Twoomey expected customs simply to accept that they were being returned because they were mechanically defective—a scenario with which customs officers were familiar and which would not arouse their suspicions.

At Limassol the crates were officially loaded on the British cargo ship *Tower Stream* for a journey to Antwerp, to be transferred to another vessel for a subsequent trip to Dublin. *Tower Stream* travelled via Haifa, London and Rotterdam to Antwerp, where the ship was boarded on the pretext that the manifest appeared to be incorrect in respect of part of the cargo. Customs officers opened the crates containing the transformers labelled as cargo on its way to Progress Electro in Dublin. It was clear that the customs officers knew exactly what they were doing; there was nothing wrong with the ship's documents. No one, not even the IRA, knows how the operation was discovered. It could have been caused by a suspicious member of the ship's crew, someone in the arms-dealing chain, or a brilliant piece of surveillance. The breakdown may have occurred in Ireland. After the cargo was seized, McCollum was arrested and Twoomey, a member of the IRA Army Council, was also caught. It is believed that the arrest of Twoomey resulted from surveillance placed on McCollum as soon as the cargo of guns and explosives was discovered.

The arms were seized in December, but in January 1978 the IRA showed that there were always other sources of weaponry. The M60 machine-gun appeared on the streets of Belfast and demonstrated its deadly firepower. The tabloid media assumed the M60 was part of another Middle-Eastern consignment. In fact a batch of M60s had been smuggled from the United States the previous year. This not only illustrated the difficulty of closing down all the sources of weapons and smuggling routes but also proved that the IRA was always exploiting all the options. From 1977 until the mid-1980s the IRA's arms-smuggling reverted to a steady stream of guns, ammunition and explosives bought mostly in the Middle East and ferried into Ireland in small quantities in cars, cargo lorries or ships. This form of smuggling has proved the most difficult to detect because of the range of options open to the IRA and the volume of traffic on land and sea which cannot all be searched.

However, the objective of smuggling a large shipment of guns and explosives remained paramount, despite the failure of the *Claudia* deal and what became known as Operation Antwerp. A large consignment would provide a range of terrorist weaponry not available in the small batches reaching Irish shores. The IRA always dreamed of having a large quantity of assault rifles, mortars, plastic explosives—and, above all, Sam or Stinger surface-to-air missiles, which they judged would change the character of the war. Since the IRA reckoned that they had already made it too difficult for troops to operate in parts of Armagh without helicopter support, surface-to-air missiles would make it impossible for them to operate there. In areas of Belfast and other major centres, the British Army would be deprived of its spy planes and helicopters with their sophisticated electronic and photographic gear.

In the early 1980s the Provisionals looked to America for the big shipment, and they almost got what they wanted. In fact they bought a massive quantity of weapons, explosives and ammunition, shipped it across
the Atlantic and transferred the cargo from the 'mother' ship to the
Marita Ann, a cargo vessel, off the Kerry coast. An Irish Navy vessel was
in the vicinity and the cargo was seized. The name of the 'mother' ship
was never revealed. The Provisionals initially attributed the failure of the
operation to a high-placed informer in their ranks. There was media speculation that the 'mother' ship had been tracked by satellite or by a British
submarine across the Atlantic and that the Irish Navy was informed after
the IRA cargo had been transferred to the *Marita Ann.* The IRA now privately admit that the story was not elaborate and that the Irish Navy
stumbled on the arms-smuggling operation as it drew to a close. Again
this escapade illustrated the resilience of the Provos and the fact that
their efforts never ceased but were unlikely ever to succeed when the
plan involved moving shipments across oceans.

Yet their persistence did pay off, because Mu'ammar al-Qadhafi came
to their aid, as did Iran, which adopted a similar attitude to Britain as
Libya. Both countries became violently anti-British as American foreign
policy under Ronald Reagan found an admiring ally in Margaret
Thatcher. The Provisionals exploited the anti-British feeling sweeping
the Middle East to mount a major arms-smuggling operation which succeeded in bringing into Ireland the largest collection of assault rifles and
plastic explosives ever assembled by the IRA. No one in the Provisional
movement will talk about it, though I was told that, despite press specu-
lations that there were three shipments, there was in fact only one, but it
was bigger than all the others which failed.

In 1987 the MV *Eksund,* which was bought and registered in Sweden,
was boarded in French waters and her crew were arrested. The *Eksund*
was found to contain a massive quantity of weapons and explosives. Her
captain and crew were from the Irish Republic, and the vessel had come
from Lebanon. The arms seizure was regarded as a major coup until it
was realised that a previous shipment of similar dimensions had got
through to the Provos. That shipment brought the Czech-made explosive
Semtex into IRA hands. The one weapon which the IRA did not acquire
was the surface-to-air missile. Its absence from the large arms shipment
is difficult to understand. The only reasonable explanation is that in
1988-9 the IRA were developing the technology to produce a surface-to-
air missile capable of evading the anti-missile devices on British Army
helicopters. Those devices were designed to eliminate the threat of
Stinger and Sam surface-to-air missiles which British intelligence knew
were in the hands of groups such as the PLO.

What was not known when the *Eksund* was seized was that a quantity of Semtex explosives had been off-loaded from the ship off the Spanish coastline. It was transferred to a smaller vessel, which took the Semtex to Puerto Banus, and it was this consignment which was later intended for use in Gibraltar. The *Eksund* was equipped with several small landing craft for unloading the cargo once the vessel reached the Irish coastline. The discovery of the *Eksund* produced a flurry of stories suggesting satellite surveillance, submarine surveillance and the use of a French reconnaissance plane to track the ship. No one may ever know the means by which the IRA operation was uncovered. Perhaps the ship was simply spotted unloading the explosives off the Spanish coast. On the other hand it may have been the result of an intricate intelligence operation. Sending the *Eksund* to one of the most dangerous and constantly scrutinised parts of the world was a risk the IRA was prepared to take. One major shipment evaded the intelligence watchers of the major Western nations, with their spies, satellites and eavesdropping equipment; maybe the second one fell foul of the intelligence traps. Neither the IRA nor the intelligence community will betray its secrets in a war where bluff and double bluff play such a part.

The IRA have the money and the resilience; and while they have the support of states such as Algeria, Libya and Iran, as well as the assistance of Palestinian terrorists, weapons and explosives will continue to reach Ireland. They may arrive constantly in small quantities, but there is always the risk that the IRA will get the 'big one'. As an IRA leader put it to me:

We are not daunted by failure. We will try and try and sooner or later the 'big one' gets through. We know what we are up against. There isn't an intelligence service that doesn't have someone in the Middle East and everything we do there has the potential for failure. Equally, while they are looking at someone else, we can escape the net. There are also many options.

The option which the British security services know they need to prevent is the one which could offer the IRA access to surface-to-air missiles.

17

Killing for Profit
Criminal Alliances and Terrorism

T he one area of the dirty war which the paramilitaries on both sides are reluctant to discuss, even with the few journalists in whom they often confide, is racketeering, which I dealt with briefly in the previous chapter. The reason for this reticence is that the rackets brought together sworn enemies who convinced their own supporters that they were constantly at war while they secretly engaged in a bizarre dialogue, unknown to the general public and to the most ardent supporters of terrorism.

Money brought groups of terrorists from both sides to a secret conference where they carved up parts of Northern Ireland, designating areas within which individual terrorist groups would operate criminal enterprises without interference from terrorists from the other community. Loyalists and Republicans entered into a joint arrangement which guaranteed protection of each other's criminal pursuits and made it possible for each side to raise enough money to purchase arms for the continuance of the war and the deaths of over 2000 innocent people. Central to this collusion was an agreement that the leaders of the terrorist organisations and rackets on both sides would not be targeted for assassination. That did not preclude the killing of civilians or members of the security forces. This agreement, which guaranteed the safety of those in both camps who were ordering the deaths of so many other people, persisted for many years.

Contrary to popular opinion, media coverage and black propaganda emanating from official sources, the genesis for this part of the dirty war rests in contacts which were established in the early to mid-1970s between Loyalists and members of the supposedly defunct Official IRA and not between Loyalists and the Provisional IRA. The contacts between Official IRA men and Loyalists took place at a time when the Workers' Party, which owes it origins to the Official IRA, was claiming that the IRA was no longer in existence and its ethos firmly consigned to the past. In fact some members of the Official IRA had established contact with people within the Loyalist community from the late 1960s and retained those relationships despite the communal violence which from 1969 separated the communities and drove many people into the paramilitary organisations. It was on the basis of the early social contacts and relations formed in prison in the early 1970s that criminal associations were subsequently developed. From the outset there was less enmity between members of the Official IRA and certain Loyalists than between most Loyalists and the emerging Provisional IRA, which appeared to be at the forefront of the tribal conflict. The initial collusion between Loyalists and Republicans was centred in West Belfast, where the communities lived in close proximity, and involved members of the Ulster Defence Association and the Official IRA. It resulted in the massive building-site fraud and extortion of monies from the business community, as described in the previous chapter. The Provisionals entered this phase of the dirty war at a later stage, but it was not they who devised it, though there is evidence to suggest that they refined it. Those members of the Official IRA who shaped a racketeering strategy changed their ideological allegiance within a few years and joined the Irish National Liberation Army, which assumed much of the control of the rackets and the contact with Loyalists. This Loyalist-Republican connection provides a fascinating insight into the way in which certain terrorists were prepared to put aside their mutual enmity in pursuit of profit. Although the profits from the rackets enabled the paramilitaries to purchase arms, pay their volunteers and support the families of prisoners, it also enabled the UDA leader, James Craig, to lead a 'champagne lifestyle' and take his bodyguards and enforcers on continental holidays.

Craig masterminded the criminal enterprises in Loyalist West Belfast. He was one of those Loyalists who was on speaking terms with members of the Official IRA before 1969 and later strengthened his relations with them when he found himself in prison for criminal offences in the early 1970s. He possessed a well-developed criminal mind and realised the potential for exploiting the lawlessness of the province by entering into an alliance with Republicans on the basis of the one thing they had in common: a lack of financial resources to fight an ongoing war. Craig also saw the advantage of developing a criminal strategy in a society where the forces of law and order were much too preocccupied with terrorism to worry about extortion and fraud. He had little difficulty in convincing several members of the Official IRA that there was much to be mutually gained from co-operation between Republican and Loyalist groups to create a criminal monopoly. As a practised criminal he perceived an opportunity to use the firepower of paramilitaries on both sides to close down the regular criminal element and create a monopoly for the UDA and the IRA.

On the Republican side there was a central figure who dealt with Craig and devised the tax-exemption fraud which was applied to building sites. Since this man has never been charged with any offence in connection with racketeering, for legal reasons I shall refer to him as Mr X. It was Mr X who had provided Craig with much-needed advice at the outset of his unholy alliance, and it was also Mr X who made use of a Belfast accountant to operate the tax-exemption fraud. The accountant fled to Dublin in the late 1970s when the RUC began to suspect his involvement, and he still resides in Dublin. Mr X also operated out of a bar close to the Markets area in Belfast city centre where he dispensed tax-exemption certificates. He visited building sites which were under the control of the Officials and later the INLA and was accompanied by a known terrorist who operated as his enforcer. I am not in a position to name the enforcer for legal reasons.

While the racketeers on both sides met to discuss their criminal enterprises, they were also obliged to meet when any terrorist action threatened to jeopardise their collusion—such as the murder or attempted murder of someone known to the racketeers or of a member of either organisation. On one occasion a Republican was shot by Loyalists in Belfast city centre. The victim was a member of the Official IRA, who immediately protested to James Craig. He had authorised the shooting in the belief that the victim was in the ranks of the Provisionals, having decided this on the basis of an RUC intelligence document which had been passed to the UDA by a disaffected policeman. Craig apologised to the Officials, explained that the shooting was a mistake, and promised that such an event would not occur again. However, he did not admit that he personally gave the orders for the killing or that he was in possession of a security forces intelligence document. The Official IRA was not satisfied with his apology or explanation and demanded a meeting at which both sides could discuss the implications of the shooting and ways of preventing a recurrence of such a mistake. Mr X told Craig that the Official IRA would not stand idly by and watch its members being assassinated and the incident could lead to an ending of their joint criminal ventures. Recognising that the cosy relationship with the IRA could be jeopardised, Craig agreed to a meeting to resolve any differences and to emphasise his regret at the shooting. Both organisations arranged to send delegates to a meeting in the Royal Bar in Ann Street in Belfast city centre. Craig and Mr X ensured that UDA and Official IRA volunteers would be placed strategically in the Ann Street vicinity so that if the meeting was discovered by the security forces the volunteers would create a diversion to allow the delegates to reach safety in their respective ghettos.

The meeting was attended by Craig with four UDA officers and Mr X with four members of the Official IRA. Prominent in the Craig grouping was 'Bucky' McCullough, who was to figure tragically in later events in Craig's life. Among the Republican delegation was a man with a patch over one eye, 'Dimple' Vallely (who has since died). Mr X and Craig did most of the talking. All of those present on the Republican side joined the INLA a short time later and removed the rackets from the control of the Official IRA. This meeting, however, was conducted over drinks in a calm atmosphere, and any differences which were apparent were quickly resolved and discussion centred on business ventures. To anyone watching from a distance, the Republican/Loyalist gathering could well have resembled a group of friends having a night on the town or builders discussing the merits of various enterprises. While this was going on people were being killed in Belfast.

That meeting was crucial in the development of the relationship between all those present. Its significance was later evaluated by the UDA's military wing, the Ulster Freedom Fighters, when they conducted a secret inquiry into the activities of Jimmy Craig. The following extract from their report stresses the significance of the Royal Bar get-together:

This was the start of a liaison which was to bring about racketeering, extortion and collusion leading to the deaths of leading Loyalists. The people involved in this and subsequent meetings became so confident that they invited each other to pubs and clubs in their respective areas. The Republicans drank in such places as the Loyalist Club, Royal Bar and Top House Bar. Loyalists in turn drank and visited such places as the Lagan Social Club in the Markets area, the Trocadero and the Manhattan Bar. All of this took place with the knowledge and permission of — [for legal reasons the author has been obliged to remove the name of a UDA leader].

While racketeering flourished, the war on the streets continued and the general public remained ignorant of the fact that some of those men who were ordering the deaths of innocent people on both sides of the tribal divide were also meeting together for drinks and meals in selected pubs and clubs. Meetings became a means not only of resolving disputes about which grouping should control a particular geographical area or building site but also of finding ways of helping each other as partners in crime. When bricklayers were required on a site controlled by Craig, for instance, the Republican delegates offered to 'bus in' bricklayers so that a particular site could be completed in a legally stipulated time, thus avoiding any penalty payments to the builder or contractor. Meanwhile many of these men left cosy meetings with their sworn enemies and ordered the deaths of soldiers, policemen, UDA men or innocent Catholics.

Not everything went smoothly with Craig's operations, partly because 'Bucky' McCullough became disillusioned with him. McCullough was not averse to using monies from the rackets to further the aims of the UDA and to purchase weapons for its military wing, the UFF, but he was opposed to the use of money for personal gain. McCullough began to suspect that Craig was taking a percentage of racketeering funds for himself, but he was frightened to confront Craig because he was so powerful and ruthless. When Craig was remanded in custody to Crumlin Road prison on extortion charges, however, McCullough had the opportunity to discover the extent to which Craig was milking the organisation's fund. He examined the UDA files on the organisation's finances in West Belfast and uncovered an internal fraud by his boss. McCullough was not discreet about his discovery and UDA men loyal to Craig informed him that 'Bucky' McCullough was demanding an internal inquiry into the misuse of UDA funds. Craig decided that his lieutenant, 'Bucky', was a serious threat to his personal ambitions and had to be removed from this world. However, it was not an easy killing to arrange and Craig knew an accusing finger would be pointed at him if it was carried out by a member of the UDA. The perfect solution lay in using his INLA contacts, particularly those who were originally members of the Official IRA and were at the Royal Bar meeting. Members of the INLA would readily kill a member of a Loyalist paramilitary organisation, unlike the Official IRA, which by this stage appeared to be defunct and at the very least had ceased hostilities against all terror organisations except the Provisionals. Craig let it be known to his INLA contacts that McCullough was deeply involved in sectarian assassinations. From all accounts McCullough did not have a history as a hit-man, but the INLA were prepared to believe Craig and to use his help in the forming of intelligence about McCullough's lifestyle and whereabouts. The INLA sent a hit-team to McCullough's home in the heart of the Shankill and shot him dead. His demise ensured that Craig did not face charges of swindling UDA funds. Henceforth Craig was determined that no one would get too close to his operations. He also established himself as undisputed UDA commander of West Belfast by cleverly engineering the departure of a man who had been the commander in that area of the city for several years.

Jimmy Craig felt secure in the knowledge that he was in overall command of the UDA in the most powerful base in the city and that the Official IRA and INLA would not order his assasination, but he also recognised that the greatest risk to his life could come from the Provisional IRA. He knew that given the slightest opportunity the Provisionals would send a hit-squad into the Shankill to kill him. Forever the opportunist and unscrupulous enough to consider any action which would guarantee his personal safety, Craig decided that he had to do a deal with the Provos. Meanwhile he was willing to co-operate with the RUC by offering them information to keep himself out of prison, as well as colluding with military intelligence, and with anyone who had the power to threaten his lifestyle or weaken his dominance of Protestant West Belfast. He reckoned, however, that to obtain an assurance from the Provisionals that he would not be at the top of their hit-list he had to offer them something they needed badly. Initially he offered to discuss changes in the criminal boundaries within Belfast that would enable all paramilitary organisations to obtain a reasonable share of the loot from racketeering; but the Provisionals were capable of creating and maintaining their own rackets and money-making schemes without relying on Craig. All they wanted from him was information on Loyalists, both members of the UDA and those of the outlawed UVF. Craig was willing to offer them the intelligence they required to target particular people.

In May 1982 the leader of the infamous Shankill Butchers gang, Lenny Murphy, was released from prison and began an orgy of killing. He was high on the Provisional IRA hit-list and they demanded that Craig provide them with the intelligence necessary for a hit-squad to stalk Murphy and kill him. Craig detested Murphy: his killing sprees brought too much police attention into the Shankill area, and this threatened Craig's criminal activities. Murphy in turn was not frightened by Craig's reputation and was prepared to set himself up in criminal pursuits which compromised Craig's operations. The UVF leadership was terrified of having to cope with Murphy and at least one member of the UVF leadership was resigned to the fact that Murphy should be assassinated. Craig therefore agreed to help the Provos but insisted that the killing could prove difficult because Murphy knew he was wanted by the IRA, was careful never to leave the safety of the Shankill and its peripheral areas, and confined knowledge of his movements to a few people, one of whom was his girlfriend. In my book *The Shankill Butchers* I wrote that I believed the Provisionals to be responsible for his assassination and I also named Craig, but I was unaware of the extent of Craig's involvement in Murphy's death in November 1982. In fact Craig used two of his lieutenants to track Murphy over a period of weeks to establish whether there was a pattern to his behaviour that would leave him exposed to an assassination attempt. They discovered that his routine was erratic but that the one constant factor in his life was his daily visit to his girlfriend, Hilary Thompson, who lived in the Glencairn housing estate, a Loyalist enclave a short distance from his family home at Brookmount Street on the Shankill Road. Craig learned that he often spent the night in the Glencairn house but was certain to visit the premises at least once a day. This information convinced IRA intelligence that there was a discernible pattern to Murphy's behaviour which left him vulnerable. However, the problem facing the IRA was how to be in the right place at the right time to shoot the 'master Butcher', as he was known to the tabloid media. Although Glencairn offered the best opportunity to kill their quarry, it also posed serious risks for a hit-squad. They would have to be present at or near Murphy's girlfriend's house at the moment he decided to call on her, and after the killing they would need a secure escape route. The IRA assessed the risks as follows:

We were faced with the problem that if we sent a hit-team into Glencairn they would be obliged to lie in wait in a car or van. Sitting in an area where strangers immediately come under suspicion was too big a risk. A hit-team would have to be there for some time and then there was the risk that they could be wiped out by the UVF or disgruntled Loyalists.

The IRA have never revealed the details of how they killed the leader of the Butchers or the part played by James Craig. In researching the rackets and the collusion which existed between Loyalists and Republicans I came across two pieces of evidence which independently confirm the way in which Craig helped the Provisionals to kill Lenny Murphy. The UFF conducted a private inquiry into allegations that Craig was central to the IRA plan which resulted in Murphy's death. In quoting what the UFF put into print I am obliged for legal reasons to replace some names with blank spaces:

The people who know about Murphy's death have no doubt who set him up. Craig and — set him up on —'s instructions using —, a Ligoniel Protestant married to a Catholic, as the contact man. Craig provided the damning evidence by telling a number of people of his part in the killing of Murphy. Craig conned people in Glencairn into showing him where Murphy parked his car.

The UFF report also contained a claim that the 9mm sub-machine-gun used in the killing was found buried in the Glencairn area in 1987. This is what I wrote about Murphy's death in *The Shankill Butchers*:

At 6.40 pm on 16 November, Murphy drove to the Glencairn housing estate and made his way to Forthriver Park, oblivious of the fact that a blue Morris Marina van was trailing him, keeping a safe distance and travelling at a steady speed. As Murphy parked at the rear of Hilary Thompson's house and turned off the engine [of his Rover car], the blue van turned slightly, with its rear facing the Rover. Suddenly the back doors of the van were thrown open and two gunmen emerged, one armed with a 9mm sub-machine-gun and the other with a .38 Special revolver. They opened fire on Murphy who, unaware of their presence, was about to open the door of his car. He was hit by twenty-six bullets in the head and body and died instantly....

The blue van used by the 'hit squad' was hired weeks earlier in the Braniel area of predominantly Protestant East Belfast. When the killers fled, the van was found burning at Forthriver and Harmony Hill, strategically placed to block anyone pursuing the gunmen. A car which was used to spirit away the gunmen into the nationalist enclave of Ligoniel was also found the same day.

I also referred to a piece of detail which puzzled police at the time: 'Close to Murphy's girlfriend's house was a gap in a hedge leading to a field, a shortcut known only to locals. Through the gap in the hedge, police found masks and gloves which they believe were used by the gunmen'. I know now that the masks and gloves were dropped by people who were supporting the Provo hit-team. Those people were Craig's men, and they also removed the weapons which fired the fatal shots so that the IRA gunmen could leave the area unarmed and if stopped by a security forces' patrol would not be in possession of incriminating evidence. Since the sub-machine-gun was an unusual design and would not have been easy to conceal or use again, Craig ordered it to be buried. The .38 revolver was never found, but I am told that Craig liked it and knew that it would not arouse notice, whereas the sub-machine-gun was of a type not used by Loyalists and would attract too much attention. The UFF investigators also traced the member of Craig's gang who burned the killer's blue van to enable them to make their escape. Their report claims that the UFF found letters which were exchanged between a Republican based in Ligoniel and a member of Craig's gang and which bore testimony to the planning by Craig and the IRA before the hit-squad made its final move against Murphy. None the less the UFF were left with a doubt about Murphy's death and they speculated that the men who killed Murphy could have been members of Craig's group who created an impression of IRA involvement to disguise Craig's participation. However, a source very close to the IRA confirmed to me that not only did an IRA team carry out the killing but they stayed in Glencairn overnight in a house owned by a person who was friendly with Craig. The source told me the following:

Craig and the Provos knew that, to hit Murphy and get out, the hit-team needed to be based in a safe-house in Glencairn. Firstly the IRA hit-men were moved from West

Belfast, where they were normally based, to Ligoniel close to Glencairn. Everything was set in motion as far as planning was concerned. The IRA didn't trust Craig and so they reached an agreement that when the time came for the hit-men to move into Glencairn to do the killing they would be obliged to remain there for at least twenty-four hours to give them a fair chance of hitting Murphy. The IRA insisted that during that crucial twenty-four hours Craig provided hostages—the same number of his men who would be held by the IRA so that in the event of the IRA team being compromised, the hostages would be wiped out and so would Jimmy Craig at a later date. It was also Craig's people who hired the van, and got rid of the gloves, masks and guns.

It was also around 1982 that Craig received phone calls to UDA headquarters on the Shankill Road from a mysterious person who always identified himself as Joe. When Craig was asked about this person he remarked that he was a prison warder whom he met while serving a sentence in Crumlin Road prison and that he was very kind and helpful. According to the UFF, Joe was a member of the Provisional IRA from Unity Flats and was Craig's IRA contact. The UFF identified Joe, and that is his Christian name, but for legal reasons I am unable to include his surname. They claim that, when a UDA officer was sent to meet Joe to deliver a cryptic message from Craig, the UDA man recognised Joe as a known Provisional.

Joe's contact with Craig led to one of the most bizarre arrangements between Craig and the IRA. Joe told Craig that the IRA needed assistance in planning the murder of Republican supergrasses who were being held in a specially constructed unit in Crumlin Road prison. The IRA were aware that Lenny Murphy had been able to poison an accomplice in Crumlin Road prison in 1973 and that Loyalist paramilitaries had several prison warders under their control. Joe explained that the IRA wanted Craig to coerce someone into gaining access to the supergrass wing or to their food. The IRA would provide poison which could be administered directly with force (as Murphy had done) or in their meals, since they had acquired a deadly substance which could be placed in food or water without discolouring the contents. Joe handed over the poison to one of Craig's men. The UFF admit that the UDA officer who was given the poison was arrested after receiving it and was held for questioning in Castlereagh Holding Centre. The poisonous substance was removed from him and he was released from police custody after several days without charge. According to the IRA, Craig deliberately sabotaged the operation at an early stage by informing the RUC. This ensured that the plot could not be attempted again and removed Craig from an obligation which would have had dangerous consequences for him. If the supergrasses had been murdered, Loyalist collusion would have been suspected. Craig, say the IRA, was shrewd and unwilling to take the risk. By informing the RUC of the plot he was doing himself a favour with his police contacts.

Part of this bargain with them was that the UDA officer who was caught with the poison be released after questioning. Craig ended the IRA plot very cleverly and successfully turned it to his advantage.

According to the UFF, Joe telephoned Craig after Gerry Adams was shot by a Loyalist hit-squad in March 1984 as he drove through Belfast city centre:

Meetings with Joe were only attended by Craig or — of the UDA. They were held in the Capstan, Royal and King Arthur bars in Belfast city centre. The IRA contacted Craig after Gerry Adams was shot and asked him what was going on and what about the agreement regarding top men. It is believed that Joe made the call. Craig was stupid to tell other people about the call. (Witness available)

The shooting of Adams was indeed a breach of a longstanding agreement that Republican and Loyalist leaders would be left off hit-lists. Craig was worried not only about this development but about a plan to kill Mr X of the INLA. The UDA leadership considered Mr X a legitimate target, and it was only Craig's intervention that prevented him being assassinated. Craig had profit in mind, but he convinced the UDA's ruling body that Mr X was providing him with useful intelligence on Republicans. However, Craig's luck was beginning to run out, because one man in the UDA leadership believed that Craig was lining his own pockets. That man was John McMichael, who aside from being a prominent political figure in the UDA was also a brigadier in the UDA's illegal military wing, the UFF. McMichael received a report from a UDA officer in West Belfast that Craig was regularly meeting his IRA contact, Joe from Unity Flats, and that Craig was 'divulging all the information to Joe and getting nothing in return'. However, according to some sources, Craig tried to get himself out of trouble by providing McMichael and the UFF with information on the INLA which could not be traced back to him. It was not enough. According to a UFF report, the Provisionals asked for a top-level meeting with the UDA leadership after the attempted murder of Gerry Adams, but this was rejected out of hand by John McMichael, who ordered Craig to abandon his contacts with Republicans. Craig ignored McMichael's orders and continued to meet members of the Provisional IRA, INLA and a breakaway faction from the INLA known as the IPLO, the Irish People's Liberation Army.

There were other people similarly interested in Craig, namely those in the intelligence community such as Special Branch and military intelligence, who were particularly keen to identify his contacts and to unravel the complex web of criminal activity which was at the root of racketeering. They placed surveillance on him, photographed and video-recorded his movements and his meetings with Republicans. This work was carried out by members of the elite E4A department of the RUC assisted by technical experts from MI5. One of the video recordings of conversations which Craig conducted in city centre bars later found its way into the hands of the UFF. It showed Craig at a meeting in the Capstan Bar in the Cornmarket area of Belfast and alongside him a member of the IRA's Northern Command. The possession of that video was an indication of the contacts the UFF had within the RUC. Such an important piece of intelligence should never have been allowed to fall into the hands of terrorists. It is worth noting that the videotape was acquired in 1988, eighteen months before major revelations about the UFF's possession of photographic documents on IRA suspects.

Before the video was received by the UFF, John McMichael was murdered by the IRA. A bomb placed under his car exploded while he was sitting behind the driving wheel of the vehicle outside his home in Lisburn in December 1987. Prior to his murder he had confronted Craig about racketeering and his contacts with Republicans. After McMichael's death there was widespread media speculation that the UDA were conducting an inquiry into McMichael's murder to establish whether there was Republican/Loyalist collusion in the killing. There was no such inquiry, but there was a change of leadership within the UDA in March 1988, when certain people in the organisation began looking in the direction of Jimmy Craig. The report of a subsequent inquiry conducted by both the UDA and the UFF makes for interesting reading, but as with all such documents I am obliged to omit names and addresses for both legal and ethical reasons:

Despite McMichael's warning, Craig continued to meet PIRA/INLA/IPLO people. Although the row before Christmas 1987 probably hastened McMichael's death it in itself did not bring it about. McMichael had confided in close colleagues that he knew that Craig had warned the Provisional IRA that — — was a UFF target. McMichael had also told UFF intelligence to drop information that Craig could pick up —, the idea being to watch for the information coming back. There is no doubt that — — and — —, both members of PIRA, were warned about the UFF targeting them. Last but not least, McMichael had reopened the issue of alleged UDA/PIRA collusion in Lenny Murphy's murder. Within two days of John McMichael's murder, sources close to senior UDA officers indicated Loyalist involvement. Rumour became rife, not least because his office in UDA HQ in Gawn Street in East Belfast was ransacked and orders issued that the office should be locked and no one allowed admittance.

Inner Council members who were not happy about the affair decided to make their own enquiries. For obvious reasons these early enquiries had to be very discreet but after leadership changes in March 1988 things began to come together. The breakthrough came in the summer when a member of the UDA Inner Council was contacted by some UDA people in England who claimed to have some information about McMichael's death. A meeting was arranged in England at which it soon became clear that what was being said there came from Northern Ireland sources using the English UDA people as a means of relaying vital information about McMichael's death.

By this stage it had been established that Craig had supplied the colour, make and number of McMichael's car as well as information on a place (not his home) where it would be parked for a certain period. It was decided to watch Craig as closely as possible not because we did not believe what we were told but because we wished to catch him out ourselves. Within limits Craig had been under almost constant surveillance since Christmas. The results of this surveillance make interesting reading. All of Craig's taxi journeys were monitored and the drivers questioned. The areas he was dropped off include the Central Information Agency in Ormeau Avenue and Apollo Road off Boucher Road as meeting places with Provisional IRA people. He nearly always used taxis for these journeys, getting out of the taxis to sit in other cars, telling the taxi drivers to wait for him as he was collecting money from builders. A short piece in the 'Who' column of the *Sunday World* newspaper asking how a leading Shankill Road Loyalist was able to walk freely about the Unity Flats complex came as no surprise to our investigators. They had twice observed Craig going into the Flats, meeting a girl and being taken to two separate addresses.

In February of 1988 Craig was in a car stopped by a Security Forces patrol in Dunmurry. The other occupant was ——, a top Provo Craig met in Crumlin Road jail. [Author's note: If this is true, the incident in Dunmurry could shed light on the fact that it was from Dunmurry police station in September 1989 that the UFF acquired documents relating to suspected members of the IRA. The person named with Craig was and remains a member of the IRA's Belfast Brigade and is a leading activist.] The Provo is the boyfriend of another leading Provo, —— of —, Glen Road (telephone number —). Craig was also observed meeting —— of Moira Street in the Short Strand area who had Provo form. Probably his last act of treachery was to tell leading Markets Provo, — (last known address 77 — —), that a Protestant builder was carrying out work for the Security Forces up the country. Craig had fallen out with the builder after he had refused to pay him for a site at Templepatrick. [Author's note: Templepatrick is an area about ten miles from Belfast and this is an indication that Craig did not limit his operations to West Belfast.] The Provo, —, let this slip to a source friendly to the UDA and Craig's meeting with the Provo was observed and a warning was passed to the builder.

The UDA and UFF were not simply interested in McMichael's death; they and the UVF were concerned that there was an informer in Loyalist circles who had set up other Loyalist leaders for assassination, and they needed to know whether it was Jimmy Craig. The Provisionals had killed not only Murphy but also UVF officers such as John Bingham, William 'Frenchie' Marchant, George Seawright (a firebrand Scots preacher who hated Catholics) and Fred Otley. IRA and IPLO hit-squads had shot each of these men in the heart of the Loyalist stronghold of Shankill. The UFF investigation into these shootings was inconclusive and produced only circumstantial evidence, though IRA sources privately point the finger at Craig. In the secret report the UFF made the following observations:

Although there is nothing to link Craig with the death of John Bingham, coincidence is stretched to the limit regarding the deaths of Frenchie Marchant, George Seawright and Fred Otley. On the day of Marchant's death Craig had arranged to meet him. Instead of Craig getting out of the car outside the Eagle to meet Frenchie, he got out outside the Inter-City furniture shop at the corner of Conway Street and stood talking for five minutes. Inside that five minutes Marchant was murdered fifty yards away.

On the day George Seawright was murdered, Craig brought two other UDA men to a meeting on Shankill Leisure Centre car park. While they were sitting in the car park, Seawright was shot fifty yards away. Fred Otley was shot in the shop at the corner of Agnes Street and Shankill Road and Craig was sitting twenty yards away in Mikhala's café. Others can be the judge of whether these three incidents were a coincidence.

What the UFF did not know was that a week before his death George Seawright met a member of the IPLO in the Europa Hotel in Belfast. According to a journalistic source, Seawright requested the meeting to discuss his personal safety and to ask that he be removed from the IPLO's list of assassination priorities. The source is of the opinion that Seawright was afraid for his life because of the manner in which Bingham and Marchant had been so easily murdered. One journalist was told by the IPLO that Seawright was willing to trade information for an assurance that he would not be on their hit-list. Since that was a ploy used by Jimmy Craig, one might speculate that Craig was instrumental in per-suading Seawright to meet with a Republican paramilitary. I am informed that one week after this meeting George Seawright was shot dead and the IPLO cynically referred to his death as a 'popular hit'.

Craig was no stranger to the Europa Hotel. According to UFF docu-ments, he attended a meeting there with Mr X of the INLA, his enforcer and a member of the INLA Brigade Staff. The UFF say that the meeting was called by the INLA to ask Craig to explain why one of their members had been shot on the Cliftonville Road in North Belfast, which was with-in Craig's territory. According to the UFF, two senior UDA officers from West Belfast attended the meeting as observers after other top-ranking officers declined invitations to be present. An internal UFF report on the matter made the following points:

The two West Belfast officers were disgusted at what went on. The INLA delegation said at the end of the meeting that they were satisfied that Craig had nothing to do with the shooting but they then put forward the names of two UVF men and said they were responsible. It must be stressed that Craig was alone with the INLA people for over half an hour before the two West Belfast officers arrived to observe the pro-ceedings. The INLA men asked if the names of the UVF men could be confirmed as the people who did the shooting. At this point our people got up and left.

The UFF also learned from another member of the UDA that Craig asked him to accompany him on a visit to a Republican club in the Markets area. Craig told this man to arm himself with a .45 revolver for the jour-ney. When they arrived at the club, Craig's companion was searched and the revolver taken from him for safekeeping, but as they were leaving the premises the revolver was returned to him. This illustrates the absurdity of some aspects of the collusion between paramilitaries, but more brutal consequences were to follow.

On 15 October 1988 Jimmy Craig was lured to a meeting with other members of the UDA at the Castle Inn in East Belfast. As he sat quietly enjoying a drink, two men in ski masks, armed with automatic weapons, entered the bar and shot him dead. The UFF had finally decided that it could no longer risk having Craig in its midst. His murder did not stop the rackets. While they remain, the contacts established across the divide will also remain, because it is through those contacts that the profits accrue to purchase the arms which keep paramilitaries in business.

Conclusion
The Dirty War Goes On

Writing this book has been an extremely difficult, dangerous and depressing task. It has been difficult because of the nature of the sources and contacts with whom one is obliged to communicate. Sources and contacts prefer to remain anonymous because of the risks to personal safety if one is judged to be in possession of certain types of information. It is easy for persons to be labelled terrorist sympathisers or supporters. Some people who supplied me with the information did so out of a sense of duty or a belief that a particular story should be told because the public had a right to know. I never felt that any of the sources or contacts sought to compromise me, and the paramilitaries I met knew I was not someone who could be easily duped. The work was at times dangerous because I was obliged to meet people to whom violence is a way of life. It was also depressing because it illustrated the immovable ideologies, prejudice and mythology which are all-pervasive in Ireland. So many questions remained unanswered owing to the nature of the conflict I was examining. However, I believe the questions are valid and, in presenting them as unanswered, I have demonstrated the need for answers from those who are combatants in the dirty war. I also feel strongly that the RUC, leaving aside Special Branch, has been hampered in its attempts to investigate many of the episodes which I have revealed and analysed.

Special Branch, military intelligence and the security services operate with a freedom which makes it virtually impossible for CID properly to investigate incidents involving personnel from any of their agencies. In reality CID has been neutered. The 'pitchfork killings' episode illustrates how CID was unable to gain access to the information and people relevant to their inquiry. The RUC has no authority on Army bases and is denied access to files relating to intelligence matters. This limiting of the central role of a police force is, I believe, damaging to society and only serves to heighten suspicion of cover-ups and conspiracies—the staple diet of a dirty war. I also learned matters which I decided not to include in the book because they would have placed people at risk and compromised ongoing security operations.

One matter over which I deliberated for a long time was the connection between certain members of the legal profession and terrorists. Solicitors and barristers do a difficult job and one does not wish to exacerbate their problems by indicating a connection between some members of the profession and terrorism. However, I felt I was obliged to reveal the nature of what I learned because this lawyer-terrorist connection is a devastating weapon in the terrorist armoury and the public has a right to know. Members of the legal profession have been shot dead, and one of them was murdered in his home in 1989, but the story I am about to tell has no relation to those men, who were innocent victims and whose lives were not tainted by unethical or criminal behaviour.

The main connection between terrorist organisations and the legal profession occurs at solicitor level, because it is a solicitor's role to deal with arrested persons from the moment they are arrested until they appear in court, when they are formally represented by barristers. This is loosely the arrangement; and it is the solicitor-client relationship that is exploited by terrorists. When a terrorist suspect is arrested, police are empowered by emergency legislation to question that person over a seven-day period. RUC interrogators have often used that period to extract statements of guilt and information about the arrested person's accomplices, terrorist structures and plans. When the terrorist suspect is out of circulation, if he or she is 'broken' by interrogators and reveals important intelligence, the security forces can act quickly on the information before terrorist groupings are aware that they have been compromised. It is therefore vital for terrorist leaders to know whether one of their number is revealing the names of accomplices, the whereabouts of weapons and explosives dumps, or plans for future operations. The only person allowed access to an arrested suspect is the suspect's solicitor. Solicitors who are 'in the pay' of a terrorist organisation can ask their clients what they have told their interrogators and can pass messages from an organisation's leadership to their clients. In other words, solicitors can establish whether clients have compromised their terrorist overlords and accomplices or whether they are in a weak mental state and likely to break under continued questioning. If several members of an organisation are interrogated by police, the solicitor is free to meet all of them and establish which one is a potential supergrass.

When I refer to these rogue solicitors as being 'in the pay' of the para-militaries I mean they are paid, not directly, but by receiving a flow of clients from a particular organisation. It has not been unknown for a terrorist suspect who has been broken by police interrogators to realise that his failure to resist interrogation will be quickly conveyed to his over-lords if he has accepted advice from a particular lawyer. I am aware of one case where a killer changed his solicitor because statements he had made to police incriminated terrorists who were free and he knew his solicitors would have access to those statements and would convey their contents to terrorist leaders; if that had happened, his life would have been at risk, even in prison. In the early 1970s, when Loyalist hit-squads were being sent out to kill Catholics, they were given the names of solic-itors to contact in the event of being apprehended before or after a killing, in order to ensure that only those solicitors who were approved by the leadership were to have access to Loyalist assassins. That is not to con-clude that solicitors who regularly represent members of paramilitary organisations are under the control of those organisations. I am alluding to a small number of solicitors who set aside professional ethics for per-sonal gain or political motives. Such people come from both sides of the conflict, and their religious persuasion determines the terrorist organisa-tions they represent.

In the course of my research I acquired documentary proof of one example of a solicitor acting in an unethical, if not criminal, fashion. I was extremely concerned about using the material without supporting evidence to indicate that it was not simply an isolated example. I spoke to police interrogators, who assured me that I was not dealing with an isolated case of one rogue solicitor. The policemen emphasised that those solicitors who were involved were few in number, but their undermining of police work had an extremely serious and damaging effect. The docu-ments which came into my possession and which contain police interro-gation notes illustrate how one solicitor was operating on behalf of a ter-rorist leadership. It is not my role to act as prosecutor, nor would I wish to single out one solicitor and place his life at risk. I have removed his name and the names of the policemen from the following extracts from relevant documents. The name of the accused has also been omitted, as well as details which might serve to identify him, his organisation and, as a result, his solicitor. In the documents I am about to reproduce, the solicitor will be referred to as A, the accused as 'defendant' and the policemen as Detective Sergeant B and Detective Sergeant C. Dashes will indicate names of terrorists mentioned by the defendant. The interroga-tion notes were taken by detectives B and C. I have arranged them in sec-tions to indicate the chronological sequence of the interrogation over a period of several days, and I include only those parts of the notes which relate to what I term the solicitor-terrorist connection:

It was put to the defendant that by reading the notes from the previous day, it appeared to us that he had not admitted any further involvement in terrorist activity. The defendant replied: 'That's right.' It was suggested to the defendant that as he had now started to tell us the truth that he might as well tell us the whole truth and clear everything up and get it off his chest. The defendant stated that he had seen his solicitor the previous day and that his solicitor, A, had told him to say nothing more. The defendant was informed that this was all very well and that he was quite within his rights to remain silent, but that some time in the future his conscience would start to trouble him, if not now, about the taking of human life, as on occasions we believed he had taken human life to further the aims of the —. The defendant replied that he did not know what to say or who to trust. He was asked to explain what he meant and he replied: 'I don't trust my solicitor because he's more interested in the — [the terrorist organisation] than what happens to me and I don't trust yous as all yous want me to do is to admit to things.' The defendant was informed that there was no question of us asking him to admit to anything that he was not involved in and we were only interested in the truth of his involvement in crimes which he had committed. The defendant replied: 'Look I've told A everything that I admitted to yous the other day, and he asked me who was interviewing me when I made the statements and I told him that it was yous.' At this stage I interrupted the defendant by holding up my hand and informed him that I did not want to know what transpired between him and his solicitor during their consultations. The defendant replied: 'I don't care. I don't trust him. I'm going to tell you.' The defendant went on to say that his solicitor, A, had told him that he knew Det. Sgt C and that he was a bad one but did not know me, Det. Sgt B, but that he would not be long in finding out. The defendant then said that A was not very pleased that he, the defendant, had withdrawn his complaint against the police interviewers because anybody arrested by the police was told by the — [the terrorist organisation] to make a complaint early on so that if anything was brought out in court, they could say that they were forced into making statements. The defendant further stated that A had told him that he, the defendant, would have to lodge his complaint again against the police as soon as possible. The defendant informed us that there was nothing in his complaint, but that he would have to make it to police authorities before he left Castlereagh Holding Centre because if he didn't he would be under suspicion of touting when he was transferred from Castlereagh to prison. The defendant added that A had told him to make the complaint as he had before. The defendant then said: 'Look! It's nothing against yous but I'll have to do it some time before I leave here.' The defendant then said that his solicitor, A, asked him if he named anybody else that was involved with him in what he had admitted to the police. The defendant stated that he told A that he hadn't named anyone else and A told him to name nobody and to say or sign nothing else and that he, the defendant, had nothing to worry about as he, A, would ensure he got off any charges on the basis that he suffered duress at the hands of the police interviewers. The defendant was asked if he thought we were not to be trusted. He replied: 'I think I would trust yous more than him.' The defendant was asked who he was referring to when he mentioned 'him' and he replied that it was his solicitor, A....

The defendant said he felt sorry for his family. He said: 'You know I will have to make a complaint before I am charged to keep me right with the boys in prison, but I intend to plead guilty in court.'

The statement commenced at 5.45 pm and terminated at 6.00 pm. When the statement was finished, the defendant tilted his chair back and folded his arms. He laughed and said: 'You know A thinks that I have gone supergrass. I told him that I hadn't but that somebody was talking as the police knew too much.' The defendant was told that he was informed at an earlier stage that what transpired between him and his solicitor had nothing to do with us. The defendant said: 'Fuck him. He is more interested in them than he is in me.' The defendant then went on to say that his solicitor, A, had asked him if he had named anybody and that he, the defendant, had denied this. The defendant stated that A told him that some of the 'boys' thought that he, the defendant, had gone supergrass. The defendant said that he told A this was not so. He then went on to say that A asked him who was interviewing him in relation to what he had admitted and that he told him it was Det. Sgt B and Det. Sgt C. The defendant said A told him to say or sign nothing more as he, A, could still get him off on the basis of police duress and A further told him to make a complaint immediately. The defendant then stated apologetically: 'I'll have to make a complaint before I go.' This interview terminated at 6.15 and the defendant was returned to his cell by uniformed staff....

The defendant was then asked if anything else had come into his mind that he had been involved in and which we had not been told since we saw him last. The defendant replied: 'No, as far as I can remember, I've told you everything.' The defendant then stated: 'A's worried.' He was asked was he referring to his solicitor and replied that he was and he went on to tell us that he had just seen A a short time earlier and that A—at this point I interrupted the defendant and told him we were not interested in what went on between him and his solicitor. The defendant replied: 'You will when you hear that he's been bought and paid for.' He went on to say that he, the defendant, had told A about admitting involvement in robbery to police. The defendant further stated that his solicitor, A, asked him if he had named anyone else and that he, the defendant, told him that he hadn't. The defendant said his solicitor, A, asked him who was interviewing him and he told him it was Det. Sgt B and Det. Sgt C. The defendant went on to say that A told him that A had met — and — the previous night [the names omitted here are those of terrorist leaders].

The defendant was asked who were these two men mentioned by his solicitor. The defendant replied that they were both members of the Brigade Staff of the — and that one of them, —, was the Brigade Provost Marshal and the —. He was asked where his solicitor met these men and he replied that he did not know and that his solicitor had not told him. The defendant said his solicitor, A, did, however, tell him that he, A, talked to the men about the situation of those in Castlereagh, including himself, the defendant. His solicitor said these men believed it was obvious that someone was talking and it sounded like whoever it was, was going supergrass and that they wanted to know what they were up against. The defendant then stated that he told his solicitor that he, the defendant, thought that — was the supergrass as there were things put to him by the police which only — could have known. The defendant asked us was he right. He was told that we were not at liberty to discuss anything of that nature with him. The defendant nodded his head and said: 'That's okay. I'll find out who it is anyway.' The defendant then informed us that his solicitor, A, had been telling him that it was important to know how deep the rot was and he, A, was going back to see — and — [terrorist leaders] again. The defendant went on to say that his solicitor, A, had also told him that when he, the defendant, got to the Crumlin Road prison, that he was to go straight to see — and tell him everything that happened in Castlereagh after A's visit. The defendant was asked who was the man in

Crumlin Road prison and he replied that he was the — commander in the prison. The
defendant went on to say that A told him that he, A, would go into prison and see the
commander before the defendant was charged in order to assure the commander
that the defendant had not talked so that he, the defendant, would be okay in prison.
The defendant was asked if he was serious about what he had just told us and he
replied: 'I'm not joking. This is what A told me today.' The defendant again stated that
his solicitor, A, told him that he must make a complaint against the police immediately and that he, A, was very annoyed with him for not having made a complaint
before now. We had a further discussion with the —.

Those extracts are a damning comment on one solicitor and they illustrate how terrorists can exploit the right of a solicitor to talk to suspects
while they are under interrogation. As I stated earlier, this is not an isolated case and it represents a much deeper malady. It happens away from
public view, and this is the first time that it has been documented.

The dirty war goes on. On 13 January 1990 three robbers were shot
dead in West Belfast by members of an Army undercover unit. The manner in which the robbers were killed revived the allegation that the security forces were operating a shoot-to-kill policy. Politicians from both the
nationalist community and the middle-of-the-road Alliance Party called
for an inquiry and expressed dismay that there appeared to have been no
effort to arrest the three men, two of whom were armed only with imitation firearms and appeared to have been shot repeatedly while they lay
on the ground.

The three robbers were members of a gang which comprised five regular associates but was often supplemented by freelance criminals who
drove getaway cars, provided safe-houses or hid stolen goods. They
called themselves the 'Hole in the Wall Gang' and operated in both
Northern Ireland and the Republic. According to police records they
were professional criminals who favoured robbing banks or post offices
but were willing to undertake other ventures provided the risks were not
too great. In other words, they were not prepared to rob premises known
to be owned or connected to paramilitary organisations. RUC detectives
who investigated some of the crimes they committed in 1988 knew they
were not connected with the IRA, did not possess weapons but did use
imitation guns. The gang rarely operated in Republican areas of Belfast
because one of their members, twenty-five-year-old Eddie Hale from the
Poleglass housing estate in West Belfast, was a casualty of the
Provisionals' policy of punishing criminals who were known to be operating in Republican areas. In 1987 Hale was abducted by the IRA from a
house in West Belfast and questioned about crimes in the west of the city.
He was then shot through the arms, legs and ankles. After shooting him
the IRA warned Hale that if they again discovered he was 'engaged in

anti-social behaviour' his punishment could well be more serious. The following year, however, he was convicted for handling stolen goods and going equipped to commit a crime; clearly he was a hardened criminal who was prepared to risk further retribution from the IRA. The did not act against him, and it is believed that their reason for not fulfilling their threat was that the crime for which he was convicted was committed outside West Belfast in an area not judged to be under IRA jurisdiction.

Two of Hale's associates in the gang were also habitual criminals with a range of convictions. Forty-two-year-old John Joseph McNeill, who was single and lived in the Oldpark area in the north of the city, had a criminal record which contained almost thirty convictions for offences including assaulting police, theft, burglary and handling stolen goods. His record dated from the late 1960s. The youngest member of the gang was twenty-one-year-old Peter Thompson, whose family lived in the Twinbrook area of West Belfast. He had six convictions and his criminal activities began when he was sixteen.

A criminal who knew them, and who like them is a Catholic, told me the following:

Those guys, like me, were generally careful not to operate in hard Republican areas, but when things are bad and you need the money, you know only one way to get it, and that is to do what you do best, even if that means risking the wrath of the Provisionals. They're a difficult lot, unlike the Loyalist paramilitaries. Catholic criminals have difficulty operating effectively as far as armed robbery is concerned because it is not easy to get the real things—I mean guns. You cannot and dare not ask the Provos, and that is why guys like Eddie Hale would resort to imitation firearms. You see it sounds crazy, but the work comprises risks anyway. If you go out with an imitation firearm you can't defend yourself and you risk getting shot dead by being mistaken for a terrorist. There's no time to shout: 'Hey lads, this is only a toy gun', or 'This Heckler is only an imitation.' Now those risks you know about so it is not much different to risk hitting a bank or post office in a Provo area. Firstly, if you're not seen and you have good security in your gang and a trustworthy fence to handle stolen goods, nobody is going to know who did the job. There are so many criminals around. However, if somebody breaks cover or is too flush with money and the Provos get to hear of it they'll pull you in for interrogation. When they ask you to talk, you talk and take the punishment. If they think you're a real bad bastard and you're prepared to lie to them or you name another thief and they later find out it was really you, they'll not have any mercy. It'll be a head job. But, for all that, if things are bad, people will operate in a Provo area. The one advantage is that the cops tend to think such jobs are carried out by the IRA. That is what annoys the IRA and is one reason why they hate ordinary criminals. The Provos have their own means of raising money and don't need to hit premises which pay protection. When a pub that is contributing to Provo funds is hit by robbers, it makes the IRA look silly and they are expected to find the culprits.

Now when it comes to Loyalist paramilitaries it is a different matter. In my criminal past I associated with people within the UDA and they were prepared to lend guns provided they got a slice of the action. They didn't care that you were a Catholic.

There was profit. If there was no profit they would just as soon cut your throat or put a bullet in your head. The UVF, like the Provos, were not prepared to offer weapons on loan to criminals. In fact the UDA also stopped this practice after the killing of Jimmy Craig, the West Belfast UDA chief.

However, Hale and his colleagues in the Hole in the Wall Gang were offered weapons from a most unusual source—two joyriders who also specialised in stealing from cars. On 9 December 1989 some young men from West Belfast stole a black Vauxhall Astra from the city centre. In a fashion common to joyriders in Belfast, they drove the Vauxhall to a car-park adjacent to the Homestead Inn on a quiet country road in the town-land of Drumboe between Belfast and Lisburn, intending to swap it for another car of their choice. There they left the Vauxhall but removed nothing from it because they saw little of obvious value to them. They spotted a Nissan Bluebird and reckoned it was the type of car they would like to drive back to Belfast; there were also two holdalls in the vehicle. After forcing entry to the vehicle and examining the holdalls, however, they decided that the car was 'too hot'. Inside the holdalls were guns and military equipment. They transferred the holdalls to the Vauxhall and returned to Belfast, where they set light to the Vauxhall on the Stewartstown Road and then went in search of someone who might pur-chase the weapons.

One holdall contained a Heckler and Koch sub-machine-gun with four loaded magazines, a 9mm Brown semi-automatic pistol with three loaded magazines, and a flash grenade of the type used by the SAS or members of the covert units within 14th Intelligence. This Army grouping origi-nated in the mid-1970s and was first stationed at Castledillon in County Armagh. It was the organisation which Robert Nairac joined and has also been referred to as 4 Field Survey Troop or the 14th Independent Company. It is tasked much like the SAS, with whom it operates, and is under the direct control of the Army but with MI5 advisers in its hierar-chy. Besides the SAS it is the most secret organisation in the British Army. Its members now number approximately 250 and they operate not only throughout Northern Ireland but also across the border in the Irish Republic. Their role is to gather intelligence and operate on it after analy-sis. In order to discover more about this organisation, to help unravel the whole incident, I sought out a source within the Army who has only ever provided me with accurate information on topics which cannot be traced to him. This source has always been careful never to give me details which if published could endanger members of the security forces and has only supplied information on matters where he believes there is a genuine pub-lic interest. What I was told places information on the record for the first time:

It is irrelevant what title should be applied to this organisation, which does a fine job in combating terrorism. It is essentially in the front line and, when the order is given, its men are obliged to take real risks. It has been operating since the mid-seventies and has developed a sophistication beyond most organisations within the security forces. It works closely with Special Branch but there are the obvious strains and stresses one associates with security in Northern Ireland. I am not simply talking about petty jealousies but about who is in control. Special Branch runs its informers/agents and this unit runs its own informers. However, Special Branch began to feel that this specialist organisation was encroaching on its territory and made representations at the very highest level and claimed that this Army grouping was getting out of control, with units operating when and where they liked without reference to Special Branch. Special Branch reinforced the complaint by saying that this grouping was recruiting people who were already Special Branch agents/informers or recruiting people who were of no use in intelligence gathering or providing information. Special Branch was listened to, and rules were established in 1989 which stipulated that before any agent or informer could be recruited by this Army organisation, Special Branch required to be informed. This led to Special Branch exercising a control which was realised in the following fashion: if these Army specialists wished to recruit an agent/informer, they would approach Special Branch and provide the name of the person. Special Branch would then say whether the said person was already a Special Branch informer/agent, and whether this person was in their opinion of any value; finally, they would give the Army grouping the authority to recruit the person. Part of the difficulty with this organisation is that it does have a degree of autonomy which is resented and it is not represented on the Task Coordinating Group, which is made up of members of the major security groupings.

My source also confirmed that the weapons stolen from the car at the Homestead belonged to two members of this organisation, which I know to be 14th Intelligence. The undercover team comprised a man and woman who were taking time off for a drink when their car was burgled and the holdalls removed. This source also confirmed two other pieces of detail, hitherto unpublished, which are crucial to an understanding of how 14th Intelligence operates and the risks it creates through carelessness:

The episode at the Homestead was a disgrace, a clear breach of security, though it must be said that lapses of this kind are inevitable for people in this organisation who are constantly under pressure. What did not come to light was that, even after this episode, there was another occurrence. Those of us within the Army were shocked, and it served to heighten awareness of Special Branch complaints. On 8 January a male/female team went to a concert in the King's Hall in Belfast featuring the Tears for Fears pop group. Afterwards they went to the Europa Hotel, booked into a room and spent the night together. They left two holdalls in their car containing equipment similar to the items stolen at the Homestead. There was absolute panic, but fortunately the car was found the next day in West Belfast with the gear untouched. The other thing which is worth noting is that this grouping now handles direct confrontations with terrorists or armed criminals. When information is acquired that a terrorist unit or armed criminals are ready to operate, these units go up against them. Generally speaking, they operate in two cars, two operatives to each car. In one car there will be a female. That will be the car which will in difficult circumstances be the one used to engage in surveillance from a stationary position. The presence of the female with a male in a stationary car is less likely to excite the interest of terrorists or criminals than two males. The second car will contain the men who will do the necessary shooting, but they will be constantly on the move until the moment when their colleagues in the stationary car indicate that the time has come to confront the armed terrorists or robbers. In circumstances where information is received which indicates that imitation firearms are going to be used, the subsequent security force operation becomes the responsibility of the RUC and in particular of CID and the uniformed branch. However, the moment it is known that real guns are to be in the hands of the criminals or terrorists, the matter is placed through Special Branch and this specialist organisation is tasked to go into action. Part of the reason is that they can cope with the firepower which terrorists or armed criminals can bring to bear in a situation like Northern Ireland. The ordinary policeman is not trained for direct confrontational eventualities. It takes special people to do that.

My source also confirmed that it was this grouping which recruited the supergrass Anthony O'Doherty and gave him specialist training. Although the source refused to be drawn on the relationship between E4 and 14th Intelligence, he hinted that 14th Intelligence were better trained and since the Stalker investigation took the primary role in difficult operations. He also suggested that security was tighter within the covert army teams, and that they did not trust the RUC undercover units to maintain absolute secrecy. I suspected, however, that what he was really saying was that 14th Intelligence preferred to retain its secret role and not to face scrutiny from any grouping with the RUC apart from its contact with Special Branch, with whom it was obliged to communicate and with whom it occasionally shared information.

He did confirm that the male/female team who spent the night together in the Europa Hotel were quickly moved out of Northern Ireland and were not available for interview by police. When CID learned of the disappearance of the weapons and sought to interview the undercover team, they were told they had left the province, but at that time the undercover operators were in fact at Army HQ in Lisburn waiting to be flown to England to face disciplinary charges and were being questioned about the nature of the documents which were in the missing car.

In the meantime, the two joyriders had quickly sold the weapons from the car at the Homestead for £200 to the Hole in the Wall Gang. The Heckler and Koch sub-machine-gun was removed to a garage at Lurgan, where, unknown to its owner, it was stored by a man who acted as a fence to the gang. He rented the garage and used it as a clearing house for stolen goods. The gun was removed to Lurgan so that if the gang decided to operate outside Belfast, they had a weapon in a place near to many rural towns and the Irish border. Within two days the RUC raided the garage in Lurgan and removed the Heckler and Koch. I have discovered from my source that the RUC was able to act so quickly because an informer who was a close associate of the gang revealed to police that Hale and his associates had acquired two guns. The informer was unable to reveal the whereabouts of the 9mm Browning pistol because it was hidden somewhere in Belfast. Information about the theft of the guns, the discovery of the Heckler and Koch and the fact that one gun was still missing was also conveyed to the 14th Intelligence but was kept secret from the media and the public, partly because police were engaged in delicate negotiations with the gang's fence and also because 14th Intelligence requested that the matter be kept secret to avoid embarrassment.

The informer led police to the weapons and also to the fence who had hired the garage. Detectives quickly established that the owner of the premises was unaware of the use being made of his garage but he was able to name the person who had hired it. Detectives and the fence reached an arrangement that, if he secured the return of the Browning pistol from those who had stolen it, no charges would be preferred against him or the joyriders and the members of the gang. It is not uncommon for police to offer such a deal; this has occurred in the past, when members of the UDA stole weapons from policemen but returned them after police approached the UDA leadership. In this instance the security forces could have traced the joyriders and the gang by placing surveillance on the fence once he tried to contact those holding the pistol, but from all accounts that was not necessary. During a twenty-two-hour police interrogation the fence was presented with the names of every member of the gang. He is alleged to have told the gang that all police wished was the return of the pistol. As a result of the interrogation and the subsequent deal the pistol was returned, but the whole matter, including the identity of the gang, was also brought to the attention of Special Branch and 14th Intelligence. It is fair to assume that both these agencies soon became intimate with police records of members of the gang and police intelligence of their activities. The police informer who enabled CID so quickly to identify those who had acquired the stolen military equipment must surely have been in a position to acquaint his handlers in CID with two other important pieces of information which I can reveal but which were not mentioned in subsequent press reports.

When the joyriders drove into Belfast with the two holdalls they parked the stolen Vauxhall Astra on the Stewartstown Road in West Belfast, removed the stolen military gear and then set the car alight to destroy fingerprints. They made their way to a house rented by the gang and used as its headquarters. Peter Thompson and Eddie Hale had been living there for four months. The house was situated in the Dunmurry district on the periphery of West Belfast and the joyriders frequently visited it to sell the gang goods taken from cars or vehicles they had stolen, which the gang used in robberies. This association of professional criminals and young joyriders who were also thieves represents a subculture of lawlessness which is prevalent within Northern Irish society and obscured by the political violence, since terrorists are often deemed responsible for offences committed by ordinary criminals. When the two joyriders arrived at the gang's hideout, the holdalls were examined by Hale, Thompson and another person. The joyriders were given £200 and told to keep the matter secret.

After the deaths of Hale, Thompson and McNeill, remaining members of the gang told Gerry Adams that one of the holdalls contained a military map and codes but had been destroyed. Could it be that the gang did not destroy the second holdall and its contents? Did the gang pass on that holdall to the IRA? Did the IRA in return provide Hale and his companions with a form of immunity from punishment if they carried out any criminal offence in a Republician neighbourhood? Were such questions in the minds of members of Special Branch and 14th Intelligence? One can reasonably conclude that the informer who tipped police off about the gang's possession of the guns would also have been able to acquaint them with the whereabouts of the second holdall, assuming that the informer resided in Belfast and was in close contact with the gang.

Whatever the truth, the fact remains that the gang were in possession of documents which contained secret codes. Whether or not they destroyed the relevant material, they certainly viewed it and discussed what they should do with it.

It is also valid to argue that persons in 14th Intelligence and Special Branch who closely monitor terrorism must have wondered whether the gang were on the periphery of the IRA and providing them with intelligence or a service which was compromising undercover units. When the second car was taken from the Europa Hotel on 8 January, five days before the three gang members were shot by soldiers, intelligence observers must have wondered whether the same joyriders were at work again. When I discovered that a second 14th Intelligence car was taken but found with everything intact, I was tempted to conclude that the thieves who left such a car and its contents untouched in West Belfast must have known that they could not fence the contents and that they could have been the same joyriders. The joyriders who stole the holdalls from the Homestead would certainly have known by 8 January that it was best not to touch such materials again. I am reliably informed that after the Homestead theft the gang told them about the police discovery of the Heckler and the return of the Browning. There may well be no connection between the second car and the Homestead thieves; coincidence in Northern Ireland is too often thought to be significant when it is not.

However, the disappearance of the car would have indicated to Special Branch and 14th Intelligence the need for urgency in examining the relations between joyriders and a gang such as the Hole in the Wall and whether gangs of this type traded stolen military materials with the IRA.

After the return of the Browning pistol the gang members became afraid for their safety. They believed they were being watched from a house opposite their hideout in Dunmurry, and on one occasion they thought they heard a security radio channel at the side of the house. Peter Thompson's parents, who are law-abiding and did not condone his criminal behaviour, said he was 'on edge' in the weeks before his death and that a young woman with an English accent made several phone calls to the family home asking to speak to Peter but was told each time that he was no longer living at home. According to Mrs Thompson the day before her son was shot dead she was followed by a young man in a red Ford Escort XR2. The Thompson family also claim that a car containing several strangers was parked outside their home at midnight one day during the Christmas period. The Thompsons also allege that a car driven by a brown-haired woman drove past the Dunmurry hideout on several occasions and sped off when challenged. This tends to confirm other evidence that the gang were under constant surveillance. There is every reason to assume that they would have been under scrutiny, since they had acquired weapons stolen from undercover soldiers and were in possession of military materials which were not returned.

It may well have been the intention of Special Branch and 14th Intelligence to bring the gang to justice. I am convinced that surveillance was mounted on the gang as soon as police located the guns but that it was restricted to members of 14th Intelligence. The surveillance of the gang ceased to be a matter for CID once Special Branch told CID that they were taking over and that another informer close to the gang was saying the gang was preparing to use real guns in a big operation. On 10 January several members of the gang met in the Dunmurry house. Among them were Hale and Thompson. They agreed that they should undertake a robbery that week and convinced themselves that the matter of the stolen guns and their suspicions about being watched should be put aside. Since several thousand pounds' worth of stolen goods were lost when police raided the garage in Lurgan, they badly needed cash. That week two unknown persons put a proposal to the gang that they should rob Sean Graham's bookmaker's premises at the junction of the Falls and Whiterock Road. The plan was that several gang members would enter the premises from the side door. A source who was aware of the gang's discussion of this proposal gave me the following account:

They discussed hitting Graham's betting shop by the side door because they were in possession of information that in that week the bins would be emptied and delivered late. The plan was to knock on the side door of the betting shop and shout 'Bins', and the door would be opened to accommodate the collection of refuse, with the result that the gang would have easy access to the place without having to walk through the front door on a main thoroughfare.

The gang decided not to undertake this robbery but instead to hijack a van transporting money to post offices in another part of the city on Friday, 12 January. That operation was aborted for reasons which have not become clear.

On Saturday, 13 January, at approximately 9 am, the gang sat in the Dunmurry house. Hale argued that they should have robbed the book-maker's. Another gang member said it was now too late, since the plan was to enter the premises at 9.30 before there were many punters present. Hale pointed out that they could still drive down the road and rob the betting shop before midday, because the Dunmurry house was less than two miles from the proposed target. The general feeling among the gang was that they should not undertake the operation, but Hale persuaded Thompson and a person whom I can only refer to as Mr X to take part. He also encouraged McNeill to act as the driver for the robbery. Two gang members who said they would not take part agreed none the less to drive two of the robbers to the Falls area and leave them in the vicinity of the betting shop. McNeill was tasked to drive an Opel Kadett which had been stolen from a car-park in the Royal Victoria Hospital on Thursday night in anticipation of the Friday hijack. The two members who opted out of the betting shop robbery also agreed to conceal three balaclava masks and two replica weapons in the city cemetery directly opposite the betting shop; the replicas were a Schmeisser sub-machine-gun and a 9mm Browning pistol.

Shortly before 11 am, McNeill drove into the city cemetery and with one of the robbers collected the masks and imitation weapons. Then he parked alongside the bookmaker's, adjacent to the side entrance. Hale and Thompson and Mr X put on the balaclava masks which were worn on the top of their heads, like what are described in Belfast as 'monkey hats'. These woollen hats fit neatly round the head and are worn by jog-gers in cold weather. When a balaclava is worn in this fashion a terrorist or criminal can pull it down over his face quickly and just as quickly pull it back up and return it to the shape of a normal hat. Hale was given the replica Schmeisser and Mr X the imitation pistol. The three chose to enter the premises from the front and not by the side door as planned. I can offer no definite explanation for this change of plan, except that they may have decided that the ruse of pretending to be binmen would not work at 11 am. Once inside the front door, they pulled down their masks, opened a second door and shouted to customers and staff to lie down on the floor facing away from them. By this stage they had also removed the imitation firearms from inside their coats. As they began scooping money into bags, they heard a banging noise and shouting at the side door. Believing they were about to be apprehended, they panicked and ran to the front entrance.

Hale and Thompson were first on to the street and were shot dead. Mr X managed to scramble back into the betting shop, where he tore off his mask and dropped the imitation pistol on the floor. He lay on the floor with other customers and later escaped in the confusion which followed the shooting.

Hale and Thompson were hit by a hail of bullets at the front of the betting shop. McNeill was shot dead as he sat at the wheel of the getaway car. Eyewitness reports carried in many newspapers and in television broadcasts appeared to confirm that the getaway driver was the first to be shot. Hale and Thompson were killed as they exited from the premises.

Most reports testified to a clinical ferocity which claimed the lives of the three robbers. Several stories that a Vauxhall Astra car containing the two soldiers who carried out the shooting parked behind the getaway car, that the soldiers emerged from the car and one armed with a Browning pistol shot McNeill. These same soldiers are believed to have shot the other two robbers, one of whom was carrying what must have appeared to be a real sub-machine-gun, the replica Schmeisser. Allegations of a shoot-to-kill policy by the security forces were reactivated when television, radio and later the newspapers carried accounts from bystanders who said they saw one of the soldiers shooting into the bodies of Hale and Thompson as they lay on the pavement. What was not immediately made known was that a second car was positioned near the betting shop and contained two undercover members of 14th Intelligence, one of them a woman.

Theories about the shootings soon emerged. *The Sunday World* newspaper carried the headline 'Car mix-up led to deaths':

A bungled IRA operation could have led to the deaths of three betting shop robbers by soldiers who thought they were a Provo team who had switched cars. Police sources have claimed that an IRA operation to kill a policeman on the Falls Road on the Friday night sparked the latest shoot to kill affair. At the last minute the gunmen abandoned their assassination bid but they drove the stolen car they were using to a shopping complex and abandoned it. Minutes later another stolen car later used by the robbers was stolen less than a quarter of a mile away. But the RUC had mistakenly put two and two together and thought that the Opel car had been taken by the same Provo hit team. Police Intelligence allege the Army undercover squad were cruising in unmarked cars in the upper Falls district when they spotted the car taken by the betting shop robbers. They thought it was the same Provo hit squad who had tried to shoot police in the area the previous night. So they moved in using summary execution methods.

Mr X and other members of the gang were terrified after the shooting and sought advice from a priest, who advised them to talk to the MP for West Belfast, Gerry Adams. They contacted Adams, who is also President of Provisional Sinn Fein, and told him about the history of the stolen guns, the deal arranged through a middle-man with the RUC, and other events leading up to the betting shop robbery. Sinn Fein sought immediately to exploit the circumstances of the shooting with a headline in its news-sheet, *An Phoblacht,* which claimed the deaths were a 'symptom of Britain's secret war'. In the story beneath this headline no mention was made of the fact that Eddie Hale was shot by the IRA in 1987. Sinn Fein accused the soldiers of ignoring Army regulations that they challenge before opening fire. This was more than ironic, coming from an organisation which advocates the summary execution of all members of the security forces and does not believe in issuing challenges to any of its victims.

The overall account in the media did not deal with the presence of informers close to the gang, or how the presence of one informer led to the identification of the gang and the recovery of the weapons. I am not firmly convinced that there was a second informer, even though my source claims that was so. I believe my source pointed me in that direction because that was the information being conveyed to the Army and most likely CID. The presence of a second informer would have enabled Special Branch to take charge of targeting the gang for surveillance on the grounds that he was saying real guns were about to be used by Hale and his associates. Is it possible that Special Branch falsely claimed to have an informer so that they could remove CID from the investigation and keep the whole matter under secret Special Branch control? I am not suggesting for one moment that Special Branch had any sinister motives. After all, they had to consider so many possibilities concerning this gang and above all needed to find out more about them. Alternatively, an informer close to the gang in Belfast may have been encouraging them to believe that a major crime was being planned involving real weapons, and any gang that was willing to buy a Heckler and Koch would have appeared to have something very serious in mind. One tends to associate criminals with sawn-off shotguns and not high-powered weapons such as a Heckler and Koch, but I believe in this case the 'Hole in the Wall Gang', as their very name suggests, were not very cunning and were prepared to accept any kind of weapon. Peter Thompson's father later remarked that the gang 'did not have much brains'. He based his judgement on their decision to rob a betting shop before midday using the stolen Opel Kadett with its Dublin registration.

What was in the minds of the soldiers who fired the fatal shots? Did they happen upon an armed robbery or were they part of an ongoing surveillance operation that ended tragically? These questions will be answered only when all the facts are known, though that is not always possible in a dirty war where secrecy is necessary.

While examining this incident I was obliged to look closely at the recent use of undercover patrols, and I came across a story of a cat-and-mouse game played between teams from 14th Int. and the IRA in East Belfast in 1989. The IRA in the Short Strand area were monitoring Army radio signals to try to discover whether there were specialist units in the area. One source explained why the IRA company were on alert:

When an Army helicopter is overhead and there are no uniformed personnel in a neighbourhood you can be sure that the Army has created a sterile area so that undercover patrols can move into the area and work without interference. You must remember that if uniformed people are in an area they may stop any car, and that could include one with undercover people in it, and that doesn't help undercover operations. To avoid that eventuality and to ensure that uniformed soldiers don't mistake their own people for IRA and end up shooting them, the area is cleared of all uniformed police, Army and UDR. IRA people on the ground know by instinct that it is happening.

As the IRA monitored radio signals, by chance they picked up communications between specialist patrols, but they could not pinpoint the exact locations of the undercover teams. The IRA commander decided to place a large number of his men unarmed on the streets of the area with orders to watch out for any suspicious persons or cars. Weapons were removed from a dump, and active service volunteers were placed on standby, ready to go into action. The IRA men scouring the neighbourhood were close to abandoning the operation when two of them passed a parked car and heard a voice calling out a message from inside the boot. It was an undercover soldier shouting to colleagues to rescue him. He had seen the IRA men approach his car and reckoned he might be in danger. When his fears were realised, he was close to panic. While the IRA men were trying to open the car boot, two back-up cars of undercover soldiers arrived in response to a radio communication from inside the boot. On seeing cars screeching into the street the IRA men ran away. The soldier in the boot was rescued. His role had been to observe the movements of people in the area through a small hole in the boot cover. He may also have been equipped with a miniature camera, though remote-controlled miniature cameras can now be placed in parked cars.

Another bizarre incident occurred in the Falls area near Sean Graham's bookmaker's shop in 1989. A young couple had just left a car parked in a side street off the Falls Road when they were approached by several teenage members of the IRA. Within seconds a car sped up and whisked the couple away. Inside the abandoned car, the young IRA men found a

Heckler and Koch sub-machine-gun. Minutes later the entire area was sealed off by uniformed soldiers, who searched every street and removed the couple's car. The next morning a slogan appeared on a nearby gable wall: 'Thanks for the Heckler.'

The dirty war appears to have no end in sight and it often generates more questions than it answers. I found the writing of this book extremely depressing because in many instances I encountered stories which illustrated the futility of the conflict and the waste of human life in alleyways, on remote hillsides or in a border forest. There appeared to me to be many players in the game—not just terrorists—who showed little regard for the sanctity of life. In a sense I felt that all the combatants in a dirty little war such as this eventually become tainted by it. I was concerned to examine the extent to which people in some of those agencies of government in the front line of this war are permitted to operate without the degree of scrutiny which a democracy of necessity must exercise to ensure that society itself does not become a victim of war in respect of its own values.

In attempting to seek an explanation for many events I concluded that if there are great conspiracies, as several observers tend to suggest, they are not to be found in the varied matters that I analysed. In fact there are numerous parts to the jigsaw which forms the dirty war, and I believe that many parts which have yet to be uncovered will fit into the jigsaw. They will not, however, come together to produce conspiracies but may create theories about the elements that make up the conflict. My role, I felt, was to prise open some of the issues, to unravel some of the stories which have become distorted by the propaganda of either side and to tease out the complexity of the backdrop to the war.

The dirty war is to be found in such events as secret burials; the use of Military Reconnaissance Force squads; the manipulation of those who become informers and inevitably the victims; the development of the sophisticated technology of surveillance; and the manner in which the public is so frequently deceived about the true nature of the conflict. It is also about heroes and villains, the collusion between members of the security forces and terrorism, and ultimately the rules by which the war is fought. These elements have made it a dirty little war. It is no longer about massive street confrontations between mobs and the security forces, or between the two communities, or large-scale gun battles in the ghettos of Belfast. The war is now won or lost in the 'game' which involves the use of agents and double agents, the placing of high-definition surveillance equipment, the bugging of weapons and explosives in terrorist dumps and the effectiveness of propaganda.

It is also about a breakdown in society and the way in which terrorism has been institutionalised, and it is this which will need to be addressed if the dirty war ever ends. The institutionalised nature of violence is to be found in the title of one of the chapters of this book, 'Killing for Profit'. Terrorism has now found its way into the profitable aspects of life where it receives acceptance at levels of society where it would normally be shunned. Through 'legitimate' businesses terrorists have the means to hire lawyers and accountants in order to ensure that their businesses run smoothly. Terrorism has now a hold on society through the ownership of pubs, clubs, shops and the distribution of those luxuries such as videos which many of us acquire. In some areas of Belfast it is possible to point to licensed premises owned by men who are or have been connected with terrorism and who acquired the capital to buy the businesses from the proceeds of racketeering. In this way terrorism may well remain an integral part of society. However, it is not all about racketeering and other criminal enterprises. It is also a war between bitterly opposing forces with a history which does not easily lend itself to change. There is an uneasy feeling that this type of war has the potential to remain a feature of life in Ireland because it is not fought on a grand scale which would constantly bring it to the attention of the world or involve a sufficiently large number of people in society. In other words, it may not ultimately disturb enough lives for society as a whole to seek to end it.

On another level it fits into the pattern of international terrorism, and for that reason it may occasionally find itself high on the agenda of a Europe which has every reason to fear terrorism. When one recognises that the IRA could have changed the course of British history this century with the bombing of the Royal Hotel at Brighton during the Tory Party Conference in 1984 one must also accept that serious measures are required to deal with the threat it poses. The central question seems to be related to what kind of measures are acceptable in defeating terrorism. I hope I have provided the reader with the means to scrutinise those rules of engagement which have been used by agencies of government over the last twenty years.

I hope I have also illustrated that there is nothing glorious about the dirty war and that it is not concerned with any great ideological conflict. The victims who have been subjected to torture or inhuman and degrading treatment before their lives have been forfeited are a testimony to the hatred, bigotry, prejudice and senselessness which provide the impetus for the continuance of the dirty war. The fact that it is a war fought without the normal rules of engagement means that at some point those who are combating terrorism use means which they believe are best suited to this type of conflict, and as a result sometimes those involved in the dirty war are compromised by it.

It would, however, be wrong to conclude that this is a statement which is inherently critical of those who are vested with the authority to deal with terrorism. I hope I have shown that the war against the terrorist is critical to society but is not easily defined in terms of what is required to deal with the type of conflict which exists in Ireland and which finds its way into other countries in Europe. I feel there is a need not simply to examine one event but to see the conflict against the history of Northern Ireland and to provide the reader with an opportunity to see the totality of the issue rather than the selective history which both communities in Northern Ireland exploit to perpetuate the prejudice that is central to much of the dirty war.

Finally, in reiterating that the dirty war often generates more questions than it answers, I hope the reader will understand that in some instances where no answer was available I included the question in the belief that the question of itself was important and that perhaps its existence may encourage someone, somewhere, to provide an answer.

Postscript

When I wrote this book, I realized that I had been dealing with the classic undercover war that takes place in most conflict situations. In this one, however, the participants, British Intelligence and the IRA, arguably one of the most proficient terrorist organizations in the world, regarded each other as highly skilled.

When troops were employed on the streets of Northern Ireland in 1969, the British with a long history of dirty wars, relied on tactics learned in colonial emergencies in Kenya, Palestine, Aden and Cyprus. In the decades following, they refined their methods, believing for some time that they could defeat the IRA. However, by the end of the 1970s, it was clear that they were dealing with an enemy that had a long history of combating the British Military, had become so sophisticated in the Intelligence War and could not be easily destroyed.

The Lower Falls Curfew in July 1970 was the event that defined the British colonial mindset and the fact that the Army was being given a free hand to apply tactics learned elsewhere. In sealing off a Catholic district with a massive use of force, the Army was using a counter-insurgency strategy that backfired. A small Catholic enclave was overrun by troops and ransacked while hundreds of people were rounded up for questioning and screening. Field Marshall Lord Michael Carver later told me that it was a crude operation, yet it also crystallized two things: firstly, the Army had quickly defined its enemy as the Catholic population and secondly, without political control it would be free to begin a Dirty War.

It can be argued that the Army was only acting under political orders and to some extent that is a valid assertion. At the time of the 1970 curfew, the attitude of the Edward Heath Government in London was that the Army could resolve a situation that politicians in London preferred to ignore. An illustration of that political mindset was a meeting of GEN 42, a secret cabinet committee in 10 Downing Street. In attendance was the Prime Minister, Edward Heath, who told his Chief of the General Staff that British soldiers were legally entitled to shoot protesters on the streets of Northern Ireland. Heath's argument was that protesters were enemies of the Crown and soldiers were lawfully entitled to fire on them. Field Marshall Carver, at that time, Chief of the Defence Staff, confronted the Prime Minister and told him there was no legal basis for his position vis-à-vis soldiers and protesters. Carver also told me that he was never informed about a Ministry of Defence plan to select some of the 1971 internees and subject them to hooding and white noise that was later described by the Human Rights Court as ill-treatment.

It was an unreal political environment in which the British Government was, in effect, hoping the Army would find a solution. It was the Army that had taken Britain out of other colonial situations. Heath's Home Secretary, Reginald Maulding, on his first brief visit to Northern Ireland described the province as 'that bloody awful country'. Like others within the British cabinet and many British politicians before him, he felt frustrated and confused by Irish politics. It was an atmosphere in which the classified military organizations in the shadows believed they had free rein to employ whatever tactics they thought would defeat the enemy.

It was in 1970 that secret dirty war operations were put in place by British Military Intelligence with the assistance of elements within the Ministry of Defence in Whitehall and other bodies within the British Intelligence structure. The first of these was known internally as 'The Whiterock Operation' but within the military, it was sometimes referred to as the 'Military Reconnaissance' or 'Military Reaction Force'. Its activities were beyond the normal rules of surveillance and information gathering, because it engaged in unattributable shootings aimed at creating sectarian tensions in order to detach the IRA from its ideology and draw it into a shooting war with the Protestants. In one episode, a Whiterock squad, armed with the type of weapons used by the IRA, fired at a group of Protestants in a West Belfast street. The objective was to leave bullets in people or brickworks so that police forensic experts would later determine that the cartridges came from IRA-type weaponry. In another episode, shots were fired from a Thompson submachine gun into a Catholic housing estate.

The intention was to drive a wedge between Provisional IRA and its counterpart, the Official IRA, hoping that they would engage in a shooting war that would weaken them and disillusion the Catholic community. The Whiterock Operation also encouraged Police Special Branch to use blackmail to recruit Catholics and Protestants who were subsequently trained and employed within Whiterock units. Some of these agents were engaged in causing explosions that were blamed on the IRA.

In the background, British Intelligence established the Information Policy Unit based at Army HQ in Lisburn, County Antrim. Its aim was to target the British and Irish media with black propaganda war about the IRA. The staff within the unit believed they were fighting a propaganda war and were prepared to concoct stories to criminalize the IRA in the minds of the Catholic population. An additional aim was to convince the British public that the British Army was fighting and winning a just war. In my view, the British lost the propaganda war because there were too many professional journalists not willing to be conned and the Provisional IRA was adept at the use of propaganda.

As for 'Whiterock/MRF', it lasted three years and was replaced by the '12/14 Independent Company' which staged its twenty- fifth anniversary at Sandburst Military College in September 1998. Like its predecessor, 12/14 Company, as it became known, created secret off-shoots to carry out the operations that could not be traced directly to the military. One of these was known as the Future Research Units. In 1990, a secret police memorandum was passed to the RUC Chief Constable linking Future Research Units to the abductions of a Catholic student from Queen's University in Belfast. The student—X—was abducted by unknown men, blindfolded, taken to a house and stripped. Electrodes were then attached to his genitals. The blindfold was removed and he was shown videos of other Queen's University students. His captors demanded to know which of the filmed students was a member of the IRA. X was later blindfolded, trussed up and driven to an alleyway in Belfast where he was left to make his way home. Among other questionable operations was the bugging of confessionals in Catholic Churches and St. Peter's Parochial House in the Lower Falls area of West Belfast.

However, it was in January 1991 that the British public was afforded a rare insight into the workings of Military Intelligence when one of the British Army's terrorist agents appeared in a Belfast courtroom charged with over twenty offenses including five of conspiracy to murder. Much to the dismay of the media who were hoping for a full trial with controversial revelations, the agent pleaded 'guilty'. The Judge, Sir Basil Kelly, a former Protestant Unionist Attorney General in the days of Stormont rule, passed a ten year sentence. The agent, 44-year-old Brian Nelson, doubled as a terrorist within the UDA/Ulster Freedom Fighters. His plea of guilty and the fact that the Director of Public Prosecutions decided to overlook two additional charges of murder, ensured that there was no detailed scrutiny of the double life led by Nelson and his British Military handlers.

In an unprecedented step, a Colonel in Military Intelligence appeared in court as a character witness for Nelson, perhaps hoping to encourage leniency in the sentencing of the Army agent. The Colonel portrayed Nelson as a 'courageous' man whose mistakes were 'understandable'. He stressed that the 'mistakes', notably conspiracy to murder Catholics, were 'very understandable', but nonetheless Nelson was always loyal to the British Army. The Colonel also told the Judge that no guidelines existed for the running of agents, who in the context of Northen Ireland were bound to become involved in criminality. Moral responsibility, he added, lay with the system that had not yet found ways of coming to terms with the problems of running an agent. It was a startling series of admissions with critical omissions. The Colonel was revealing that in over twenty years, no rules applied to running agents, which begged the question of how many others like Nelson were involved in murder. By definition, he was also defending a Protestant agent's instinct to kill Catholics. What the Colonel omitted to say was that Nelson, a British Army soldier, was controlled by the Military who provided him with his targets. Nelson passed Intelligence on those targets to hit squads within the Ulster Freedom Fighters. Many of the targets were members of the Republican Movement whom the Army wanted killed.

Nelson was an operative in the tradition of two decades of undercover war. He informed his handlers of all his activities including the offenses to which he pleaded guilty. In fact, his activities were reminiscent of the English criminals, the Littlejohn brothers, who were sent to Ireland not only to spy but to get involved in terrorism. The story of Albert Walker Baker, another British soldier who claimed he cruelly tortured and killed Catholics while working for the British, appears believable in the context of Nelson's revelations. Nelson's history as an agent, like Baker's, also began in the 1970s and was interrupted when Nelson took his family to Germany in the early 1980s and was employed in manual labour. At the beginning of 1987, MI5 persuaded Military Intelligence to arrange a meeting with him in a London hotel. They persuaded him to return to Belfast where he became Coordinator of Intelligence for the Ulster Freedom Fighters. His handlers provided him with files on the lifestyles and movements of important members of Sinn Fein/IRA. He stored them in his computer in order to pass relevant information to UFF gunmen. Nelson kept his handlers up to date with targets independently selected by the IRA and no attempt was made to pass on this data to the police who could have prevented killings. Before he was arrested in a police operation, Nelson received a tip-off and destroyed his computerized files. An English policeman, John Stevens, was given the task of investigating Nelson's activities and discovered that he was in the middle of a dirty war. Stevens interviewed members of Special Branch and Military Intelligence, assembling classified files on Nelson only to find that they were destroyed in a fire. The files were kept in a heavily guarded police building with specially installed electronic surveillance safeguards. Forensic experts were unable to determine the cause of the fire. We may never know the full extent of Nelson's involvement in approved killings or how many other agents acted in a similar capacity. The Colonel who gave evidence on his behalf opened the door to the belief that throughout the conflict, British Military Intelligence and other parts of the British Intelligence apparatus acted unlawfully. The question that will remain a closely guarded secret is how much of their work was approved by those in political control in 10 Downing Street.

One of the killings for which Nelson was not charged was that of Catholic solicitor, Pat Finucane, who represented the families of the IRA trio shot dead by the SAS in 1988 in Gibraltar. Nelson knew the killers were en route to Finucane's home in North Belfast in February 1989—as did Military Intelligence—but that information was not passed onto the RUC who might have been able to prevent the death of the solicitor at the hands of the UFF. Finucane was an extremely able lawyer who frequently represented Republicans or the families of killed IRA members. In a divided society like Northern Ireland, lawyers acted without prejudice for the paramilitaries on both sides. Finucane had been extremely successful in controversial cases involving IRA suspects. I believe his ability, rather than his religious persuasion, was the cause of his death. Several of my contacts within the RUC were convinced that the orders for his assassination were passed to Nelson by Military Intelligence and subsequently to the UFF. One RUC source told me: 'We were angry about the failure of Military Intelligence to inform us about Finucane and other people whom their agent, Nelson, was targeting. But then why should they have confided in us? We would have stopped it and that was not their objective.'

From any reasonable analysis, one would have to conclude that the classic undercover war, from a British perspective, was a failure because the enemy understood how to combat it. The IRA responded to British strategies by establishing tightlyknit cells. By building a tough, ruthless internal security structure to root out informers, agents and double agents, and by encouraging IRA activists to offer themselves as British agents. Contrary to the British tabloid newspaper portrayal of the IRA as a 'bunch of criminals and psychopaths', there were many within the IRA intelligence who were skilled operators admired by their British counterparts.

In the 1980s, I met a senior figure from within the IRA's Internal Security organization who was also instrumental in setting up the

'England Department' cell structure that carried out the bombing campaign in Britain. He was an astute, clinical person who told me:

British Intelligence can be brilliant but it is not consistently so. Arrogance is its great weakness plus the tendency to believe that we will act predictably. It is also unwieldy with too many organizations with their fingers in the pie. The inter-agency rivalry helped us because shared intelligence was compromised by a desire to claim victory. We learned a lot when we exposed their operations. We kept files on the interrogation of their agents whom we captured. That enabled us to constantly update our intelligence on the way they operated. Every one of our people interrogated by them was debriefed on his release so that we knew what kind of people conducted their question sessions. Through that process we identified their interrogators, learned what they were interested in and what they thought they knew. It was a game…a dangerous game.

In effect, it was a process in which people were sacrificed by both sides and innocent victims were wrongly accused of working for one side or the other.

In 1992, while staying in a Belfast Hotel, I was approached by a chambermaid whose father was tortured and killed by the IRA who branded him an Army agent. 'My father was a bomber for the IRA', she told me, 'but he was never an informer. They tortured him and forced so much alcohol into his system that he died. My family has had to live with the humiliation that my father was a traitor to the Cause'. One of the IRA men who initially identified her father was Brendan Davison who, unknown to his superiors, was an agent for the British. It is my contention that Davison, whom I wrote about in this book, pointed an accusing finger at another person in order to deflect attention from himself. The IRA accorded Davison the status of hero and a paramilitary funeral with a place in the Republican plot in Milltown Cemetery in Belfast. His name was inscribed on a headstone alongside other IRA men who were killed on 'active service'. When this book was published, I received death threats from Davison's associates and it was only five years later that senior figures in IRA Intelligence privately acknowledged that my assertion about him was correct. By that stage, the IRA was unwilling to admit that one of the members of his Internal Security structure was a British agent. It would not have benefited the Republican cause by such an admission, which would have required the scratching of his name from the headstone and the burial of his remains in another part of Milltown Cemetry.

Another dimension to the book that presented me with personal security problems were the revelations about the IRA secret burials and the naming of people involved in that process. In the Autumn of 1995, the RUC set up a special detective squad to investigate what was termed 'The

Disappeared'—people murdered and buried by the IRA. A detective from the squad asked for my help, which I refused because the terms of reference for his enquiry were loaded against Republicans. I asked him why his brief did not include an examination of those who were killed by Protestant terrorists and also buried in unmarked graves. I pointed out to him that while writing the history of the Loyalist terrorist, Michael Stone, and examining statements made by Albert Walker Baker, it was evident that the IRA was not alone in adopting this practice. The detective in question was unable to provide me with an answer. I also asked if his terms of reference included a search for the body of Captain Robert Nairac, the only British soldier of the conflict whose body remains missing. I received a reply to the effect that the 'Nairac issue was too politically sensitive'. I made private enquiries that confirmed that Nairac was not on the squad's agenda because any discussion about his death and the disappearance of his remains would rekindle issues about his part in the dirty war. My principle was that all the disappeared should be included in the investigation and, until that was done, I was not prepared to be part of something that could be validly deemed politically partisan. I was aware that Robert Nairac's sister, in the company of a former IRA Chief of Staff, met members of the IRA Army Council who told her that her brother's remains would not be 'handed over' until the conflict ended. They justified their decision on the basis that Robert Nairac was responsible for the assassination of a leading IRA captain and other Republicans. Contrary to British Military black propaganda that the corpse was fed to pigs, the IRA buried Nairac along the railway line that runs from Newry in Northern Ireland to Dundalk in the Irish Republic.

After publication of this book, I was approached by the mothers of two young men who were believed to have been abducted by the IRA in the 1970s and killed. Their crime was that they burgled an illegal drinking club run by IRA figures in the Andersonstown area of Belfast. What is not in doubt is that the two young men were interrogated by the IRA, released and days later disappeared. In response to a plea for help from the mothers, I took the unprecedented step of using my role as a BBC program editor to use the airwaves to ask the IRA where the two young men were buried. The IRA did not respond even though the mothers subsequently appealed to Gerry Adams, the President of Provisional Sinn Fein. A priest from Clonard Monastery in Belfast made a secret trip to Dublin where he met the Army Council who told him they knew nothing of the disappearance of the young men. I subsequently received this letter from Margaret McKinney that illustrates that a dirty war leaves its own mark on many people:

Dear Martin,

I had the privilege of meeting you when you gave me the opportunity to tell my story on the BBC. It was the first time I was ever able to talk about what happened about Brain and John McClory. If you can recall, they were kidnapped and murdered by the IRA. I will always be grateful for you for giving me that chance and everyone knows it has been great therapy for me. Before that, no one wanted to know the real truth. Over the last few weeks, it has been said that they were buried on the Glen Road in what used to be a building site when the housing estate was being built. I got a phone call from a prisoner who was talking to an inmate who told him the story about it so he was involved. I am praying so hard that I will get his body soon so that I can put him to rest and then maybe I can get on with my life because it's been haunting me for all these seventeen years. They have a campaign now for the release of the bodies...maybe up to twenty. I am sending you blue ribbons to wear for the campaign and I would be privileged if you would wear them as they are nonpolitical. Once again, I thank you from the bottom of my heart.

Signed, Margaret McKinney

At the time of writing this postscript, Margaret and the other relatives of the 'disappeared' have not had their hopes realized.

In Margaret's case, one can only hope that something mysterious happened and her son and his friend fled to another part of the world where they have been frightened to contact their relatives. That is a forlorn hope in the context of the undercover war.

Perhaps another dimension to it is that we may never know the truth about some of the killings that were attributed to terrorist organizations or whether all of those 'executed' as traitors by the IRA and the Loyalist paramilitaries were guilty. The Dirty War often created a paranoia within paramilitary ranks where there was a constant search for traitors. In this aspect of the conflict, the British Government failed to scrutinize or curb the excesses of secret bodies within the Intelligence apparatus. There were no rules or guidelines, as the British Army Colonel pointed out in the Nelson case.

One of the reasons why there was an attempt to discredit the English Policeman, John Stalker, was that he was 'dangerously' close to unraveling unlawful aspects of the British undercover war.

I learned that the Intelligence hierarchy feared that Stalker's investigation would expose the use of agent provocateurs and a willingness to permit terrorist agents to engage in murder to protect their secret agent roles.

The unofficial excesses within the Dirty War were curbed when MI5 was given the supremacy role in security in the early 1990s. Their brief was to put the 'British Intelligence House' in order in regard to the Northern Ireland conflict. They quickly centralized intelligence gathering, restricting the flow of information so that it could not be used for unlawful purposes. Their first task was to ensure that Military Intelligence ceased to independently run operations that were not overseen by MI5. MI5, or the Security Service as it is commonly known, gained the supremacy role in security with a clever Intelligence sting of its own. Using a journalist agent, it finally, through a series of episodes, exposed the Military's use of Brian Nelson as a terrorist and agent. The public awareness of the fact that Nelson was a killer and that the undercover war was not only dirty, but without guidelines in respect of the running of agents, strengthened MI5's advice to government that greater controls were required in the Intelligence War. MI5 also secretly argued that the Intelligence apparatus had failed to stop the IRA bombing Britain because too many parts of the Intelligence structure did not share Intelligence on terrorists. When MI5 took over in 1992, it quickly set up a chain of command whereby all information was channeled through its staff. This angered many people within the security industry, especially members of the Anti-Terrorist Squad at Scotland Yard who found that their access to Intelligence was confined and they were obliged to seek permission from MI5 for operations or ongoing data and surveillance on the IRA. MI5's tactics did prove fruitful in the years after the 1992 decision to give them the overseeing role. They were more successful in damaging the IRA's England cell structure and in reshaping the Intelligence apparatus in Northern Ireland.

However, it is my contention that in such a conflict, the war behind the headlines will always be a dirty war irrespective of who is in control of the Official Intelligence dimension to it. The running of agents within terrorist organizations cannnot be achieved without permitting those agents to act as terrorists and therefore act outside of the law. Secondly, one of the lessons learned by the British was that the panoply of dirty tricks they used and the technology of surveillance they devised were never as successful as basic techniques of espionage such as man-to-man surveillance and terrorist agents. Successful penetration of the terrorist groupings was achieved by recruiting people from within the ranks and man-to-man surveillance led to identifying the whereabouts of senior terrorist operatives before bombings or shootings took place.

In an overall assessment of the Dirty War, none of the combatants emerged unscathed and in many respects it was a standoff, which is why the IRA and British Intelligence regarded the other as highly skilled. This war, fought in the shadows in which blackmail, torture and murder were employed, produced its own victims, some of them sacrificed for a long-term objective or wrongly judged because of the atmosphere of all-pervasive paranoia.

Appendix
The Green Book

What follows is the constitution, aims, objectives and disciplinary procedures of the IRA. Known as 'The Green Book', it is the IRA's official handbook. It has not been edited or altered in any way, and is printed here, in its recent edition, for the first time. Any errors of grammar or of sense can be attributed to the original.

CONSTITUTION OF OGLAIGH NA hEIREANN

1. Title:
The Army shall be known as Oglaigh na hEireann.

2. Membership:
1 Enlistment in Oglaigh na hEireann shall be open to all those over the age of 17 who accept its objects as stated in the Constitution and who make the following pledge:
'I.... (name).... promise that I will promote the objects of Oglaigh na hEireann to the best of my knowledge and ability and that I will obey all orders and regulations issued to me by the Army Authority and by my superior officer.'
2 Participation in Stormont or Westminister and in any other subservient parliament, if any, is strictly forbidden.
3 Enlistment shall be at the discretion of the Army Authority.

3. Objects:
1 To guard the honour and uphold the sovereignty and unity of the Republic of Ireland.
2 To support the establishment of an Irish Socialist Republic based on the 1916 Proclamation.
3 To support the establishment of, and uphold, a lawful government in sole and absolute control of the Republic.
4 To secure and defend civil and religious liberties and equal rights and equal opportunities for all citizens.
5 To promote the revival of the Irish language as the everyday language of the people.

4. Means:

1 To organise Oglaigh na hEireann for victory.

2 To build on a spirit of comradeship.

3 To wage revolutionary armed struggle.

4 To encourage popular resistance, political mobilisation and political action in support of these objectives.

5 To assist, as directed by the Army Authority, all organisations working for the same objectives.

5. Army Control:

1 The General Army Convention shall be the Supreme Army Authority.

2 The Army Council shall be the Supreme Authority when a General Convention is not in session.

3 The Army Council, only after Convention, shall have power to delegate its powers to a government which is actively endeavouring to function as the de facto government of the Republic.

4 When a government is functioning as the de facto government of the Republic, a General Army Convention shall be convened to give the allegiance of Oglaigh na hEireann to such a government.

5 All personnel and all armaments, equipment and other resources of Oglaigh na hEireann shall be at the disposal of and subject to the Army Authority, to be employed and utilised as the Army Authority shall direct.

6. General Army Convention:

1 A General Army Convention of Delegates (selected as set out hereinafter) shall meet every two years unless the majority of these delegates notify the Army Council that they it better for military purposes to postpone it. When a General Army Convention is postponed, it shall be summoned to meet as soon as the majority of the delegates shall notify the Army Council that they deem it advisable.

2 An Extraordinary General Army Convention and that the urgency of the issue for the Convention does not permit of the selection of delegates as prescribed, that the delegates to the previous General Army Convention constitute the Extraordinary General Army Convention. When for any reason a delegate to the previous General Army Convention has become ineligible, or is not available, the Battalion Council shall elect a delegate in his/her stead. Every active Volunteer in the Battalion shall be eligible to stand as a delegate.

4 When the Army is engaged on active service, no Unit or General Army Convention shall be held until a reasonable time after hostilities have terminated, unless the Army Authority decides otherwise.

5 An Executive of twelve members shall be elected by ballot at the General Army Convention: at least eight of these members shall be delegates to the Convention: Four members may be elected from active Volunteers who are not delegates. The next six in line shall, however, be eligible as subsitutes to the Executive in order of their election. The Executive shall always have six substitutes in readiness.

6 No member of the Executive may also be a member of the Army Council and members of the Executive subsequently elected to the Army Council will resign from the Executive. Vacant positions on the Executive arising in such a way shall be filled by those substitutes next in line from the Convention elections.

7 The following shall be entitled to attend and vote at the General Army Convention:

Delegates selected by Battalion Convention.

Delegates selected by General Headquarters Staff and Staffs of Brigades, Divisions and Commands.

Two members of the Executive.

All members of the Army Council.

The Chief of Staff, the Adjutant-General and the Quartermaster-General.

8 Only Volunteers on the Active List shall be eligible as delegates to the General Army Convention.

9 A majority of the General Army Convention may invite anyone whom they wish to attend to speak.

10 The Chairperson of the General Army Convention shall be chosen by the General Convention.

7. Duties and Powers of the Executive:

1 The Chairperson of the General Army Convention or his/her representative shall, within forty-eight hours of the termination of the Conventions, summon a meeting of the Army Executive over which he/she shall preside during the election of a Chairperson and Secretary. The Army Executive shall then proceed with the election of an Army Council of seven members.

2 The Army Executive shall meet at least once every six months. The Secretary of the Executive shall be responsible for the summoning of the members.

3 It shall be the duty of the Executive to advise the Army Council on all matters concerning the Army

4 The Executive shall have powers, by a majority vote, to summon an Extraordinary General Army Convention.

5 A member of the Executive who, for any reason, ceases to be an active member of Oglaigh na hEireann shall cease to be a member of the Executive.

6 Casual vacancies on the Executive shall be filled by co-operation after any substitutes that may be elected by the General Army Convention have been exhausted. Vacancies shall be filled within a period of one month.

7 The Executive shall hold office until the following General Army Convention shall elect a new Executive.

8 An extraordinary meeting of the Executive shall be summoned by the secretary of the Executive when a majority of the Army Council or a majority of the Executive so decide.

9 Two-thirds of the available members shall constitute a quorum of the Executive, for co-option purposes only. Full Executive powers shall not be vested in less than five members.

8. Duties and Powers of the Army Council:

1 The Chairperson of the Army Executive or his/her representative shall, as soon as possible after the election of the Army Council, summon a meeting of the Army Council, over which he/she shall preside, until a Chairperson and Secretary have been elected.

2 The Army Council shall meet at least once a month.

3 Vacancies occuring in the Army Council shall be filled from substitutes elected by the Executive or co-opted by the Army Council in advance. Co-options by the Army Council must be ratified by the Executive at its next meeting.

4 Any active Volunteer shall be eligible for membership of the Army Council. The Army Council shall have power to:

1 Conclude peace or declare war when a majority of the Council so decide. The conclusion of peace must be ratified by a Convention.

2 Appoint a Chief of Staff and ratify all appointments to the Commissioned ranks.

3 Make regulations regarding organisation, training, discipline, equipment and operations, such as will ensure that the Army will be as efficient as possible.

4 Take all necessary steps to secure co-ordination with other republican organisations.

5 Keep in touch with all foreign organisations and countries which may help the Army in any way.

6 Arrange for the care of wounded Volunteers and their dependants and the dependants of Volunteers killed, imprisoned or on active-service.

The Chief of Staff, Adjutant-General and Quartermaster-General shall be entitled to attend and speak at all meetings of the Army Council but not be entitled to vote unless they are members of the Army Council.

Four members shall constitute a quorum of the Army Council.

A member of the Army Council who, for any reason, ceases to be an active Volunteer, shall cease to be a member of the Army Council.

9. Selection of Delegates:
Delegates to the Command Conventions shall be elected by ballot as follows:

1 At each parade called for the purpose, each unit in Command Area shall elect a delegate to attend the Command Convention.

2 One member of the Command Staff, elected by the Staff at a special meeting called for the purpose.

3 The Command OC shall be entitled to attend and vote at the Command Convention.

4 Each Command Convention shall meet when instructed by the Army Authority and elect one delegate when the total number of Volunteers who parade for Unit Conventions do not exceed twenty, and two when the number of Volunteers do not exceed fifty, and one delegate for each twenty additional Volunteers on parade at Unit Conventions.

Brigade Conventions:

Where the Independent Unit is a Brigade, a Brigade Convention may be held consisting of the delegates elected by the Units, Battalion Staffs and the Brigade Staff, with the power to pass or reject any resolution brought forward by these delegates. The delegates from each Battalion shall each elect their own delegates to the Army Convention.

Election of Brigade, Divisional and Command Staff delegates to the General army Convention.

Two delegates shall be elected at a meeting of General Headquarters Staff officers, with the exception of the Chief of Staff, Adjutant-General and Quartermaster-General.

Resolutions to General Army Convention:

Command Conventions and the meetings of GHQ Staff for the election of delegates to General Army Convention shall have power to discuss any matter relating to the Army or to the Nation and to pass resolutions regarding such matters. These resolutions shall be forwarded to GHQ within the time specified by the Army Authority and shall appear on the agenda for the General Army Convention.

10. Changes to the Constitution:
It shall require a two-thirds majority of a General Army Convention to change articles in this Constitution.

OGLAIGH NA hEIREANN (IRISH REPUBLICAN ARMY)
GENERAL HEADQUARTERS GENERAL ARMY ORDERS
(REVISED 1987)

General Order No. 1

1 Membership of the Army is only possible through being an active member of any army Unit or directly attached to General Headquarters. Any person who ceases to be an active member of a Unit or working directly with General Headquarters, automatically ceases to be a member of the Army. There is no reserve in the Army. All Volunteers must be active.

2 The duties of a Volunteer shall be at the discretion of the Unit Commander. If for a good and genuine reason a Volunteer is unable to carry out the normal duties and routine which obtains in the Unit, the OC may allot him/her some special duties. So long as he/she performs these duties satisfactorily and makes regular reports he/she shall be considered as an active Volunteer.

3 Leave of absence may be granted to a Volunteer in the case of illness or for other valid reason.

4 A Volunteer who, for any reason, ceases to maintain contact with his/her Unit or with General Headquarters for a period of three months shall automatically cease to be a member of the Army.

5 The provision of this General Order does not apply to Volunteers in prison.

General Order No. 2

Volunteers when making the Army Declaration promise '...to obey all orders and regulations issued by the Army Authority and any superior officers.'

1 Where an order issued by a duly accredited officer has been disobeyed, the Volunteer in question must be suspended immediately, pending investigation of the case.

2 Any Volunteer carrying out an unofficial operation is automatically dismissed from the Army and is liable to immidate repudiation.

Minimum penalty for breach of this order: Dismissal.

General Order No. 3

1 All applications for re-admission by those who were dismissed or who resigned from the Army, must be submitted to the Army Council or delegated authority, who alone have the power to sanction reinstatement.

2 Where a Volunteer is summarily dismissed from the Army he/she may apply to his/her Unit OC to have his/her case tried by Court-martial. Such application must be made within seven days from the date of receipt of notification of dismissal.

3 Once a Court-martial has confirmed such a dismissal, then as in all other cases, any further appeal or application for reinstatement must be forwarded to the Army Council through the Unit Commander.

General Order No. 4

No member of Oglaigh na hEireann may be a member of a political party which recognises the partition institutions of government as sovereign authorities for the Irish people.

General Order No. 5

part 1

A Volunteer shall not:

1 Swear or pledge allegiance or recognition to the partition institutions of government of the Six or Twenty Six County states.

2 Swear or pledge recognition of their legitimacy as sovereign governing bodies for the Irish people.

3 Swear or pledge himself/herself in any way to refrain from using arms or other methods of struggle to overthrow British rule in Ireland.
Minimum penalty for breaches: Dismissal.

part 2
When arrested a Volunteer shall:
1 Remain silent.
2 Refuse to give any account of his/her movements, activities or associates, when any of these have any relation to the organisation or personnel of Oglaigh na hEireann.
3 Refuse to make or sign any statements.

part 3
A Volunteer shall:
1 Refuse to obey any order issued by the partitionist authorities requiring him/her to leave Ireland or reside inside or outside a specified area in Ireland.
2 Refuse to give any undertakings about his/her future behaviour. Volunteers released from prison on ticket-of-leave are bound by this.
Minimum penalty for breaches: Dismissal.

part 4
Any Volunteer committed to prison forfeits all previous rank and shall report into the Oglaigh na hEireann structure for de-briefing and further instructions.
A Volunteer's attitude in court shall be at the discretion of the Army Authority. Maximum penalty for breaches which are not also a breach of orders in Part 1: Dismissal with ignominy.

part 5
No Volunteer should succumb to approaches or overtures, blackmail or bribery attempts, made by the enemy and should report such approaches as soon as possible.
Volunteers who engage in loose talk shall be dismissed.
Volunteers found guilty of treason face the death penalty.

General Order No. 6
Committees under Army control will have their terms of references clearly laid out for them. They will adhere strictly to these terms of reference. In case of departure from these the individual or individuals responsible will be removed from the Committee. The Army Authority has the right to remove any member of such Committees from the Committee at any time.

General Order No. 7
Volunteers are forbidden to undertake hunger-strikes without the express sanction of General Headquarters.
Maximum penalty for breach: Dismissal.

General Order No. 8
1 Volunteers are strictly forbidden to take any military action against 26 County forces under any circumstances whatsoever. The importance of this order in present circumstances especially in the border areas cannot be over-emphasised.

2 Minimum arms shall be used in training in the 26 County area. In the event of a raid, every effort shall be made to get the arms away safely. If this fails, the arms shall be rendered useless and abandoned.

3 Maximum security precautions must be taken when training. Scouts must always be posted to warn of emergency. Volunteers arrested during the training or in possession of arms will point out that the arms were for use against the British forces of occupation only. This statement should be repeated at all subsequent Court proceedings.

4 At all times Volunteers must make it clear that the policy of the Army is to drive the British forces of occupation out of Ireland.

General Order No. 9

Firing parties at funerals are only allowed in the case of Volunteers who die on active service or as a direct result of enemy action. General Headquarters permission must be obtained.

General Order No. 10

No member of Oglaigh na hEireann shall make any statement either verbally or in writing to the Press or Mass Media without General Headquarters permission. Volunteers are forbidden to advocate anything inconsistent with Army policy. Minimum penalty for breaches: Dismissal with ignominy.

General Order No. 11

Any Volunteer who seizes or is party to the seizure of arms, ammunition or explosives which are being held under Army control, shall be deemed guilty of treachery. A duly constituted Court-martial shall try all cases.

Penalty for breach of this order: Death.

NOTE: As in all other cases of death penalty, sentence must be ratified by the Army Council.

General Order No. 12

A Volunteer with knowledge of the whereabouts of Army property which is not under Army control shall report such information immediately to his/her OC. Minimum penalty for failure to do this: Dismissal.

General Order No. 13

1 Any Volunteer who attempts to lower the morals or undermine the confidence of other Volunteers in Army leadership or in any individual in the Army control shall be deemed guily of treachery.

2 Any Volunteer taking part in a campaign of slander and denigration against another Volunteer thereby weakening authority and discipline, and bringing the Army into disrepute, shall likewise be deemed guilty of treachery. Minimum penalty: Dismissal with ignominy.

3 All Volunteers are expected to act in an honourable way so as the struggle is not harmed or undermined.

Any Volunteer who brings the Army into disrepute by his/her behaviour may be guilty of a breach of his/her duties and responsibilities as a Volunteer in Oglaigh na hEireann and may be dismissed.

General Order No. 14

Oglaigh na hEireann is a voluntary organisation and Volunteers resign membership by giving notice to the relevant Army authority. However, no Volunteer or former Volunteer may join any other military organisation where his/her training, experience and knowledge gained in Oglaigh na hEireann could be used by that organisation.

General Order No. 15
No Volunteer convicted by a Court-martial on a capital offence can be executed if that Volunteer can show that he did not receive instructions in the Green Book. The officer(s) responsible for recruiting this Volunteer and clearing his/her application shall be held responsible for neglect and being in breach of this order.

COURTS OF INQUIRY
1. A Court of Inquiry may be set up to investigate allegations against any member of the Army, any alleged irregularity, or any other matter affecting the Army.
2. The Court may be convened by the OC or any Unit or by the CS. The Convening Authority should supply the Court with specific terms of reference in writing, setting out the precise nature of the matters to be investigated.
3. The Court shall consist of three members, one of who will be appointed President by the Convening Officer of his/her representative. Any active Volunteer may be appointed to sit on a Court of Inquiry.
4. The powers and duties of a Court of Inquiry are: to examine all witnesses who appear before it and having considered all the evidence, to make specific recommendations to the Convening Authority. It has no power to bring in any verdict or to pass any sentence. It may recommend Court-martial proceedings, but decision on this point rests with the Convening Authority.
NOTE: The powers and duties of the Court of Inquiry should be made clear to the members of the Court and to all witnesses appearing before it, by the Convening Authority or his/her representative.
5. The members of the Court, should be supplied with copies of all General Army Orders, as they may be required for the drawing up of recommendations
6. Witnesses summoned to appear before the Court should be accommodated in a separate room to that in which the Court is held. They should be cautioned before hand that they are not to discuss the matters being investigated, among themselves. An officer should be detailed to remain in the room with the witnesses. The witnesses will be called singly before the Court to testify.
7. Evidence should be taken on oath which will be administered to each witness by the President. Should a witness object to testifying on oath, he/she must state the objections, to the Court. Unsworn testimony may be taken, but will not carry the same weight as sworn testimony. Once a witness has been examined, he/she may be recalled as often as the Court requires, to answer any further questions the Court wishes to put. For this reason, witnesses will not be allowed to leave the precincts of the Court except with express permission of the Court.
8. If the Court so decided, it may call for additional witnesses to those summoned by the Convening Authority.
9. The recommendations of the Court shall be made in writing and signed by the three members of the Court. These recommendations together with a record of the proceedings and all documents connected with the inquiry, shall be forwarded to the Competent Authority by the President.
NOTE: The President appoints one member of the Court to record the proceedings unless a note-take or other means of recording is specially provided by the Competent Authority.

OATHS FOR COURTS OF INQUIRY

To be taken by each member of the court.

I...swear by the Almight God that I will conduct this Inquiry without fear, favour or affection.

And I swear that I will not disclose the vote or opinion of any member of the court unless required to do so by the Competent Authority. And I swear not to disclose the recommendations of the Court until they have disclosed by the Competent Authority.

To be taken by each witness:

I...swear by Almighty God that my evidence to the Court shall be the truth, the whole truth and nothing but the truth.

To be taken by the official note-taker:

I...swear by Almighty God that I will maintain inviolate the proceedings of this Court, and that I will not disclose its proceedings unless required to do so by the Competent Authority.

COURT MARTIAL

1. A Court-martial is set up by the OC of any Unit or by the CS, to try any Volunteer on a specific charge or charges.

2. The Court shall consist of three members of equal rank or higher than the accused.

3. The Convening Officer will appoint one member of the Court as President.

4. When a Court-martial is set up by a Unit OC, the Adjutant of the Unit, or some members of the Unit delegated by the Adjutant to do so, will act as Prosecuting Council. When the Convening Authority is the CS, he/she may appoint any officer other than the Adjutant-General to act as Prosecuting Counsel.

5. The accused may call on any Volunteer to act as his/her Defence Counsel, or if he/she desires, may defend the case himself/herself.

6. A copy of the charge shall be supplied to the accused in reasonable time before the case is heard to enable him/her to prepare defence. The Convening Authority may either supply the accused with a summary of the evidence it is proposed to place before the Court, or arrange for a preliminary hearing at which witnesses for the prosecution will give on oath, a summary of their testimony. At such preliminary hearings, neither defence nor prosecution counsel will be present, but the accused may cross-examine the witnesses. The evidence shall be taken down in writing from each witness, shall be read over to the accused and shall be signed by him/her. If the accused wishes to make a statement or give evidence on oath, he/she must be cautioned that anything he/she says may be taken down and used in evidence at any subsequent hearing of the case.

7. If the accused objects to any of the three officers comprising the Court, the objection will be examined by the remaining two members and, if upheld, the member objected to will be replaced.

8. The Convening Authority will supply the Court with a copy of the charges and with copies of General Army Orders.

9. The Convening Authority will ensure that the Prosecuting Counsel is in possession of all the facts relevant to the case and that all prosecution witnesses are present at the Court.

10. During the hearing of the case, all witnesses will be kept in separate rooms as in the case of a Court of Inquiry. The only persons present in the Court shall be the members of the Court, the accused, the Defence Counsel (if any), Prosecuting Counsel and note-taker (if any) and the witness under examination.

11. Evidence should be taken on oath which will be administered to each witness by the President. Should a witness object to testifying on oath, he/she must state the objections, to the Court. Unsworn testimony may be taken, but will not carry the same weight as sworn testimony. Once a witness has been examined, he/she may be recalled as often as the Court requires, to answer any further questions the Court wishes to put. For this reason, witnesses will not be allowed to leave the precincts of the Court except with the express permission of the Court.

12. At the start of the case, the President will read each charge to the accused and ask the accused if he/she pleads guilty to the charge.

13. Witnesses when called to testify will be cross-examined first by the Prosecuting Counsel and then by the Defence Counsel, or by the accused if conducting his/her own defence. Witnesses may be questioned by any member of the Court. Should either Counsel wish to recall a witness who has already testified, permission of the Court must first be obtained. The Court may recall any witness. Witnesses may not leave the precincts of the Court without permission from the Court.

14. At any time it so desires, the Court may go into private session to decide on points which may arise, such as the admissability of evidence.

15. When all witnesses have testified. Defence Counsel will sum up and make closing address to Court. This will be followed by summing up and closing address of the Prosecuting Counsel. The Court then goes into private session to consider its verdict and sentence.

16. For a breach of any General Army Order, the Court shall not have power to impose a lesser penalty than that laid down in such order.

17. The verdict and sentence of the Court shall be set down in writing and signed by the three members. This, together with a summary of the evidence must be forwarded by the President of the Convening Authority. Sentence is subject to the ratification of the Convening Authority.

NOTE: In the case of the death penalty sentence must be ratified by the A/C. (Army Council)

18. The accused may forward an appeal against the verdict or sentence or both to the Adjutant-General who will place it before the Competent Authority. The appeal should be forwarded by accused through his/her OC, who in turn will forward it to the Adjutant-General with a signed copy of verdict and sentence and a summary of the evidence. The Competent Authority may order a new trial or reduce the penalty, but may not increase the penalty imposed by the Court. NOTE: The President appoints one member of the Court to as recorder, unless a note-taker or other means of recording the proceedings is specially provided by the Convening Authority.

OATHS FOR COURT-MARTIAL

To be taken by each member of the court:

I...swear by Almighty God that I will try the accused on the issues presented to the Court without fear, favour or affection.

And I swear that I will not disclose the vote or opinion of any member of the Court or any proceedings of the Court unless required to do so by the Competent Authority.

And I swear not to disclose the verdict or sentence of the Court until they have been disclosed by the Competent Authority.

To be taken by each witness:
I...swear by Almighty God that my evidence to the Court shall be the truth, the whole truth and nothing but the truth.

To be taken by the official note-taker:
I...swear by Almighty God that I will maintain inviolate the proceedings of this Court and that I will not disclose its proceedings unless required to do so by the Competent Authority.

NOTES FOR COURT-MARTIAL

1. On the Court assembling, the Convening Authority or his/her representative reads the order convening the Court.

2. The President asks the accused if he/she has any objection to any member of the Court. Members of the Court retire and consider any objections, and decide whether objection is to be upheld or rejected.

3. If any objection is upheld, the Convening Authority or his/her representative nominates another member.

4. The President appoints one member of the Court to record the proceedings, unless a note-taker is specially appointed by the Convening Authority.

5. The President then reads the charge or charges to the accused and asks him/her to plead to each separate charge.

6. The Prosecutor presents his/her authority to the Court and makes the opening statement for the prosecution, outlining the charges.

7. The Prosecutor then calls witnesses to substantiate case for the prosecution.

8. Accused or his/her Counsel cross-examine witness for the prosecution.

9. When evidence for the prosecution is closed, the accused or his/her Counsel makes opening statement for the defence.

10. Witnesses for the defence are then called.

11. Accused or his/her Counsel makes closing statement for the Defence.

12. Prosecutor makes closing statement for the prosecution.

13. Court may ask for records as to the character and record of the accused.

14. The Court retires to consider the findings on each charge and to award the sentence. The Court may award a separate sentence or punishment on each charge on which the accused is found guilty of, or one sentence or punishment, to cover more than one charge.

15. Where different sentences are proposed, the Court shall vote first on the lesser sentence proposed.

16. Members of the Court shall vote on sentence according to their seniority, the junior members voting first.

17. The President of the Court shall be responsible for forwarding to the Competent Authority.

(a) The written records or other records of the proceedings of the Court and all documents connected with the trial.

(b) The findings and sentence of the Court.

18. The oath to witnesses shall be administered by the President of the Court.

CODE OF CONDUCT
(Issued in 1987)

No serious guerrilla organisation can exist or hope to achieve victory without a number of prerequisites.

One one side of the coin these include comradeship, an internal structure (or infra-structure), rules and regulations, an ability to recruit, and a brief in achieving objectives. On the other side there has to be public support and the commanding of the admiration and respect of the public.

Where comradeship is lacking and where there are no rules and regulations one can see from past INLA feuds how disagreements can degenerate into anarchy and demoralise one's base of support.

The Irish Republican Army is one of the oldest and surviving guerilla armies in the world. It has a long tradition of struggle but at certain times in its history a number of the prerequisites for success were absent—conditions were not right, but most importantly nationalist opinion in the North was not ripe for a sustained armed struggle. All this changed in the 1960s with the attempted repression of the Civil Rights Movement and from then until now the struggle has taken on a steady momentum of its own.

The IRA's objectives are set down in a written constitution (which can only be amended by General Army Convention: the last IRA Convention was in 1986). The IRA however, is regulated by a set of General Army Orders (which can be amended at any time by an Army Council). Volunteers have always been expected to be familiar with the Constitution and General Army Orders, but in recent years familiar also with the Green Book which is a further breakdown of the aims and objectives of the organisation, the tactics of how to conduct oneself during interrogation.

Enemy

The British government has attempted to undermine the struggle, deter people from fighting and sap the morale of Volunteers and supporters through a number of measures.

It kills people, it jails people, it consistently repeats that it will not give way to the IRA, it ridicules one's objectives as being unrealistic and unachievable. It attacks the methods such as the commandeering of cars, the taking over houses, fighting a war in the streets in which people live, the execution of informers, etc. All of this is so much hypocrisy compared to the commandeering of a country and British institutionalised violence and sectarianism. Most objective people—and not necessarily sympathetic people—can see through this hypocrisy, and only ongoing politicisation and publicity can really counter it.

It is IRA successes that demoralise the British and undermine their case. Ongoing IRA successes reinforce the belief in victory which in turn will lead to increased support.

Behaviour

No organisation and no organisation's members are above reproach. The behaviour of Volunteers on operations and how republicans conduct themselves in their private lives will, where exploitable, be used by the British, the media, and the SDLP, and the Movement's other detractors to undermine the Movement in the minds of the general public.

When Mao's Red Army was fighting the revolution in China its Code of Conduct was summed up succinctly, (if idealistically) as follows:

Three General Rules of Discipline
1. Obey orders in all actions.

2. Do not take a single needle or piece of thread from the people.
3. Hand all booty over to headquarters.

And the Eight Reminders
1. Talk to people politely.
2. Be fair in all business dealings.
3. Return everything you have borrowed.
4. Pay for anything you have damaged.
5. Don't beat or bully people.
6. Don't damage crops.
7. Don't flirt with women.
8. Don't illtreat prisoners of war.

This is somewhat idealistic but one gets the drift about striving for the optimum in good behaviour and the necessity of avoiding scandal. Given the pervasiveness of the media in everyone's lives nowadays it is therefore even more essential for republicans to consider the effect of their attitudes and behaviour on supporters. To be conscious of how their behaviour could be used to ridicule the Movement and thus unjustifiably bring the struggle into disrepute.

The Republican Movement relies on a voluntary code of conduct (through Volunteers can still be dismissed under General Army Orders for blatant actions which bring the Movement into disrepute) and below are some of the guidelines expected of members:

1. Republican Volunteers are expected to be truthful in their dealings with other comrades and other sections of the Movement.

2. They are expected to be honest in all matters relating to the public, both in terms of official and private business. Whilst the majority of members are from working-class backgrounds, a business-person (who is also a known republican activist) who provides a poor serviced to the public or who exploits the public in business dealings is no asset to the republican cause.

3. Republicanism stands for equality and an end to sexism. Male Volunteers who mistreat or exploit their partners are flying in the face of this principle. Volunteers must practice domestically what the Movement preaches publicly.

4. Anyone promoting sectarianism or displaying sectarian attitudes should immediately be disciplined.

5. Republicanism has an international dimension which means respecting as equals other nationalities and races. Anyone who pays lip service to international solidarity and then slips into mimicking the racist attitudes which are typical of an imperialist mentality should be immediately upbraided. All people are equal and everyone has an international duty to oppose racism and oppression from wherever it emanates.

6. Our culture is something of which we should be proud, it is part of our identity and it can also be used, not in a chauvanistic sense, but against the British to show the separateness of our identity as an individual nation. Republicans who do not subscribe, to Irish culture, or who have no interest in promoting the Irish language, should respect those who are making progress on this front against considerable odds. It is simply laziness which prevents people from attempting to learn their native language: no-one is that busy!

7. The Green Book makes reference to people who take alcohol urging them to be extremely careful. Under excessive drinking people's tongues loosen, people whom one wouldn't normally trust become 'great friends', and one is vulnerable to the temptation of engaging in 'loose talk'.

Apart from the security risk, a drunken republican is hardly the best example of a freedom fighter, he or she is open to ridicule from the Movement's detractors. The activities of republicans even engaged in innocent celebrations would be used by the enemy, so vulnerable are ambassadors of freedom struggle on this issue! So be moderate and be careful and remember what you represent. If you need to 'let off steam' then be discreet.

8. Alcohol affects different people in different ways, turning some aggressive people into affectionate doves, and making some normally pleasant people nasty and unbearable!

Under alcohol people's attitudes can also undergo unpleasant changes: respect towards others, one's partner, the Movement, can temporarily diminish leaving one with a lot of apologising and more than a hangover the following day. Dependency on alcohol is also a major weakness which the Special Branch will be quick to exploit.

The code set out here represents mere commonsense and is a reminder to all activists of their responsibilities. No-one has been press-ganged into republicanism. If you cannot do the struggle the honour of your service, then do not do it the dishonour of a disservice. It is as simple as that.

Volunteers' Rights
(issued in 1988)

Volunteers should be well versed in General Army Orders and Court of Inquiry and Court Martial procedures. They should understand that they are aimed not only at ensuring the IRA runs smoothly within these agreed disciplinary codes, but also at protecting the rights of Volunteers. While everyone is accountabled to disciplinary process under General Army Orders, this is not their only function. They are there to protect the Army and as the Army is its Volunteers, they must serve to protect the Volunteers as well.

Communications within the Army are of vital importance. Thus all Volunteers should: be aware of how the Army structure works and of how a Volunteer can and should pass grievances or observations upwards. The onus is on the Volunteer to do this in a non-disruptive way, working through and using the proper channels all the time. All Volunteers should have access to their immediate superiors. This is through normal Army channels to GHQ. If this is unsatisfactory then there is access through GHQ to Army Council. The onus is on each tier, if requested, to pass requests upwards.

Security permitting, a Volunteer should always get an answer. Whether the Volunteer agrees with the answer is irrelevant: once Volunteers exhaust the channels, Army discipline demands that the answer be accepted. Final redress can be sought through the Army Council. Issues which are not important enough to warrant this should not be permitted to cause disruption or harmful dissensions. The onus is on the Volunteers to behave at all times in a correct, positive and responsible manner avoiding personal conflict or diversions from our main task.

Suspension of Volunteers should be conducted sparingly. Where suspensions are necessary they should not be of lengthy duration. Except in special circumstances Volunteers should not normally be suspended, unless facing charges, eg a Volunteer facing a court of inquiry should not normally be suspended. However, when a court of inquiry decided to press charges, this would normally involve suspension until the charges are adjudicated on. Special circumstances where a volunteer could be suspended by a competent senior authority could for example, include a refusal to obey an Army Order.

The above deals with suspension of membership of the Army. Suspension of a

Volunteer from specific duties or a position in the Army is permissable at the discretion of a competent senior authority. Again the normal right to appeal applies. Summary dismissal of a Volunteer should be avoided except in the most extreme circumstances. Every Volunteer has the right to a court of inquiry. It should be noted that such a court, arising out of a summary dismissal, is a court, where those responsible for the dismissal will have to stand over their actions. They are not permitted to introduce new evidence other than that on which the dismissal was based. Volunteers summarily dismissed have seven days in which to appeal against the dismissal.

Courts are established by the Army Authority. Thus recommendations by courts must be agreed on by the Army Authority before they are acted on, or made known to other Volunteers.

All of the above places a heavy responsibility on those holding positions within the Army. The Adjutant General is responsible for discipline. The Adjutant General or those to whom he/she has delegated responsibility should be consulted in all cases involving the possible dismissal of Volunteers.

An organisation like ours which seeks political objectives based upon the principles of justice and freedom, must ensure that these principles are applied internally and in our dealings with one and other.

Volunteers, and this includes everyone from the CS to the Unit Volunteer, must be treated in a fair and overhand way.

Index